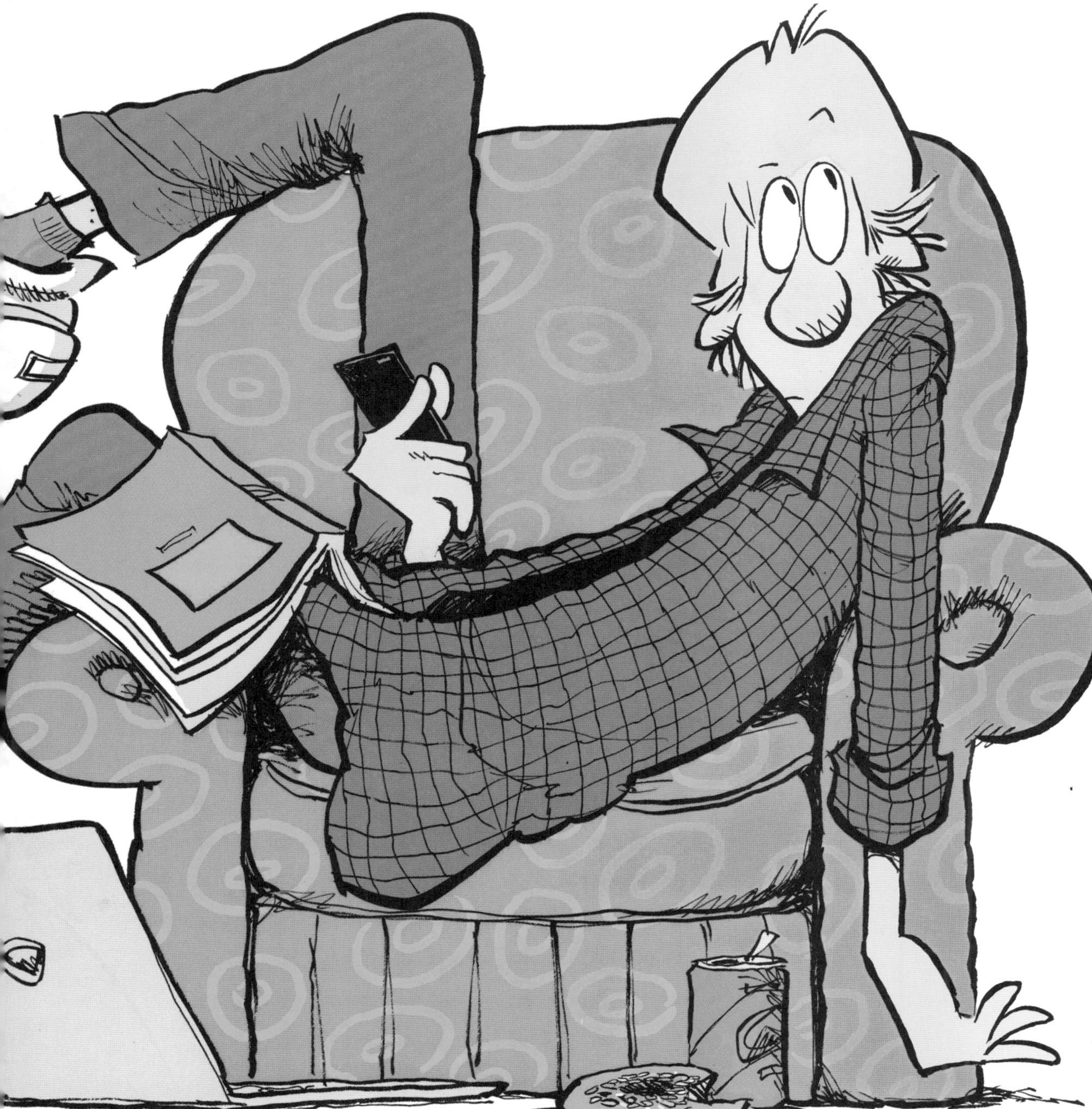

WHAT WAS THAT ALL ABOUT?

ALSO BY JERRY SCOTT AND JIM BORGMAN

Zits: Sketchbook 1

Growth Spurt: Zits Sketchbook 2

Don't Roll Your Eyes at Me, Young Man!: Zits Sketchbook 3

Are We an "Us"?: Zits Sketchbook 4

Zits Unzipped: Zits Sketchbook 5

Busted!: Zits Sketchbook 6

Road Trip: Zits Sketchbook 7

Teenage Tales: Zits Sketchbook 8

Thrashed: Zits Sketchbook No. 9

Pimp My Lunch: Zits Sketchbook No. 10

Are We Out of the Driveway Yet?: Zits Sketchbook No. 11

Rude, Crude, and Tattooed: Zits Sketchbook No. 12

Jeremy and Mom

Pierced

Lust and Other Uses for Spare Hormones

Jeremy & Dad

You're Making That Face Again

Drive!

Triple Shot, Double Pump, No Whip Zits

Zits en Concert

Peace, Love, and Wi-Fi

Zits Apocalypse

Extra Cheesy Zits

TREASURIES

Humongous Zits

Big Honkin' Zits

Zits: Supersized

Random Zits

Crack of Noon

Alternative Zits

My Bad

Sunday Brunch

GIFT BOOK

A Zits Guide to Living with Your Teenager

WHAT WAS THAT ALL ABOUT?

20 Years of Strips and Stories

JERRY SCOTT and **JIM BORGMAN**

Andrews McMeel
PUBLISHING®

To our remarkable families,
without whom this book would have been
a lot thinner and less funny.

J.S. J.B.

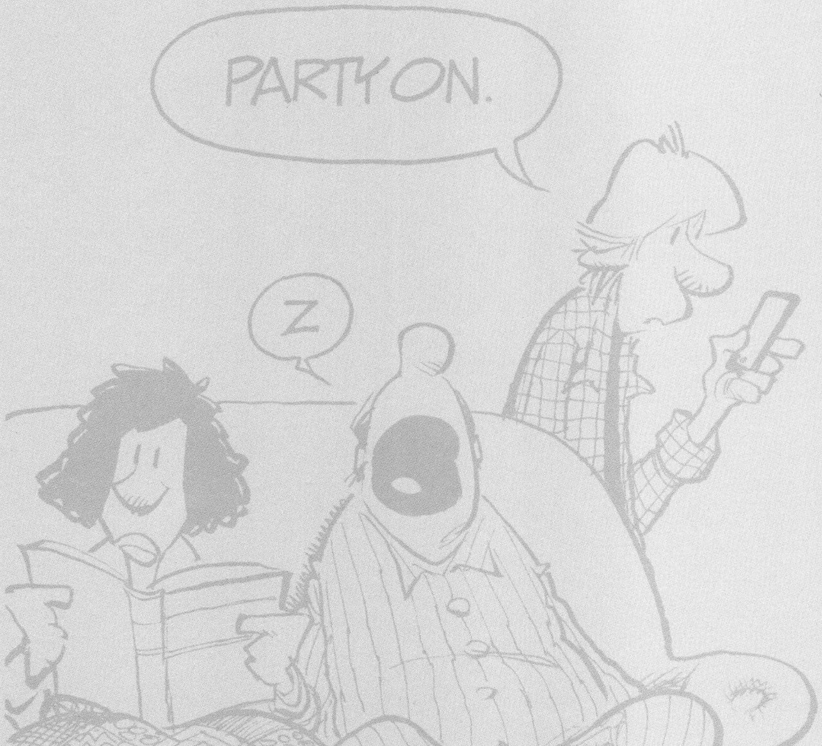
PARTY ON.
Z

CONTENTS

ELONGATED SLUGGOS

Jerry Scott

In February of 1995, when I was living in Cave Creek, a small town north of Phoenix, Arizona, I got a call from Jim Borgman, the Pulitzer Prize–winning editorial cartoonist for the *Cincinnati Enquirer* and a guy I barely knew. We had served on the board of directors of the National Cartoonists Society together. And by "served" I mean we kept our heads down when work was being assigned and volunteers sought.

Jim had been invited to speak at the Arizona Press Club and, it being February and all, was looking for an excuse not to get back to the Midwest too quickly. He asked me what he should do to kill some time in the sun, and I suggested he try a place I knew of near Sedona. Garlands Resort is a little gem in the Oak Creek Canyon area with individual cabins, great food, and plenty of nothing to do. I described it in such glowing detail and mouthwatering terms that by the end of the phone call I had invited myself to come along. The only rule was that there was to be no cartooning work done . . . just hanging around, hiking, and eating good meals while unwinding from deadlines.

So we did that for a couple of days, and then I broke the rule. I had been fired from the *Nancy* comic strip a few weeks before this and was frantically working on an idea for a new strip. The new one was supposed to be about a teenager, but all of my drawings looked less like teenage boys than freakishly elongated Sluggos. So I grabbed a few beers (a recognized currency among cartoonists) and ambled over to Jim's cabin, sketchbook in hand.

"Funny stuff," he said. "But your teenagers look like elongated Sluggos." We talked about all the reasons a strip about a teenager wouldn't work, and then Jim said, "If you're asking me how I would draw a teenager, I'd just draw my son."

Dylan Borgman was fifteen years old at the time, and Jim explained that boys that age don't just occupy space . . . they drape, slouch, crowd, and dominate it. Then he drew this:

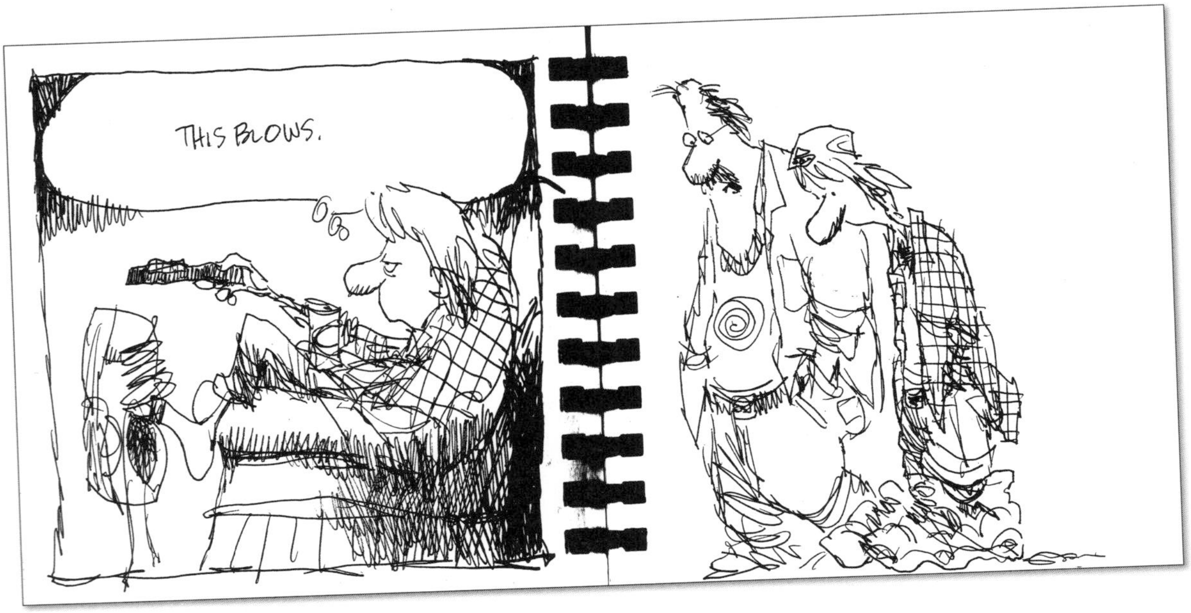
THIS BLOWS.

And this:

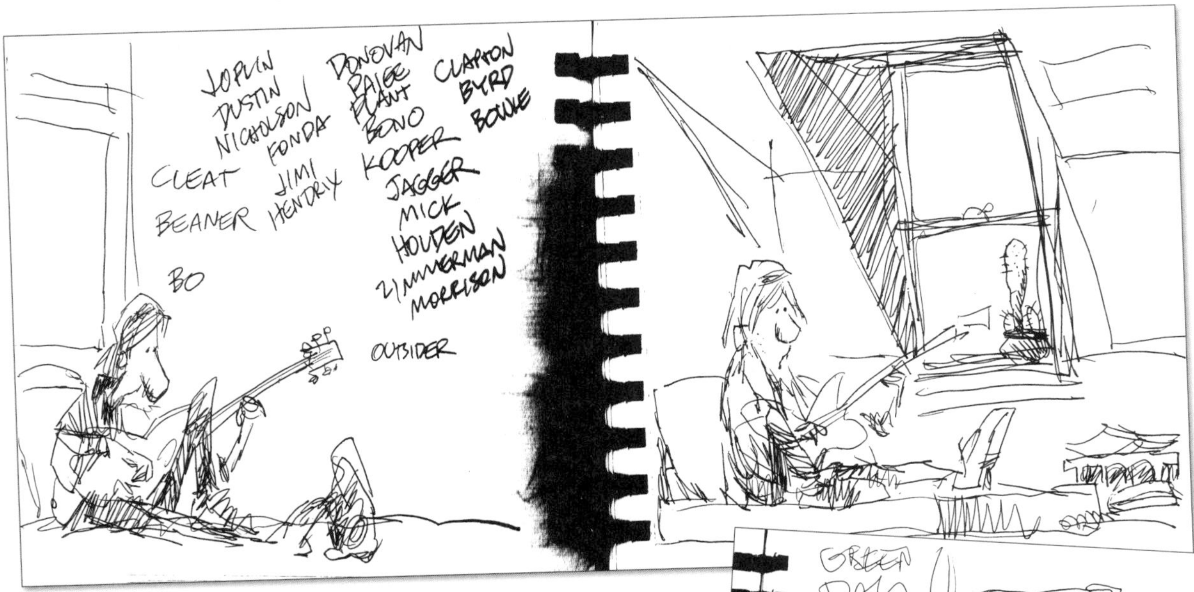
JOPLIN
DUSTIN
NICHOLSON
CLEAT
BEANER
BO
FONDA
JIMI
HENDRIX
DONOVAN
PAIGE
PLANT
BONO
KOOPER
JAGGER
MICK
HOLDEN
MORRISON
CLAPTON
BYRD
BOWIE
OUTSIDER

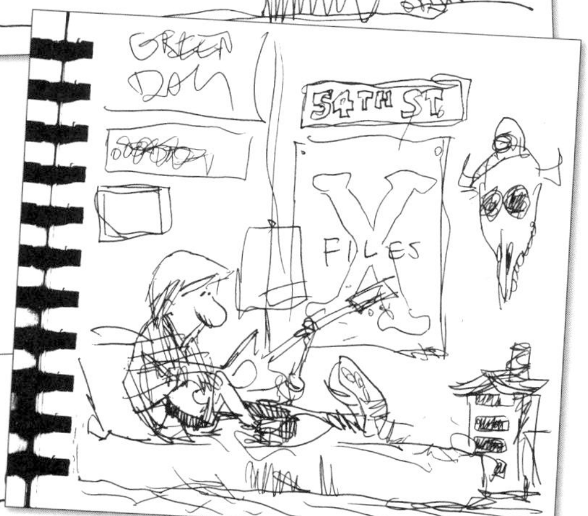
GREEN DAY
54TH ST.
FILES

By beer two I knew that something was happening. Or might happen. This idea of mine suddenly had a brilliant new look and a deeper sensibility with the prospect of two creators contributing to it.

Then we decided to forget the whole thing and go home.

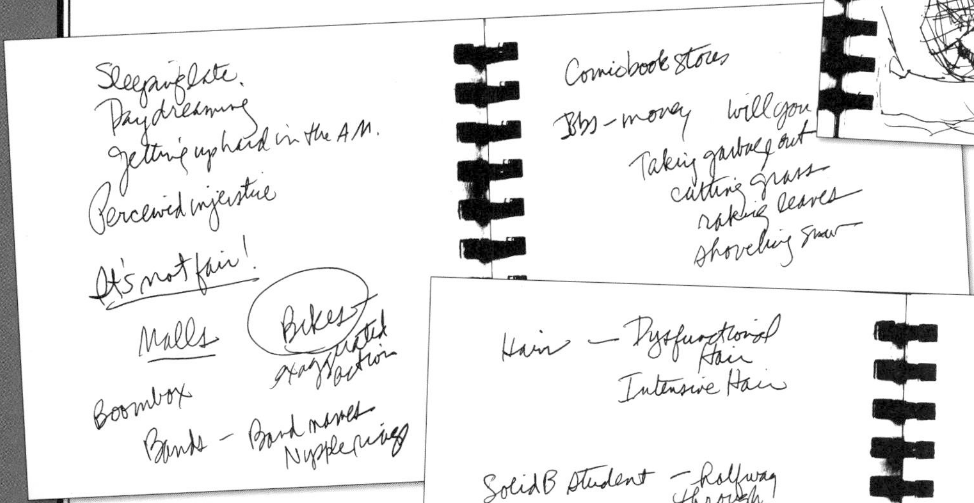
Sleeping late.
Daydreaming
getting up hard in the A.M.
Perceived injustice
It's not fair!
Malls
Bikes
exaggerated action
Boombox
Bands - Band names
Comicbook stores
Jobs - money
will you
Taking garbage out
cutting grass
raking leaves
shoveling snow

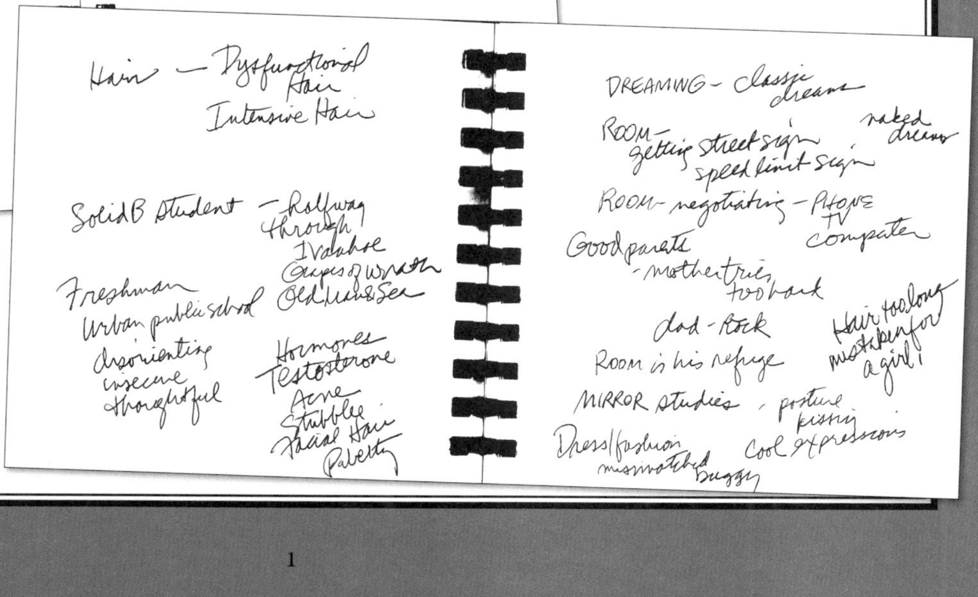
Hair - Dysfunctional Hair
Intensive Hair
Solid B Student
Ivanhoe
Grapes of Wrath
Old Man & Sea
Freshman
Urban public school
disorienting
insecure
thoughtful
Hormones
Testosterone
Acne
Stubble
Facial Hair
Puberty
DREAMING - classic dreams
naked dreams
ROOM - getting street sign
speed limit sign
ROOM - negotiating - PHONE
TV
computer
Good parents
- mother tries too hard
dad - Rock
Hair too long mistaken for a girl!
Room is his refuge
MIRROR studies - posture
kissing
Cool expressions
Dress/fashion
mismatched
baggy

July 7, 1997

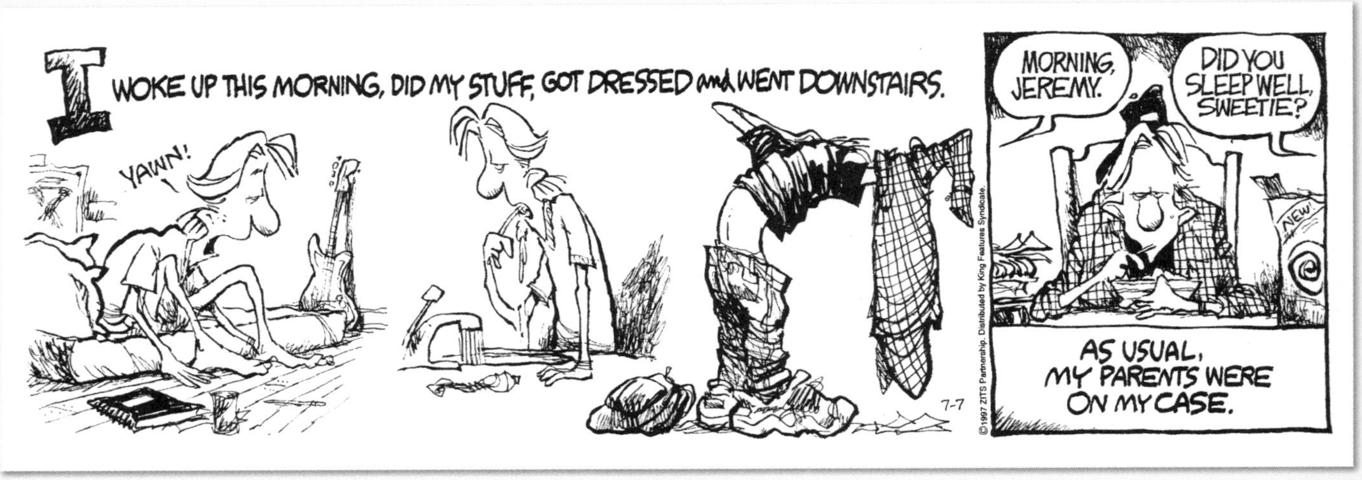
I WOKE UP THIS MORNING, DID MY STUFF, GOT DRESSED and WENT DOWNSTAIRS.
YAWN!
7-7
©1997 ZITS Partnership. Distributed by King Features Syndicate.
MORNING, JEREMY.
DID YOU SLEEP WELL, SWEETIE?
NEW!
AS USUAL, MY PARENTS WERE ON MY CASE.

July 9, 1997

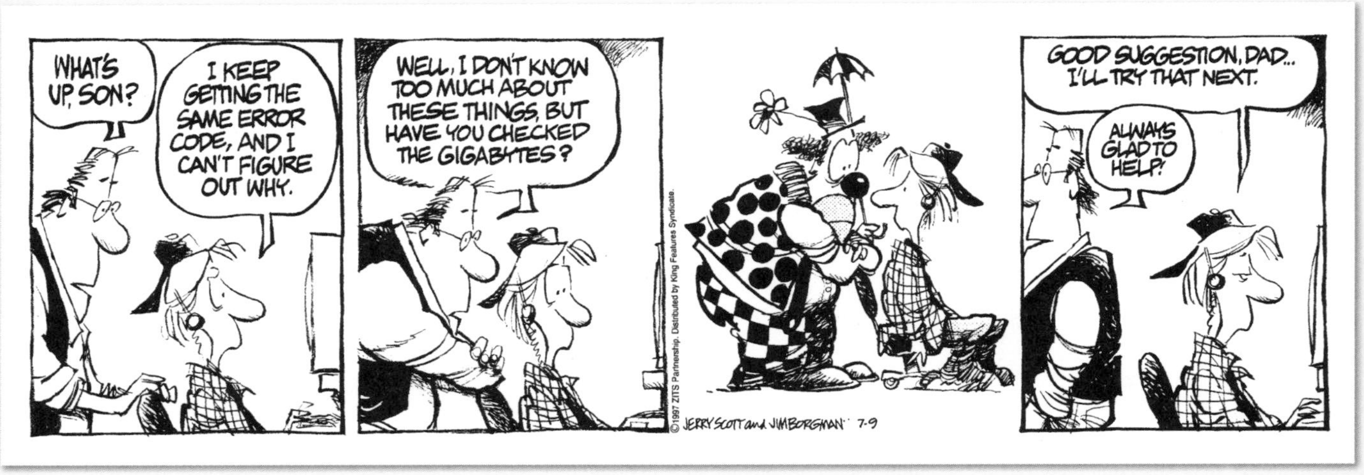
WHAT'S UP, SON?
I KEEP GETTING THE SAME ERROR CODE, AND I CAN'T FIGURE OUT WHY.
WELL, I DON'T KNOW TOO MUCH ABOUT THESE THINGS, BUT HAVE YOU CHECKED THE GIGABYTES?
©1997 ZITS Partnership. Distributed by King Features Syndicate.
JERRY SCOTT and JIM BORGMAN 7-9
GOOD SUGGESTION, DAD... I'LL TRY THAT NEXT.
ALWAYS GLAD TO HELP!

July 10, 1997

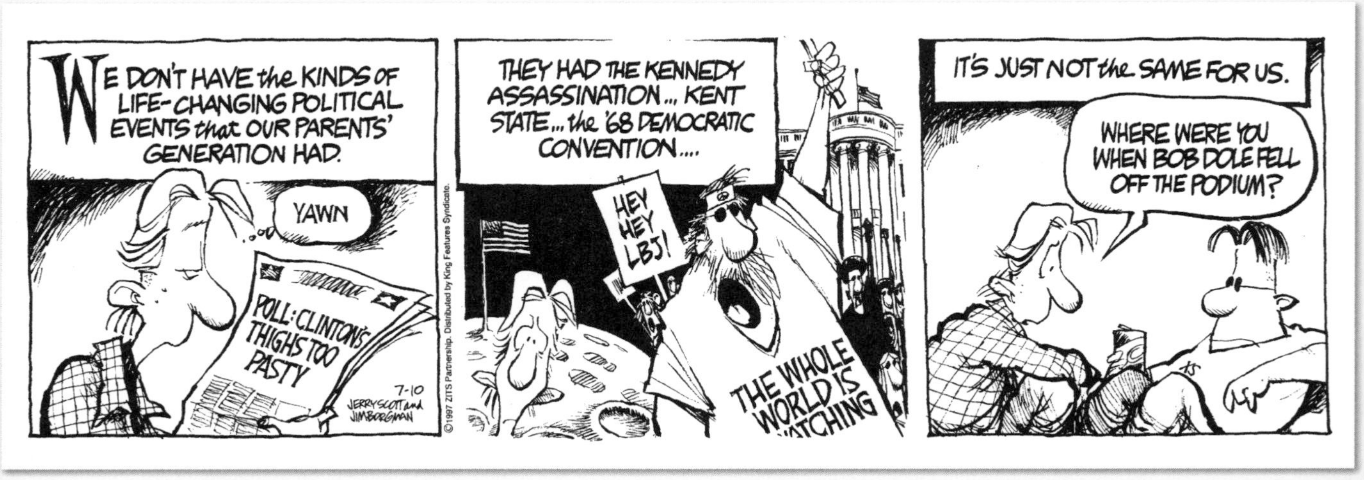
WE DON'T HAVE the KINDS OF LIFE-CHANGING POLITICAL EVENTS that OUR PARENTS' GENERATION HAD.
YAWN
POLL: CLINTON'S THIGHS TOO PASTY
7-10
JERRY SCOTT and JIM BORGMAN
©1997 ZITS Partnership. Distributed by King Features Syndicate.
THEY HAD THE KENNEDY ASSASSINATION..., KENT STATE... the '68 DEMOCRATIC CONVENTION....
HEY HEY LBJ!
THE WHOLE WORLD IS WATCHING
IT'S JUST NOT the SAME FOR US.
WHERE WERE YOU WHEN BOB DOLE FELL OFF THE PODIUM?

July 17, 1997

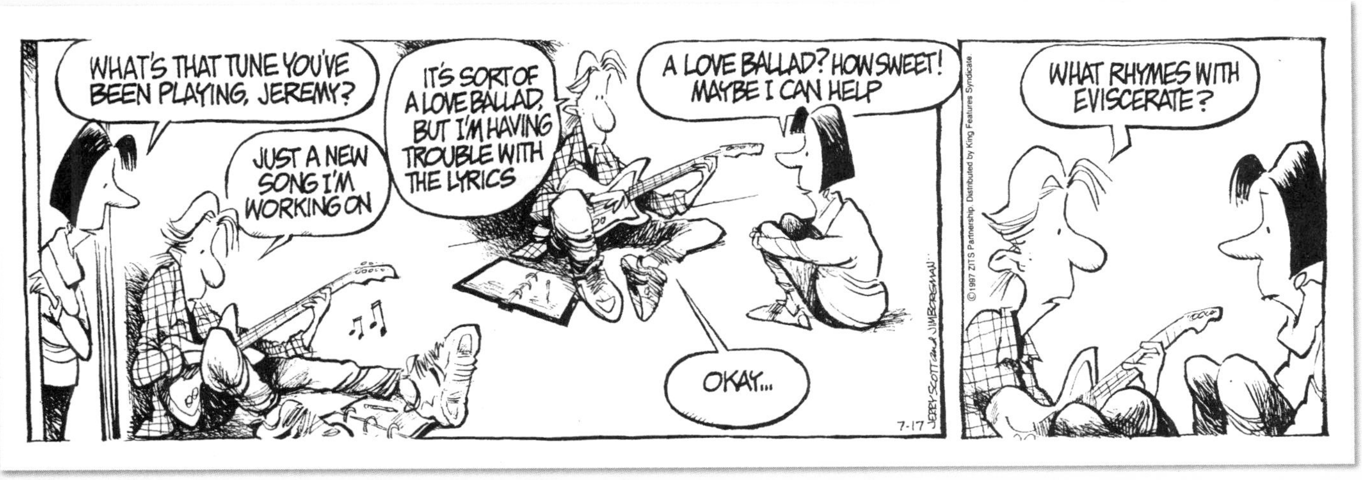
WHAT'S THAT TUNE YOU'VE BEEN PLAYING, JEREMY?
JUST A NEW SONG I'M WORKING ON
IT'S SORT OF A LOVE BALLAD, BUT I'M HAVING TROUBLE WITH THE LYRICS
A LOVE BALLAD? HOW SWEET! MAYBE I CAN HELP
OKAY...
WHAT RHYMES WITH EVISCERATE?
JERRY SCOTT and JIM BORGMAN 7-17
©1997 ZITS Partnership. Distributed by King Features Syndicate

July 18, 1997

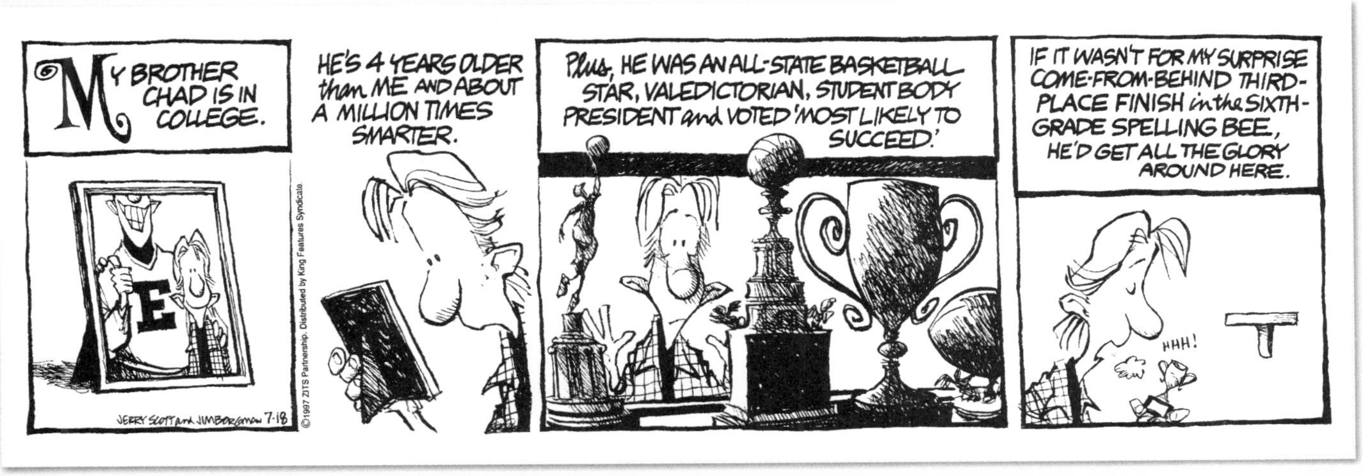
MY BROTHER CHAD IS IN COLLEGE.
JERRY SCOTT and JIM BORGMAN 7-18
©1997 ZITS Partnership. Distributed by King Features Syndicate.
HE'S 4 YEARS OLDER than ME AND ABOUT A MILLION TIMES SMARTER.
Plus, HE WAS AN ALL-STATE BASKETBALL STAR, VALEDICTORIAN, STUDENT BODY PRESIDENT and VOTED 'MOST LIKELY TO SUCCEED.'
IF IT WASN'T FOR MY SURPRISE COME-FROM-BEHIND THIRD-PLACE FINISH in the SIXTH-GRADE SPELLING BEE, HE'D GET ALL THE GLORY AROUND HERE.
HHH!

July 22, 1997

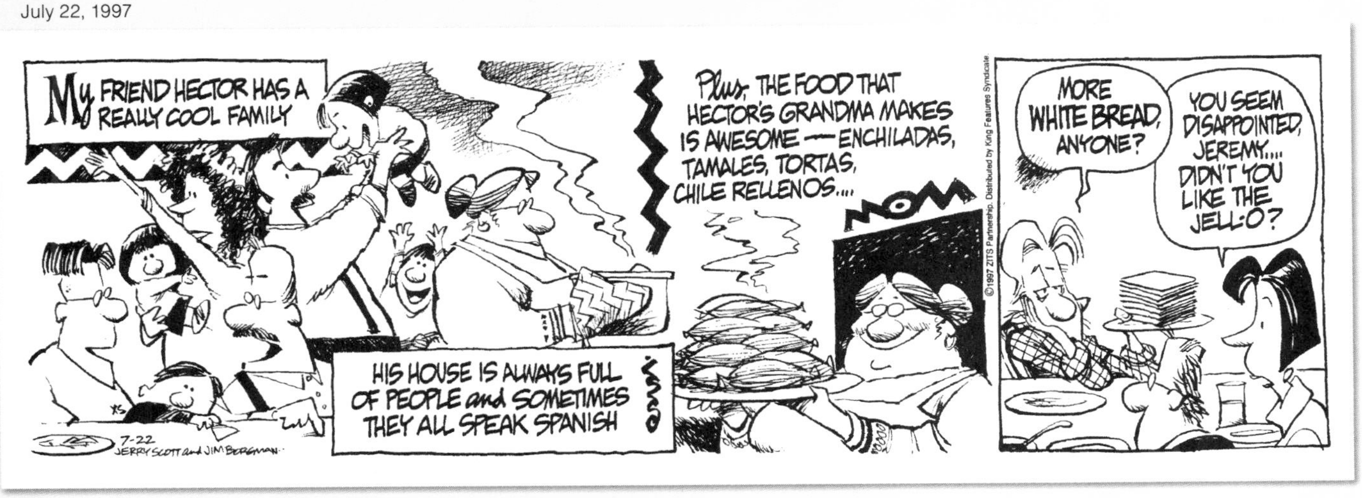
MY FRIEND HECTOR HAS A REALLY COOL FAMILY
HIS HOUSE IS ALWAYS FULL OF PEOPLE and SOMETIMES THEY ALL SPEAK SPANISH
7-22 JERRY SCOTT and JIM BORGMAN
Plus, THE FOOD THAT HECTOR'S GRANDMA MAKES IS AWESOME — ENCHILADAS, TAMALES, TORTAS, CHILE RELLENOS....
MOM
©1997 ZITS Partnership. Distributed by King Features Syndicate
MORE WHITE BREAD, ANYONE?
YOU SEEM DISAPPOINTED, JEREMY.... DIDN'T YOU LIKE THE JELL-O?

July 20, 1997

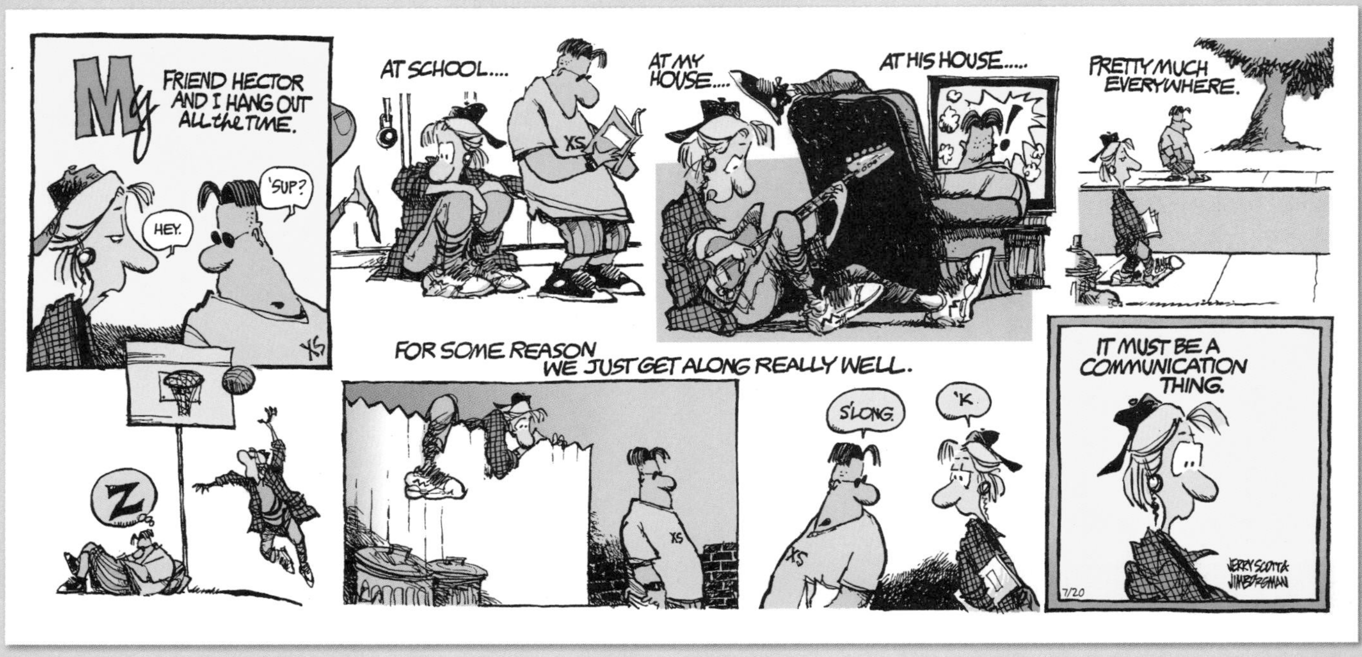
MY FRIEND HECTOR AND I HANG OUT ALL the TIME.
HEY.
'SUP?
XS
AT SCHOOL....
XS
AT MY HOUSE....
AT HIS HOUSE.....
PRETTY MUCH EVERYWHERE.
FOR SOME REASON WE JUST GET ALONG REALLY WELL.
Z
XS
S'LONG.
'K.
XS
IT MUST BE A COMMUNICATION THING.
JERRY SCOTT & JIMBORGMAN
7/20

July 27, 1997

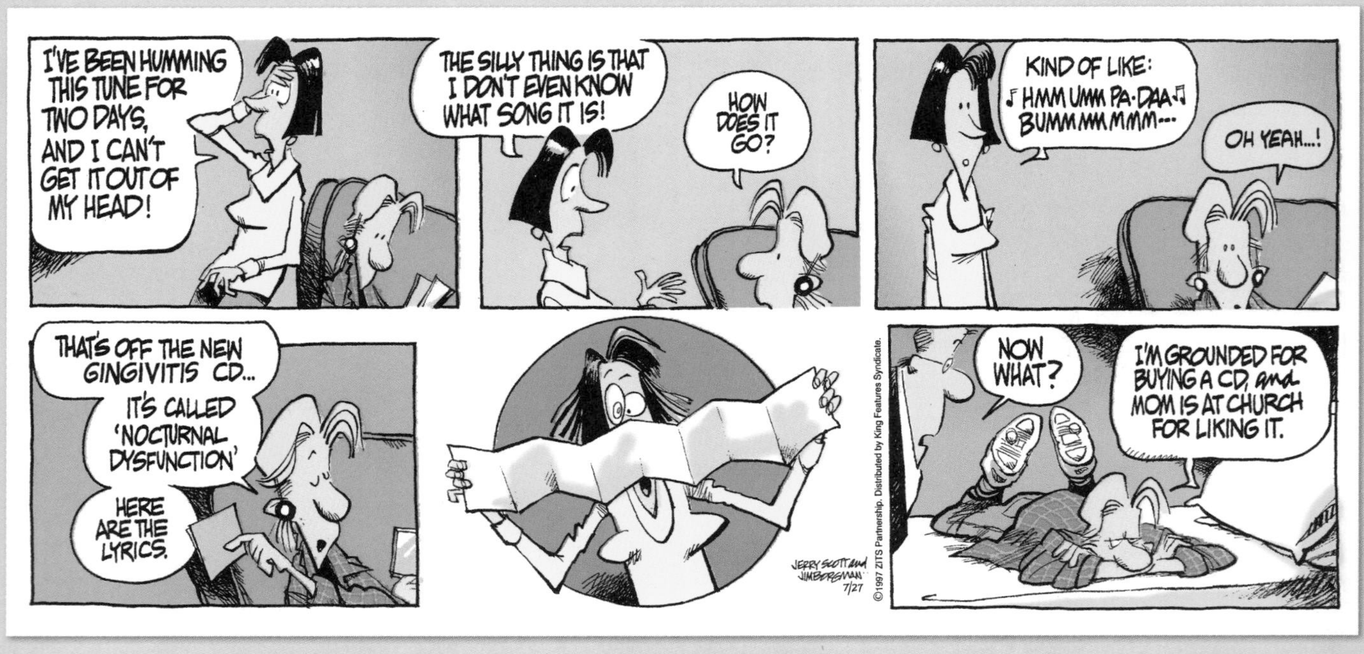
I'VE BEEN HUMMING THIS TUNE FOR TWO DAYS, AND I CAN'T GET IT OUT OF MY HEAD!
THE SILLY THING IS THAT I DON'T EVEN KNOW WHAT SONG IT IS!
HOW DOES IT GO?
KIND OF LIKE: ♫ HMM UMM PA-DAA ♫ BUMMMMMMM---
OH YEAH...!
THAT'S OFF THE NEW GINGIVITIS CD...
IT'S CALLED 'NOCTURNAL DYSFUNCTION'
HERE ARE THE LYRICS.
JERRY SCOTT and JIMBORGMAN 7/27
©1997 ZITS Partnership. Distributed by King Features Syndicate.
NOW WHAT?
I'M GROUNDED FOR BUYING A CD, and MOM IS AT CHURCH FOR LIKING IT.

July 24, 1997

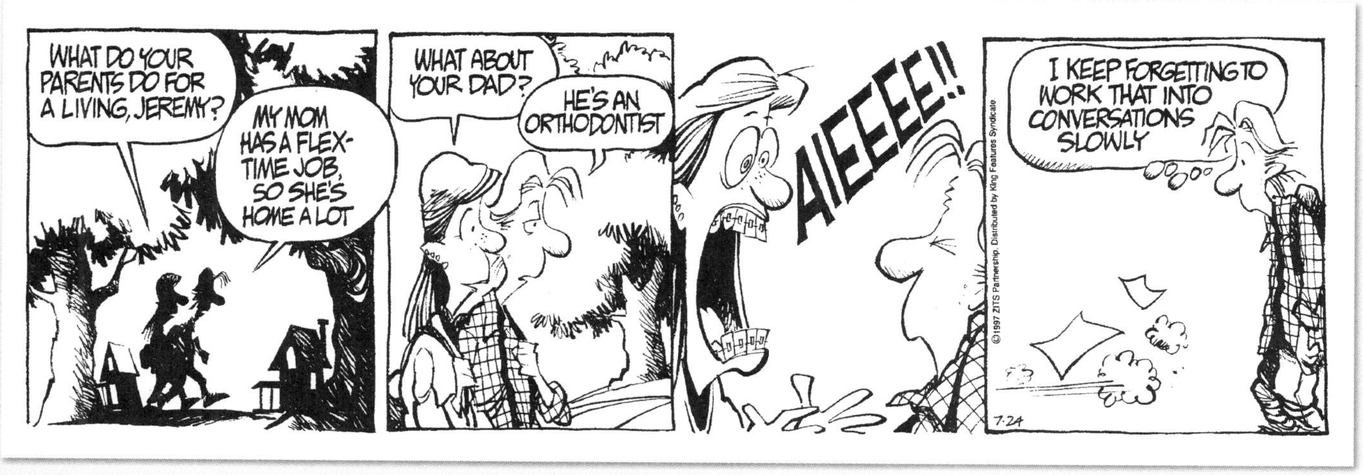
WHAT DO YOUR PARENTS DO FOR A LIVING, JEREMY?
MY MOM HAS A FLEX-TIME JOB, SO SHE'S HOME A LOT
WHAT ABOUT YOUR DAD?
HE'S AN ORTHODONTIST
AIEEEE!!
I KEEP FORGETTING TO WORK THAT INTO CONVERSATIONS SLOWLY
©1997 ZITS Partnership. Distributed by King Features Syndicate.
7·24

July 26, 1997

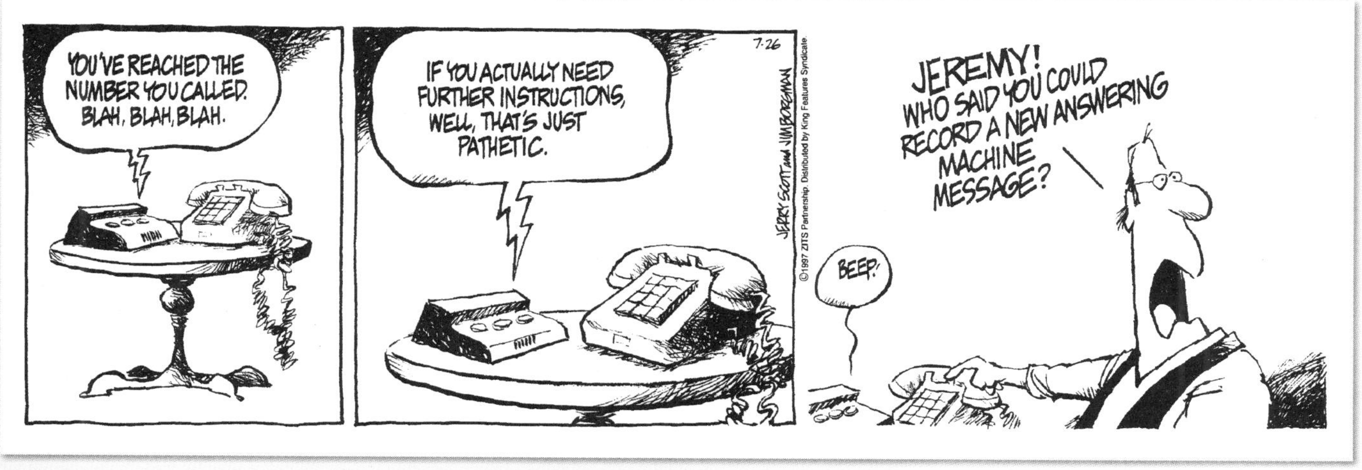
YOU'VE REACHED THE NUMBER YOU CALLED. BLAH, BLAH, BLAH.
IF YOU ACTUALLY NEED FURTHER INSTRUCTIONS, WELL, THAT'S JUST PATHETIC.
7·26
JERRY SCOTT and JIM BORGMAN
©1997 ZITS Partnership. Distributed by King Features Syndicate.
BEEP!
JEREMY! WHO SAID YOU COULD RECORD A NEW ANSWERING MACHINE MESSAGE?

July 29, 1997

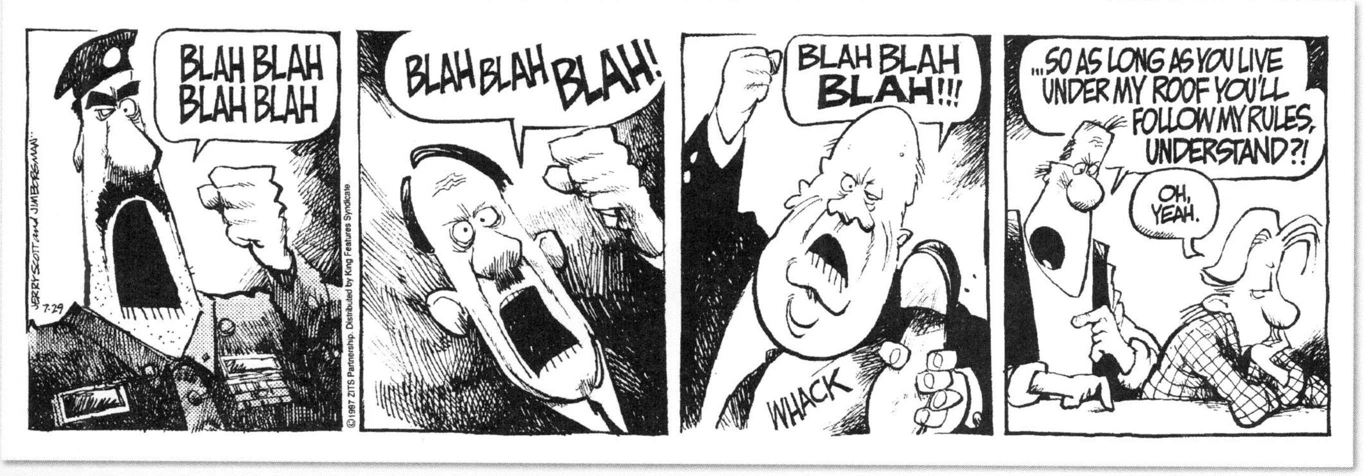
BLAH BLAH BLAH BLAH
JERRY SCOTT and JIM BORGMAN
7·29
BLAH BLAH BLAH!
©1997 ZITS Partnership. Distributed by King Features Syndicate
BLAH BLAH BLAH!!!
WHACK
...SO AS LONG AS YOU LIVE UNDER MY ROOF YOU'LL FOLLOW MY RULES, UNDERSTAND?!
OH, YEAH.

August 5, 1997

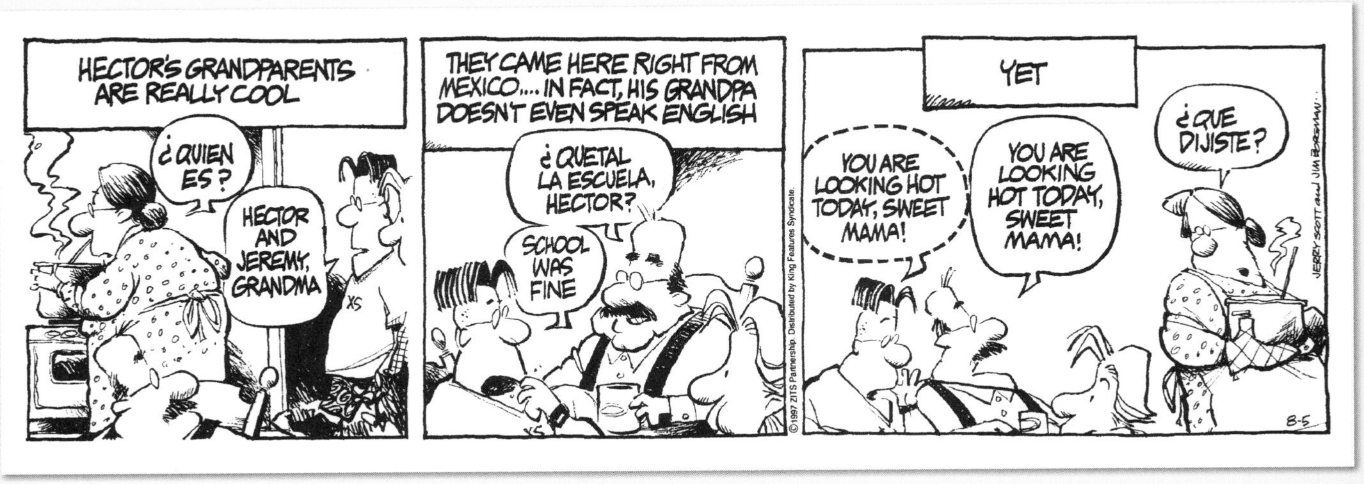
HECTOR'S GRANDPARENTS ARE REALLY COOL
¿QUIEN ES?
HECTOR AND JEREMY, GRANDMA
THEY CAME HERE RIGHT FROM MEXICO.... IN FACT, HIS GRANDPA DOESN'T EVEN SPEAK ENGLISH
¿QUETAL LA ESCUELA, HECTOR?
SCHOOL WAS FINE
YET
YOU ARE LOOKING HOT TODAY, SWEET MAMA!
YOU ARE LOOKING HOT TODAY, SWEET MAMA!
¿QUE DIJISTE?
© 1997 ZITS Partnership. Distributed by King Features Syndicate.
JERRY SCOTT and JIM BORGMAN
8-5

August 9, 1997

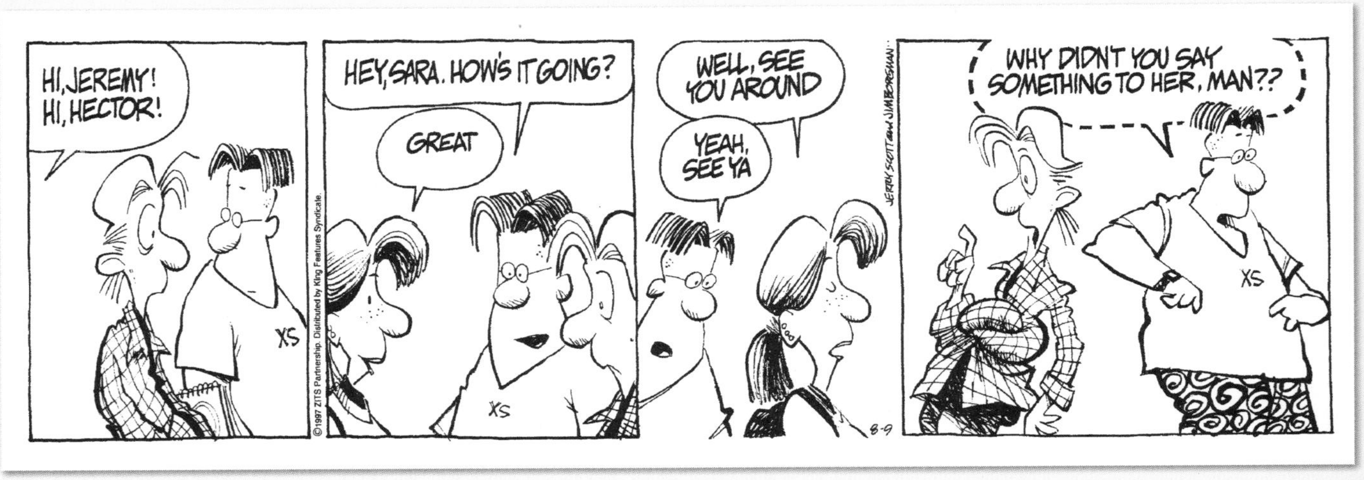
HI, JEREMY! HI, HECTOR!
HEY, SARA. HOW'S IT GOING?
GREAT
WELL, SEE YOU AROUND
YEAH, SEE YA
WHY DIDN'T YOU SAY SOMETHING TO HER, MAN??
© 1997 ZITS Partnership. Distributed by King Features Syndicate.
JERRY SCOTT and JIM BORGMAN
8-9

August 14, 1997

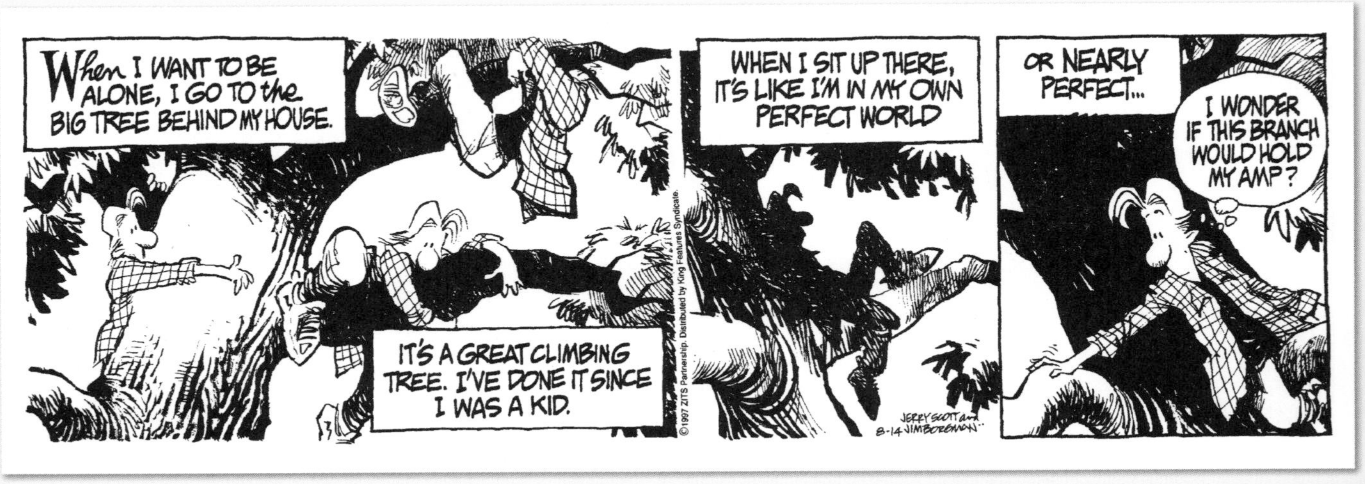
When I WANT TO BE ALONE, I GO TO the BIG TREE BEHIND MY HOUSE.
IT'S A GREAT CLIMBING TREE. I'VE DONE IT SINCE I WAS A KID.
WHEN I SIT UP THERE, IT'S LIKE I'M IN MY OWN PERFECT WORLD
OR NEARLY PERFECT...
I WONDER IF THIS BRANCH WOULD HOLD MY AMP?
© 1997 ZITS Partnership. Distributed by King Features Syndicate.
JERRY SCOTT and JIM BORGMAN
8-14

August 19, 1997

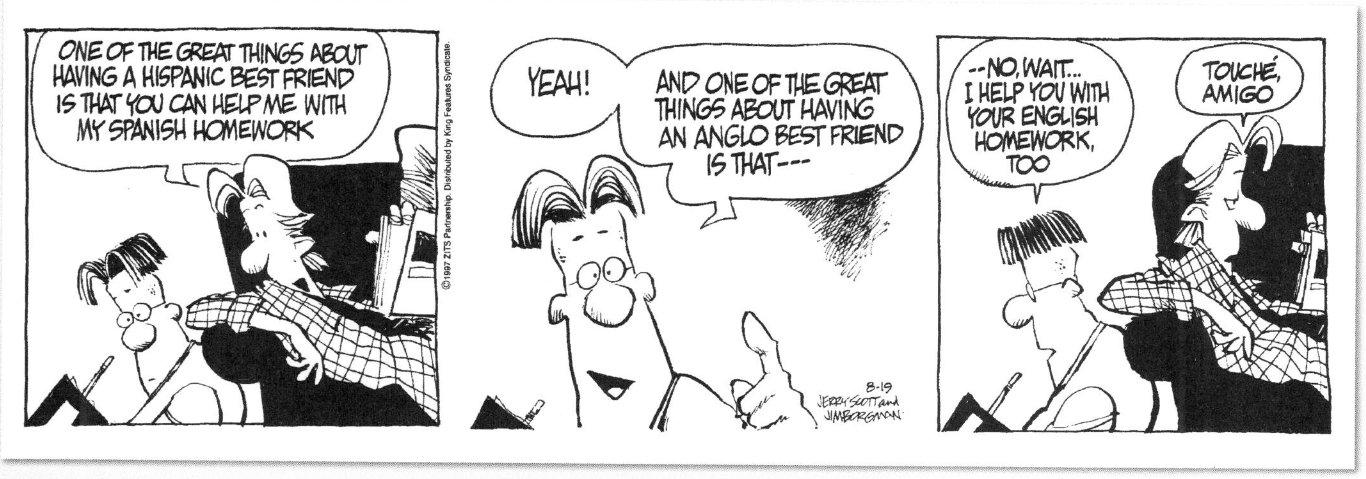

ONE OF THE GREAT THINGS ABOUT HAVING A HISPANIC BEST FRIEND IS THAT YOU CAN HELP ME WITH MY SPANISH HOMEWORK
©1997 ZITS Partnership. Distributed by King Features Syndicate.
YEAH!
AND ONE OF THE GREAT THINGS ABOUT HAVING AN ANGLO BEST FRIEND IS THAT---
8-19 JERRY SCOTT and JIMBORGMAN
--NO, WAIT... I HELP YOU WITH YOUR ENGLISH HOMEWORK, TOO
TOUCHÉ, AMIGO

August 26, 1997

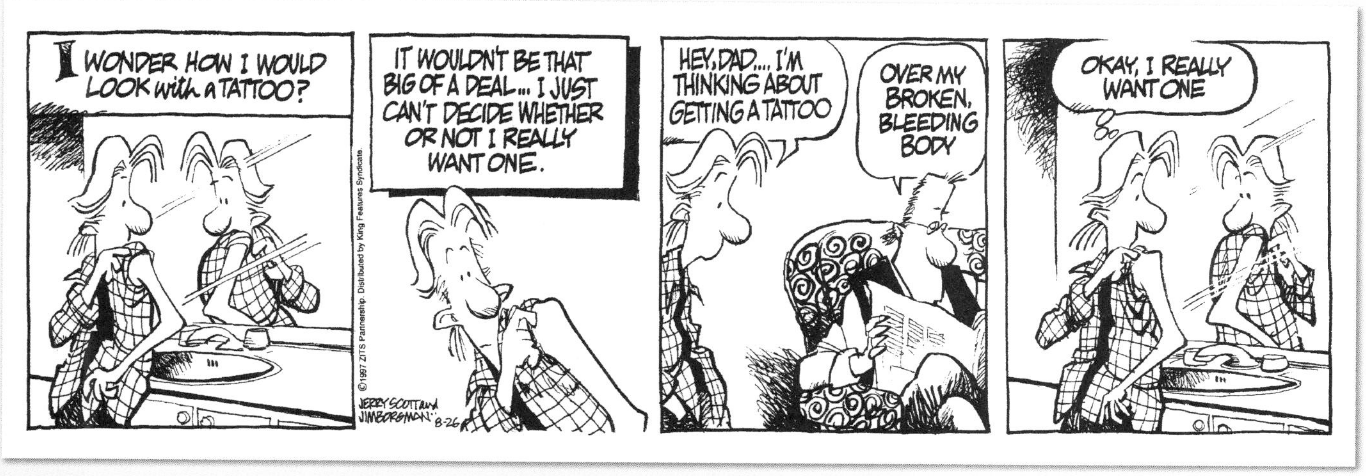

I WONDER HOW I WOULD LOOK with a TATTOO?
©1997 ZITS Partnership. Distributed by King Features Syndicate.
JERRY SCOTT and JIMBORGMAN 8-26
IT WOULDN'T BE THAT BIG OF A DEAL... I JUST CAN'T DECIDE WHETHER OR NOT I REALLY WANT ONE.
HEY, DAD.... I'M THINKING ABOUT GETTING A TATTOO
OVER MY BROKEN, BLEEDING BODY
OKAY, I REALLY WANT ONE

September 12, 1997

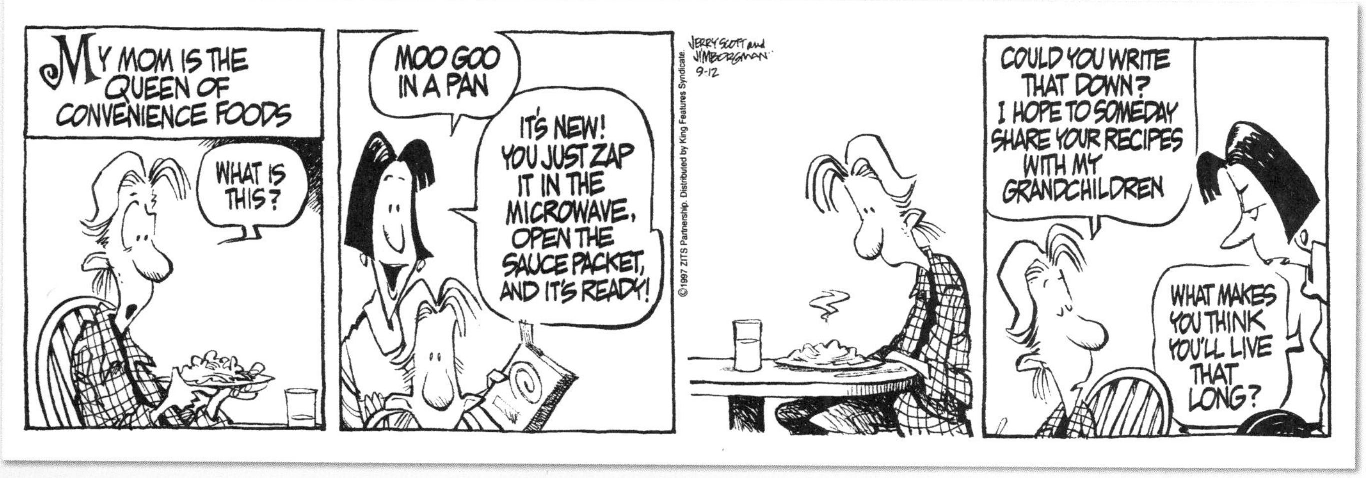

MY MOM IS THE QUEEN OF CONVENIENCE FOODS
WHAT IS THIS?
MOO GOO IN A PAN
IT'S NEW! YOU JUST ZAP IT IN THE MICROWAVE, OPEN THE SAUCE PACKET, AND IT'S READY!
©1997 ZITS Partnership. Distributed by King Features Syndicate.
JERRY SCOTT and JIMBORGMAN 9-12
COULD YOU WRITE THAT DOWN? I HOPE TO SOMEDAY SHARE YOUR RECIPES WITH MY GRANDCHILDREN
WHAT MAKES YOU THINK YOU'LL LIVE THAT LONG?

August 10, 1997

JERRY SCOTT and JIMBORGMAN 8/10
©1997 ZITS Partnership. Distributed by King Features Syndicate.
RING!
HELLO?

December 14, 1997

©1997 ZITS Partnership. Distributed by King Features Syndicate.
GNAW! GULP!
CRUNCH!
SLURP!
WHAT HAPPENED TO THE HO-HOs I BOUGHT YESTERDAY?
ALL I KNOW IS, JEREMY HAD SOME FRIENDS OVER AFTER SCHOOL.
JERRY SCOTT and JIMBORGMAN
12/14

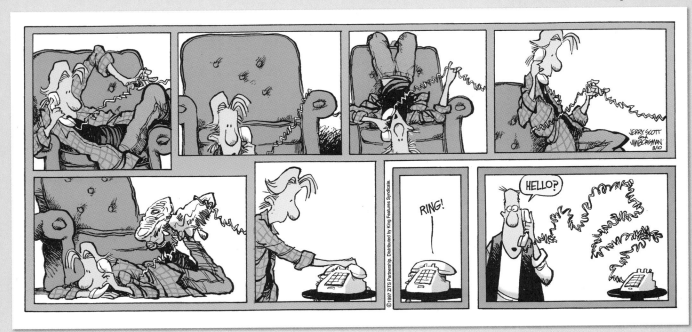

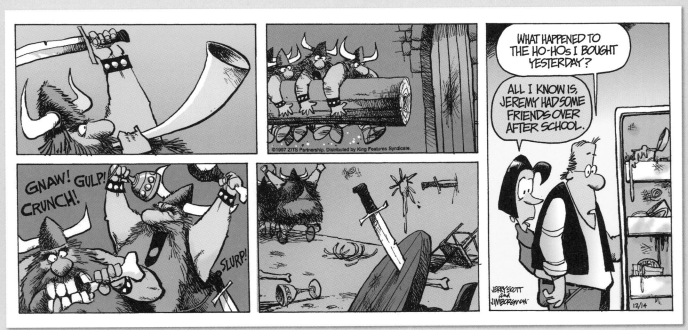

September 26, 1997

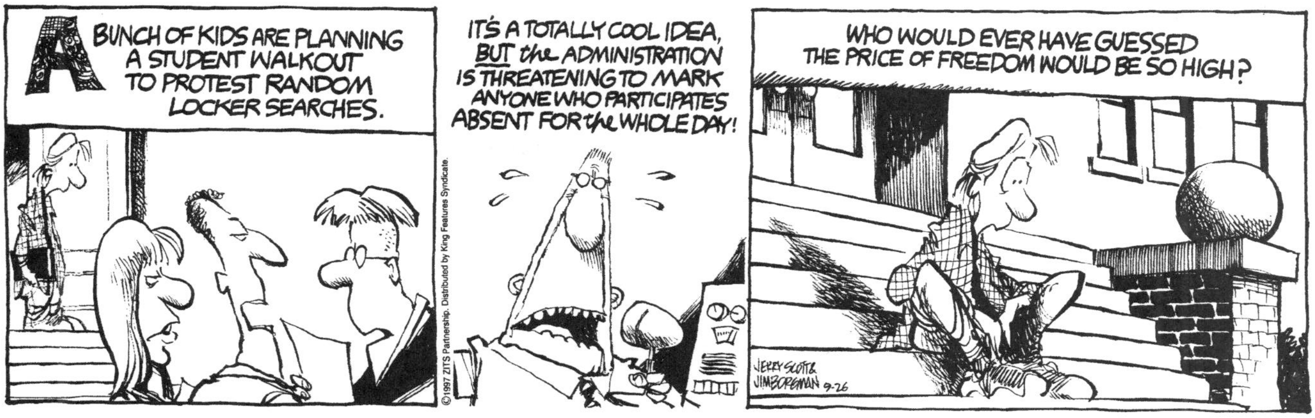
A BUNCH OF KIDS ARE PLANNING A STUDENT WALKOUT TO PROTEST RANDOM LOCKER SEARCHES.
IT'S A TOTALLY COOL IDEA, BUT the ADMINISTRATION IS THREATENING TO MARK ANYONE WHO PARTICIPATES ABSENT FOR the WHOLE DAY!
WHO WOULD EVER HAVE GUESSED THE PRICE OF FREEDOM WOULD BE SO HIGH?
© 1997 ZITS Partnership. Distributed by King Features Syndicate.
JERRY SCOTT & JIMBORGMAN 9-26

October 3, 1997

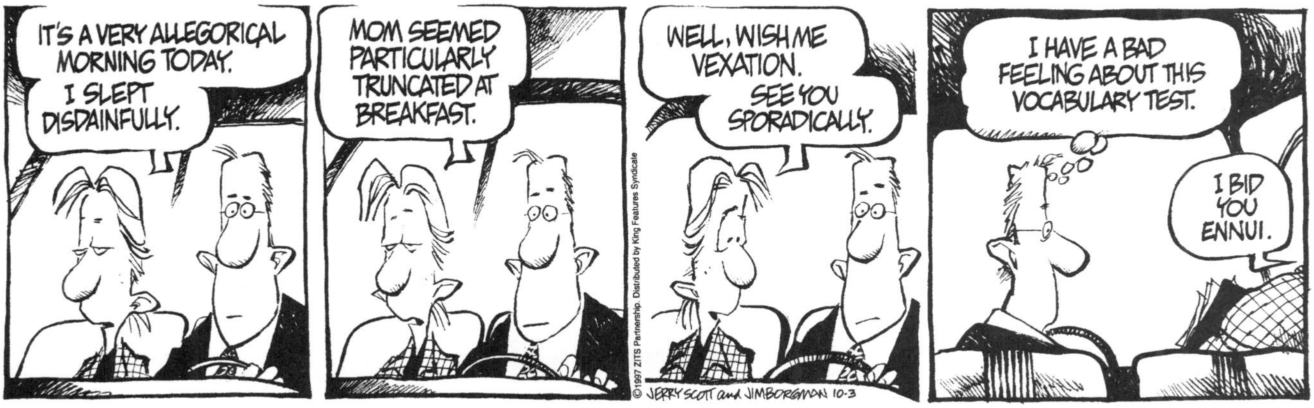
IT'S A VERY ALLEGORICAL MORNING TODAY. I SLEPT DISDAINFULLY.
MOM SEEMED PARTICULARLY TRUNCATED AT BREAKFAST.
WELL, WISH ME VEXATION. SEE YOU SPORADICALLY.
I HAVE A BAD FEELING ABOUT THIS VOCABULARY TEST.
I BID YOU ENNUI.
© 1997 ZITS Partnership. Distributed by King Features Syndicate
JERRY SCOTT and JIMBORGMAN 10-3

October 20, 1997

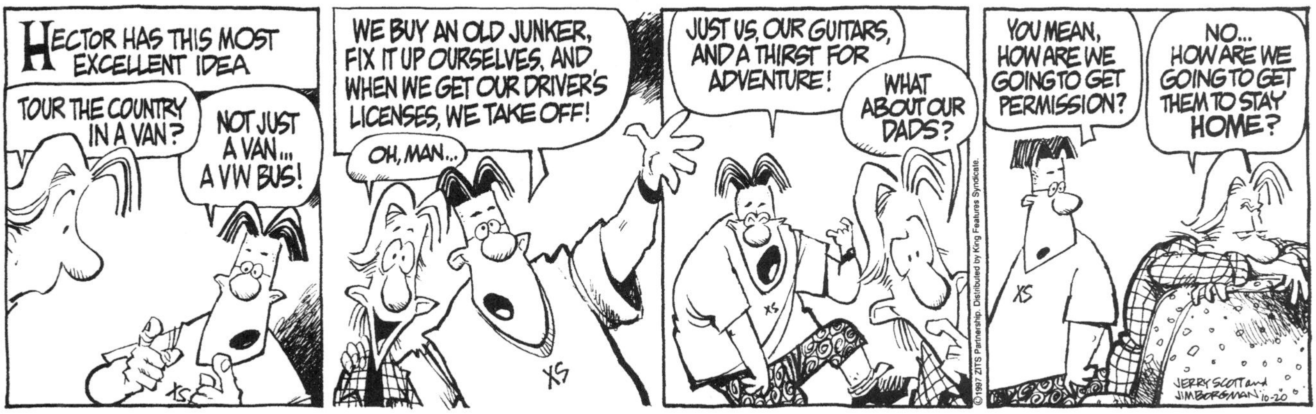
HECTOR HAS THIS MOST EXCELLENT IDEA
TOUR THE COUNTRY IN A VAN?
NOT JUST A VAN... A VW BUS!
WE BUY AN OLD JUNKER, FIX IT UP OURSELVES, AND WHEN WE GET OUR DRIVER'S LICENSES, WE TAKE OFF!
OH, MAN...
JUST US, OUR GUITARS, AND A THIRST FOR ADVENTURE!
WHAT ABOUT OUR DADS?
YOU MEAN, HOW ARE WE GOING TO GET PERMISSION?
NO... HOW ARE WE GOING TO GET THEM TO STAY HOME?
© 1997 ZITS Partnership. Distributed by King Features Syndicate.
JERRY SCOTT and JIMBORGMAN 10-20

November 7, 1997

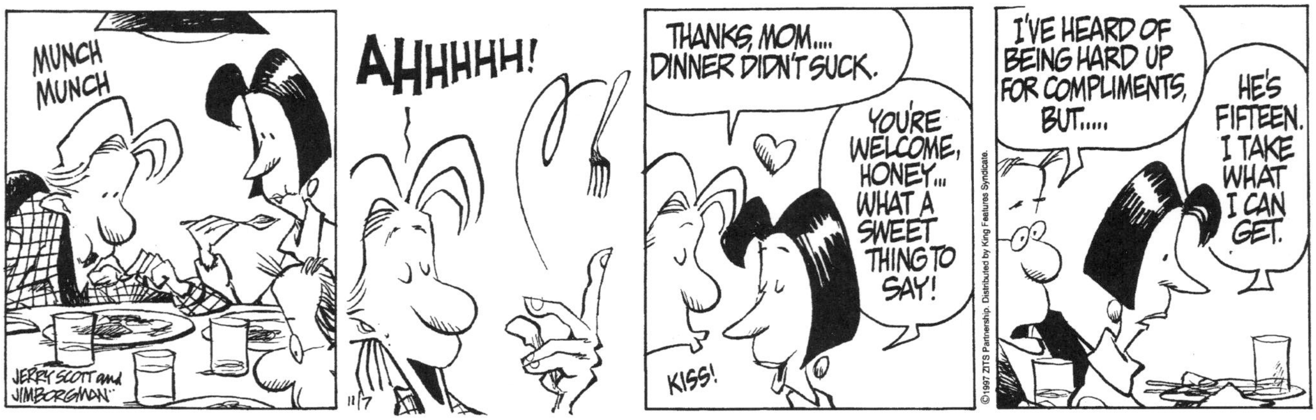
MUNCH MUNCH
JERRY SCOTT and JIM BORGMAN
AHHHHH!
11/7
THANKS, MOM.... DINNER DIDN'T SUCK.
YOU'RE WELCOME, HONEY... WHAT A SWEET THING TO SAY!
KISS!
I'VE HEARD OF BEING HARD UP FOR COMPLIMENTS, BUT.....
HE'S FIFTEEN. I TAKE WHAT I CAN GET.
©1997 ZITS Partnership. Distributed by King Features Syndicate.

December 25, 1997

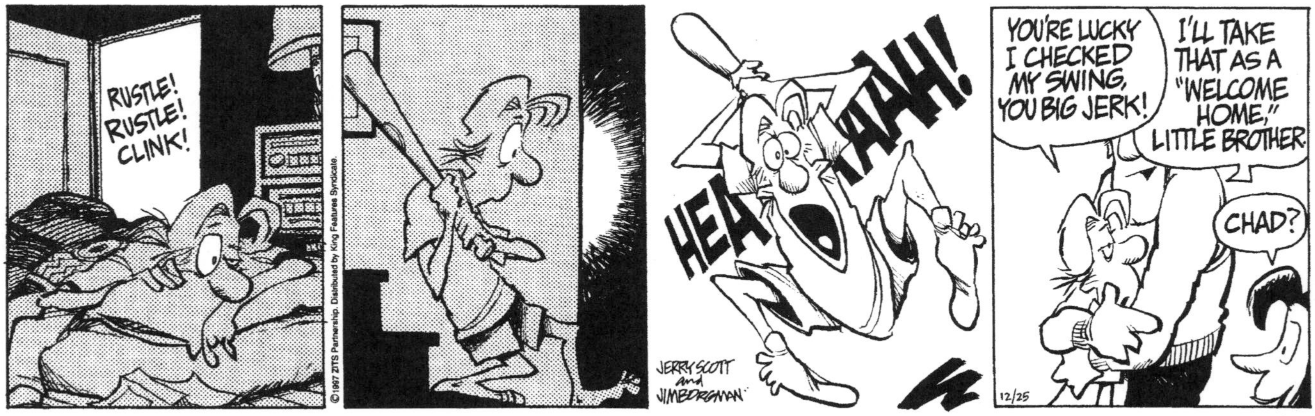
RUSTLE! RUSTLE! CLINK!
©1997 ZITS Partnership. Distributed by King Features Syndicate.
HEAAAAH!
JERRY SCOTT and JIM BORGMAN
YOU'RE LUCKY I CHECKED MY SWING, YOU BIG JERK!
I'LL TAKE THAT AS A "WELCOME HOME," LITTLE BROTHER.
CHAD?
12/25

December 30, 1997

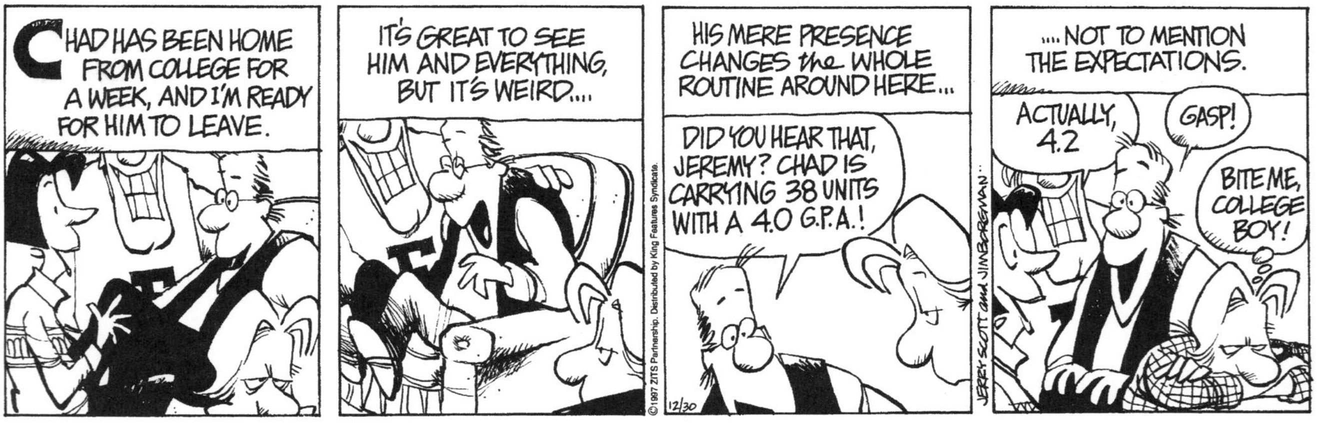
CHAD HAS BEEN HOME FROM COLLEGE FOR A WEEK, AND I'M READY FOR HIM TO LEAVE.
IT'S GREAT TO SEE HIM AND EVERYTHING, BUT IT'S WEIRD....
©1997 ZITS Partnership. Distributed by King Features Syndicate.
HIS MERE PRESENCE CHANGES the WHOLE ROUTINE AROUND HERE...
DID YOU HEAR THAT, JEREMY? CHAD IS CARRYING 38 UNITS WITH A 4.0 G.P.A.!
12/30
....NOT TO MENTION THE EXPECTATIONS.
ACTUALLY, 4.2
GASP!
BITE ME, COLLEGE BOY!
JERRY SCOTT and JIM BORGMAN

Jeremy's House

Jim Borgman

As Jerry and I began to wrap our minds around the world we were creating in *Zits*, there were a lot of questions to answer. Where do these characters live? What sort of school do Jeremy and his friends attend? What does his house look like? Should we identify these things or leave them vague?

Cartoonists have supplied varying degrees of detail in their comic strips. After all these years, do we know anything about Dagwood's work besides the desk where he naps? *Peanuts* barely nodded to the entire adult world. On the other hand, longtime readers could probably draw a detailed blueprint of the Pattersons' house in *For Better or For Worse*.

I naturally draw with a lot of detail, so I needed to have a pretty good idea of what Jeremy's world looked like. We decided the Duncans live in the Midwest, where seasons change, and Jeremy goes to a big public high school, somewhere in or around Cincinnati, where I've lived most of my life. I would have no trouble, then, fleshing out almost any scene. Most of these specifics can go unsaid, leaving readers to see their own lives in *Zits*, but they have to be fairly clear in our heads.

On the other hand, we also believe in an elastic cartoon universe, and things can stretch to accommodate the needs of any given idea. Jeremy's room, for example, contains these elements: a mattress on the floor, a puffy quilt, a window with the blinds askew that leads out to a roof he hangs out on, a dresser with clothes draped over it, a heaping laundry basket, some band posters on the walls, boxes containing half-eaten pizzas, and nine cubic yards of other crap strewn about. I've never quite figured out where all of these things are in relation to each other. They move about according to the needs of that day's idea. But his room is immediately identifiable nonetheless.

On a brainstorming visit to my home in Cincinnati early on, Jerry and I rode bikes through the suburb of Wyoming. We came upon a certain house that just had the right feel. I made these drawings in my sketchbook, and they became the loose model for the Duncans' home.

Not sure about that igloo, though.

January 11, 1998

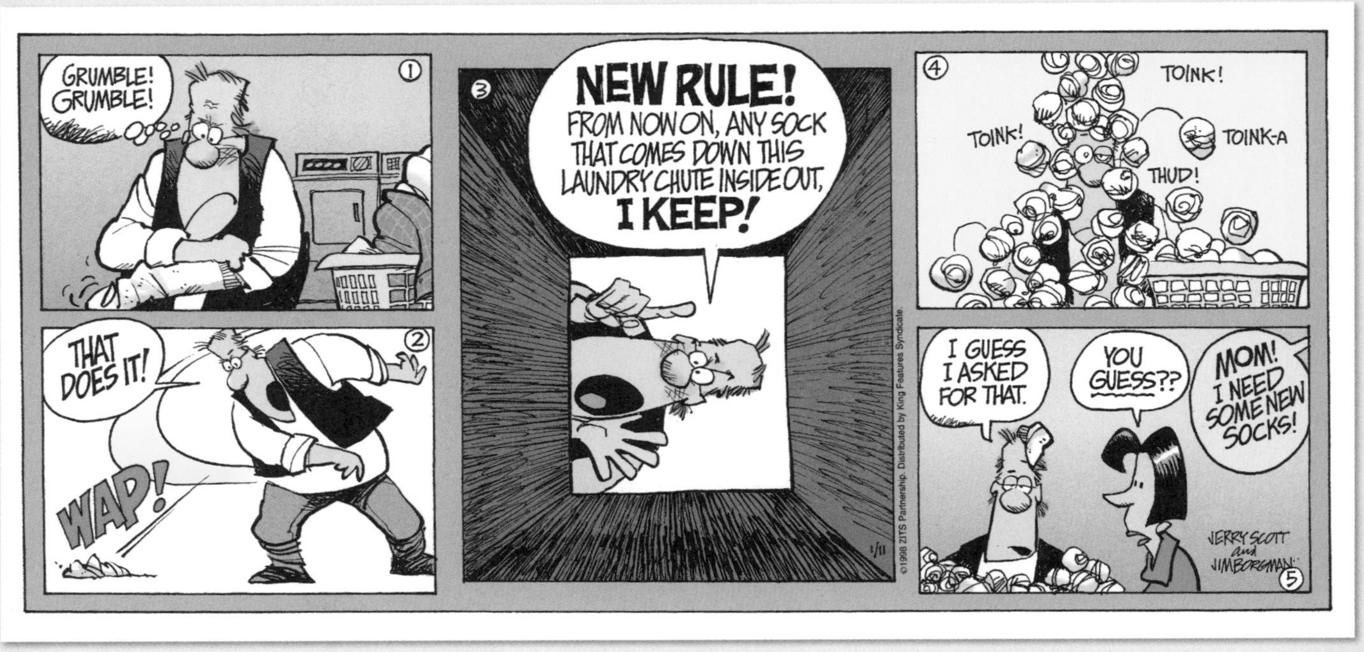
GRUMBLE! GRUMBLE!
THAT DOES IT!
WAP!
NEW RULE! FROM NOW ON, ANY SOCK THAT COMES DOWN THIS LAUNDRY CHUTE INSIDE OUT, I KEEP!
TOINK!
TOINK!
TOINK-A
THUD!
I GUESS I ASKED FOR THAT.
YOU GUESS??
MOM! I NEED SOME NEW SOCKS!
JERRY SCOTT and JIM BORGMAN
©1998 ZITS Partnership. Distributed by King Features Syndicate.

January 18, 1998

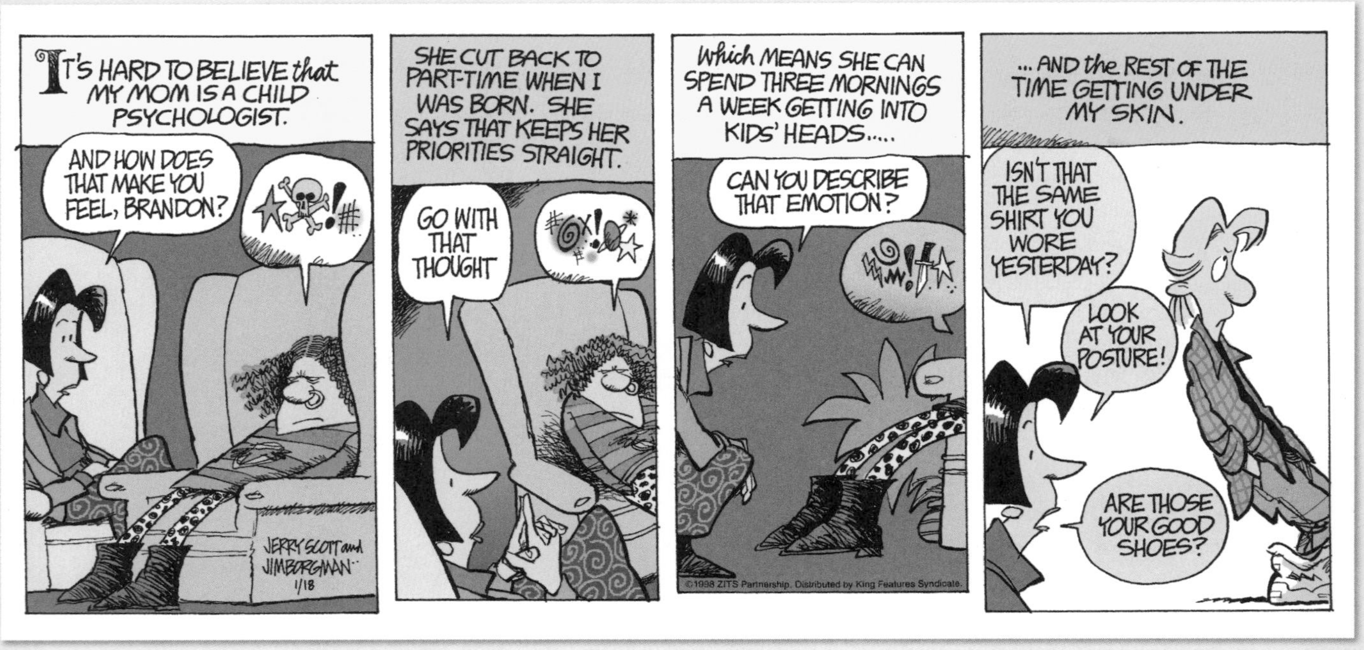
IT'S HARD TO BELIEVE that MY MOM IS A CHILD PSYCHOLOGIST.
AND HOW DOES THAT MAKE YOU FEEL, BRANDON?
SHE CUT BACK TO PART-TIME WHEN I WAS BORN. SHE SAYS THAT KEEPS HER PRIORITIES STRAIGHT.
GO WITH THAT THOUGHT
Which MEANS SHE CAN SPEND THREE MORNINGS A WEEK GETTING INTO KIDS' HEADS.....
CAN YOU DESCRIBE THAT EMOTION?
... AND the REST OF THE TIME GETTING UNDER MY SKIN.
ISN'T THAT THE SAME SHIRT YOU WORE YESTERDAY?
LOOK AT YOUR POSTURE!
ARE THOSE YOUR GOOD SHOES?
JERRY SCOTT and JIM BORGMAN 1/18
©1998 ZITS Partnership. Distributed by King Features Syndicate.

February 16, 1998

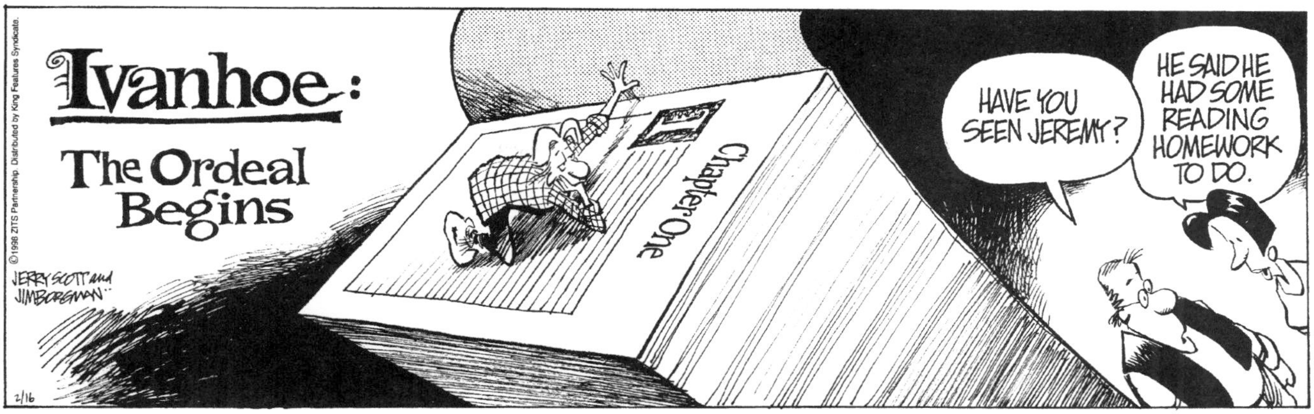
Ivanhoe:
The Ordeal Begins
Chapter One
HAVE YOU SEEN JEREMY?
HE SAID HE HAD SOME READING HOMEWORK TO DO.
JERRY SCOTT and JIM BORGMAN
©1998 ZITS Partnership. Distributed by King Features Syndicate.

February 18, 1998

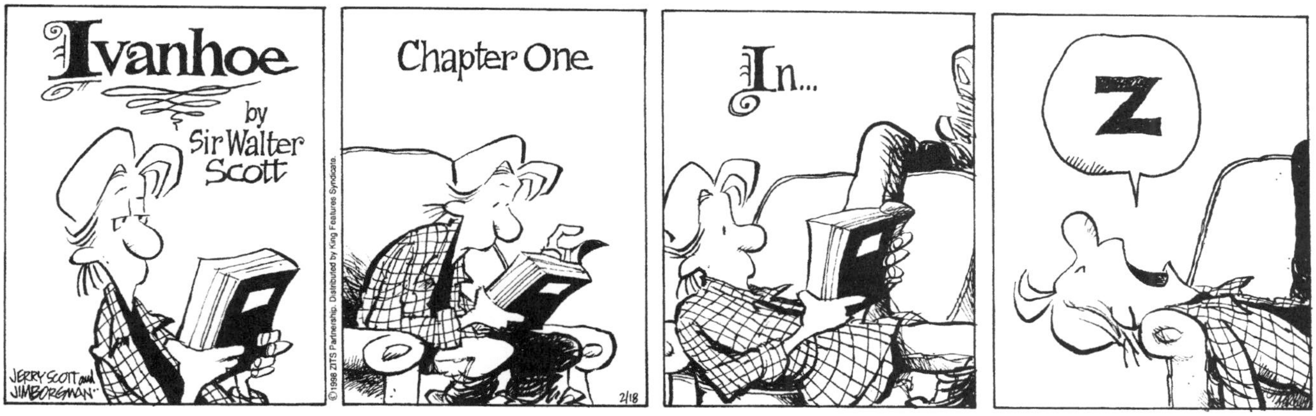
Ivanhoe
by Sir Walter Scott
Chapter One
In...
Z
JERRY SCOTT and JIM BORGMAN
©1998 ZITS Partnership. Distributed by King Features Syndicate.

February 20, 1998

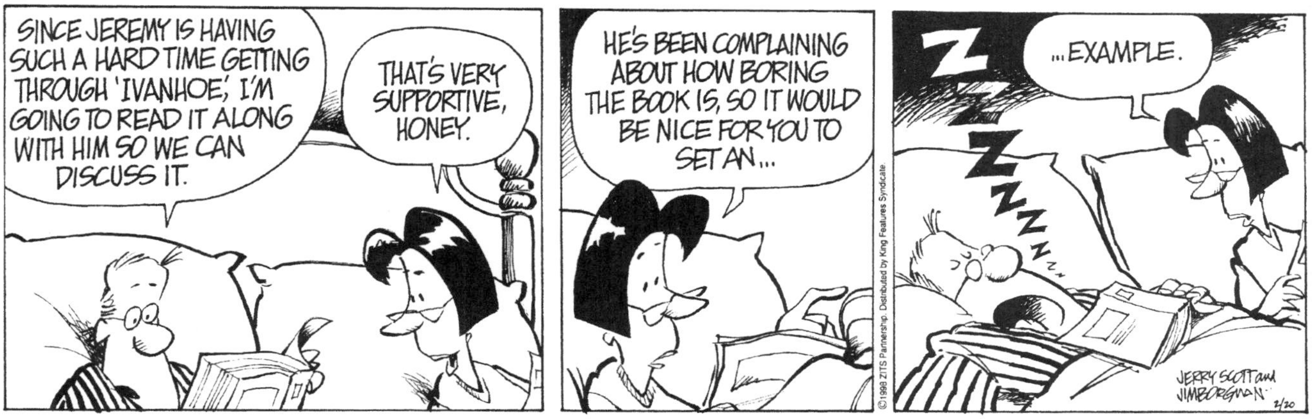
SINCE JEREMY IS HAVING SUCH A HARD TIME GETTING THROUGH 'IVANHOE,' I'M GOING TO READ IT ALONG WITH HIM SO WE CAN DISCUSS IT.
THAT'S VERY SUPPORTIVE, HONEY.
HE'S BEEN COMPLAINING ABOUT HOW BORING THE BOOK IS, SO IT WOULD BE NICE FOR YOU TO SET AN...
ZZZZZZ
...EXAMPLE.
JERRY SCOTT and JIM BORGMAN
©1998 ZITS Partnership. Distributed by King Features Syndicate.

April 6, 1998

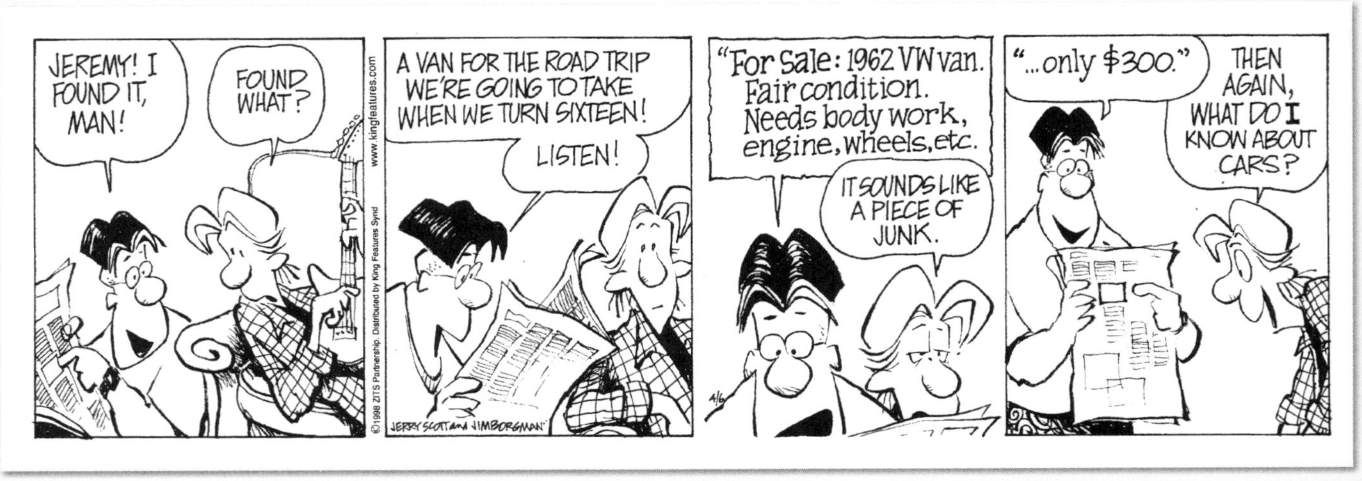
JEREMY! I FOUND IT, MAN!
FOUND WHAT?
©1998 ZITS Partnership. Distributed by King Features Synd
www.kingfeatures.com
A VAN FOR THE ROAD TRIP WE'RE GOING TO TAKE WHEN WE TURN SIXTEEN!
LISTEN!
JERRY SCOTT and JIM BORGMAN
"For Sale: 1962 VW van. Fair condition. Needs body work, engine, wheels, etc.
IT SOUNDS LIKE A PIECE OF JUNK.
4/6
"...only $300."
THEN AGAIN, WHAT DO I KNOW ABOUT CARS?

April 11, 1998

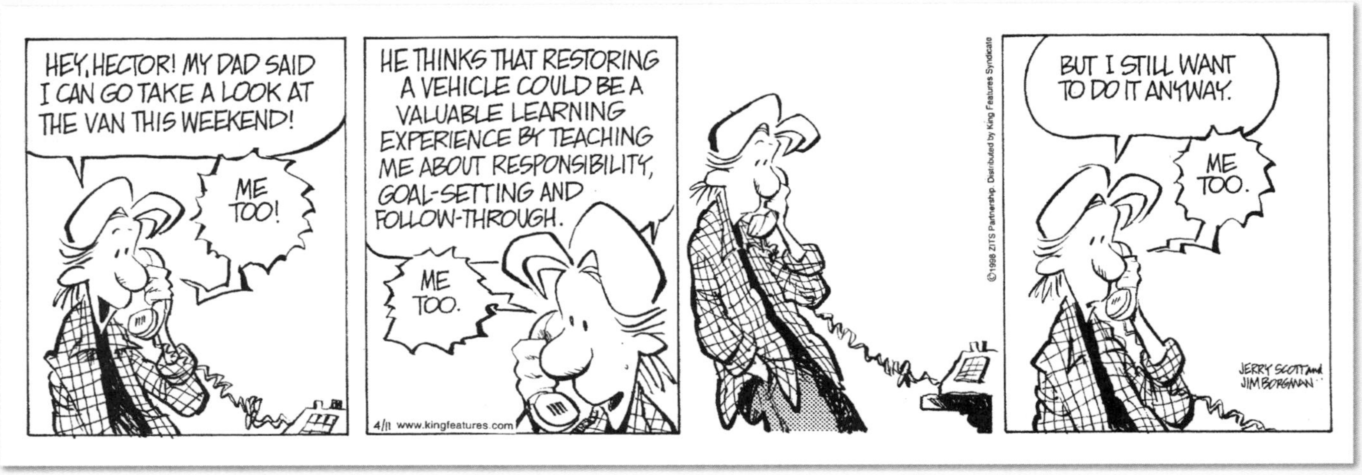
HEY, HECTOR! MY DAD SAID I CAN GO TAKE A LOOK AT THE VAN THIS WEEKEND!
ME TOO!
HE THINKS THAT RESTORING A VEHICLE COULD BE A VALUABLE LEARNING EXPERIENCE BY TEACHING ME ABOUT RESPONSIBILITY, GOAL-SETTING AND FOLLOW-THROUGH.
ME TOO.
4/11 www.kingfeatures.com
©1998 ZITS Partnership. Distributed by King Features Syndicate
BUT I STILL WANT TO DO IT ANYWAY.
ME TOO.
JERRY SCOTT and JIM BORGMAN

April 14, 1998

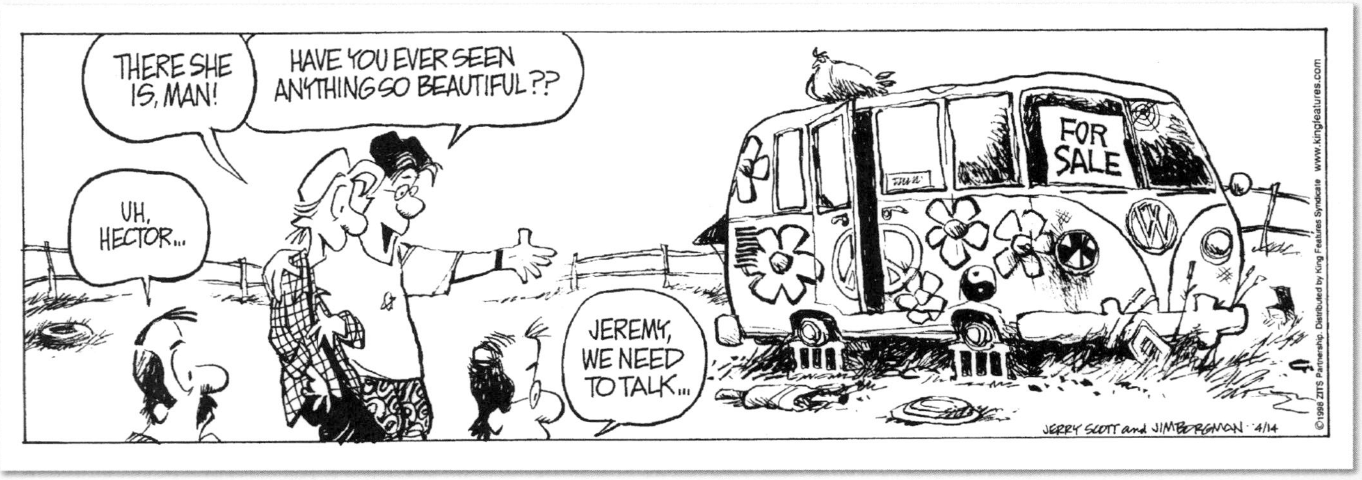
THERE SHE IS, MAN!
HAVE YOU EVER SEEN ANYTHING SO BEAUTIFUL??
UH, HECTOR...
JEREMY, WE NEED TO TALK...
FOR SALE
JERRY SCOTT and JIM BORGMAN 4/14
©1998 ZITS Partnership. Distributed by King Features Syndicate www.kingfeatures.com

April 16, 1998

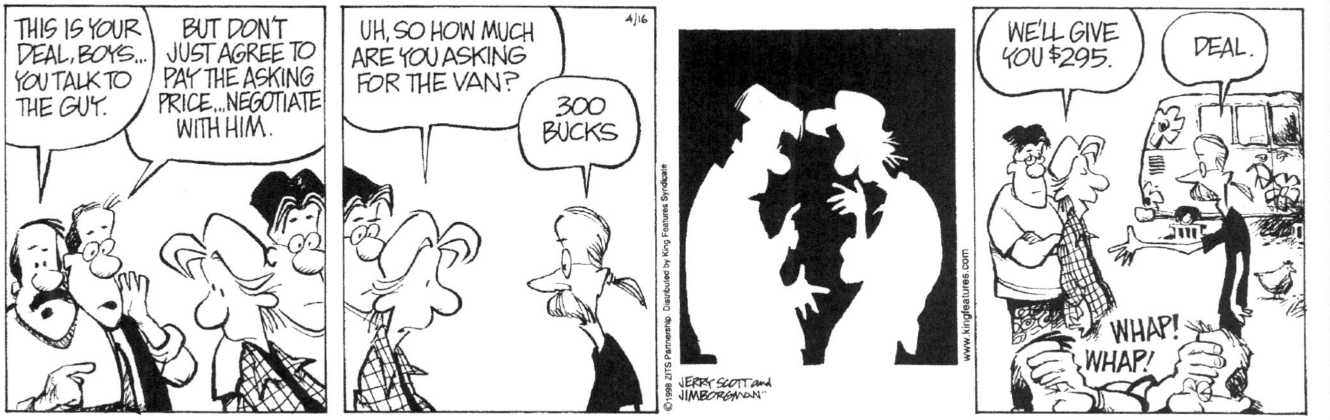

THIS IS YOUR DEAL, BOYS... YOU TALK TO THE GUY.
BUT DON'T JUST AGREE TO PAY THE ASKING PRICE...NEGOTIATE WITH HIM.
UH, SO HOW MUCH ARE YOU ASKING FOR THE VAN?
300 BUCKS
WE'LL GIVE YOU $295.
DEAL.
WHAP! WHAP!
©1998 ZITS Partnership. Distributed by King Features Syndicate
JERRY SCOTT and JIM BORGMAN
www.kingfeatures.com

May 6, 1998

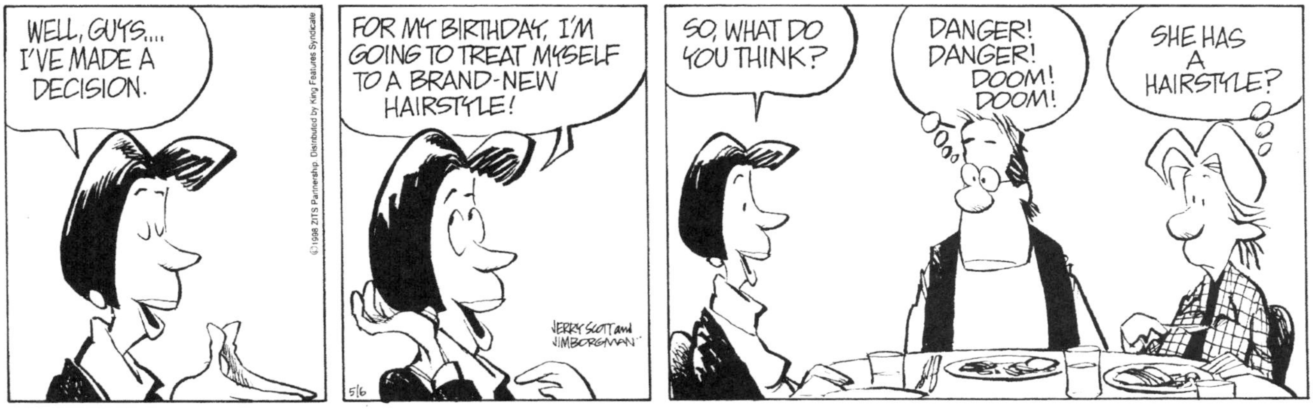

WELL, GUYS.... I'VE MADE A DECISION.
FOR MY BIRTHDAY, I'M GOING TO TREAT MYSELF TO A BRAND-NEW HAIRSTYLE!
SO, WHAT DO YOU THINK?
DANGER! DANGER! DOOM! DOOM!
SHE HAS A HAIRSTYLE?
©1998 ZITS Partnership. Distributed by King Features Syndicate
JERRY SCOTT and JIM BORGMAN

June 17, 1998

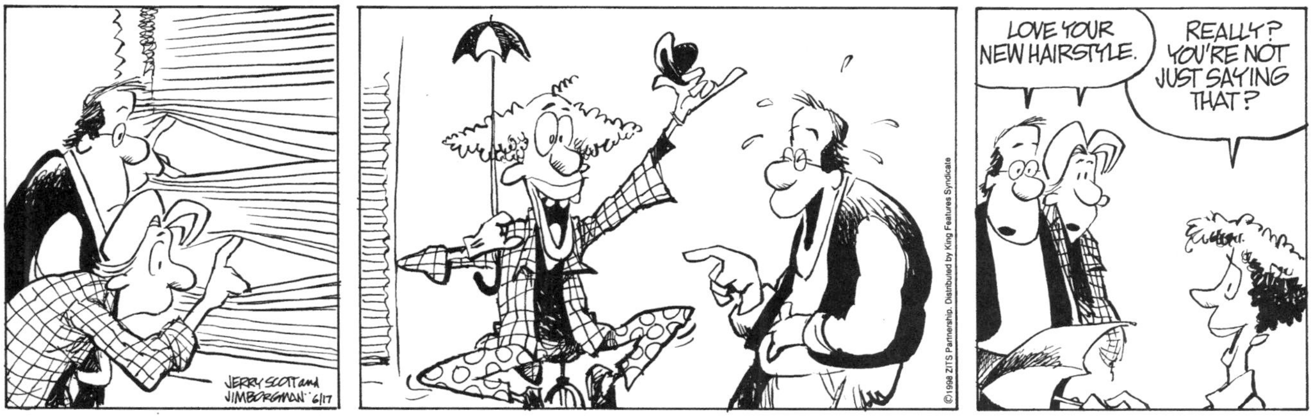

LOVE YOUR NEW HAIRSTYLE.
REALLY? YOU'RE NOT JUST SAYING THAT?
JERRY SCOTT and JIM BORGMAN
©1998 ZITS Partnership. Distributed by King Features Syndicate

June 10, 1998

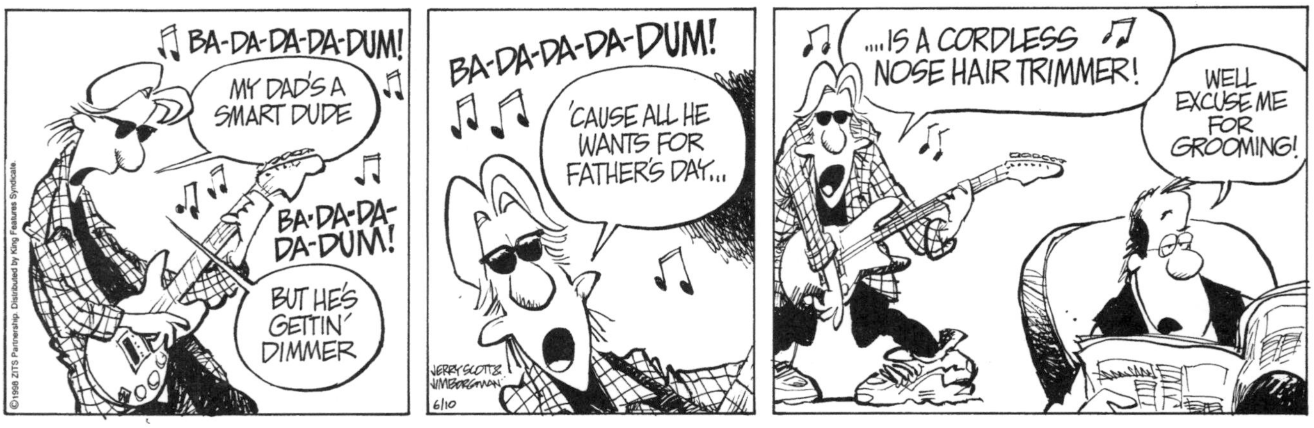
BA-DA-DA-DA-DUM!
MY DAD'S A SMART DUDE
BA-DA-DA-DA-DUM!
BUT HE'S GETTIN' DIMMER
©1998 ZITS Partnership. Distributed by King Features Syndicate.
BA-DA-DA-DA-DUM!
'CAUSE ALL HE WANTS FOR FATHER'S DAY...
JERRY SCOTT & JIM BORGMAN 6/10
....IS A CORDLESS NOSE HAIR TRIMMER!
WELL EXCUSE ME FOR GROOMING!

January 23, 1998

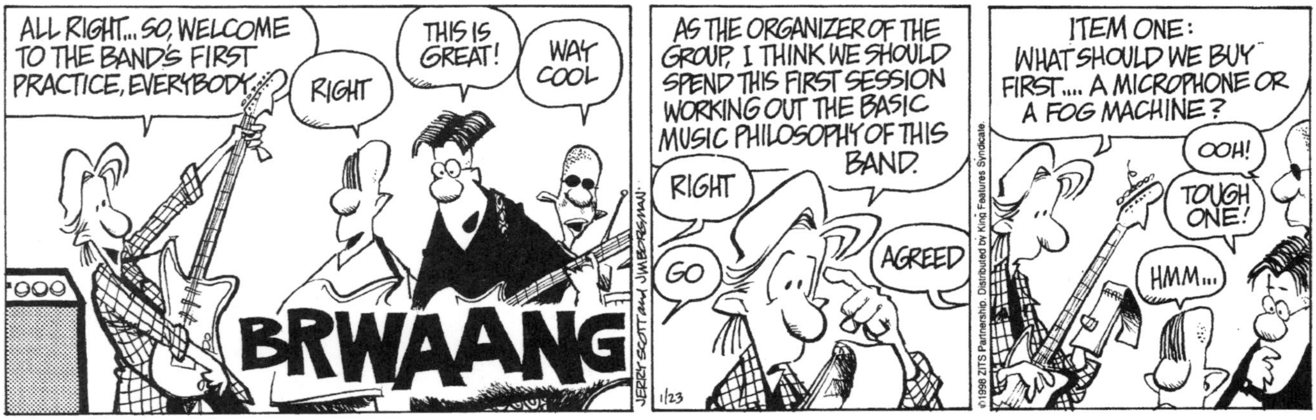
ALL RIGHT... SO, WELCOME TO THE BAND'S FIRST PRACTICE, EVERYBODY.
RIGHT
THIS IS GREAT!
WAY COOL
BRWAANG
JERRY SCOTT and JIM BORGMAN 1/23
AS THE ORGANIZER OF THE GROUP, I THINK WE SHOULD SPEND THIS FIRST SESSION WORKING OUT THE BASIC MUSIC PHILOSOPHY OF THIS BAND.
RIGHT
GO
AGREED
©1998 ZITS Partnership. Distributed by King Features Syndicate.
ITEM ONE: WHAT SHOULD WE BUY FIRST.... A MICROPHONE OR A FOG MACHINE?
OOH!
TOUGH ONE!
HMM...

August 5, 1998

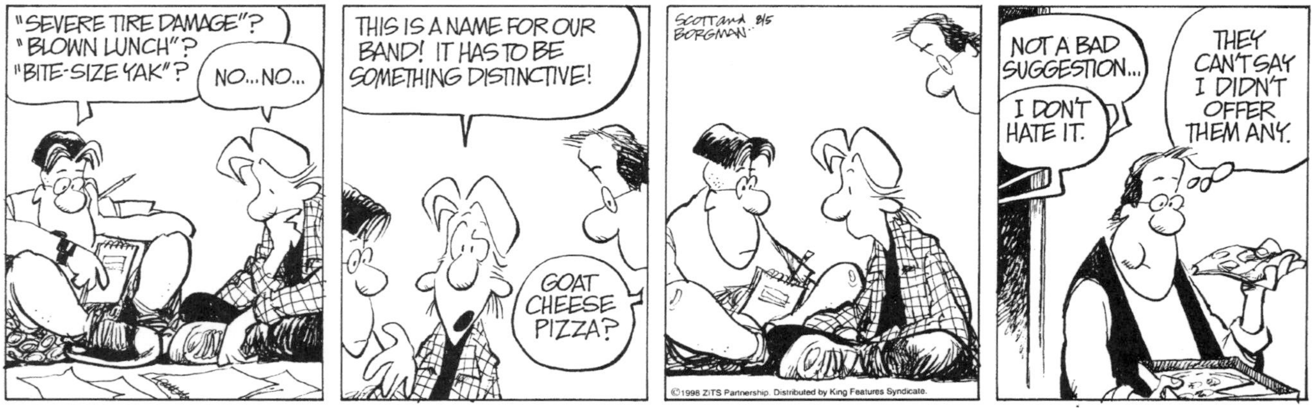
"SEVERE TIRE DAMAGE"? "BLOWN LUNCH"? "BITE-SIZE YAK"?
NO...NO...
THIS IS A NAME FOR OUR BAND! IT HAS TO BE SOMETHING DISTINCTIVE!
GOAT CHEESE PIZZA?
SCOTT and BORGMAN 8/5
©1998 ZITS Partnership. Distributed by King Features Syndicate.
NOT A BAD SUGGESTION...
I DON'T HATE IT.
THEY CAN'T SAY I DIDN'T OFFER THEM ANY.

June 21, 1998

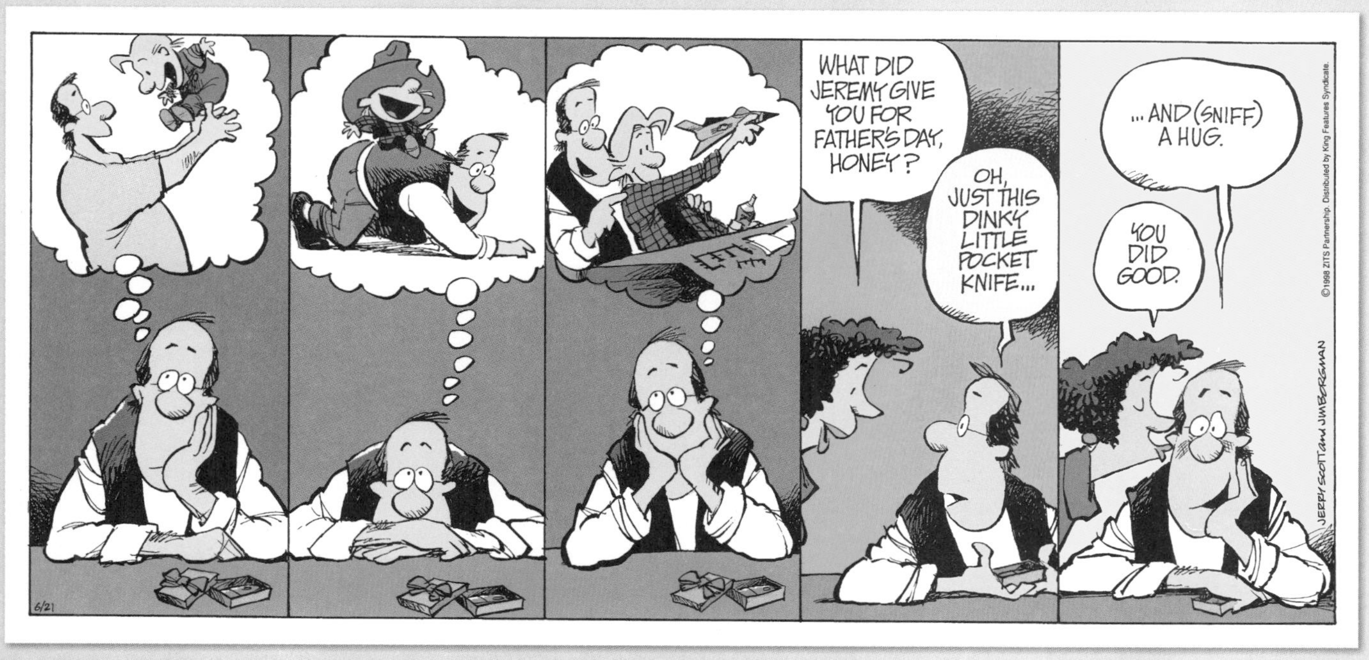
WHAT DID JEREMY GIVE YOU FOR FATHER'S DAY, HONEY?
OH, JUST THIS DINKY LITTLE POCKET KNIFE...
...AND (SNIFF) A HUG.
YOU DID GOOD.
6/21
JERRY SCOTT and JIMBORGMAN
©1998 ZITS Partnership. Distributed by King Features Syndicate.

August 16, 1998

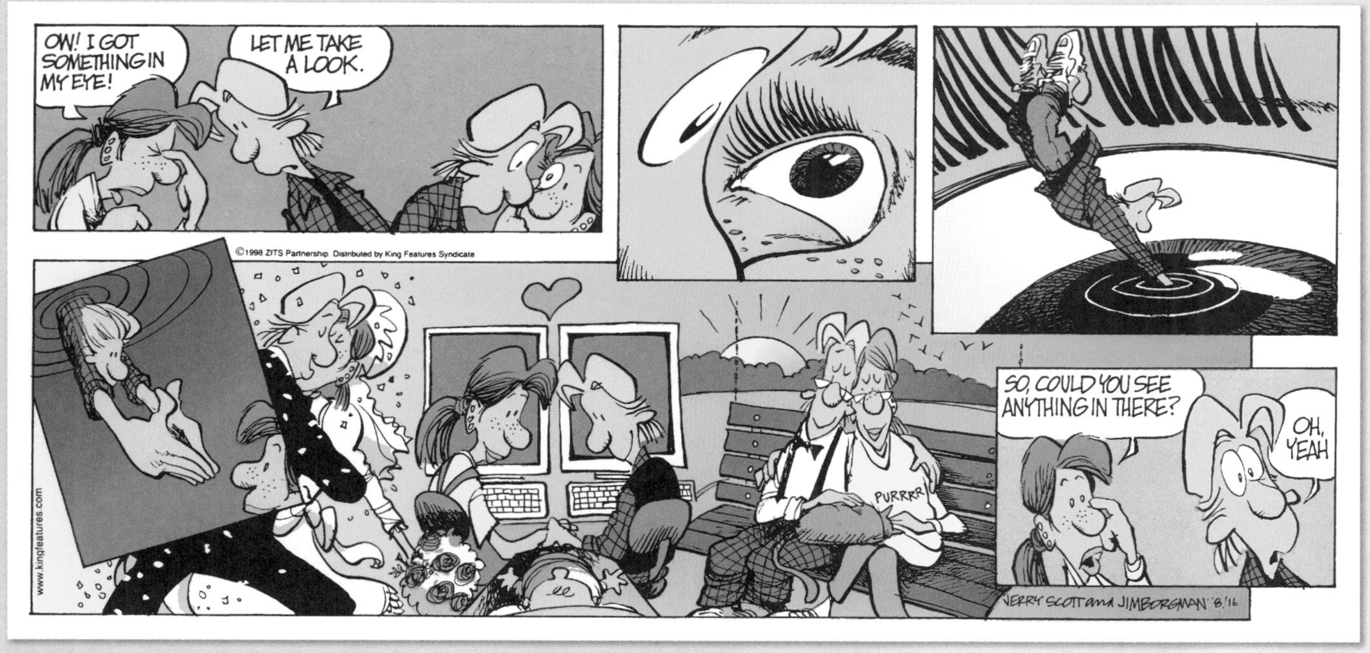
OW! I GOT SOMETHING IN MY EYE!
LET ME TAKE A LOOK.
©1998 ZITS Partnership. Distributed by King Features Syndicate
PURRRR
SO, COULD YOU SEE ANYTHING IN THERE?
OH, YEAH
JERRY SCOTT and JIMBORGMAN '8'16
www.kingfeatures.com

August 27, 1998

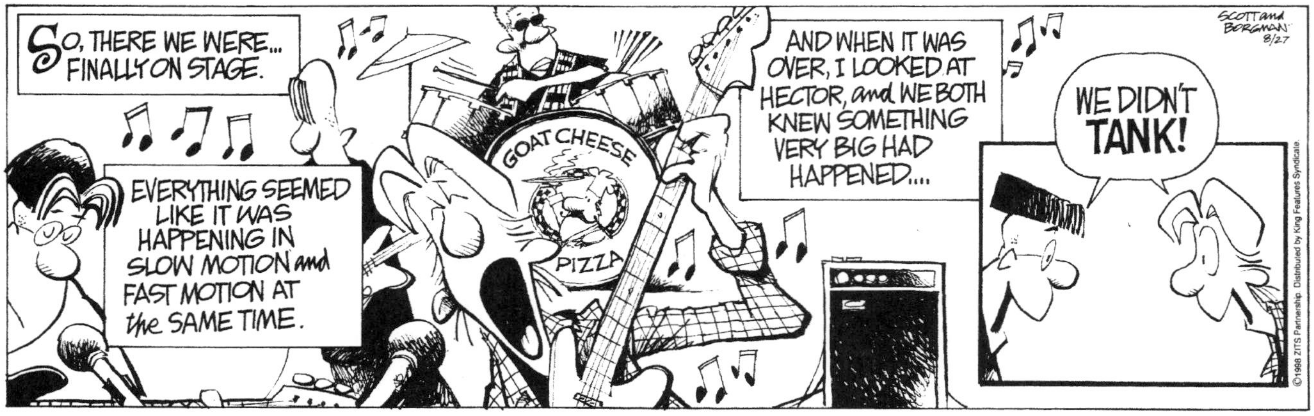
SO, THERE WE WERE... FINALLY ON STAGE.
EVERYTHING SEEMED LIKE IT WAS HAPPENING IN SLOW MOTION and FAST MOTION AT the SAME TIME.
GOAT CHEESE PIZZA
AND WHEN IT WAS OVER, I LOOKED AT HECTOR, and WE BOTH KNEW SOMETHING VERY BIG HAD HAPPENED....
WE DIDN'T TANK!
SCOTT and BORGMAN 8/27
©1998 ZITS Partnership. Distributed by King Features Syndicate.

August 28, 1998

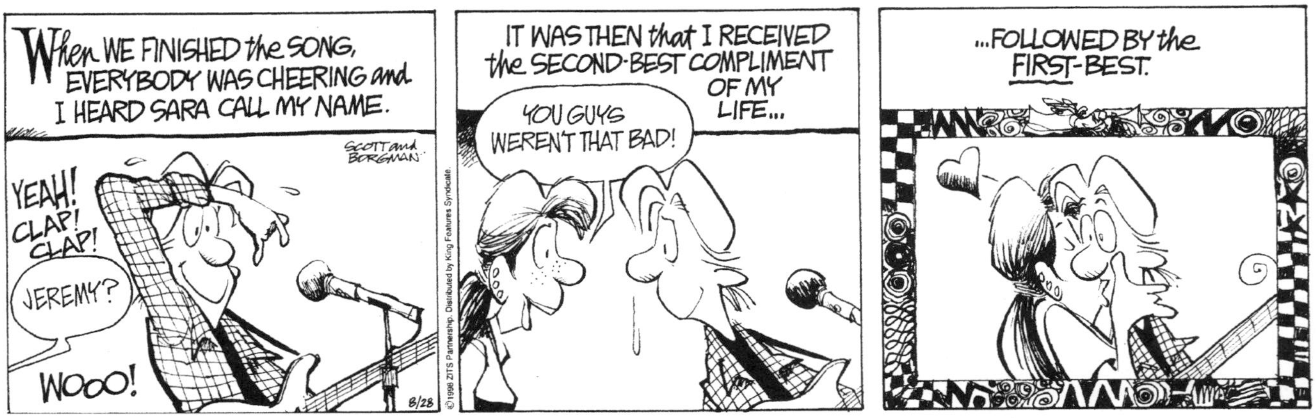
When WE FINISHED the SONG, EVERYBODY WAS CHEERING and I HEARD SARA CALL MY NAME.
YEAH! CLAP! CLAP!
JEREMY?
WOOO!
SCOTT and BORGMAN 8/28
©1998 ZITS Partnership. Distributed by King Features Syndicate.
IT WAS THEN that I RECEIVED the SECOND-BEST COMPLIMENT OF MY LIFE...
YOU GUYS WEREN'T THAT BAD!
...FOLLOWED BY the FIRST-BEST.

November 10, 1998

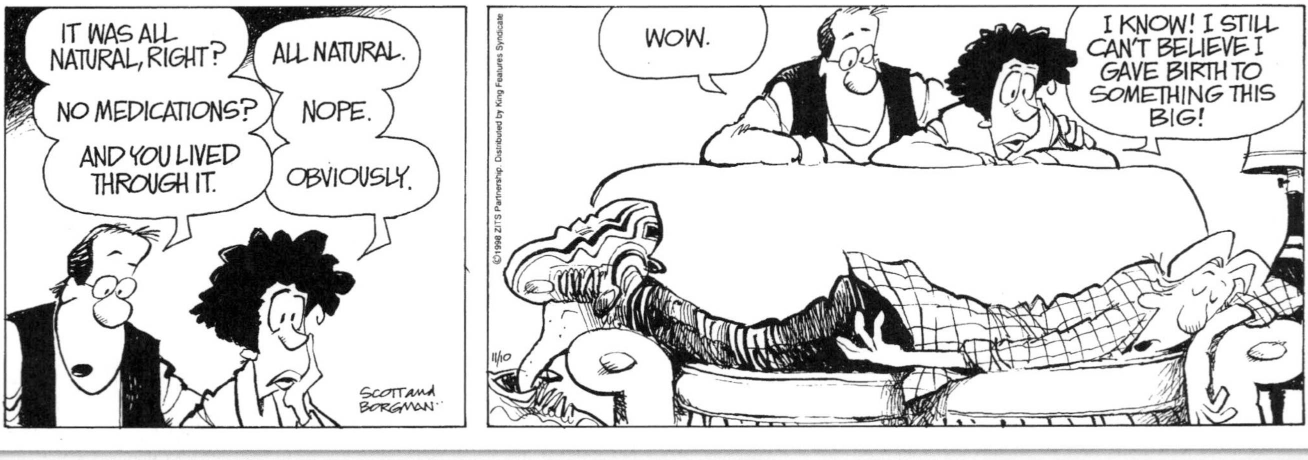
IT WAS ALL NATURAL, RIGHT?
ALL NATURAL.
NO MEDICATIONS?
NOPE.
AND YOU LIVED THROUGH IT.
OBVIOUSLY.
SCOTT and BORGMAN
©1998 ZITS Partnership. Distributed by King Features Syndicate.
WOW.
I KNOW! I STILL CAN'T BELIEVE I GAVE BIRTH TO SOMETHING THIS BIG!
11/10

October 26, 1998

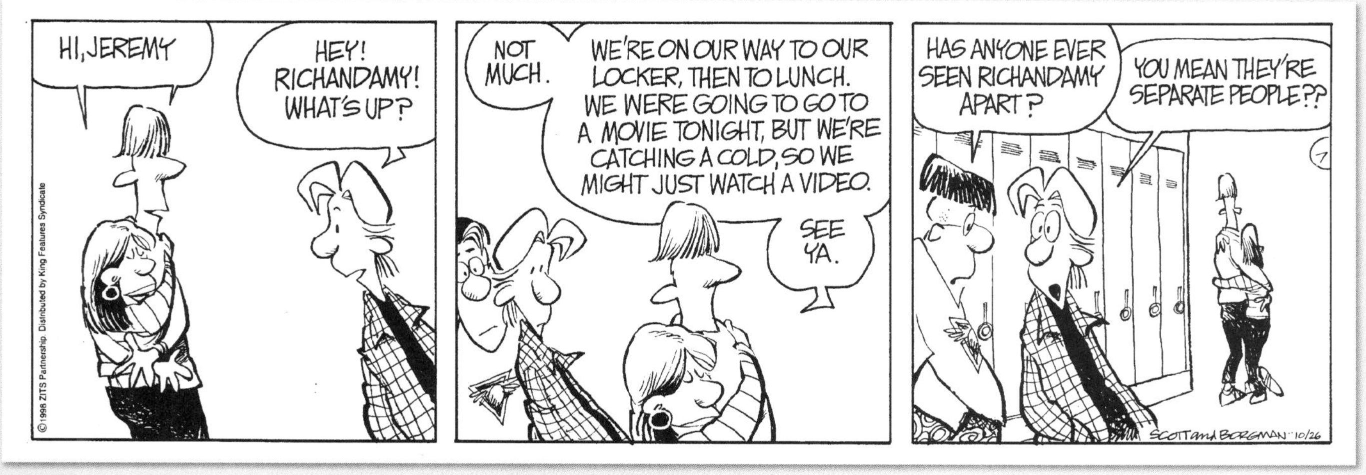

HI, JEREMY
HEY! RICHANDAMY! WHAT'S UP?
NOT MUCH.
WE'RE ON OUR WAY TO OUR LOCKER, THEN TO LUNCH. WE WERE GOING TO GO TO A MOVIE TONIGHT, BUT WE'RE CATCHING A COLD, SO WE MIGHT JUST WATCH A VIDEO.
SEE YA.
HAS ANYONE EVER SEEN RICHANDAMY APART?
YOU MEAN THEY'RE SEPARATE PEOPLE??
© 1998 ZITS Partnership. Distributed by King Features Syndicate
SCOTT and BORGMAN 10/26

October 27, 1998

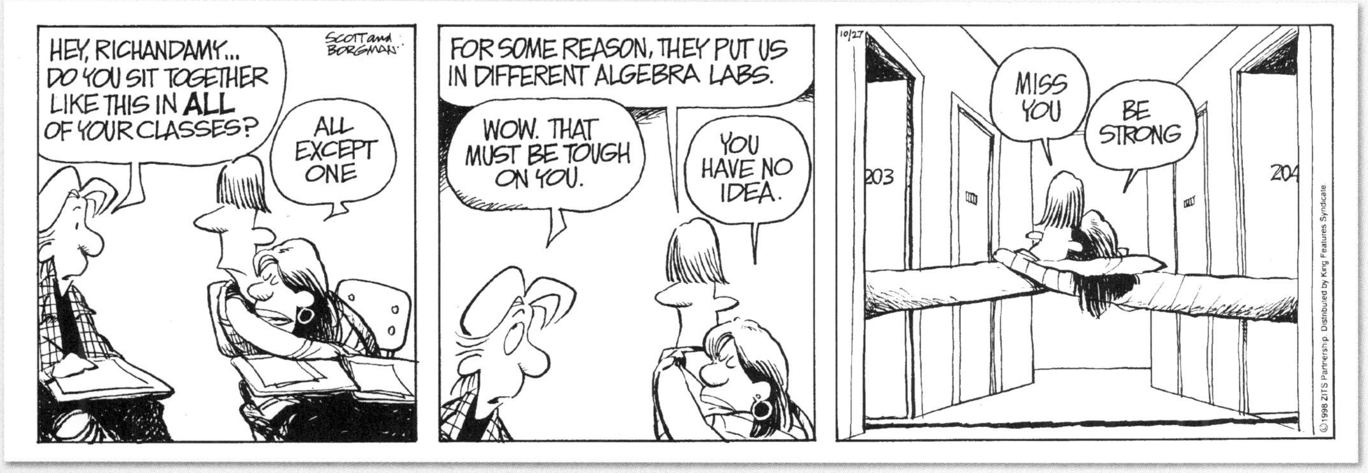

HEY, RICHANDAMY... DO YOU SIT TOGETHER LIKE THIS IN **ALL** OF YOUR CLASSES?
ALL EXCEPT ONE
SCOTT and BORGMAN
FOR SOME REASON, THEY PUT US IN DIFFERENT ALGEBRA LABS.
WOW. THAT MUST BE TOUGH ON YOU.
YOU HAVE NO IDEA.
10/27
MISS YOU
BE STRONG
203
204
© 1998 ZITS Partnership. Distributed by King Features Syndicate.

October 29, 1998

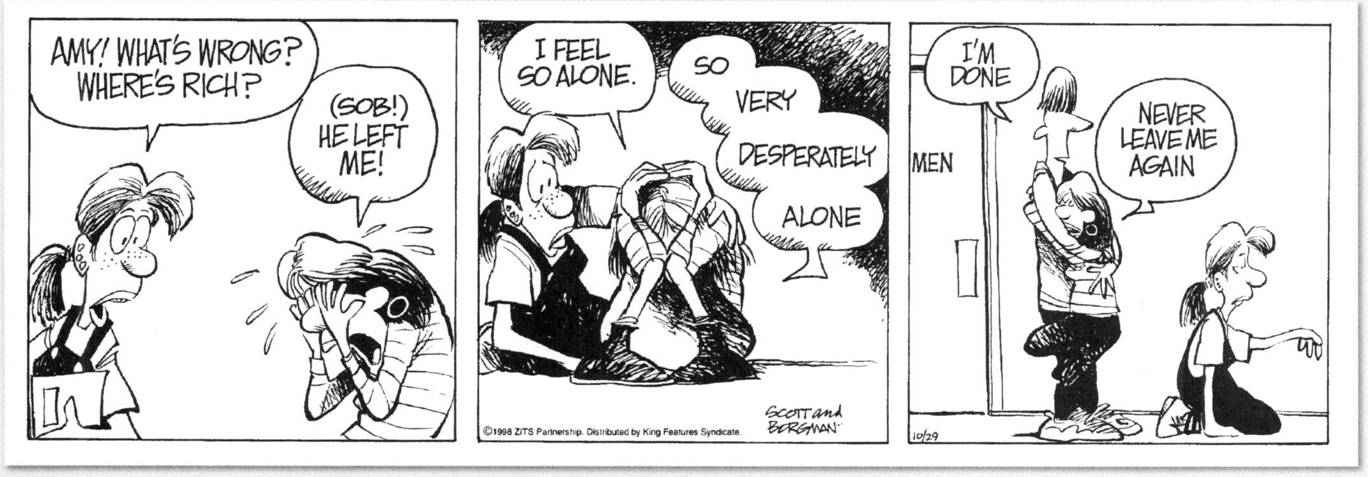

AMY! WHAT'S WRONG? WHERE'S RICH?
(SOB!) HE LEFT ME!
I FEEL SO ALONE.
SO
VERY
DESPERATELY
ALONE
©1998 ZITS Partnership. Distributed by King Features Syndicate.
SCOTT and BORGMAN
I'M DONE
MEN
NEVER LEAVE ME AGAIN
10/29

August 30, 1998

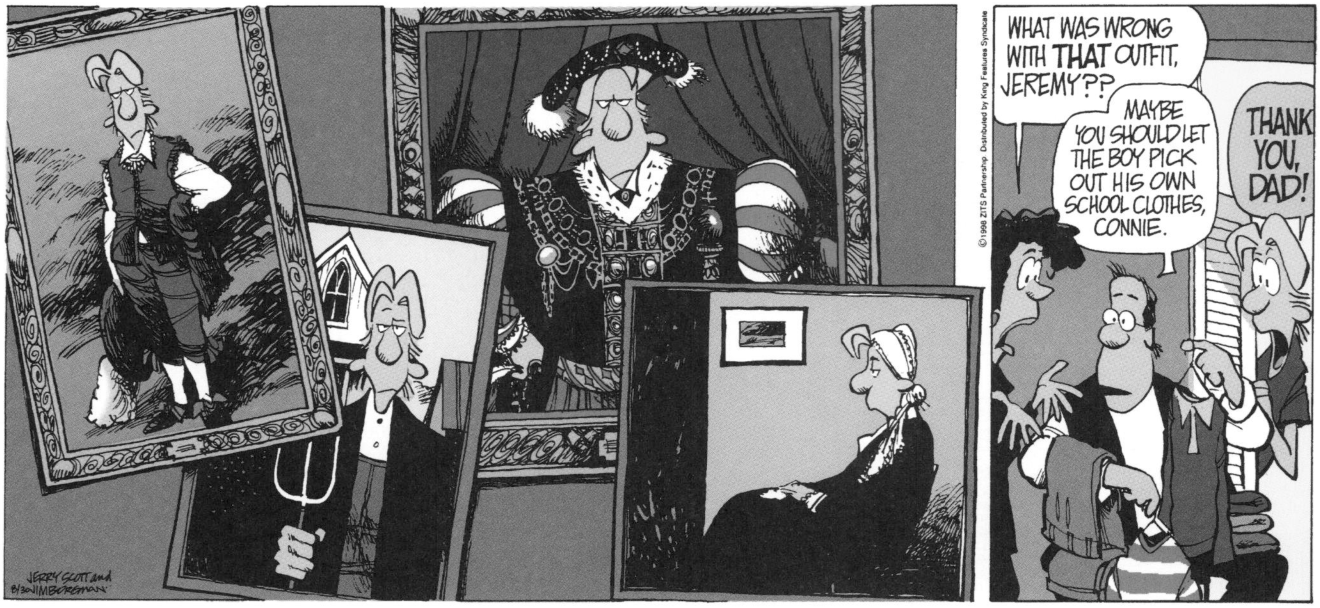
JERRY SCOTT and 8/30 JIM BORGMAN
© 1998 ZITS Partnership. Distributed by King Features Syndicate
WHAT WAS WRONG WITH **THAT** OUTFIT, JEREMY??
MAYBE YOU SHOULD LET THE BOY PICK OUT HIS OWN SCHOOL CLOTHES, CONNIE.
THANK YOU, DAD!

September 13, 1998

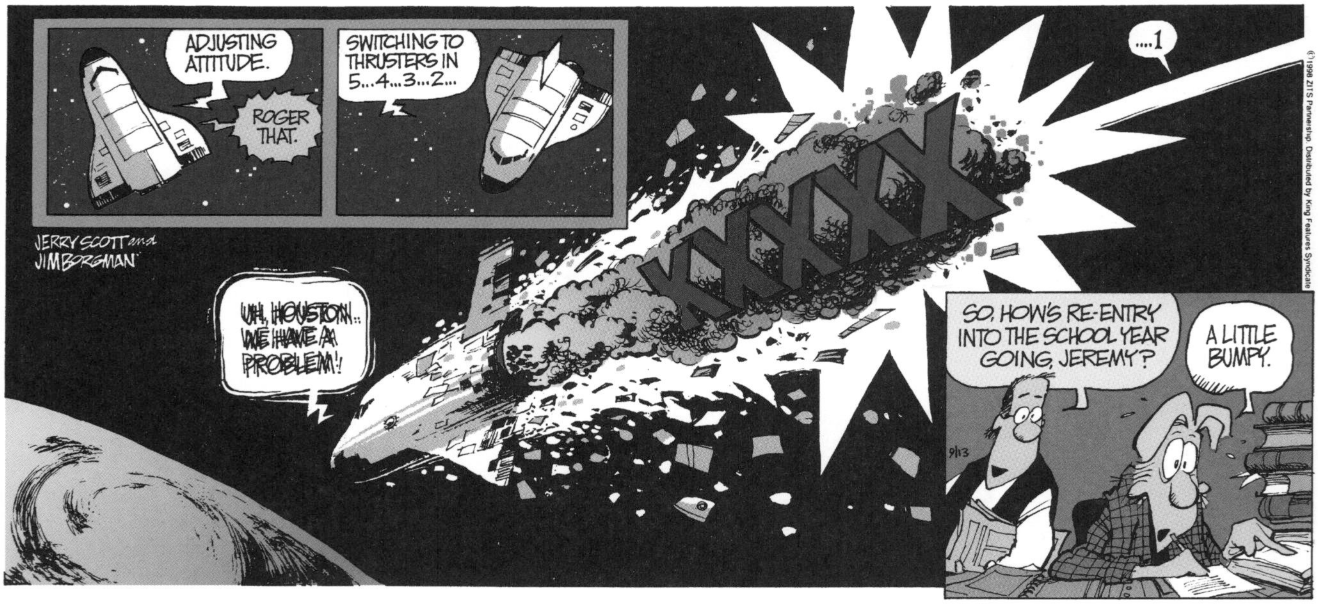
ADJUSTING ATTITUDE.
ROGER THAT.
SWITCHING TO THRUSTERS IN 5...4...3...2...
....1
JERRY SCOTT and JIM BORGMAN
© 1998 ZITS Partnership. Distributed by King Features Syndicate
XXXXX
UH, HOUSTON... WE HAVE A PROBLEM!
SO, HOW'S RE-ENTRY INTO THE SCHOOL YEAR GOING, JEREMY?
A LITTLE BUMPY.
9/13

September 20, 1998

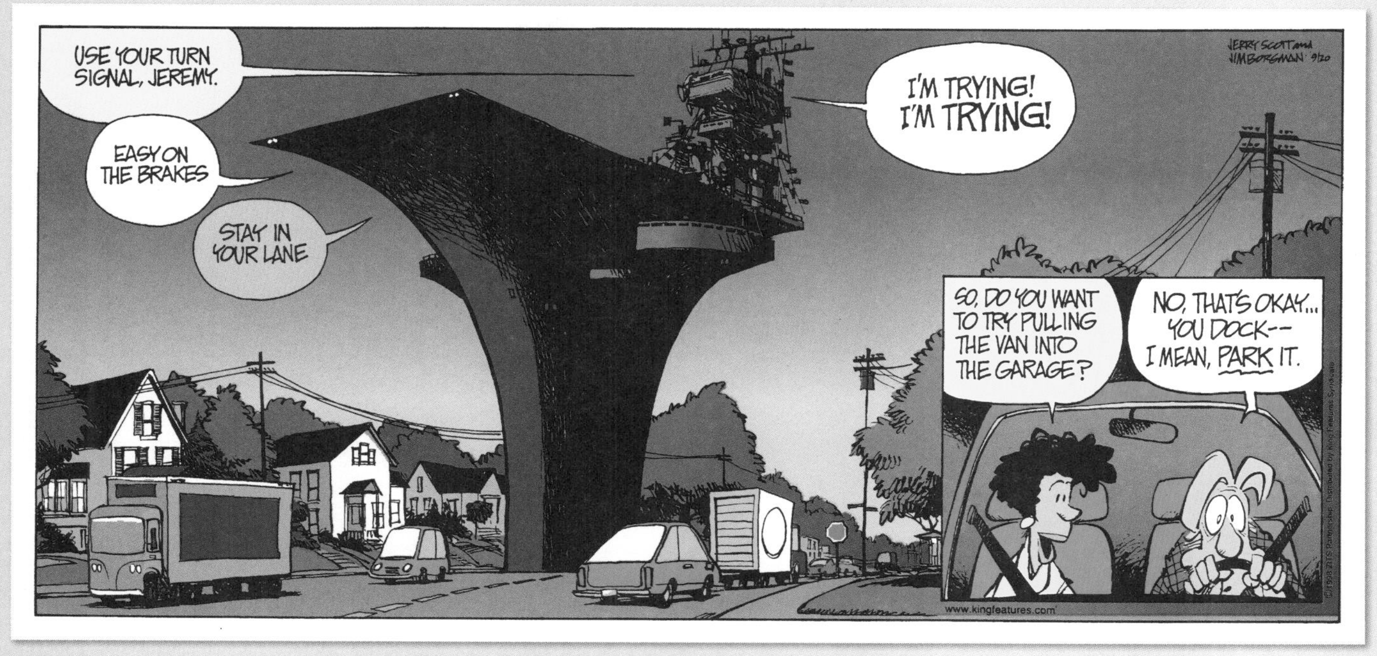
USE YOUR TURN SIGNAL, JEREMY.
EASY ON THE BRAKES
STAY IN YOUR LANE
I'M TRYING! I'M TRYING!
JERRY SCOTT and JIM BORGMAN 9/20
SO, DO YOU WANT TO TRY PULLING THE VAN INTO THE GARAGE?
NO, THAT'S OKAY... YOU DOCK-- I MEAN, PARK IT.
©1998 ZITS Partnership. Distributed by King Features Syndicate
www.kingfeatures.com

November 1, 1998

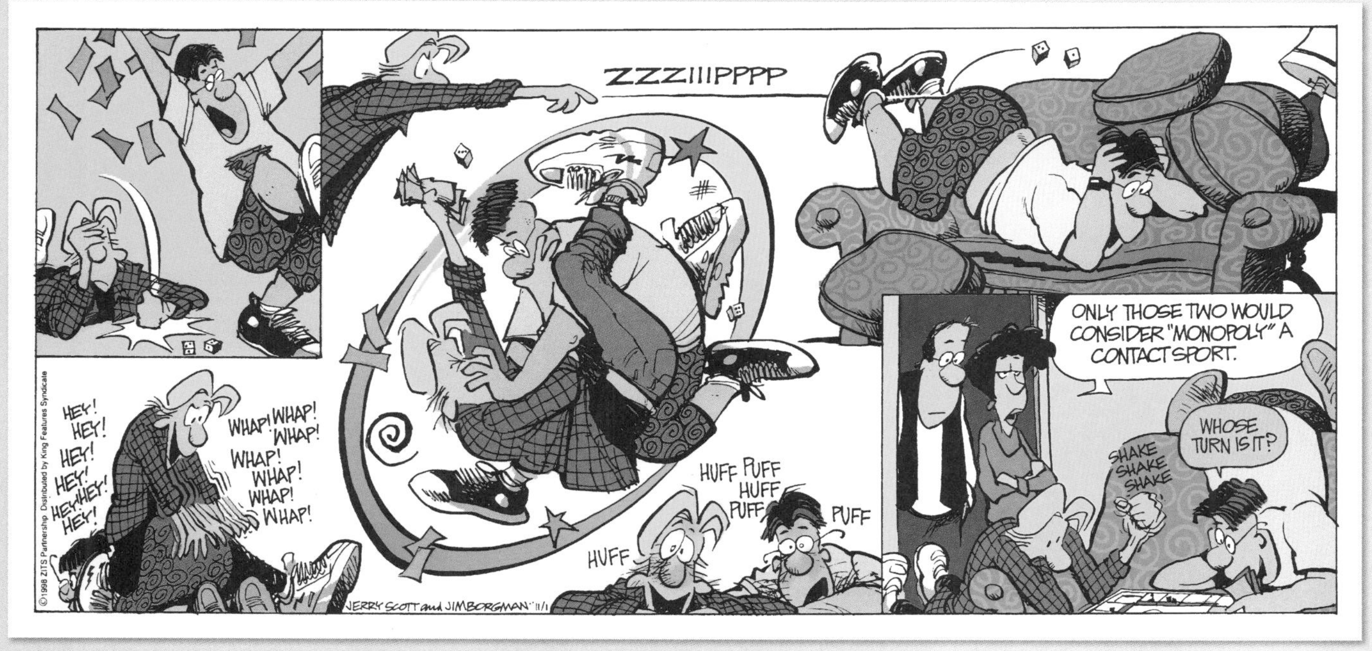
ZZZIIIPPPP
©1998 ZITS Partnership Distributed by King Features Syndicate
HEY! HEY! HEY! HEY! HEY! HEY! HEY!
WHAP! WHAP! WHAP! WHAP! WHAP! WHAP! WHAP!
HUFF PUFF HUFF PUFF
PUFF
HUFF
JERRY SCOTT and JIM BORGMAN 11/1
ONLY THOSE TWO WOULD CONSIDER "MONOPOLY" A CONTACT SPORT.
SHAKE SHAKE SHAKE
WHOSE TURN IS IT?

December 4, 1998

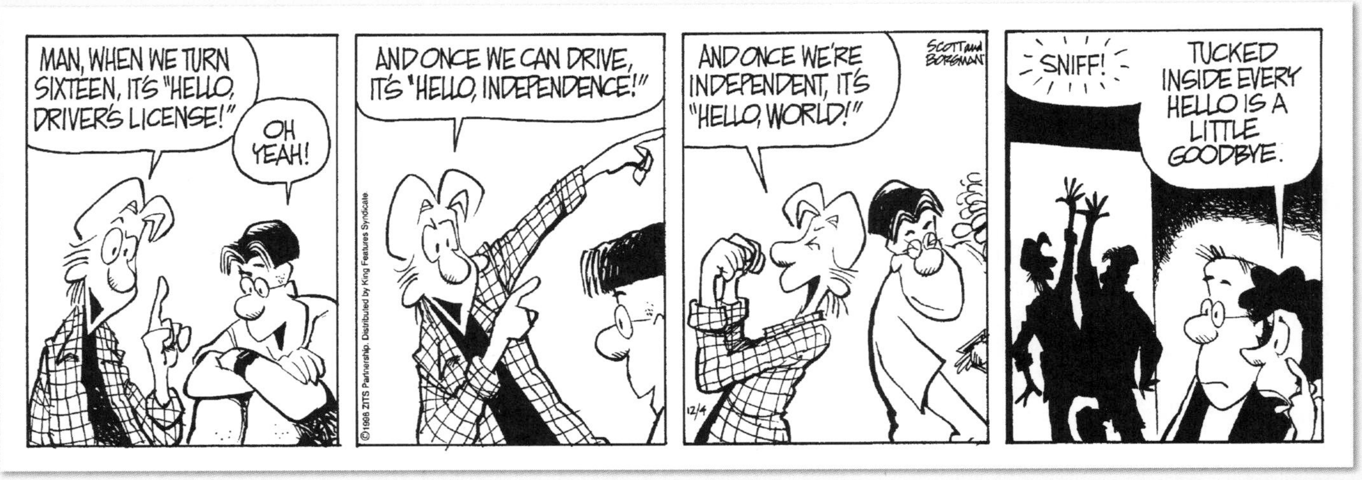
MAN, WHEN WE TURN SIXTEEN, IT'S "HELLO, DRIVER'S LICENSE!"
OH YEAH!
AND ONCE WE CAN DRIVE, IT'S "HELLO, INDEPENDENCE!"
AND ONCE WE'RE INDEPENDENT, IT'S "HELLO, WORLD!"
SNIFF!
TUCKED INSIDE EVERY HELLO IS A LITTLE GOODBYE.
SCOTT and BORGMAN
©1998 ZITS Partnership. Distributed by King Features Syndicate.

December 14, 1998

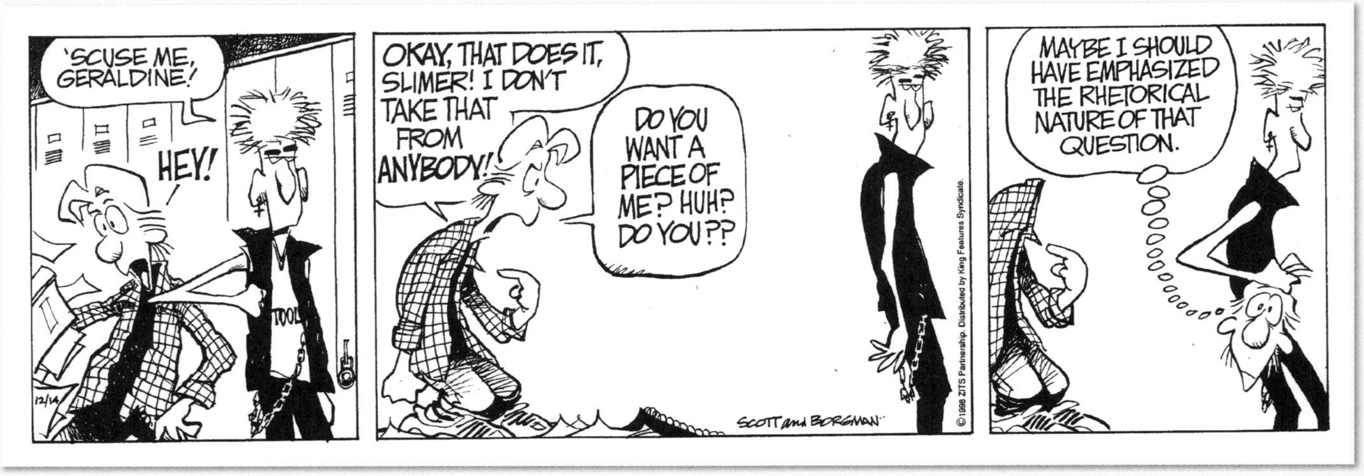
'SCUSE ME, GERALDINE!
HEY!
TOOL
OKAY, THAT DOES IT, SLIMER! I DON'T TAKE THAT FROM ANYBODY!
DO YOU WANT A PIECE OF ME? HUH? DO YOU??
SCOTT and BORGMAN
©1998 ZITS Partnership. Distributed by King Features Syndicate.
MAYBE I SHOULD HAVE EMPHASIZED THE RHETORICAL NATURE OF THAT QUESTION.

December 16, 1998

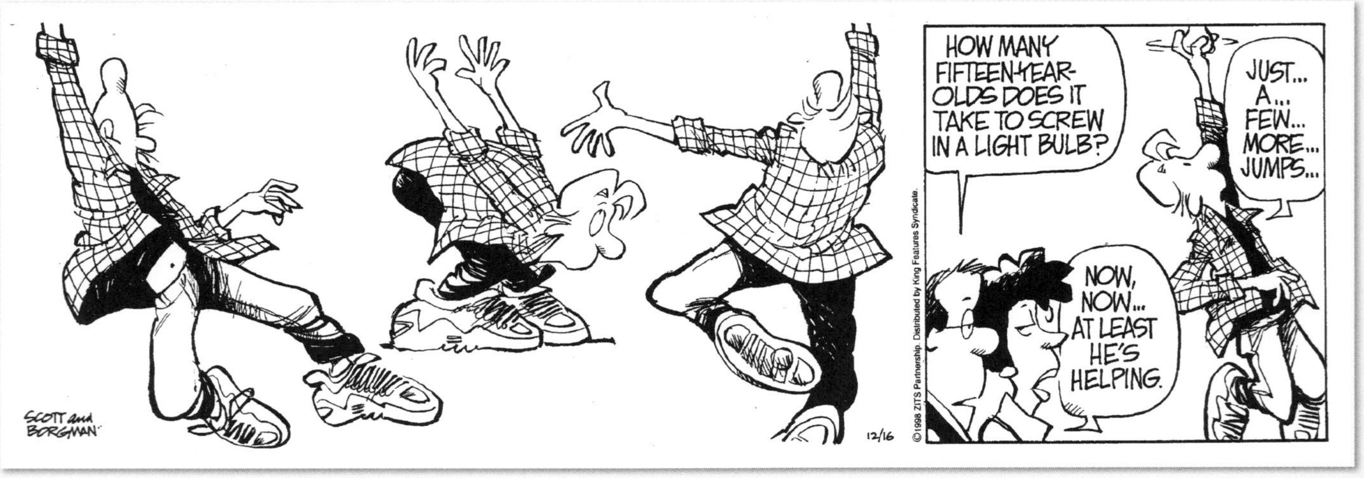
SCOTT and BORGMAN
©1998 ZITS Partnership. Distributed by King Features Syndicate.
HOW MANY FIFTEEN-YEAR-OLDS DOES IT TAKE TO SCREW IN A LIGHT BULB?
JUST... A... FEW... MORE... JUMPS...
NOW, NOW... AT LEAST HE'S HELPING.

December 6, 1998

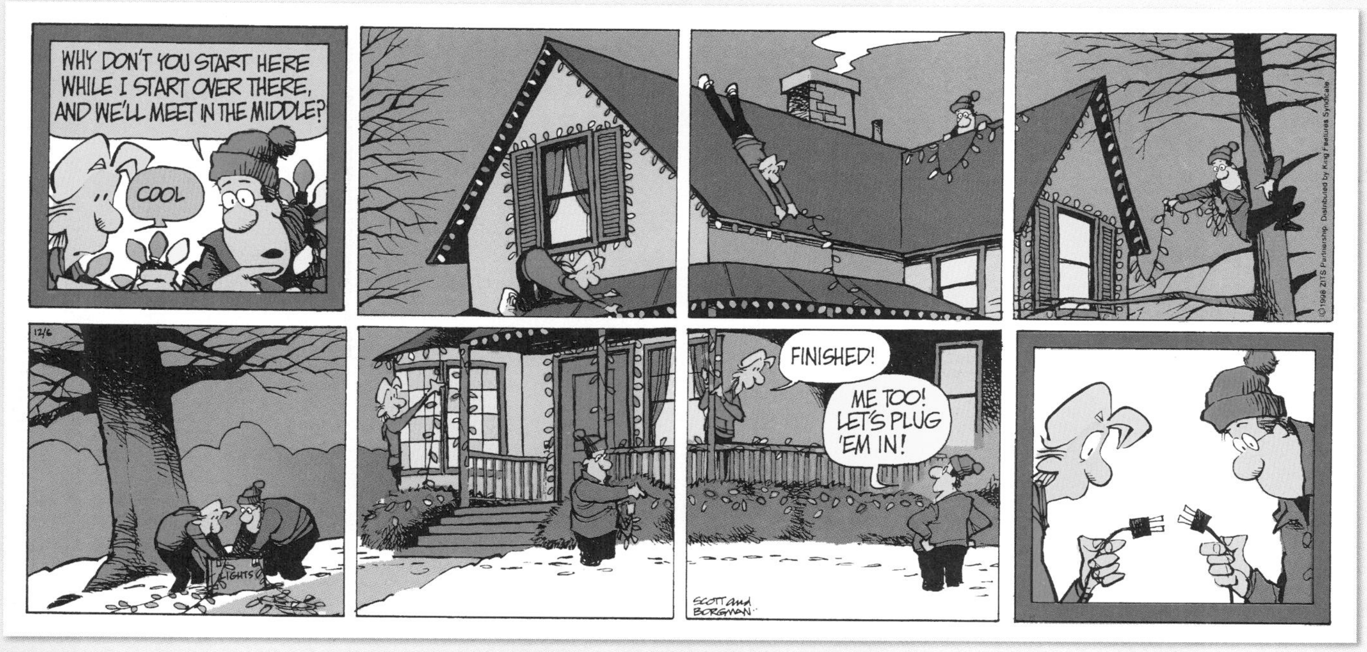
WHY DON'T YOU START HERE WHILE I START OVER THERE, AND WE'LL MEET IN THE MIDDLE?
COOL
©1998 ZITS Partnership. Distributed by King Features Syndicate
12/6
LIGHTS
FINISHED!
ME TOO! LET'S PLUG 'EM IN!
SCOTT AND BORGMAN

December 27, 1998

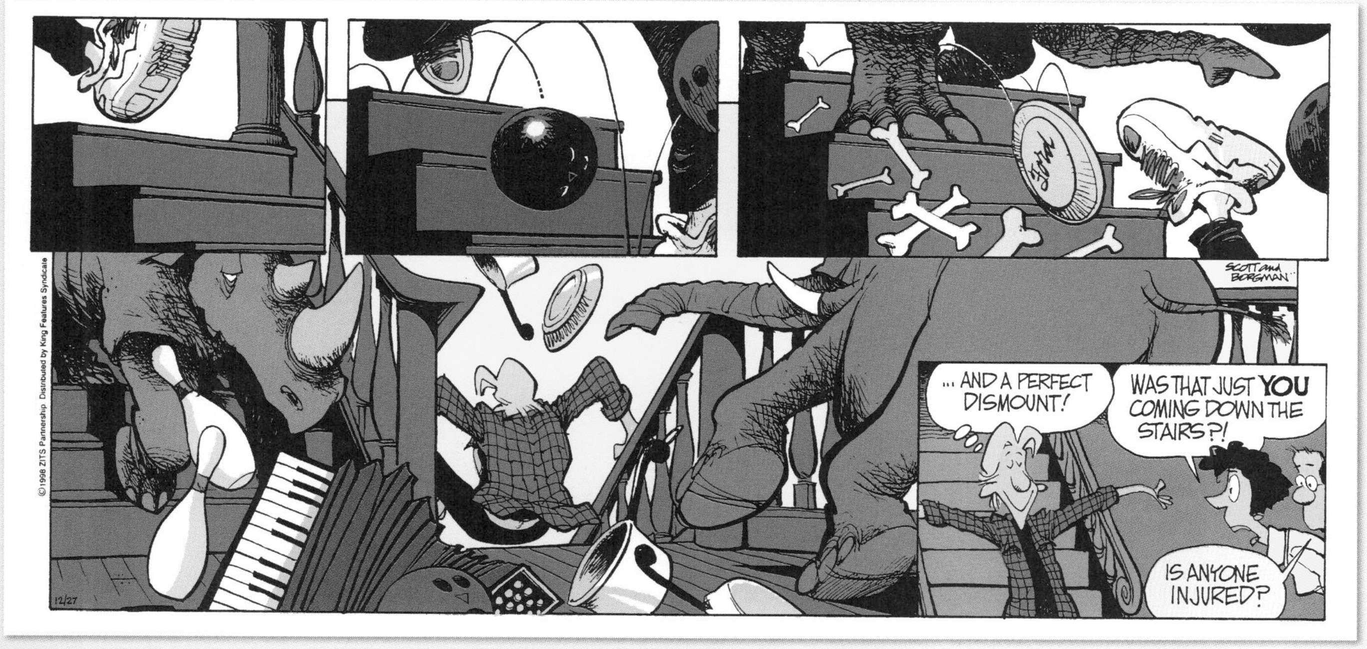
©1998 ZITS Partnership. Distributed by King Features Syndicate
SCOTT AND BORGMAN
... AND A PERFECT DISMOUNT!
WAS THAT JUST **YOU** COMING DOWN THE STAIRS?!
IS ANYONE INJURED?
12/27

MAKING the SUITS SQUIRM

Jerry Scott

After a year of writing, rewriting, drawing, re-drawing, despairing, and re-despairing, the comic strip was starting to take the shape of something King Features was willing to put before the public. The characters were gaining consistency, a voice was emerging, and the funny was happening. Just about everything, including the sales brochure, was in place. All we needed was a title to slap on the thing. Sort of like all Hannibal needed was to just hop over the Alps with those elephants.

Naming a comic strip is a big deal for a lot of reasons. For one thing, you're stuck with whatever name you choose for the life of the strip . . . and comic strips have been known to live longer than some Galapagos tortoises. Our editor, the late Jay Kennedy, lectured us at length about the importance of the title in a series of phone calls, but nothing we were coming up with was very descriptive or memorable. During the last phone discussion on the subject, Jay was getting desperate for us to make a decision. "Remember," he said, "The title has to send a message about the content and the attitude of the strip. It has to say 'teenager,' 'angst,' and ideally, it should be just one or two words." Attempting to lighten the mood, I blurted,"Why don't we just call it *Zits*?" Everybody laughed (Jay more nervously than Jim or me), and then Jay said, "No, seriously." And we said, "No . . . SERIOUSLY. That's a good title."

There were a series of meetings about this among Hearst executives (honest!), and against their better judgment, they finally okayed the title. We didn't really know it was the right one until Charles M. Schulz (the creator of Charlie Brown and Snoopy and a godlike figure to most cartoonists) said to Jim, "*Zits* is the worst name for a comic strip since *Peanuts*."

(Mic drop)

JEREMY
JEREMY'S WORLD
JEREMY and STUFF
STUFF
STUFF ABOUT ME
WHATEVER.
WHY ME?
WHY NOT?
CHILL.
BACK OFF.
DUH.
WORK in PROGRESS.
YO.
MY SO-CALLED LIFE and STUFF
GROUNDED
GROUNDED FOR LIFE
CROSSROADS
MONKEY PARTS
GET OFF MY CASE!
Planet Jeremy
AS IF!
Cowboy
Supposedly MY LIFE
Supposedly ME
CHAO and JEREMY
LIFE and STUFF
BOWEL OBSTRUCTION
STOMACH CONTENTS
ZITS

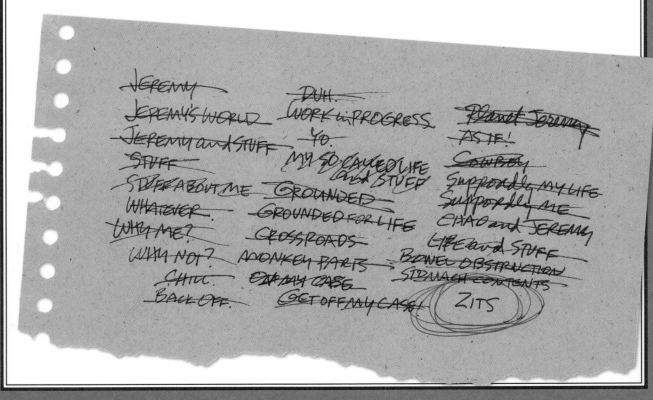

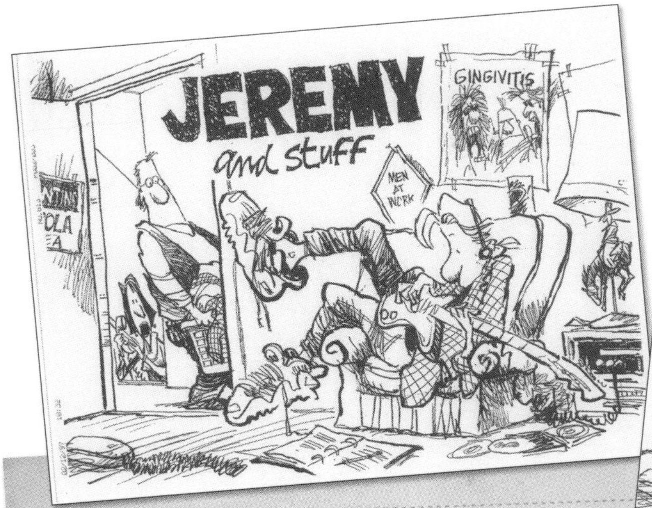
JEREMY
and stuff
GINGIVITIS
MEN AT WORK

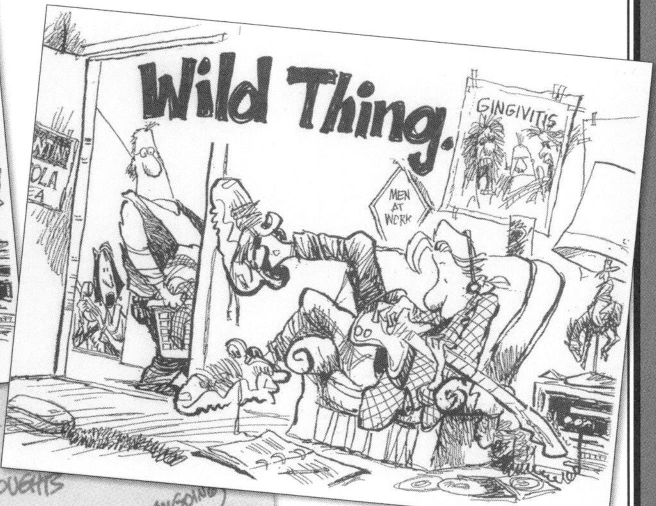
Wild Thing.
GINGIVITIS
MEN AT WORK

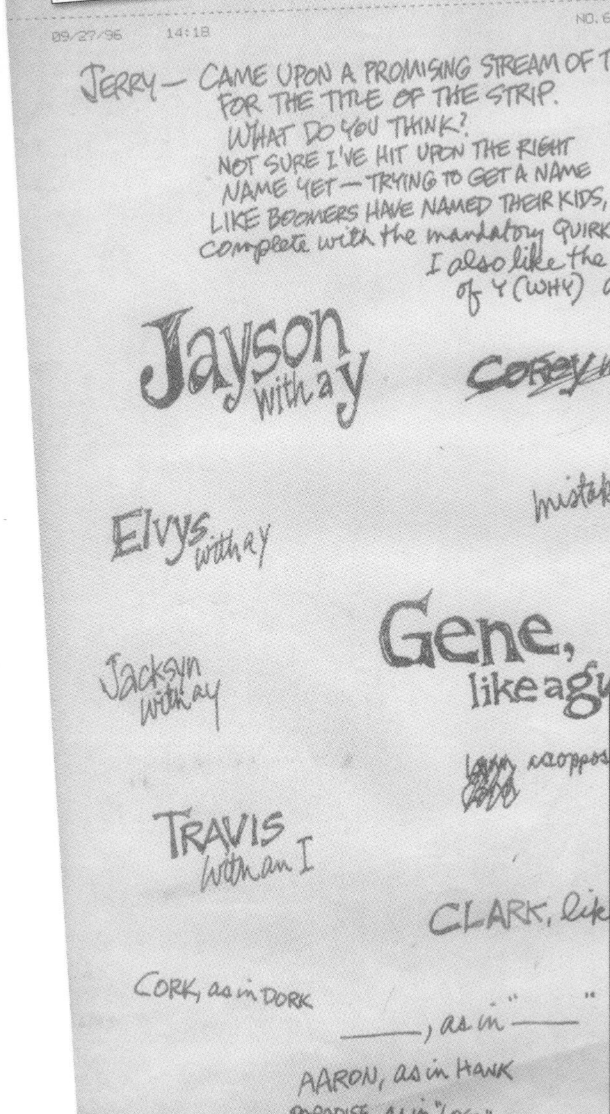
09/27/96 14:18 NO.614

JERRY— CAME UPON A PROMISING STREAM OF THOUGHTS FOR THE TITLE OF THE STRIP. WHAT DO YOU THINK?
NOT SURE I'VE HIT UPON THE RIGHT NAME YET — TRYING TO GET A NAME LIKE BOOMERS HAVE NAMED THEIR KIDS, compleete with the mandatory QUIRKY SPELLING.
I also like the double-meaning of Y (WHY) and I (EYE).
—Jim

ONGOING
Practicing signature all the time

Jayson with a y

Corey with a y

mistaken for a girl— crushing!! at 13

Elvys with a y

Gene, like a guy

Jacksyn with a y

TRAVIS with an I

CLARK, like

CORK, as in DORK

———, as in "———"

AARON, as in HANK
PARADISE, as in "LOST"

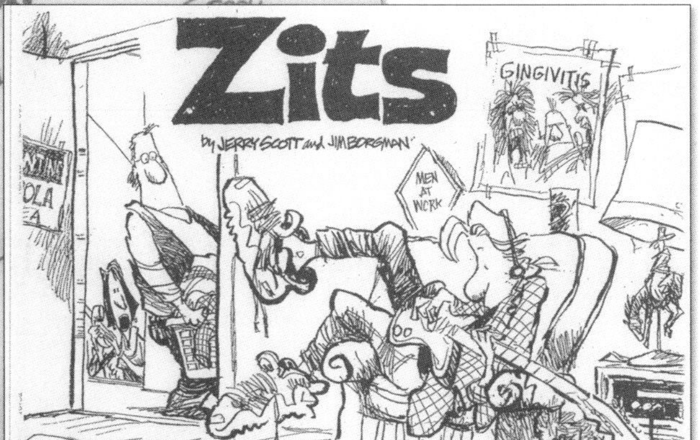
Zits
by JERRY SCOTT and JIM BORGMAN
GINGIVITIS
MEN AT WORK

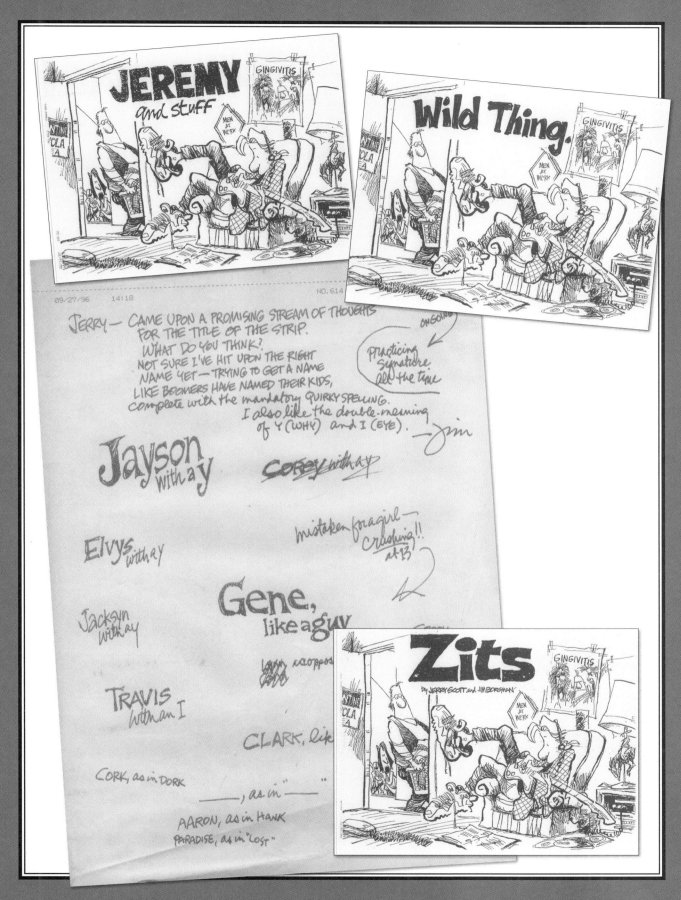

January 10, 1999

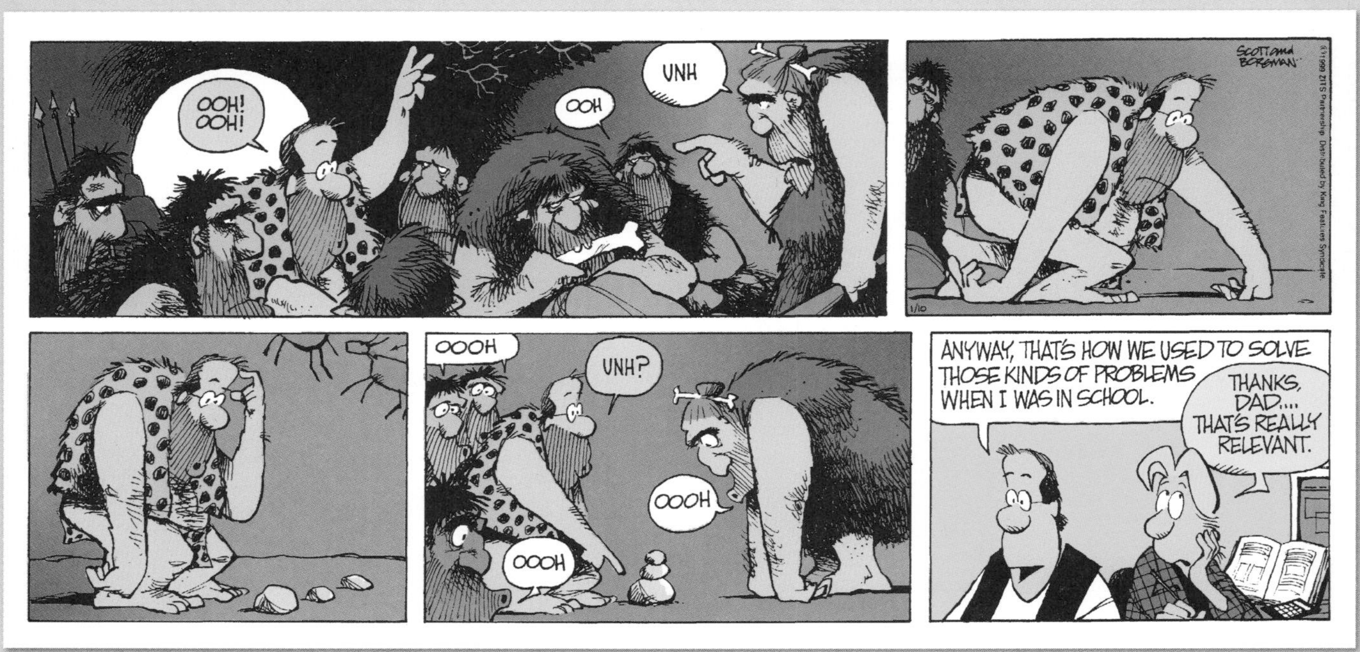

OOH! OOH!
OOH
UNH
SCOTT and BORGMAN
©1999 ZITS Partnership. Distributed by King Features Syndicate.
1/10
OOOH
UNH?
OOOH
OOOH
ANYWAY, THAT'S HOW WE USED TO SOLVE THOSE KINDS OF PROBLEMS WHEN I WAS IN SCHOOL.
THANKS, DAD.... THAT'S REALLY RELEVANT.

January 17, 1999

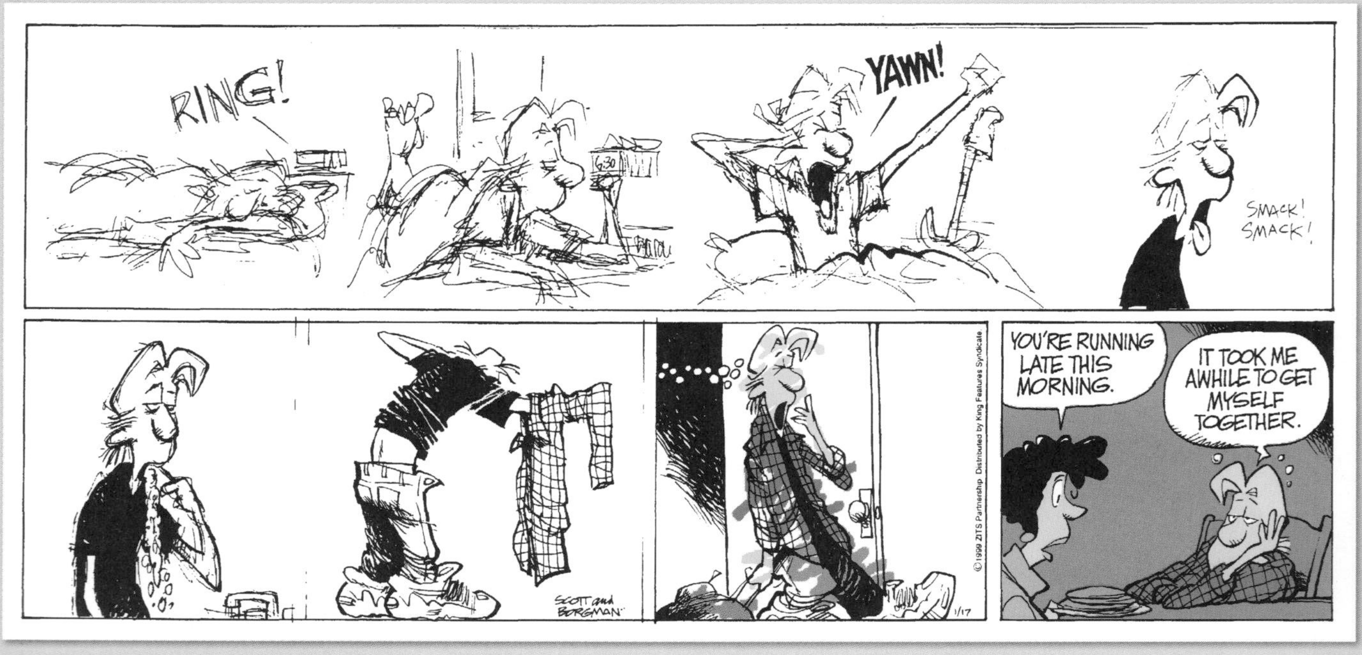

RING!
6:30
YAWN!
SMACK! SMACK!
SCOTT and BORGMAN
© 1999 ZITS Partnership. Distributed by King Features Syndicate
1/17
YOU'RE RUNNING LATE THIS MORNING.
IT TOOK ME AWHILE TO GET MYSELF TOGETHER.

January 15, 1999

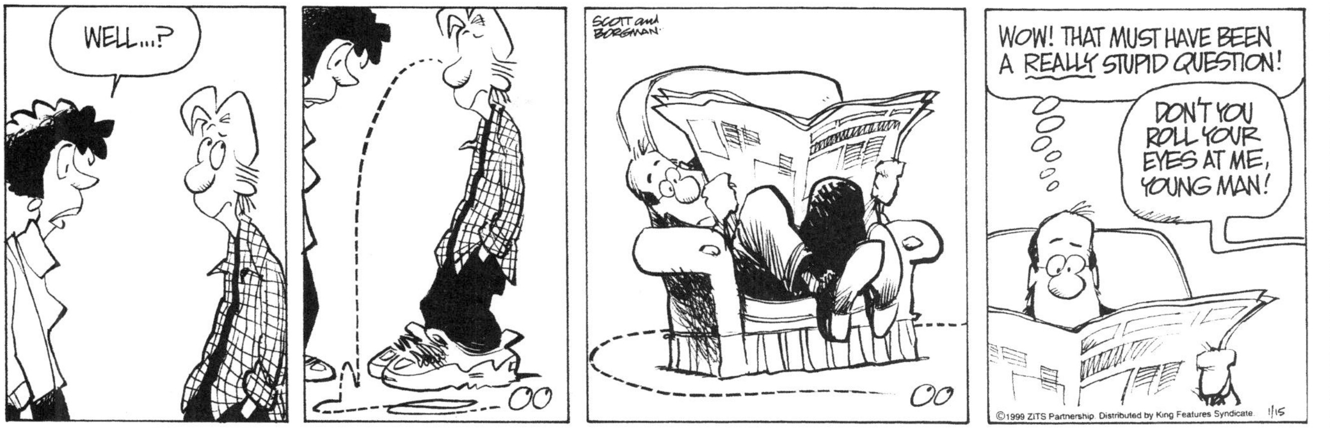
WELL...?
SCOTT and BORGMAN
WOW! THAT MUST HAVE BEEN A REALLY STUPID QUESTION!
DON'T YOU ROLL YOUR EYES AT ME, YOUNG MAN!
©1999 ZITS Partnership. Distributed by King Features Syndicate.
1/15

January 23, 1999

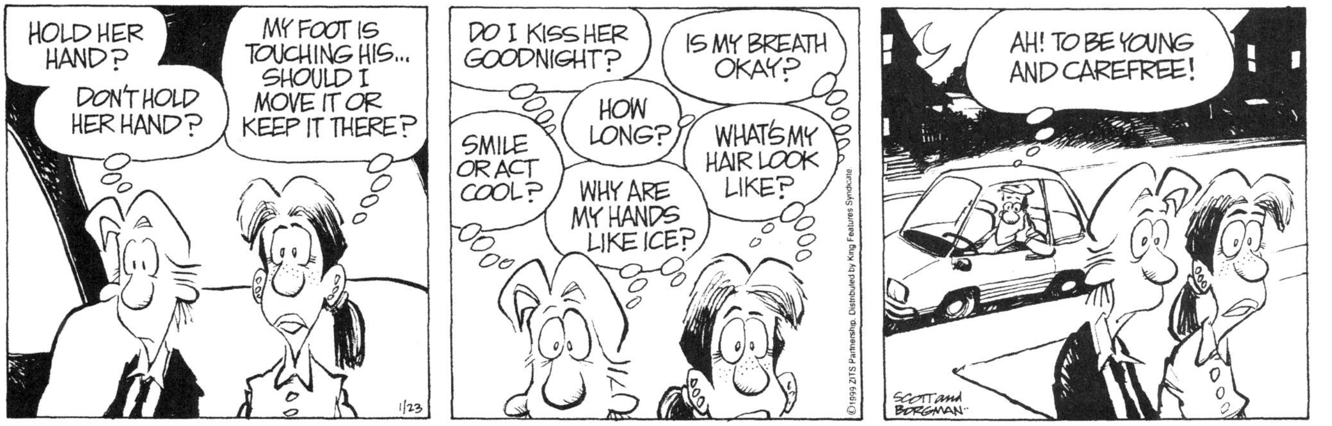
HOLD HER HAND?
DON'T HOLD HER HAND?
MY FOOT IS TOUCHING HIS... SHOULD I MOVE IT OR KEEP IT THERE?
1/23
DO I KISS HER GOODNIGHT?
IS MY BREATH OKAY?
HOW LONG?
SMILE OR ACT COOL?
WHAT'S MY HAIR LOOK LIKE?
WHY ARE MY HANDS LIKE ICE?
©1999 ZITS Partnership. Distributed by King Features Syndicate
AH! TO BE YOUNG AND CAREFREE!
SCOTT and BORGMAN

February 2, 1999

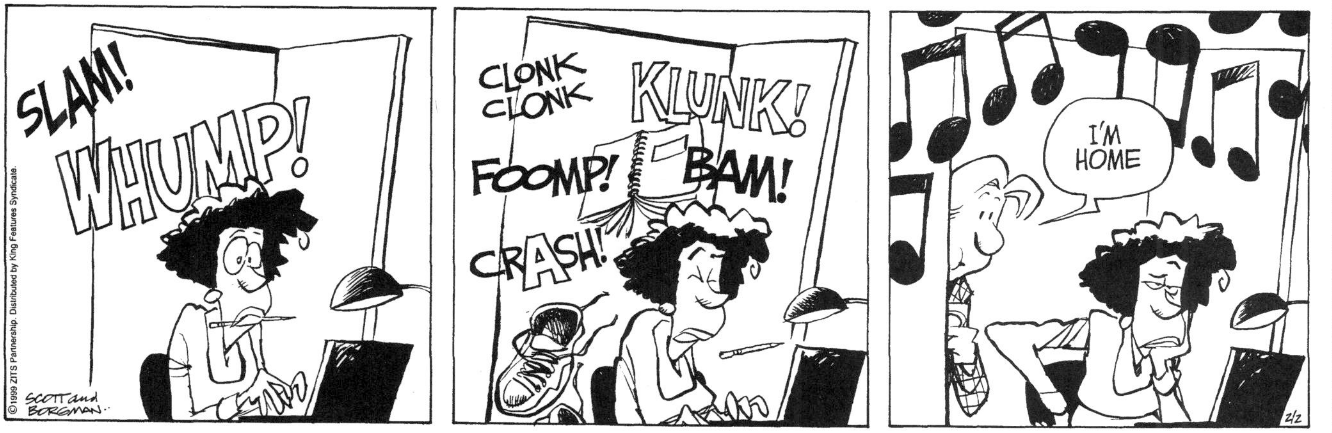
SLAM!
WHUMP!
©1999 ZITS Partnership. Distributed by King Features Syndicate.
SCOTT and BORGMAN
CLONK CLONK
KLUNK!
FOOMP!
BAM!
CRASH!
I'M HOME
2/2

February 8, 1999

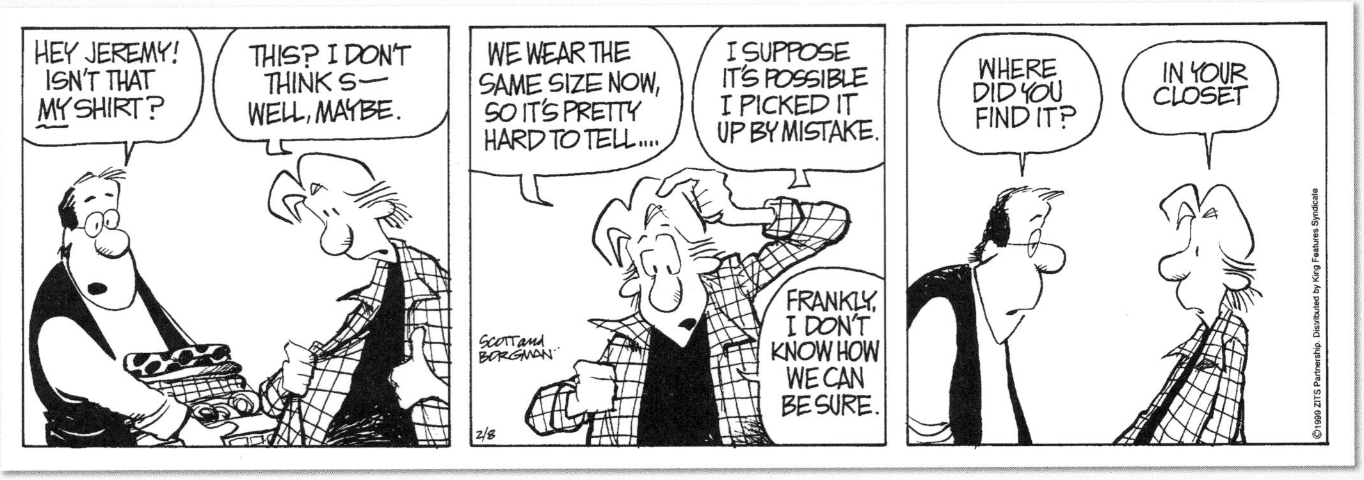
HEY JEREMY! ISN'T THAT MY SHIRT?
THIS? I DON'T THINK S— WELL, MAYBE.
WE WEAR THE SAME SIZE NOW, SO IT'S PRETTY HARD TO TELL....
I SUPPOSE IT'S POSSIBLE I PICKED IT UP BY MISTAKE.
FRANKLY, I DON'T KNOW HOW WE CAN BE SURE.
SCOTT and BORGMAN
2/8
WHERE DID YOU FIND IT?
IN YOUR CLOSET
©1999 ZITS Partnership. Distributed by King Features Syndicate

March 9, 1999

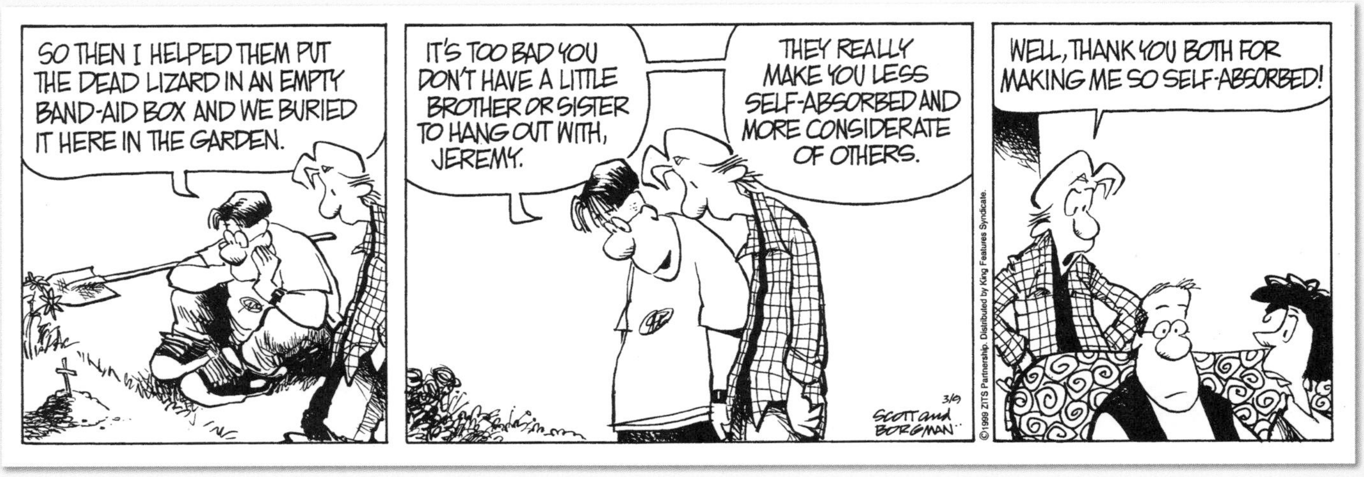
SO THEN I HELPED THEM PUT THE DEAD LIZARD IN AN EMPTY BAND-AID BOX AND WE BURIED IT HERE IN THE GARDEN.
IT'S TOO BAD YOU DON'T HAVE A LITTLE BROTHER OR SISTER TO HANG OUT WITH, JEREMY.
THEY REALLY MAKE YOU LESS SELF-ABSORBED AND MORE CONSIDERATE OF OTHERS.
3/9
SCOTT and BORGMAN
©1999 ZITS Partnership. Distributed by King Features Syndicate.
WELL, THANK YOU BOTH FOR MAKING ME SO SELF-ABSORBED!

March 15, 1999

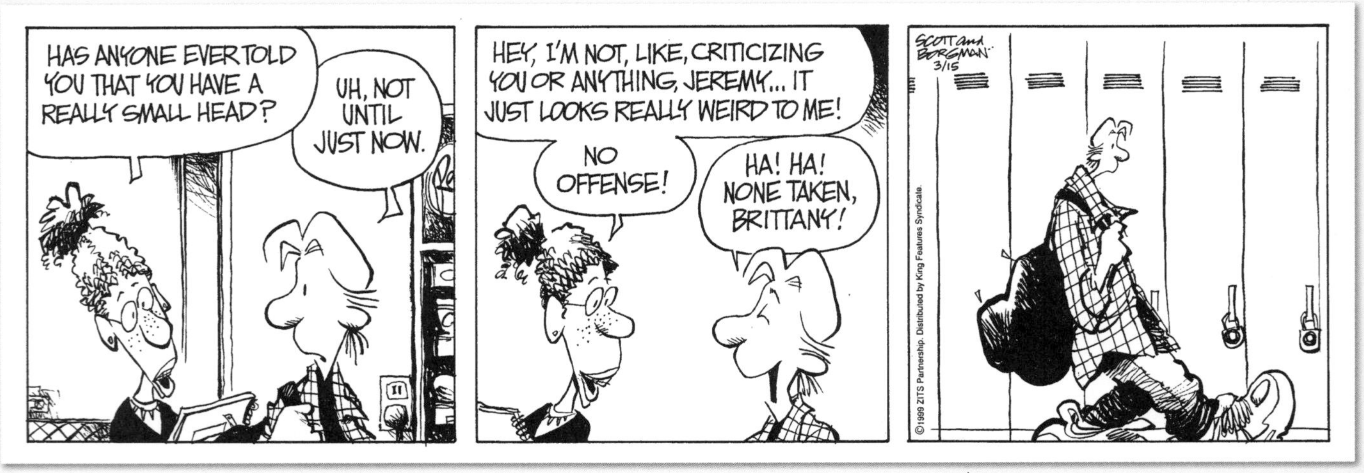
HAS ANYONE EVER TOLD YOU THAT YOU HAVE A REALLY SMALL HEAD?
UH, NOT UNTIL JUST NOW.
HEY, I'M NOT, LIKE, CRITICIZING YOU OR ANYTHING, JEREMY... IT JUST LOOKS REALLY WEIRD TO ME!
NO OFFENSE!
HA! HA! NONE TAKEN, BRITTANY!
©1999 ZITS Partnership. Distributed by King Features Syndicate.
SCOTT and BORGMAN
3/15

March 21, 1999

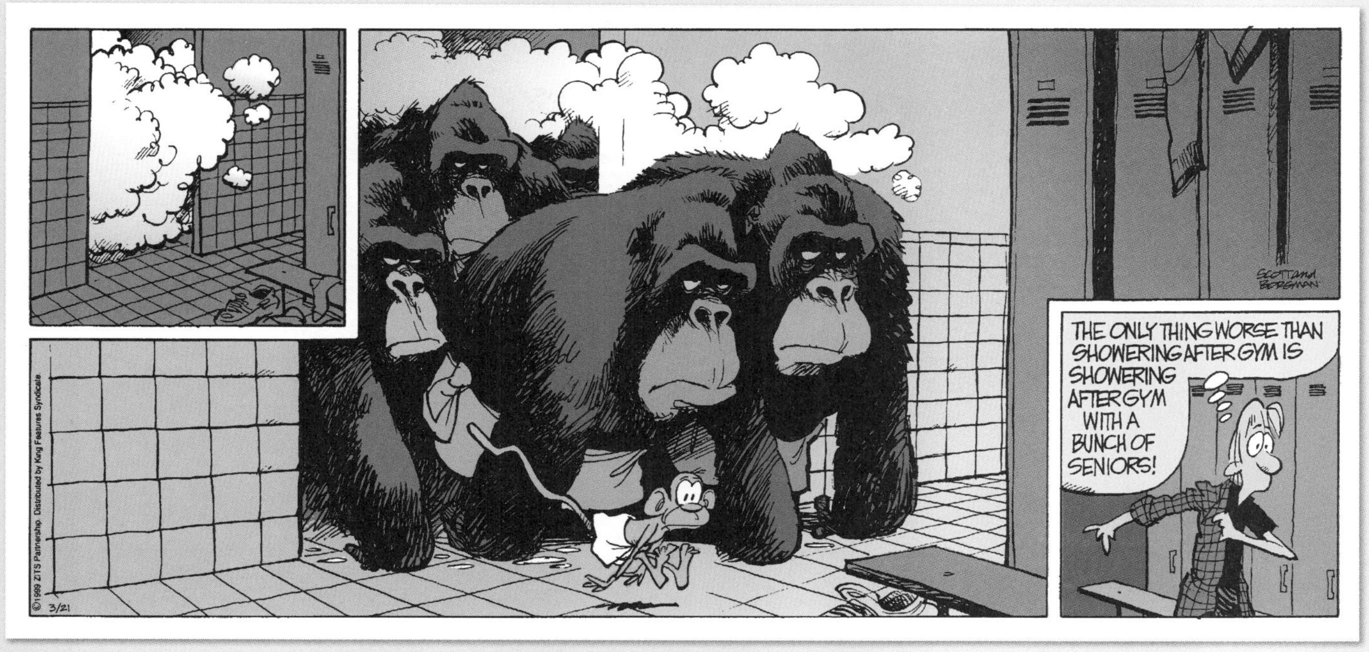
THE ONLY THING WORSE THAN SHOWERING AFTER GYM IS SHOWERING AFTER GYM WITH A BUNCH OF SENIORS!
SCOTT AND BORGMAN
©1999 ZITS Partnership. Distributed by King Features Syndicate.
3/21

May 9, 1999

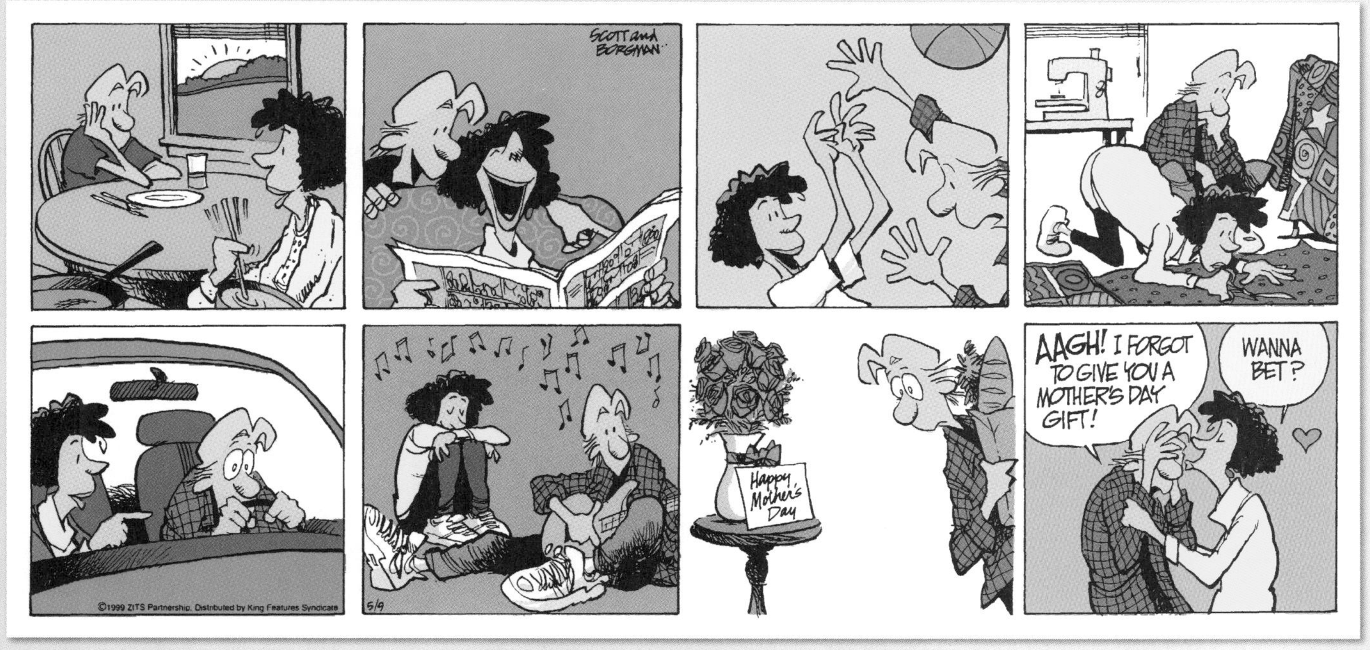
SCOTT AND BORGMAN
Happy Mother's Day
AAGH! I FORGOT TO GIVE YOU A MOTHER'S DAY GIFT!
WANNA BET?
©1999 ZITS Partnership. Distributed by King Features Syndicate
5/9

May 4, 1999

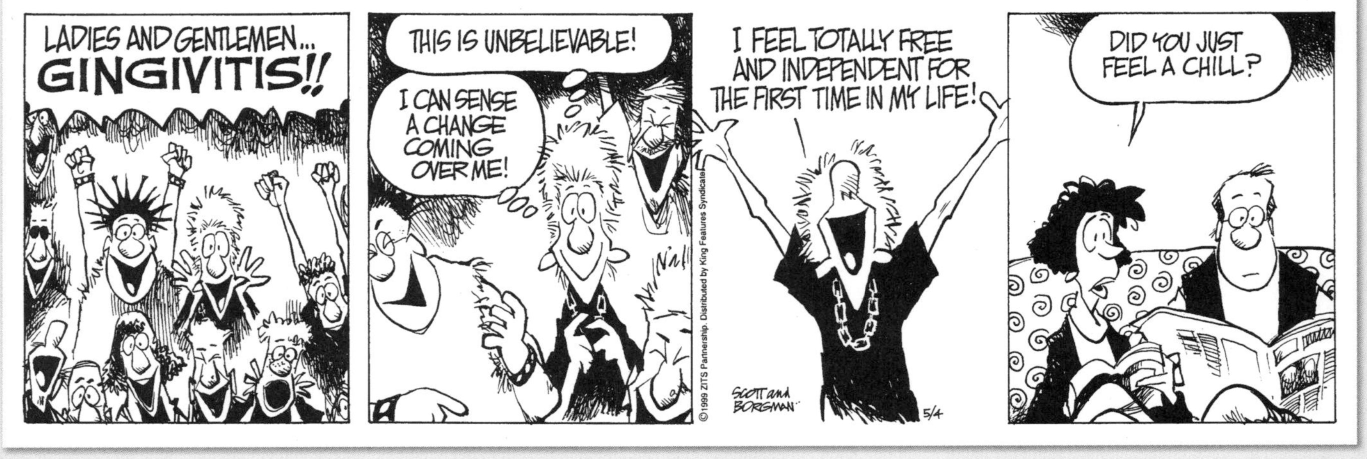
LADIES AND GENTLEMEN... GINGIVITIS!!
THIS IS UNBELIEVABLE!
I CAN SENSE A CHANGE COMING OVER ME!
© 1999 ZITS Partnership. Distributed by King Features Syndicate.
I FEEL TOTALLY FREE AND INDEPENDENT FOR THE FIRST TIME IN MY LIFE!
SCOTT and BORGMAN
5/4
DID YOU JUST FEEL A CHILL?

May 5, 1999

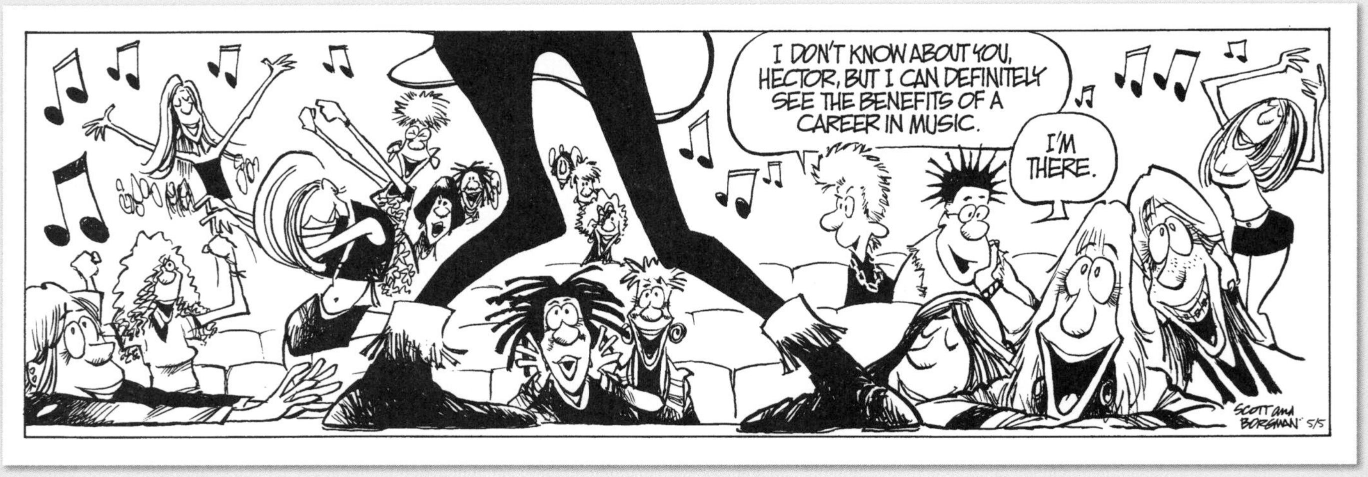
I DON'T KNOW ABOUT YOU, HECTOR, BUT I CAN DEFINITELY SEE THE BENEFITS OF A CAREER IN MUSIC.
I'M THERE.
SCOTT and BORGMAN 5/5

May 6, 1999

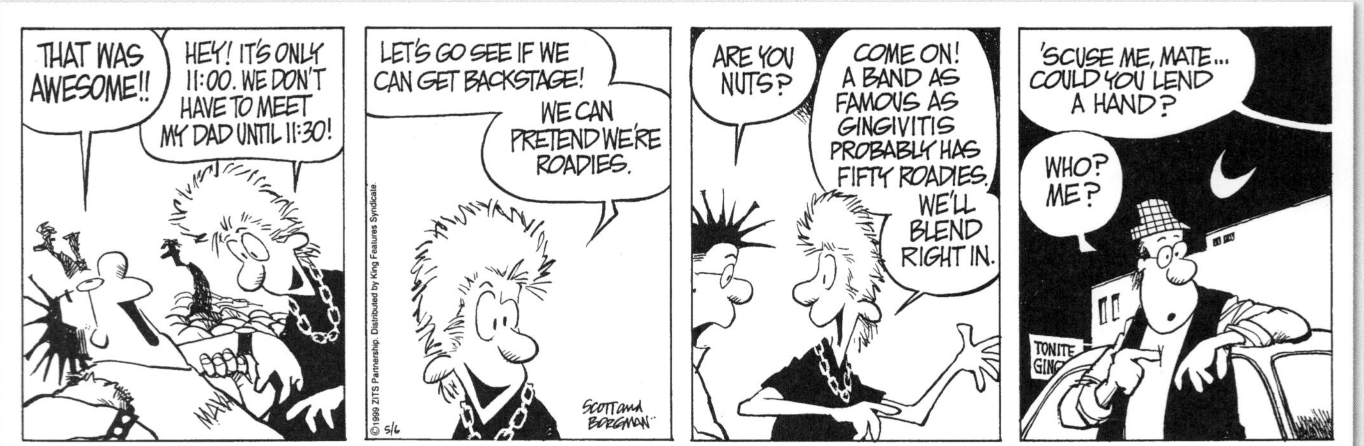
THAT WAS AWESOME!!
HEY! IT'S ONLY 11:00. WE DON'T HAVE TO MEET MY DAD UNTIL 11:30!
LET'S GO SEE IF WE CAN GET BACKSTAGE!
WE CAN PRETEND WE'RE ROADIES.
© 1999 ZITS Partnership. Distributed by King Features Syndicate.
5/6
SCOTT and BORGMAN
ARE YOU NUTS?
COME ON! A BAND AS FAMOUS AS GINGIVITIS PROBABLY HAS FIFTY ROADIES.
WE'LL BLEND RIGHT IN.
'SCUSE ME, MATE... COULD YOU LEND A HAND?
WHO? ME?
TONITE
GING

May 7, 1999

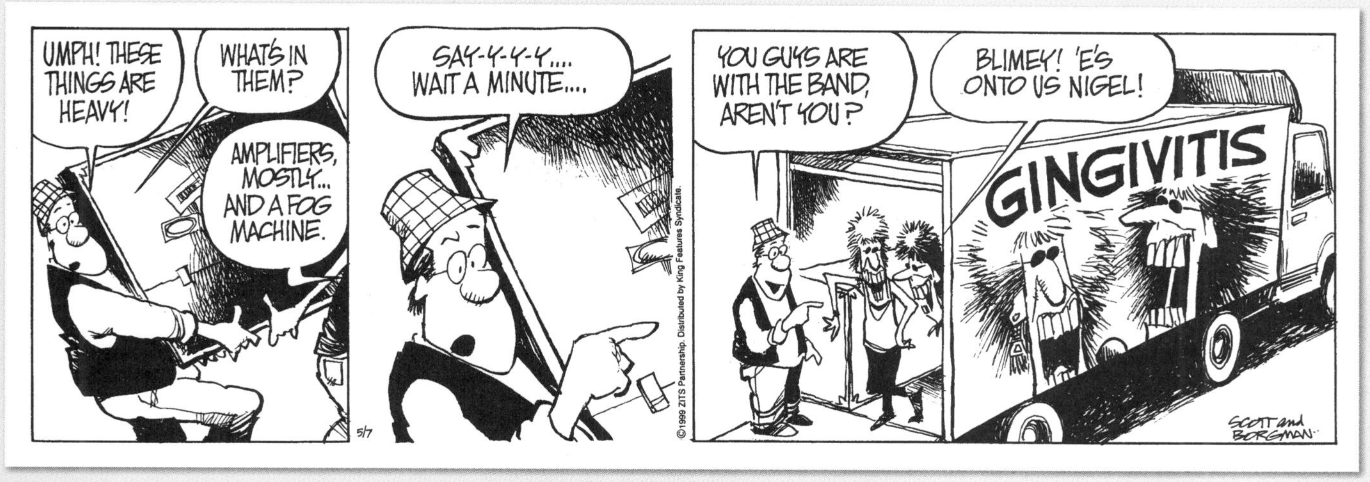
UMPH! THESE THINGS ARE HEAVY!
WHAT'S IN THEM?
AMPLIFIERS, MOSTLY... AND A FOG MACHINE.
SAY-Y-Y-Y.... WAIT A MINUTE....
YOU GUYS ARE WITH THE BAND, AREN'T YOU?
BLIMEY! 'E'S ONTO US NIGEL!
GINGIVITIS
© 1999 ZITS Partnership. Distributed by King Features Syndicate.
SCOTT and BORGMAN

May 10, 1999

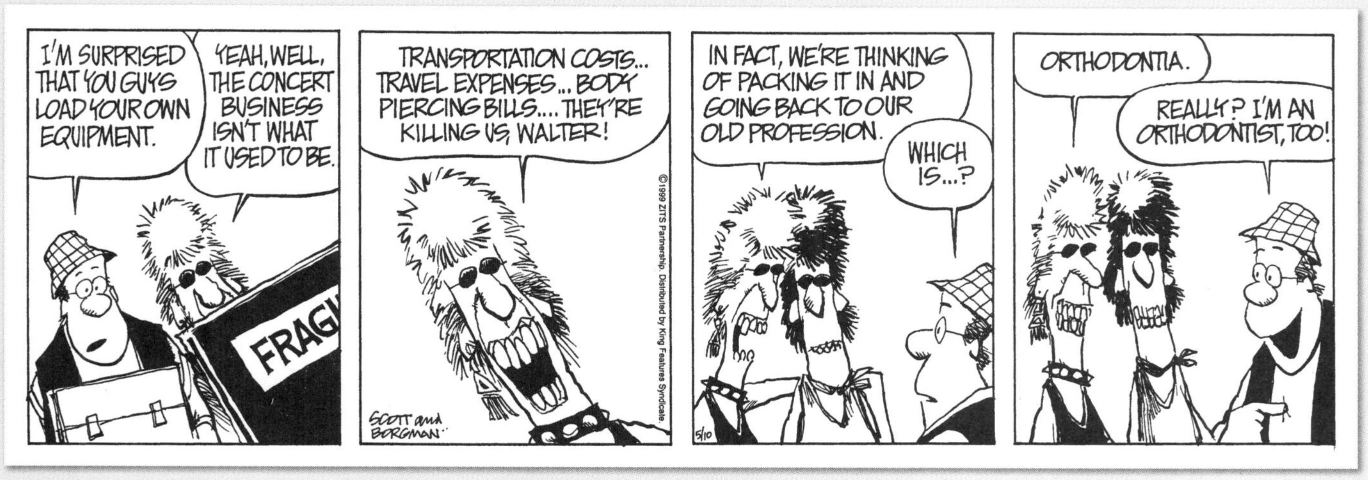
I'M SURPRISED THAT YOU GUYS LOAD YOUR OWN EQUIPMENT.
YEAH, WELL, THE CONCERT BUSINESS ISN'T WHAT IT USED TO BE.
FRAG
TRANSPORTATION COSTS... TRAVEL EXPENSES... BODY PIERCING BILLS.... THEY'RE KILLING US, WALTER!
SCOTT and BORGMAN
© 1999 ZITS Partnership. Distributed by King Features Syndicate.
IN FACT, WE'RE THINKING OF PACKING IT IN AND GOING BACK TO OUR OLD PROFESSION.
WHICH IS...?
ORTHODONTIA.
REALLY? I'M AN ORTHODONTIST, TOO!

May 11, 1999

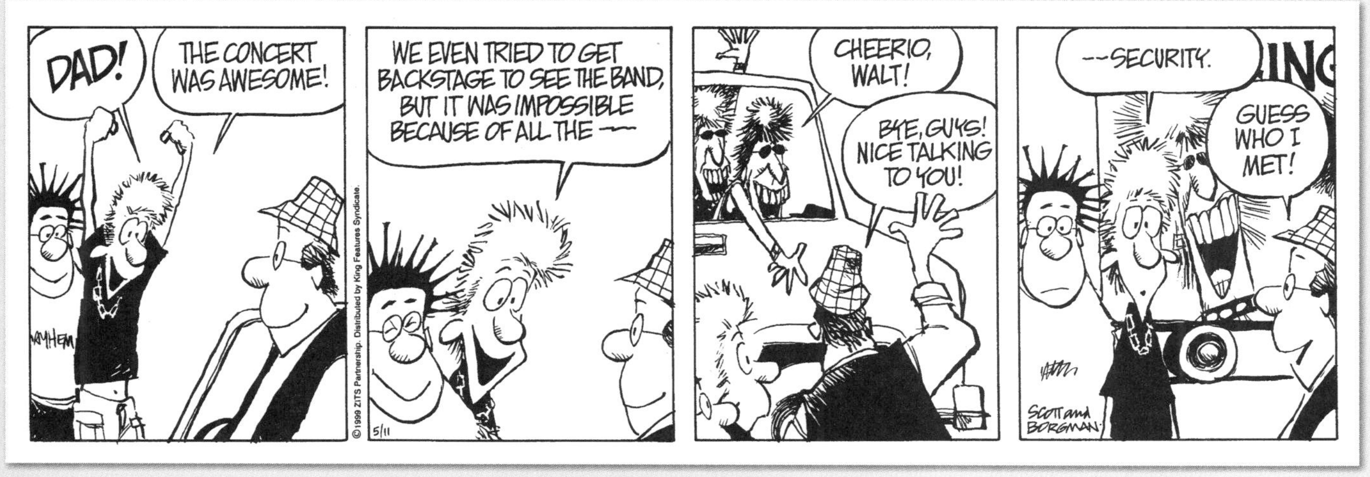
DAD!
THE CONCERT WAS AWESOME!
MAYHEM
© 1999 ZITS Partnership. Distributed by King Features Syndicate.
WE EVEN TRIED TO GET BACKSTAGE TO SEE THE BAND, BUT IT WAS IMPOSSIBLE BECAUSE OF ALL THE —
CHEERIO, WALT!
BYE, GUYS! NICE TALKING TO YOU!
--SECURITY.
GUESS WHO I MET!
SCOTT and BORGMAN

March 24, 1999

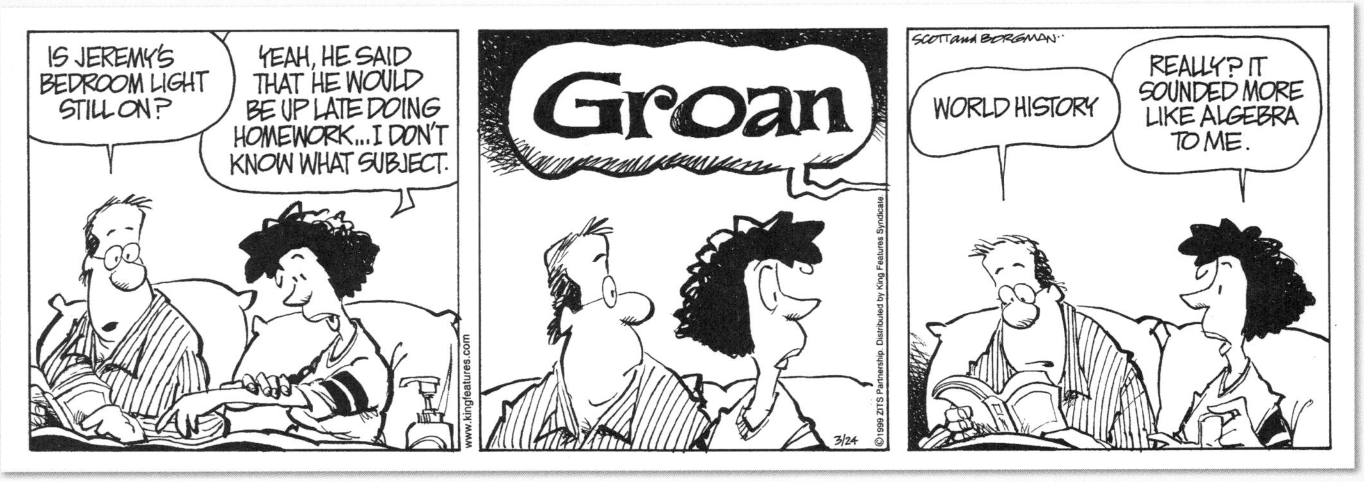
IS JEREMY'S BEDROOM LIGHT STILL ON?
YEAH, HE SAID THAT HE WOULD BE UP LATE DOING HOMEWORK...I DON'T KNOW WHAT SUBJECT.
Groan
WORLD HISTORY
REALLY? IT SOUNDED MORE LIKE ALGEBRA TO ME.

November 26, 1999

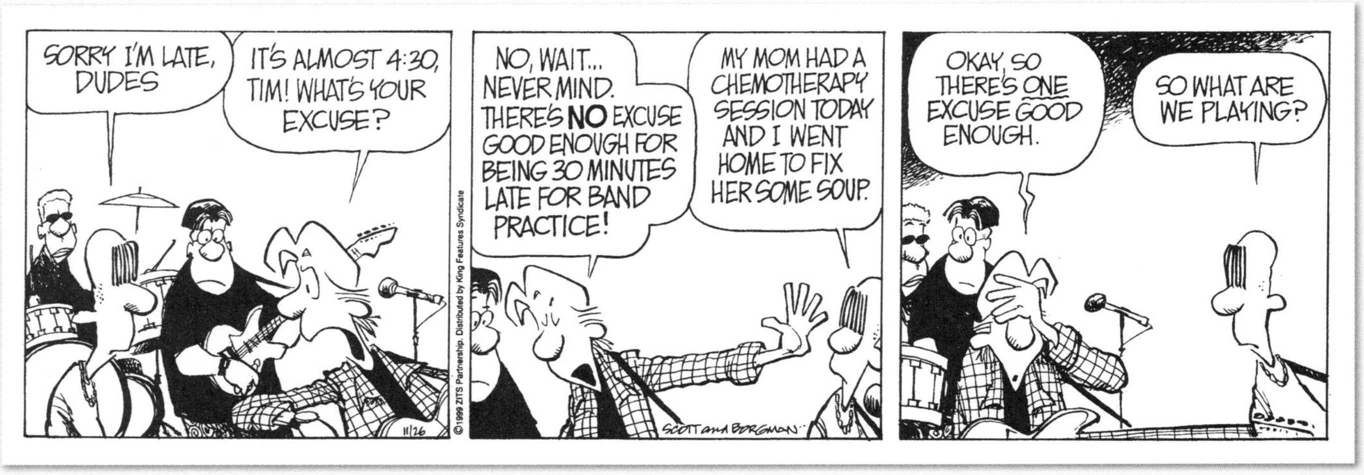
SORRY I'M LATE, DUDES
IT'S ALMOST 4:30, TIM! WHAT'S YOUR EXCUSE?
NO, WAIT... NEVER MIND. THERE'S NO EXCUSE GOOD ENOUGH FOR BEING 30 MINUTES LATE FOR BAND PRACTICE!
MY MOM HAD A CHEMOTHERAPY SESSION TODAY AND I WENT HOME TO FIX HER SOME SOUP.
OKAY, SO THERE'S ONE EXCUSE GOOD ENOUGH.
SO WHAT ARE WE PLAYING?

December 13, 1999

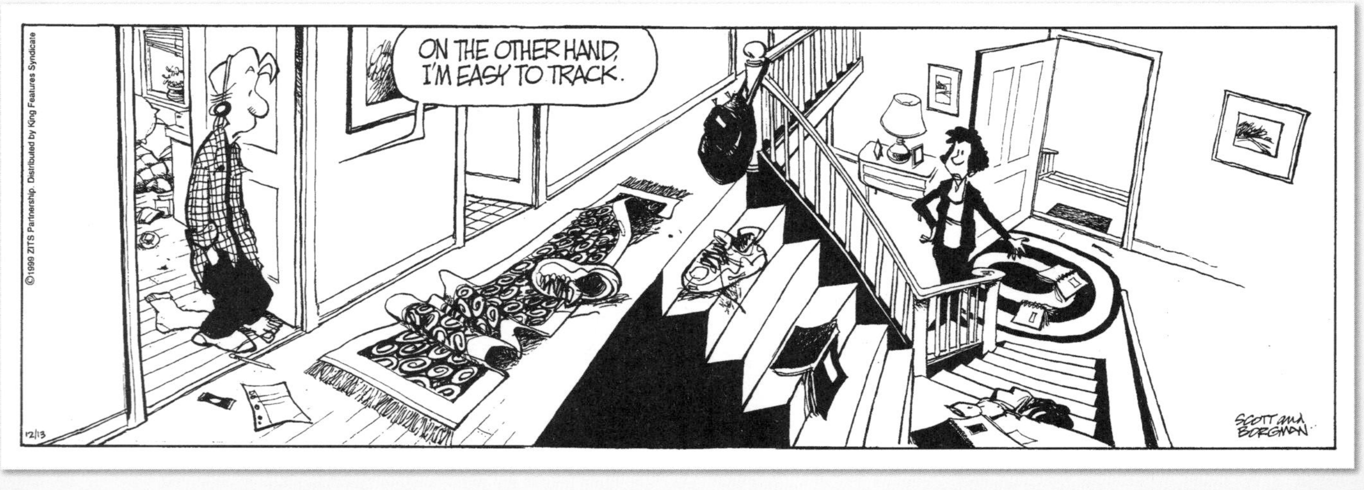
ON THE OTHER HAND, I'M EASY TO TRACK.

May 23, 1999

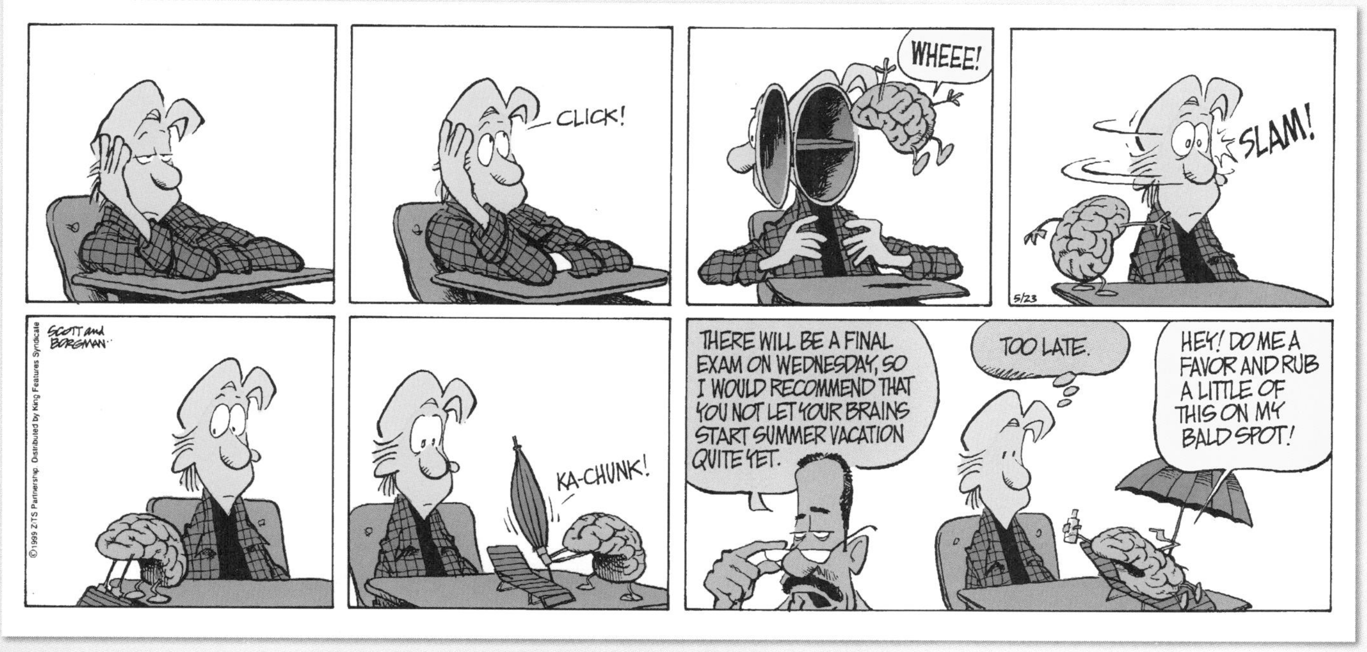
CLICK!
WHEEE!
SLAM!
5/23
SCOTT and BORGMAN
© 1999 ZITS Partnership. Distributed by King Features Syndicate
KA-CHUNK!
THERE WILL BE A FINAL EXAM ON WEDNESDAY, SO I WOULD RECOMMEND THAT YOU NOT LET YOUR BRAINS START SUMMER VACATION QUITE YET.
TOO LATE.
HEY! DO ME A FAVOR AND RUB A LITTLE OF THIS ON MY BALD SPOT!

September 12, 1999

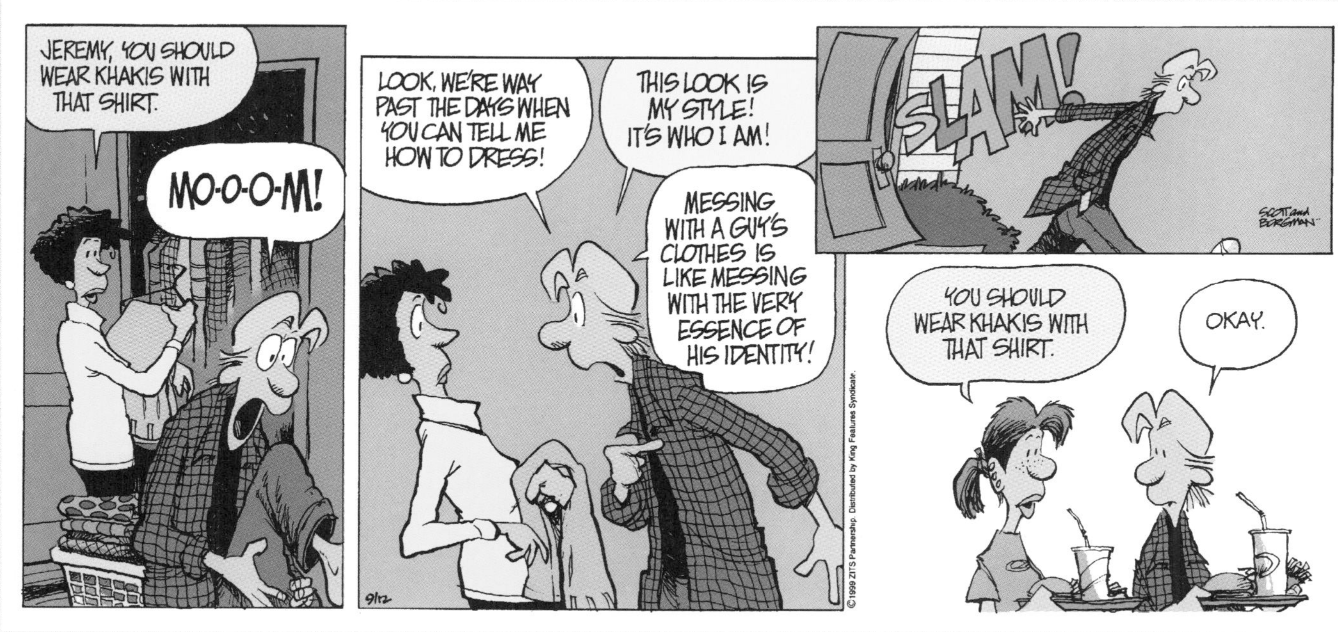
JEREMY, YOU SHOULD WEAR KHAKIS WITH THAT SHIRT.
MO-O-O-M!
LOOK, WE'RE WAY PAST THE DAYS WHEN YOU CAN TELL ME HOW TO DRESS!
THIS LOOK IS MY STYLE! IT'S WHO I AM!
MESSING WITH A GUY'S CLOTHES IS LIKE MESSING WITH THE VERY ESSENCE OF HIS IDENTITY!
9/12
© 1999 ZITS Partnership. Distributed by King Features Syndicate.
SLAM!
SCOTT and BORGMAN
YOU SHOULD WEAR KHAKIS WITH THAT SHIRT.
OKAY.

September 26, 1999

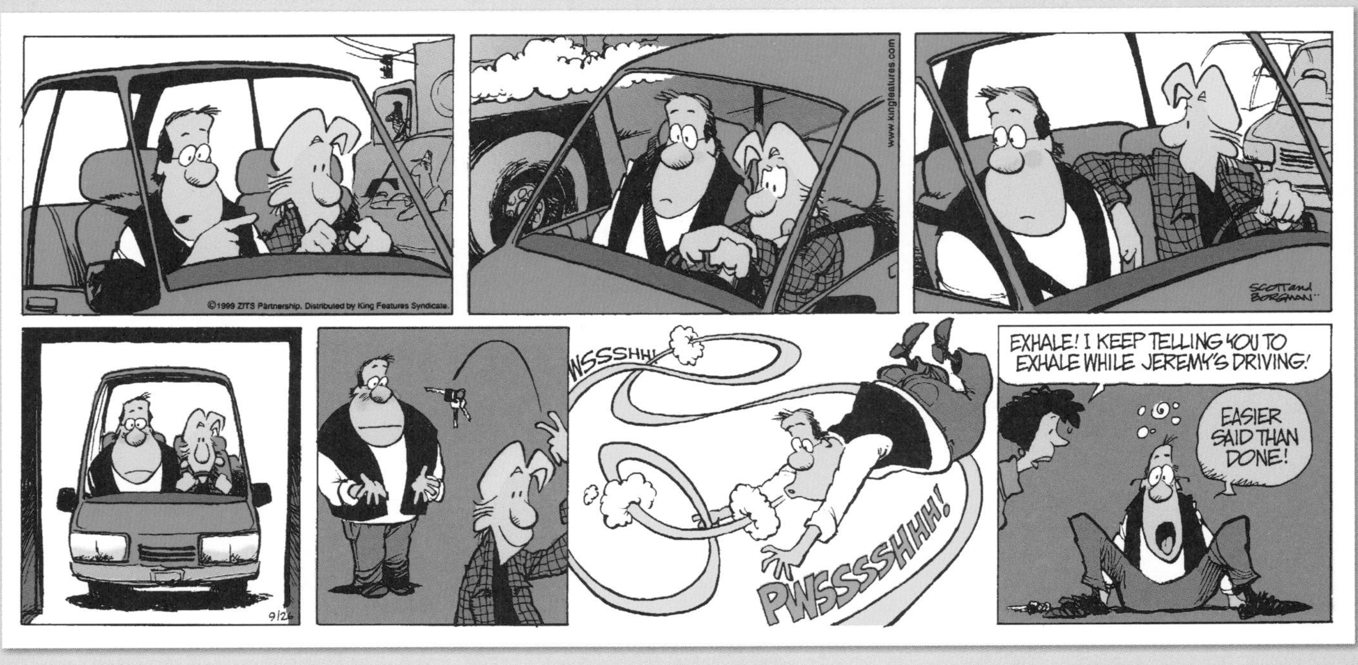
©1999 ZITS Partnership. Distributed by King Features Syndicate.
www.kingfeatures.com
SCOTT and BORGMAN
9/26
WSSSHH!
PWSSSSHHH!
EXHALE! I KEEP TELLING YOU TO EXHALE WHILE JEREMY'S DRIVING!
EASIER SAID THAN DONE!

October 10, 1999

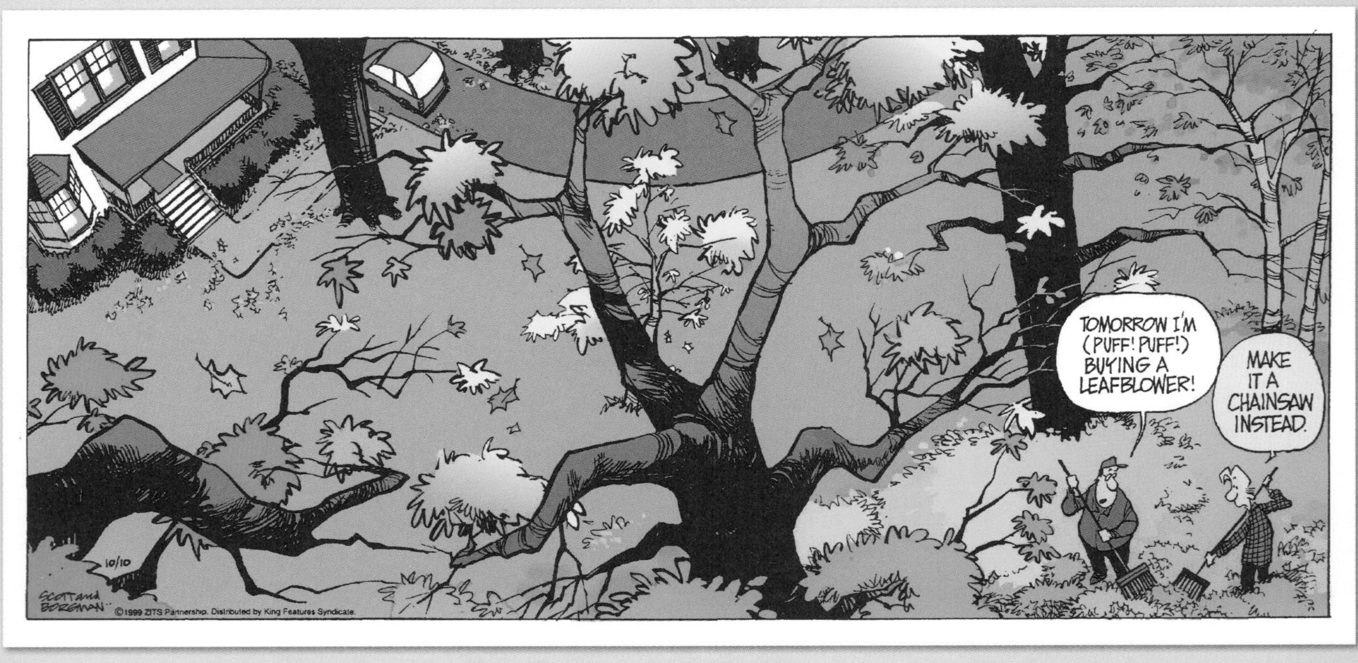
TOMORROW I'M (PUFF! PUFF!) BUYING A LEAFBLOWER!
MAKE IT A CHAINSAW INSTEAD.
10/10
SCOTT and BORGMAN
©1999 ZITS Partnership. Distributed by King Features Syndicate.

November 21, 1999

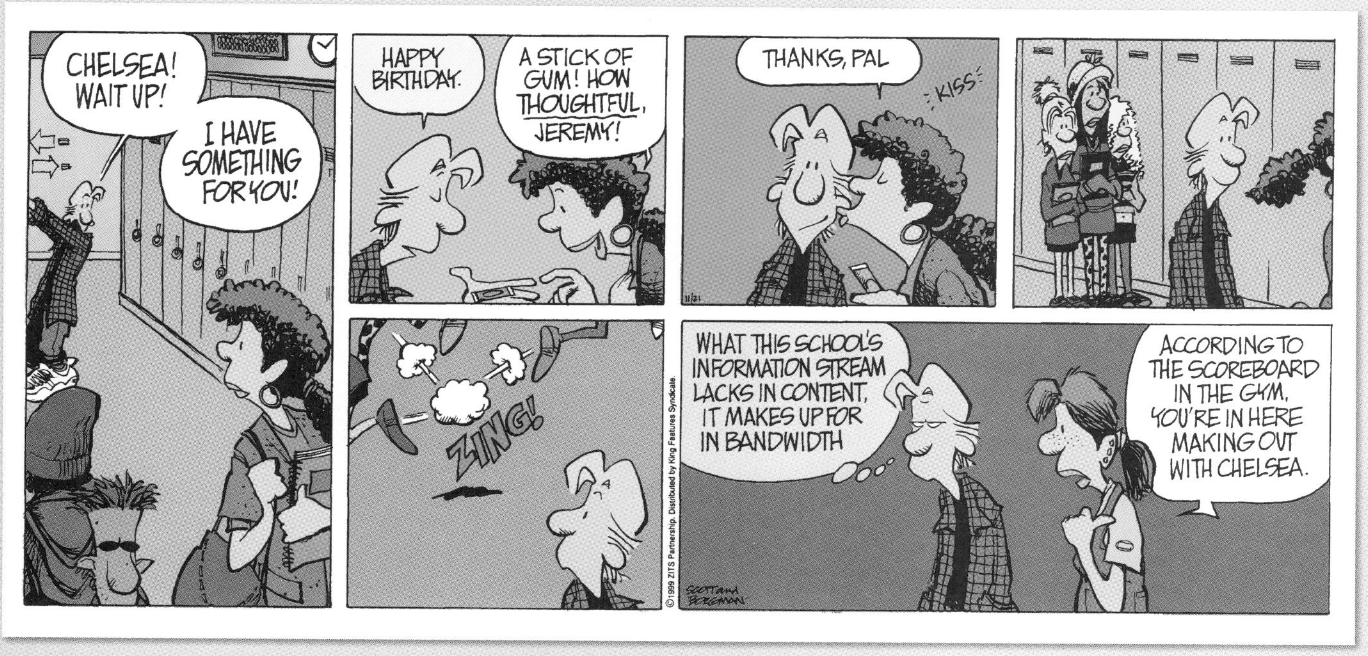
CHELSEA! WAIT UP!
I HAVE SOMETHING FOR YOU!
HAPPY BIRTHDAY.
A STICK OF GUM! HOW THOUGHTFUL, JEREMY!
THANKS, PAL
KISS
ZING!
WHAT THIS SCHOOL'S INFORMATION STREAM LACKS IN CONTENT, IT MAKES UP FOR IN BANDWIDTH
ACCORDING TO THE SCOREBOARD IN THE GYM, YOU'RE IN HERE MAKING OUT WITH CHELSEA.
© 1999 ZITS Partnership. Distributed by King Features Syndicate.
SCOTT and BORGMAN

November 28, 1999

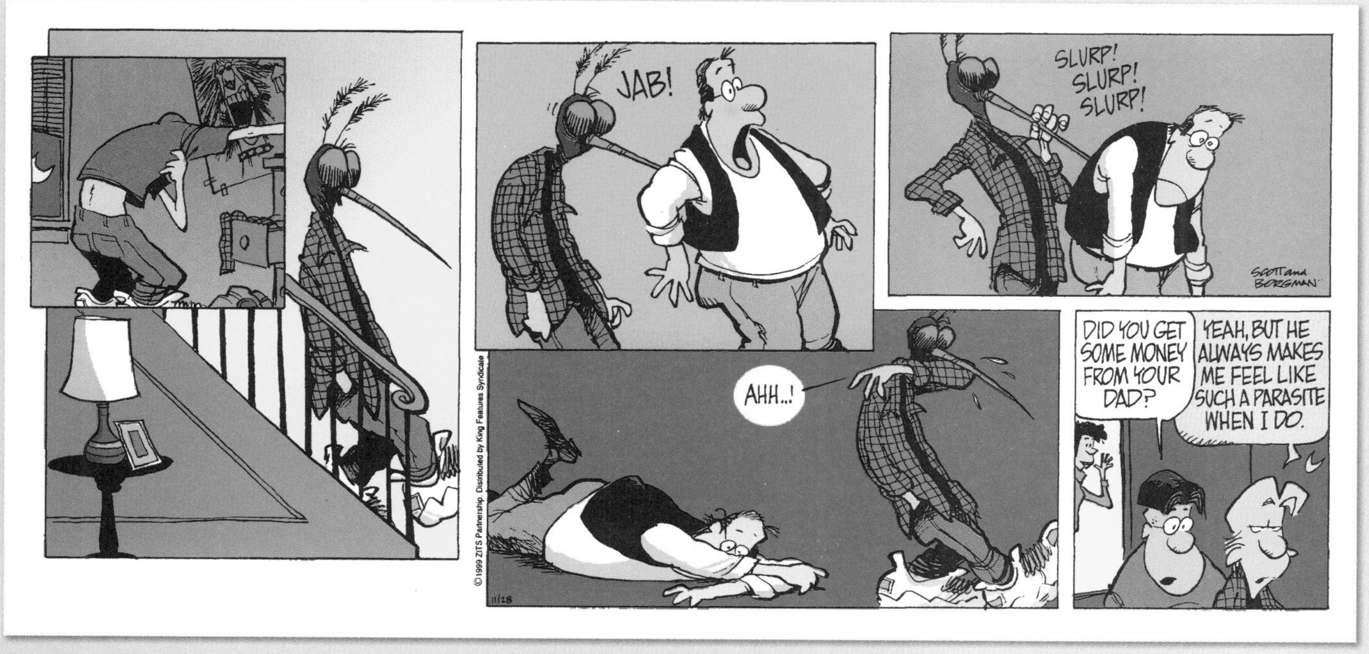
JAB!
SLURP! SLURP! SLURP!
SCOTT and BORGMAN
AHH...!
DID YOU GET SOME MONEY FROM YOUR DAD?
YEAH, BUT HE ALWAYS MAKES ME FEEL LIKE SUCH A PARASITE WHEN I DO.
© 1999 ZITS Partnership. Distributed by King Features Syndicate

April 19, 1999

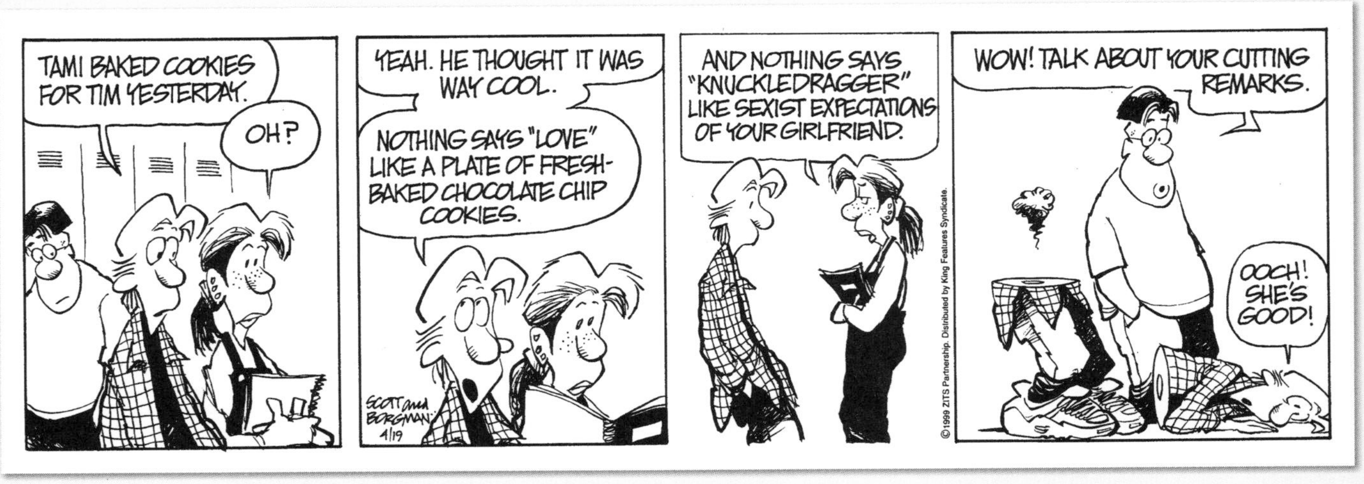

TAMI BAKED COOKIES FOR TIM YESTERDAY.
OH?
YEAH. HE THOUGHT IT WAS WAY COOL.
NOTHING SAYS "LOVE" LIKE A PLATE OF FRESH-BAKED CHOCOLATE CHIP COOKIES.
SCOTT and BORGMAN 4/19
AND NOTHING SAYS "KNUCKLEDRAGGER" LIKE SEXIST EXPECTATIONS OF YOUR GIRLFRIEND.
©1999 ZITS Partnership. Distributed by King Features Syndicate.
WOW! TALK ABOUT YOUR CUTTING REMARKS.
OOCH! SHE'S GOOD!

December 21, 1999

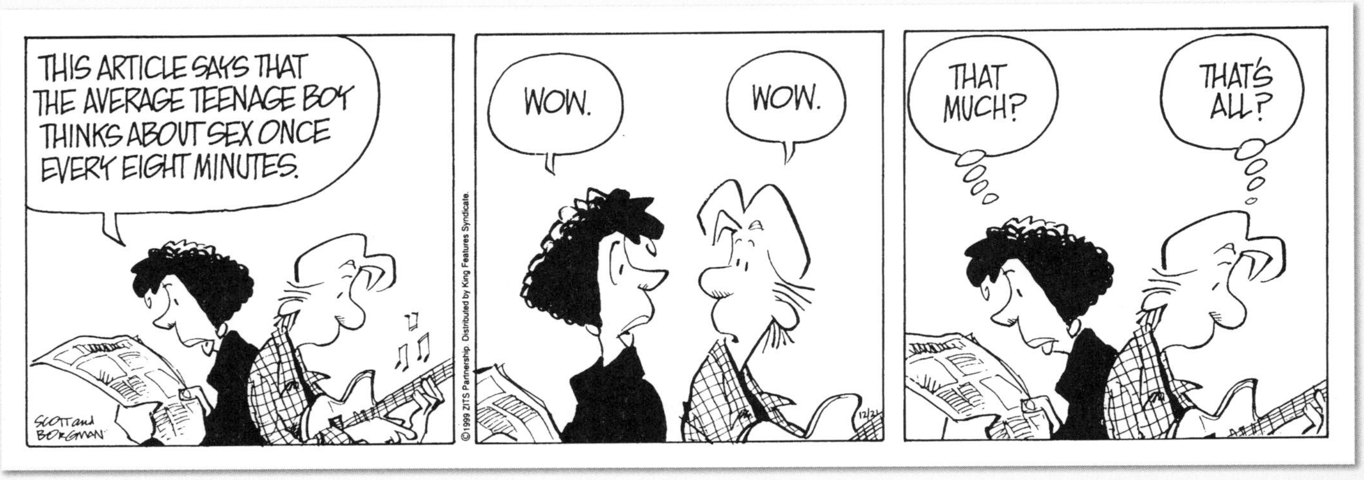

THIS ARTICLE SAYS THAT THE AVERAGE TEENAGE BOY THINKS ABOUT SEX ONCE EVERY EIGHT MINUTES.
SCOTT and BORGMAN
©1999 ZITS Partnership. Distributed by King Features Syndicate.
WOW.
WOW.
12/21
THAT MUCH?
THAT'S ALL?

December 25, 1999

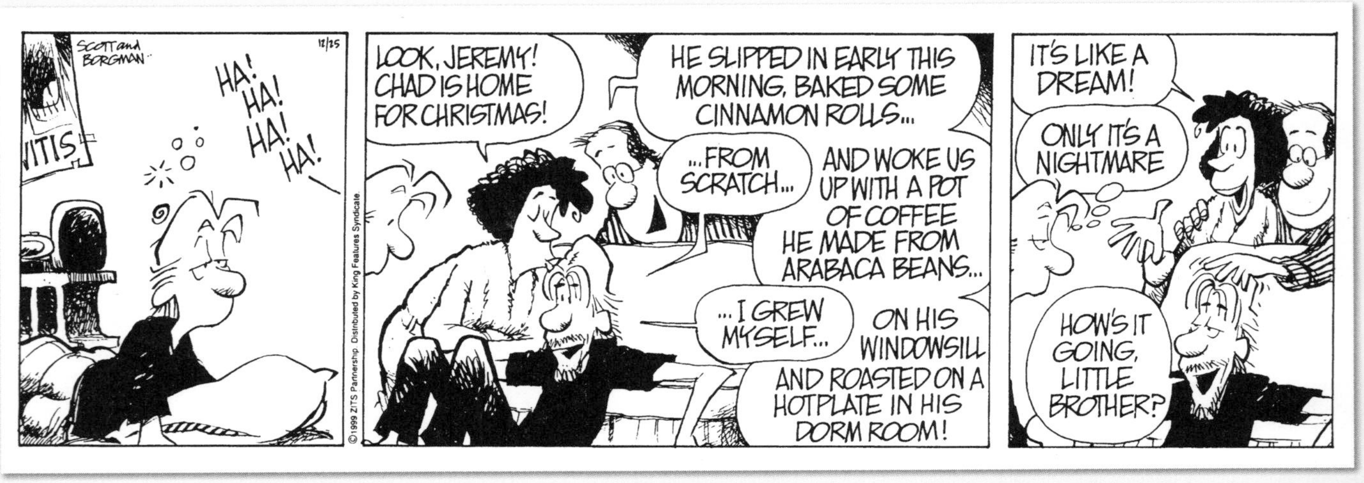

SCOTT and BORGMAN
12/25
HA! HA! HA! HA!
ZITS
©1999 ZITS Partnership. Distributed by King Features Syndicate.
LOOK, JEREMY! CHAD IS HOME FOR CHRISTMAS!
HE SLIPPED IN EARLY THIS MORNING, BAKED SOME CINNAMON ROLLS...
...FROM SCRATCH...
AND WOKE US UP WITH A POT OF COFFEE HE MADE FROM ARABACA BEANS...
...I GREW MYSELF...
ON HIS WINDOWSILL
AND ROASTED ON A HOTPLATE IN HIS DORM ROOM!
IT'S LIKE A DREAM!
ONLY IT'S A NIGHTMARE
HOW'S IT GOING, LITTLE BROTHER?

German 101

Jerry Scott

So I got a call in early 2000 from somebody who said that *Zits* was to be awarded the Max & Moritz Prize for Best Comic Strip by the International Comics Shows folks in Erlangen, Germany. For some reason, Jim wasn't available to go, so my wife, Kim, and I decided to make the trip.

The thing about the Max & Moritz Prize is that you don't just show up and get a medal. No, you show up, are handed a medal, and then expected to give a funny speech to several hundred non-English-speaking attendees while holding two heavy loaves of bread baked in the shape of two boys (it's complicated—Google it).

Since I was doing all of the heavy lifting (sorry) on this adventure, Jim offered to write my speech. He happened to have a close friend who is fluent in German, so they concocted a plan. My acceptance speech would consist of simply reading a letter written to the Max & Moritz officials and attendees from Jim Borgman . . . in German. I don't speak German, so they wrote it out phonetically for me. After explaining all this to the folks at the ceremony, and apologizing for not knowing what I was about to say, I read the letter. Here's what it looked like:

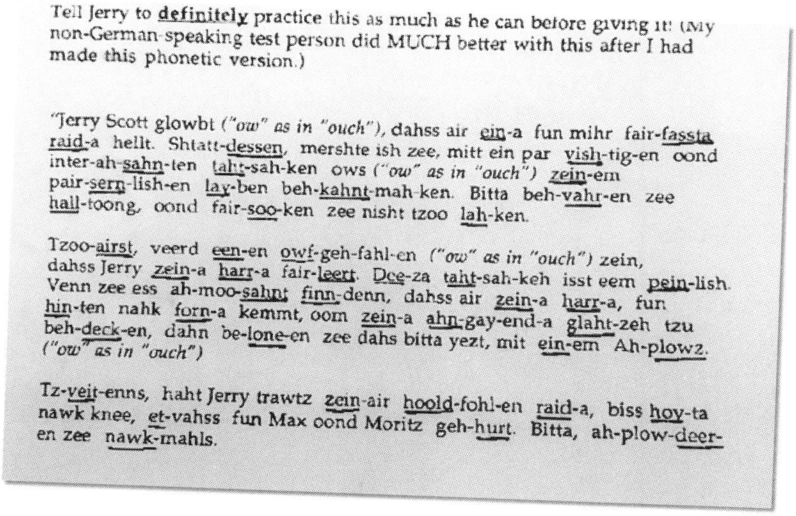

Tell Jerry to **definitely** practice this as much as he can before giving it! (My non-German-speaking test person did MUCH better with this after I had made this phonetic version.)

"Jerry Scott glowbt (*"ow" as in "ouch"*), dahss air ein-a fun mihr fair-fassta raid-a hellt. Shtatt-dessen, mershte ish zee, mitt ein par vish-tig-en oond inter-ah-sahn-ten taht-sah-ken ows (*"ow" as in "ouch"*) zein-em pair-sern-lish-en lay-ben beh-kahnt-mah-ken. Bitta beh-vahr-en zee hall-toong, oond fair-soo-ken zee nisht tzoo lah-ken.

Tzoo-airst, veerd een-en owf-geh-fahl-en (*"ow" as in "ouch"*) zein, dahss Jerry zein-a harr-a fair-leert. Dee-za taht-sah-keh isst eem pein-lish. Venn zee ess ah-moo-sahnt finn-denn, dahss air zein-a harr-a, fun hin-ten nahk forn-a kemmt, oom zein-a ahn-gay-end-a glaht-zeh tzu beh-deck-en, dahn be-lone-en zee dahs bitta yezt, mit ein-em Ah-plowz. (*"ow" as in "ouch"*)

Tz-veit-enns, haht Jerry trawtz zein-air hoold-fohl-en raid-a, biss hoy-ta nawk knee, et-vahss fun Max oond Moritz geh-hurt. Bitta, ah-plow-deer-en zee nawk-mahls.

And here's what I was saying:

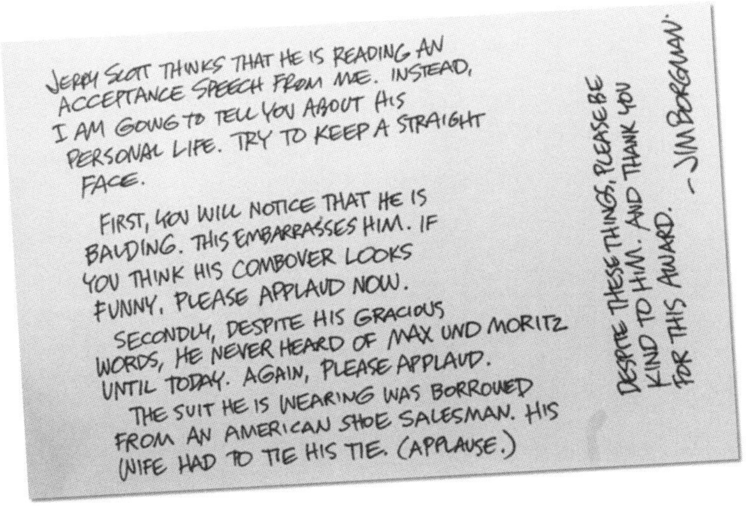

JERRY SCOTT THINKS THAT HE IS READING AN ACCEPTANCE SPEECH FROM ME. INSTEAD, I AM GOING TO TELL YOU ABOUT HIS PERSONAL LIFE. TRY TO KEEP A STRAIGHT FACE.

FIRST, YOU WILL NOTICE THAT HE IS BALDING. THIS EMBARRASSES HIM. IF YOU THINK HIS COMBOVER LOOKS FUNNY, PLEASE APPLAUD NOW.

SECONDLY, DESPITE HIS GRACIOUS WORDS, HE NEVER HEARD OF MAX UND MORITZ UNTIL TODAY. AGAIN, PLEASE APPLAUD.

THE SUIT HE IS WEARING WAS BORROWED FROM AN AMERICAN SHOE SALESMAN. HIS WIFE HAD TO TIE HIS TIE. (APPLAUSE.)

DESPITE THESE THINGS, PLEASE BE KIND TO HIM. AND THANK YOU FOR THIS AWARD.

– JIM BORGMAN

The crowd went wild, Kim and I ate some of the bread before dumping the rest in a trash can in the Munich Airport, and comic fans in Germany think I'm an idiot. That's a win in my book.

January 17, 2000

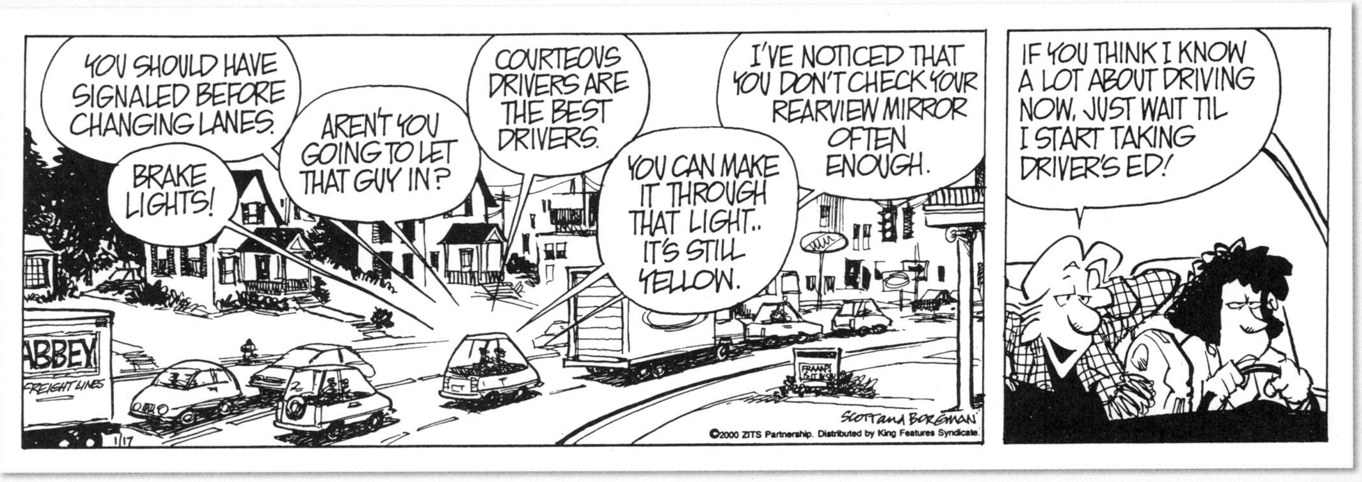
YOU SHOULD HAVE SIGNALED BEFORE CHANGING LANES.
BRAKE LIGHTS!
AREN'T YOU GOING TO LET THAT GUY IN?
COURTEOUS DRIVERS ARE THE BEST DRIVERS.
YOU CAN MAKE IT THROUGH THAT LIGHT.. IT'S STILL YELLOW.
I'VE NOTICED THAT YOU DON'T CHECK YOUR REARVIEW MIRROR OFTEN ENOUGH.
ABBEY
FREIGHT LINES
1/17
SCOTT and BORGMAN
©2000 ZITS Partnership. Distributed by King Features Syndicate.
IF YOU THINK I KNOW A LOT ABOUT DRIVING NOW, JUST WAIT TIL I START TAKING DRIVER'S ED!

January 24, 2000

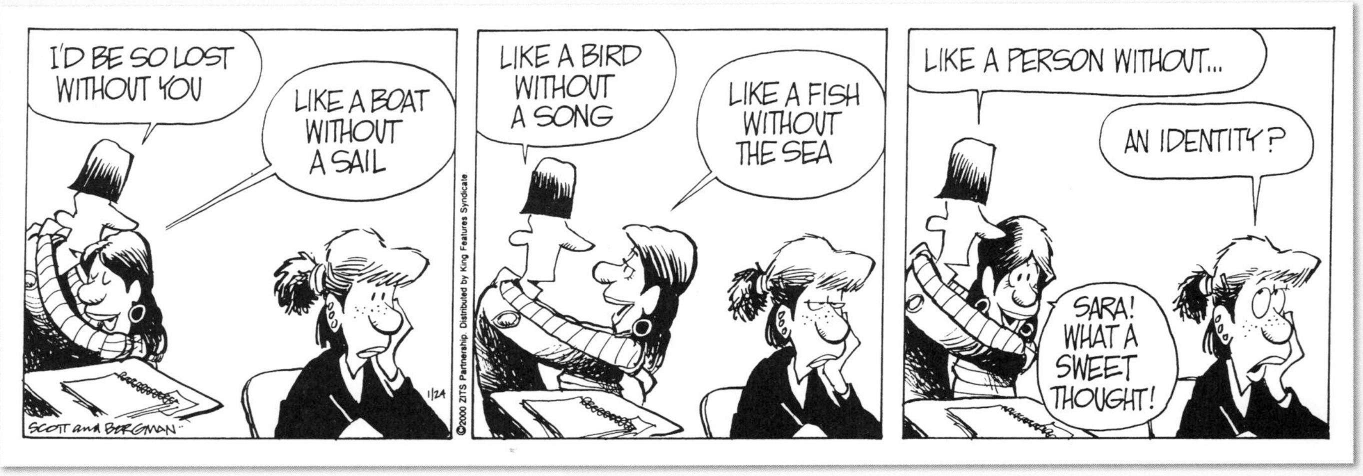
I'D BE SO LOST WITHOUT YOU
LIKE A BOAT WITHOUT A SAIL
SCOTT and BORGMAN
1/24
©2000 ZITS Partnership. Distributed by King Features Syndicate
LIKE A BIRD WITHOUT A SONG
LIKE A FISH WITHOUT THE SEA
LIKE A PERSON WITHOUT...
AN IDENTITY?
SARA! WHAT A SWEET THOUGHT!

April 10, 2000

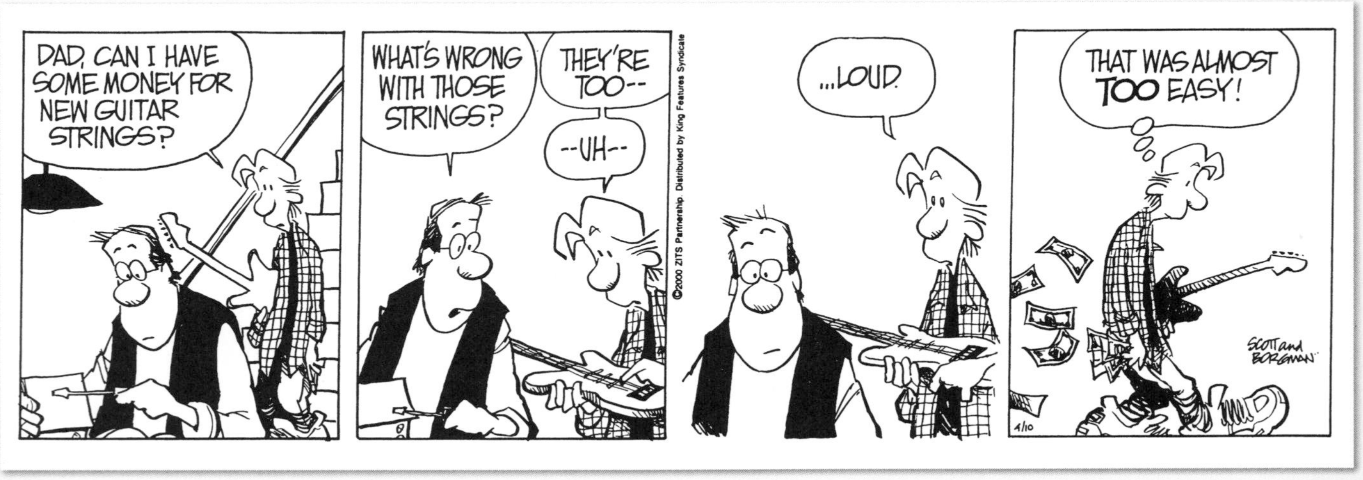
DAD, CAN I HAVE SOME MONEY FOR NEW GUITAR STRINGS?
WHAT'S WRONG WITH THOSE STRINGS?
THEY'RE TOO--
--UH--
©2000 ZITS Partnership. Distributed by King Features Syndicate
...LOUD.
THAT WAS ALMOST TOO EASY!
SCOTT and BORGMAN
4/10

February 14, 2000

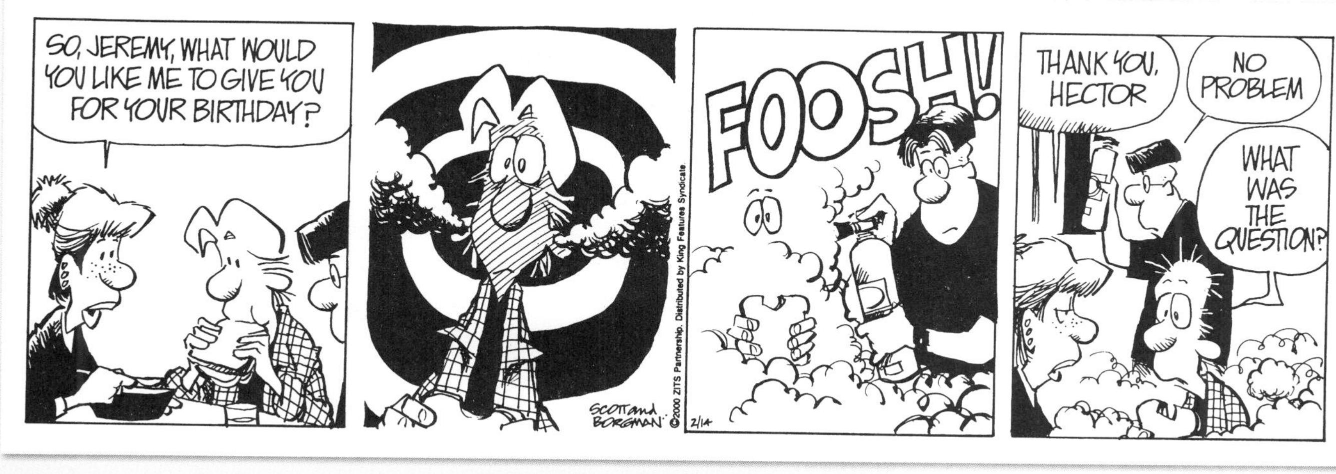
SO, JEREMY, WHAT WOULD YOU LIKE ME TO GIVE YOU FOR YOUR BIRTHDAY?
FOOSH!
THANK YOU, HECTOR
NO PROBLEM
WHAT WAS THE QUESTION?
SCOTT and BORGMAN
©2000 ZITS Partnership. Distributed by King Features Syndicate
2/14

March 23, 2000

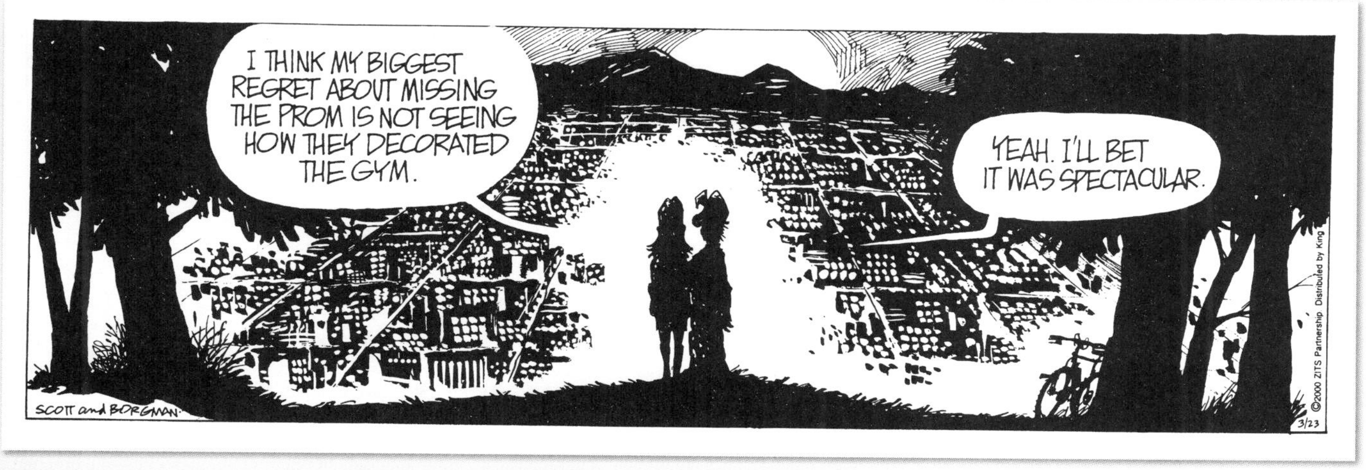
I THINK MY BIGGEST REGRET ABOUT MISSING THE PROM IS NOT SEEING HOW THEY DECORATED THE GYM.
YEAH. I'LL BET IT WAS SPECTACULAR.
SCOTT and BORGMAN
©2000 ZITS Partnership. Distributed by King
3/23

April 13, 2000

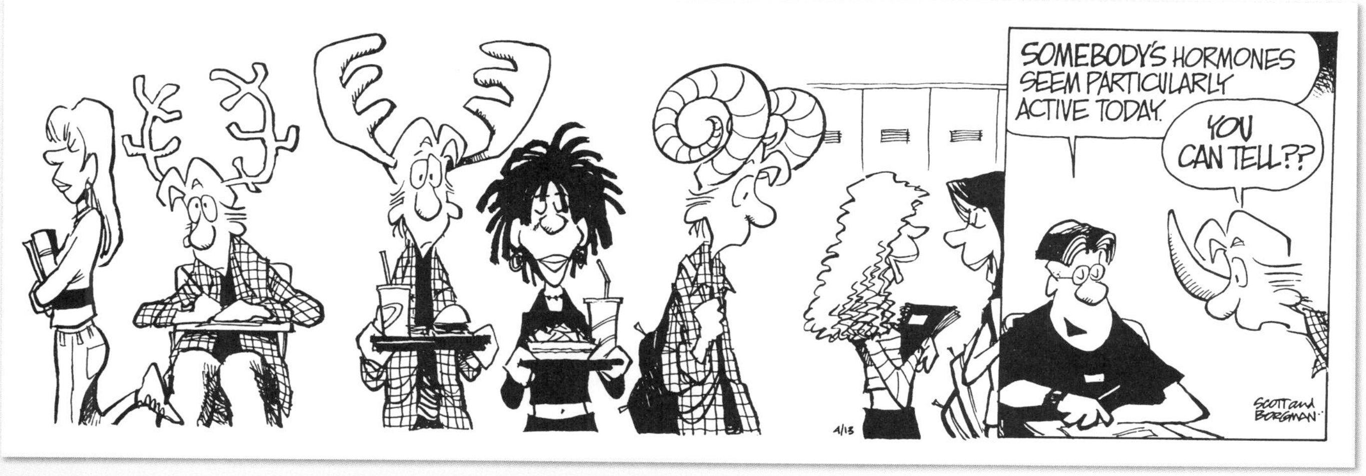
SOMEBODY'S HORMONES SEEM PARTICULARLY ACTIVE TODAY.
YOU CAN TELL??
4/13
SCOTT and BORGMAN

February 20, 2000

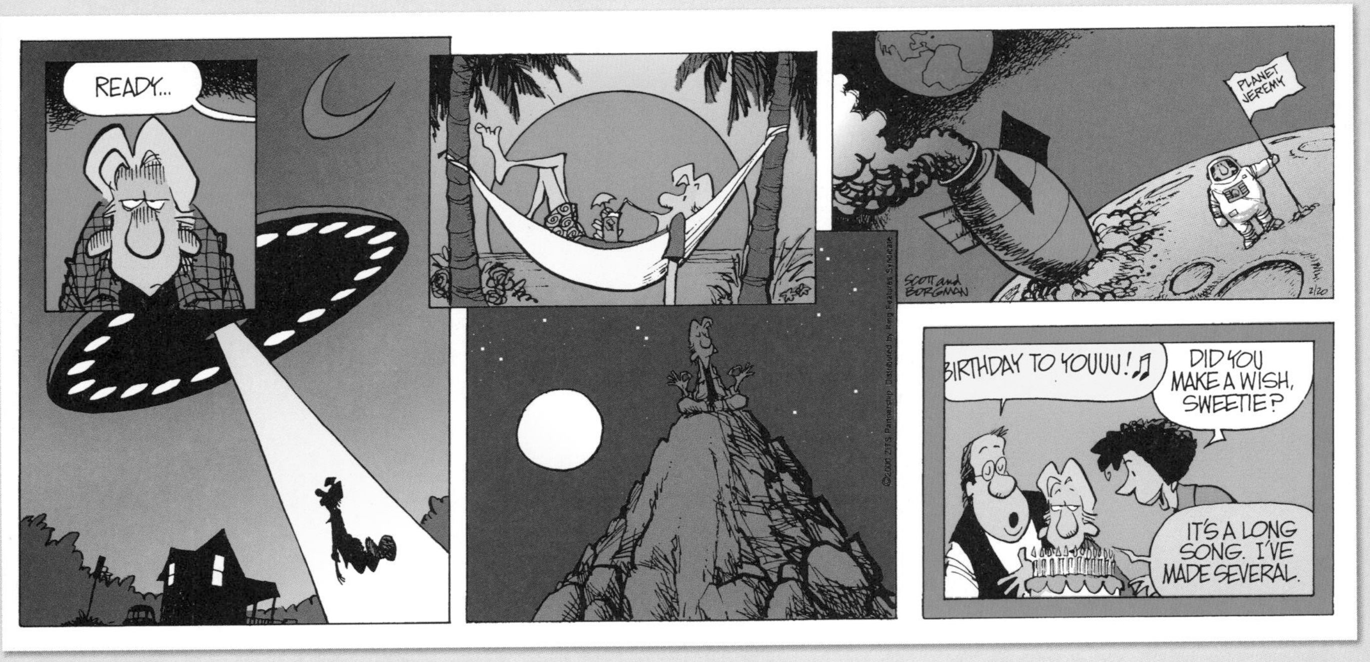
READY...
PLANET JEREMY
BIRTHDAY TO YOUUU!
DID YOU MAKE A WISH, SWEETIE?
IT'S A LONG SONG. I'VE MADE SEVERAL.
©2000 ZITS Partnership. Distributed by King Features Syndicate
SCOTT and BORGMAN

May 28, 2000

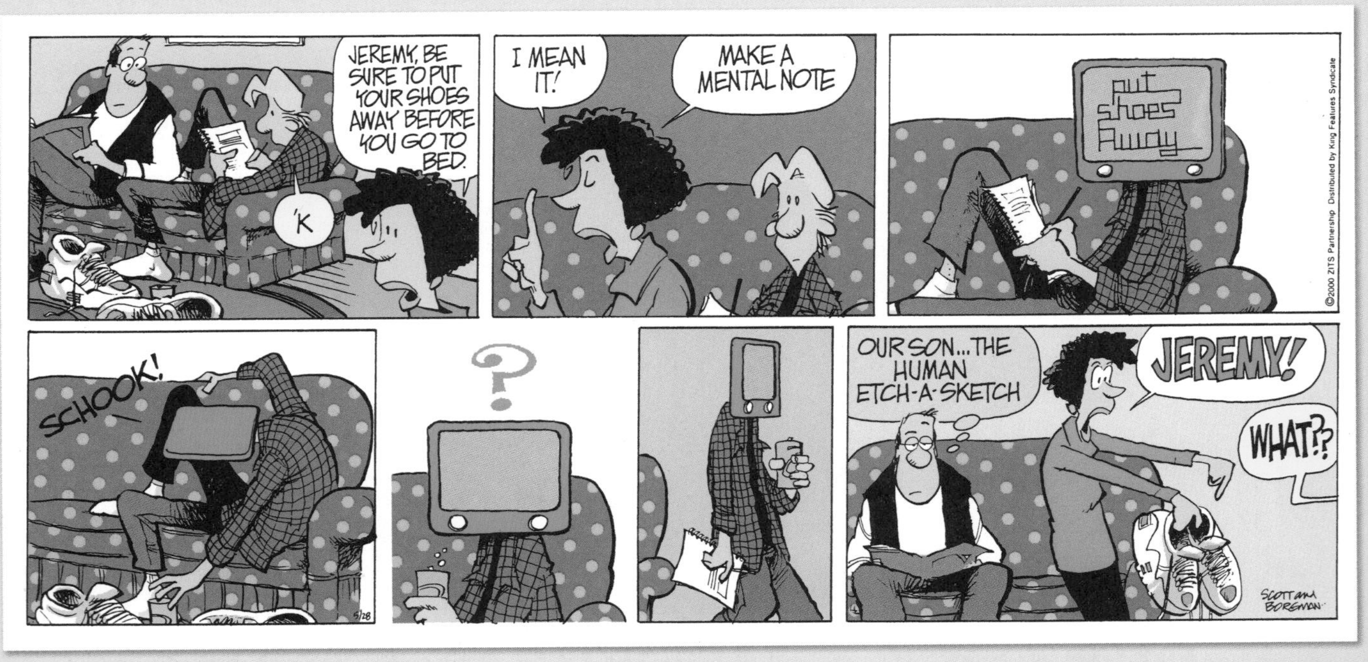
JEREMY, BE SURE TO PUT YOUR SHOES AWAY BEFORE YOU GO TO BED.
'K
I MEAN IT!
MAKE A MENTAL NOTE
put shoes Away
©2000 ZITS Partnership. Distributed by King Features Syndicate
SCHOOK!
?
OUR SON...THE HUMAN ETCH-A-SKETCH
JEREMY!
WHAT?!?
SCOTT and BORGMAN

April 25, 2000

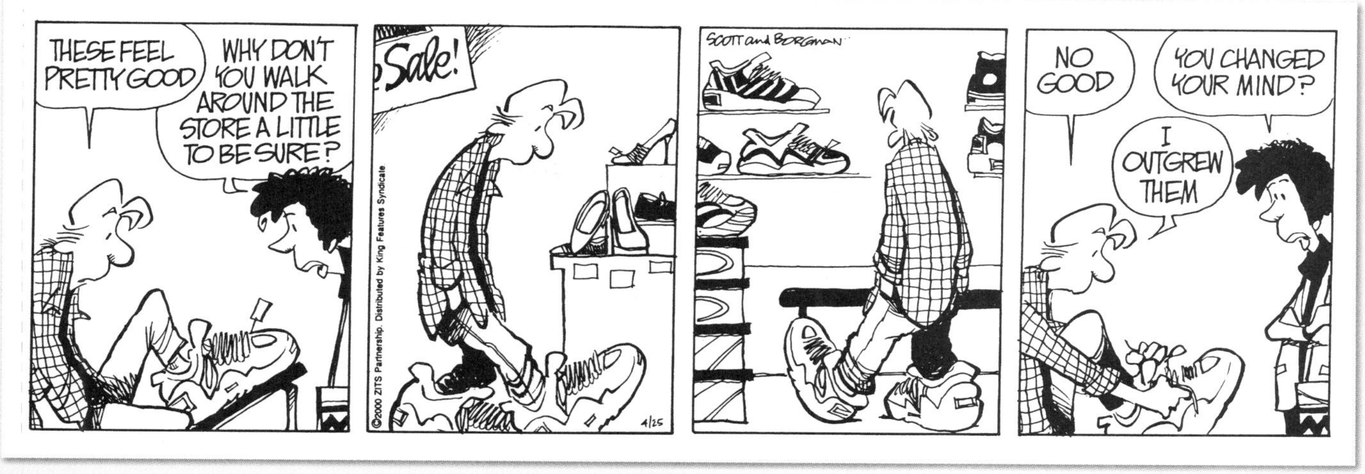
THESE FEEL PRETTY GOOD
WHY DON'T YOU WALK AROUND THE STORE A LITTLE TO BE SURE?
Sale!
SCOTT and BORGMAN
©2000 ZITS Partnership. Distributed by King Features Syndicate
4/25
NO GOOD
YOU CHANGED YOUR MIND?
I OUTGREW THEM

May 1, 2000

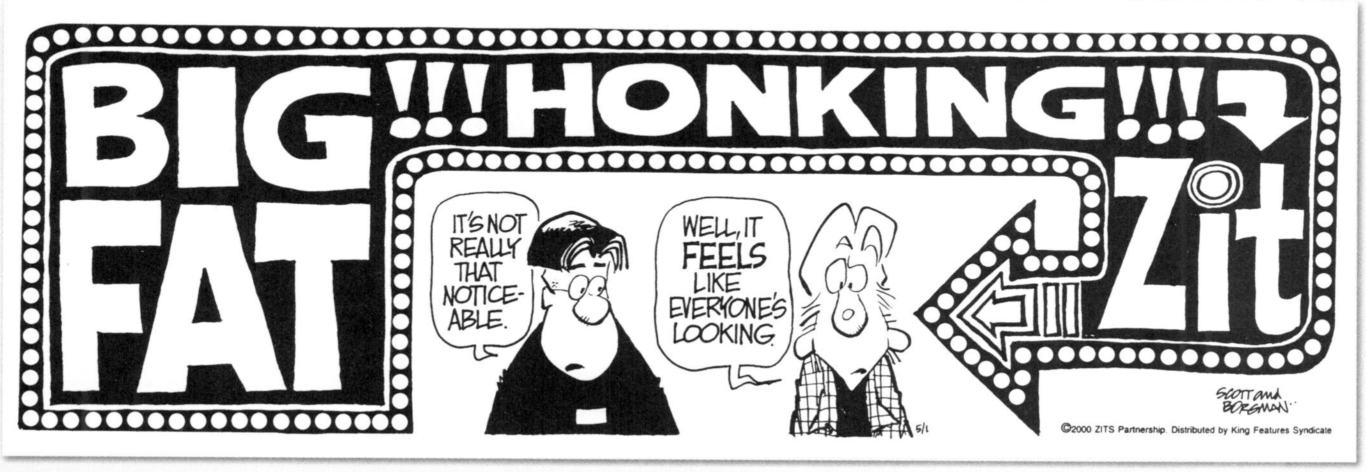
BIG!!! HONKING!!! FAT Zit
IT'S NOT REALLY THAT NOTICE-ABLE.
WELL, IT FEELS LIKE EVERYONE'S LOOKING.
5/1
SCOTT and BORGMAN
©2000 ZITS Partnership. Distributed by King Features Syndicate

May 3, 2000

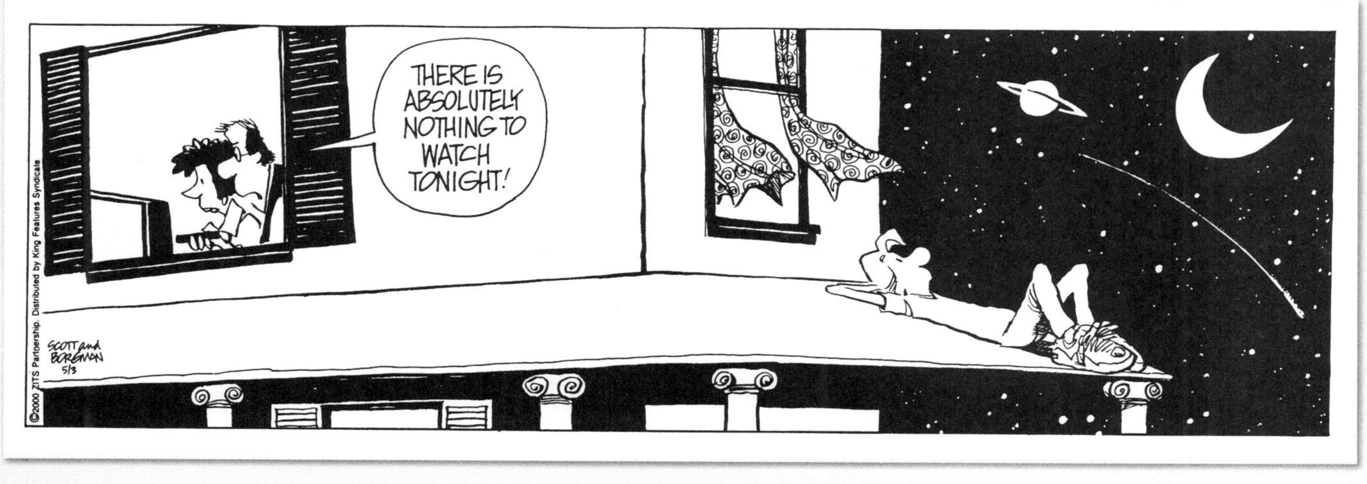
THERE IS ABSOLUTELY NOTHING TO WATCH TONIGHT!
SCOTT and BORGMAN 5/3
©2000 ZITS Partnership. Distributed by King Features Syndicate

June 18, 2000

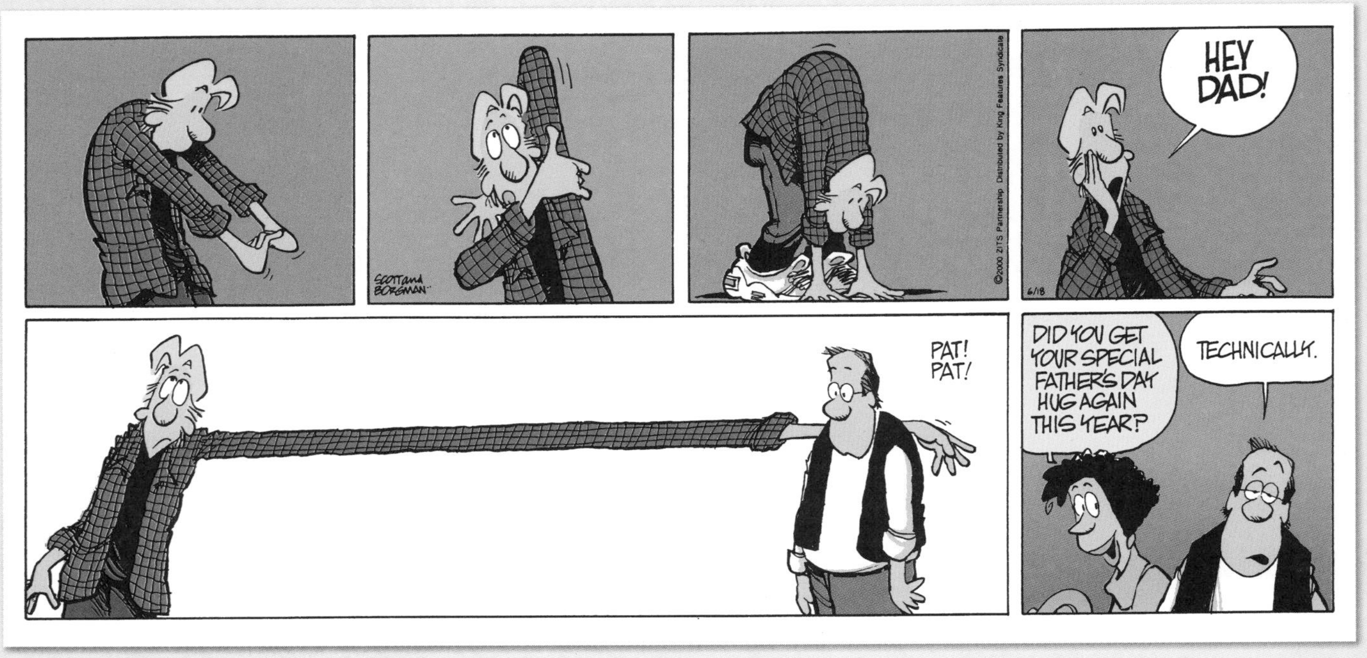

SCOTT AND BORGMAN
©2000 ZITS Partnership. Distributed by King Features Syndicate
6/18
HEY DAD!
PAT! PAT!
DID YOU GET YOUR SPECIAL FATHER'S DAY HUG AGAIN THIS YEAR?
TECHNICALLY.

July 30, 2000

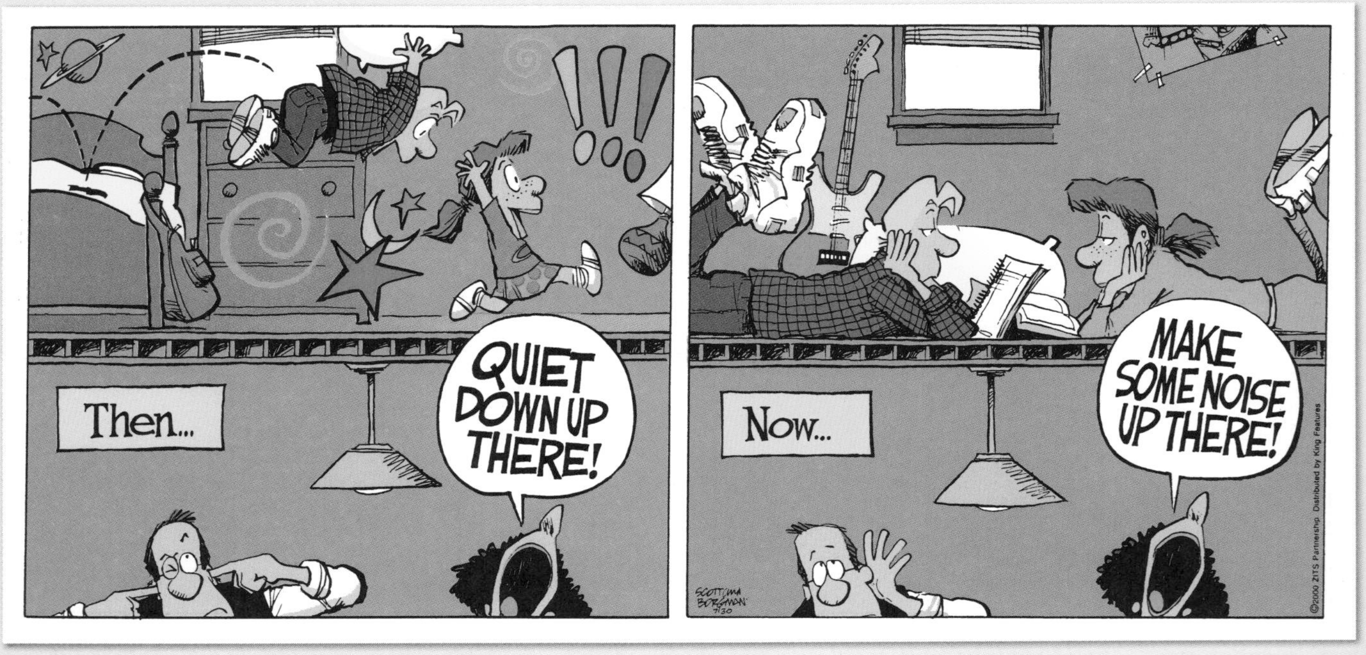

Then...
QUIET DOWN UP THERE!
Now...
MAKE SOME NOISE UP THERE!
SCOTT AND BORGMAN 7/30
©2000 ZITS Partnership. Distributed by King Features

June 26, 2000

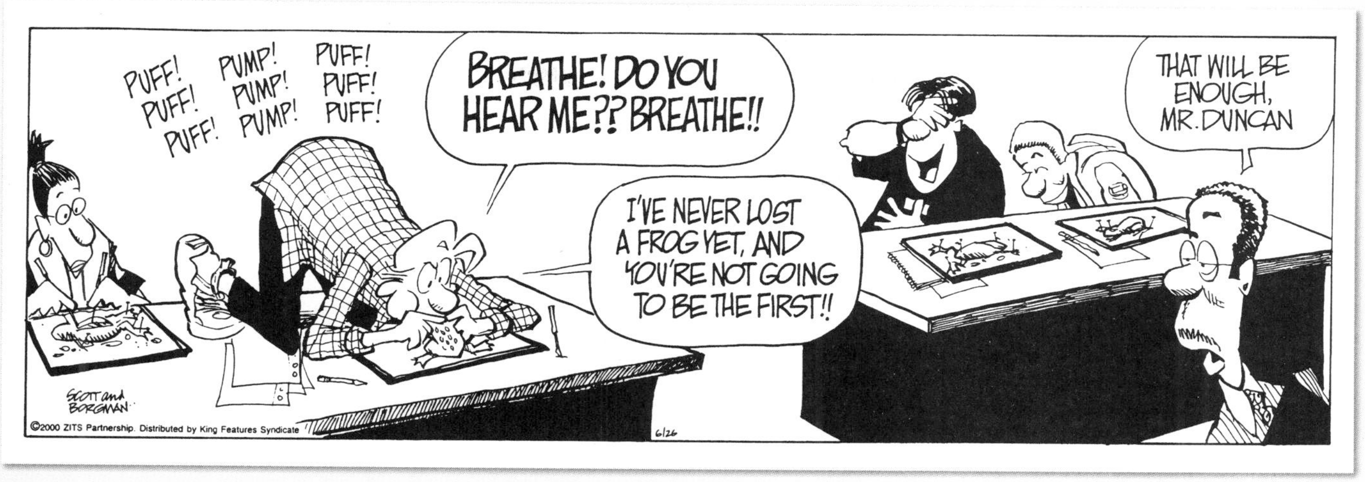

PUFF! PUFF! PUFF! PUMP! PUMP! PUMP! PUFF! PUFF! PUFF!
BREATHE! DO YOU HEAR ME?? BREATHE!!
I'VE NEVER LOST A FROG YET, AND YOU'RE NOT GOING TO BE THE FIRST!!
THAT WILL BE ENOUGH, MR. DUNCAN
SCOTT and BORGMAN
©2000 ZITS Partnership. Distributed by King Features Syndicate

July 10, 2000

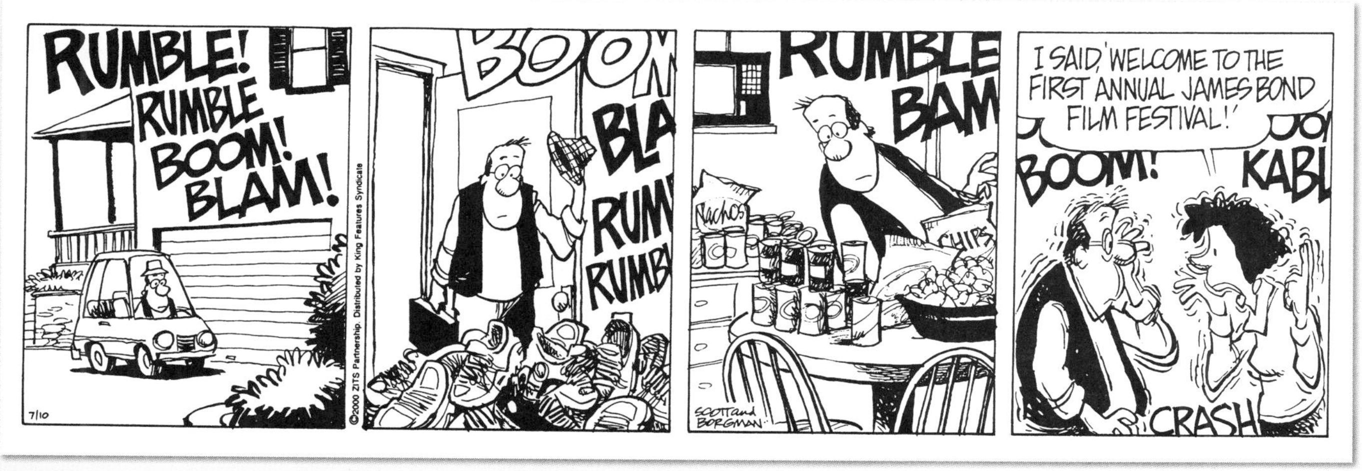

RUMBLE! RUMBLE BOOM! BLAM!
BOO
BLA
RUM
RUMB
©2000 ZITS Partnership. Distributed by King Features Syndicate
RUMBLE
BAM
NACHOS
CHIPS
SCOTT and BORGMAN
I SAID, 'WELCOME TO THE FIRST ANNUAL JAMES BOND FILM FESTIVAL!'
BOOM!
KABL
CRASH

July 19, 2000

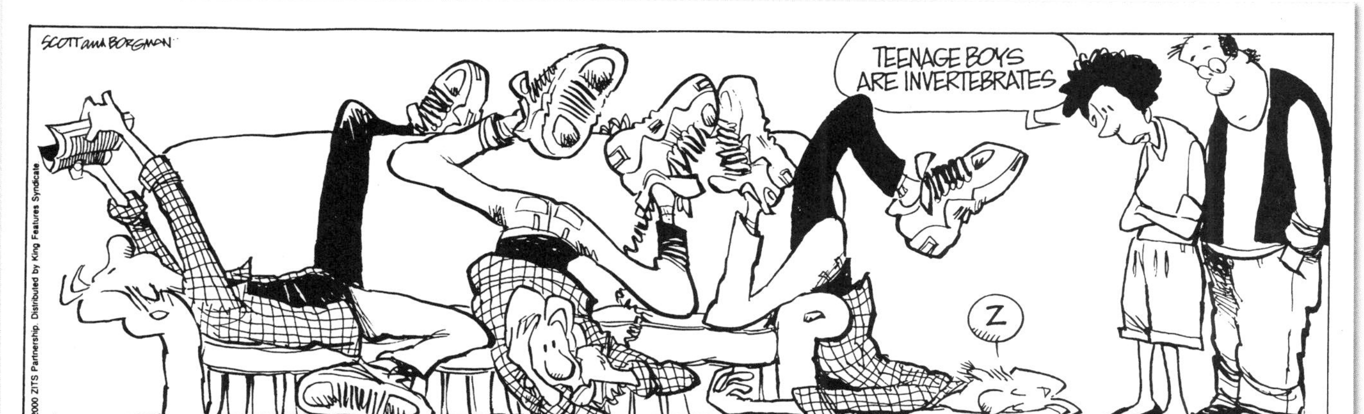

SCOTT and BORGMAN
TEENAGE BOYS ARE INVERTEBRATES
Z
©2000 ZITS Partnership. Distributed by King Features Syndicate

July 26, 2000

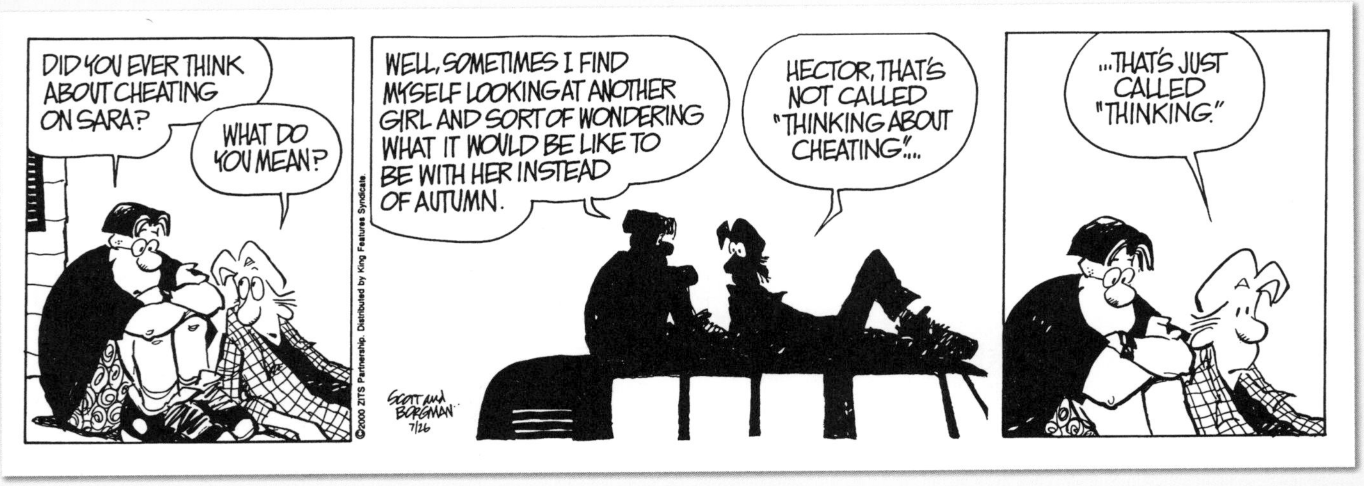

DID YOU EVER THINK ABOUT CHEATING ON SARA?
WHAT DO YOU MEAN?
WELL, SOMETIMES I FIND MYSELF LOOKING AT ANOTHER GIRL AND SORT OF WONDERING WHAT IT WOULD BE LIKE TO BE WITH HER INSTEAD OF AUTUMN.
HECTOR, THAT'S NOT CALLED "THINKING ABOUT CHEATING"...
...THAT'S JUST CALLED "THINKING."
©2000 ZITS Partnership. Distributed by King Features Syndicate.
SCOTT AND BORGMAN 7/26

August 24, 2000

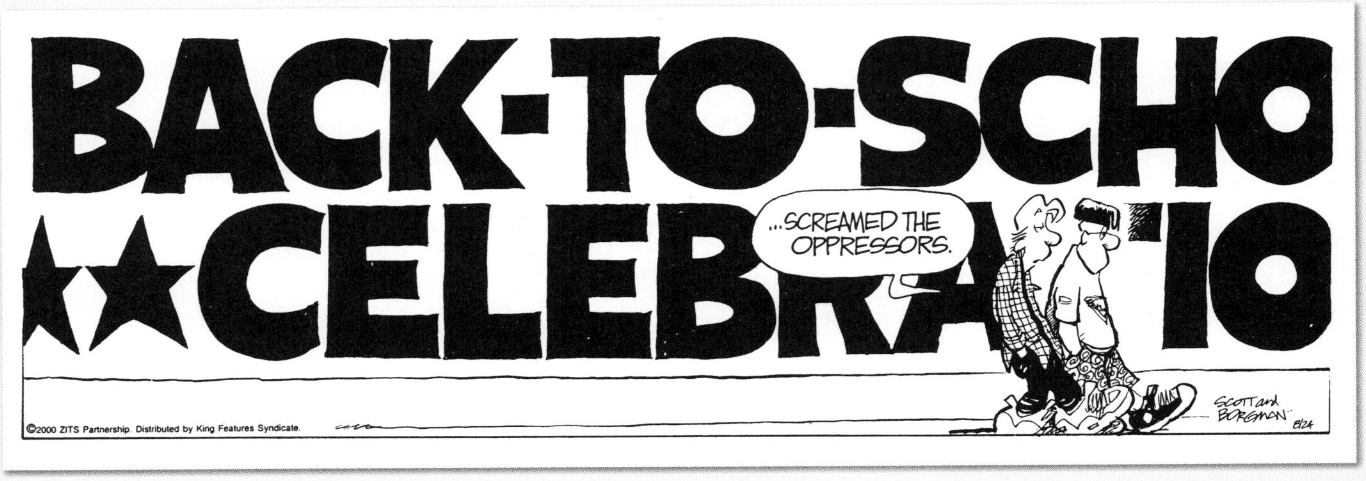

BACK-TO-SCHO
★★CELEBRA'IO
...SCREAMED THE OPPRESSORS.
©2000 ZITS Partnership. Distributed by King Features Syndicate.
SCOTT AND BORGMAN 8/24

September 1, 2000

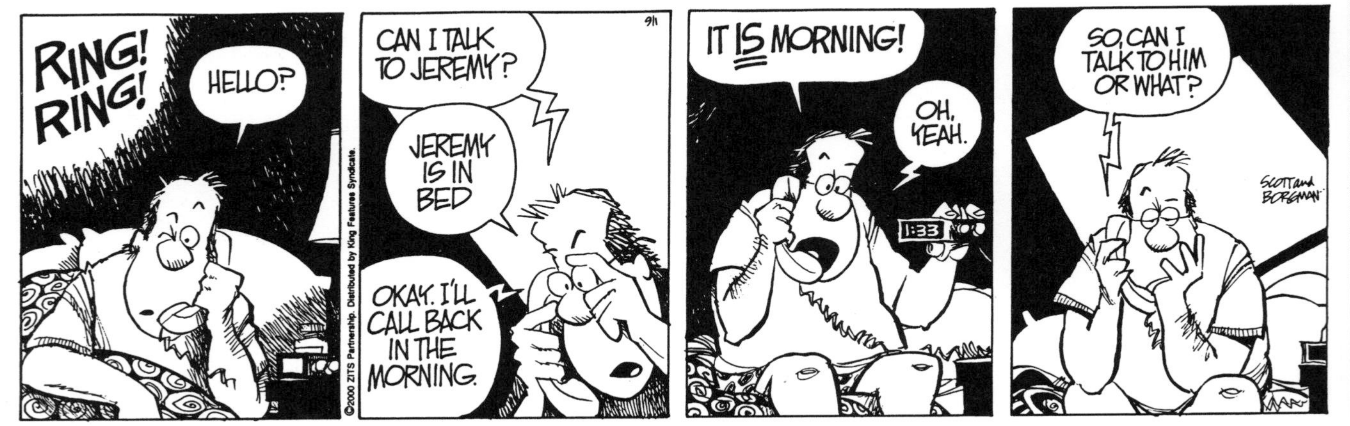

RING! RING!
HELLO?
CAN I TALK TO JEREMY?
JEREMY IS IN BED
OKAY. I'LL CALL BACK IN THE MORNING.
©2000 ZITS Partnership. Distributed by King Features Syndicate.
9/1
IT IS MORNING!
OH, YEAH.
1:33
SO, CAN I TALK TO HIM OR WHAT?
SCOTT AND BORGMAN

August 27, 2000

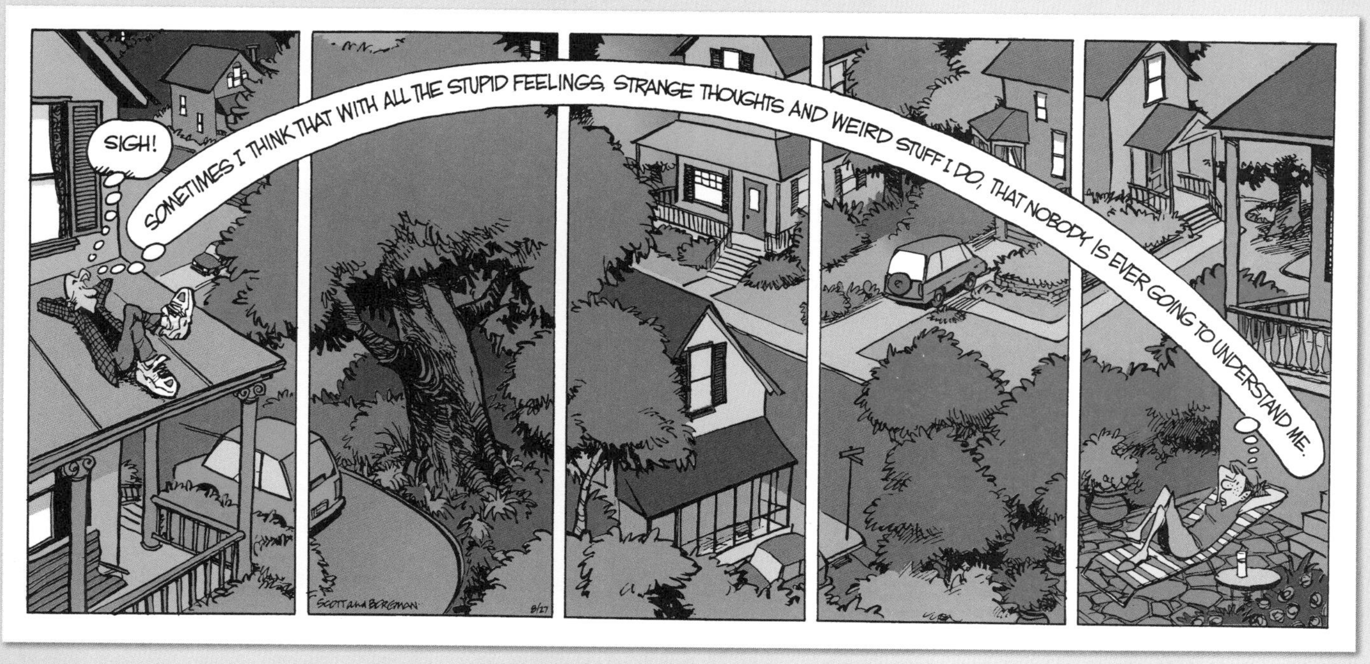

SIGH!
SOMETIMES I THINK THAT WITH ALL THE STUPID FEELINGS, STRANGE THOUGHTS AND WEIRD STUFF I DO, THAT NOBODY IS EVER GOING TO UNDERSTAND ME.
SCOTT and BORGMAN
8/27

October 29, 2000

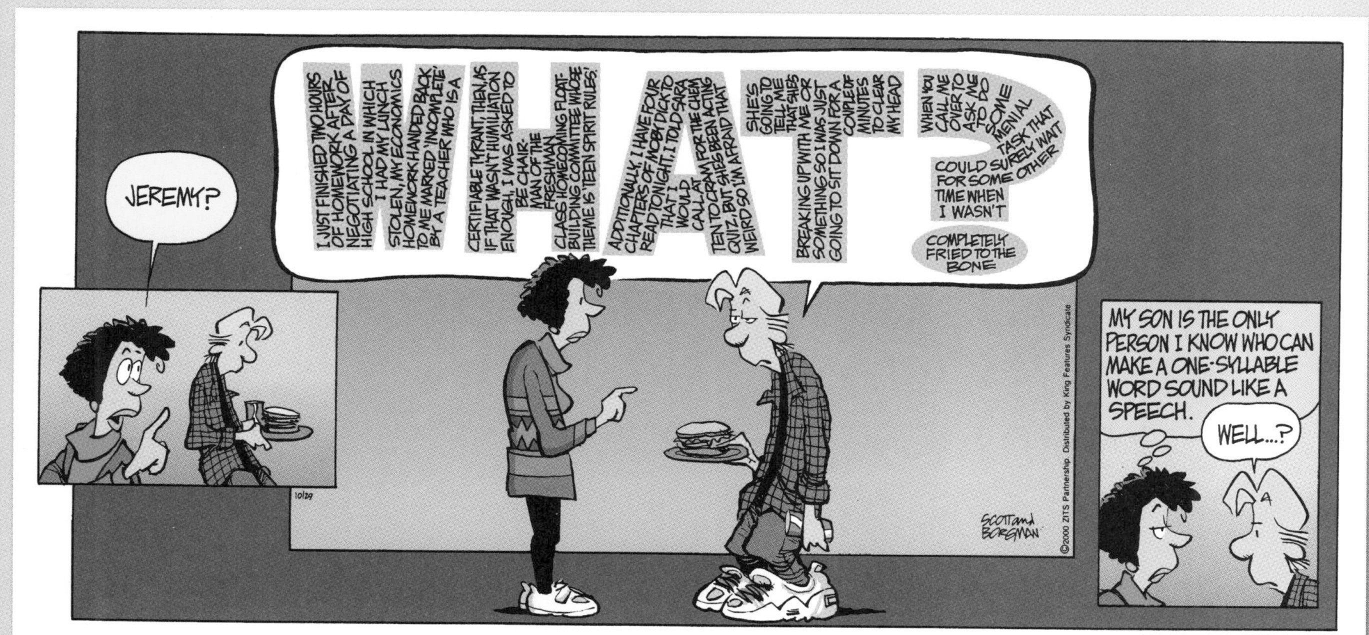

JEREMY?
10/29
WHAT?
I JUST FINISHED TWO HOURS OF HOMEWORK AFTER NEGOTIATING A DAY OF HIGH SCHOOL IN WHICH I HAD MY LUNCH STOLEN, MY ECONOMICS HOMEWORK HANDED BACK TO ME MARKED 'INCOMPLETE' BY A TEACHER WHO IS A CERTIFIABLE TYRANT. THEN, AS IF THAT WASN'T HUMILIATION ENOUGH, I WAS ASKED TO BE CHAIRMAN OF THE FRESHMAN CLASS HOMECOMING FLOAT-BUILDING COMMITTEE WHOSE THEME IS 'TEEN SPIRIT RULES.'
ADDITIONALLY, I HAVE FOUR CHAPTERS OF MOBY DICK TO READ TONIGHT. I TOLD SARA THAT I WOULD CALL AT TEN TO CRAM FOR THE CHEM QUIZ, BUT SHE'S BEEN ACTING WEIRD SO I'M AFRAID THAT SHE'S GOING TO TELL ME THAT SHE'S BREAKING UP WITH ME OR SOMETHING SO I WAS JUST GOING TO SIT DOWN FOR A COUPLE OF MINUTES TO CLEAR MY HEAD
WHEN YOU CALL ME OVER TO ASK ME TO DO SOME MENIAL TASK THAT COULD SURELY WAIT FOR SOME OTHER TIME WHEN I WASN'T
COMPLETELY FRIED TO THE BONE
SCOTT and BORGMAN
©2000 ZITS Partnership. Distributed by King Features Syndicate
MY SON IS THE ONLY PERSON I KNOW WHO CAN MAKE A ONE-SYLLABLE WORD SOUND LIKE A SPEECH.
WELL...?

September 12, 2000

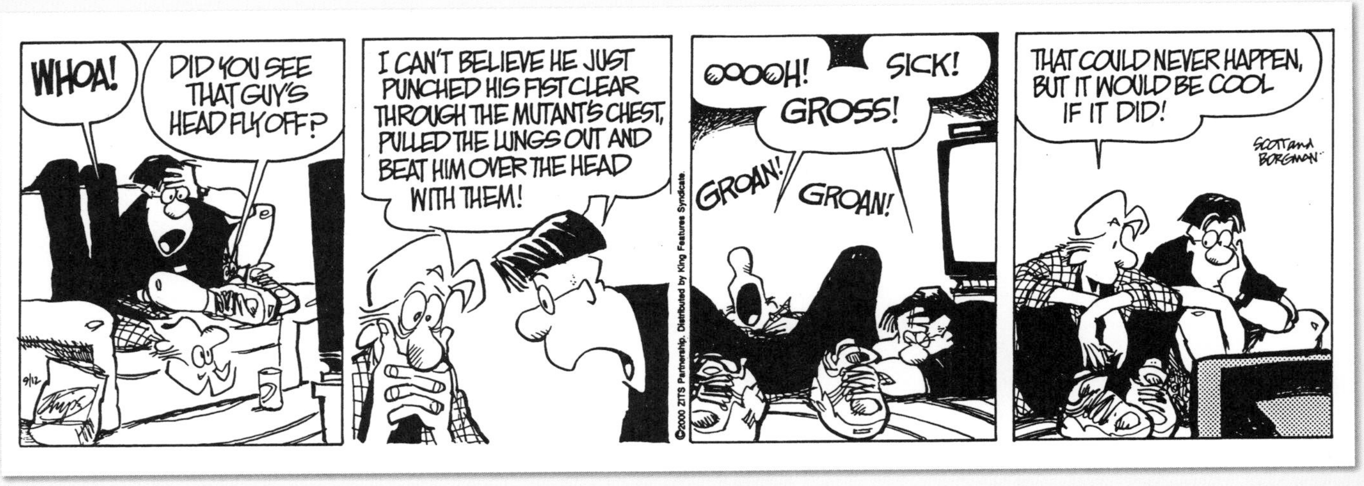
WHOA!
DID YOU SEE THAT GUY'S HEAD FLY OFF?
I CAN'T BELIEVE HE JUST PUNCHED HIS FIST CLEAR THROUGH THE MUTANT'S CHEST, PULLED THE LUNGS OUT AND BEAT HIM OVER THE HEAD WITH THEM!
©2000 ZITS Partnership. Distributed by King Features Syndicate.
OOOOH!
SICK!
GROSS!
GROAN!
GROAN!
THAT COULD NEVER HAPPEN, BUT IT WOULD BE COOL IF IT DID!
SCOTT AND BORGMAN

October 21, 2000

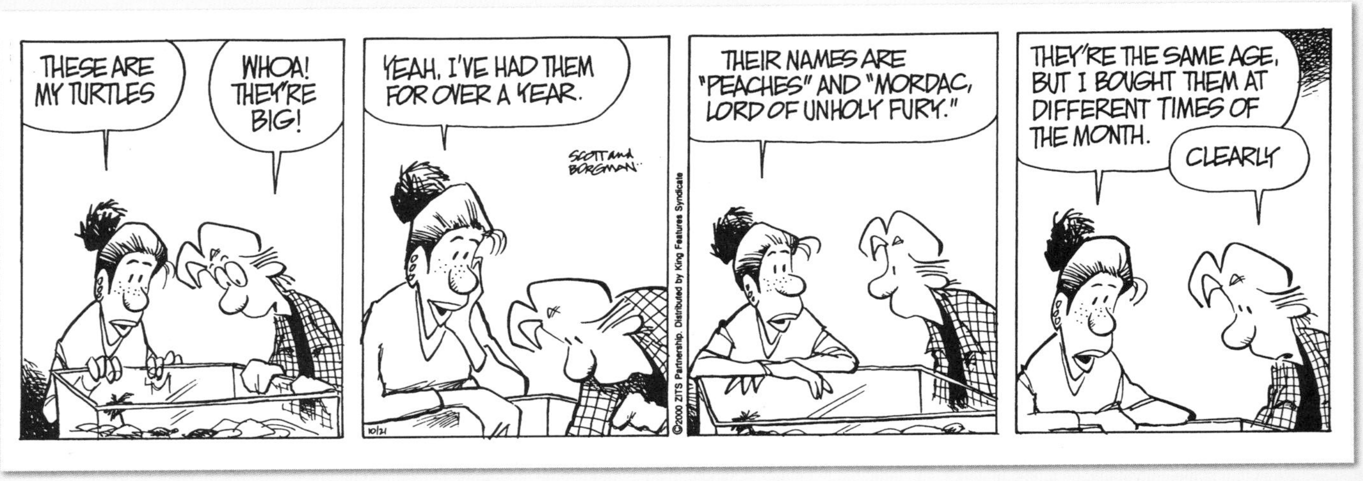
THESE ARE MY TURTLES
WHOA! THEY'RE BIG!
YEAH, I'VE HAD THEM FOR OVER A YEAR.
SCOTT AND BORGMAN
©2000 ZITS Partnership. Distributed by King Features Syndicate
THEIR NAMES ARE "PEACHES" AND "MORDAC, LORD OF UNHOLY FURY."
THEY'RE THE SAME AGE, BUT I BOUGHT THEM AT DIFFERENT TIMES OF THE MONTH.
CLEARLY

October 25, 2000

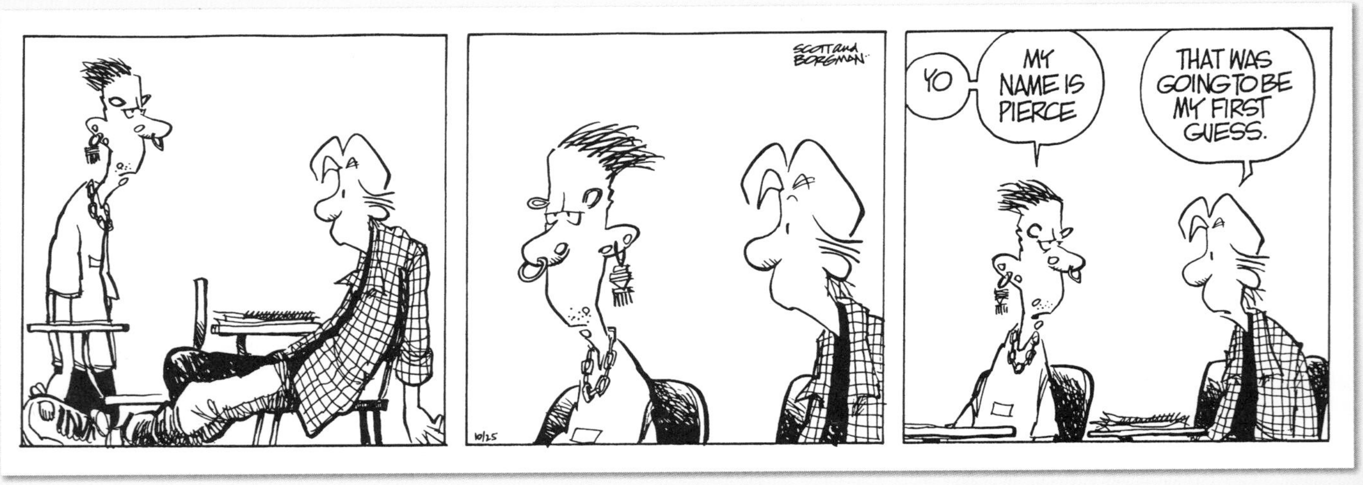
SCOTT AND BORGMAN
YO
MY NAME IS PIERCE
THAT WAS GOING TO BE MY FIRST GUESS.

November 21, 2000

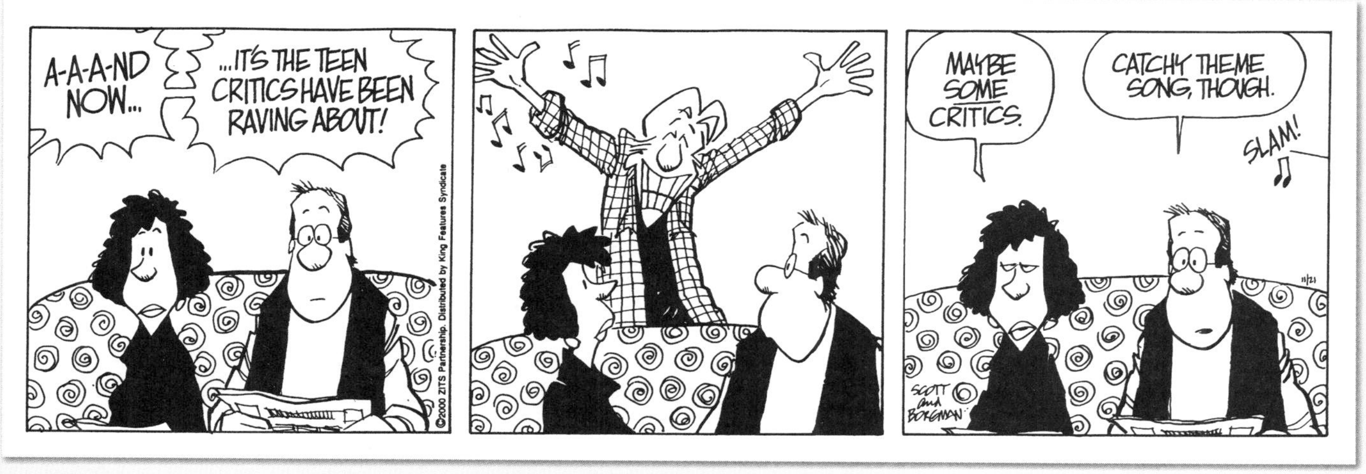
A-A-A-ND NOW...
...IT'S THE TEEN CRITICS HAVE BEEN RAVING ABOUT!
MAYBE SOME CRITICS.
CATCHY THEME SONG, THOUGH.
SLAM!
©2000 ZITS Partnership. Distributed by King Features Syndicate
SCOTT and BORGMAN

November 27, 2000

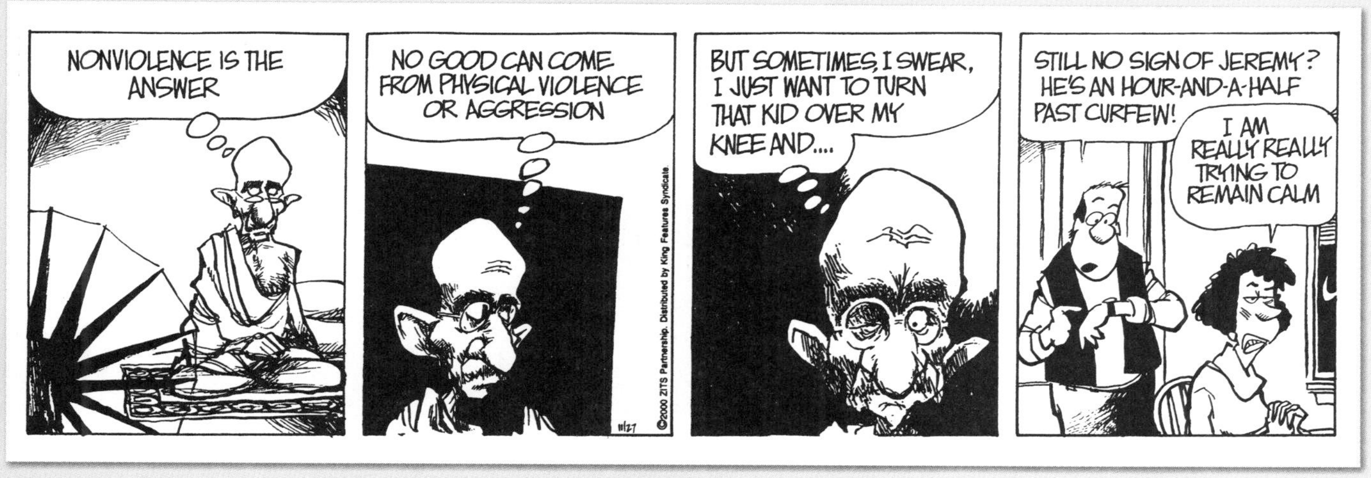
NONVIOLENCE IS THE ANSWER
NO GOOD CAN COME FROM PHYSICAL VIOLENCE OR AGGRESSION
BUT SOMETIMES, I SWEAR, I JUST WANT TO TURN THAT KID OVER MY KNEE AND....
STILL NO SIGN OF JEREMY? HE'S AN HOUR-AND-A-HALF PAST CURFEW!
I AM REALLY REALLY TRYING TO REMAIN CALM
©2000 ZITS Partnership. Distributed by King Features Syndicate.

December 8, 2000

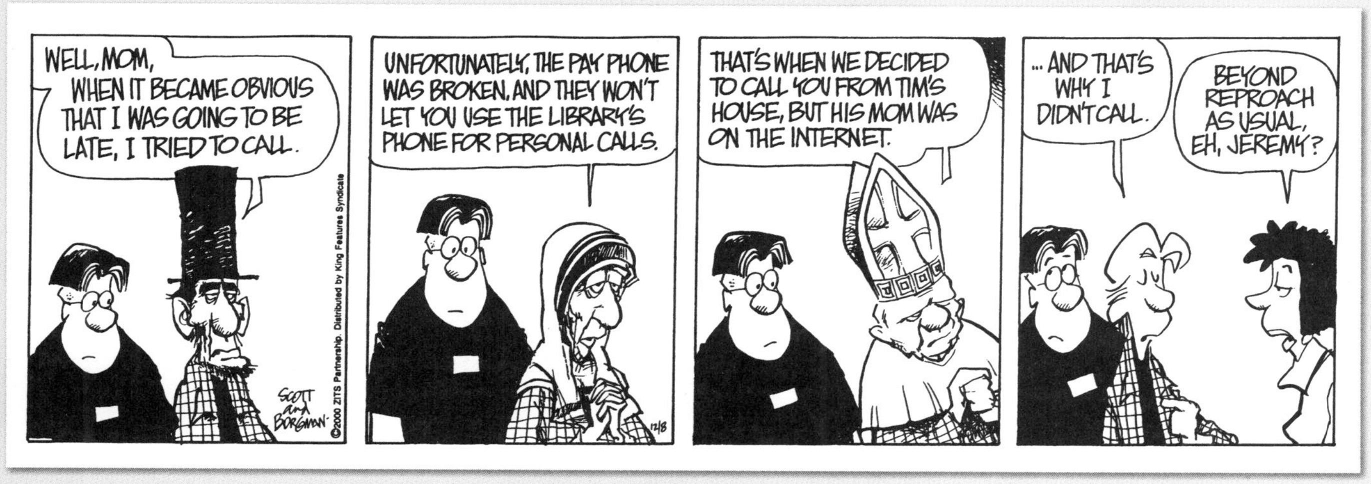
WELL, MOM, WHEN IT BECAME OBVIOUS THAT I WAS GOING TO BE LATE, I TRIED TO CALL.
UNFORTUNATELY, THE PAY PHONE WAS BROKEN, AND THEY WON'T LET YOU USE THE LIBRARY'S PHONE FOR PERSONAL CALLS.
THAT'S WHEN WE DECIDED TO CALL YOU FROM TIM'S HOUSE, BUT HIS MOM WAS ON THE INTERNET.
...AND THAT'S WHY I DIDN'T CALL.
BEYOND REPROACH AS USUAL, EH, JEREMY?
©2000 ZITS Partnership. Distributed by King Features Syndicate
SCOTT and BORGMAN

December 3, 2000

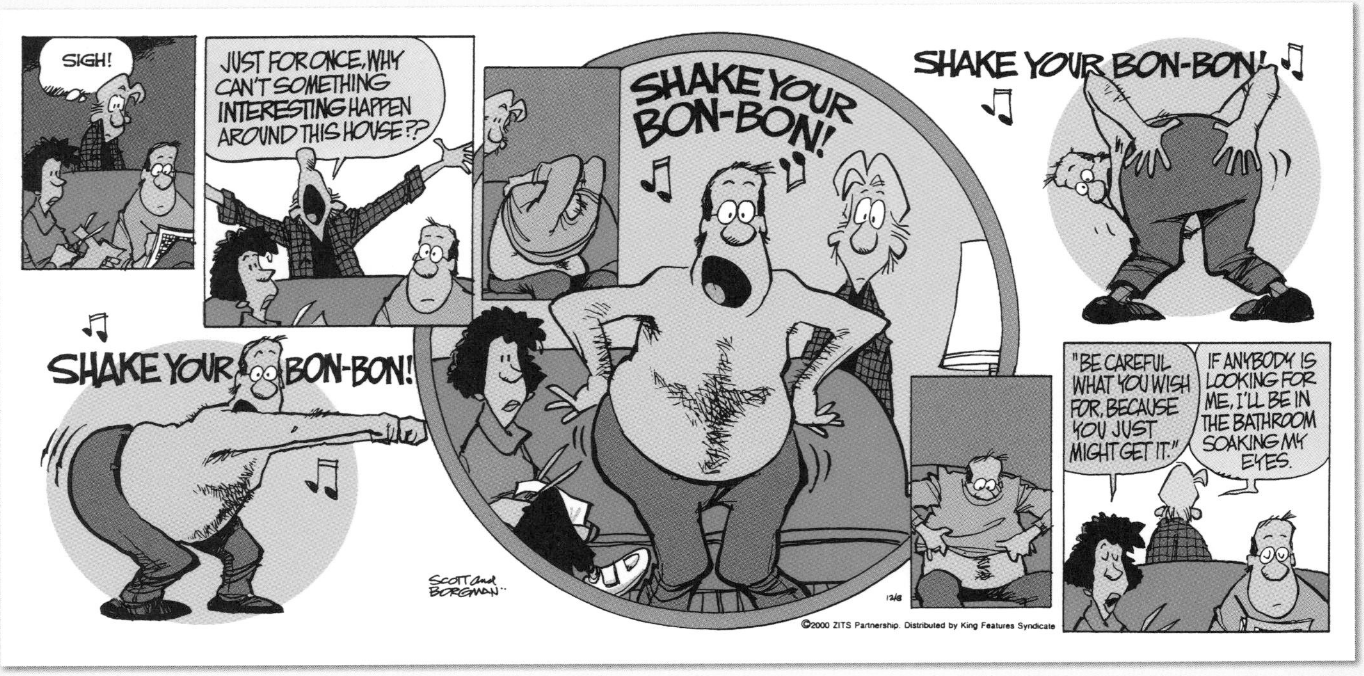
SIGH!
JUST FOR ONCE, WHY CAN'T SOMETHING INTERESTING HAPPEN AROUND THIS HOUSE??
SHAKE YOUR BON-BON!
SHAKE YOUR BON-BON!
SHAKE YOUR BON-BON!
"BE CAREFUL WHAT YOU WISH FOR, BECAUSE YOU JUST MIGHT GET IT."
IF ANYBODY IS LOOKING FOR ME, I'LL BE IN THE BATHROOM SOAKING MY EYES.
SCOTT and BORGMAN
12/3
©2000 ZITS Partnership. Distributed by King Features Syndicate

December 4, 2000

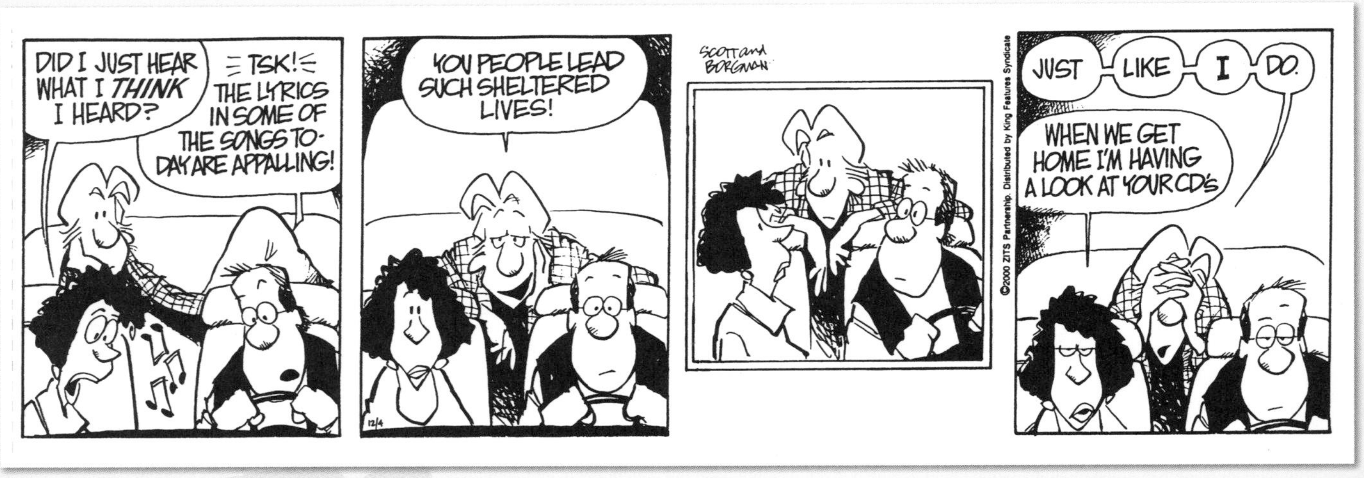
DID I JUST HEAR WHAT I *THINK* I HEARD?
TSK! THE LYRICS IN SOME OF THE SONGS TODAY ARE APPALLING!
YOU PEOPLE LEAD SUCH SHELTERED LIVES!
SCOTT and BORGMAN
12/4
©2000 ZITS Partnership. Distributed by King Features Syndicate
JUST LIKE I DO.
WHEN WE GET HOME I'M HAVING A LOOK AT YOUR CD's

The WRONG Question

Jim Borgman

Q. Hi my name is Kris, and I am a fan and have been for some time now. Because of that, I have been inspired to create my own strip. I'm looking for a program to create my comics. I'm looking for the easiest and cheapest way possible. One with layouts, fonts, and a path tool to help with the inking aspect. I wish to only use one program from start to finish. What program do you use? Hopefully you can help me out; I will appreciate it.

• • •

A. Hi, Kris,

You've come to the wrong place and, with, I believe, the wrong question.

I draw *Zits* traditionally, ink on Strathmore paper, using Winsor & Newton series 7 number 3 Kolinsky brushes. It takes hours and hours to draw each strip. I measure out the borders with a cardboard template. I letter every word by hand with several weights of pen, trying to reflect the feeling of the words and the way they are being spoken in the lettering. I draw first in pencil, then in ink, touching up with Pigma Microns and whiting-out mistakes with Pelikan Graphic White. I work hard on perspectives, backgrounds, lighting, and camera angles to keep the viewer's interest. When the drawing is finished, I scan it and continue to refine it in Photoshop.

I'm sure there are many more technologically adept ways to draw a comic strip, and I am open to new tools and techniques—artists throughout history have used any means available to them to put their vision in front of their audience. I'm sure if you continue to ask around, you will find the program you are looking for.

It's the nature of your question that bothers me and prompts this long response. Forgive me for being old-fashioned, but seeking the "easiest way possible" should not be your goal. You should be challenging yourself to stretch beyond your comfort zone, to imagine ever more nuanced ways of expressing yourself. Putting something singular and remarkable into the world takes time and thought, usually many attempts, and the patience to stay with it when the first ten tries fail. You should be thinking about working late into the night when everyone else has gone to bed and sometimes watching the sun come up as you put on the finishing touches. This is how cartoonists create worlds for their characters to live in and that seize the imaginations of their readers. It's a beautiful feeling. And readers deserve your best efforts in exchange for spending time with your ideas each day.

Good luck in all you do!

JIM BORGMAN

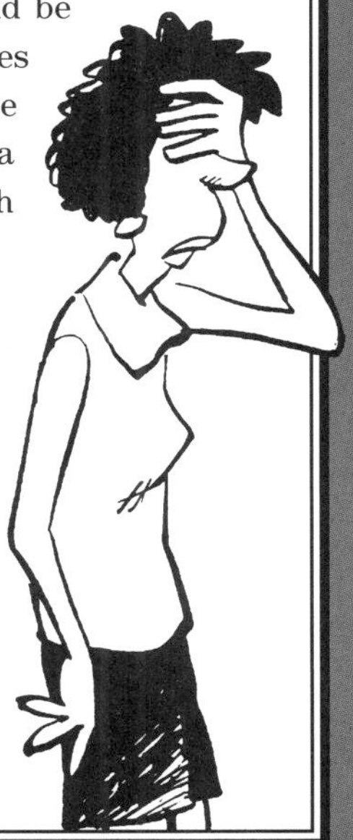

February 26, 2001

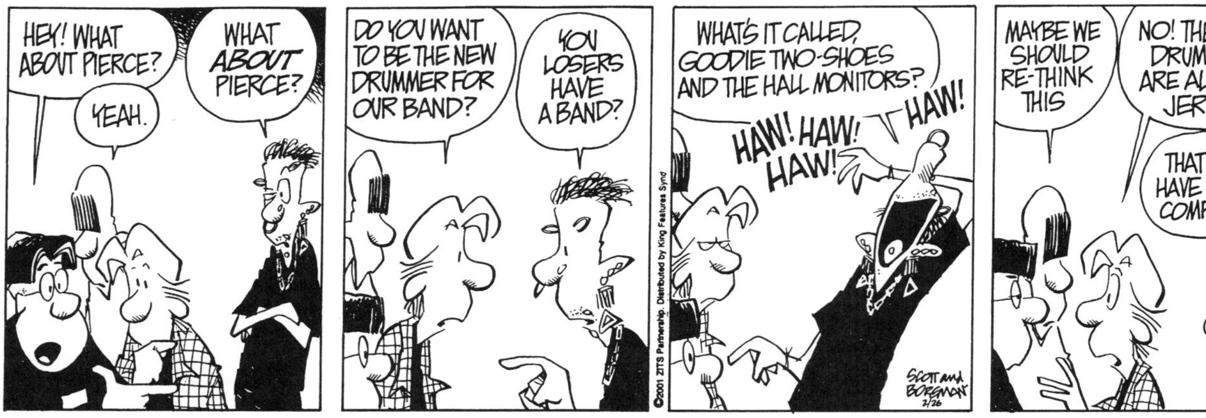

HEY! WHAT ABOUT PIERCE?
YEAH.
WHAT ABOUT PIERCE?
DO YOU WANT TO BE THE NEW DRUMMER FOR OUR BAND?
YOU LOSERS HAVE A BAND?
WHAT'S IT CALLED, GOODIE TWO-SHOES AND THE HALL MONITORS?
HAW! HAW! HAW! HAW!
MAYBE WE SHOULD RE-THINK THIS
NO! THE GOOD DRUMMERS ARE ALWAYS JERKS!
THAT BETTER HAVE BEEN A COMPLIMENT.
©2001 ZITS Partnership. Distributed by King Features Synd.
SCOTT AND BORGMAN 2/26

March 7, 2001

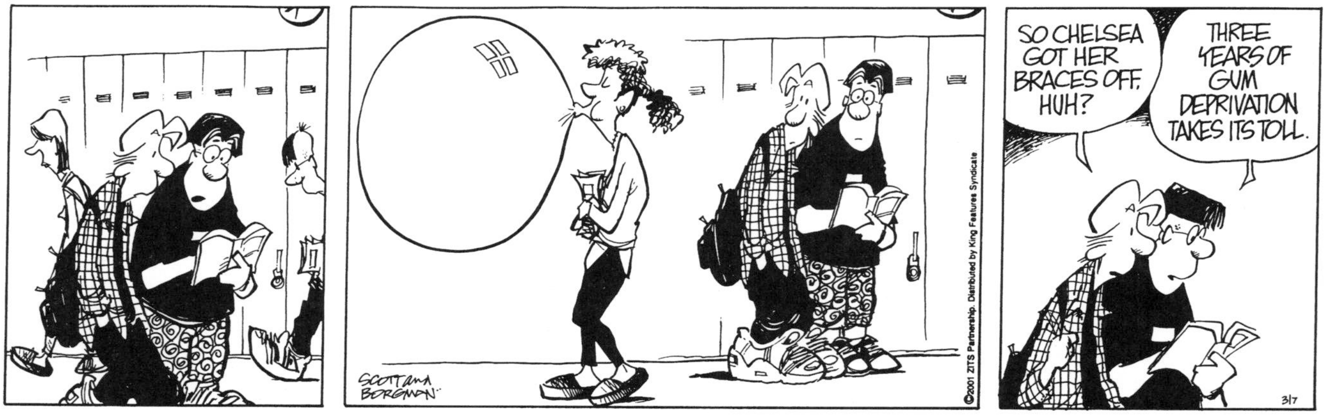

SCOTT AND BORGMAN
©2001 ZITS Partnership. Distributed by King Features Syndicate
SO CHELSEA GOT HER BRACES OFF, HUH?
THREE YEARS OF GUM DEPRIVATION TAKES ITS TOLL.
3/7

March 9, 2001

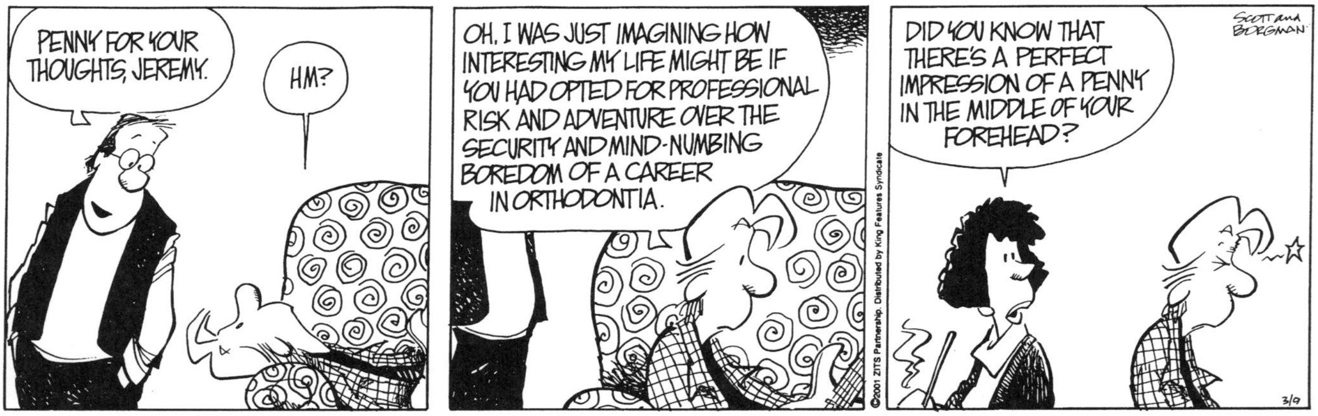

PENNY FOR YOUR THOUGHTS, JEREMY.
HM?
OH, I WAS JUST IMAGINING HOW INTERESTING MY LIFE MIGHT BE IF YOU HAD OPTED FOR PROFESSIONAL RISK AND ADVENTURE OVER THE SECURITY AND MIND-NUMBING BOREDOM OF A CAREER IN ORTHODONTIA.
©2001 ZITS Partnership. Distributed by King Features Syndicate
DID YOU KNOW THAT THERE'S A PERFECT IMPRESSION OF A PENNY IN THE MIDDLE OF YOUR FOREHEAD?
SCOTT AND BORGMAN
3/9

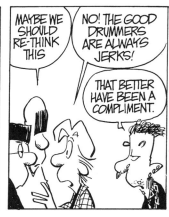

March 26, 2001

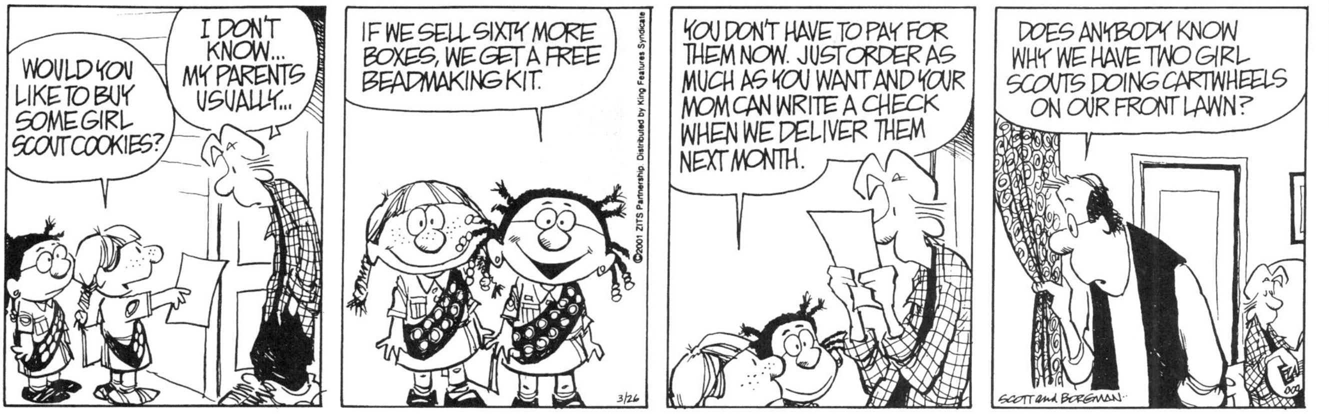
WOULD YOU LIKE TO BUY SOME GIRL SCOUT COOKIES?
I DON'T KNOW... MY PARENTS USUALLY...
IF WE SELL SIXTY MORE BOXES, WE GET A FREE BEADMAKING KIT.
©2001 ZITS Partnership. Distributed by King Features Syndicate
3/26
YOU DON'T HAVE TO PAY FOR THEM NOW. JUST ORDER AS MUCH AS YOU WANT AND YOUR MOM CAN WRITE A CHECK WHEN WE DELIVER THEM NEXT MONTH.
DOES ANYBODY KNOW WHY WE HAVE TWO GIRL SCOUTS DOING CARTWHEELS ON OUR FRONT LAWN?
SCOTT and BORGMAN

May 11, 2001

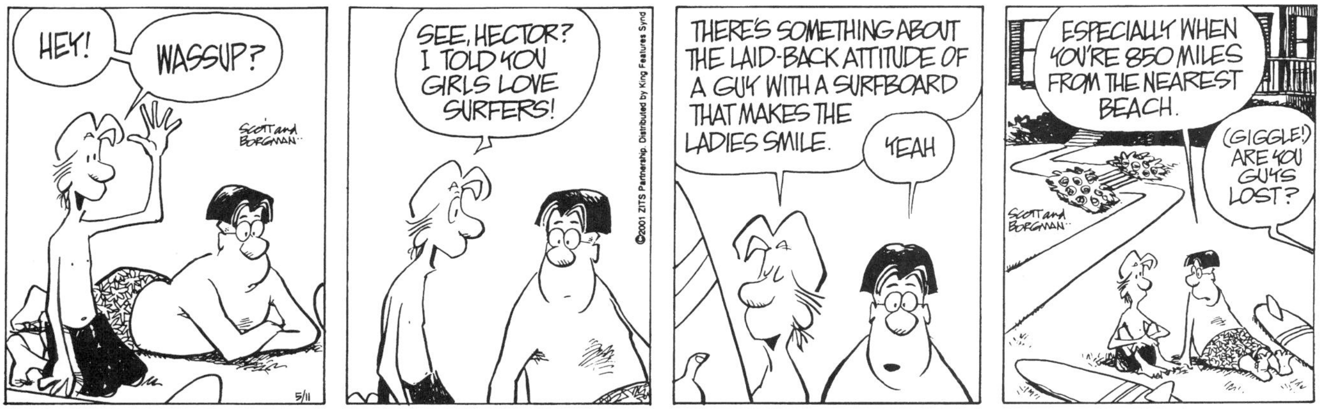
HEY!
WASSUP?
SCOTT and BORGMAN
5/11
SEE, HECTOR? I TOLD YOU GIRLS LOVE SURFERS!
©2001 ZITS Partnership. Distributed by King Features Synd.
THERE'S SOMETHING ABOUT THE LAID-BACK ATTITUDE OF A GUY WITH A SURFBOARD THAT MAKES THE LADIES SMILE.
YEAH
ESPECIALLY WHEN YOU'RE 850 MILES FROM THE NEAREST BEACH.
(GIGGLE!) ARE YOU GUYS LOST?
SCOTT and BORGMAN

July 2, 2001

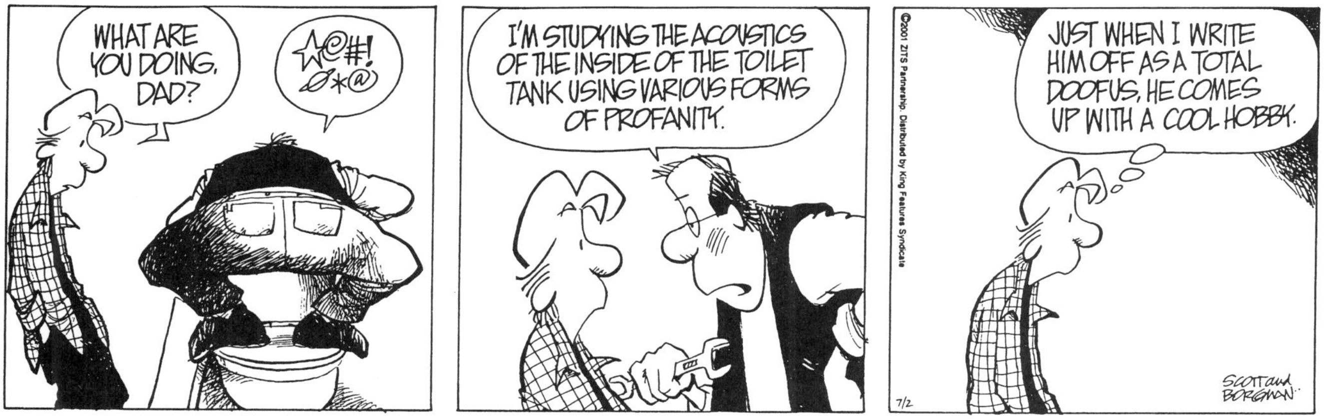
WHAT ARE YOU DOING, DAD?
☆@#! ∅*@
I'M STUDYING THE ACOUSTICS OF THE INSIDE OF THE TOILET TANK USING VARIOUS FORMS OF PROFANITY.
©2001 ZITS Partnership. Distributed by King Features Syndicate
7/2
JUST WHEN I WRITE HIM OFF AS A TOTAL DOOFUS, HE COMES UP WITH A COOL HOBBY.
SCOTT and BORGMAN

February 25, 2001

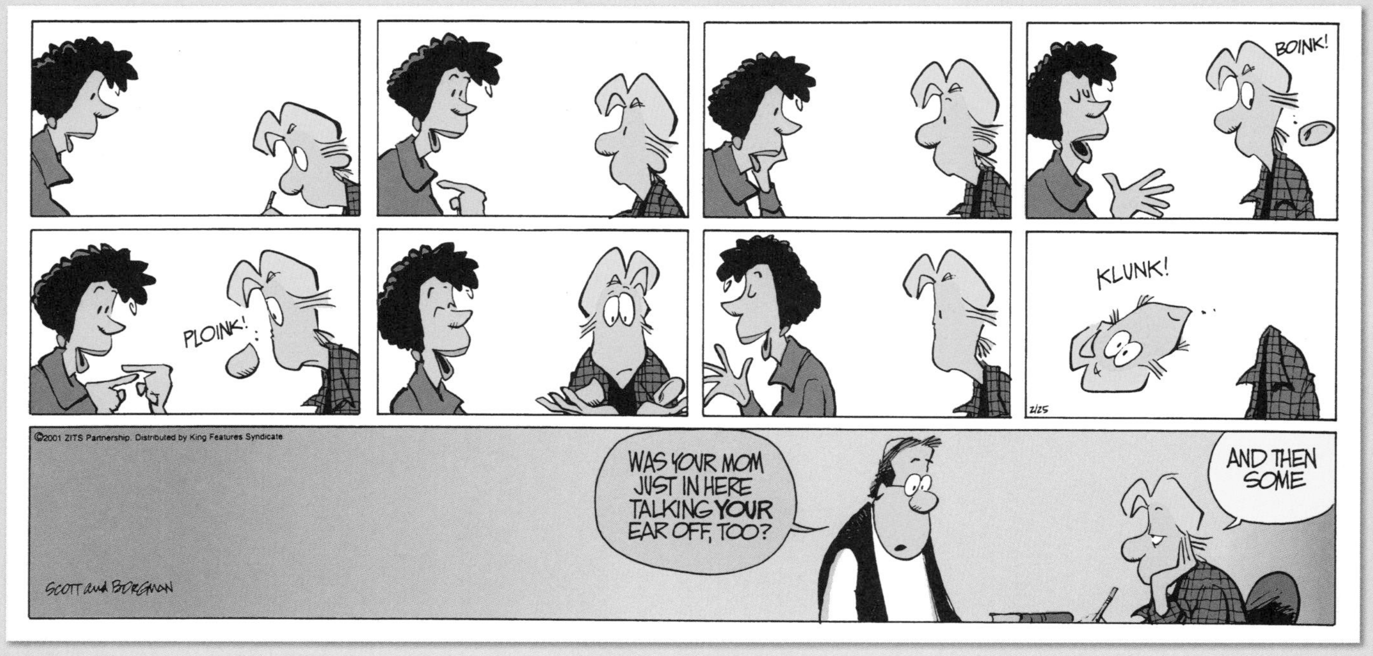
BOINK!
PLOINK!
KLUNK!
2/25
©2001 ZITS Partnership. Distributed by King Features Syndicate
WAS YOUR MOM JUST IN HERE TALKING YOUR EAR OFF, TOO?
AND THEN SOME
SCOTT and BORGMAN

April 8, 2001

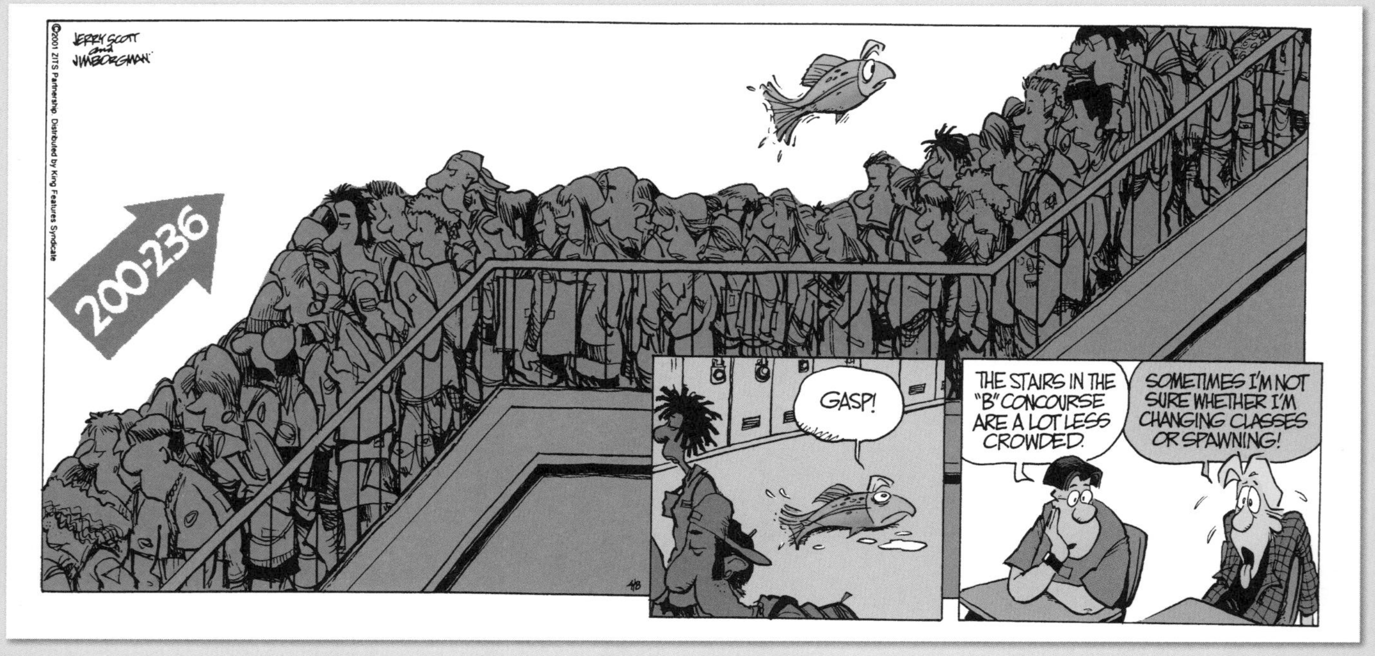
©2001 ZITS Partnership. Distributed by King Features Syndicate
JERRY SCOTT and JIM BORGMAN
200-236
4/8
GASP!
THE STAIRS IN THE "B" CONCOURSE ARE A LOT LESS CROWDED.
SOMETIMES I'M NOT SURE WHETHER I'M CHANGING CLASSES OR SPAWNING!

July 12, 2001

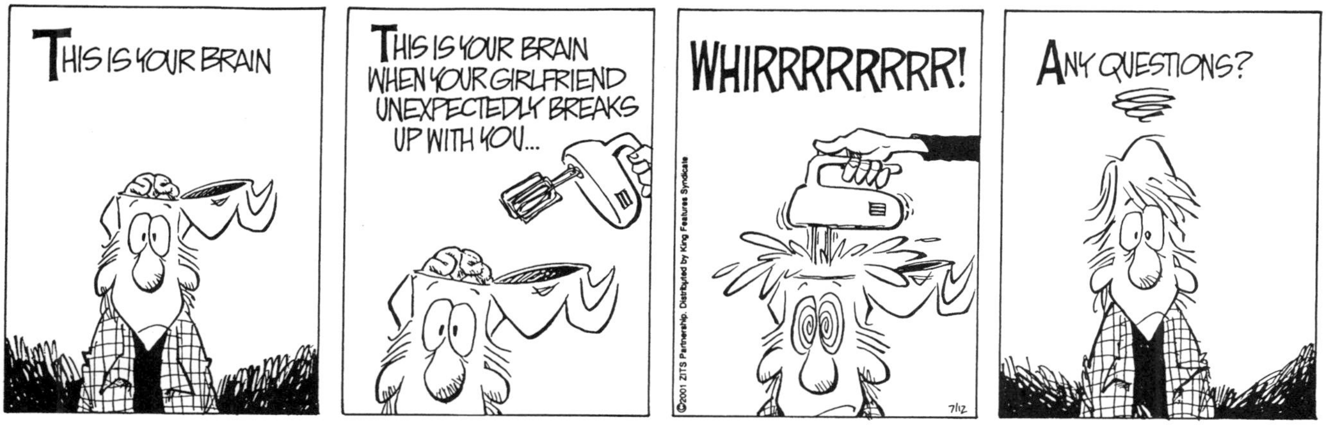
THIS IS YOUR BRAIN
THIS IS YOUR BRAIN WHEN YOUR GIRLFRIEND UNEXPECTEDLY BREAKS UP WITH YOU...
WHIRRRRRRRR!
ANY QUESTIONS?
©2001 ZITS Partnership. Distributed by King Features Syndicate
7/12

July 31, 2001

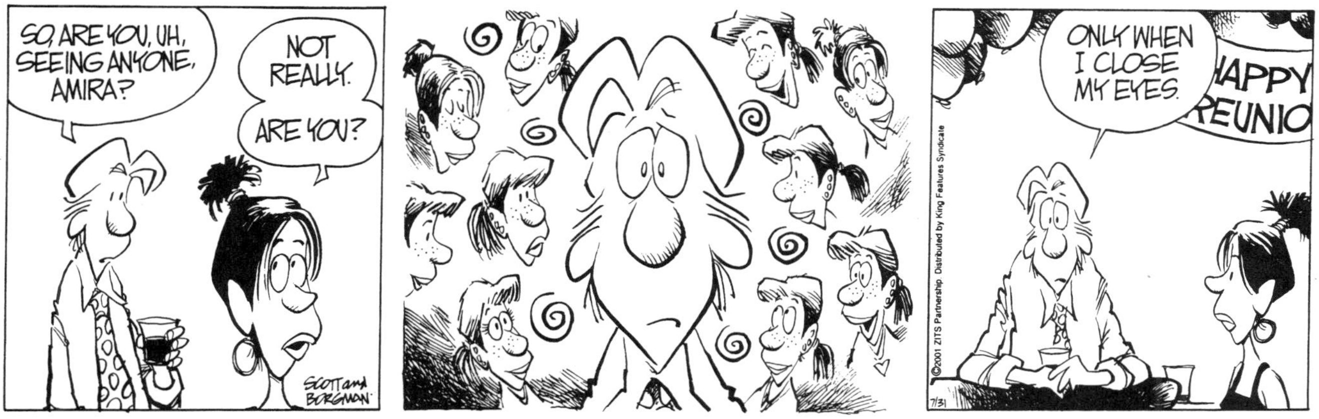
SO, ARE YOU, UH, SEEING ANYONE, AMIRA?
NOT REALLY.
ARE YOU?
SCOTT AND BORGMAN
ONLY WHEN I CLOSE MY EYES.
HAPPY REUNIO
©2001 ZITS Partnership. Distributed by King Features Syndicate
7/31

August 1, 2001

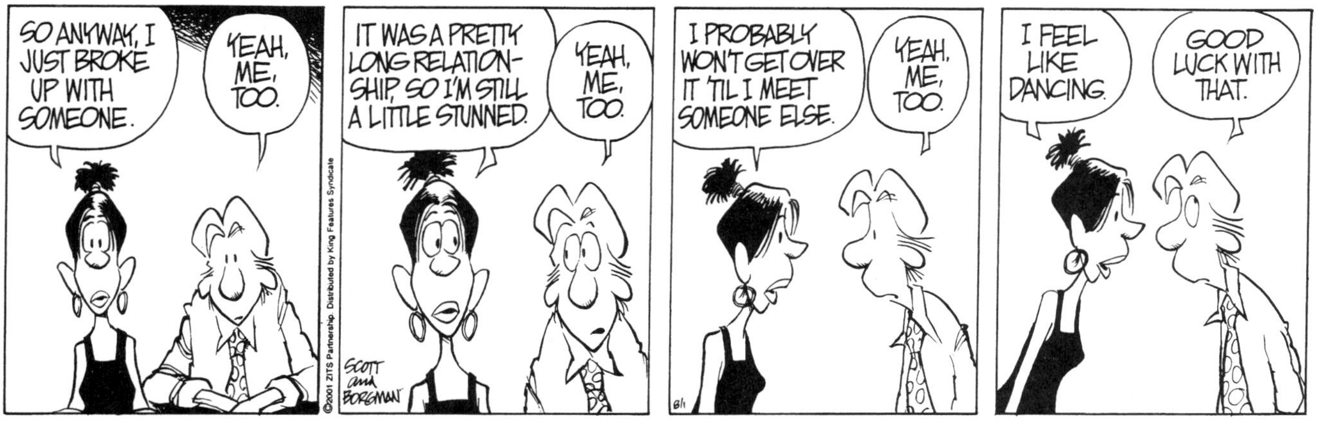
SO ANYWAY, I JUST BROKE UP WITH SOMEONE.
YEAH, ME, TOO.
©2001 ZITS Partnership. Distributed by King Features Syndicate
IT WAS A PRETTY LONG RELATION-SHIP, SO I'M STILL A LITTLE STUNNED.
YEAH, ME, TOO.
SCOTT AND BORGMAN
I PROBABLY WON'T GET OVER IT 'TIL I MEET SOMEONE ELSE.
YEAH, ME, TOO.
8/1
I FEEL LIKE DANCING.
GOOD LUCK WITH THAT.

August 2, 2001

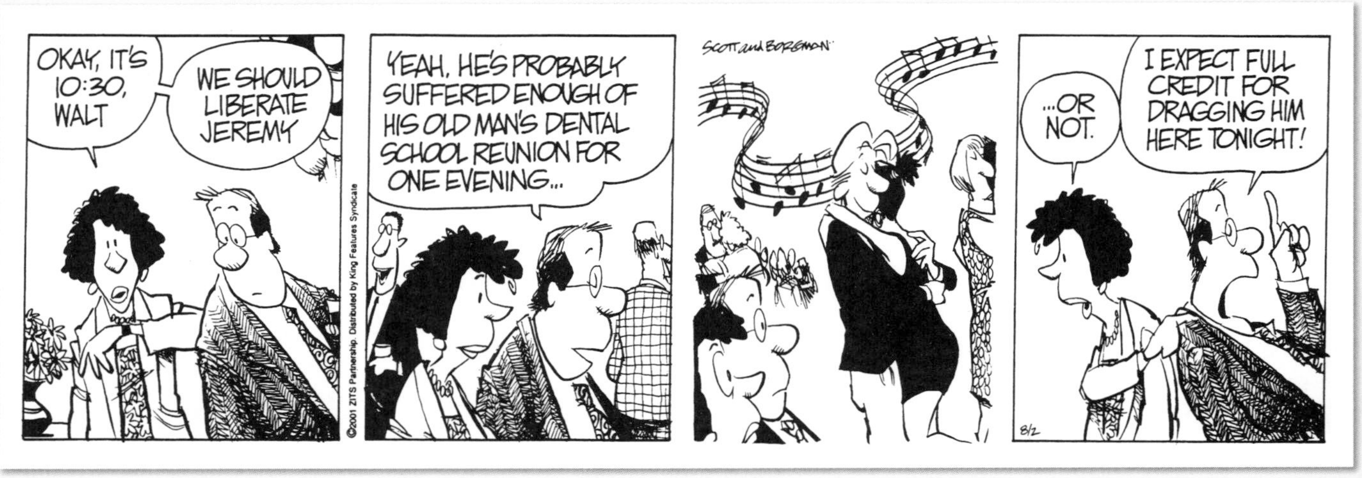
OKAY, IT'S 10:30, WALT
WE SHOULD LIBERATE JEREMY
YEAH, HE'S PROBABLY SUFFERED ENOUGH OF HIS OLD MAN'S DENTAL SCHOOL REUNION FOR ONE EVENING...
...OR NOT.
I EXPECT FULL CREDIT FOR DRAGGING HIM HERE TONIGHT!

August 3, 2001

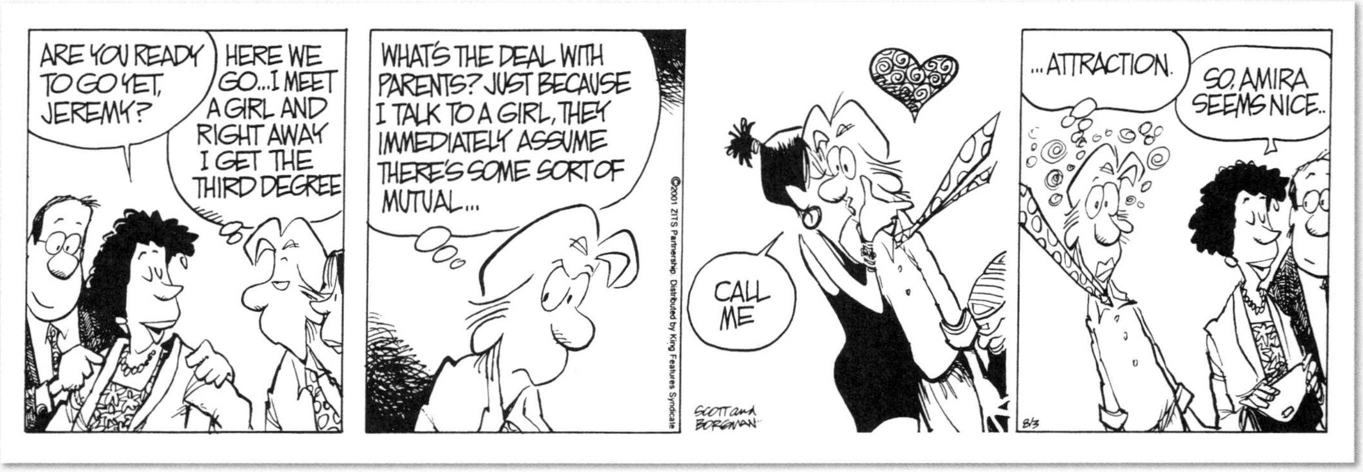
ARE YOU READY TO GO YET, JEREMY?
HERE WE GO...I MEET A GIRL AND RIGHT AWAY I GET THE THIRD DEGREE
WHAT'S THE DEAL WITH PARENTS? JUST BECAUSE I TALK TO A GIRL, THEY IMMEDIATELY ASSUME THERE'S SOME SORT OF MUTUAL...
CALL ME
...ATTRACTION.
SO, AMIRA SEEMS NICE..

August 4, 2001

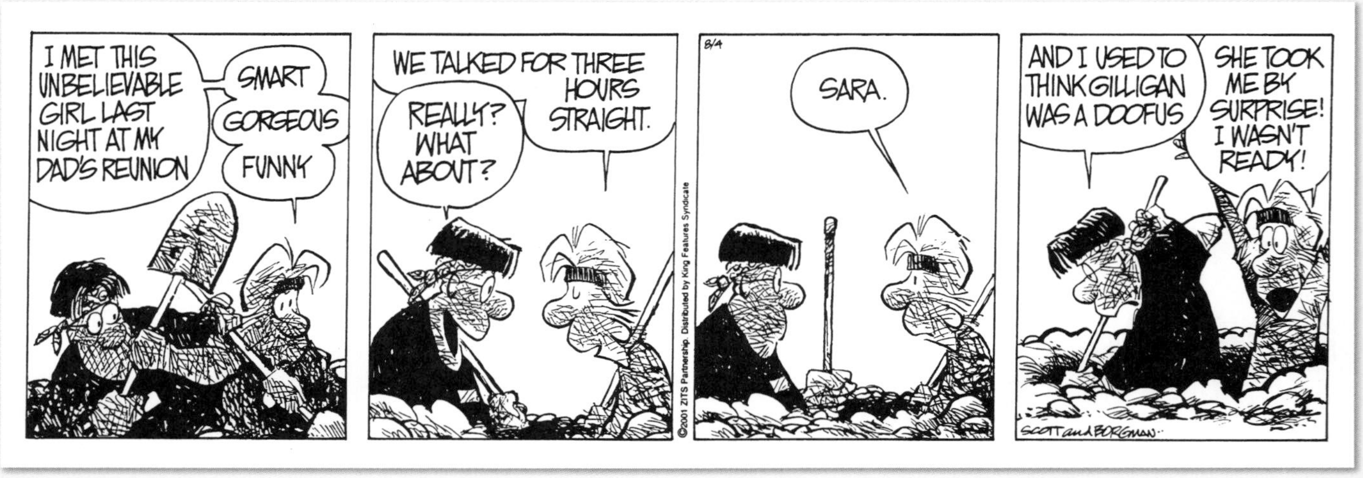
I MET THIS UNBELIEVABLE GIRL LAST NIGHT AT MY DAD'S REUNION
SMART
GORGEOUS
FUNNY
WE TALKED FOR THREE HOURS STRAIGHT.
REALLY? WHAT ABOUT?
SARA.
AND I USED TO THINK GILLIGAN WAS A DOOFUS
SHE TOOK ME BY SURPRISE! I WASN'T READY!

August 10, 2001

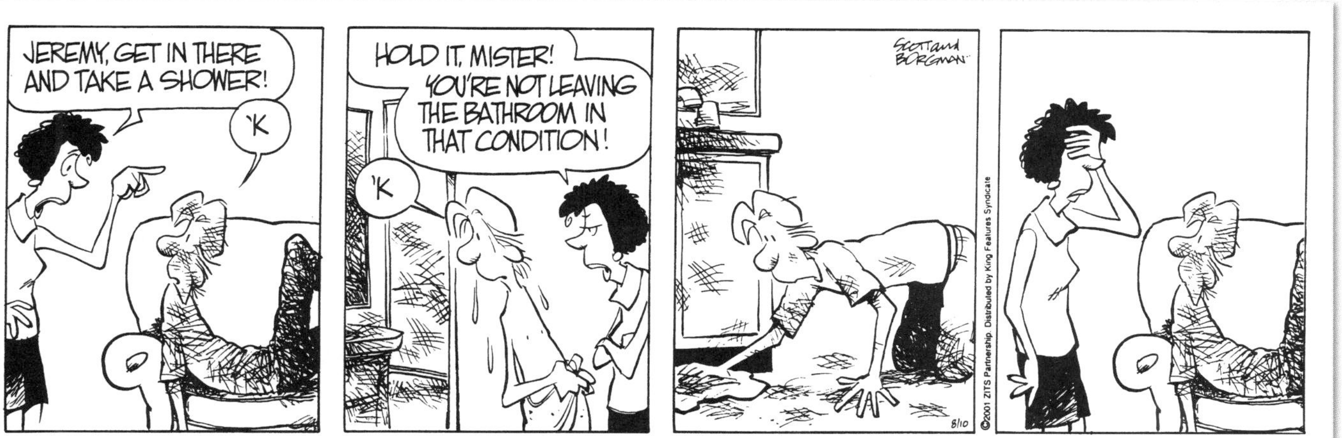
JEREMY, GET IN THERE AND TAKE A SHOWER!
'K
HOLD IT, MISTER!
YOU'RE NOT LEAVING THE BATHROOM IN THAT CONDITION!
'K
SCOTT and BORGMAN
©2001 ZITS Partnership. Distributed by King Features Syndicate
8/10

August 31, 2001

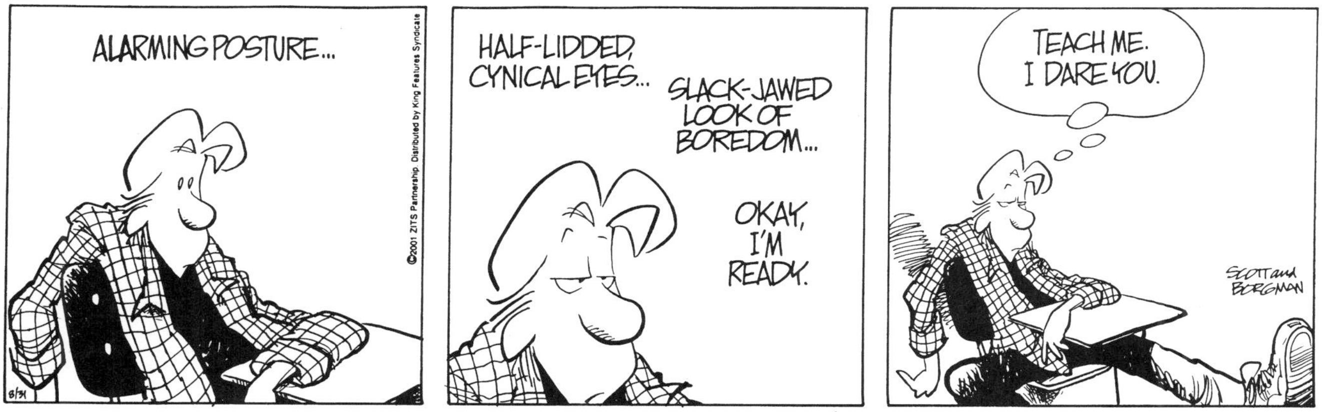
ALARMING POSTURE...
©2001 ZITS Partnership. Distributed by King Features Syndicate
8/31
HALF-LIDDED, CYNICAL EYES...
SLACK-JAWED LOOK OF BOREDOM...
OKAY, I'M READY.
TEACH ME. I DARE YOU.
SCOTT and BORGMAN

July 19, 2001

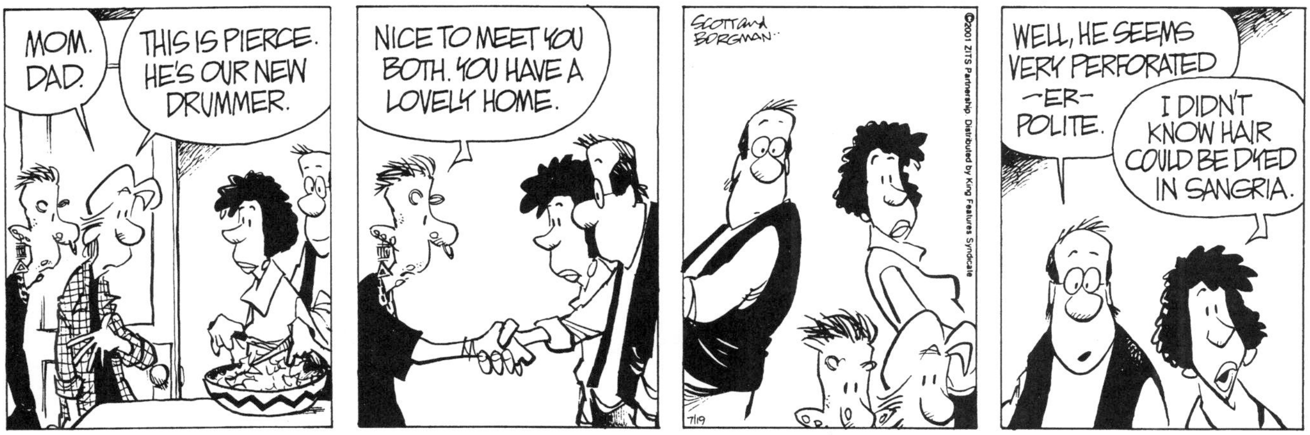
MOM. DAD.
THIS IS PIERCE. HE'S OUR NEW DRUMMER.
NICE TO MEET YOU BOTH. YOU HAVE A LOVELY HOME.
SCOTT and BORGMAN
©2001 ZITS Partnership. Distributed by King Features Syndicate
7/19
WELL, HE SEEMS VERY PERFORATED —ER— POLITE.
I DIDN'T KNOW HAIR COULD BE DYED IN SANGRIA.

May 27, 2001

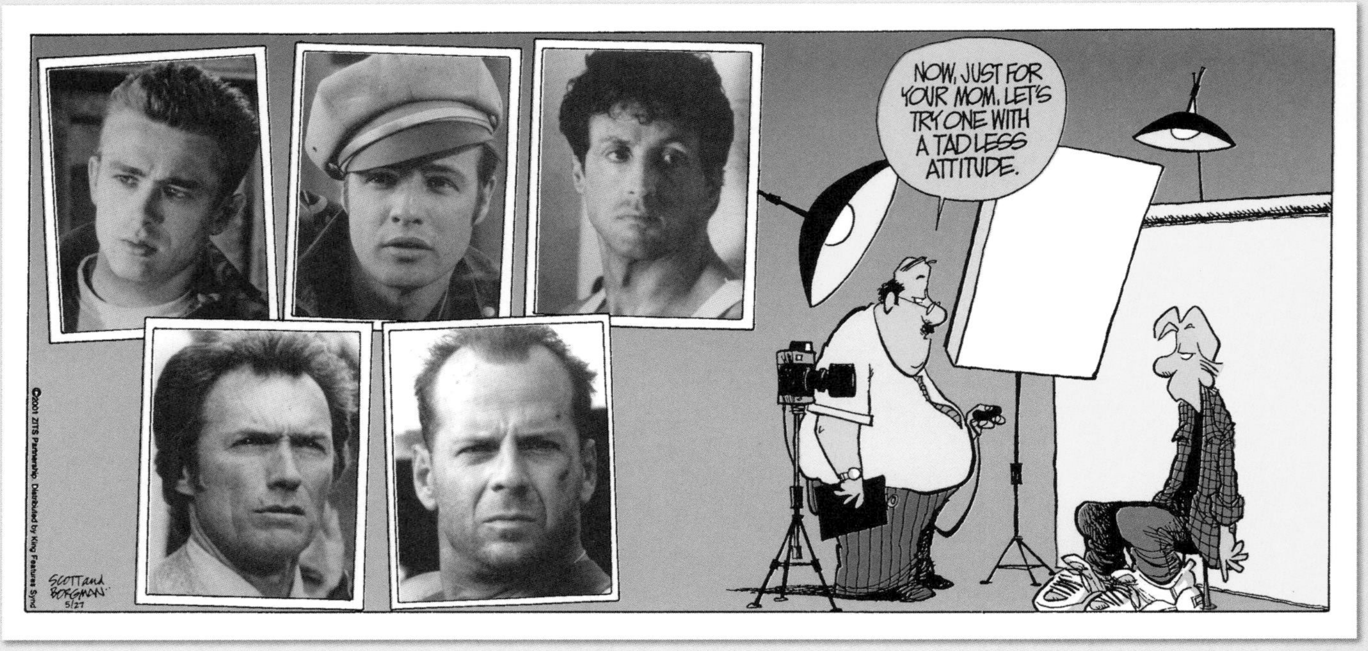
NOW, JUST FOR YOUR MOM, LET'S TRY ONE WITH A TAD LESS ATTITUDE.
SCOTT and BORGMAN 5/27
©2001 ZITS Partnership. Distributed by King Features Synd.

July 15, 2001

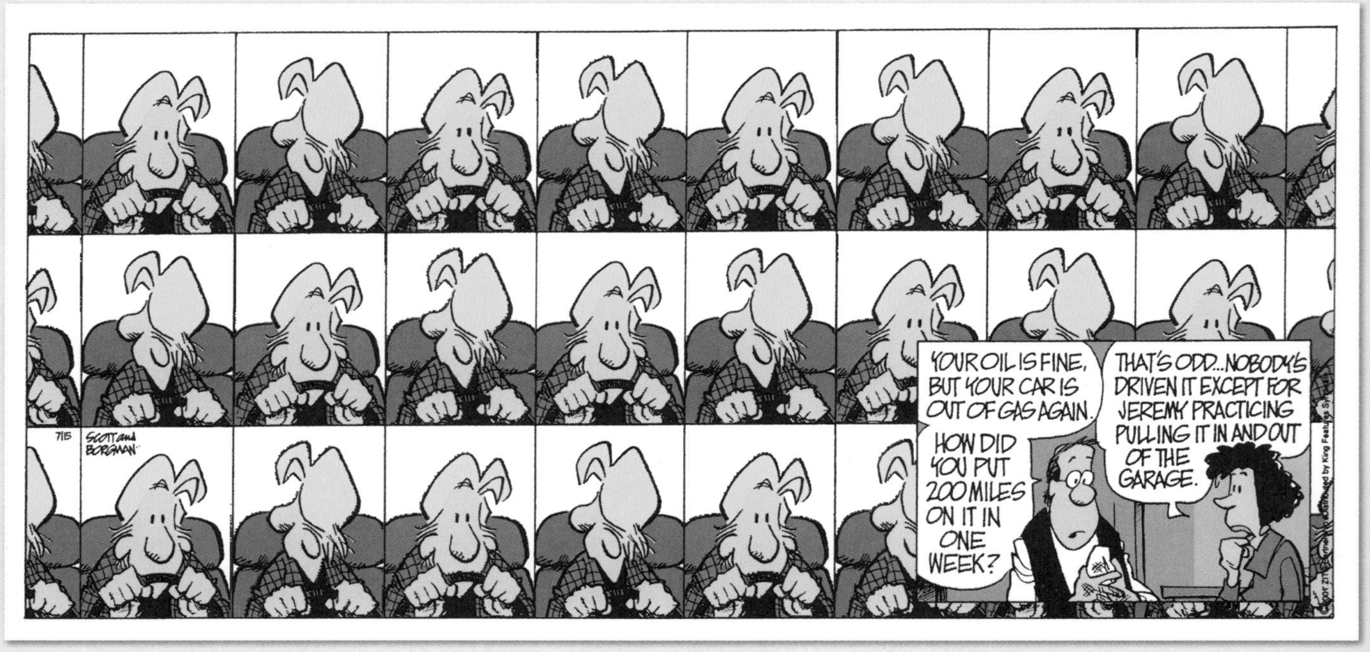
7/15 SCOTT and BORGMAN
YOUR OIL IS FINE, BUT YOUR CAR IS OUT OF GAS AGAIN.
HOW DID YOU PUT 200 MILES ON IT IN ONE WEEK?
THAT'S ODD...NOBODY'S DRIVEN IT EXCEPT FOR JEREMY PRACTICING PULLING IT IN AND OUT OF THE GARAGE.

September 22, 2001

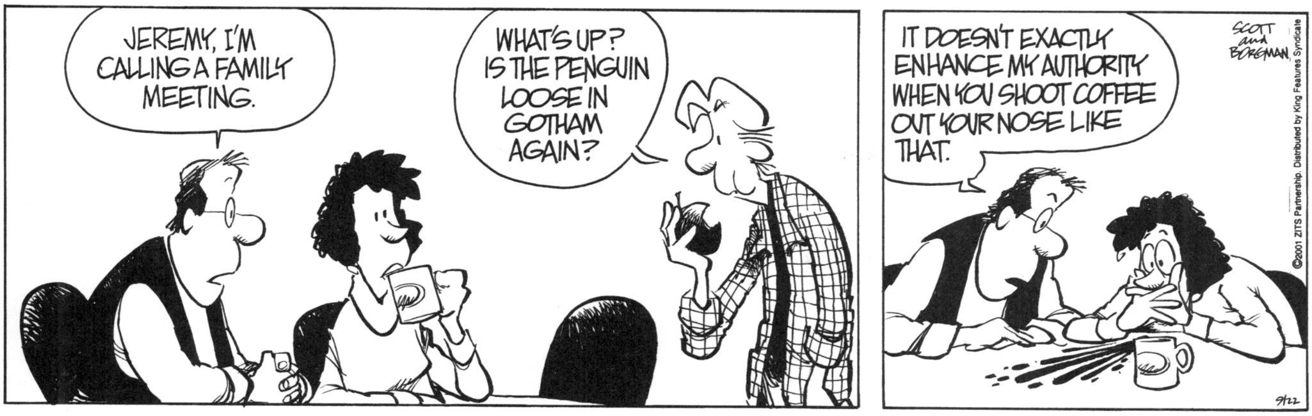
JEREMY, I'M CALLING A FAMILY MEETING.
WHAT'S UP? IS THE PENGUIN LOOSE IN GOTHAM AGAIN?
IT DOESN'T EXACTLY ENHANCE MY AUTHORITY WHEN YOU SHOOT COFFEE OUT YOUR NOSE LIKE THAT.
SCOTT and BORGMAN
©2001 ZITS Partnership. Distributed by King Features Syndicate
9/22

October 1, 2001

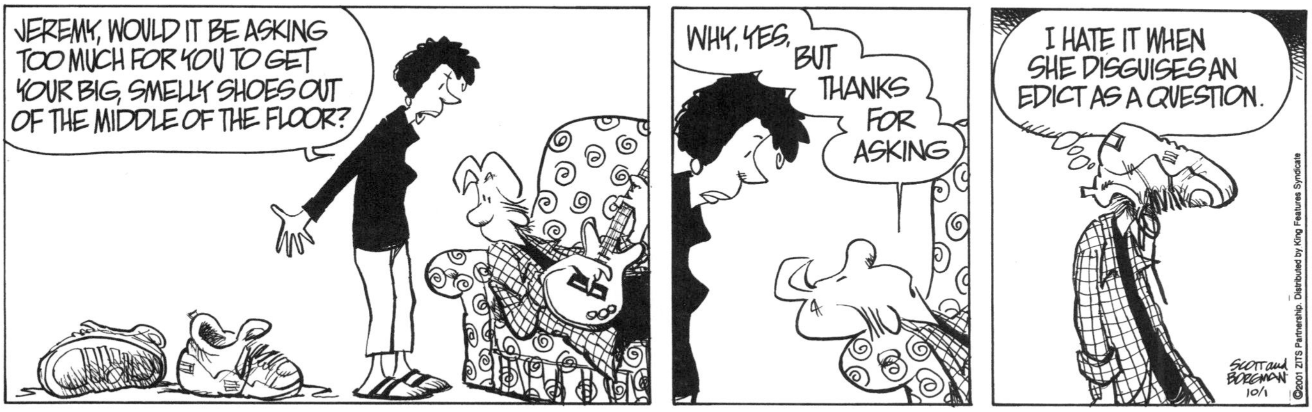
JEREMY, WOULD IT BE ASKING TOO MUCH FOR YOU TO GET YOUR BIG, SMELLY SHOES OUT OF THE MIDDLE OF THE FLOOR?
WHY, YES,
BUT THANKS FOR ASKING
I HATE IT WHEN SHE DISGUISES AN EDICT AS A QUESTION.
©2001 ZITS Partnership. Distributed by King Features Syndicate
SCOTT and BORGMAN 10/1

November 15, 2001

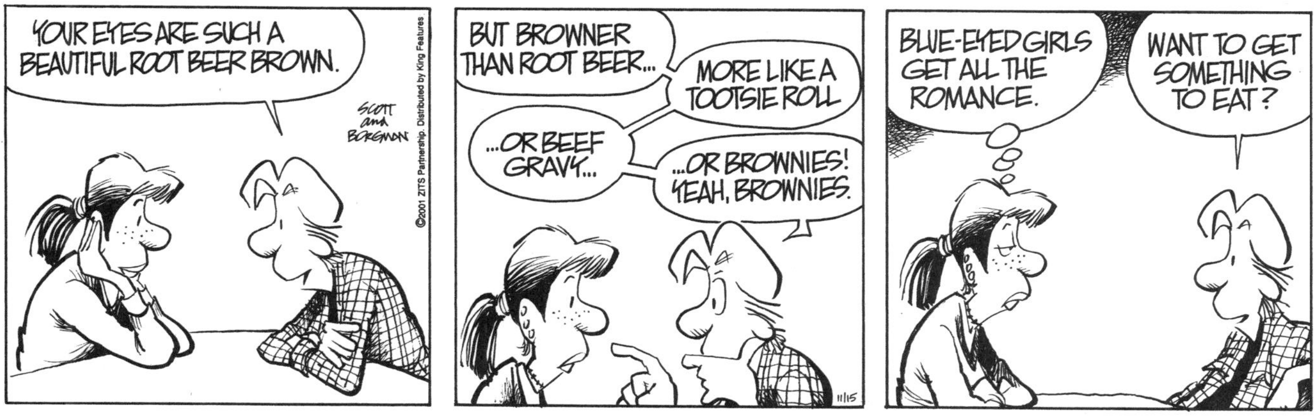
YOUR EYES ARE SUCH A BEAUTIFUL ROOT BEER BROWN.
SCOTT and BORGMAN
©2001 ZITS Partnership. Distributed by King Features
BUT BROWNER THAN ROOT BEER...
MORE LIKE A TOOTSIE ROLL
...OR BEEF GRAVY...
...OR BROWNIES! YEAH, BROWNIES.
11/15
BLUE-EYED GIRLS GET ALL THE ROMANCE.
WANT TO GET SOMETHING TO EAT?

July 22, 2001

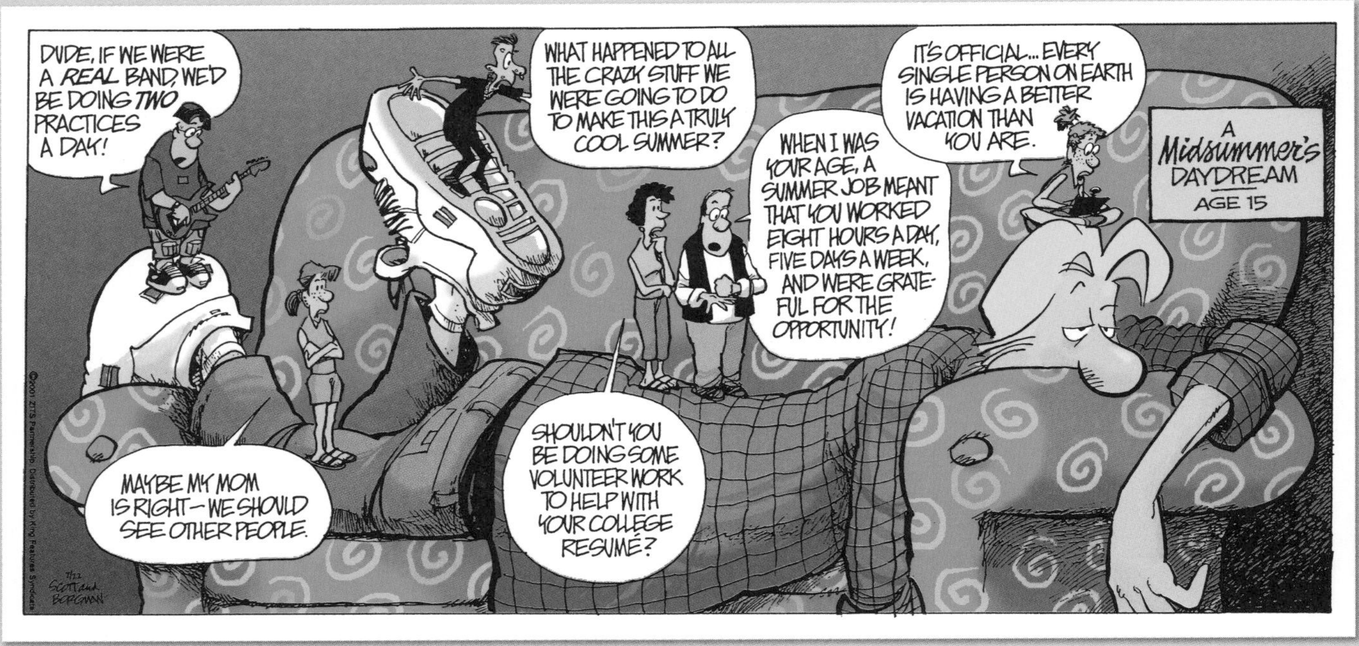
DUDE, IF WE WERE A *REAL* BAND, WE'D BE DOING *TWO* PRACTICES A DAY!
MAYBE MY MOM IS RIGHT—WE SHOULD SEE OTHER PEOPLE.
WHAT HAPPENED TO ALL THE CRAZY STUFF WE WERE GOING TO DO TO MAKE THIS A TRULY COOL SUMMER?
SHOULDN'T YOU BE DOING SOME VOLUNTEER WORK TO HELP WITH YOUR COLLEGE RESUMÉ?
WHEN I WAS YOUR AGE, A SUMMER JOB MEANT THAT YOU WORKED EIGHT HOURS A DAY, FIVE DAYS A WEEK, AND WERE GRATEFUL FOR THE OPPORTUNITY!
IT'S OFFICIAL... EVERY SINGLE PERSON ON EARTH IS HAVING A BETTER VACATION THAN YOU ARE.
A *Midsummer's* DAYDREAM AGE 15
©2001 ZITS Partnership. Distributed by King Features Syndicate
SCOTT and BORGMAN

October 21, 2001

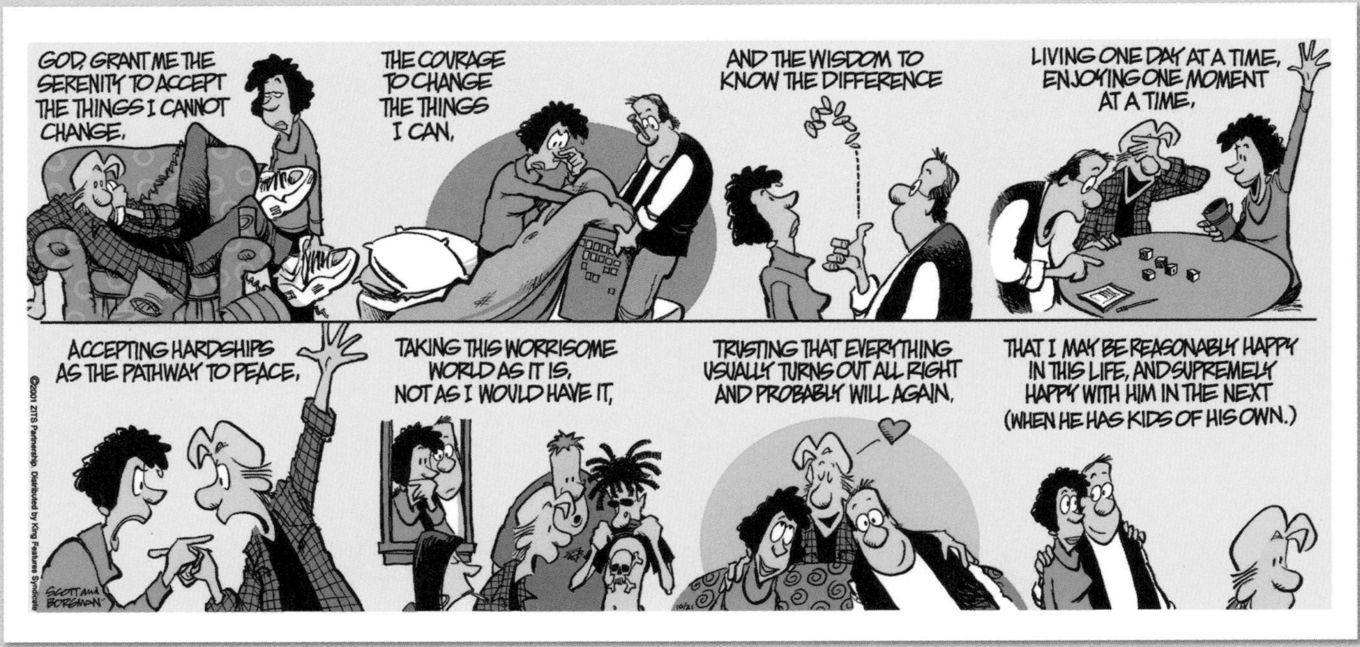
GOD, GRANT ME THE SERENITY TO ACCEPT THE THINGS I CANNOT CHANGE,
THE COURAGE TO CHANGE THE THINGS I CAN,
AND THE WISDOM TO KNOW THE DIFFERENCE
LIVING ONE DAY AT A TIME, ENJOYING ONE MOMENT AT A TIME,
ACCEPTING HARDSHIPS AS THE PATHWAY TO PEACE,
TAKING THIS WORRISOME WORLD AS IT IS, NOT AS I WOULD HAVE IT,
TRUSTING THAT EVERYTHING USUALLY TURNS OUT ALL RIGHT AND PROBABLY WILL AGAIN,
THAT I MAY BE REASONABLY HAPPY IN THIS LIFE, AND SUPREMELY HAPPY WITH HIM IN THE NEXT (WHEN HE HAS KIDS OF HIS OWN.)
©2001 ZITS Partnership. Distributed by King Features Syndicate
SCOTT and BORGMAN

November 4, 2001

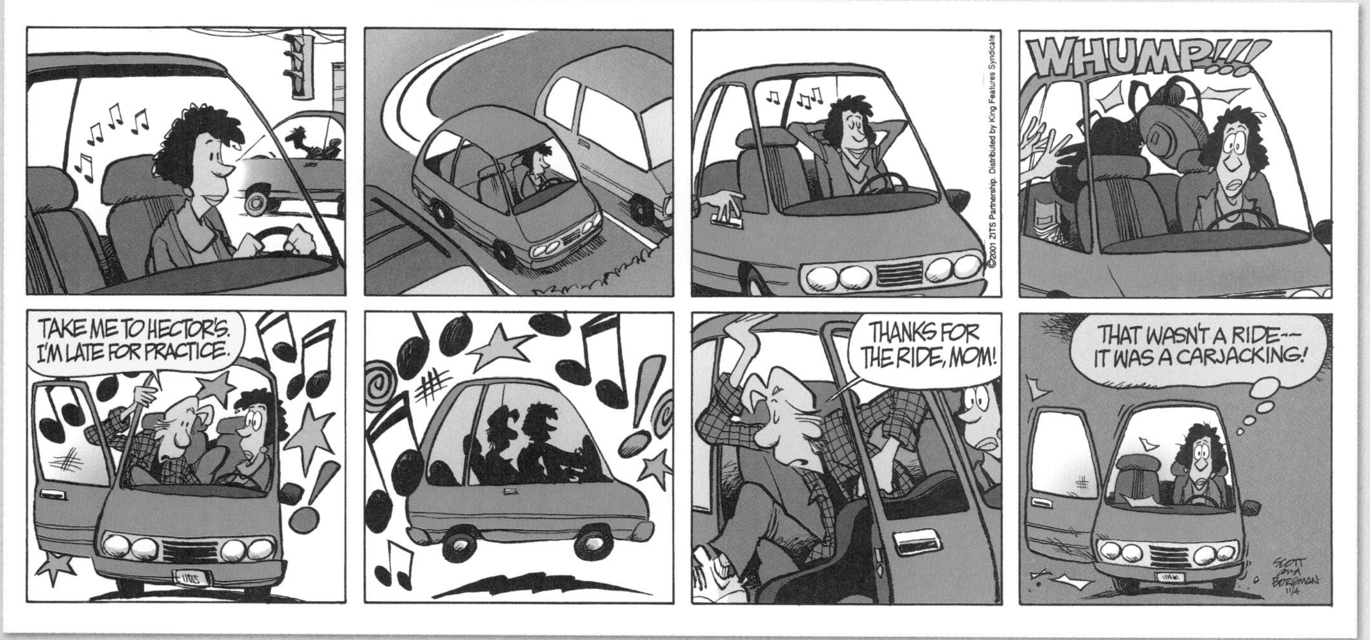
WHUMP!!!
TAKE ME TO HECTOR'S. I'M LATE FOR PRACTICE.
THANKS FOR THE RIDE, MOM!
THAT WASN'T A RIDE--IT WAS A CARJACKING!
©2001 ZITS Partnership. Distributed by King Features Syndicate
SCOTT and BORGMAN 11/4

December 9, 2001

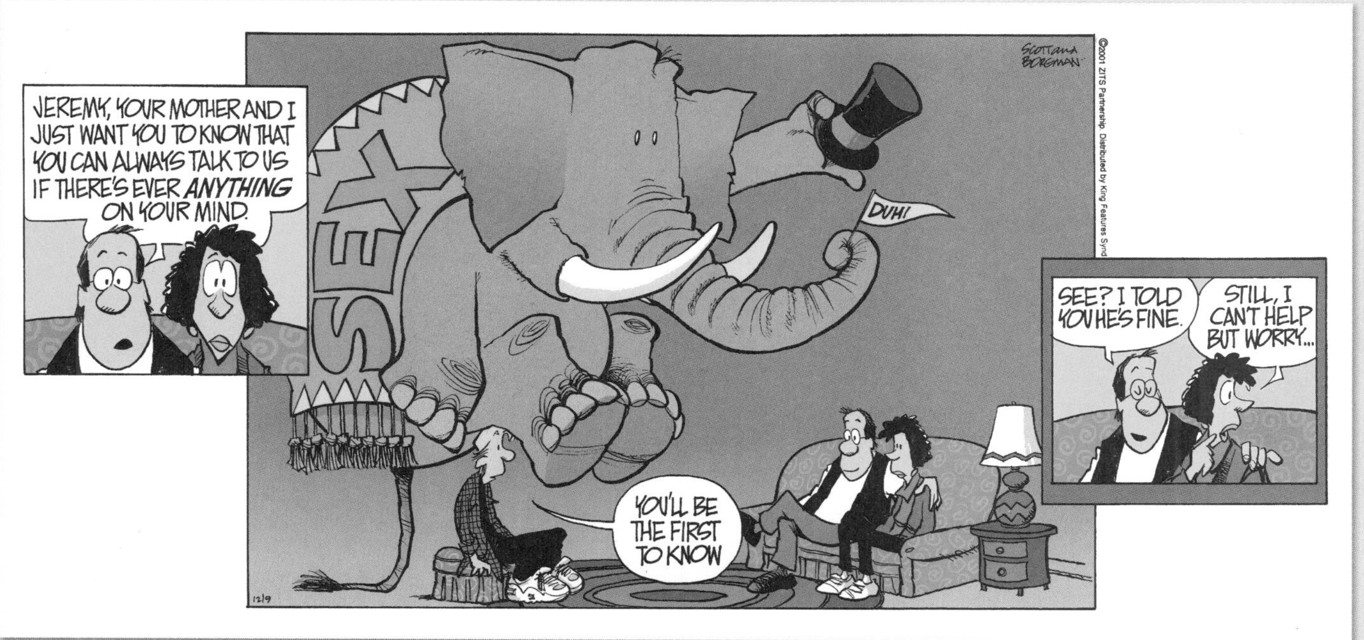
JEREMY, YOUR MOTHER AND I JUST WANT YOU TO KNOW THAT YOU CAN ALWAYS TALK TO US IF THERE'S EVER *ANYTHING* ON YOUR MIND.
SEX
DUH!
YOU'LL BE THE FIRST TO KNOW
SEE? I TOLD YOU HE'S FINE.
STILL, I CAN'T HELP BUT WORRY...
SCOTT and BORGMAN
12/9

June 18, 2001

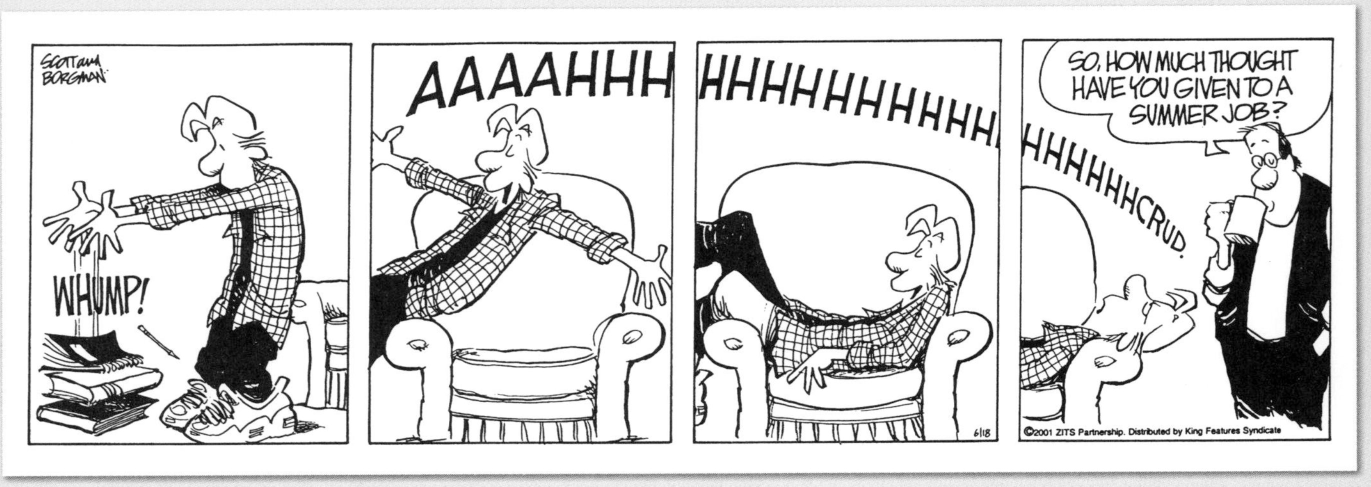
SCOTT and BORGMAN
WHUMP!
AAAAHHH
HHHHHHHHHHHH
HHHHHHHCRUD.
SO, HOW MUCH THOUGHT HAVE YOU GIVEN TO A SUMMER JOB?
6/18
©2001 ZITS Partnership. Distributed by King Features Syndicate

June 19, 2001

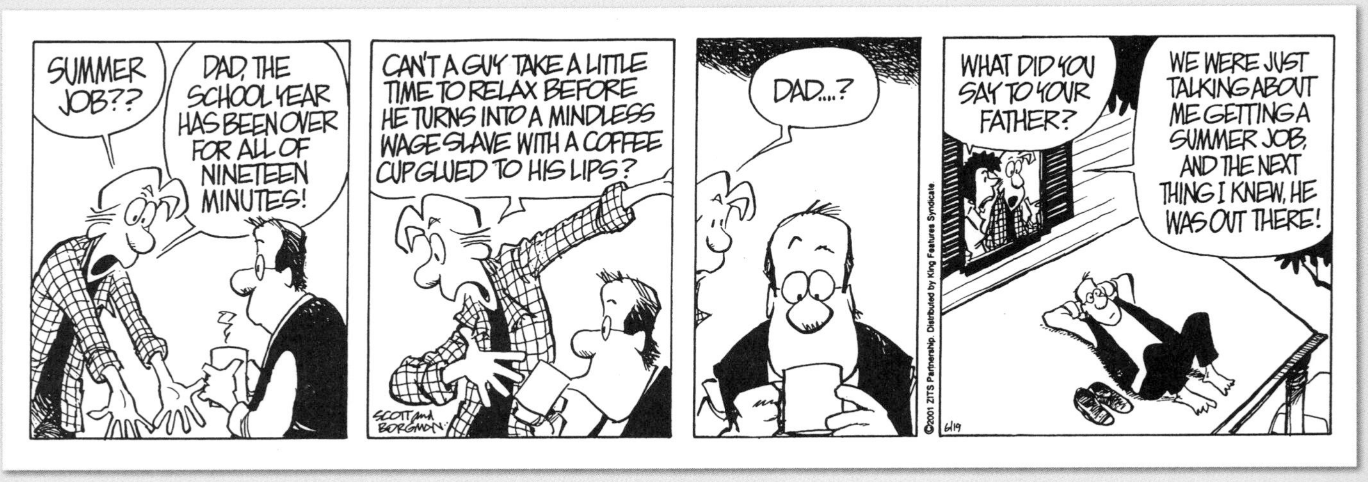
SUMMER JOB??
DAD, THE SCHOOL YEAR HAS BEEN OVER FOR ALL OF NINETEEN MINUTES!
CAN'T A GUY TAKE A LITTLE TIME TO RELAX BEFORE HE TURNS INTO A MINDLESS WAGE SLAVE WITH A COFFEE CUP GLUED TO HIS LIPS?
SCOTT and BORGMAN
DAD...?
WHAT DID YOU SAY TO YOUR FATHER?
WE WERE JUST TALKING ABOUT ME GETTING A SUMMER JOB, AND THE NEXT THING I KNEW, HE WAS OUT THERE!
©2001 ZITS Partnership. Distributed by King Features Syndicate
6/19

November 20, 2001

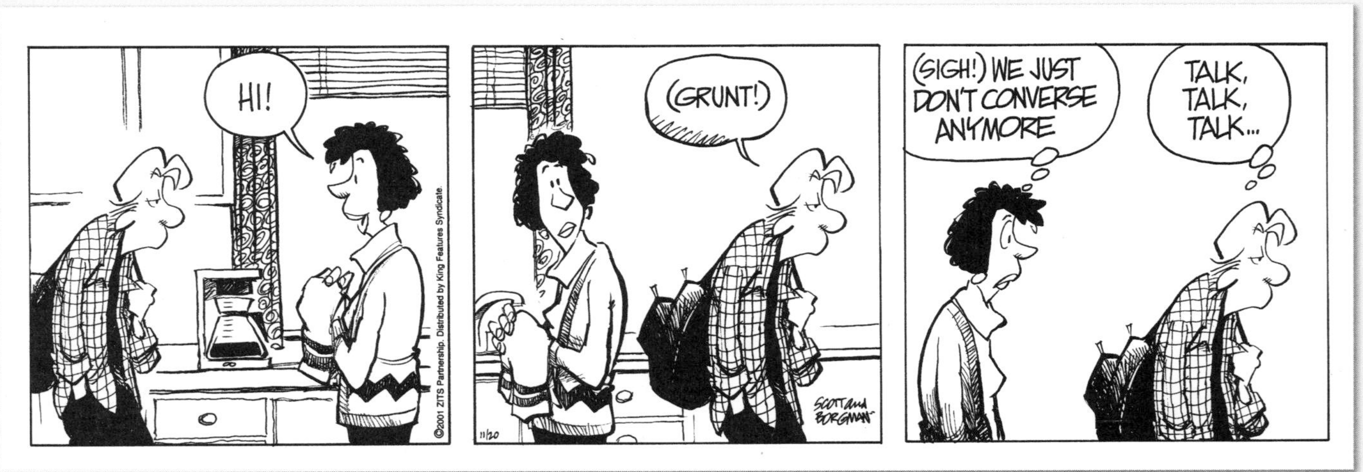
HI!
©2001 ZITS Partnership. Distributed by King Features Syndicate.
(GRUNT!)
11/20
SCOTT and BORGMAN
(SIGH!) WE JUST DON'T CONVERSE ANYMORE
TALK, TALK, TALK...

November 28, 2001

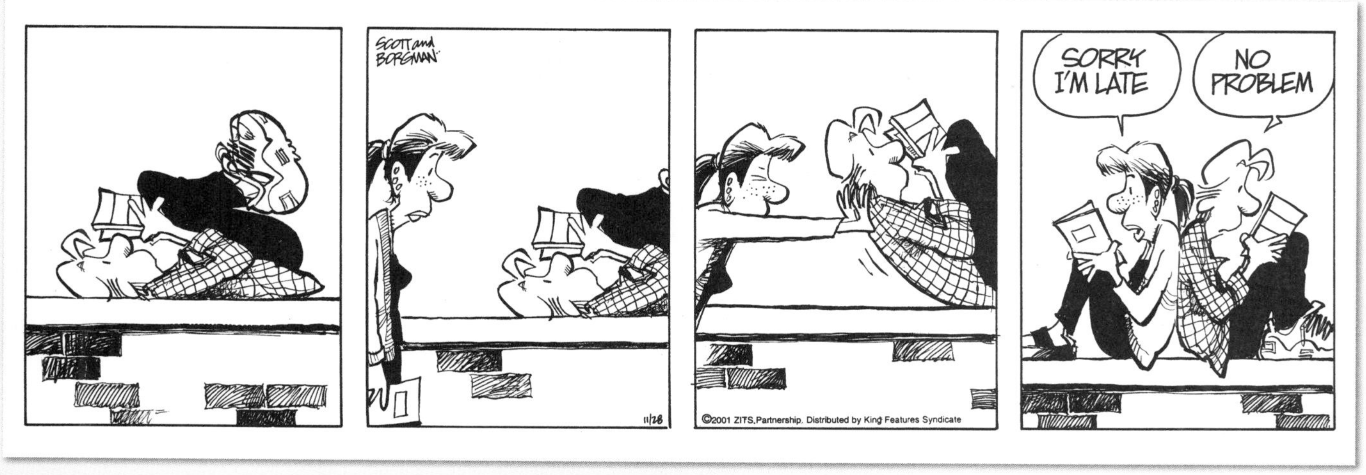
SCOTT and BORGMAN
11/28
©2001 ZITS Partnership. Distributed by King Features Syndicate
SORRY I'M LATE
NO PROBLEM

December 8, 2001

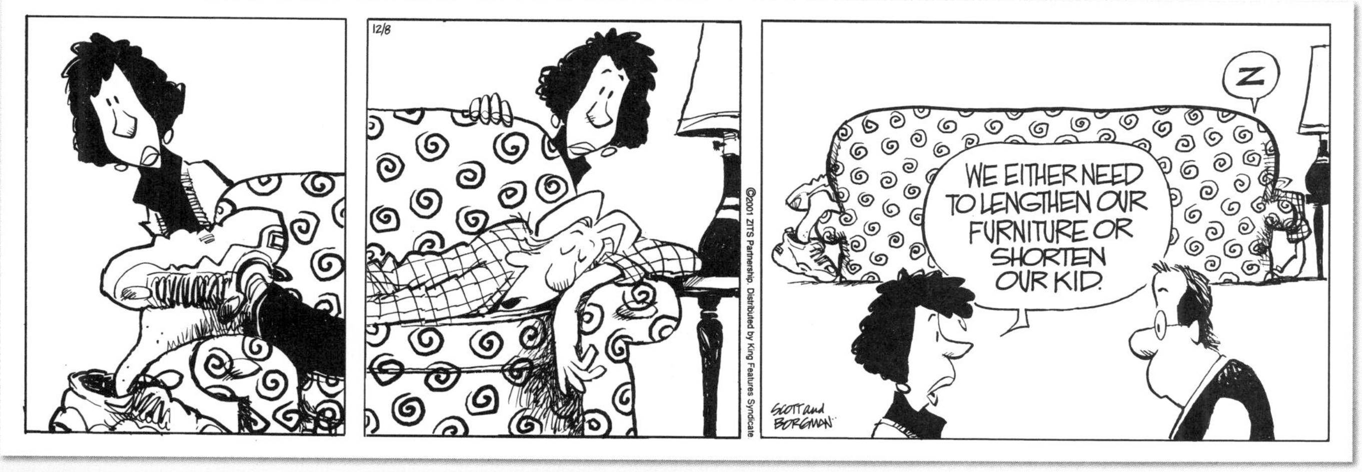
12/8
©2001 ZITS Partnership. Distributed by King Features Syndicate
Z
WE EITHER NEED TO LENGTHEN OUR FURNITURE OR SHORTEN OUR KID.
SCOTT and BORGMAN

December 31, 2001

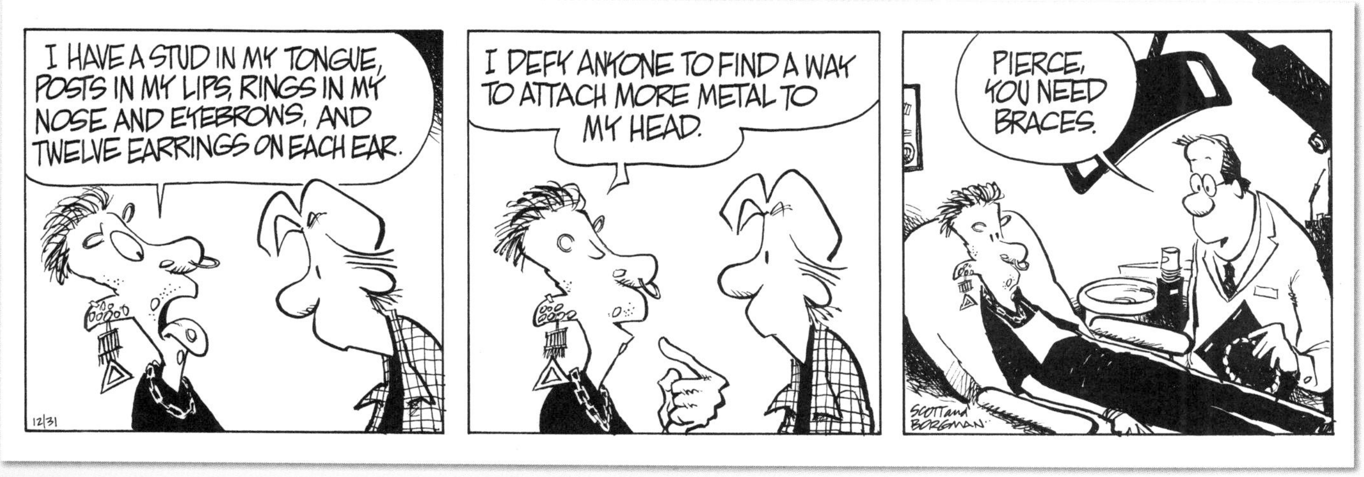
I HAVE A STUD IN MY TONGUE, POSTS IN MY LIPS, RINGS IN MY NOSE AND EYEBROWS, AND TWELVE EARRINGS ON EACH EAR.
12/31
I DEFY ANYONE TO FIND A WAY TO ATTACH MORE METAL TO MY HEAD.
PIERCE, YOU NEED BRACES.
SCOTT and BORGMAN

SPOT the CARTOONIST

Jerry Scott

My career suits me well. I like the work, and I like the independence, which I sometimes flaunt by wearing ratty clothes, not shaving, and hanging around coffee shops while I scribble away in my black wire-bound sketchbook.

I was doing exactly that one morning when a homeless guy I often see panhandling around town sat down at the next table. I noticed his ratty clothes and scraggly beard as he reached into his backpack and pulled out a wire-bound sketchbook and started happily scribbling away.

I should stay out of coffee shops.

January 2, 2002

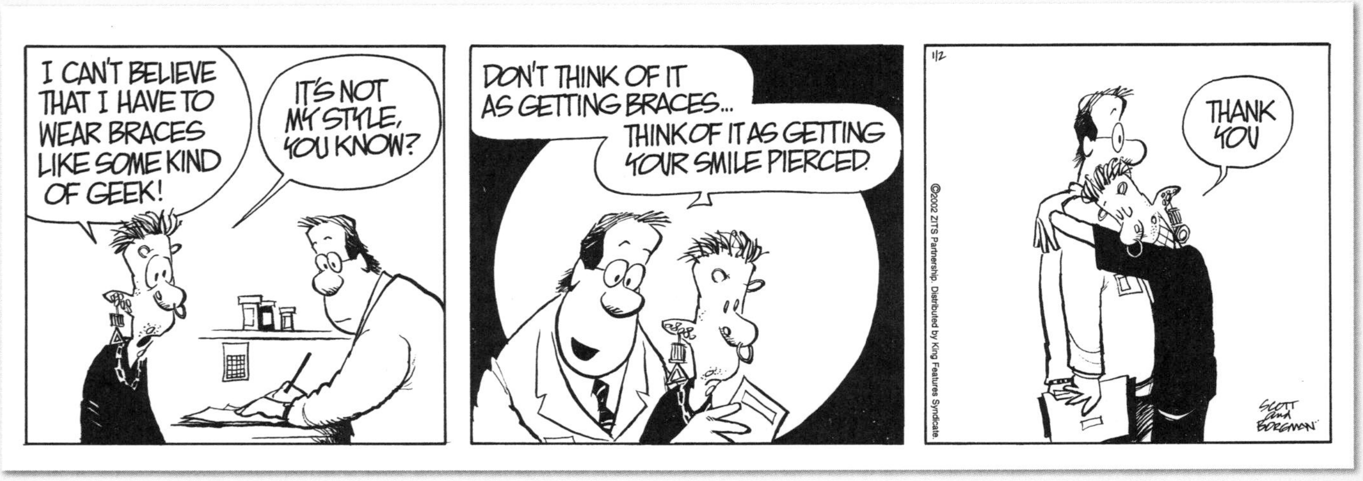
I CAN'T BELIEVE THAT I HAVE TO WEAR BRACES LIKE SOME KIND OF GEEK!
IT'S NOT MY STYLE, YOU KNOW?
DON'T THINK OF IT AS GETTING BRACES...
THINK OF IT AS GETTING YOUR SMILE PIERCED.
THANK YOU
©2002 ZITS Partnership. Distributed by King Features Syndicate.
SCOTT AND BORGMAN

January 8, 2002

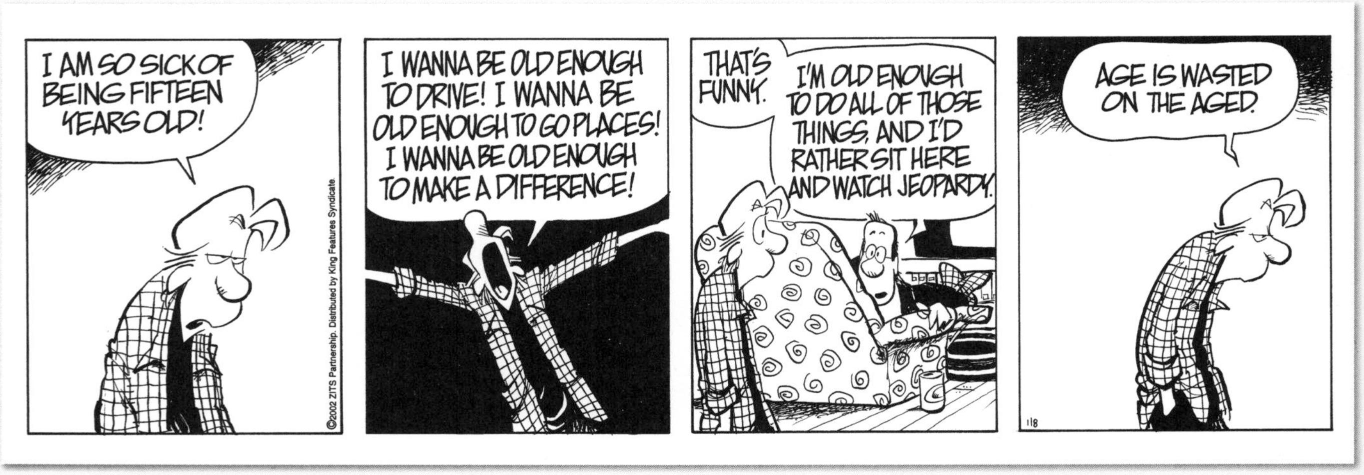
I AM SO SICK OF BEING FIFTEEN YEARS OLD!
I WANNA BE OLD ENOUGH TO DRIVE! I WANNA BE OLD ENOUGH TO GO PLACES! I WANNA BE OLD ENOUGH TO MAKE A DIFFERENCE!
THAT'S FUNNY.
I'M OLD ENOUGH TO DO ALL OF THOSE THINGS, AND I'D RATHER SIT HERE AND WATCH JEOPARDY.
AGE IS WASTED ON THE AGED.
©2002 ZITS Partnership. Distributed by King Features Syndicate.

March 1, 2002

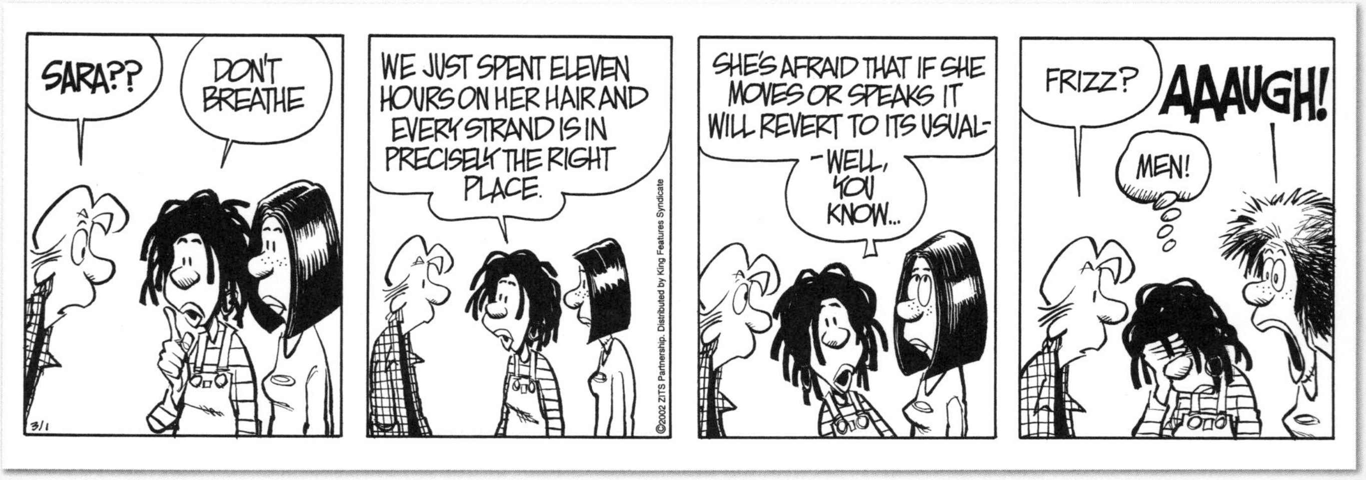
SARA??
DON'T BREATHE
WE JUST SPENT ELEVEN HOURS ON HER HAIR AND EVERY STRAND IS IN PRECISELY THE RIGHT PLACE.
SHE'S AFRAID THAT IF SHE MOVES OR SPEAKS IT WILL REVERT TO ITS USUAL-
-WELL, YOU KNOW...
FRIZZ?
AAAUGH!
MEN!
©2002 ZITS Partnership. Distributed by King Features Syndicate

January 13, 2002

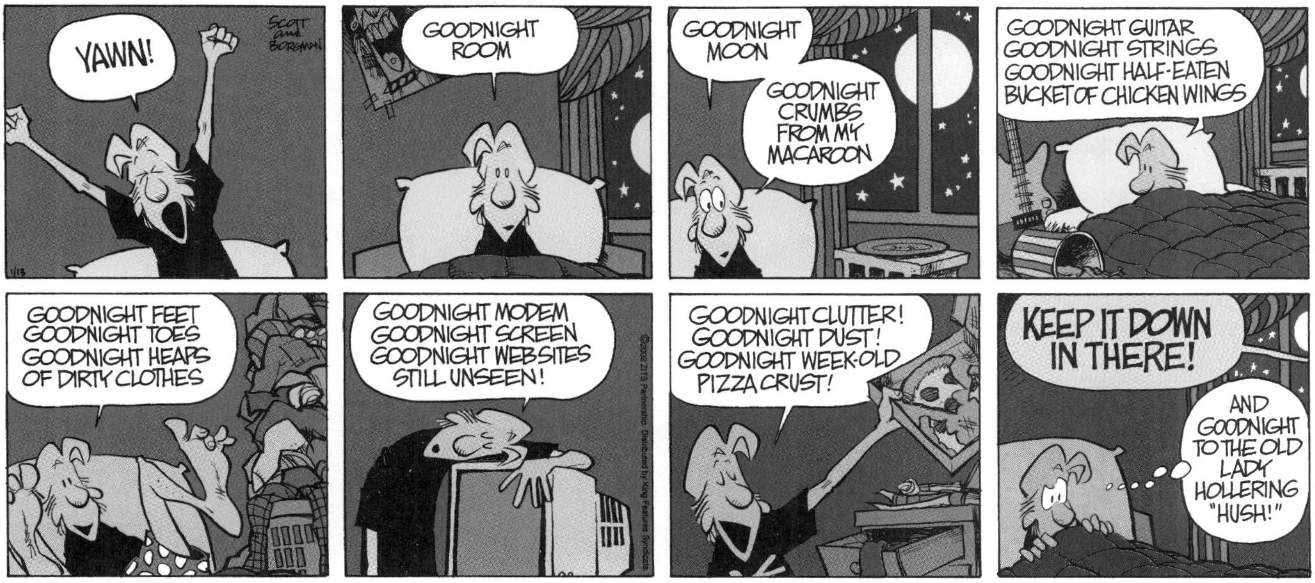
SCOTT and BORGMAN
YAWN!
1/13
GOODNIGHT ROOM
GOODNIGHT MOON
GOODNIGHT CRUMBS FROM MY MACAROON
GOODNIGHT GUITAR GOODNIGHT STRINGS GOODNIGHT HALF-EATEN BUCKET OF CHICKEN WINGS
GOODNIGHT FEET GOODNIGHT TOES GOODNIGHT HEAPS OF DIRTY CLOTHES
GOODNIGHT MODEM GOODNIGHT SCREEN GOODNIGHT WEBSITES STILL UNSEEN!
©2002 ZITS Partnership. Distributed by King Features Syndicate.
GOODNIGHT CLUTTER! GOODNIGHT DUST! GOODNIGHT WEEK-OLD PIZZA CRUST!
KEEP IT DOWN IN THERE!
AND GOODNIGHT TO THE OLD LADY HOLLERING "HUSH!"

June 2, 2002

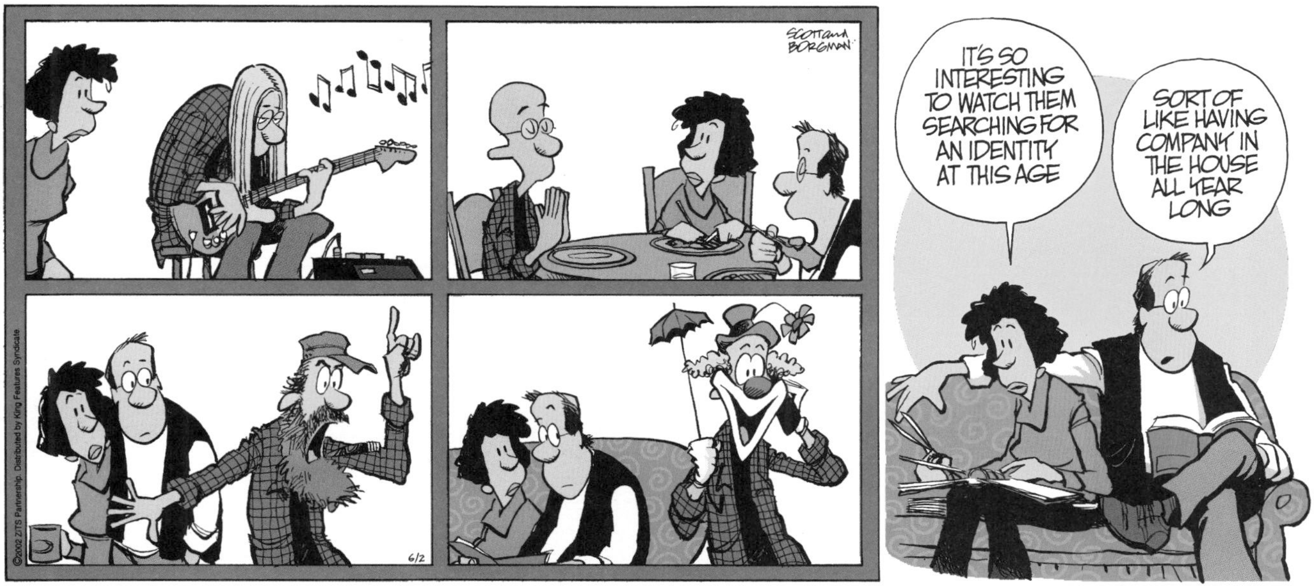
SCOTT and BORGMAN
©2002 ZITS Partnership. Distributed by King Features Syndicate
6/2
IT'S SO INTERESTING TO WATCH THEM SEARCHING FOR AN IDENTITY AT THIS AGE
SORT OF LIKE HAVING COMPANY IN THE HOUSE ALL YEAR LONG

March 15, 2002

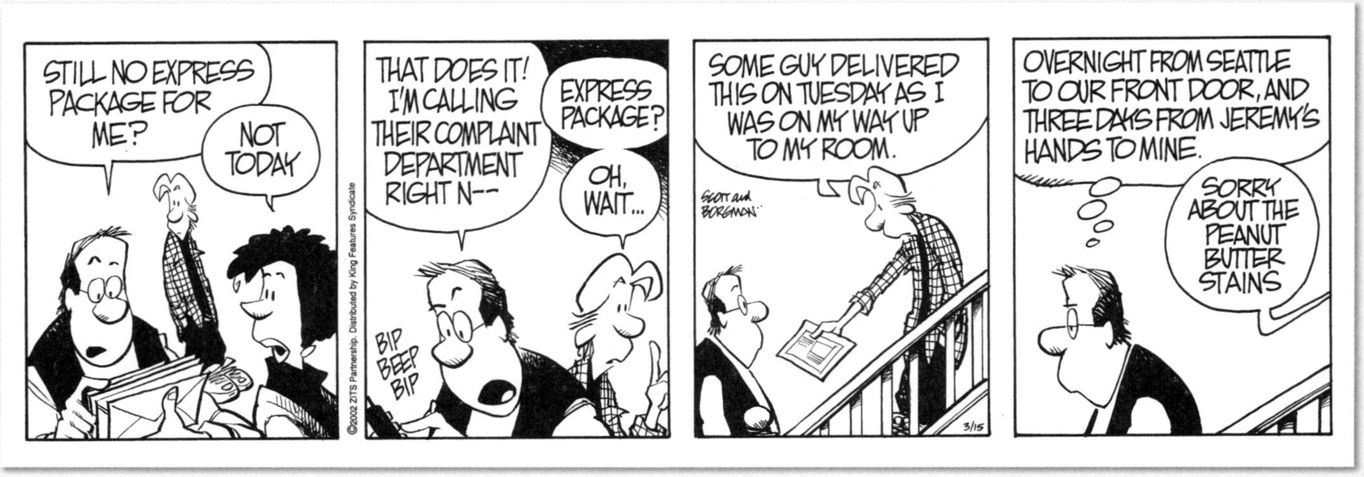
STILL NO EXPRESS PACKAGE FOR ME?
NOT TODAY
THAT DOES IT! I'M CALLING THEIR COMPLAINT DEPARTMENT RIGHT N--
BIP BEEP BIP
EXPRESS PACKAGE?
OH, WAIT...
©2002 ZITS Partnership. Distributed by King Features Syndicate
SOME GUY DELIVERED THIS ON TUESDAY AS I WAS ON MY WAY UP TO MY ROOM.
SCOTT and BORGMAN
3/15
OVERNIGHT FROM SEATTLE TO OUR FRONT DOOR, AND THREE DAYS FROM JEREMY'S HANDS TO MINE.
SORRY ABOUT THE PEANUT BUTTER STAINS

March 18, 2002

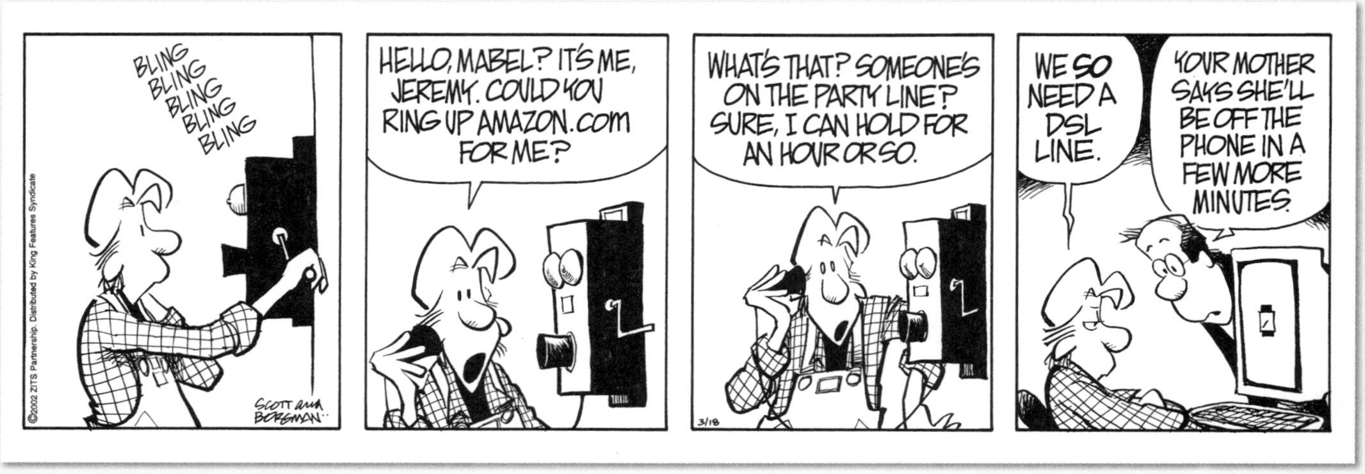
BLING BLING BLING BLING BLING
©2002 ZITS Partnership. Distributed by King Features Syndicate
SCOTT and BORGMAN
HELLO, MABEL? IT'S ME, JEREMY. COULD YOU RING UP AMAZON.COM FOR ME?
WHAT'S THAT? SOMEONE'S ON THE PARTY LINE? SURE, I CAN HOLD FOR AN HOUR OR SO.
3/18
WE SO NEED A DSL LINE.
YOUR MOTHER SAYS SHE'LL BE OFF THE PHONE IN A FEW MORE MINUTES.

March 22, 2002

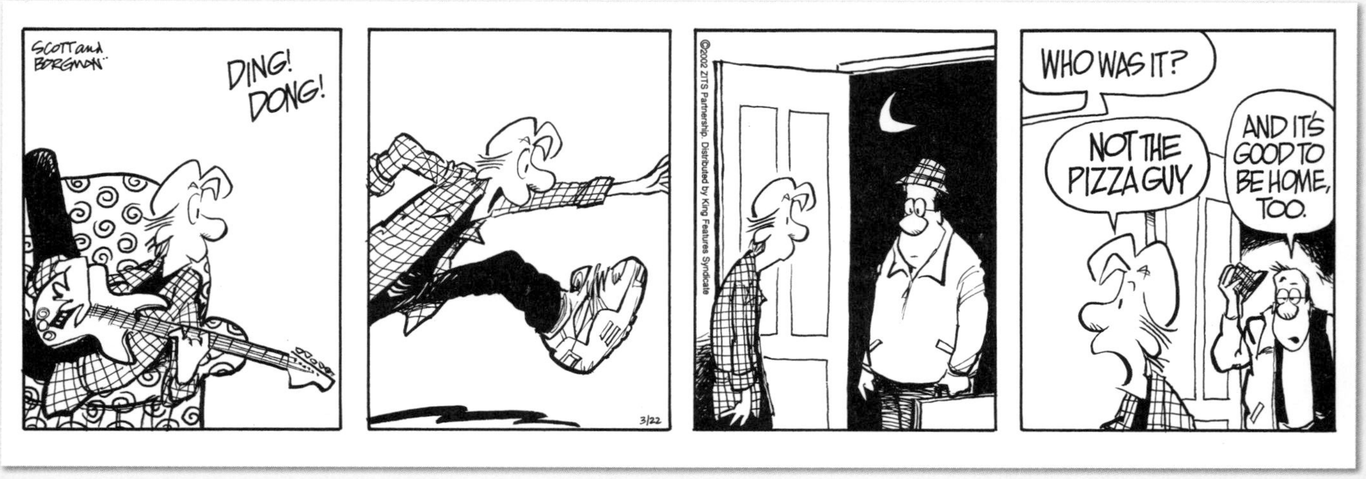
SCOTT and BORGMAN
DING! DONG!
3/22
©2002 ZITS Partnership. Distributed by King Features Syndicate
WHO WAS IT?
NOT THE PIZZA GUY
AND IT'S GOOD TO BE HOME, TOO.

March 30, 2002

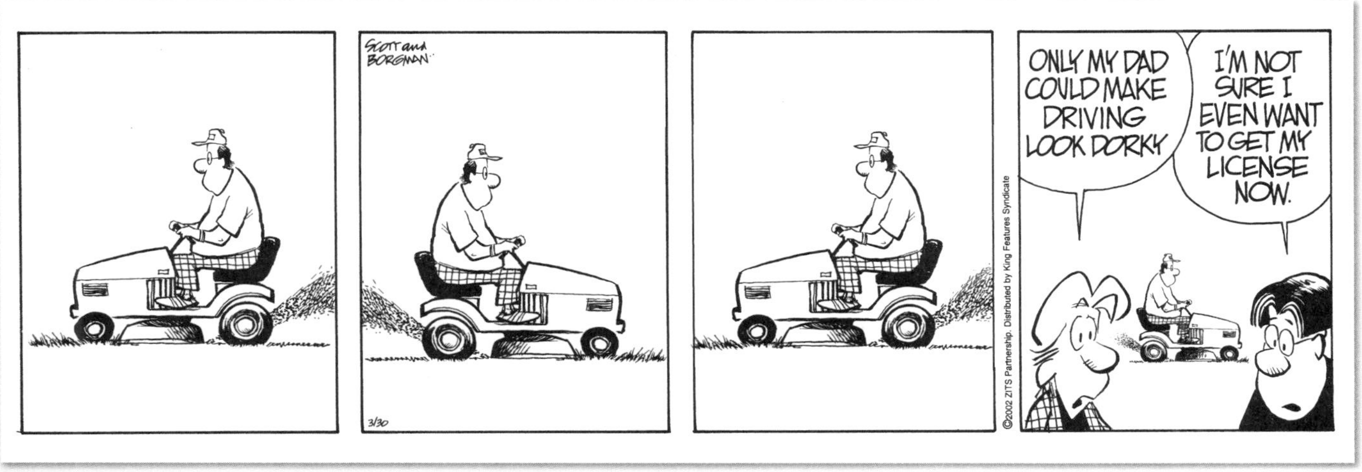
SCOTT and BORGMAN
3/30
ONLY MY DAD COULD MAKE DRIVING LOOK DORKY
I'M NOT SURE I EVEN WANT TO GET MY LICENSE NOW.
©2002 ZITS Partnership. Distributed by King Features Syndicate

April 24, 2002

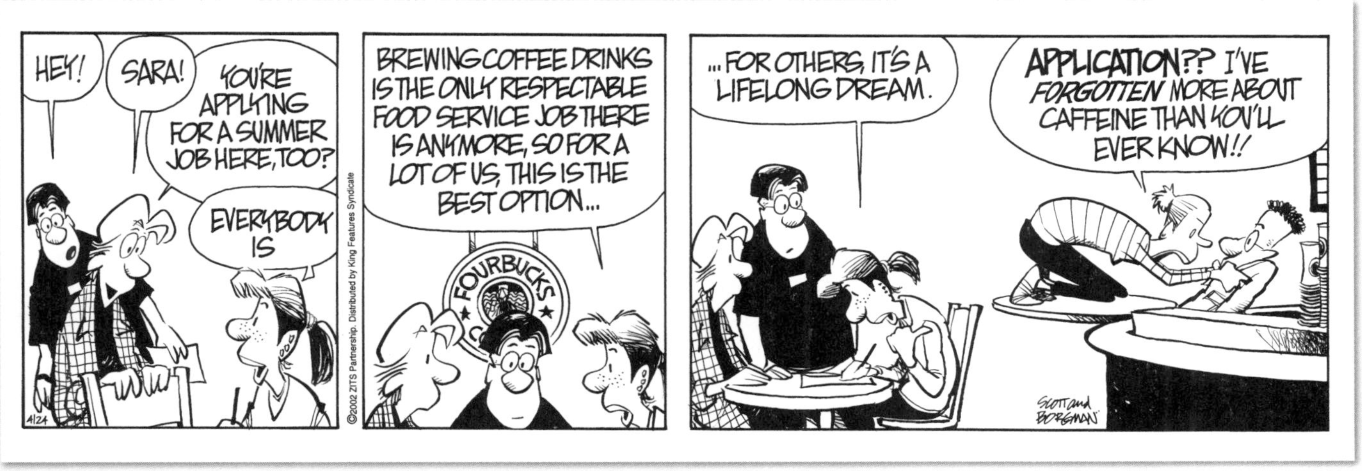
HEY!
SARA!
YOU'RE APPLYING FOR A SUMMER JOB HERE, TOO?
EVERYBODY IS
4/24
©2002 ZITS Partnership. Distributed by King Features Syndicate
BREWING COFFEE DRINKS IS THE ONLY RESPECTABLE FOOD SERVICE JOB THERE IS ANYMORE, SO FOR A LOT OF US, THIS IS THE BEST OPTION...
FOURBUCKS
...FOR OTHERS, IT'S A LIFELONG DREAM.
APPLICATION?? I'VE FORGOTTEN MORE ABOUT CAFFEINE THAN YOU'LL EVER KNOW!!
SCOTT and BORGMAN

May 3, 2002

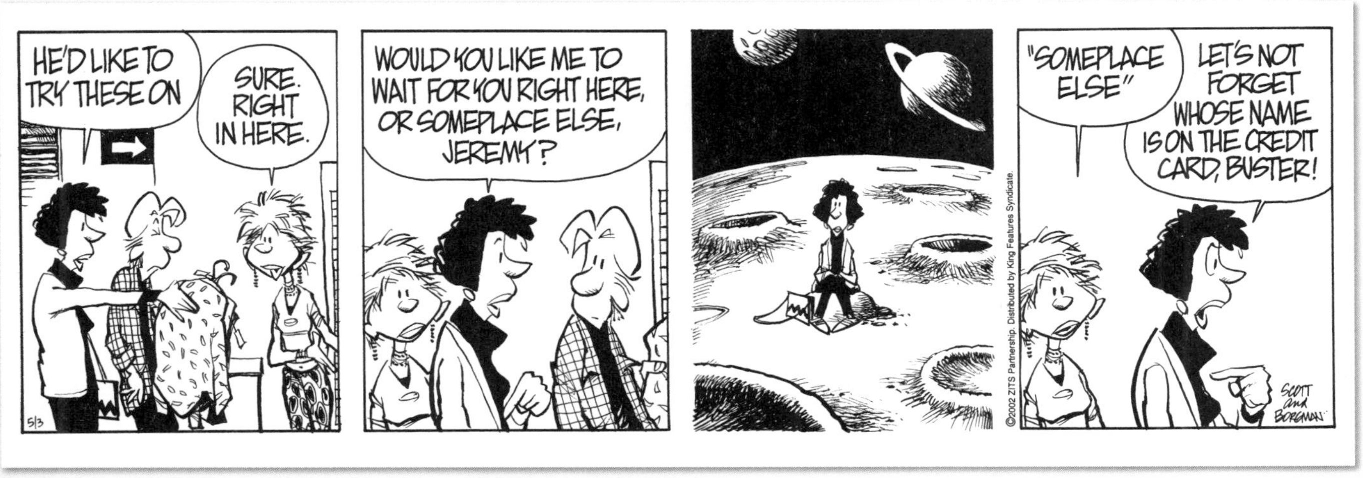
HE'D LIKE TO TRY THESE ON
SURE. RIGHT IN HERE.
5/3
WOULD YOU LIKE ME TO WAIT FOR YOU RIGHT HERE, OR SOMEPLACE ELSE, JEREMY?
©2002 ZITS Partnership. Distributed by King Features Syndicate.
"SOMEPLACE ELSE"
LET'S NOT FORGET WHOSE NAME IS ON THE CREDIT CARD, BUSTER!
SCOTT and BORGMAN

May 10, 2002

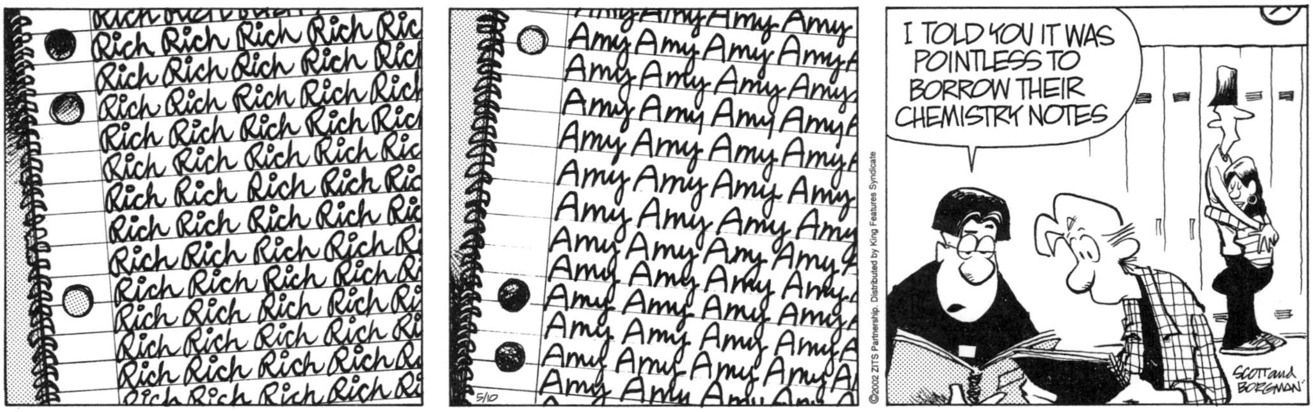
Rich Rich Rich Rich
Amy Amy Amy Amy
I TOLD YOU IT WAS POINTLESS TO BORROW THEIR CHEMISTRY NOTES
©2002 ZITS Partnership. Distributed by King Features Syndicate
SCOTT and BORGMAN
5/10

May 16, 2002

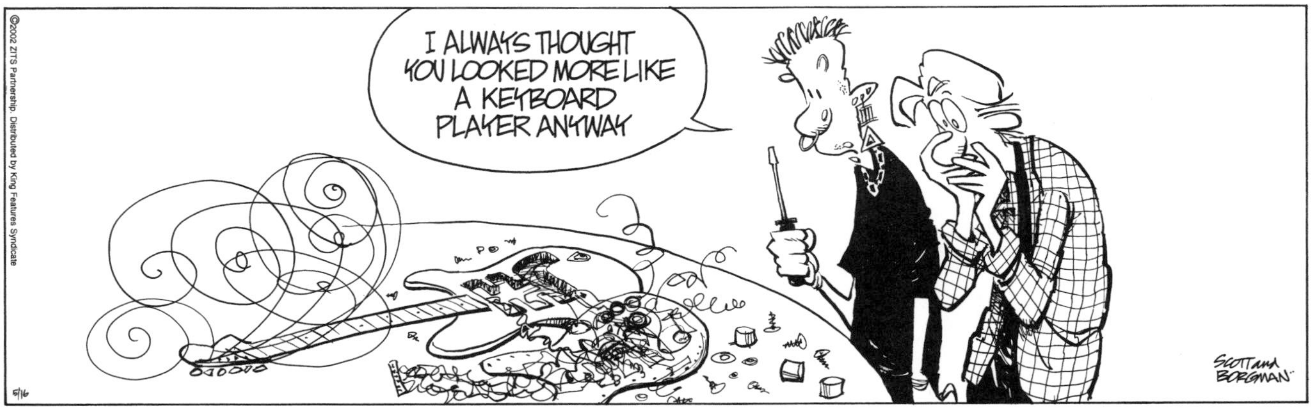
I ALWAYS THOUGHT YOU LOOKED MORE LIKE A KEYBOARD PLAYER ANYWAY
©2002 ZITS Partnership. Distributed by King Features Syndicate
SCOTT and BORGMAN
5/16

August 1, 2002

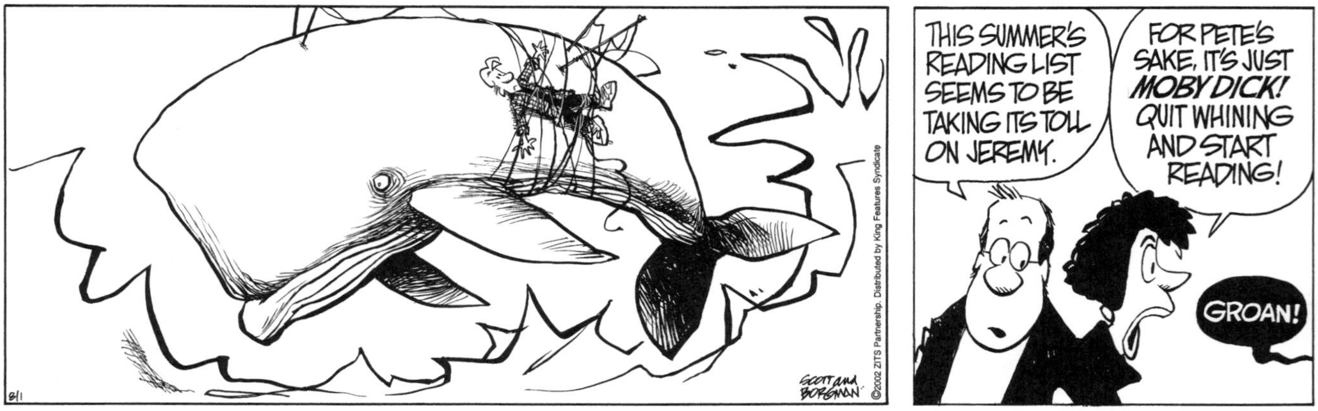
THIS SUMMER'S READING LIST SEEMS TO BE TAKING ITS TOLL ON JEREMY.
FOR PETE'S SAKE, IT'S JUST *MOBY DICK!* QUIT WHINING AND START READING!
GROAN!
©2002 ZITS Partnership. Distributed by King Features Syndicate
SCOTT and BORGMAN
8/1

June 30, 2002

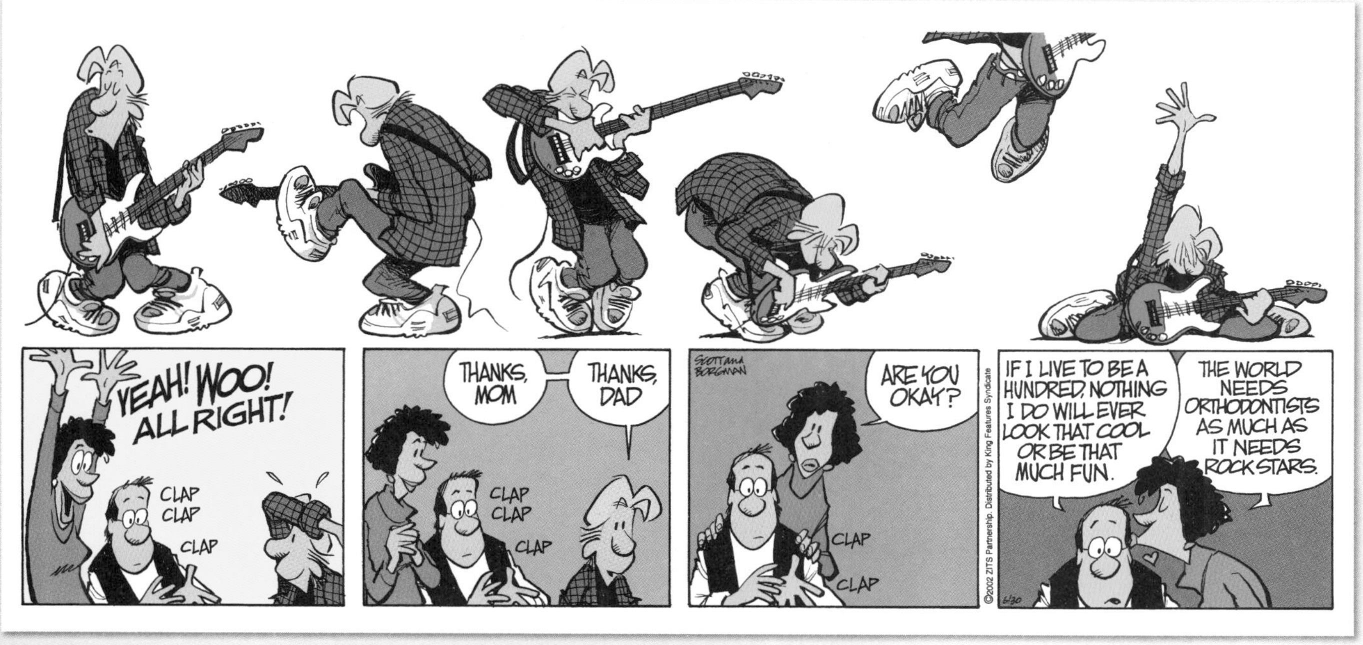
YEAH! WOO! ALL RIGHT!
CLAP CLAP
CLAP
THANKS, MOM
THANKS, DAD
CLAP CLAP
CLAP
SCOTT AND BORGMAN
ARE YOU OKAY?
CLAP
CLAP
©2002 ZITS Partnership. Distributed by King Features Syndicate
6/30
IF I LIVE TO BE A HUNDRED, NOTHING I DO WILL EVER LOOK THAT COOL OR BE THAT MUCH FUN.
THE WORLD NEEDS ORTHODONTISTS AS MUCH AS IT NEEDS ROCK STARS.

July 28, 2002

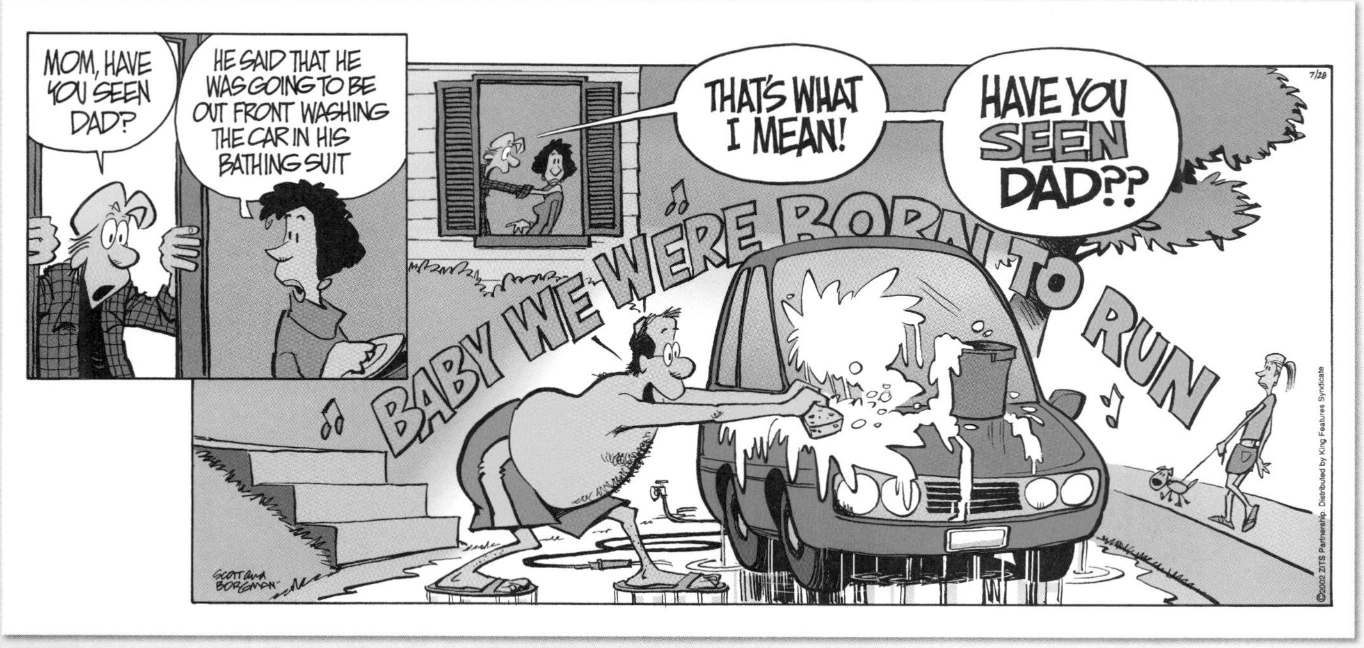
MOM, HAVE YOU SEEN DAD?
HE SAID THAT HE WAS GOING TO BE OUT FRONT WASHING THE CAR IN HIS BATHING SUIT
THAT'S WHAT I MEAN!
HAVE YOU SEEN DAD??
7/28
BABY WE WERE BORN TO RUN
SCOTT AND BORGMAN
©2002 ZITS Partnership. Distributed by King Features Syndicate

August 8, 2002

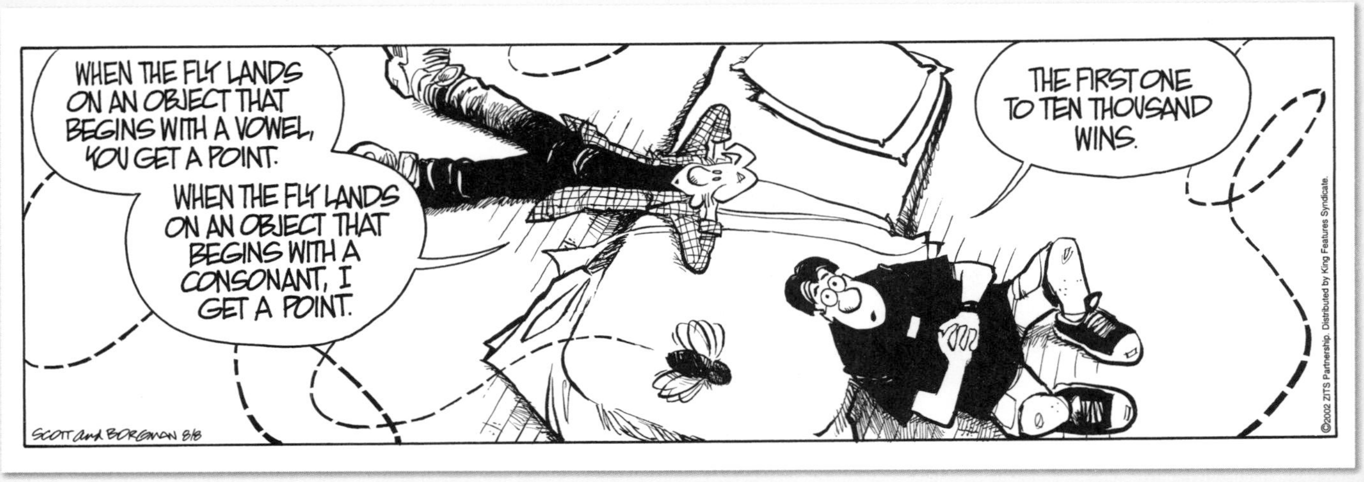
WHEN THE FLY LANDS ON AN OBJECT THAT BEGINS WITH A VOWEL, YOU GET A POINT.
WHEN THE FLY LANDS ON AN OBJECT THAT BEGINS WITH A CONSONANT, I GET A POINT.
THE FIRST ONE TO TEN THOUSAND WINS.
SCOTT and BORGMAN 8/8
©2002 ZITS Partnership. Distributed by King Features Syndicate.

August 14, 2002

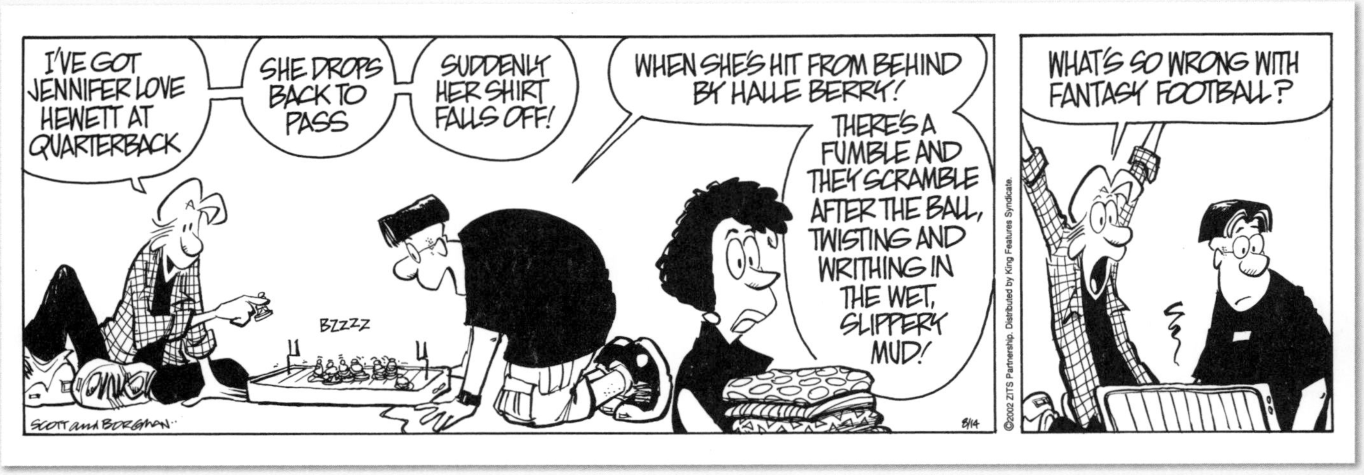
I'VE GOT JENNIFER LOVE HEWETT AT QUARTERBACK
SHE DROPS BACK TO PASS
SUDDENLY HER SHIRT FALLS OFF!
WHEN SHE'S HIT FROM BEHIND BY HALLE BERRY!
THERE'S A FUMBLE AND THEY SCRAMBLE AFTER THE BALL, TWISTING AND WRITHING IN THE WET, SLIPPERY MUD!
BZZZZ
WHAT'S SO WRONG WITH FANTASY FOOTBALL?
SCOTT and BORGMAN 8/14
©2002 ZITS Partnership. Distributed by King Features Syndicate.

August 27, 2002

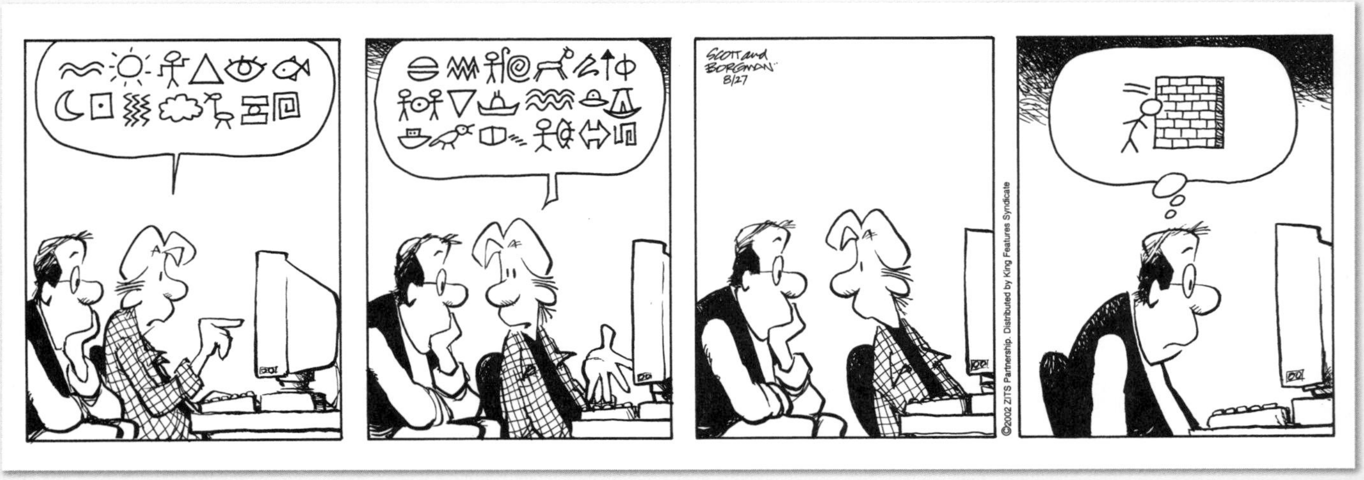
SCOTT and BORGMAN 8/27
©2002 ZITS Partnership. Distributed by King Features Syndicate

August 4, 2002

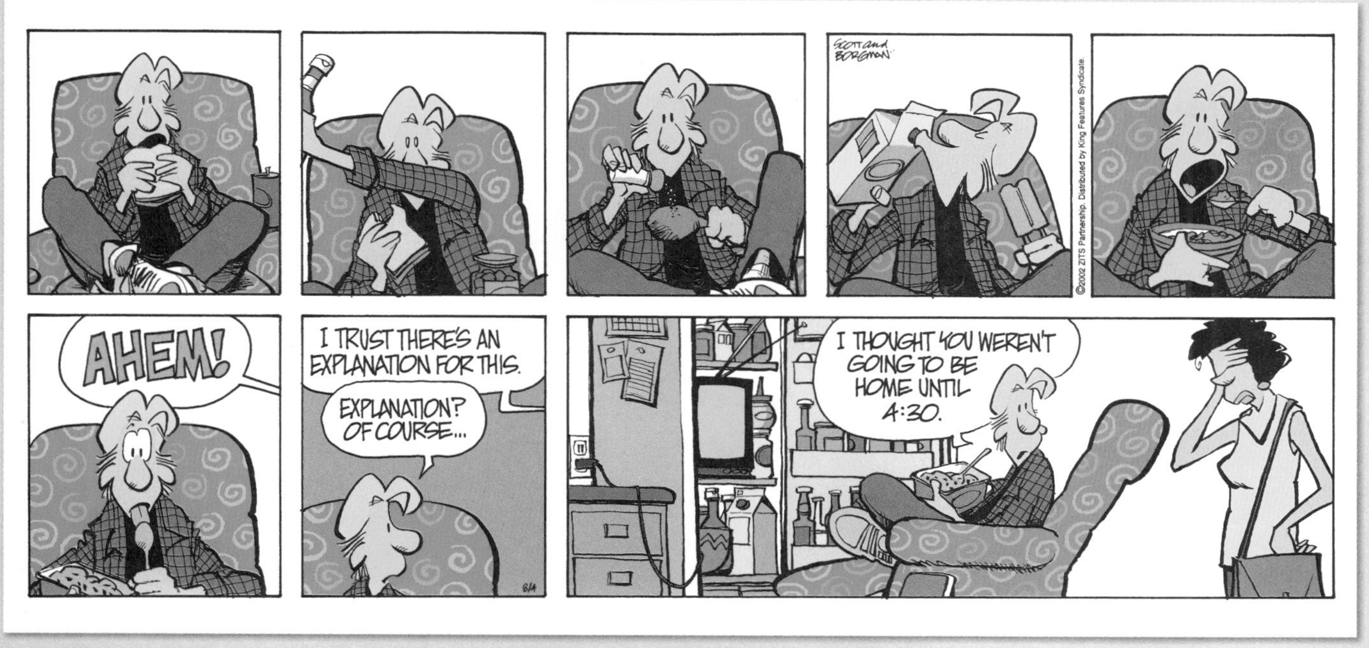
SCOTT and BORGMAN
©2002 ZITS Partnership. Distributed by King Features Syndicate.
AHEM!
I TRUST THERE'S AN EXPLANATION FOR THIS.
EXPLANATION? OF COURSE...
I THOUGHT YOU WEREN'T GOING TO BE HOME UNTIL 4:30.

October 13, 2002

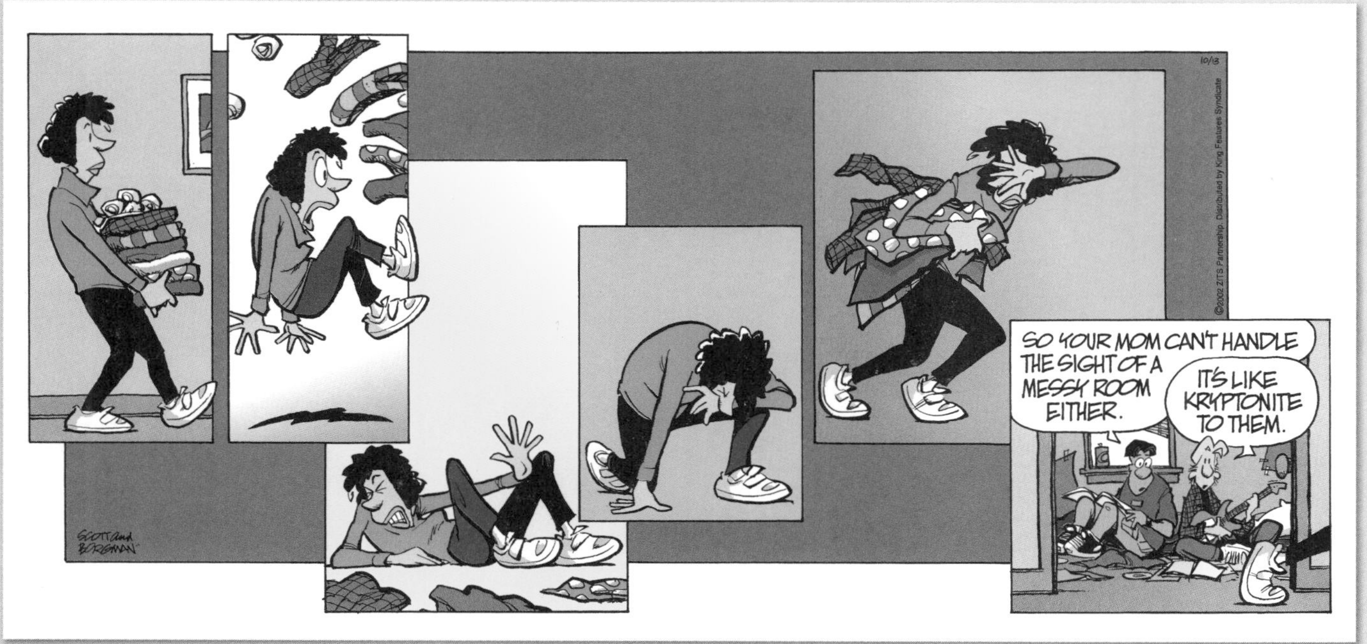
©2002 ZITS Partnership. Distributed by King Features Syndicate
SCOTT and BORGMAN
SO YOUR MOM CAN'T HANDLE THE SIGHT OF A MESSY ROOM EITHER.
IT'S LIKE KRYPTONITE TO THEM.

September 5, 2002

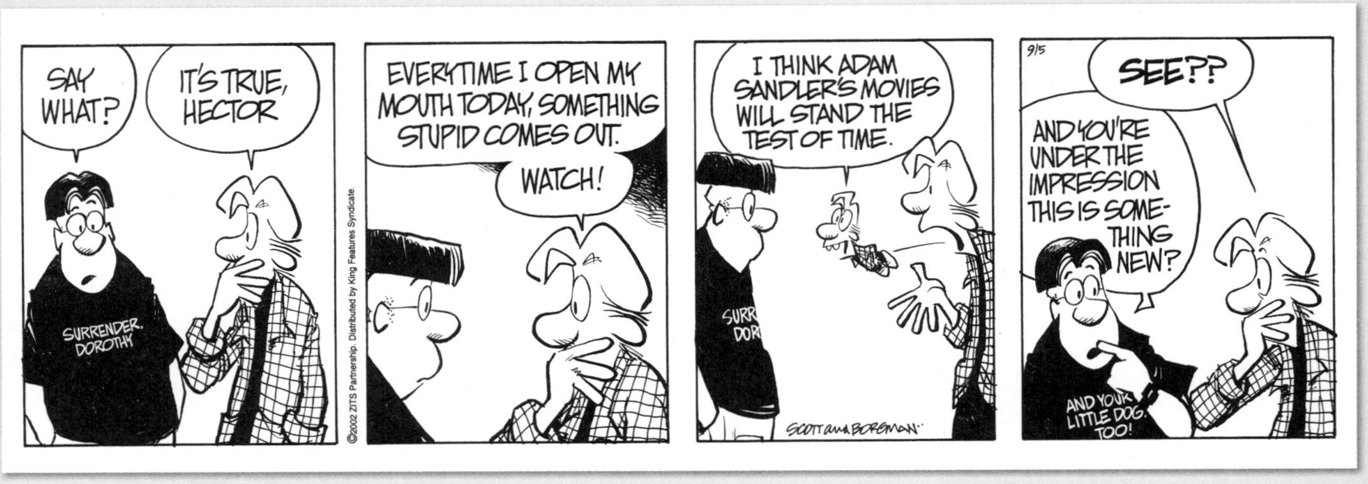

SAY WHAT?
IT'S TRUE, HECTOR
SURRENDER, DOROTHY
©2002 ZITS Partnership. Distributed by King Features Syndicate.
EVERYTIME I OPEN MY MOUTH TODAY, SOMETHING STUPID COMES OUT.
WATCH!
I THINK ADAM SANDLER'S MOVIES WILL STAND THE TEST OF TIME.
SCOTT and BORGMAN
9/5
SEE??
AND YOU'RE UNDER THE IMPRESSION THIS IS SOMETHING NEW?
AND YOUR LITTLE DOG, TOO!

September 7, 2002

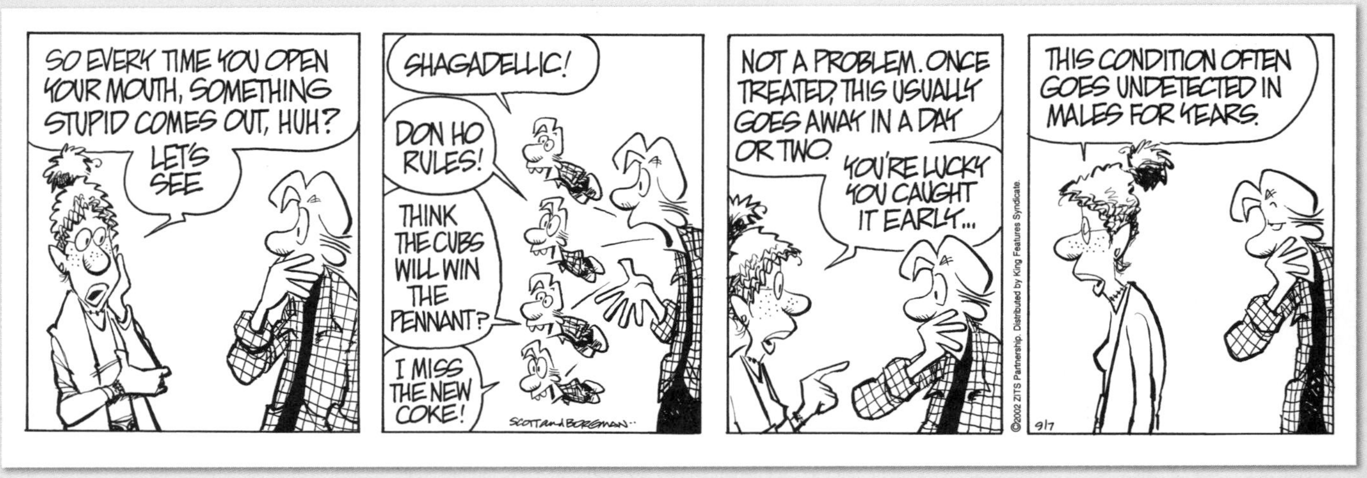

SO EVERY TIME YOU OPEN YOUR MOUTH, SOMETHING STUPID COMES OUT, HUH?
LET'S SEE
SHAGADELLIC!
DON HO RULES!
THINK THE CUBS WILL WIN THE PENNANT?
I MISS THE NEW COKE!
SCOTT and BORGMAN
NOT A PROBLEM. ONCE TREATED, THIS USUALLY GOES AWAY IN A DAY OR TWO.
YOU'RE LUCKY YOU CAUGHT IT EARLY...
©2002 ZITS Partnership. Distributed by King Features Syndicate.
9/7
THIS CONDITION OFTEN GOES UNDETECTED IN MALES FOR YEARS.

October 11, 2002

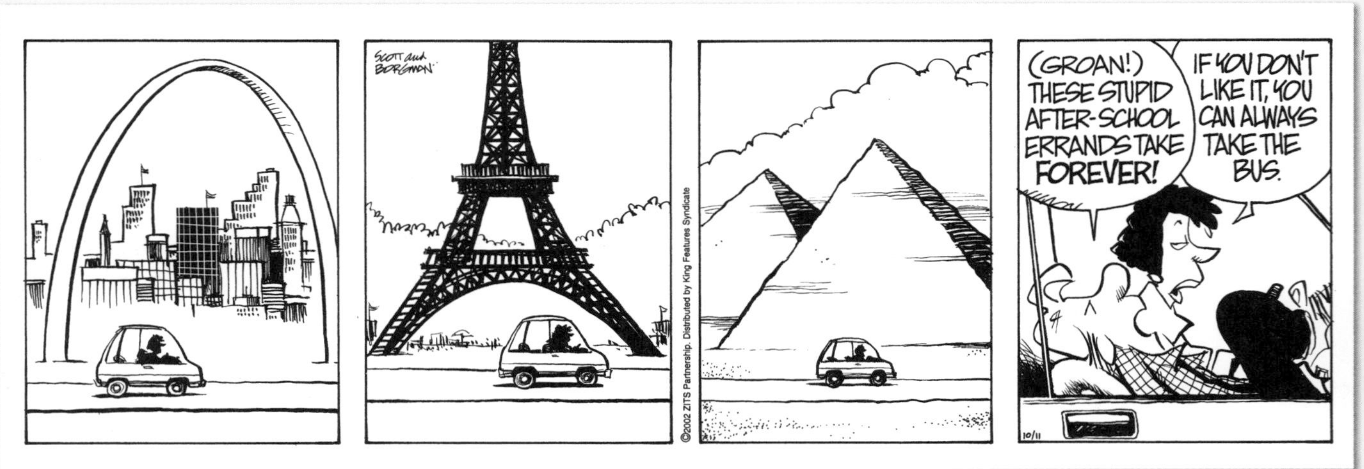

SCOTT and BORGMAN
©2002 ZITS Partnership. Distributed by King Features Syndicate
(GROAN!) THESE STUPID AFTER-SCHOOL ERRANDS TAKE FOREVER!
IF YOU DON'T LIKE IT, YOU CAN ALWAYS TAKE THE BUS.
10/11

October 18, 2002

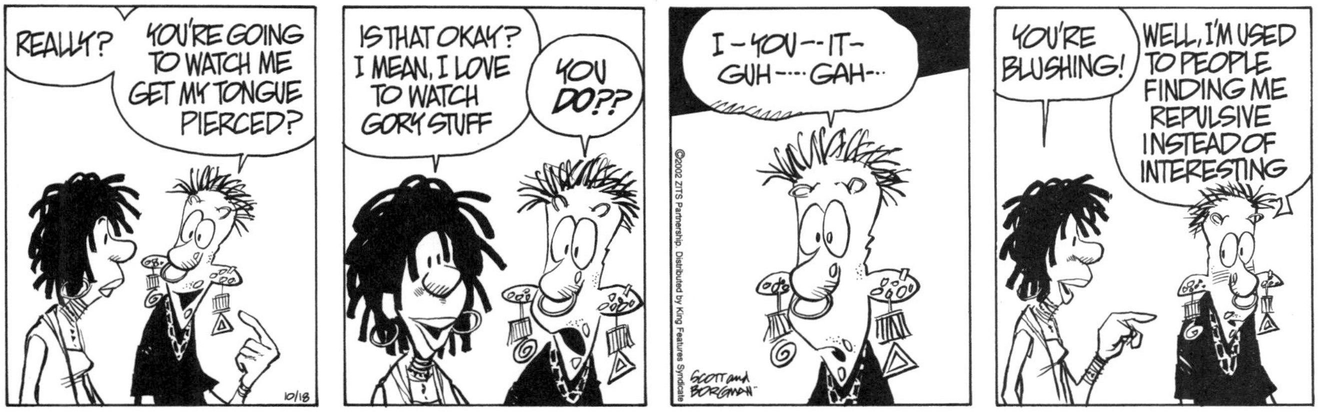
REALLY?
YOU'RE GOING TO WATCH ME GET MY TONGUE PIERCED?
IS THAT OKAY? I MEAN, I LOVE TO WATCH GORY STUFF
YOU DO??
I - YOU -- IT- GUH ---- GAH--
YOU'RE BLUSHING!
WELL, I'M USED TO PEOPLE FINDING ME REPULSIVE INSTEAD OF INTERESTING
©2002 ZITS Partnership. Distributed by King Features Syndicate
SCOTT and BORGMAN
10/18

October 19, 2002

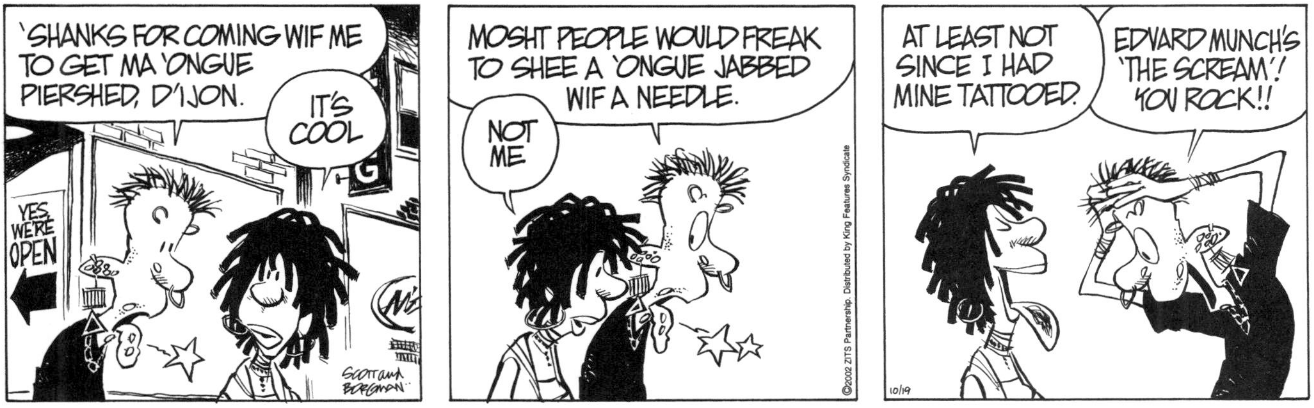
'SHANKS FOR COMING WIF ME TO GET MA 'ONGUE PIERSHED, D'IJON.
IT'S COOL
YES, WE'RE OPEN
G
MOSHT PEOPLE WOULD FREAK TO SHEE A 'ONGUE JABBED WIF A NEEDLE.
NOT ME
AT LEAST NOT SINCE I HAD MINE TATTOOED.
EDVARD MUNCH'S 'THE SCREAM'! YOU ROCK!!
©2002 ZITS Partnership. Distributed by King Features Syndicate
SCOTT and BORGMAN
10/19

October 25, 2002

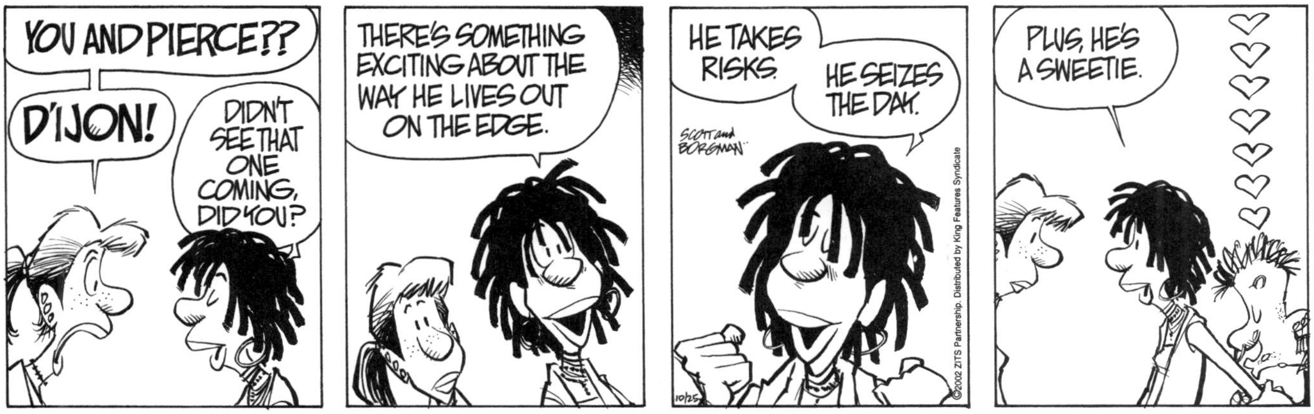
YOU AND PIERCE??
D'IJON!
DIDN'T SEE THAT ONE COMING, DID YOU?
THERE'S SOMETHING EXCITING ABOUT THE WAY HE LIVES OUT ON THE EDGE.
HE TAKES RISKS.
HE SEIZES THE DAY.
PLUS, HE'S A SWEETIE.
©2002 ZITS Partnership. Distributed by King Features Syndicate
SCOTT and BORGMAN
10/25

November 3, 2002

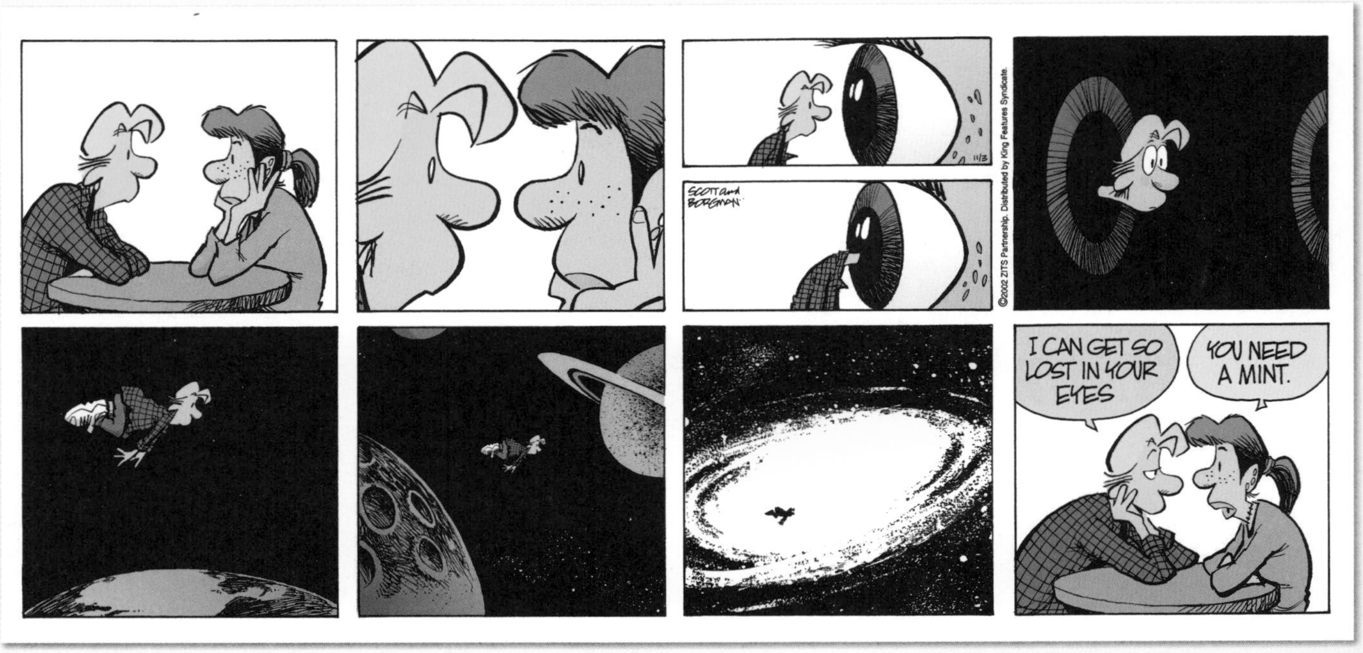
SCOTT and BORGMAN
©2002 ZITS Partnership. Distributed by King Features Syndicate.
I CAN GET SO LOST IN YOUR EYES
YOU NEED A MINT.

December 26, 2002

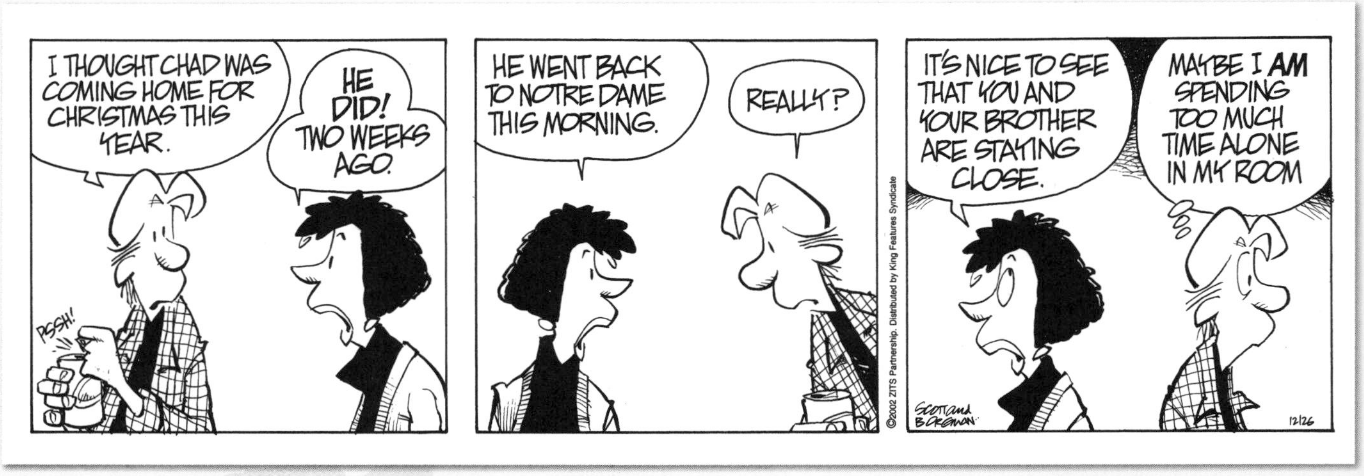
I THOUGHT CHAD WAS COMING HOME FOR CHRISTMAS THIS YEAR.
HE DID! TWO WEEKS AGO.
PSSH!
HE WENT BACK TO NOTRE DAME THIS MORNING.
REALLY?
©2002 ZITS Partnership. Distributed by King Features Syndicate
IT'S NICE TO SEE THAT YOU AND YOUR BROTHER ARE STAYING CLOSE.
MAYBE I **AM** SPENDING TOO MUCH TIME ALONE IN MY ROOM
SCOTT and BORGMAN
12/26

November 17, 2002

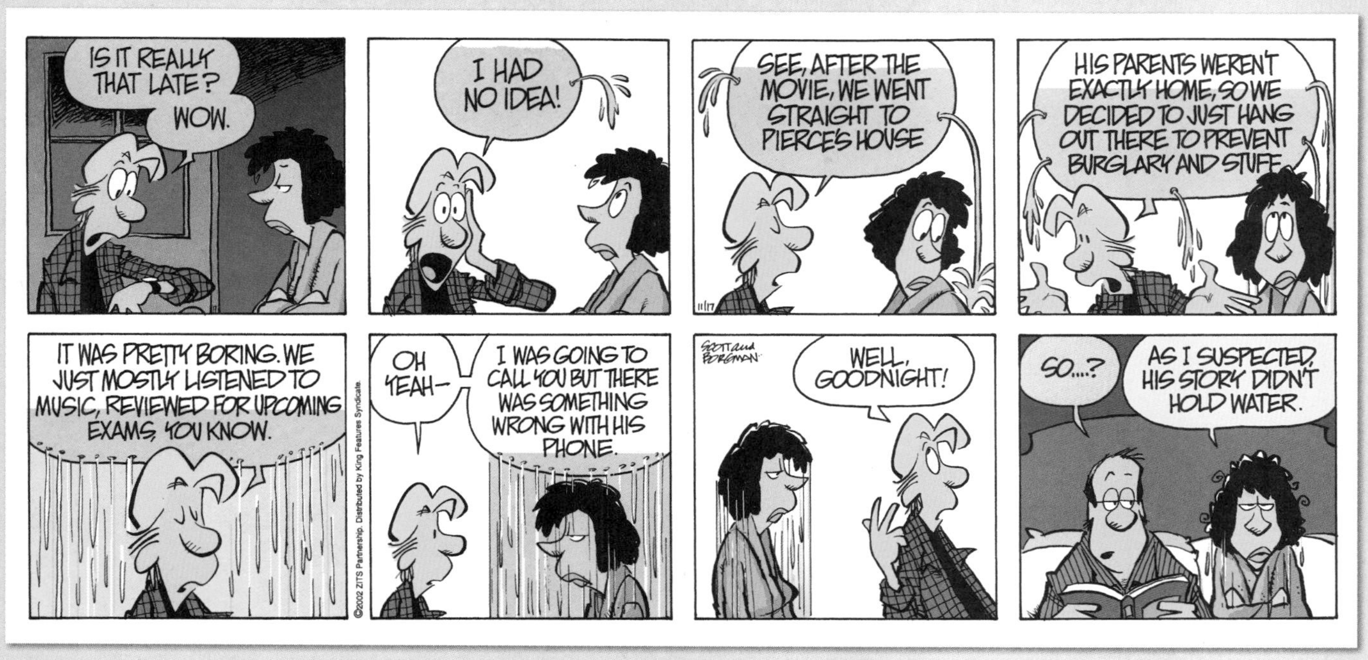
IS IT REALLY THAT LATE? WOW.
I HAD NO IDEA!
SEE, AFTER THE MOVIE, WE WENT STRAIGHT TO PIERCE'S HOUSE
HIS PARENTS WEREN'T EXACTLY HOME, SO WE DECIDED TO JUST HANG OUT THERE TO PREVENT BURGLARY AND STUFF
IT WAS PRETTY BORING. WE JUST MOSTLY LISTENED TO MUSIC, REVIEWED FOR UPCOMING EXAMS, YOU KNOW.
OH YEAH–
I WAS GOING TO CALL YOU BUT THERE WAS SOMETHING WRONG WITH HIS PHONE.
WELL, GOODNIGHT!
SO....?
AS I SUSPECTED, HIS STORY DIDN'T HOLD WATER.
©2002 ZITS Partnership. Distributed by King Features Syndicate.

December 8, 2002

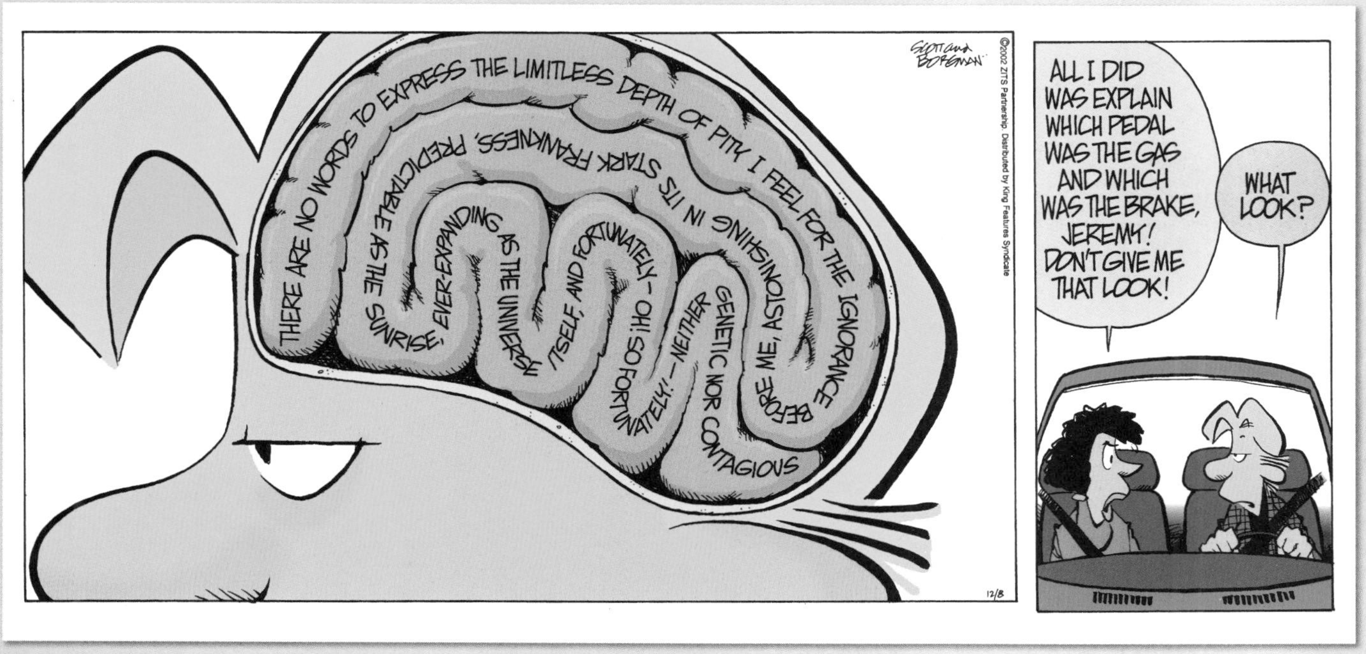
THERE ARE NO WORDS TO EXPRESS THE LIMITLESS DEPTH OF PITY I FEEL FOR THE IGNORANCE BEFORE ME, ASTONISHING IN ITS STARK FRANKNESS, PREDICTABLE AS THE SUNRISE, EVER-EXPANDING AS THE UNIVERSE ITSELF, AND FORTUNATELY– OH! SO FORTUNATELY!–NEITHER GENETIC NOR CONTAGIOUS
ALL I DID WAS EXPLAIN WHICH PEDAL WAS THE GAS AND WHICH WAS THE BRAKE, JEREMY! DON'T GIVE ME THAT LOOK!
WHAT LOOK?
©2002 ZITS Partnership. Distributed by King Features Syndicate

September 29, 2002

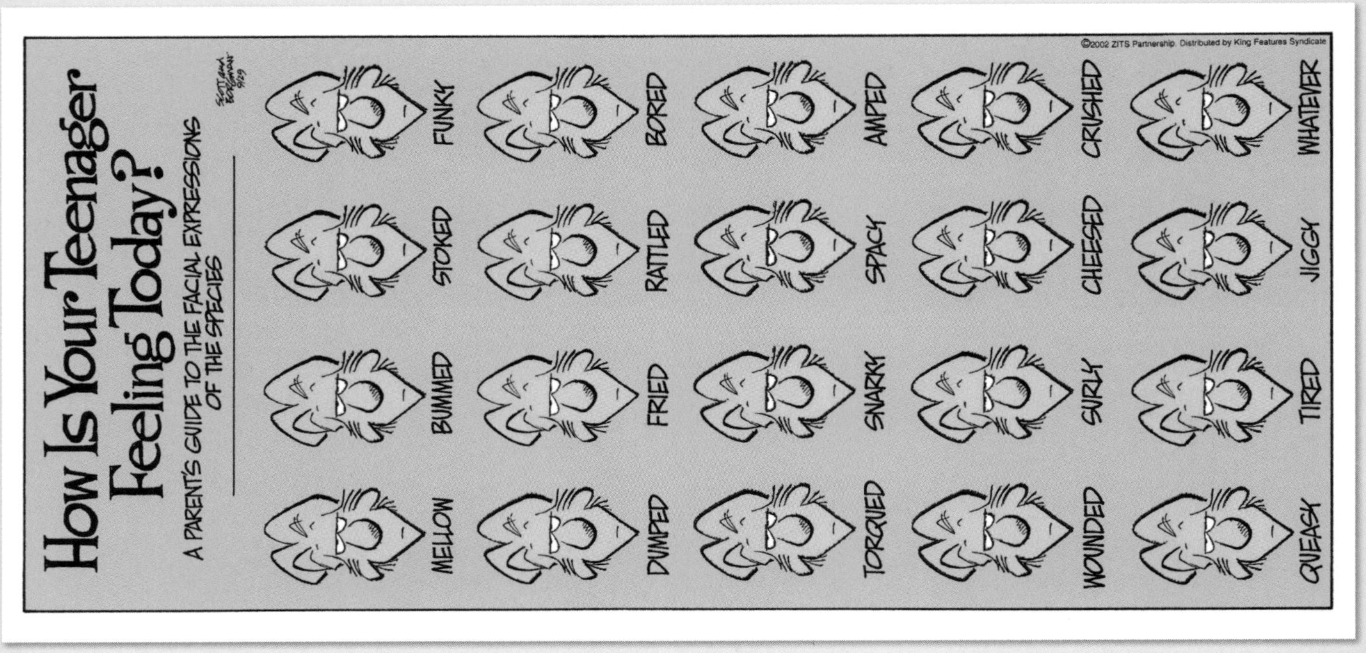

How Is Your Teenager Feeling Today?
A PARENT'S GUIDE TO THE FACIAL EXPRESSIONS OF THE SPECIES
MELLOW
BUMMED
STOKED
FUNKY
DUMPED
FRIED
RATTLED
BORED
TORQUED
SNARKY
SPACY
AMPED
WOUNDED
SURLY
CHEESED
CRUSHED
QUEASY
TIRED
JIGGY
WHATEVER
©2002 ZITS Partnership. Distributed by King Features Syndicate

November 10, 2002

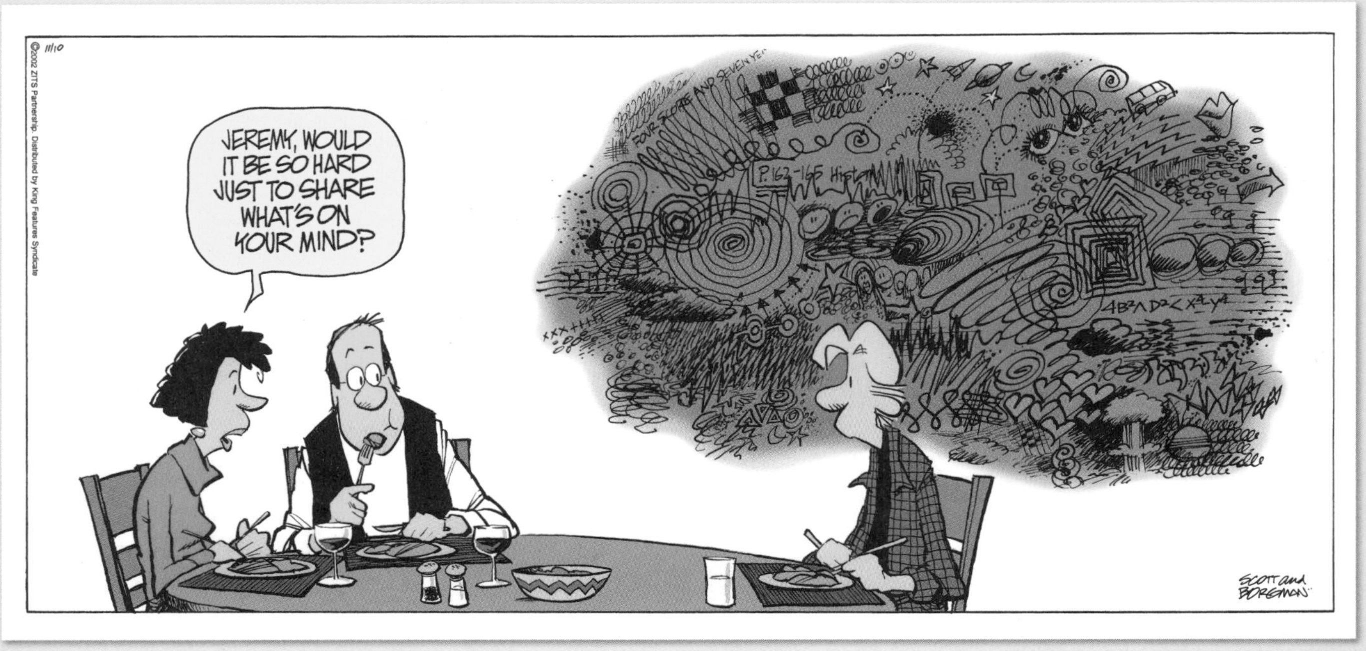

JEREMY, WOULD IT BE SO HARD JUST TO SHARE WHAT'S ON YOUR MIND?
©2002 ZITS Partnership. Distributed by King Features Syndicate
SCOTT and BORGMAN

Deadline Drama

Jim Borgman

Comic strip lore is full of stories of cartoonists playing with deadline fire. Before digital filing of our strips, you'd hear about cartoonists going to any length to get strips to the syndicates on time.

In fact, here's one: In the early years of working with Rick Kirkman on *Baby Blues*, Jerry tells a story of one desperate Thursday night. They get the strips to the FedEx office just as the employees are locking the door. Despite Kirkman's desperate plea and best puppy dog eyes, they are turned away. Through the mail slot in the door, a FedEx employee suggests they go to the airport office, which was open thirty minutes later than the other offices in town. Kirkman and Scott take off in whatever substandard car they were driving back then, hellbent on making the forty-minute drive in thirty. They made it in thirty-one. Screeching up to the airport FedEx office, they find the lights out and the door locked. But through the chainlink fence, they spot the FedEx jet warming up on the tarmac and the pilot is walking toward the plane. Somehow (and don't ask me how) they get the attention of the pilot and toss their precious package of comics over the fence to him. He gives a little salute, and the rest is near-missed deadline history.

With *Zits*, Jerry and I have mellowed into deadline choirboys, never more than a week ahead of or behind the syndicate's calendar. Deadline drama is a young man's game. If you're going to survive in this profession you've got to learn how to deliver your stuff on time-ish.

But I've always figured that if I flaked out for a month and suddenly had to deliver a lot of work really fast, I'd get a hotel room.

I work really well in hotel rooms. The first thing I do upon checking in is to rearrange the whole room. I move the desk so that it's perpendicular to the window and pull any available tables and lamps near so as to lay out sketchbooks and my computer and get a decent orientation to the TV. I fill the bathroom glasses with water—one for ink, one for whiteout. I grab wads of tissues as wipe rags and pull the couch into position for room service trays. It's not exactly The Who, but it's my cartoonist's version of trashing a hotel room.

I'm in a San Diego hotel right now, working in the room while my wife attends a conference downstairs. She's a professor and attends conferences several times a year. Since I'm a bum cartoonist, I go with her and redecorate her hotel rooms. I lucked out here. This one's got ESPN, a killer view of the harbor, and an in-room coffeemaker. I'm golden.

March 16, 2003

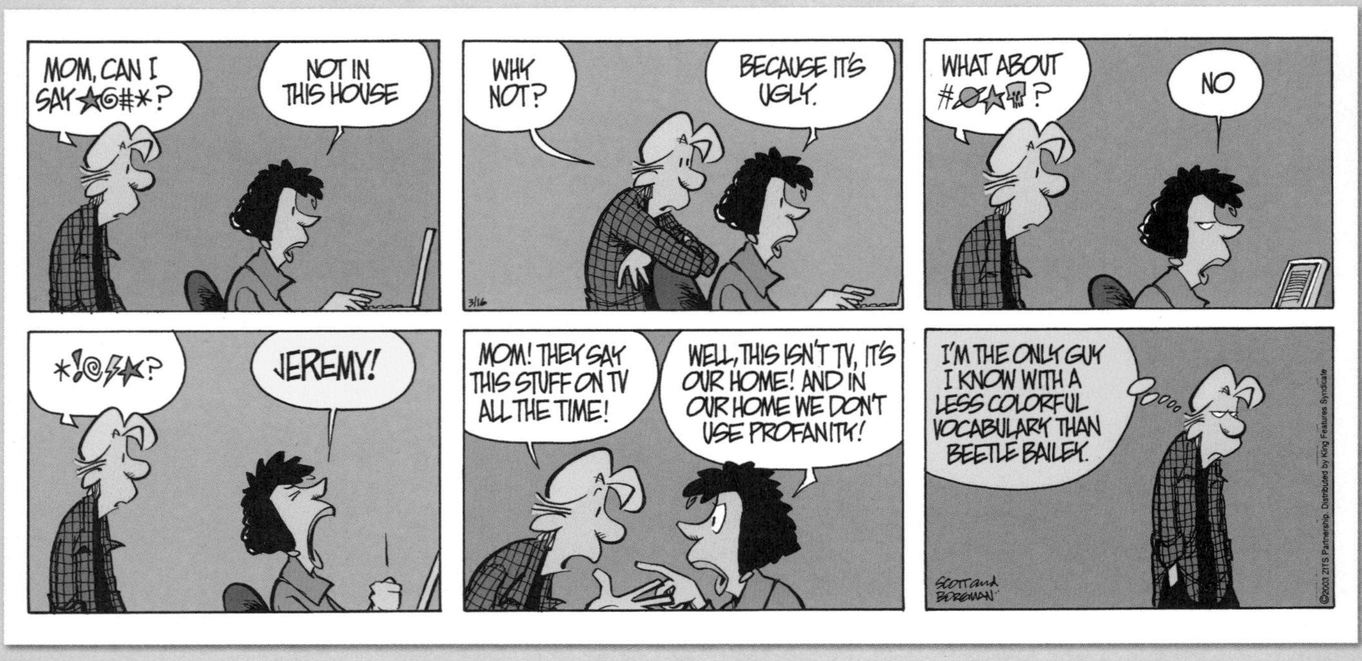
MOM, CAN I SAY ★@#*?
NOT IN THIS HOUSE
WHY NOT?
BECAUSE IT'S UGLY.
WHAT ABOUT #@★? ?
NO
*!@★? ?
JEREMY!
MOM! THEY SAY THIS STUFF ON TV ALL THE TIME!
WELL, THIS ISN'T TV, IT'S OUR HOME! AND IN OUR HOME WE DON'T USE PROFANITY!
I'M THE ONLY GUY I KNOW WITH A LESS COLORFUL VOCABULARY THAN BEETLE BAILEY.
SCOTT and BORGMAN
©2003 ZITS Partnership. Distributed by King Features Syndicate

March 30, 2003

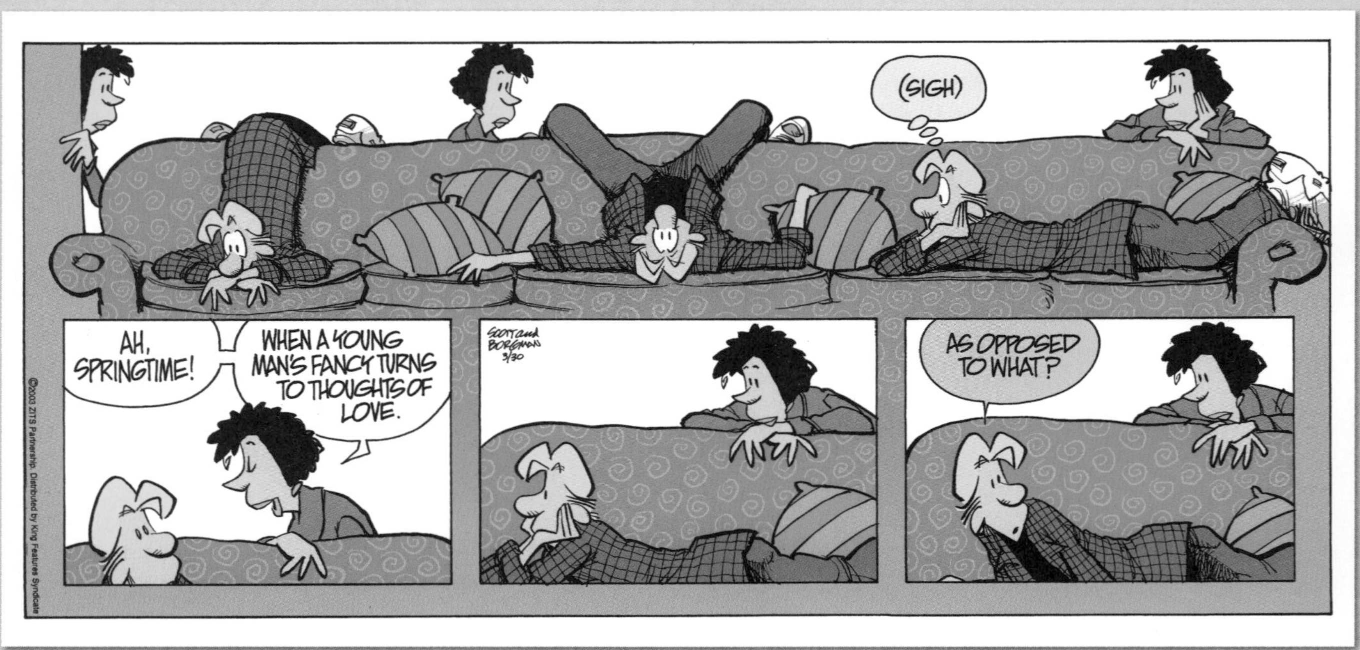
(SIGH)
AH, SPRINGTIME!
WHEN A YOUNG MAN'S FANCY TURNS TO THOUGHTS OF LOVE.
SCOTT and BORGMAN 3/30
AS OPPOSED TO WHAT?
©2003 ZITS Partnership. Distributed by King Features Syndicate

April 5, 2003

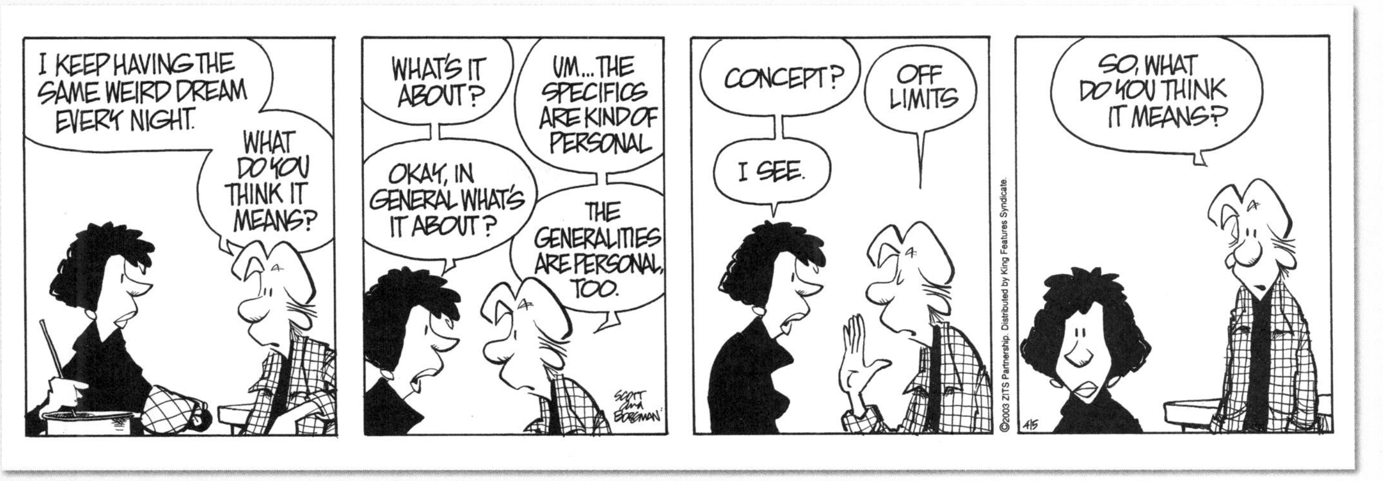
I KEEP HAVING THE SAME WEIRD DREAM EVERY NIGHT.
WHAT DO YOU THINK IT MEANS?
WHAT'S IT ABOUT?
UM... THE SPECIFICS ARE KIND OF PERSONAL
OKAY, IN GENERAL WHAT'S IT ABOUT?
THE GENERALITIES ARE PERSONAL, TOO.
CONCEPT?
OFF LIMITS
I SEE.
SO, WHAT DO YOU THINK IT MEANS?
©2003 ZITS Partnership. Distributed by King Features Syndicate.

April 15, 2003

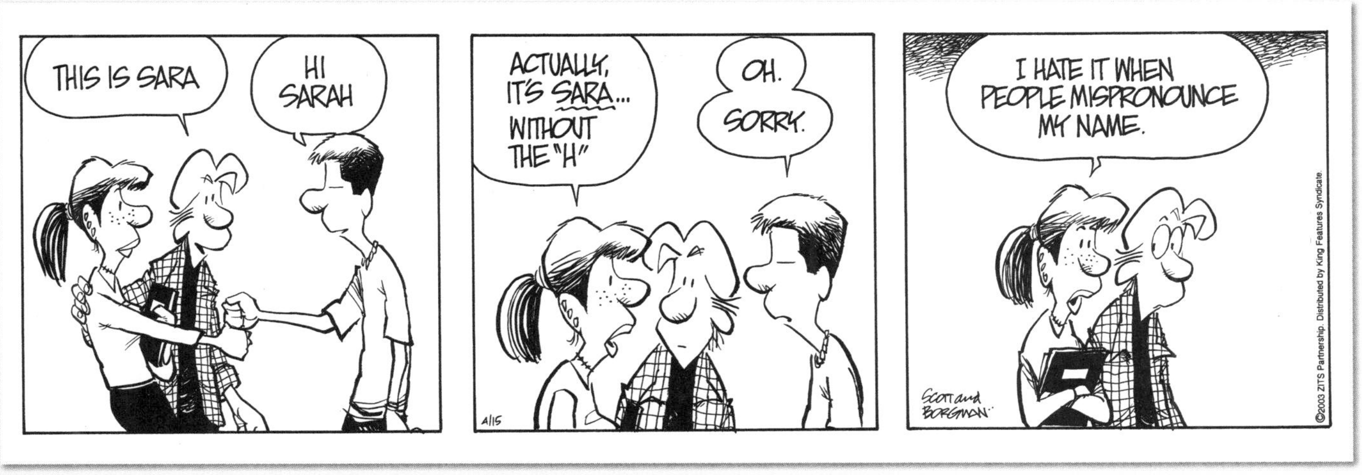
THIS IS SARA
HI SARAH
ACTUALLY, IT'S SARA... WITHOUT THE "H"
OH.
SORRY.
I HATE IT WHEN PEOPLE MISPRONOUNCE MY NAME.
©2003 ZITS Partnership. Distributed by King Features Syndicate.

June 18, 2003

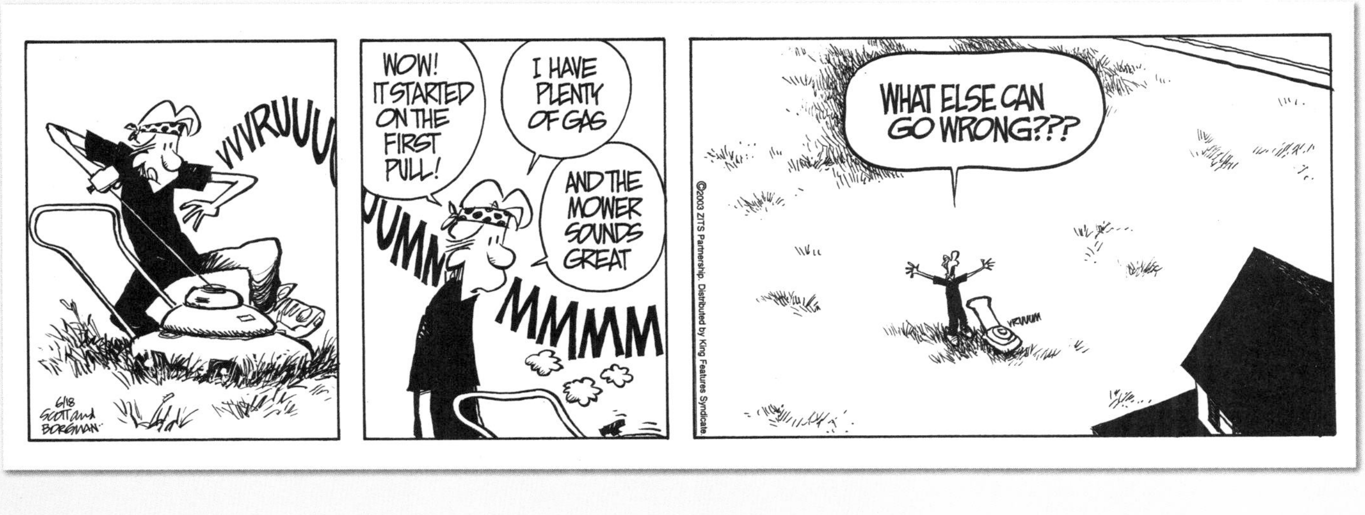
VVVRUUUU
UUMMMMMMMM
WOW! IT STARTED ON THE FIRST PULL!
I HAVE PLENTY OF GAS
AND THE MOWER SOUNDS GREAT
WHAT ELSE CAN GO WRONG???
©2003 ZITS Partnership. Distributed by King Features Syndicate.

May 12, 2003

IT FEELS WEIRD TO SIT HERE CONTEMPLATING MURDER
FISHING IS NOT MURDER!
©2003 ZITS Partnership. Distributed by King Features Syndicate.

May 13, 2003

(AHEM!)
©2003 ZITS Partnership. Distributed by King Features Syndicate.
SPEAKING OF SEX...
I KNEW IT!

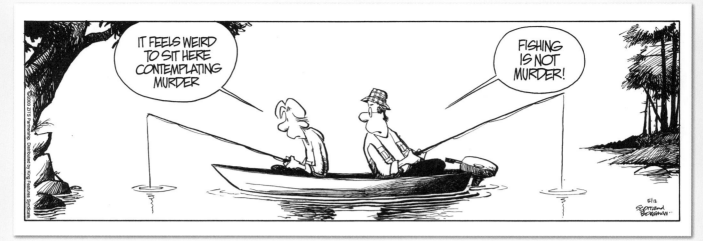

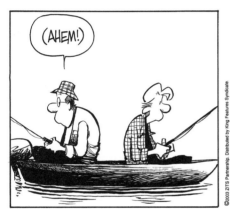

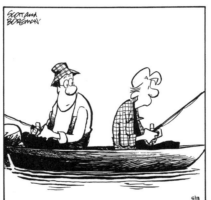

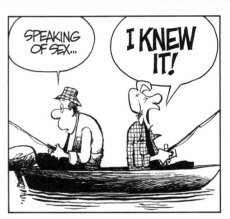

May 15, 2003

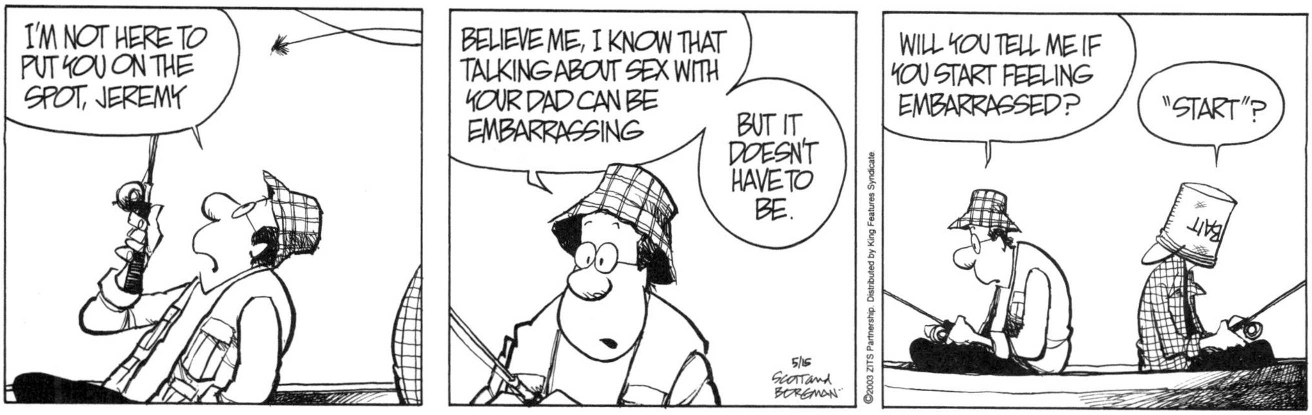
I'M NOT HERE TO PUT YOU ON THE SPOT, JEREMY
BELIEVE ME, I KNOW THAT TALKING ABOUT SEX WITH YOUR DAD CAN BE EMBARRASSING
BUT IT DOESN'T HAVE TO BE.
5/15 SCOTT and BORGMAN
©2003 ZITS Partnership. Distributed by King Features Syndicate
WILL YOU TELL ME IF YOU START FEELING EMBARRASSED?
"START"?
BAIT

May 16, 2003

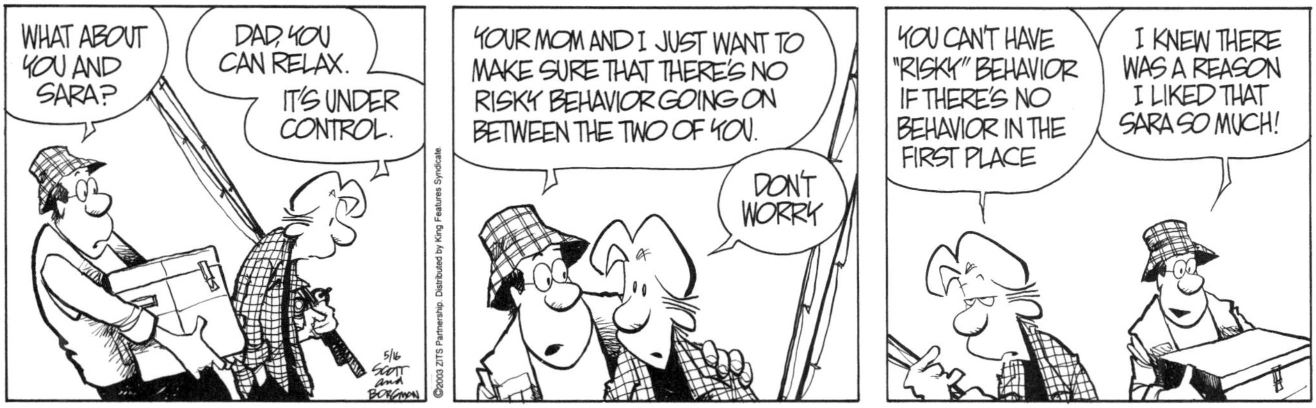
WHAT ABOUT YOU AND SARA?
DAD, YOU CAN RELAX.
IT'S UNDER CONTROL.
5/16 SCOTT and BORGMAN
©2003 ZITS Partnership. Distributed by King Features Syndicate.
YOUR MOM AND I JUST WANT TO MAKE SURE THAT THERE'S NO RISKY BEHAVIOR GOING ON BETWEEN THE TWO OF YOU.
DON'T WORRY
YOU CAN'T HAVE "RISKY" BEHAVIOR IF THERE'S NO BEHAVIOR IN THE FIRST PLACE
I KNEW THERE WAS A REASON I LIKED THAT SARA SO MUCH!

May 19, 2003

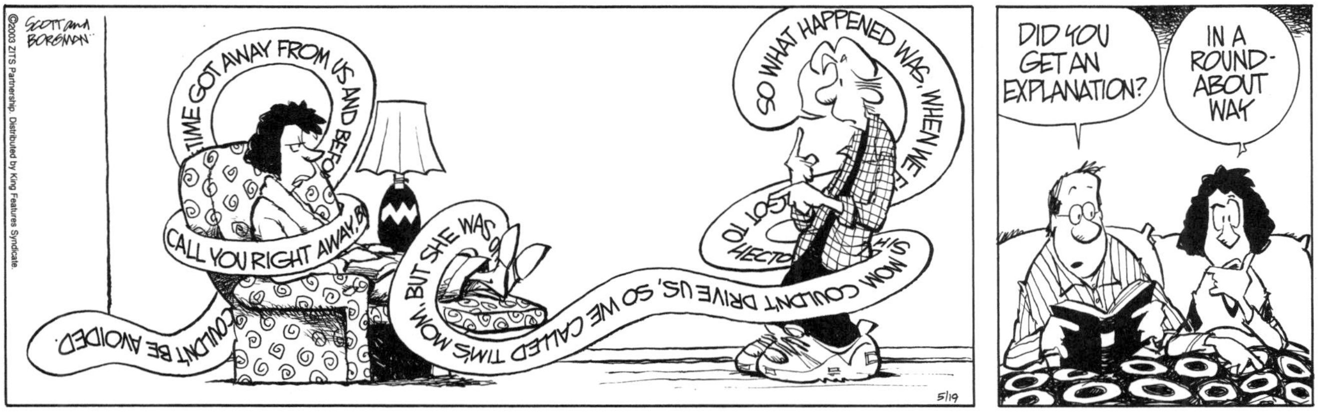
SCOTT and BORGMAN
©2003 ZITS Partnership. Distributed by King Features Syndicate.
SO WHAT HAPPENED WAS, WHEN WE
GOT TO
HECTO
HIS MOM COULDN'T DRIVE US, SO WE CALLED TIM'S MOM, BUT SHE WAS
TIME GOT AWAY FROM US AND BEFO
CALL YOU RIGHT AWAY, B
COULDN'T BE AVOIDED.
5/19
DID YOU GET AN EXPLANATION?
IN A ROUND-ABOUT WAY

April 6, 2003

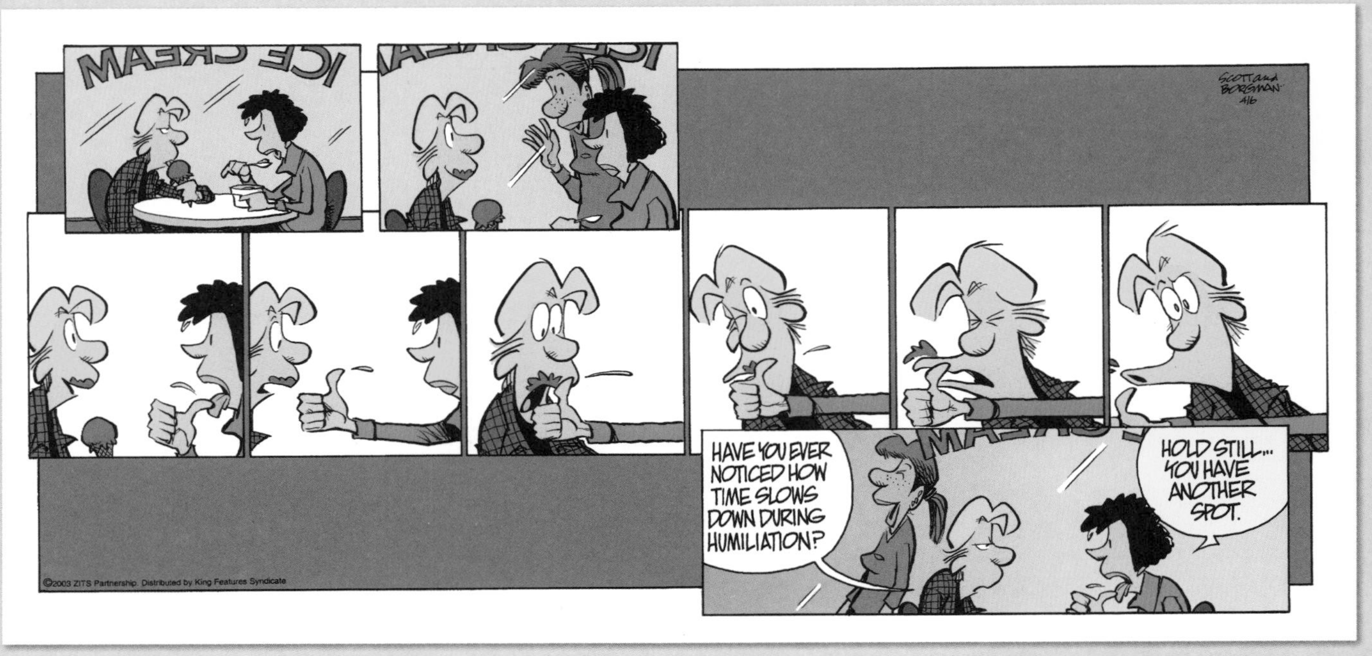
ICE CREAM
SCOTT and BORGMAN 4/6
HAVE YOU EVER NOTICED HOW TIME SLOWS DOWN DURING HUMILIATION?
HOLD STILL... YOU HAVE ANOTHER SPOT.
©2003 ZITS Partnership. Distributed by King Features Syndicate

April 20, 2003

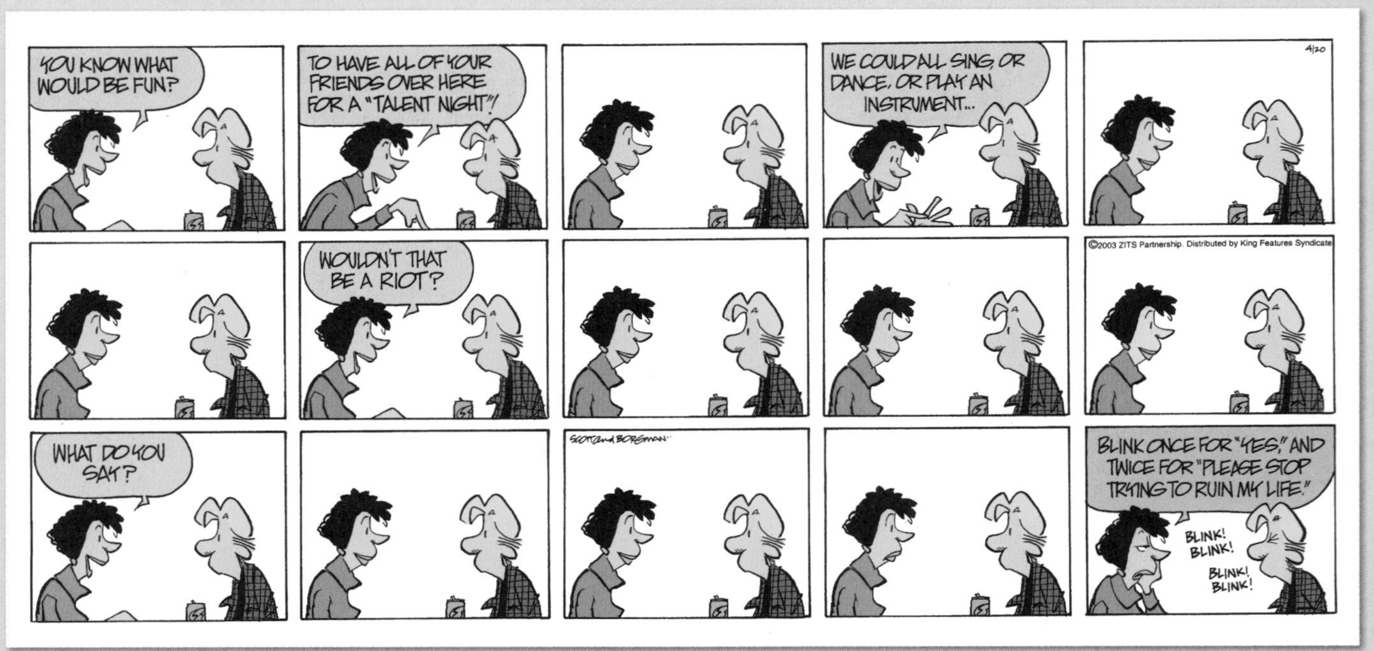
YOU KNOW WHAT WOULD BE FUN?
TO HAVE ALL OF YOUR FRIENDS OVER HERE FOR A "TALENT NIGHT"!
WE COULD ALL SING, OR DANCE, OR PLAY AN INSTRUMENT...
4/20
©2003 ZITS Partnership. Distributed by King Features Syndicate
WOULDN'T THAT BE A RIOT?
WHAT DO YOU SAY?
SCOTT and BORGMAN
BLINK ONCE FOR "YES," AND TWICE FOR "PLEASE STOP TRYING TO RUIN MY LIFE."
BLINK! BLINK!
BLINK! BLINK!

May 11, 2003

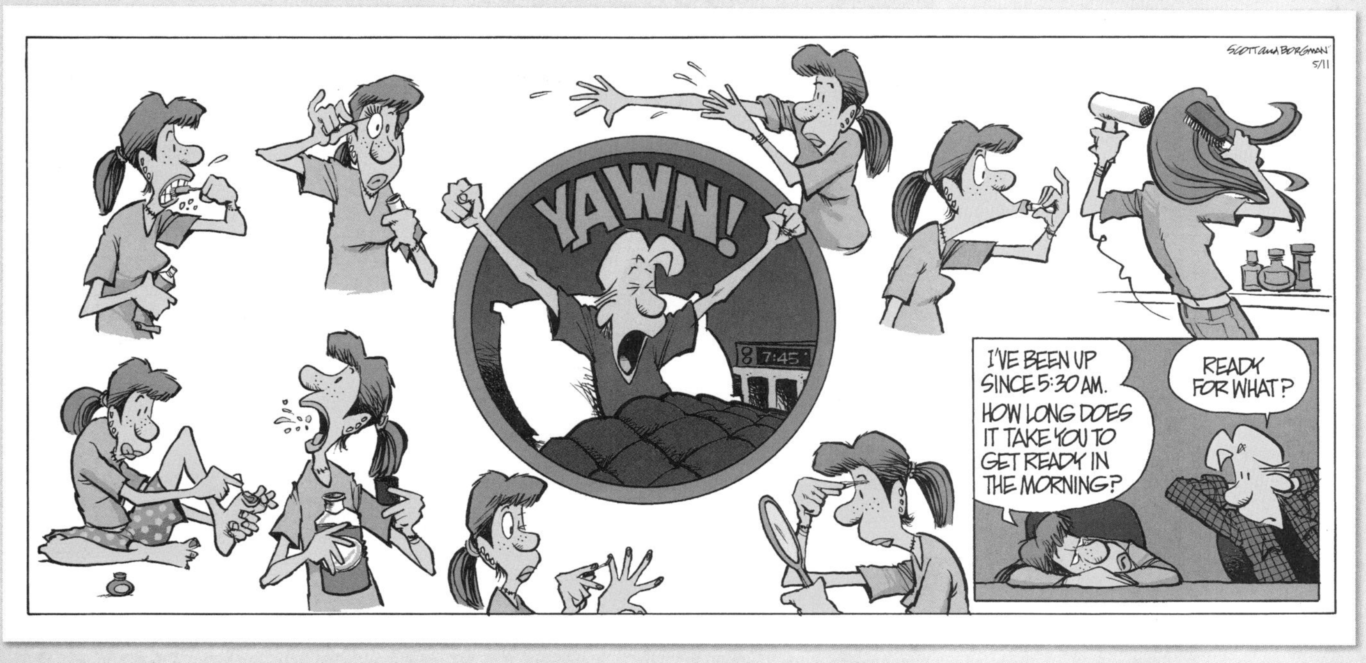

YAWN!
7:45
I'VE BEEN UP SINCE 5:30 AM. HOW LONG DOES IT TAKE YOU TO GET READY IN THE MORNING?
READY FOR WHAT?

July 6, 2003

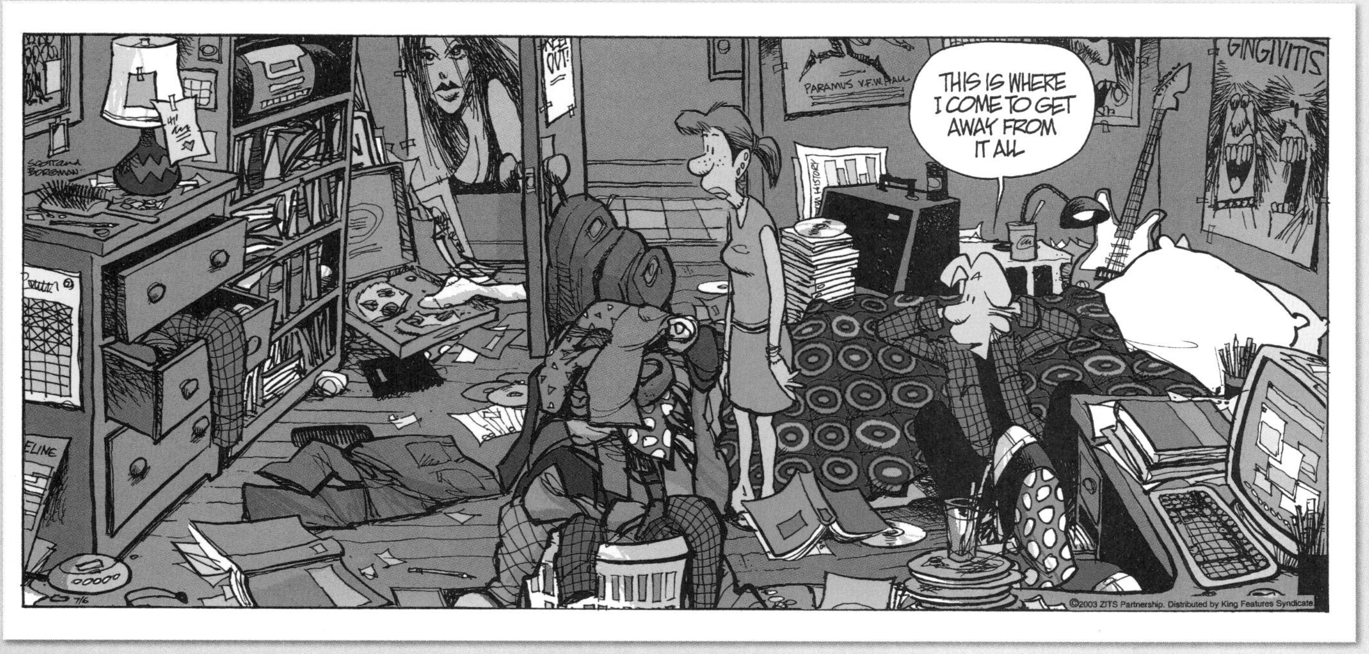

THIS IS WHERE I COME TO GET AWAY FROM IT ALL
PARAMUS V.F.W. HALL
GINGIVITIS
©2003 ZITS Partnership. Distributed by King Features Syndicate.

June 20, 2003

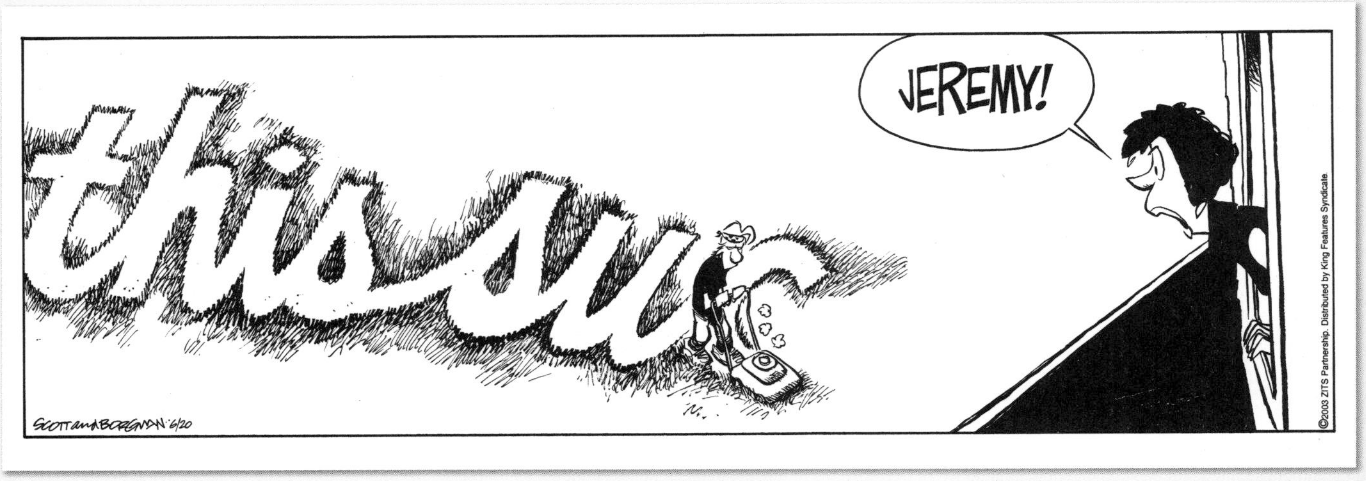
this su
JEREMY!
SCOTT and BORGMAN 6/20
©2003 ZITS Partnership. Distributed by King Features Syndicate.

June 27, 2003

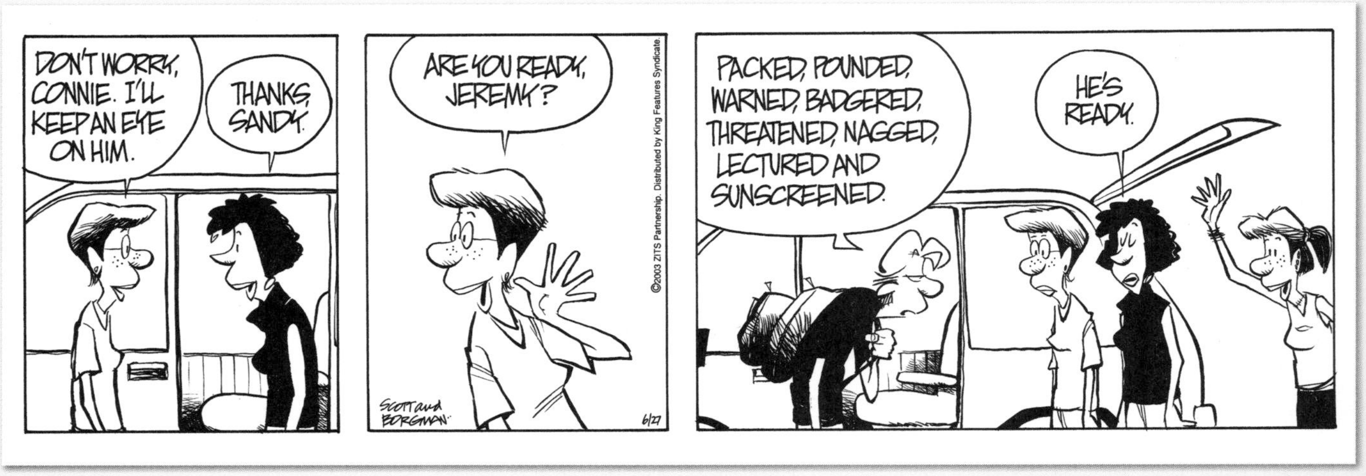
DON'T WORRY, CONNIE. I'LL KEEP AN EYE ON HIM.
THANKS, SANDY.
ARE YOU READY, JEREMY?
SCOTT and BORGMAN
6/27
©2003 ZITS Partnership. Distributed by King Features Syndicate.
PACKED, POUNDED, WARNED, BADGERED, THREATENED, NAGGED, LECTURED AND SUNSCREENED.
HE'S READY.

July 2, 2003

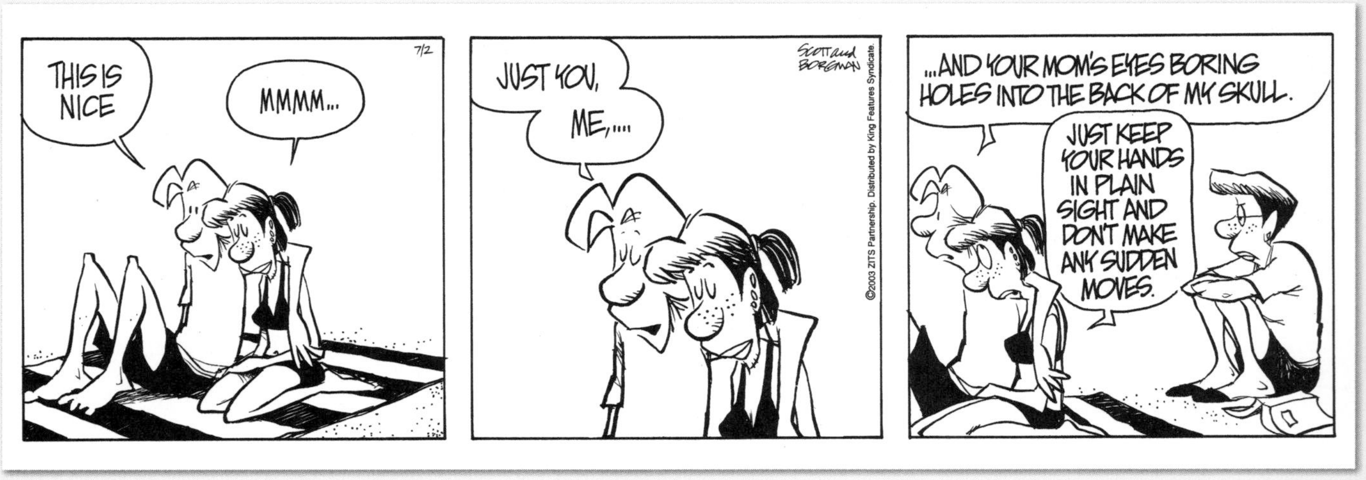
THIS IS NICE
MMMM...
7/2
JUST YOU,
ME,....
SCOTT and BORGMAN
©2003 ZITS Partnership. Distributed by King Features Syndicate.
...AND YOUR MOM'S EYES BORING HOLES INTO THE BACK OF MY SKULL.
JUST KEEP YOUR HANDS IN PLAIN SIGHT AND DON'T MAKE ANY SUDDEN MOVES.

July 13, 2003

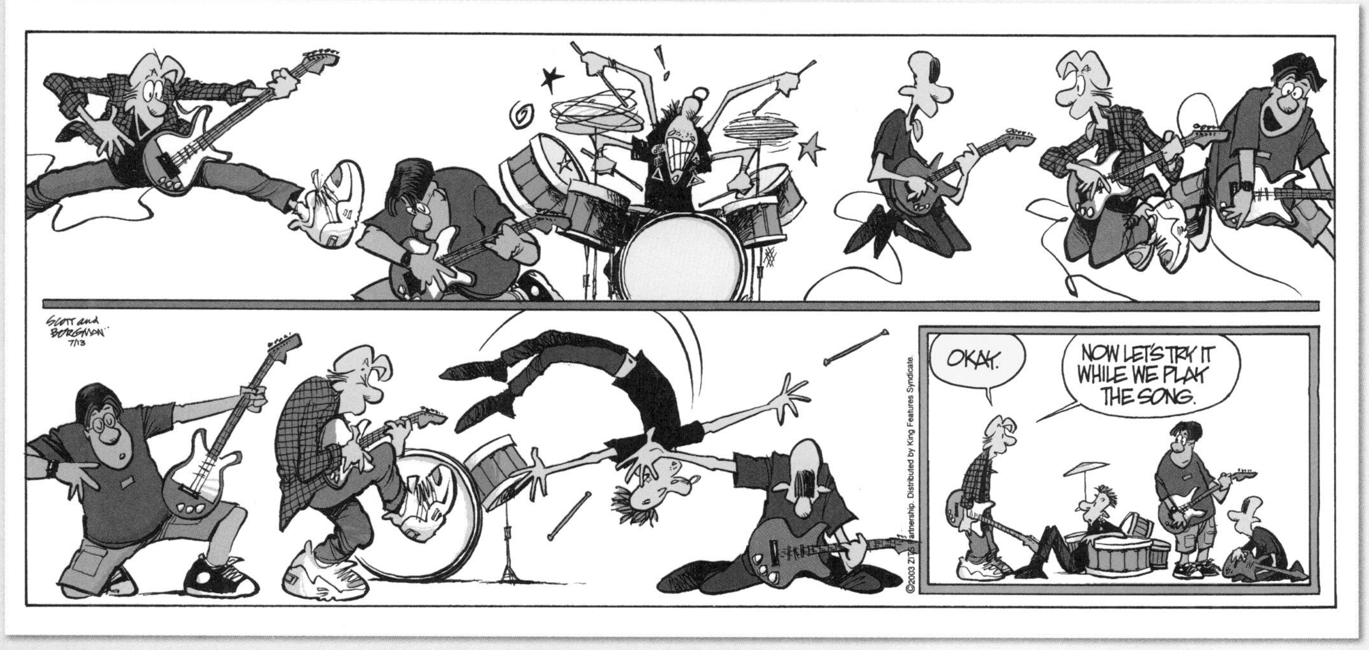
SCOTT and BORGMAN 7/13
OKAY.
NOW LET'S TRY IT WHILE WE PLAY THE SONG.
©2003 ZITS Partnership. Distributed by King Features Syndicate.

November 30, 2003

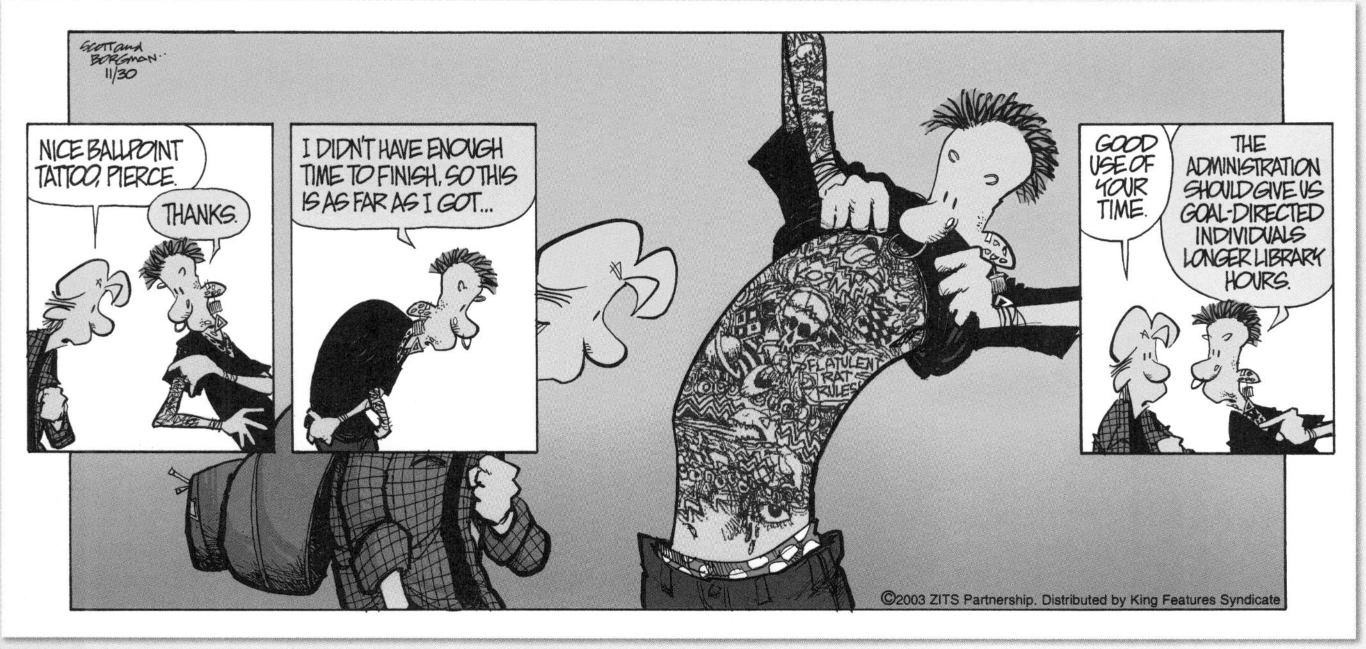
SCOTT and BORGMAN 11/30
NICE BALLPOINT TATTOO, PIERCE.
THANKS.
I DIDN'T HAVE ENOUGH TIME TO FINISH, SO THIS IS AS FAR AS I GOT...
FLATULENT RAT RULES
GOOD USE OF YOUR TIME.
THE ADMINISTRATION SHOULD GIVE US GOAL-DIRECTED INDIVIDUALS LONGER LIBRARY HOURS.
©2003 ZITS Partnership. Distributed by King Features Syndicate

October 1, 2003

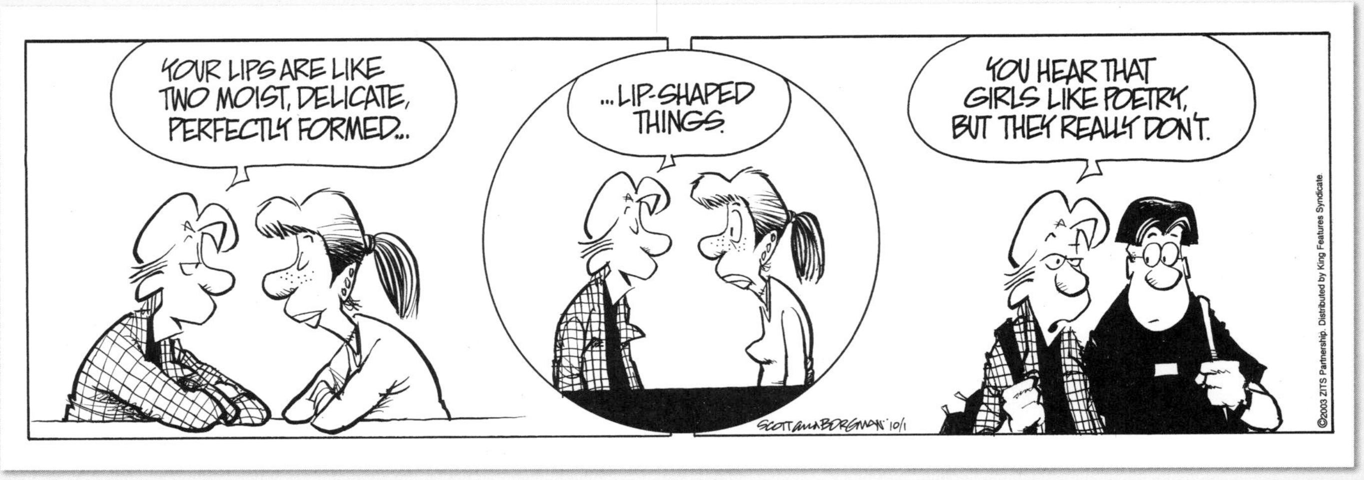
YOUR LIPS ARE LIKE TWO MOIST, DELICATE, PERFECTLY FORMED...
...LIP-SHAPED THINGS.
YOU HEAR THAT GIRLS LIKE POETRY, BUT THEY REALLY DON'T.
SCOTT AND BORGMAN 10/1
©2003 ZITS Partnership. Distributed by King Features Syndicate.

October 22, 2003

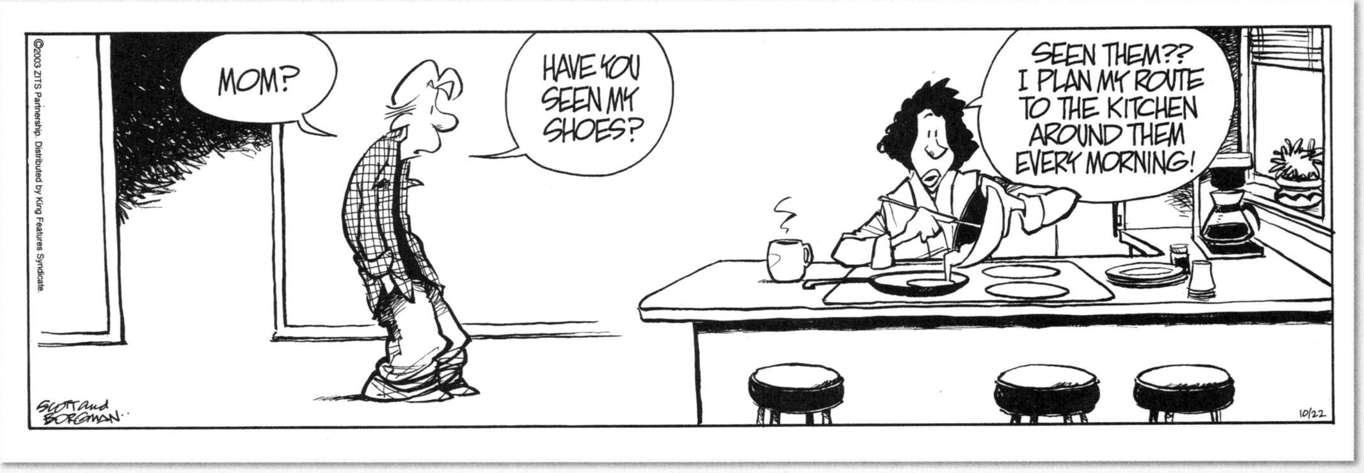
MOM?
HAVE YOU SEEN MY SHOES?
SEEN THEM?? I PLAN MY ROUTE TO THE KITCHEN AROUND THEM EVERY MORNING!
SCOTT and BORGMAN
10/22
©2003 ZITS Partnership. Distributed by King Features Syndicate.

November 27, 2003

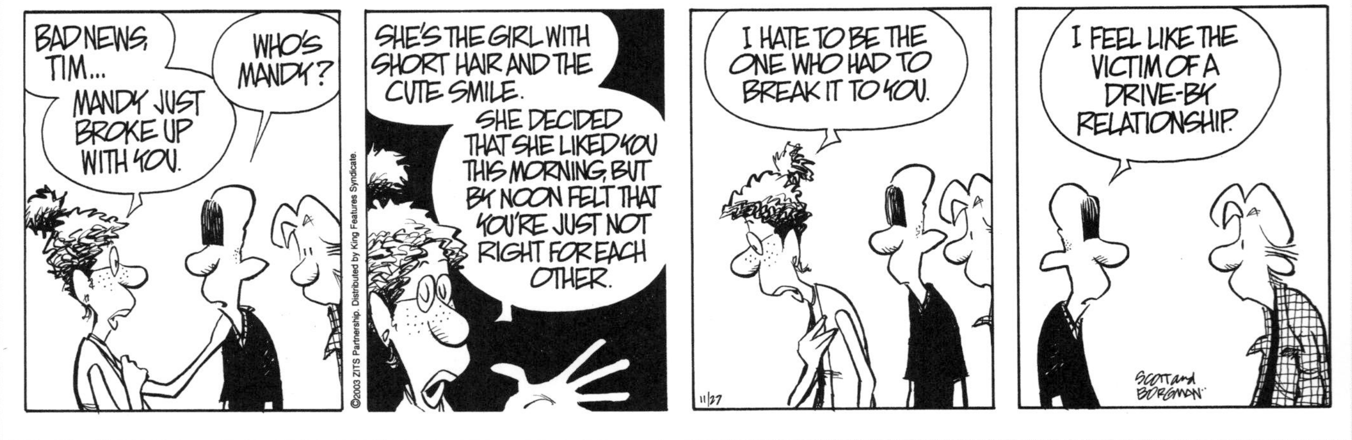
BAD NEWS, TIM...
MANDY JUST BROKE UP WITH YOU.
WHO'S MANDY?
SHE'S THE GIRL WITH SHORT HAIR AND THE CUTE SMILE.
SHE DECIDED THAT SHE LIKED YOU THIS MORNING, BUT BY NOON FELT THAT YOU'RE JUST NOT RIGHT FOR EACH OTHER.
I HATE TO BE THE ONE WHO HAD TO BREAK IT TO YOU.
I FEEL LIKE THE VICTIM OF A DRIVE-BY RELATIONSHIP.
11/27
SCOTT and BORGMAN
©2003 ZITS Partnership. Distributed by King Features Syndicate.

December 5, 2003

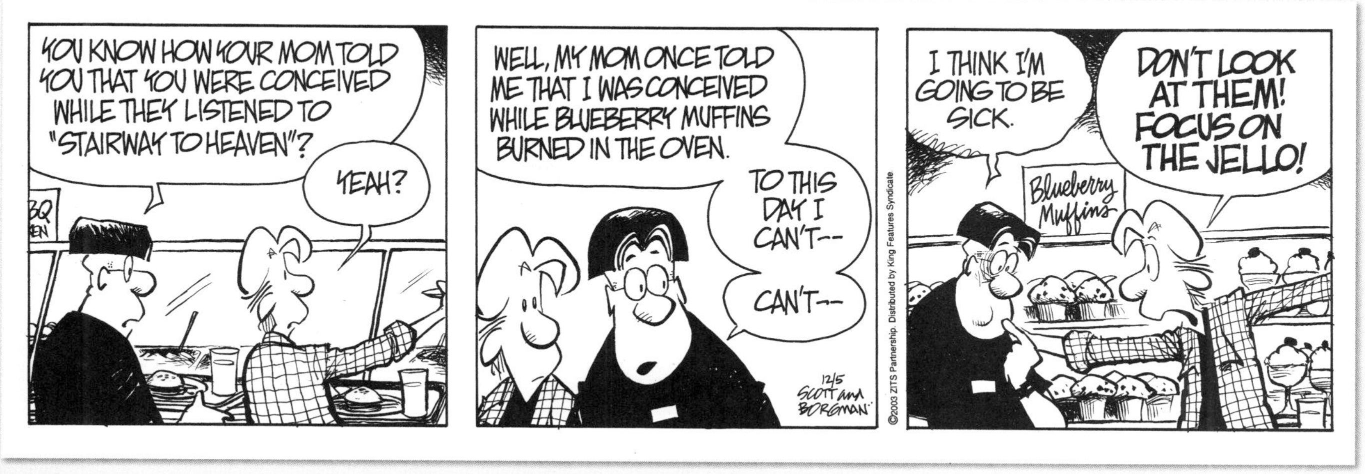
YOU KNOW HOW YOUR MOM TOLD YOU THAT YOU WERE CONCEIVED WHILE THEY LISTENED TO "STAIRWAY TO HEAVEN"?
YEAH?
WELL, MY MOM ONCE TOLD ME THAT I WAS CONCEIVED WHILE BLUEBERRY MUFFINS BURNED IN THE OVEN.
TO THIS DAY I CAN'T--
CAN'T--
12/5 SCOTT AND BORGMAN
©2003 ZITS Partnership. Distributed by King Features Syndicate
I THINK I'M GOING TO BE SICK.
DON'T LOOK AT THEM! FOCUS ON THE JELLO!
Blueberry Muffins

December 6, 2003

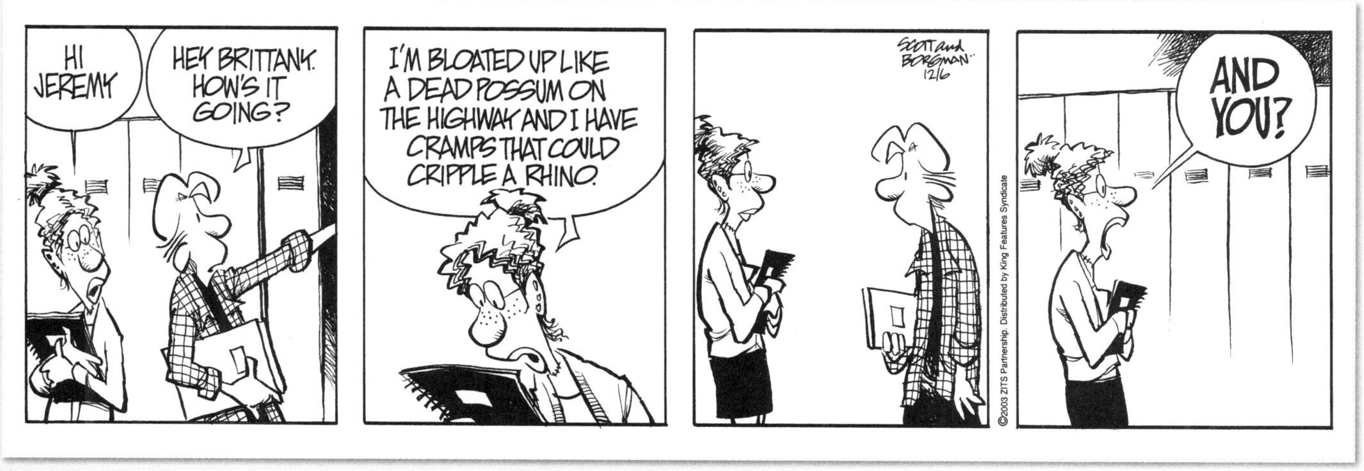
HI JEREMY
HEY BRITTANY. HOW'S IT GOING?
I'M BLOATED UP LIKE A DEAD POSSUM ON THE HIGHWAY AND I HAVE CRAMPS THAT COULD CRIPPLE A RHINO.
SCOTT AND BORGMAN 12/6
AND YOU?
©2003 ZITS Partnership. Distributed by King Features Syndicate

December 16, 2003

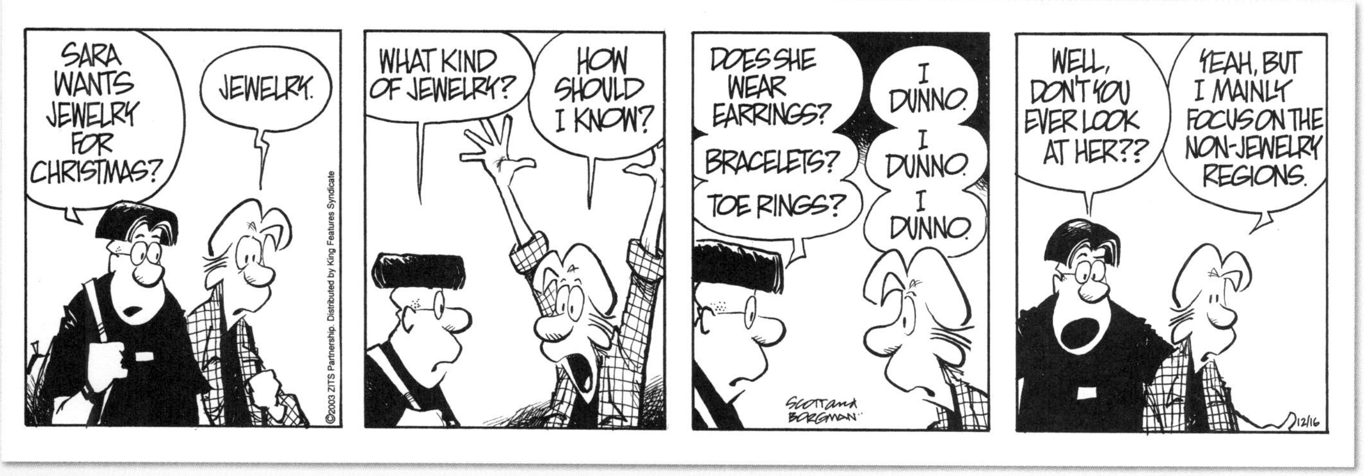
SARA WANTS JEWELRY FOR CHRISTMAS?
JEWELRY.
©2003 ZITS Partnership. Distributed by King Features Syndicate
WHAT KIND OF JEWELRY?
HOW SHOULD I KNOW?
DOES SHE WEAR EARRINGS?
I DUNNO.
BRACELETS?
I DUNNO.
TOE RINGS?
I DUNNO.
SCOTT AND BORGMAN
WELL, DON'T YOU EVER LOOK AT HER??
YEAH, BUT I MAINLY FOCUS ON THE NON-JEWELRY REGIONS.
12/16

December 14, 2003

I LIKE YOUR SWEATER
I HATE THIS SWEATER
WELL, IT LOOKS GOOD WITH YOUR HAIR
I HATE MY HAIR
WHAT'S WRONG WITH YOUR HAIR?
IT'S ALL FRIZZY, WHICH DRAWS ATTENTION TO MY CHIPMUNK CHEEKS, WHICH LEADS THE EYE TO MY NOSE.
SCOTT AND BORGMAN
AND YOU HATE YOUR NOSE.
WHAT'S WRONG WITH MY NOSE??
NOTHING! I JUST ASSUMED THAT--
ASSUMED WHAT??
ASSUMED THAT NOBODY COULD WANT A NOSE LIKE THIS? WELL, I HAPPEN TO LOVE MY NOSE, AND MANY OTHER PARTS OF MY ANATOMY, AS WELL!
ME TOO! I'M SORRY! I DIDN'T MEAN ANYTHING!
I LIKE EVERYTHING ABOUT YOU...
©2003 ZITS Partnership. Distributed by King Features Syndicate
...RIGHT DOWN TO YOUR D.N.A.
I HATE MY D.N.A.
12/14

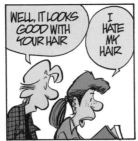

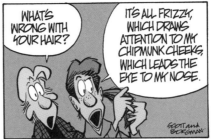

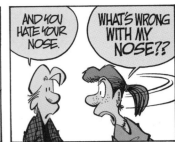

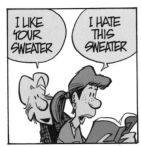

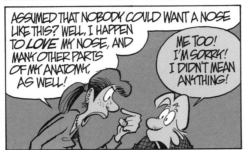

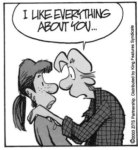

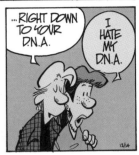

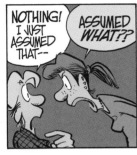

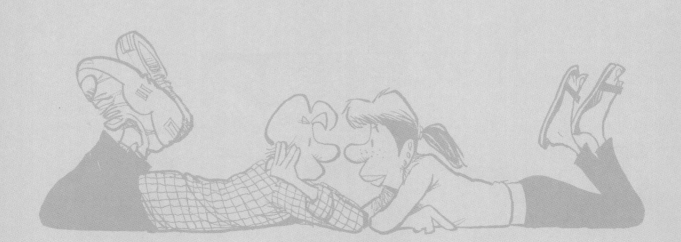

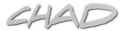

CHAD

Many comic strips have their false starts, elements that seemed funny at the time but feel off base as the strip finds its legs. Dagwood started off as an heir to a fortune who gave up his inheritance to marry Blondie; Nancy was the niece and a bit player in the moderately successful strip *Fritzi Ritz*; and *Baby Blues* started off as a strip about two talking eyeballs (not really—I just made that one up to fill space).

Meet Chad. Chad is Jeremy's perfect older brother. In the beginning, Jeremy seemed like a kid brother with the thankless job of living in his shadow. Chad would be off at college, president of Phi Beta Kappa, an engineering whiz maybe, forming a start-up that he'd sell for millions by his junior year. He and his 4.0 would drop in for a cameo from time to time. Jeremy would suffer by constant comparison.

Problem was every time we brought Chad back onto the scene, the air went out of the strip. Perfect isn't funny. And with the spotlight off Jeremy, *Zits* seemed to lose focus.

So Chad is off at college for good now. Nope, he probably isn't coming back. His family never thinks about him, and he will never graduate.

Longtime readers still bring him up. "Whatever happened to the older brother?" they ask. Sometimes I answer, "He died. Thanks for bringing it up." But it's harder to kill off a character than you'd think. Readers have long memories.

CHAD! YOU'RE HOME! HOW LONG ARE YOU STAYING?
DUDE, I'VE BEEN HERE FOR TWO WEEKS! MY PLANE LEAVES IN THREE HOURS.
REALLY?
I'VE GOT TO START PAYING MORE ATTENTION AROUND HERE!
THAT'S WHAT I KEEP TELLING YOUR SISTER.
©2006 ZITS Partnership. Distributed by King Features Syndicate
12/27
SCOTT and BORGMAN

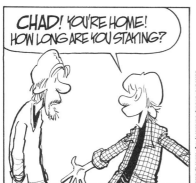

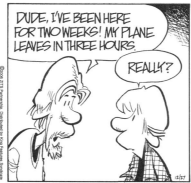

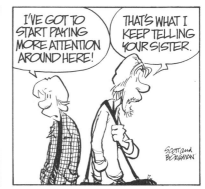

January 22, 2004

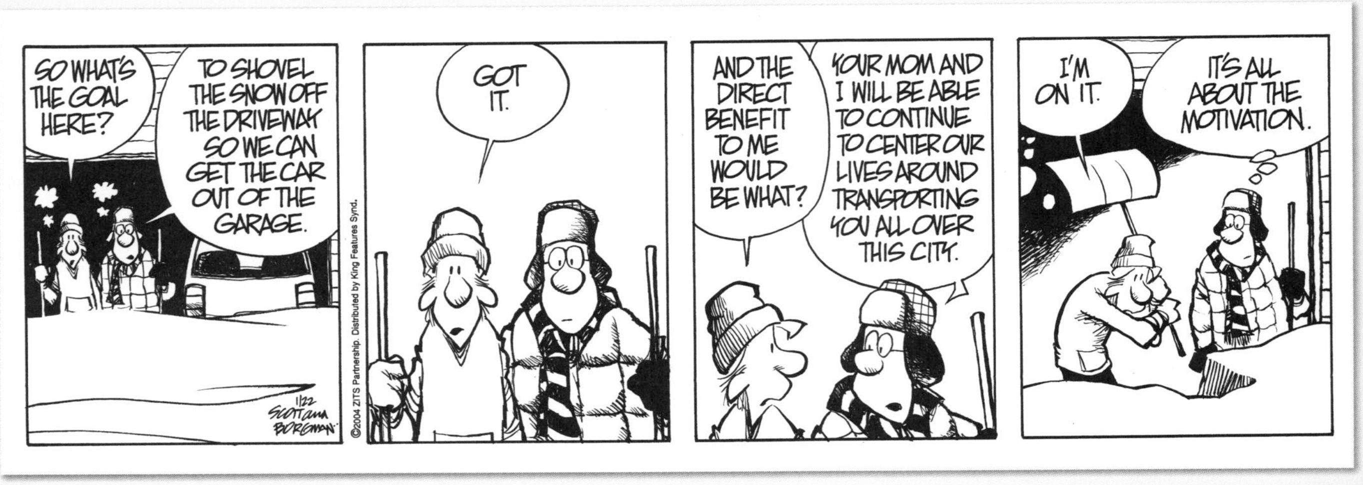
SO WHAT'S THE GOAL HERE?
TO SHOVEL THE SNOW OFF THE DRIVEWAY SO WE CAN GET THE CAR OUT OF THE GARAGE.
1/22 SCOTT and BORGMAN
©2004 ZITS Partnership. Distributed by King Features Synd.
GOT IT.
AND THE DIRECT BENEFIT TO ME WOULD BE WHAT?
YOUR MOM AND I WILL BE ABLE TO CONTINUE TO CENTER OUR LIVES AROUND TRANSPORTING YOU ALL OVER THIS CITY.
I'M ON IT.
IT'S ALL ABOUT THE MOTIVATION.

February 17, 2004

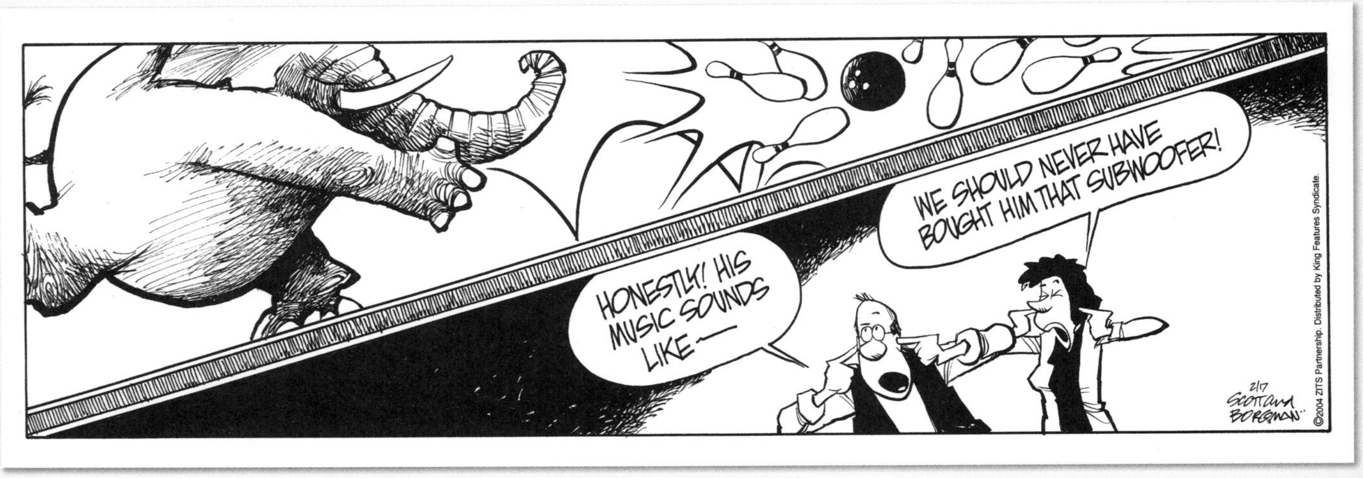
HONESTLY! HIS MUSIC SOUNDS LIKE—
WE SHOULD NEVER HAVE BOUGHT HIM THAT SUBWOOFER!
2/17 SCOTT and BORGMAN
©2004 ZITS Partnership. Distributed by King Features Syndicate.

February 19, 2004

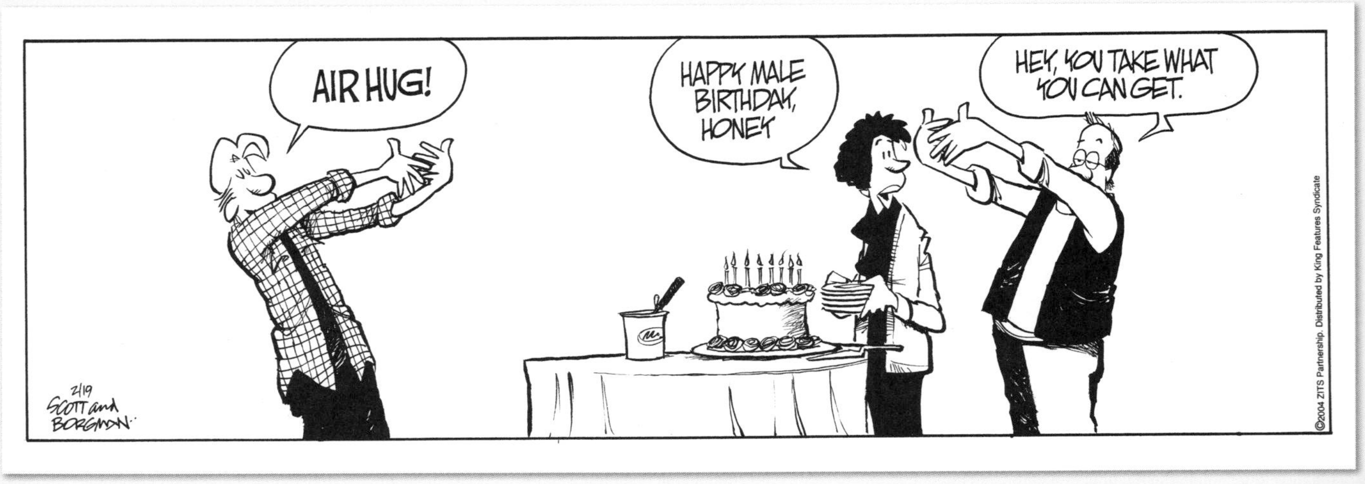
AIR HUG!
HAPPY MALE BIRTHDAY, HONEY
HEY, YOU TAKE WHAT YOU CAN GET.
2/19 SCOTT and BORGMAN
©2004 ZITS Partnership. Distributed by King Features Syndicate

February 29, 2004

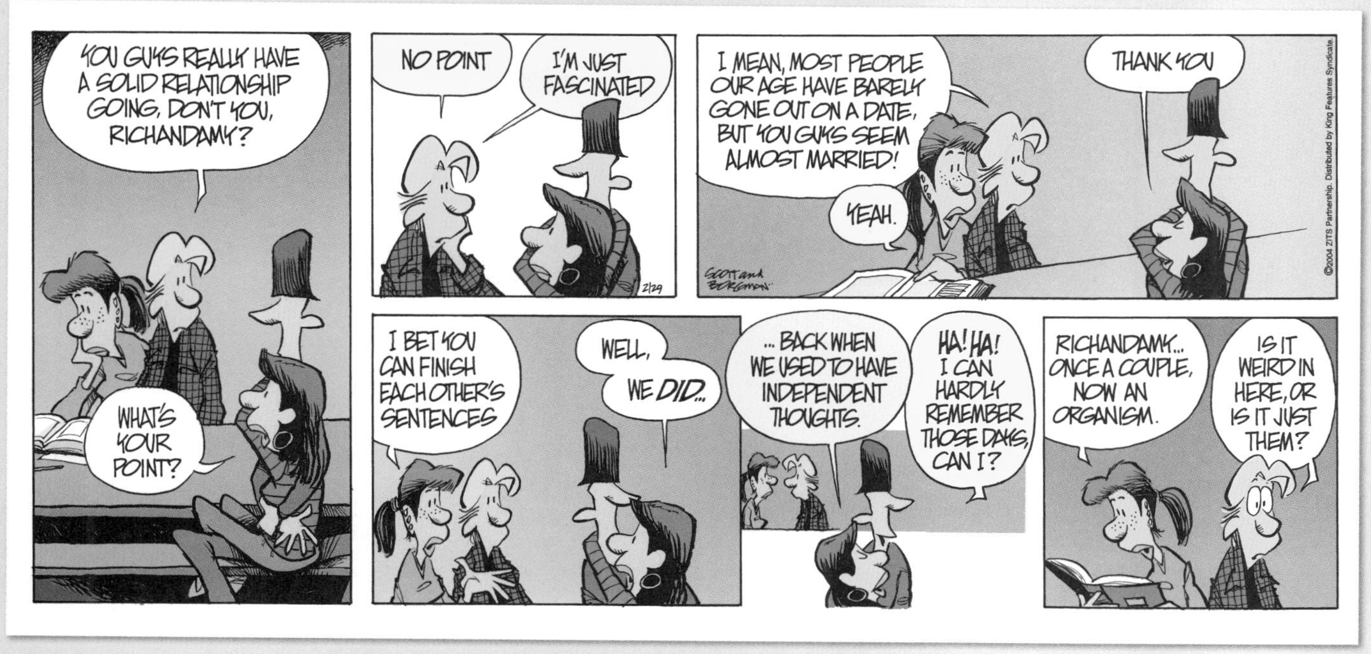
YOU GUYS REALLY HAVE A SOLID RELATIONSHIP GOING, DON'T YOU, RICHANDAMY?
WHAT'S YOUR POINT?
NO POINT
I'M JUST FASCINATED
I MEAN, MOST PEOPLE OUR AGE HAVE BARELY GONE OUT ON A DATE, BUT YOU GUYS SEEM ALMOST MARRIED!
YEAH.
THANK YOU
I BET YOU CAN FINISH EACH OTHER'S SENTENCES
WELL,
WE DID...
... BACK WHEN WE USED TO HAVE INDEPENDENT THOUGHTS.
HA! HA! I CAN HARDLY REMEMBER THOSE DAYS, CAN I?
RICHANDAMY... ONCE A COUPLE, NOW AN ORGANISM.
IS IT WEIRD IN HERE, OR IS IT JUST THEM?
SCOTT and BORGMAN 2/29
©2004 ZITS Partnership. Distributed by King Features Syndicate.

March 21, 2004

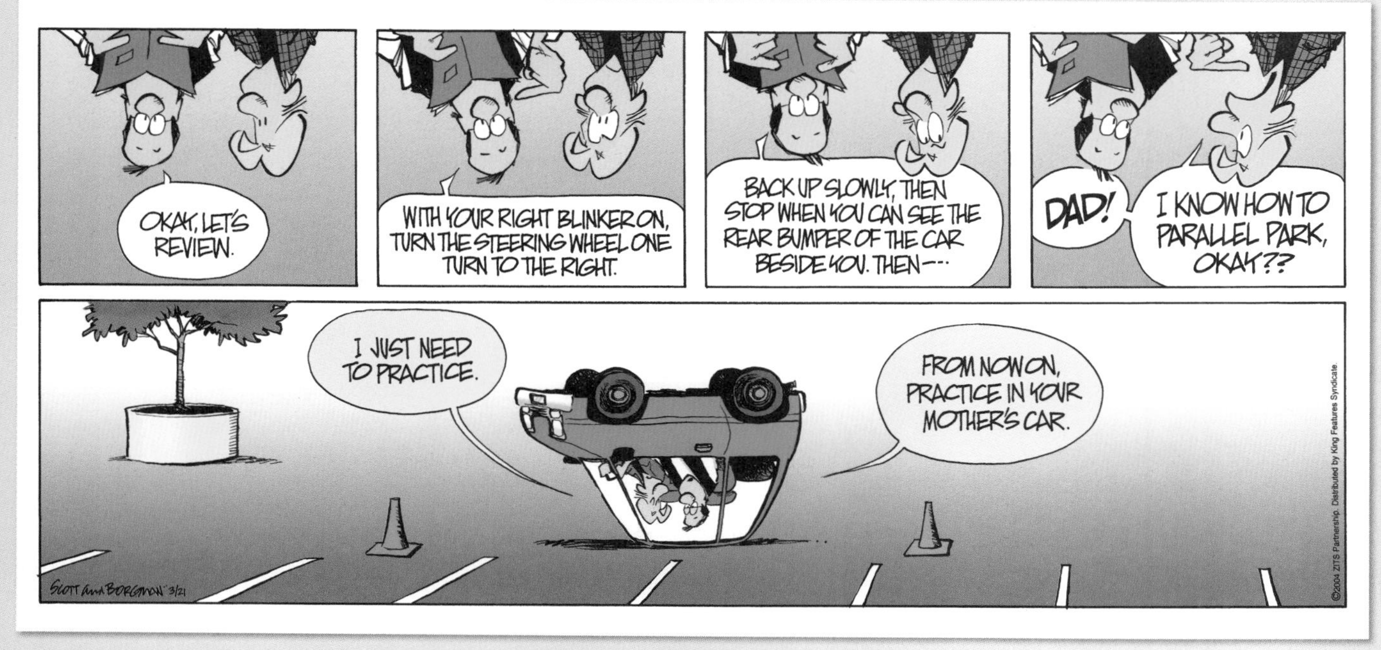
OKAY, LET'S REVIEW.
WITH YOUR RIGHT BLINKER ON, TURN THE STEERING WHEEL ONE TURN TO THE RIGHT.
BACK UP SLOWLY, THEN STOP WHEN YOU CAN SEE THE REAR BUMPER OF THE CAR BESIDE YOU. THEN---
DAD!
I KNOW HOW TO PARALLEL PARK, OKAY??
I JUST NEED TO PRACTICE.
FROM NOW ON, PRACTICE IN YOUR MOTHER'S CAR.
SCOTT and BORGMAN 3/21
©2004 ZITS Partnership. Distributed by King Features Syndicate.

March 28, 2004

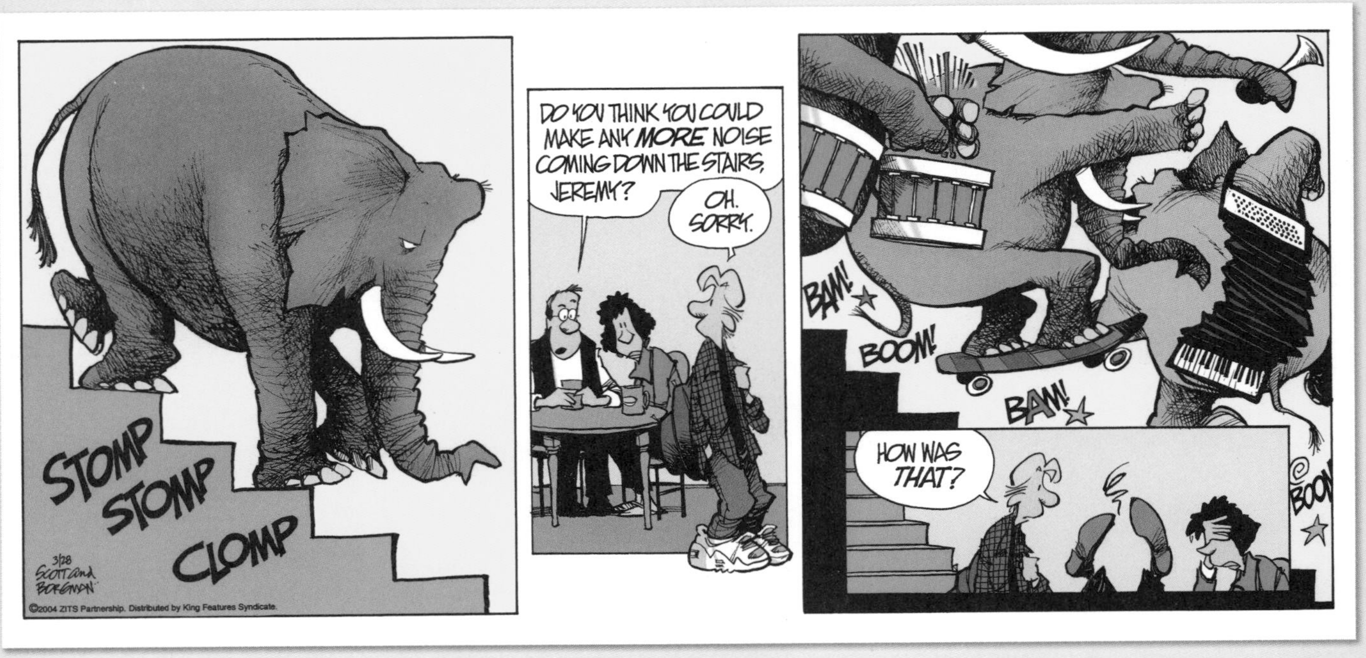
STOMP
STOMP
CLOMP
3/28 SCOTT and BORGMAN
©2004 ZITS Partnership. Distributed by King Features Syndicate.
DO YOU THINK YOU COULD MAKE ANY MORE NOISE COMING DOWN THE STAIRS, JEREMY?
OH. SORRY.
BAM!
BOOM!
BAM!
BOOM
HOW WAS THAT?

August 29, 2004

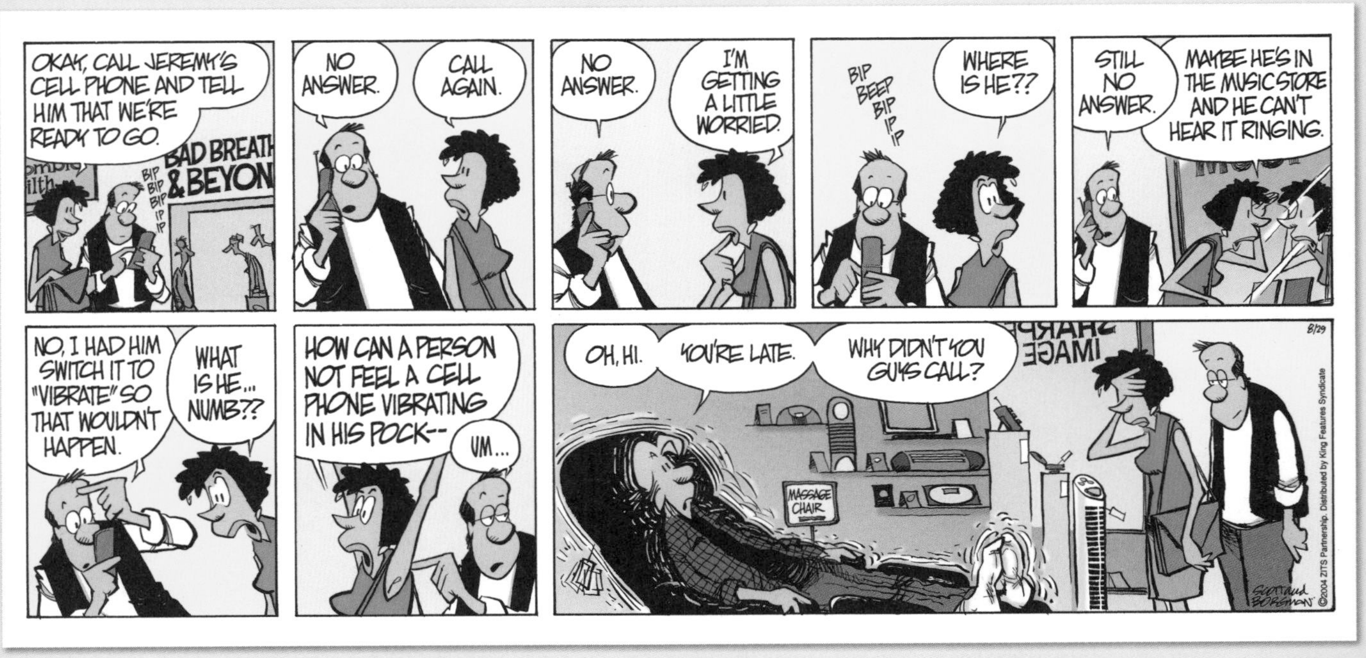
OKAY, CALL JEREMY'S CELL PHONE AND TELL HIM THAT WE'RE READY TO GO.
BIP BIP BIP IP IP
BAD BREATH & BEYON
NO ANSWER.
CALL AGAIN.
NO ANSWER.
I'M GETTING A LITTLE WORRIED.
BIP BEEP BIP IP IP
WHERE IS HE??
STILL NO ANSWER.
MAYBE HE'S IN THE MUSIC STORE AND HE CAN'T HEAR IT RINGING.
NO, I HAD HIM SWITCH IT TO "VIBRATE" SO THAT WOULDN'T HAPPEN.
WHAT IS HE... NUMB??
HOW CAN A PERSON NOT FEEL A CELL PHONE VIBRATING IN HIS POCK--
UM...
OH, HI.
YOU'RE LATE.
WHY DIDN'T YOU GUYS CALL?
SHARP IMAGE
MASSAGE CHAIR
8/29
SCOTT and BORGMAN
©2004 ZITS Partnership. Distributed by King Features Syndicate

April 5, 2004

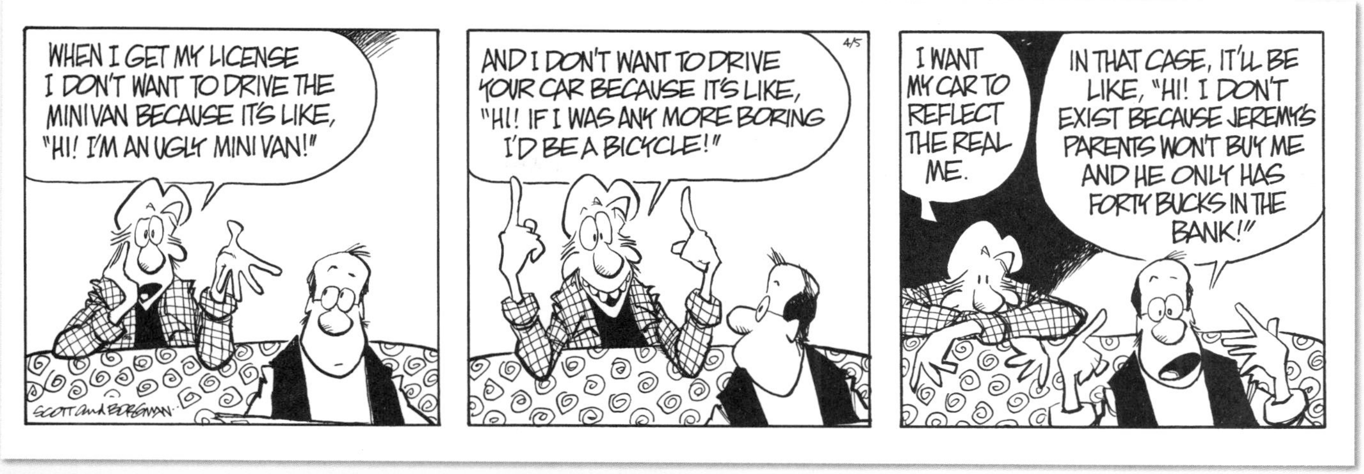
WHEN I GET MY LICENSE I DON'T WANT TO DRIVE THE MINIVAN BECAUSE IT'S LIKE, "HI! I'M AN UGLY MINIVAN!"
SCOTT and BORGMAN
AND I DON'T WANT TO DRIVE YOUR CAR BECAUSE IT'S LIKE, "HI! IF I WAS ANY MORE BORING I'D BE A BICYCLE!"
4/5
I WANT MY CAR TO REFLECT THE REAL ME.
IN THAT CASE, IT'LL BE LIKE, "HI! I DON'T EXIST BECAUSE JEREMY'S PARENTS WON'T BUY ME AND HE ONLY HAS FORTY BUCKS IN THE BANK!"

April 13, 2004

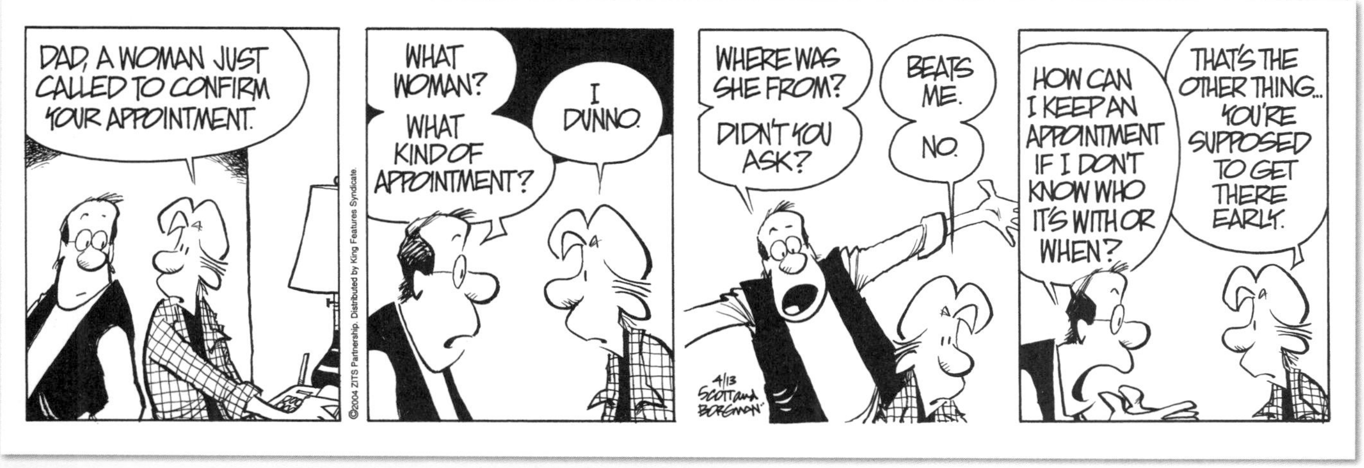
DAD, A WOMAN JUST CALLED TO CONFIRM YOUR APPOINTMENT.
©2004 ZITS Partnership. Distributed by King Features Syndicate.
WHAT WOMAN?
WHAT KIND OF APPOINTMENT?
I DUNNO.
WHERE WAS SHE FROM?
BEATS ME.
DIDN'T YOU ASK?
NO.
4/13 SCOTT and BORGMAN
HOW CAN I KEEP AN APPOINTMENT IF I DON'T KNOW WHO IT'S WITH OR WHEN?
THAT'S THE OTHER THING... YOU'RE SUPPOSED TO GET THERE EARLY.

May 29, 2004

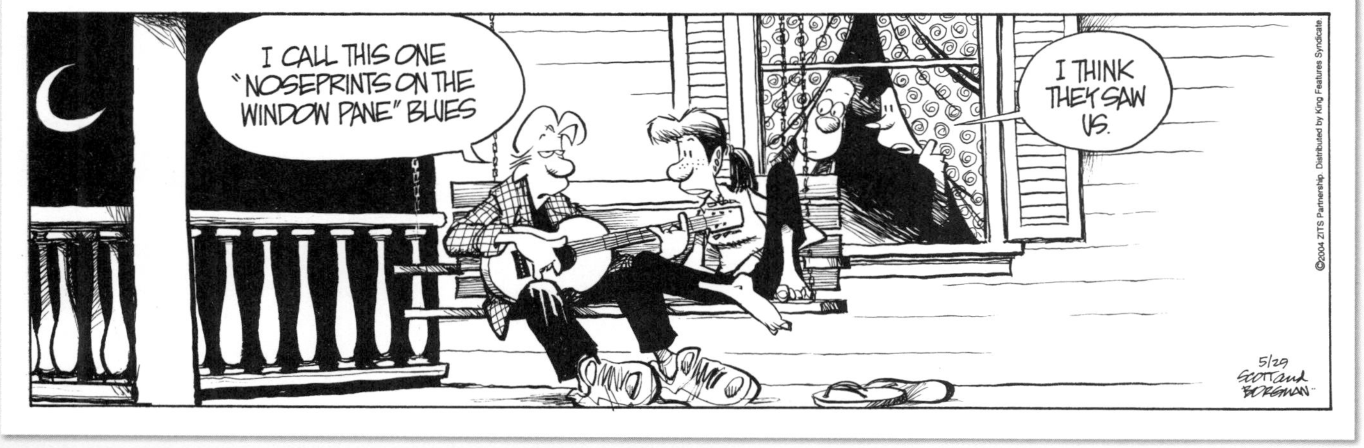
I CALL THIS ONE "NOSEPRINTS ON THE WINDOW PANE" BLUES
I THINK THEY SAW US.
©2004 ZITS Partnership. Distributed by King Features Syndicate.
5/29 SCOTT and BORGMAN

May 10, 2004

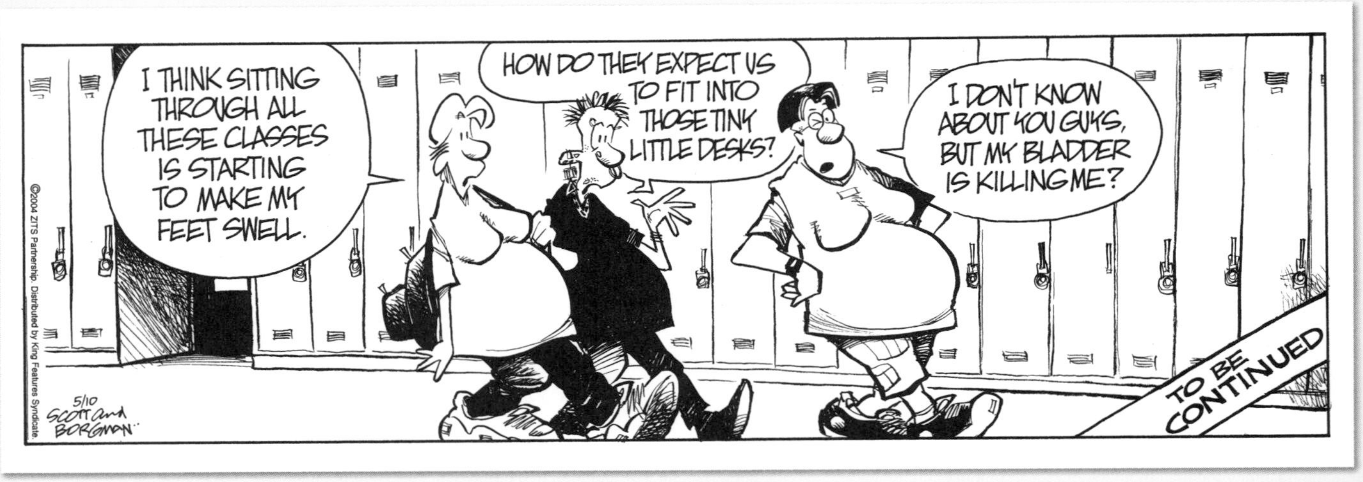
I THINK SITTING THROUGH ALL THESE CLASSES IS STARTING TO MAKE MY FEET SWELL.
HOW DO THEY EXPECT US TO FIT INTO THOSE TINY LITTLE DESKS?
I DON'T KNOW ABOUT YOU GUYS, BUT MY BLADDER IS KILLING ME?
TO BE CONTINUED
©2004 ZITS Partnership. Distributed by King Features Syndicate.
5/10 SCOTT and BORGMAN

May 13, 2004

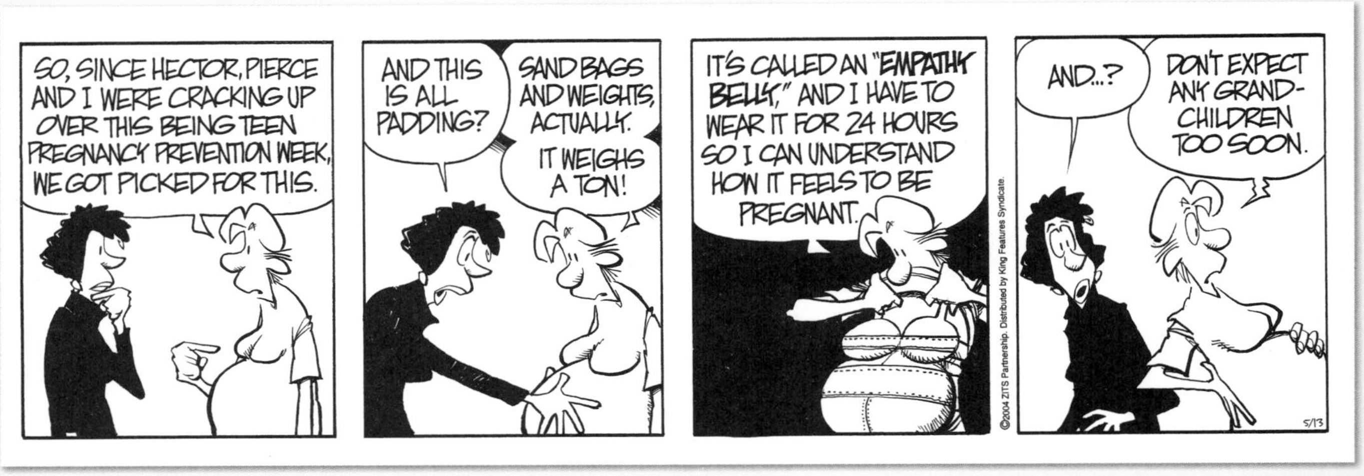
SO, SINCE HECTOR, PIERCE AND I WERE CRACKING UP OVER THIS BEING TEEN PREGNANCY PREVENTION WEEK, WE GOT PICKED FOR THIS.
AND THIS IS ALL PADDING?
SAND BAGS AND WEIGHTS, ACTUALLY.
IT WEIGHS A TON!
IT'S CALLED AN "EMPATHY BELLY," AND I HAVE TO WEAR IT FOR 24 HOURS SO I CAN UNDERSTAND HOW IT FEELS TO BE PREGNANT.
AND...?
DON'T EXPECT ANY GRAND-CHILDREN TOO SOON.
©2004 ZITS Partnership. Distributed by King Features Syndicate.
5/13

May 14, 2004

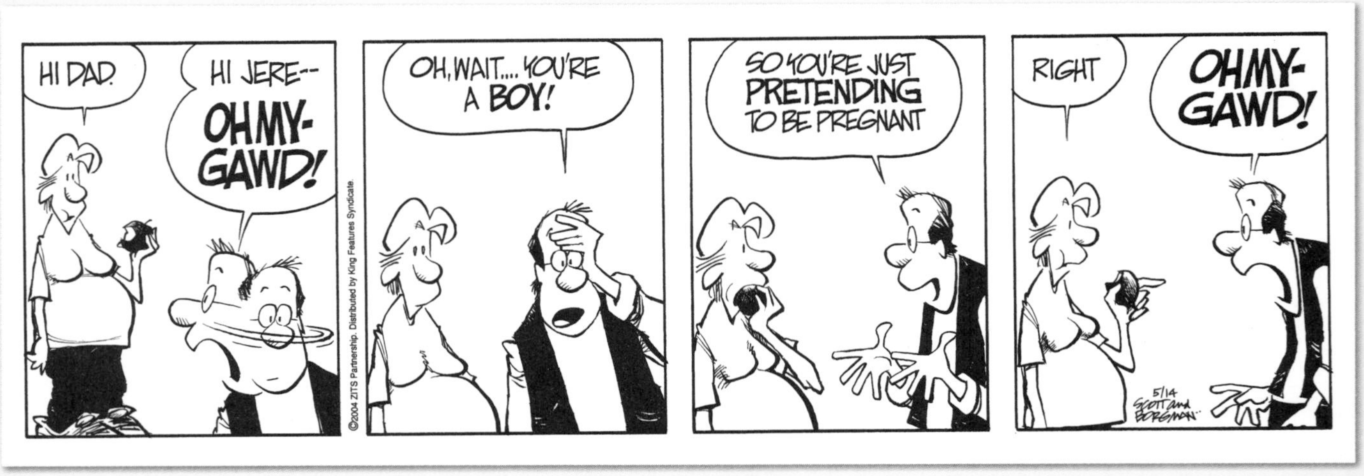
HI DAD.
HI JERE-- OHMY-GAWD!
OH, WAIT.... YOU'RE A BOY!
SO YOU'RE JUST PRETENDING TO BE PREGNANT
RIGHT
OHMY-GAWD!
©2004 ZITS Partnership. Distributed by King Features Syndicate.
5/14 SCOTT and BORGMAN

May 18, 2004

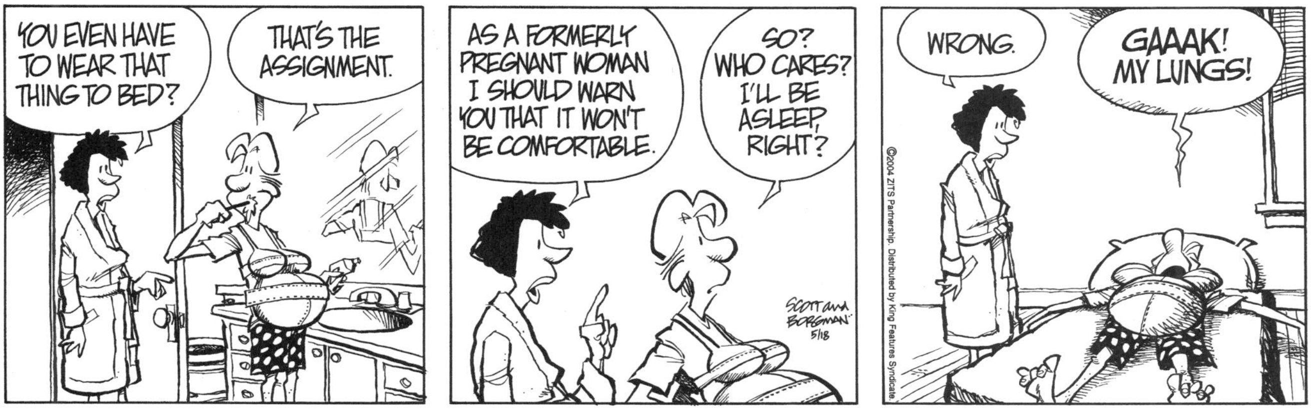
YOU EVEN HAVE TO WEAR THAT THING TO BED?
THAT'S THE ASSIGNMENT.
AS A FORMERLY PREGNANT WOMAN I SHOULD WARN YOU THAT IT WON'T BE COMFORTABLE.
SO? WHO CARES? I'LL BE ASLEEP, RIGHT?
SCOTT AND BORGMAN 5/18
©2004 ZITS Partnership. Distributed by King Features Syndicate.
WRONG.
GAAAK! MY LUNGS!

May 20, 2004

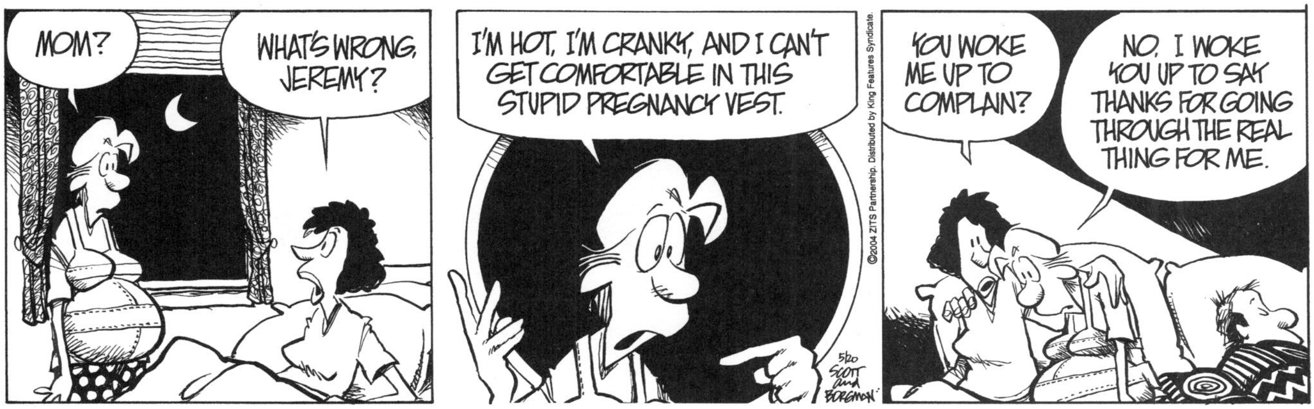
MOM?
WHAT'S WRONG, JEREMY?
I'M HOT, I'M CRANKY, AND I CAN'T GET COMFORTABLE IN THIS STUPID PREGNANCY VEST.
5/20 SCOTT AND BORGMAN
©2004 ZITS Partnership. Distributed by King Features Syndicate.
YOU WOKE ME UP TO COMPLAIN?
NO, I WOKE YOU UP TO SAY THANKS FOR GOING THROUGH THE REAL THING FOR ME.

May 31, 2004

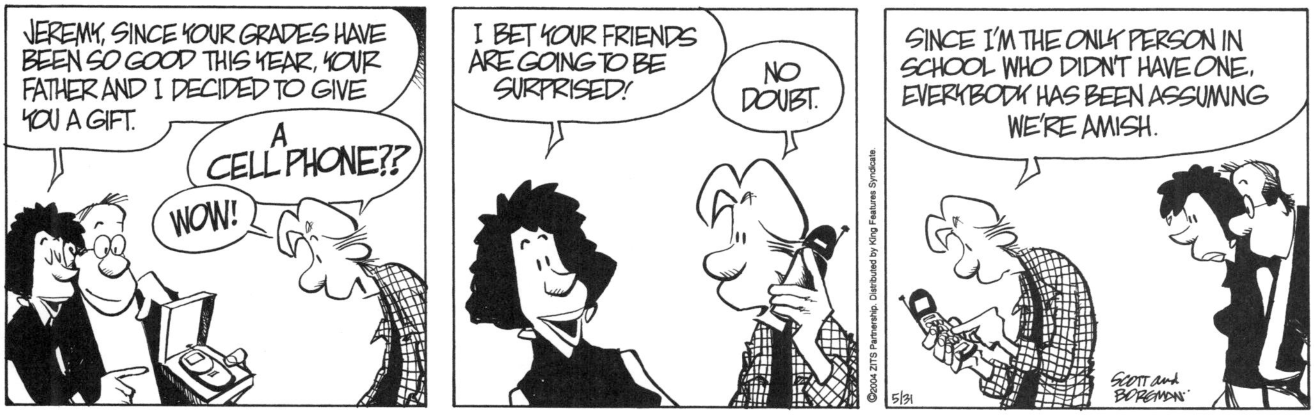
JEREMY, SINCE YOUR GRADES HAVE BEEN SO GOOD THIS YEAR, YOUR FATHER AND I DECIDED TO GIVE YOU A GIFT.
A CELL PHONE??
WOW!
I BET YOUR FRIENDS ARE GOING TO BE SURPRISED!
NO DOUBT.
©2004 ZITS Partnership. Distributed by King Features Syndicate.
SINCE I'M THE ONLY PERSON IN SCHOOL WHO DIDN'T HAVE ONE, EVERYBODY HAS BEEN ASSUMING WE'RE AMISH.
5/31
SCOTT AND BORGMAN

July 4, 2004

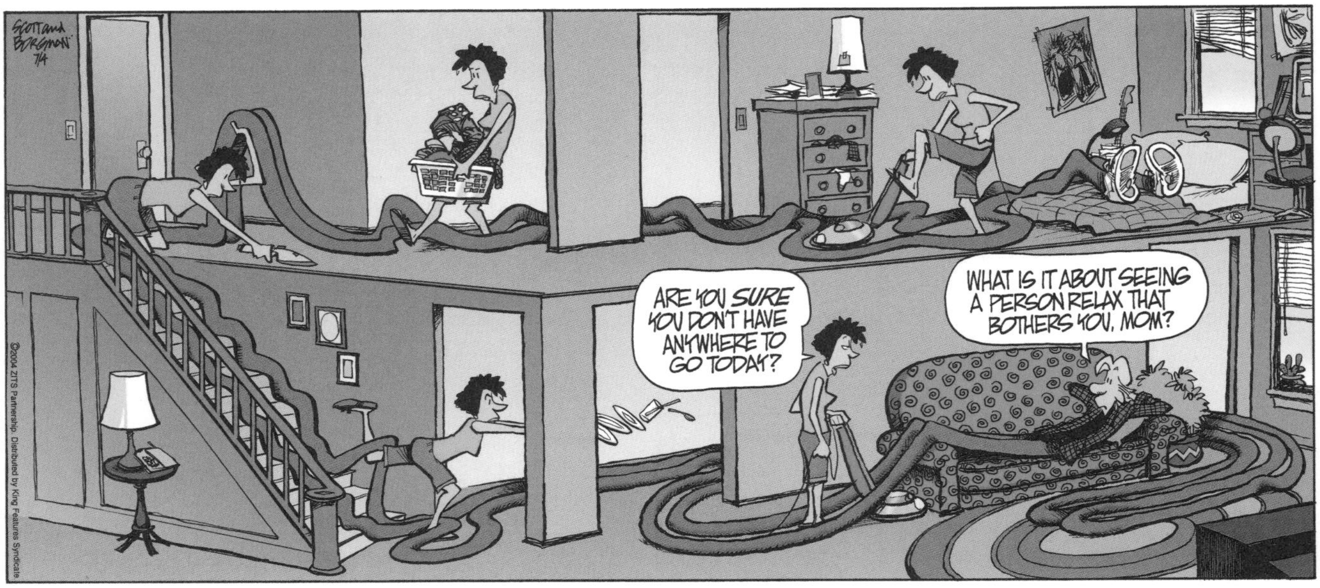
SCOTT AND BORGMAN 7/4
ARE YOU SURE YOU DON'T HAVE ANYWHERE TO GO TODAY?
WHAT IS IT ABOUT SEEING A PERSON RELAX THAT BOTHERS YOU, MOM?
©2004 ZITS Partnership. Distributed by King Features Syndicate

July 18, 2004

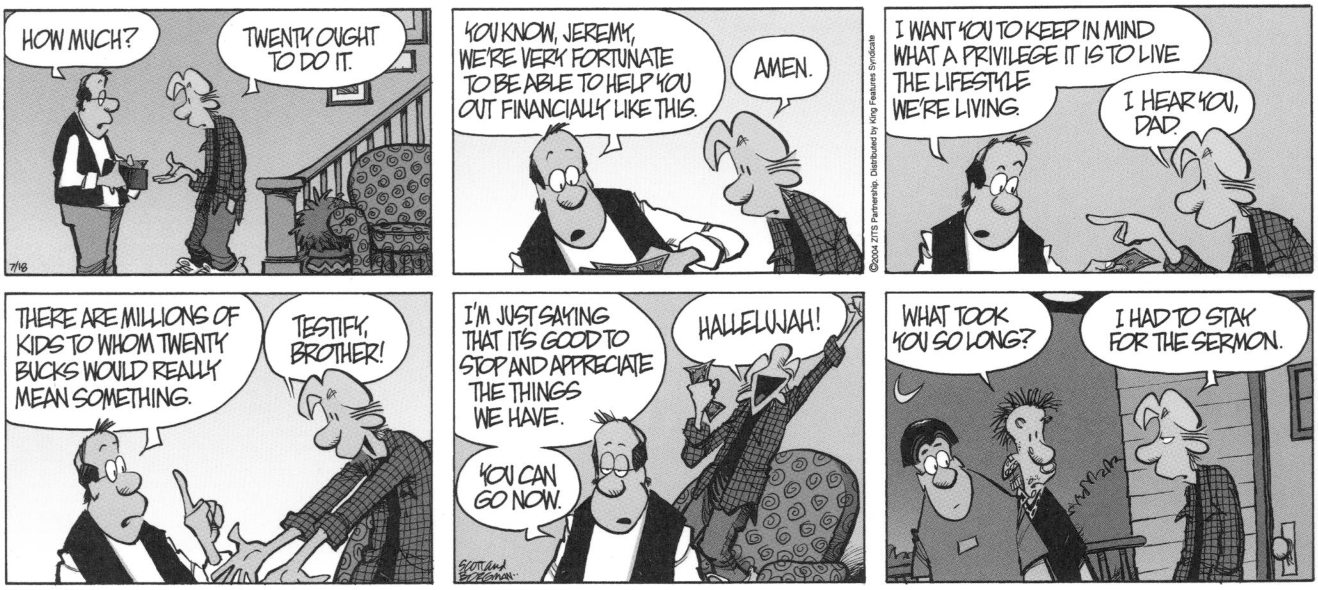
HOW MUCH?
TWENTY OUGHT TO DO IT.
YOU KNOW, JEREMY, WE'RE VERY FORTUNATE TO BE ABLE TO HELP YOU OUT FINANCIALLY LIKE THIS.
AMEN.
I WANT YOU TO KEEP IN MIND WHAT A PRIVILEGE IT IS TO LIVE THE LIFESTYLE WE'RE LIVING.
I HEAR YOU, DAD.
THERE ARE MILLIONS OF KIDS TO WHOM TWENTY BUCKS WOULD REALLY MEAN SOMETHING.
TESTIFY, BROTHER!
I'M JUST SAYING THAT IT'S GOOD TO STOP AND APPRECIATE THE THINGS WE HAVE.
HALLELUJAH!
YOU CAN GO NOW.
WHAT TOOK YOU SO LONG?
I HAD TO STAY FOR THE SERMON.
©2004 ZITS Partnership. Distributed by King Features Syndicate

June 19, 2004

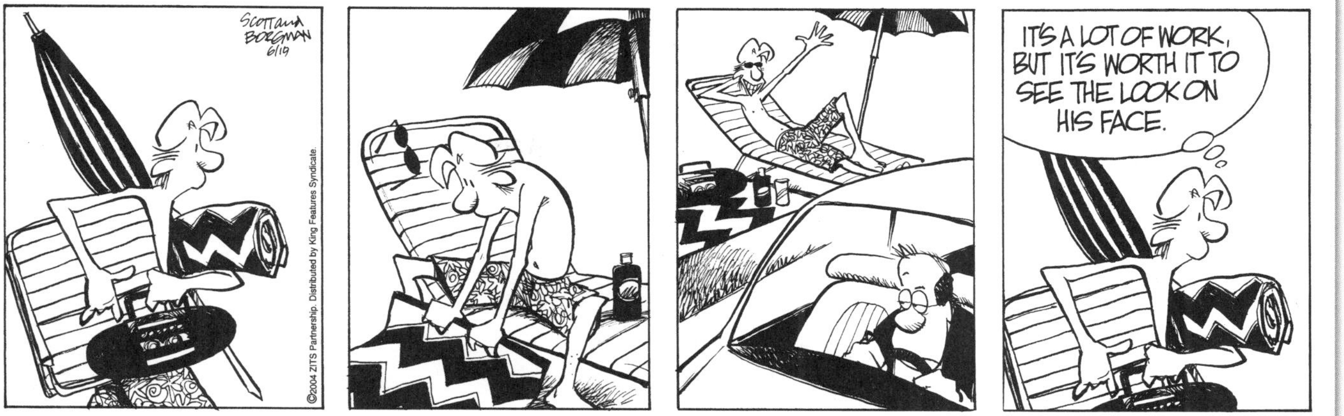
SCOTT and BORGMAN 6/19
©2004 ZITS Partnership. Distributed by King Features Syndicate.
IT'S A LOT OF WORK, BUT IT'S WORTH IT TO SEE THE LOOK ON HIS FACE.

July 5, 2004

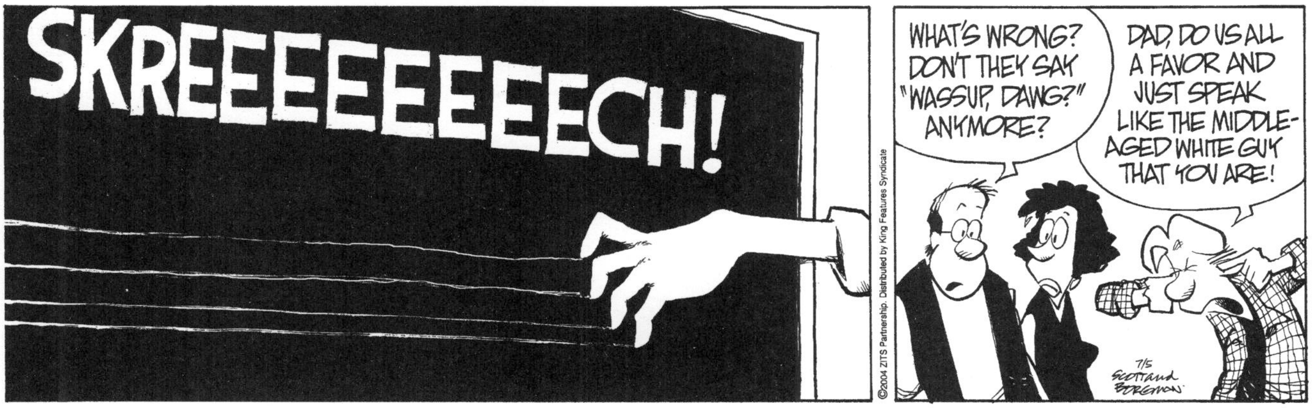
SKREEEEEEEEEECH!
©2004 ZITS Partnership. Distributed by King Features Syndicate
WHAT'S WRONG? DON'T THEY SAY "WASSUP, DAWG?" ANYMORE?
DAD, DO US ALL A FAVOR AND JUST SPEAK LIKE THE MIDDLE-AGED WHITE GUY THAT YOU ARE!
7/5 SCOTT and BORGMAN

July 9, 2004

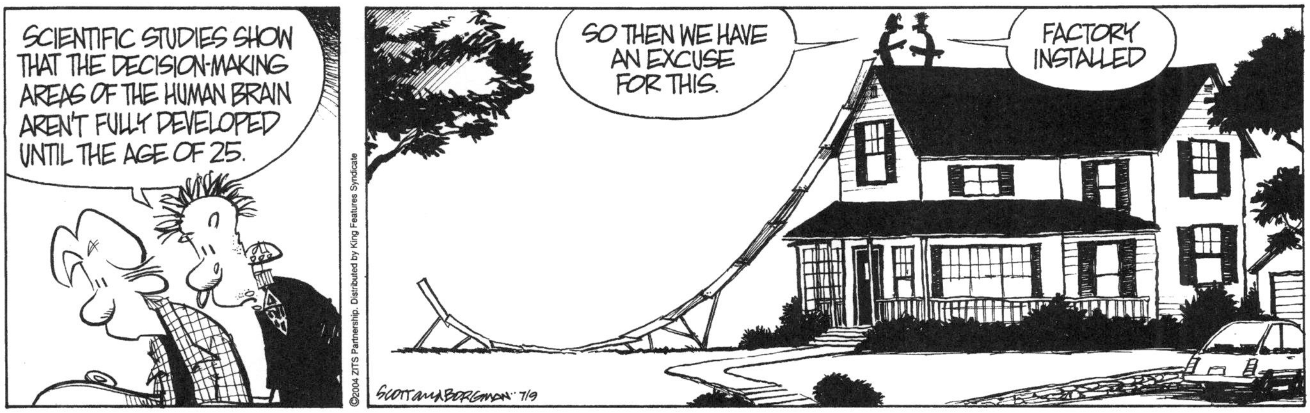
SCIENTIFIC STUDIES SHOW THAT THE DECISION-MAKING AREAS OF THE HUMAN BRAIN AREN'T FULLY DEVELOPED UNTIL THE AGE OF 25.
©2004 ZITS Partnership. Distributed by King Features Syndicate
SO THEN WE HAVE AN EXCUSE FOR THIS.
FACTORY INSTALLED
SCOTT and BORGMAN 7/9

July 25, 2004

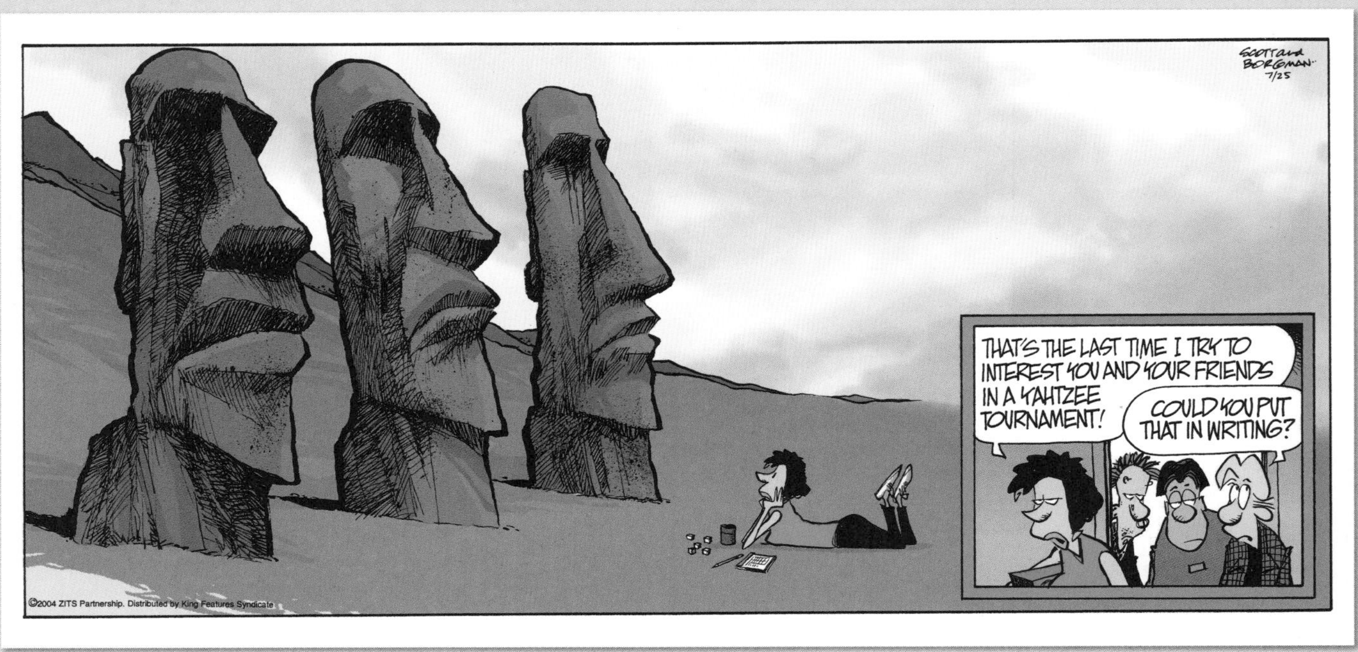
SCOTT and BORGMAN 7/25
THAT'S THE LAST TIME I TRY TO INTEREST YOU AND YOUR FRIENDS IN A YAHTZEE TOURNAMENT!
COULD YOU PUT THAT IN WRITING?
©2004 ZITS Partnership. Distributed by King Features Syndicate

October 24, 2004

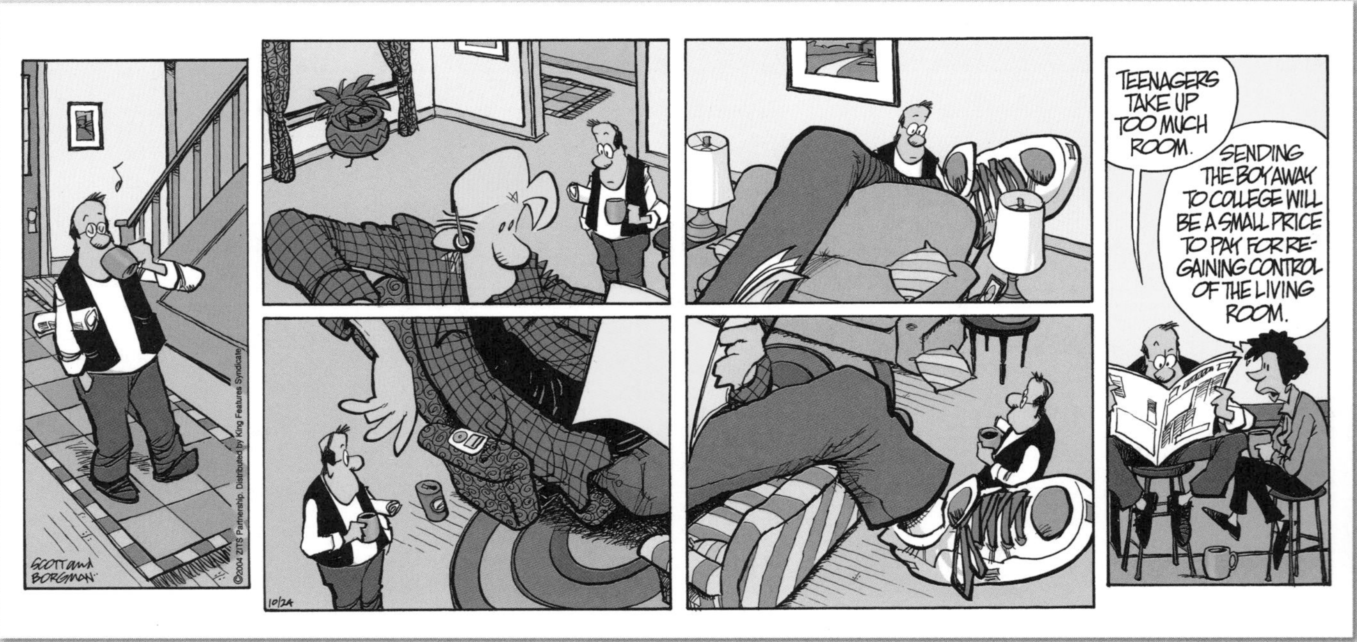
SCOTT and BORGMAN
©2004 ZITS Partnership. Distributed by King Features Syndicate
10/24
TEENAGERS TAKE UP TOO MUCH ROOM.
SENDING THE BOY AWAY TO COLLEGE WILL BE A SMALL PRICE TO PAY FOR RE-GAINING CONTROL OF THE LIVING ROOM.

July 24, 2004

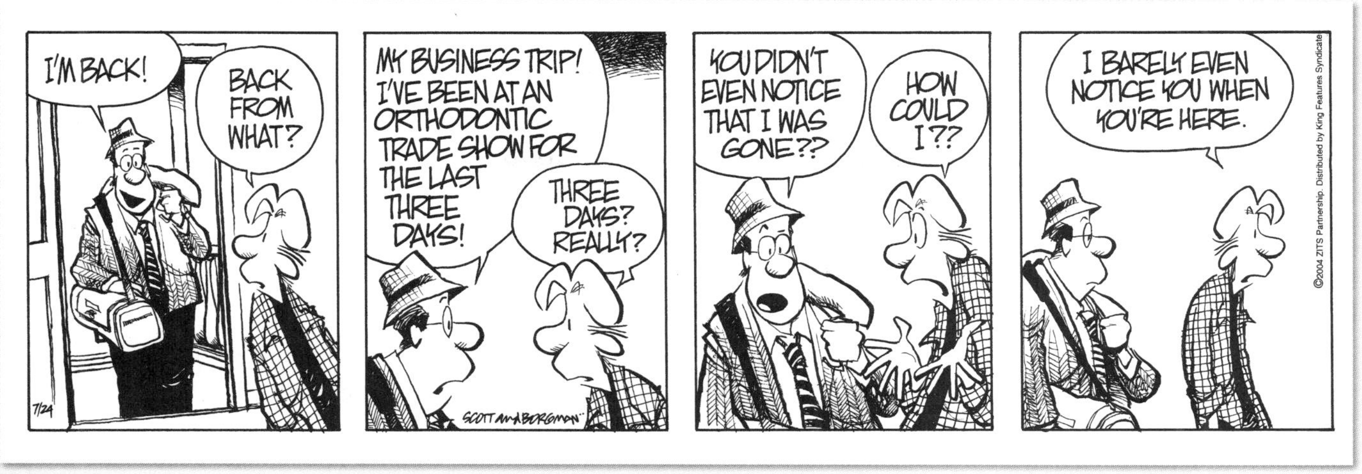
I'M BACK!
BACK FROM WHAT?
MY BUSINESS TRIP! I'VE BEEN AT AN ORTHODONTIC TRADE SHOW FOR THE LAST THREE DAYS!
THREE DAYS? REALLY?
YOU DIDN'T EVEN NOTICE THAT I WAS GONE??
HOW COULD I??
I BARELY EVEN NOTICE YOU WHEN YOU'RE HERE.
SCOTT AND BORGMAN
©2004 ZITS Partnership. Distributed by King Features Syndicate

September 1, 2004

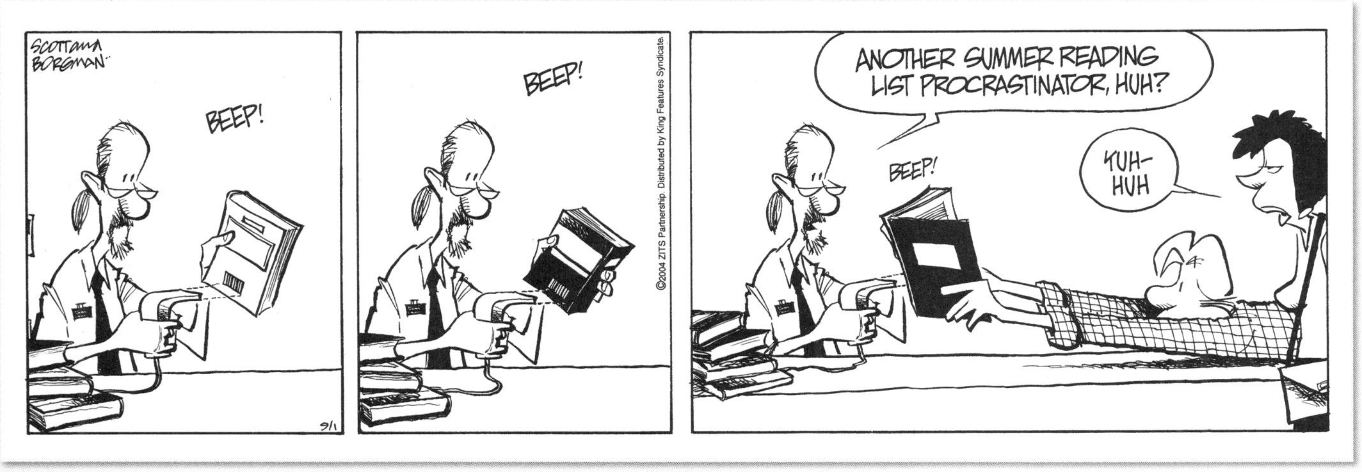
SCOTT AND BORGMAN
BEEP!
BEEP!
©2004 ZITS Partnership. Distributed by King Features Syndicate.
ANOTHER SUMMER READING LIST PROCRASTINATOR, HUH?
BEEP!
YUH-HUH

October 1, 2004

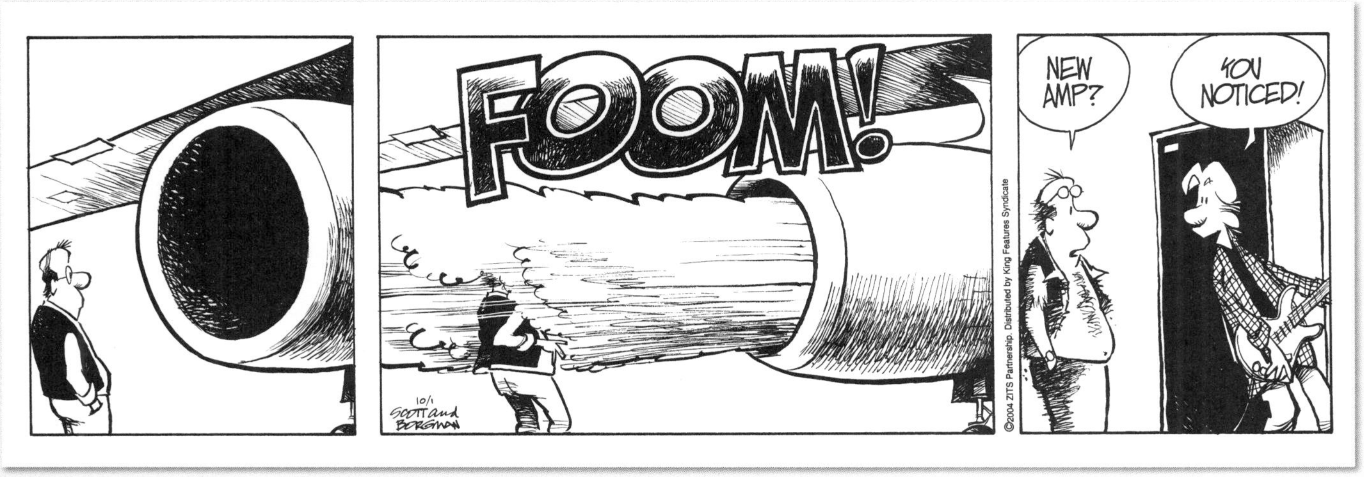
FOOM!
SCOTT AND BORGMAN
©2004 ZITS Partnership. Distributed by King Features Syndicate
NEW AMP?
YOU NOTICED!

October 6, 2004

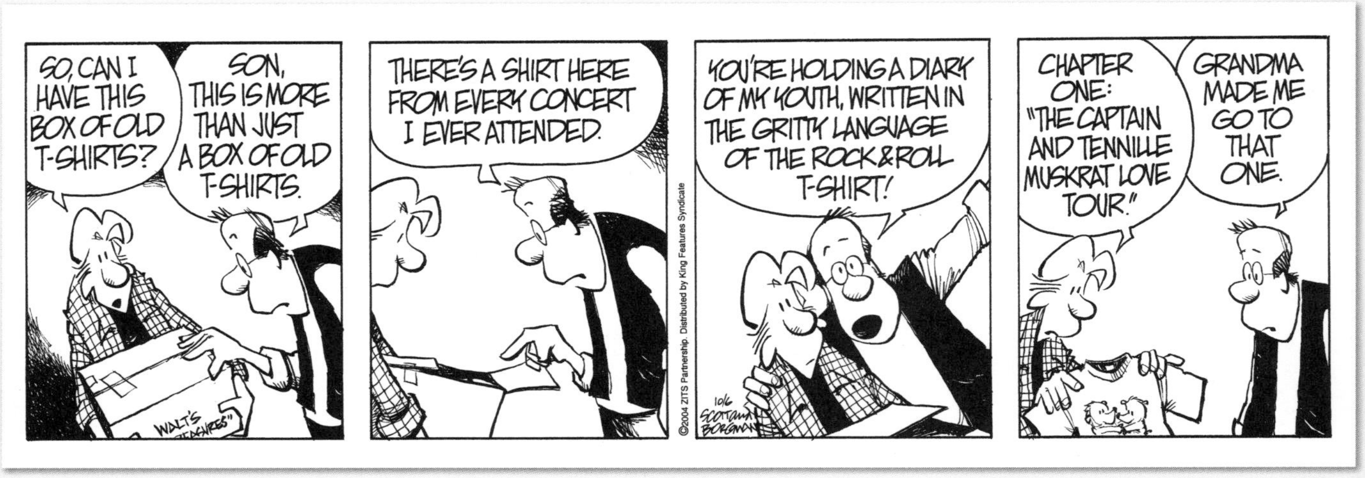
SO, CAN I HAVE THIS BOX OF OLD T-SHIRTS?
SON, THIS IS MORE THAN JUST A BOX OF OLD T-SHIRTS.
WALT'S TREASURES
THERE'S A SHIRT HERE FROM EVERY CONCERT I EVER ATTENDED.
YOU'RE HOLDING A DIARY OF MY YOUTH, WRITTEN IN THE GRITTY LANGUAGE OF THE ROCK & ROLL T-SHIRT!
©2004 ZITS Partnership. Distributed by King Features Syndicate
10/6 SCOTT AND BORGMAN
CHAPTER ONE: "THE CAPTAIN AND TENNILLE MUSKRAT LOVE TOUR."
GRANDMA MADE ME GO TO THAT ONE.

November 29, 2004

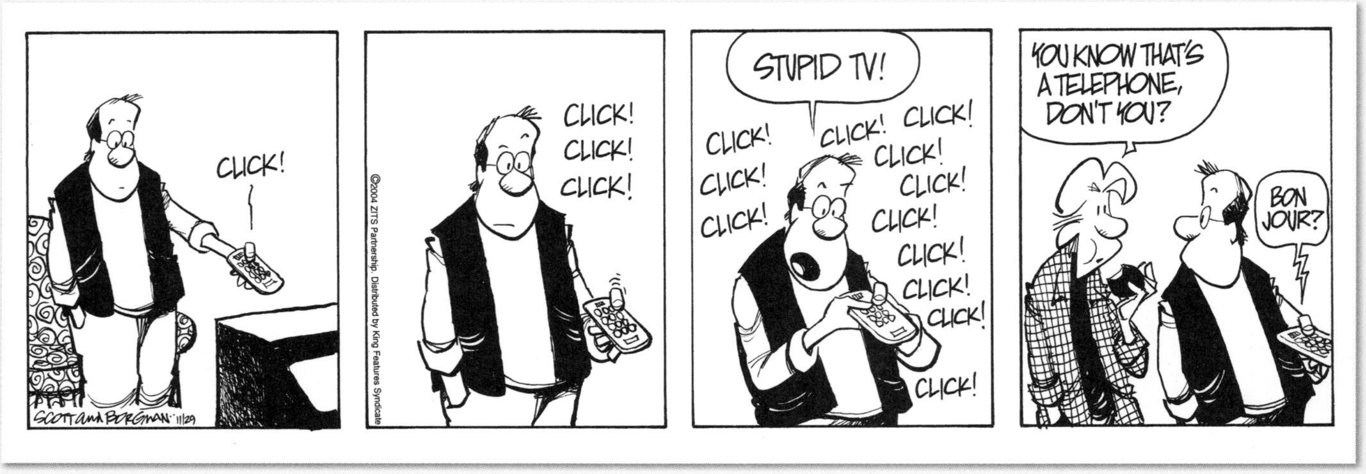
CLICK!
SCOTT AND BORGMAN 11/29
©2004 ZITS Partnership. Distributed by King Features Syndicate
CLICK! CLICK! CLICK!
STUPID TV!
CLICK! CLICK! CLICK! CLICK! CLICK! CLICK! CLICK! CLICK! CLICK! CLICK! CLICK! CLICK!
YOU KNOW THAT'S A TELEPHONE, DON'T YOU?
BON JOUR?

December 13, 2004

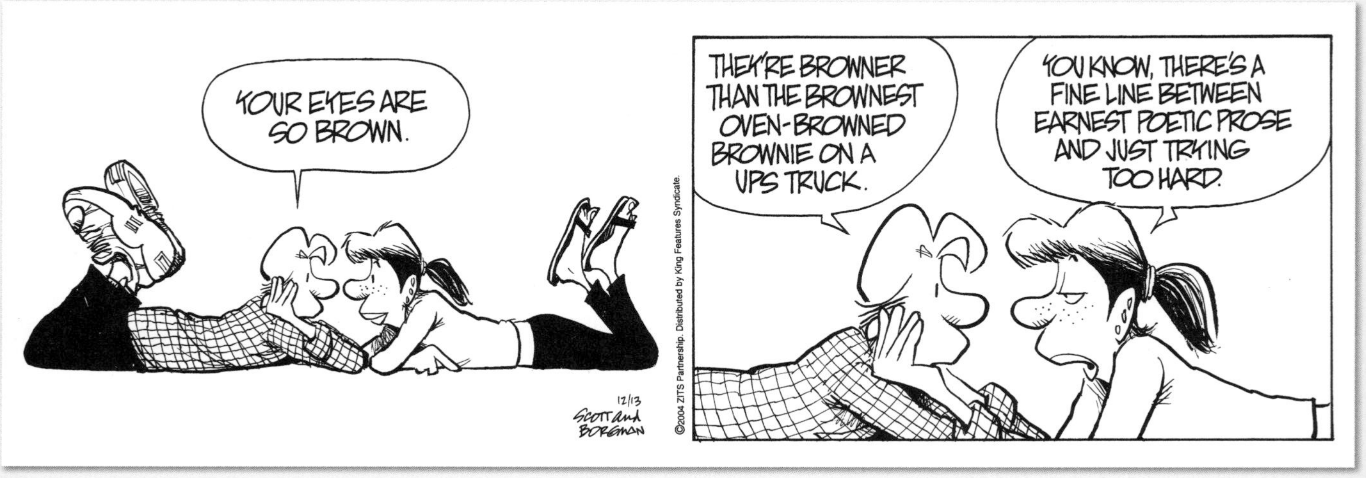
YOUR EYES ARE SO BROWN.
12/13 SCOTT AND BORGMAN
©2004 ZITS Partnership. Distributed by King Features Syndicate.
THEY'RE BROWNER THAN THE BROWNEST OVEN-BROWNED BROWNIE ON A UPS TRUCK.
YOU KNOW, THERE'S A FINE LINE BETWEEN EARNEST POETIC PROSE AND JUST TRYING TOO HARD.

December 26, 2004

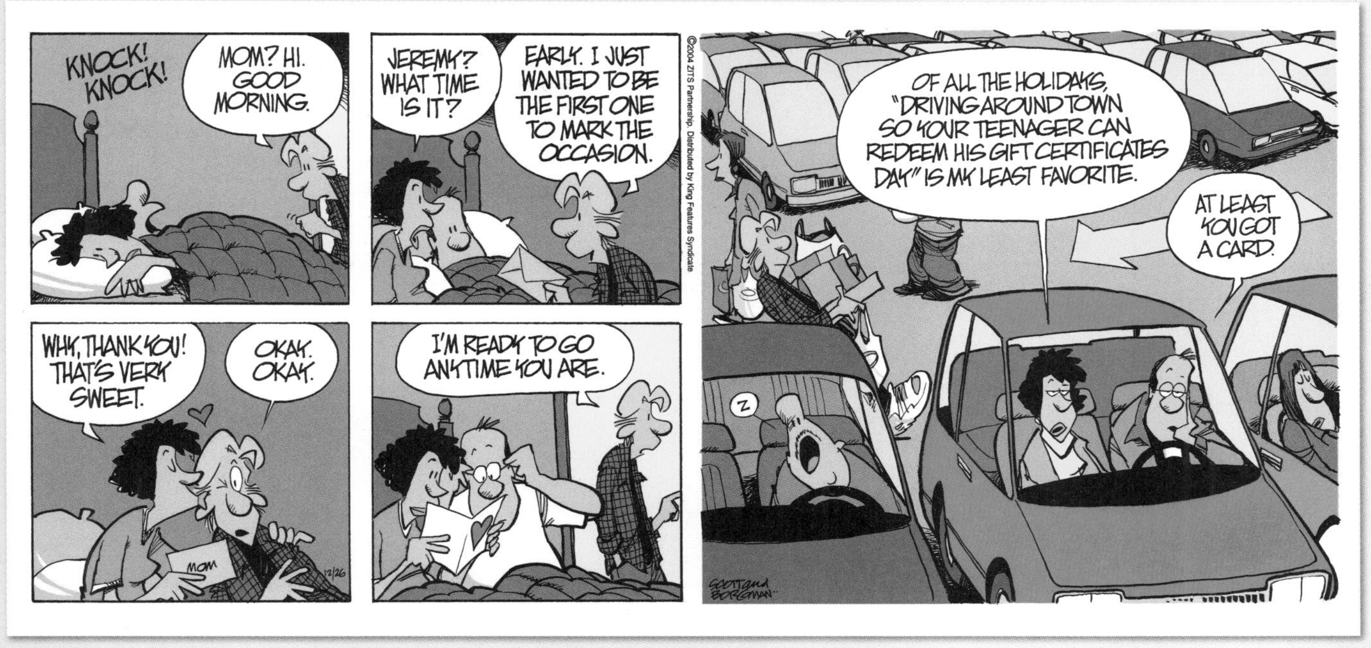

KNOCK! KNOCK!
MOM? HI. GOOD MORNING.
JEREMY? WHAT TIME IS IT?
EARLY. I JUST WANTED TO BE THE FIRST ONE TO MARK THE OCCASION.
©2004 ZITS Partnership. Distributed by King Features Syndicate
WHY, THANK YOU! THAT'S VERY SWEET.
OKAY. OKAY.
MOM
12/26
I'M READY TO GO ANYTIME YOU ARE.
OF ALL THE HOLIDAYS, "DRIVING AROUND TOWN SO YOUR TEENAGER CAN REDEEM HIS GIFT CERTIFICATES DAY" IS MY LEAST FAVORITE.
AT LEAST YOU GOT A CARD.
Z
SCOTT and BORGMAN

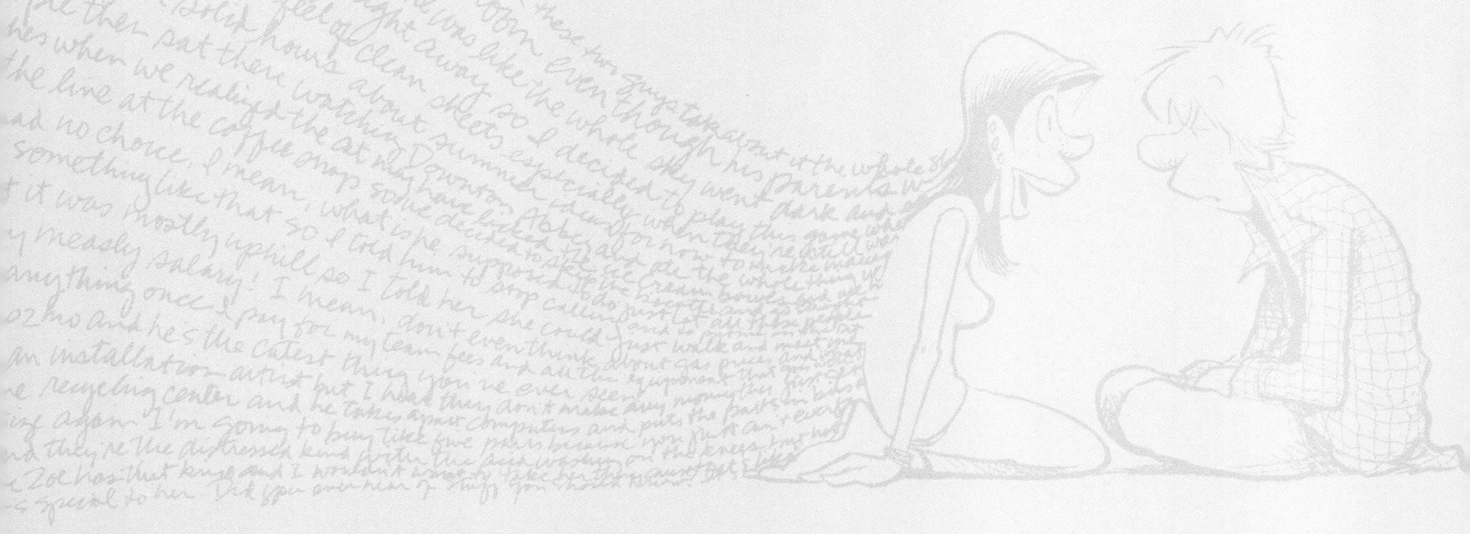

March 7, 2004

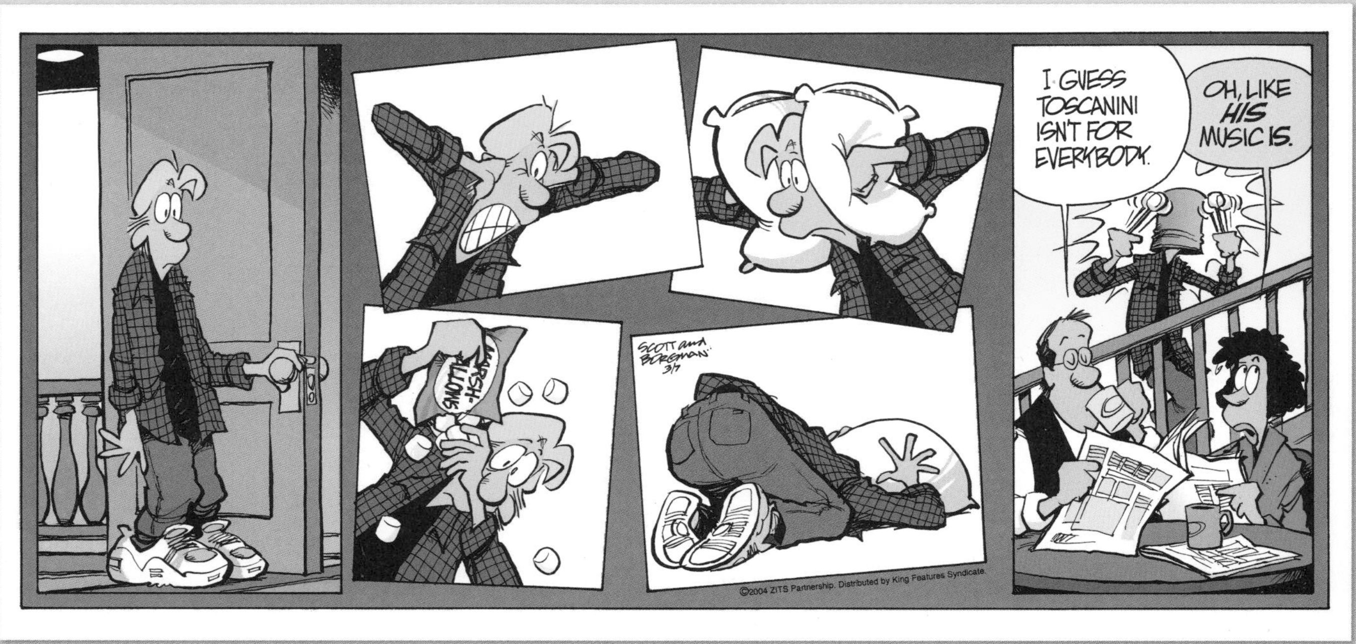
MARSH-MALLOWS
SCOTT and BORGMAN 3/7
©2004 ZITS Partnership. Distributed by King Features Syndicate.
I GUESS TOSCANINI ISN'T FOR EVERYBODY.
OH, LIKE *HIS* MUSIC IS.

June 20, 2004

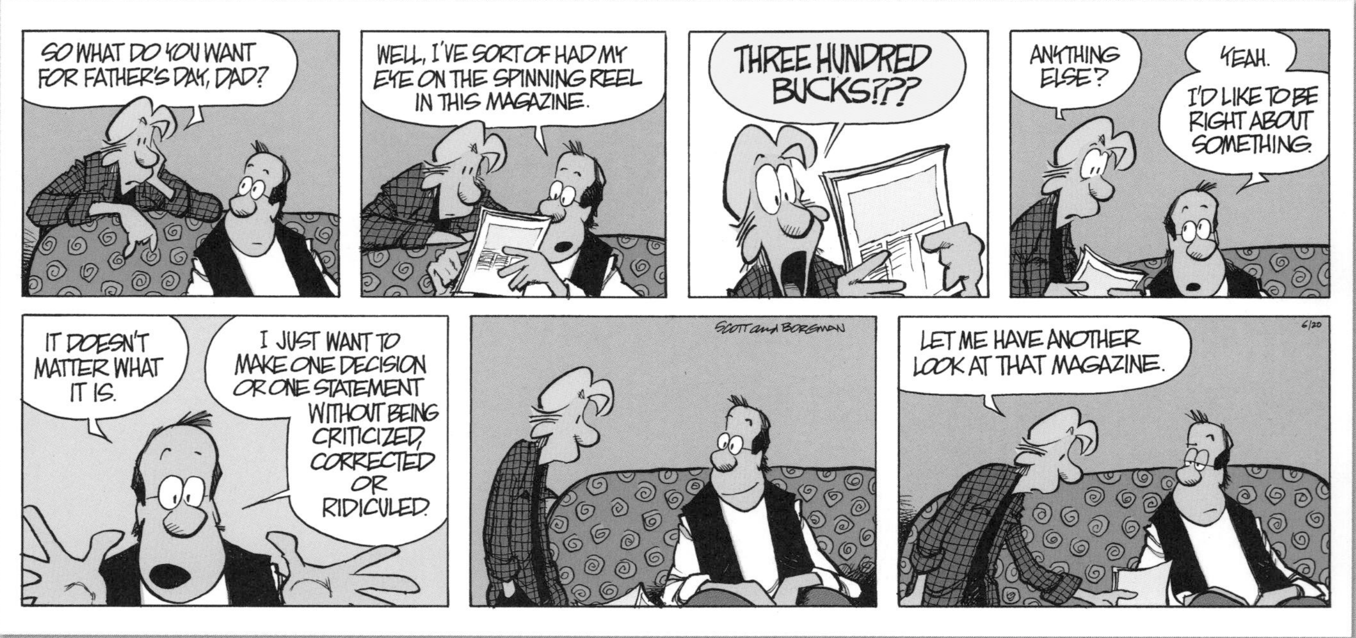
SO WHAT DO YOU WANT FOR FATHER'S DAY, DAD?
WELL, I'VE SORT OF HAD MY EYE ON THE SPINNING REEL IN THIS MAGAZINE.
THREE HUNDRED BUCKS!??
ANYTHING ELSE?
YEAH.
I'D LIKE TO BE RIGHT ABOUT SOMETHING.
IT DOESN'T MATTER WHAT IT IS.
I JUST WANT TO MAKE ONE DECISION OR ONE STATEMENT WITHOUT BEING CRITICIZED, CORRECTED OR RIDICULED.
SCOTT and BORGMAN
6/20
LET ME HAVE ANOTHER LOOK AT THAT MAGAZINE.

HAPPY FESTIVUS, or whatever

Jim Borgman

My wife noted (with a certain pointedness) that we didn't do a strip themed to Mother's Day one year. "Don't look for one on Father's Day either," I murmured. We sort of skated past those holidays that year in the commotion of assembling our giant *Sunday Brunch* book. Our little brains have only so much room.

Maybe she was right, though. In a strip like *Zits* we can choose to ignore most American holidays, like Thanksgiving, the Fourth of July, or Festivus, but Mother's Day and Father's Day are right down the middle of our plate. Maybe we look clueless when Hi is taking Lois to brunch beside us on the comics page. On the other hand, those holiday strip ideas can get hackneyed, and I've sometimes wondered whether readers appreciate a departure from the expected theme. "Plus, who ever really eats breakfast in bed?" I asked my wife, to no avail.

When Jerry and I work on *Zits*, we seldom think about the publication date beyond a vague sense of the flow of the year. Jeremy gets out of school sometime in the late spring and starts back to school in the late summer. We acknowledge Christmas because it's too big to ignore and often nod to Halloween because it's on a teenager's radar screen, but other holidays pass without mention. I could tell you it's because of our international clients (*Zits* runs in forty-five different countries in fifteen different languages), but really it's just because holiday strips mostly suck.

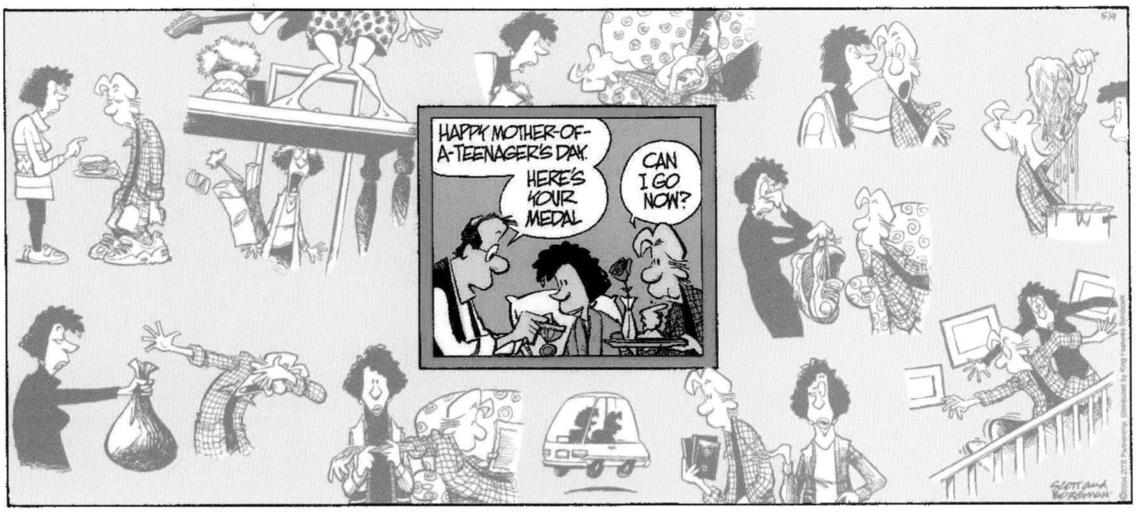
HAPPY MOTHER-OF-A-TEENAGER'S DAY.
HERE'S YOUR MEDAL
CAN I GO NOW?
SCOTT AND BORGMAN

January 9, 2005

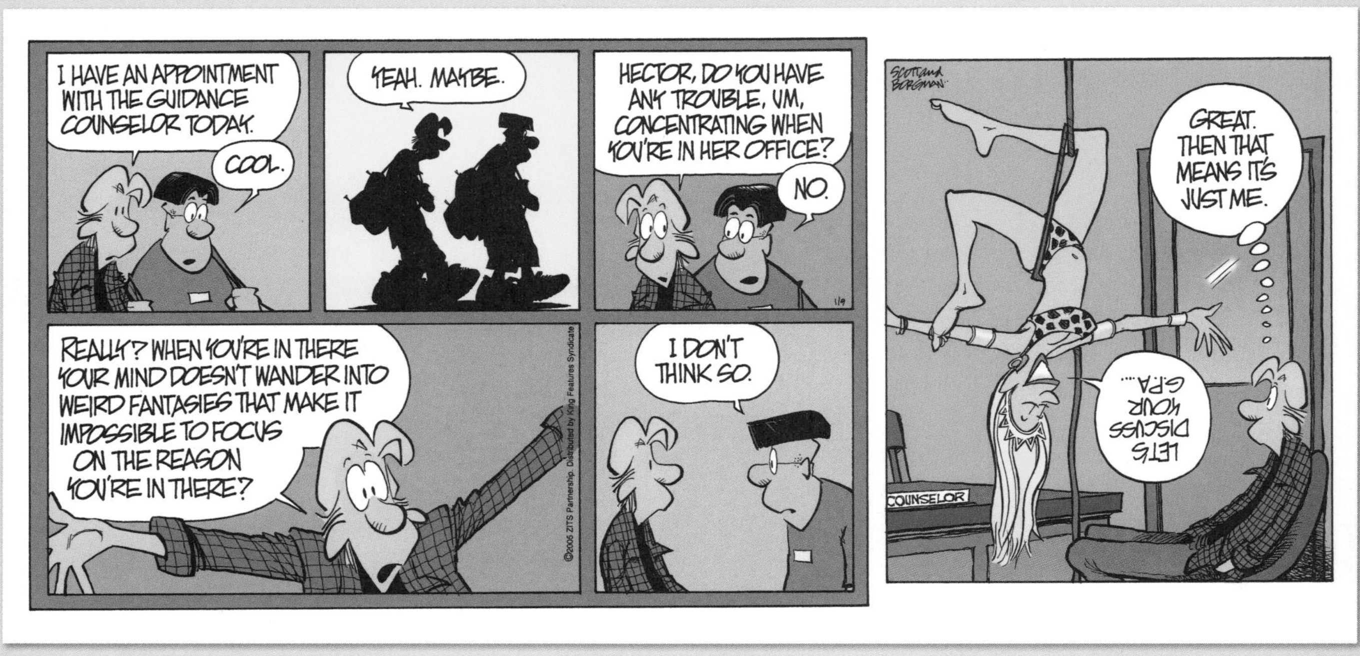
I HAVE AN APPOINTMENT WITH THE GUIDANCE COUNSELOR TODAY.
COOL.
YEAH. MAYBE.
HECTOR, DO YOU HAVE ANY TROUBLE, UM, CONCENTRATING WHEN YOU'RE IN HER OFFICE?
NO.
REALLY? WHEN YOU'RE IN THERE YOUR MIND DOESN'T WANDER INTO WEIRD FANTASIES THAT MAKE IT IMPOSSIBLE TO FOCUS ON THE REASON YOU'RE IN THERE?
I DON'T THINK SO.
LET'S DISCUSS YOUR G.P.A....
GREAT. THEN THAT MEANS IT'S JUST ME.
COUNSELOR
©2005 ZITS Partnership. Distributed by King Features Syndicate
SCOTT and BORGMAN

April 10, 2005

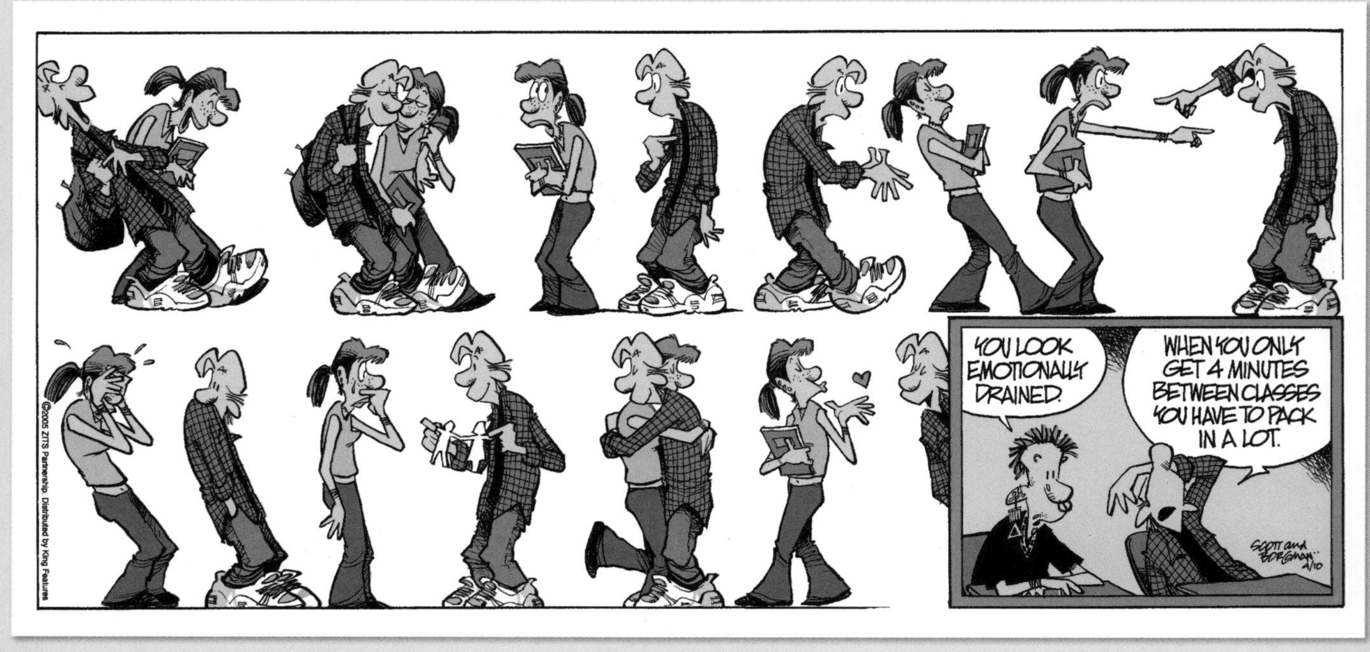
YOU LOOK EMOTIONALLY DRAINED.
WHEN YOU ONLY GET 4 MINUTES BETWEEN CLASSES YOU HAVE TO PACK IN A LOT.
©2005 ZITS Partnership. Distributed by King Features
SCOTT and BORGMAN

April 20, 2005

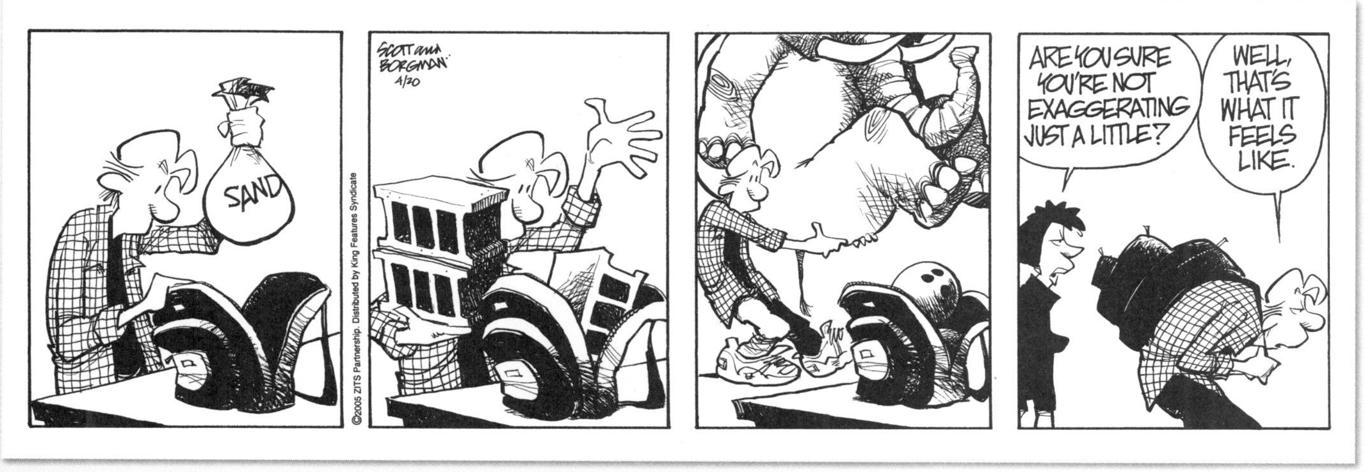
SAND
SCOTT and BORGMAN 4/20
©2005 ZITS Partnership. Distributed by King Features Syndicate
ARE YOU SURE YOU'RE NOT EXAGGERATING JUST A LITTLE?
WELL, THAT'S WHAT IT FEELS LIKE.

April 27, 2005

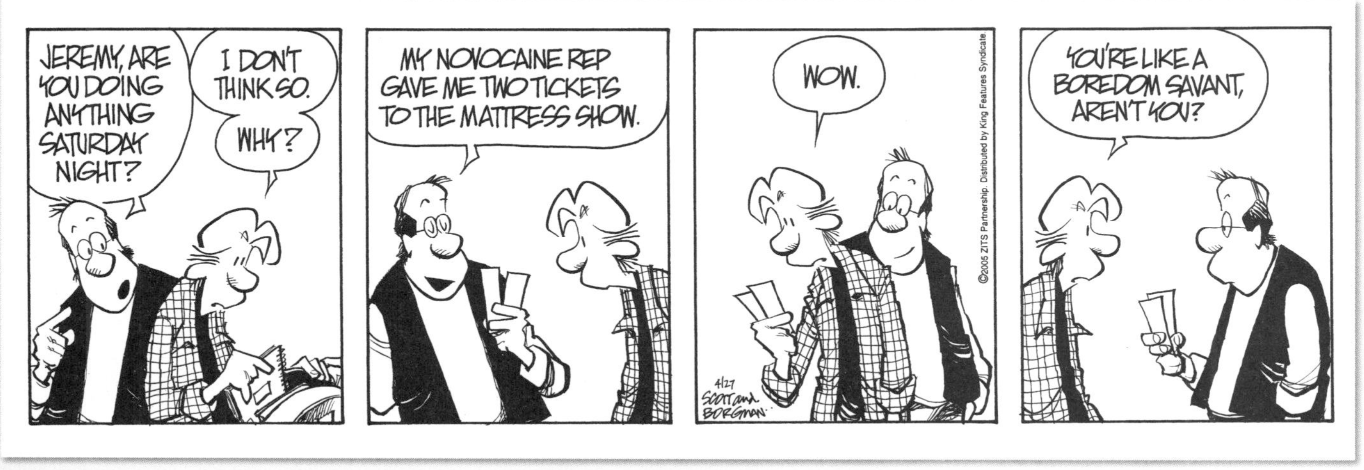
JEREMY, ARE YOU DOING ANYTHING SATURDAY NIGHT?
I DON'T THINK SO.
WHY?
MY NOVOCAINE REP GAVE ME TWO TICKETS TO THE MATTRESS SHOW.
WOW.
©2005 ZITS Partnership. Distributed by King Features Syndicate
4/27 SCOTT and BORGMAN
YOU'RE LIKE A BOREDOM SAVANT, AREN'T YOU?

April 28, 2005

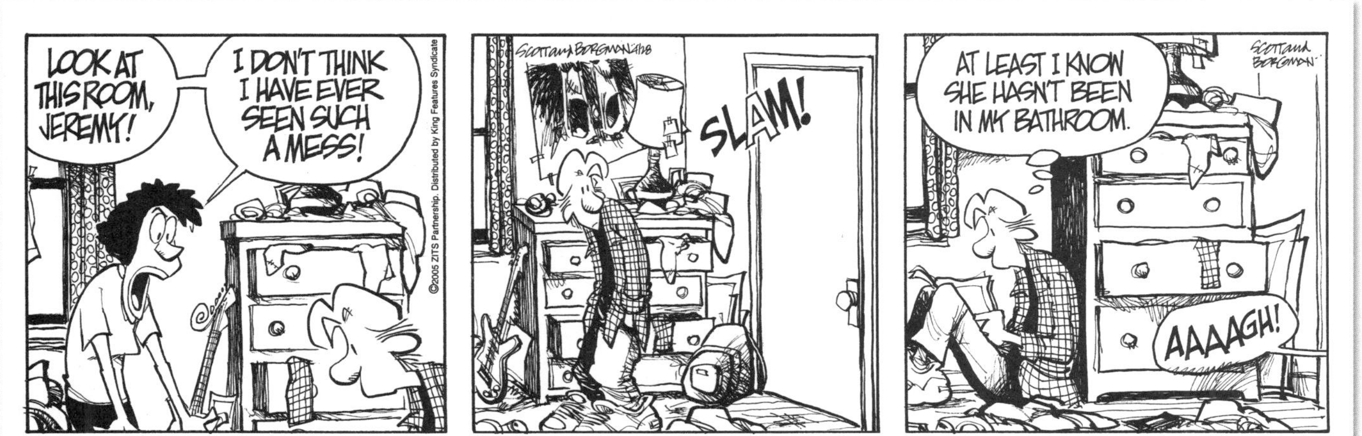
LOOK AT THIS ROOM, JEREMY!
I DON'T THINK I HAVE EVER SEEN SUCH A MESS!
©2005 ZITS Partnership. Distributed by King Features Syndicate
SCOTT and BORGMAN 4/28
SLAM!
AT LEAST I KNOW SHE HASN'T BEEN IN MY BATHROOM.
SCOTT and BORGMAN
AAAAGH!

April 30, 2005

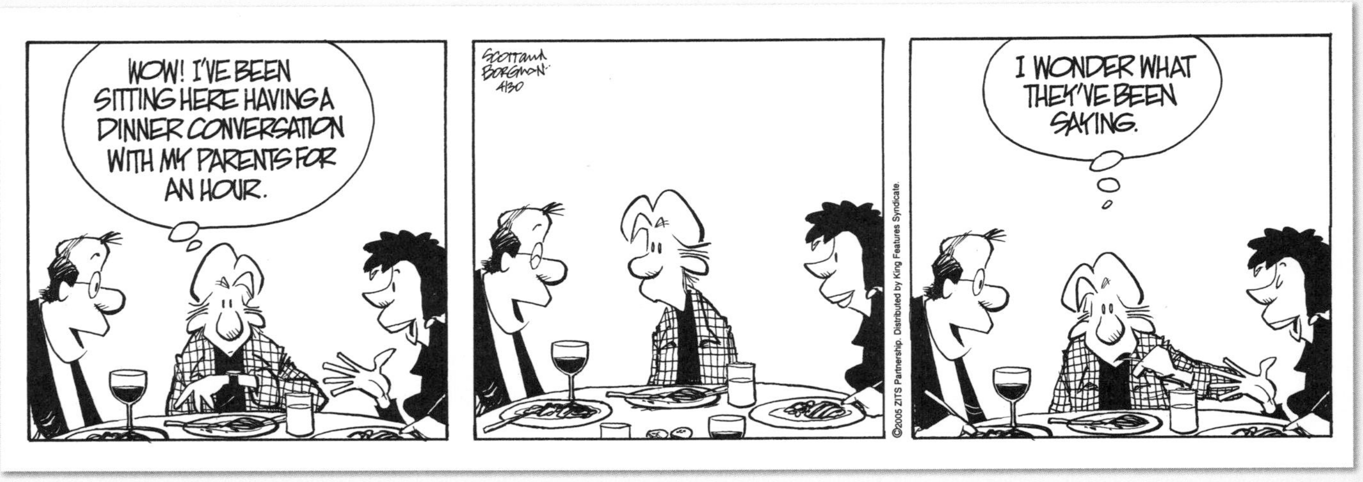
WOW! I'VE BEEN SITTING HERE HAVING A DINNER CONVERSATION WITH MY PARENTS FOR AN HOUR.
I WONDER WHAT THEY'VE BEEN SAYING.
©2005 ZITS Partnership. Distributed by King Features Syndicate.

July 18, 2005

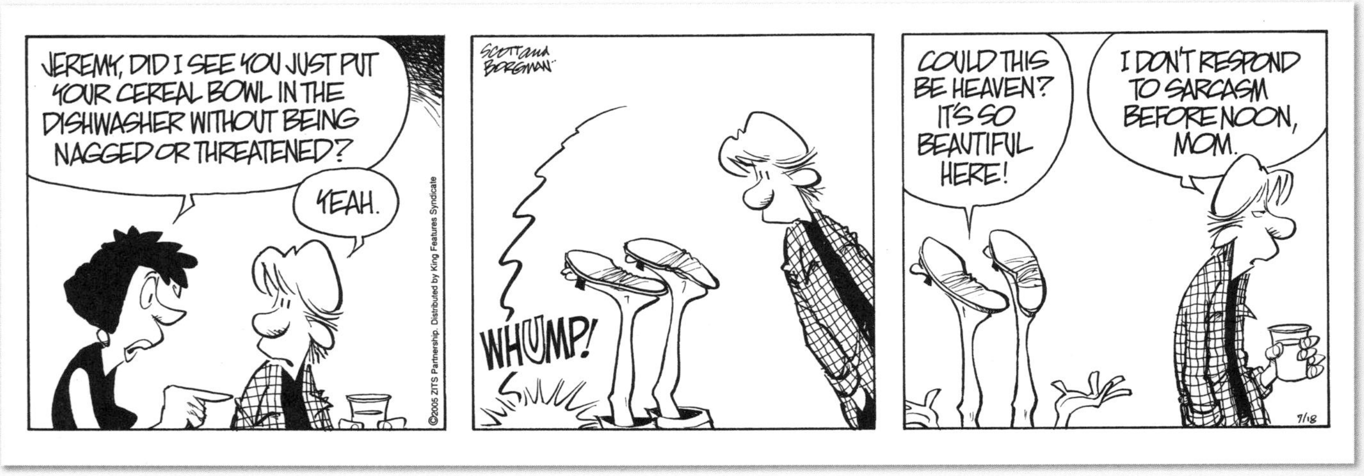
JEREMY, DID I SEE YOU JUST PUT YOUR CEREAL BOWL IN THE DISHWASHER WITHOUT BEING NAGGED OR THREATENED?
YEAH.
©2005 ZITS Partnership. Distributed by King Features Syndicate
WHUMP!
COULD THIS BE HEAVEN? IT'S SO BEAUTIFUL HERE!
I DON'T RESPOND TO SARCASM BEFORE NOON, MOM.

August 1, 2005

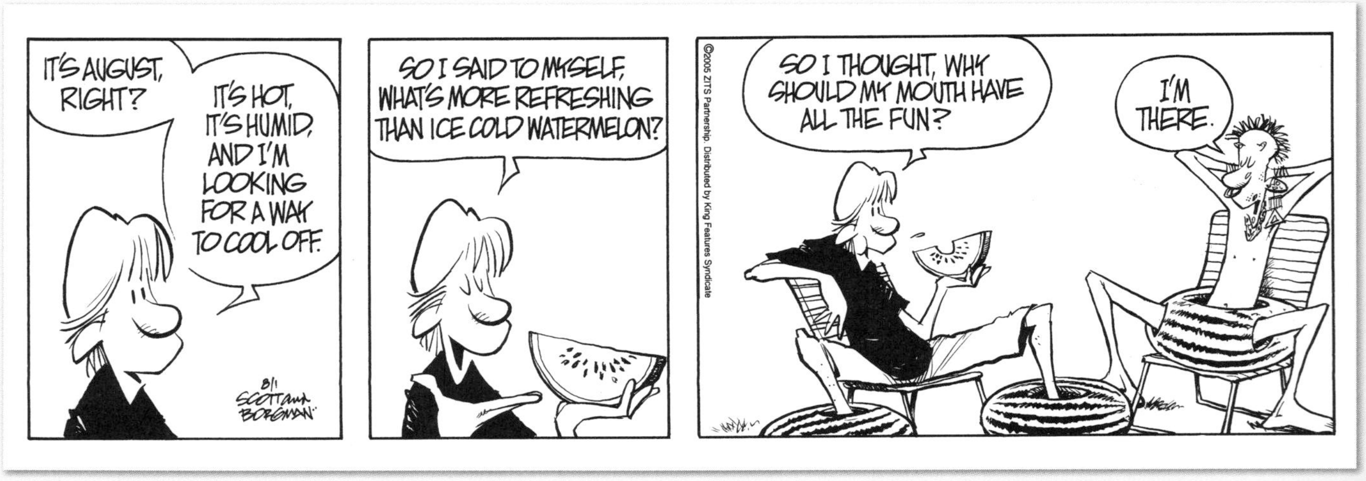
IT'S AUGUST, RIGHT?
IT'S HOT, IT'S HUMID, AND I'M LOOKING FOR A WAY TO COOL OFF.
SO I SAID TO MYSELF, WHAT'S MORE REFRESHING THAN ICE COLD WATERMELON?
©2005 ZITS Partnership. Distributed by King Features Syndicate
SO I THOUGHT, WHY SHOULD MY MOUTH HAVE ALL THE FUN?
I'M THERE.

June 5, 2005

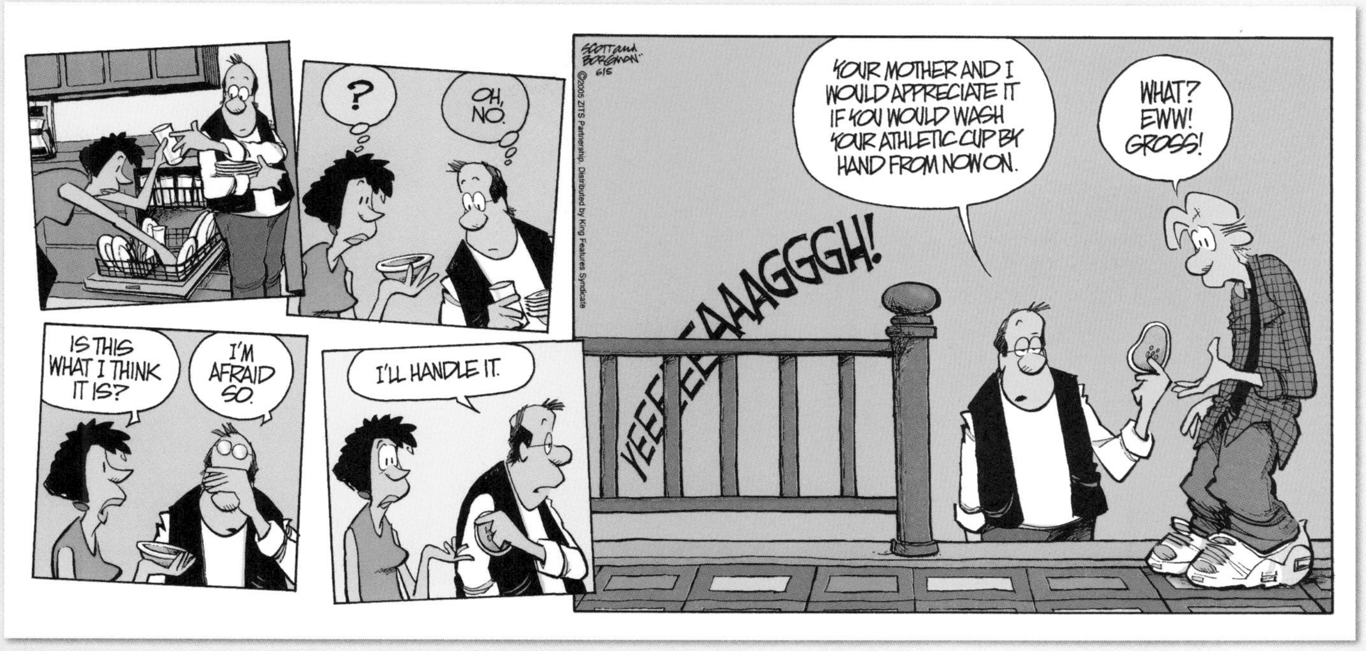
?
OH, NO.
IS THIS WHAT I THINK IT IS?
I'M AFRAID SO.
I'LL HANDLE IT.
YEEEEEEAAAGGGH!
YOUR MOTHER AND I WOULD APPRECIATE IT IF YOU WOULD WASH YOUR ATHLETIC CUP BY HAND FROM NOW ON.
WHAT? EWW! GROSS!
SCOTT and BORGMAN 6/5
©2005 ZITS Partnership. Distributed by King Features Syndicate

July 3, 2005

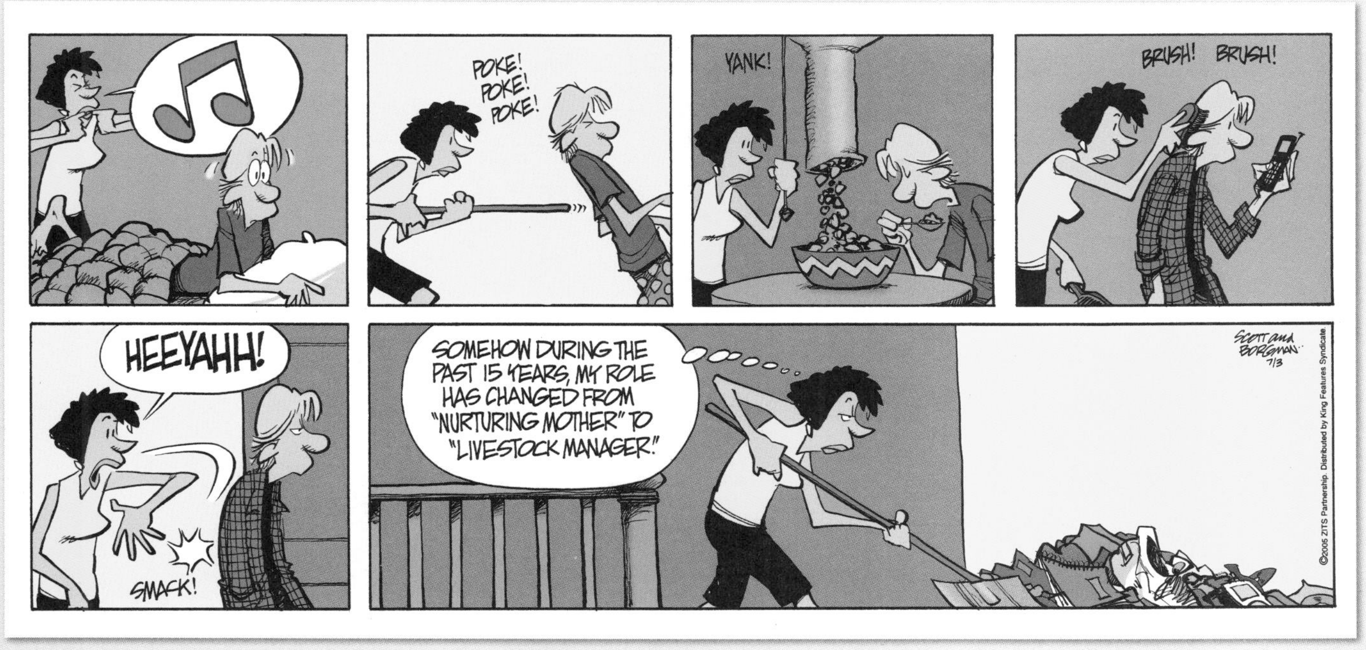
POKE! POKE! POKE!
YANK!
BRUSH! BRUSH!
HEEYAHH!
SMACK!
SOMEHOW DURING THE PAST 15 YEARS, MY ROLE HAS CHANGED FROM "NURTURING MOTHER" TO "LIVESTOCK MANAGER."
SCOTT and BORGMAN 7/3
©2005 ZITS Partnership. Distributed by King Features Syndicate

August 9, 2005

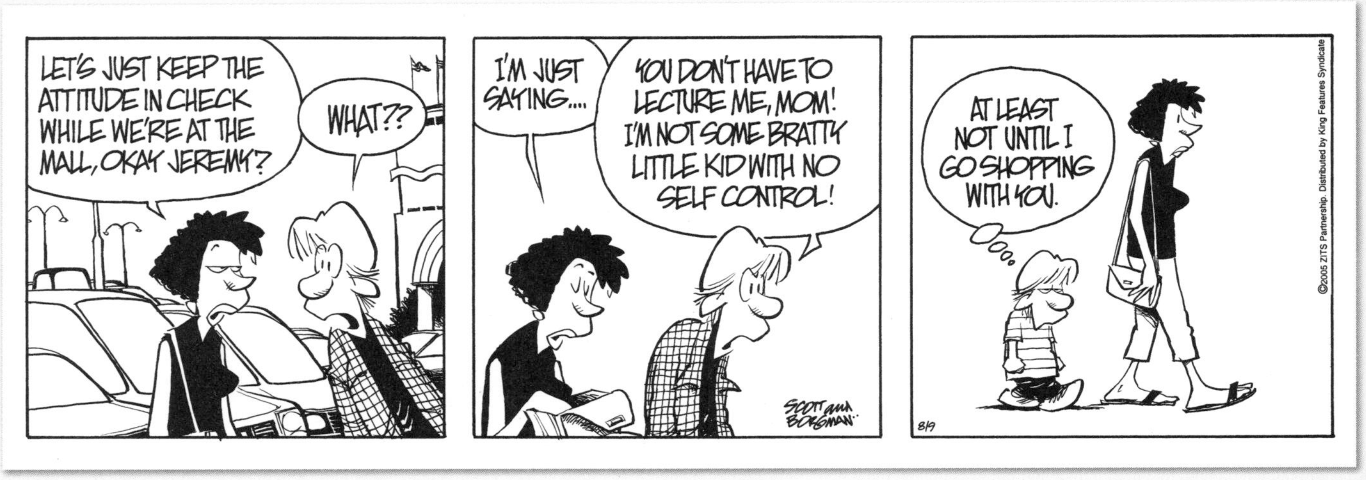
LET'S JUST KEEP THE ATTITUDE IN CHECK WHILE WE'RE AT THE MALL, OKAY JEREMY?
WHAT??
I'M JUST SAYING....
YOU DON'T HAVE TO LECTURE ME, MOM! I'M NOT SOME BRATTY LITTLE KID WITH NO SELF CONTROL!
AT LEAST NOT UNTIL I GO SHOPPING WITH YOU.
©2005 ZITS Partnership. Distributed by King Features Syndicate
SCOTT and BORGMAN
8/9

August 13, 2005

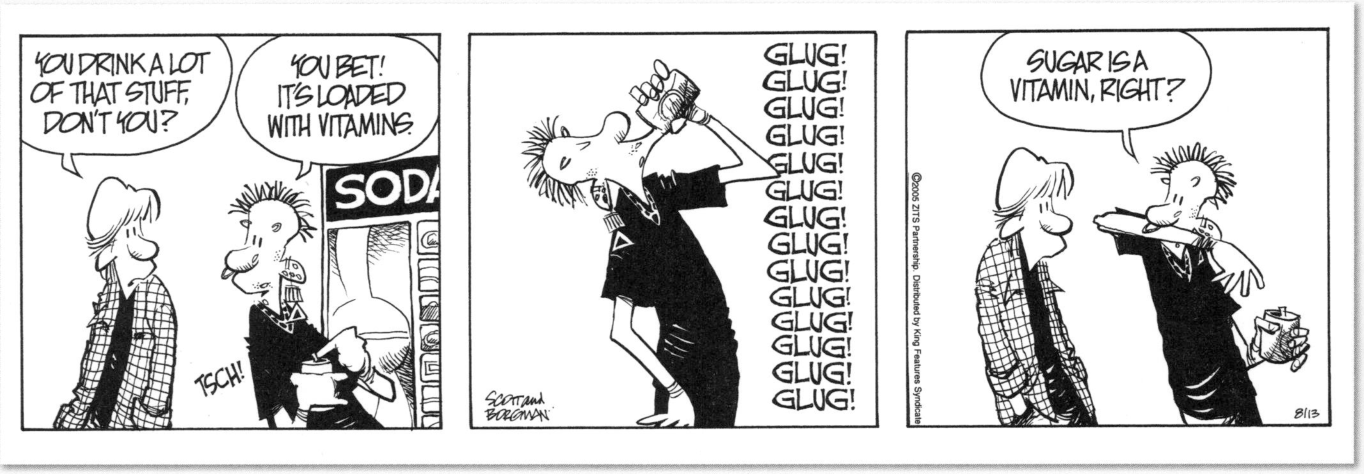
YOU DRINK A LOT OF THAT STUFF, DON'T YOU?
YOU BET! IT'S LOADED WITH VITAMINS.
SODA
TSCH!
GLUG! GLUG! GLUG! GLUG! GLUG! GLUG! GLUG! GLUG! GLUG! GLUG! GLUG! GLUG! GLUG! GLUG!
SUGAR IS A VITAMIN, RIGHT?
©2005 ZITS Partnership. Distributed by King Features Syndicate
SCOTT and BORGMAN
8/13

August 30, 2005

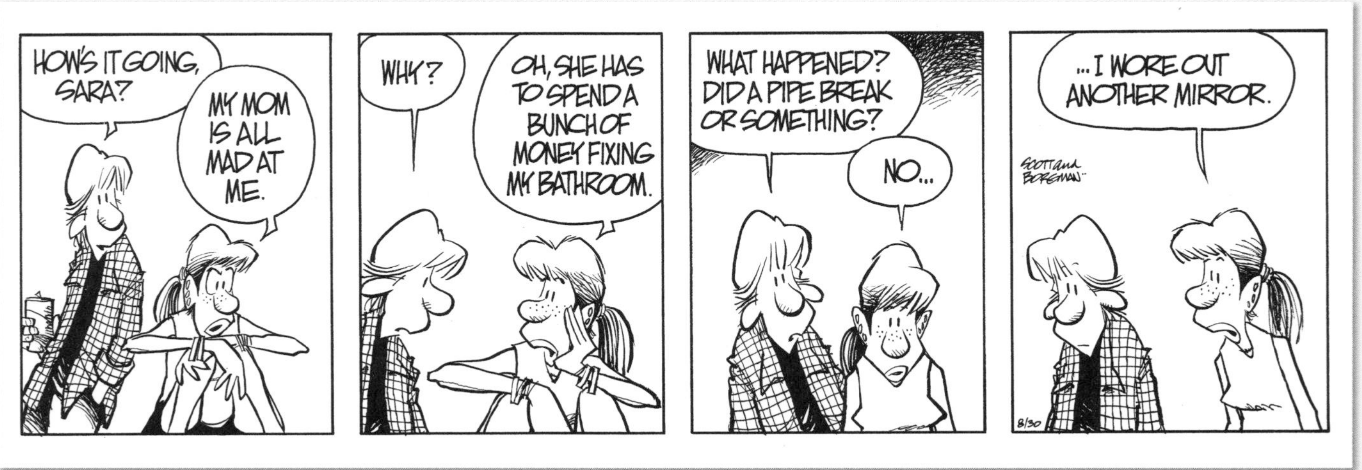
HOW'S IT GOING, SARA?
MY MOM IS ALL MAD AT ME.
WHY?
OH, SHE HAS TO SPEND A BUNCH OF MONEY FIXING MY BATHROOM.
WHAT HAPPENED? DID A PIPE BREAK OR SOMETHING?
NO...
...I WORE OUT ANOTHER MIRROR.
SCOTT and BORGMAN
8/30

August 28, 2005

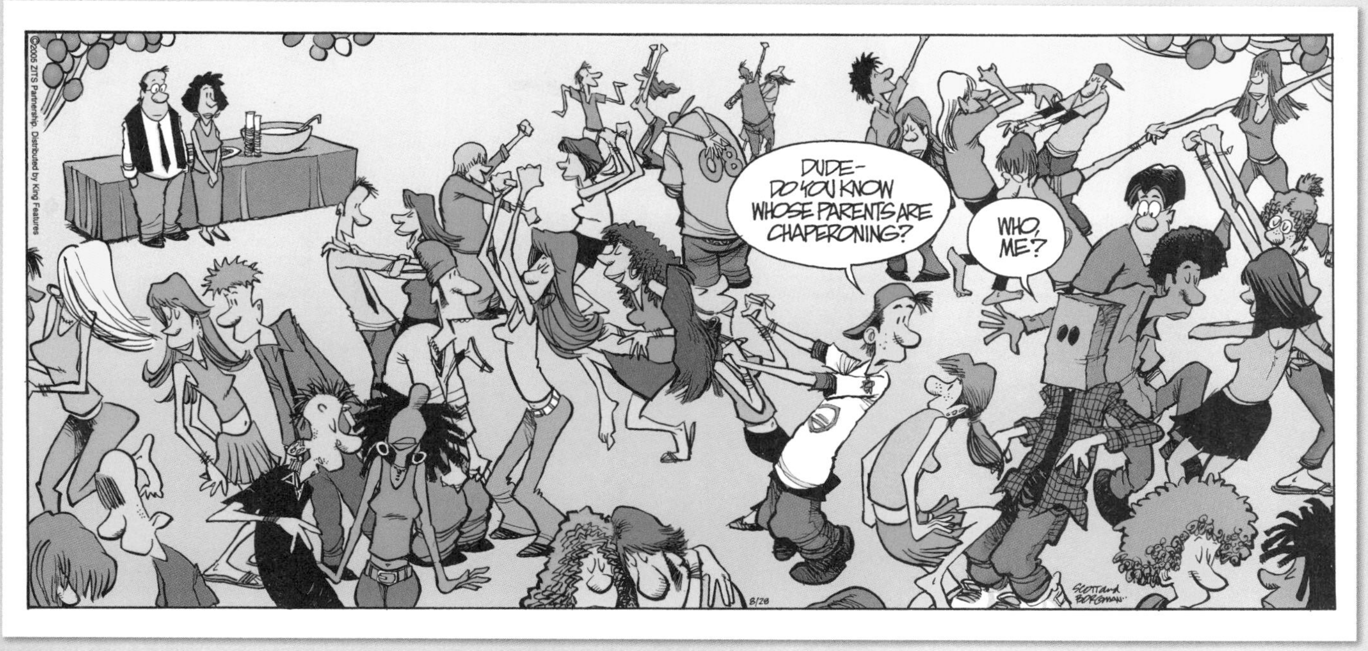
©2005 ZITS Partnership. Distributed by King Features
DUDE- DO YOU KNOW WHOSE PARENTS ARE CHAPERONING?
WHO, ME?
8/28
SCOTT and BORGMAN

October 30, 2005

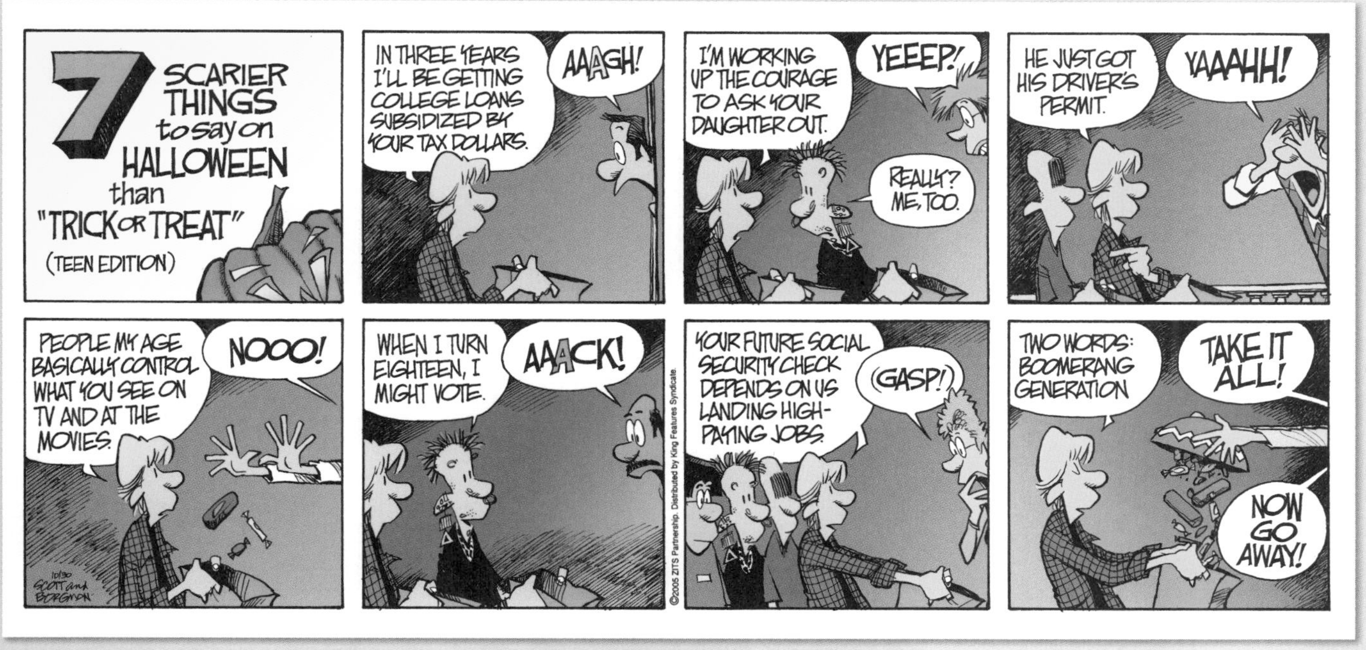
7 SCARIER THINGS to say on HALLOWEEN than "TRICK OR TREAT" (TEEN EDITION)
IN THREE YEARS I'LL BE GETTING COLLEGE LOANS SUBSIDIZED BY YOUR TAX DOLLARS.
AAAGH!
I'M WORKING UP THE COURAGE TO ASK YOUR DAUGHTER OUT.
YEEEP!
REALLY? ME, TOO.
HE JUST GOT HIS DRIVER'S PERMIT.
YAAAHH!
PEOPLE MY AGE BASICALLY CONTROL WHAT YOU SEE ON TV AND AT THE MOVIES.
NOOO!
10/30 SCOTT and BORGMAN
WHEN I TURN EIGHTEEN, I MIGHT VOTE.
AAACK!
©2005 ZITS Partnership. Distributed by King Features Syndicate.
YOUR FUTURE SOCIAL SECURITY CHECK DEPENDS ON US LANDING HIGH-PAYING JOBS.
(GASP!)
TWO WORDS: BOOMERANG GENERATION
TAKE IT ALL!
NOW GO AWAY!

September 3, 2005

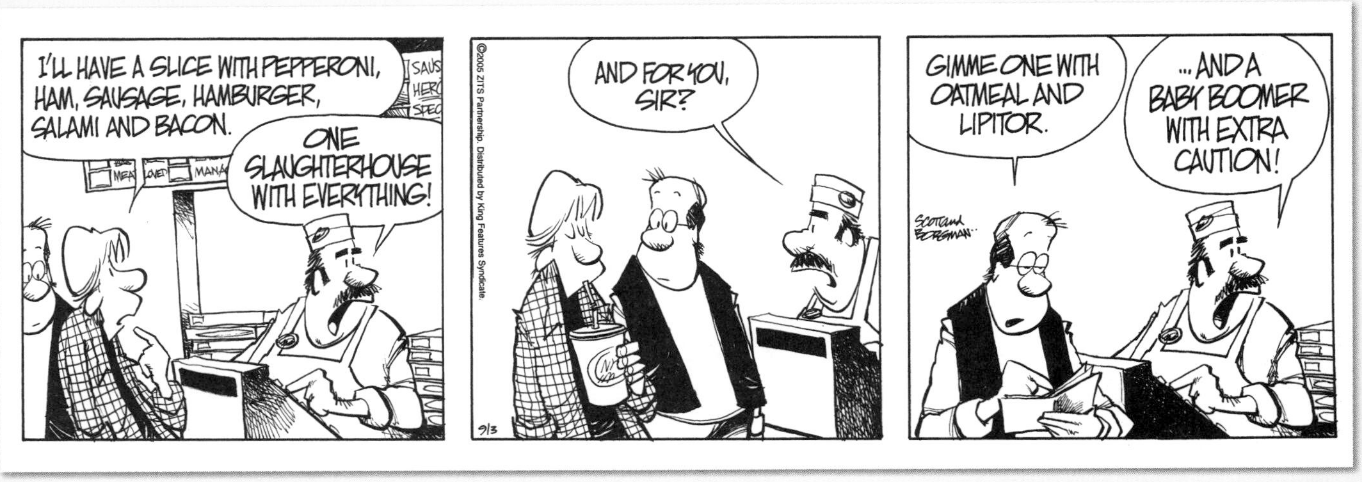
I'LL HAVE A SLICE WITH PEPPERONI, HAM, SAUSAGE, HAMBURGER, SALAMI AND BACON.
ONE SLAUGHTERHOUSE WITH EVERYTHING!
©2005 ZITS Partnership. Distributed by King Features Syndicate
AND FOR YOU, SIR?
GIMME ONE WITH OATMEAL AND LIPITOR.
...AND A BABY BOOMER WITH EXTRA CAUTION!
SCOTT and BORGMAN

September 6, 2005

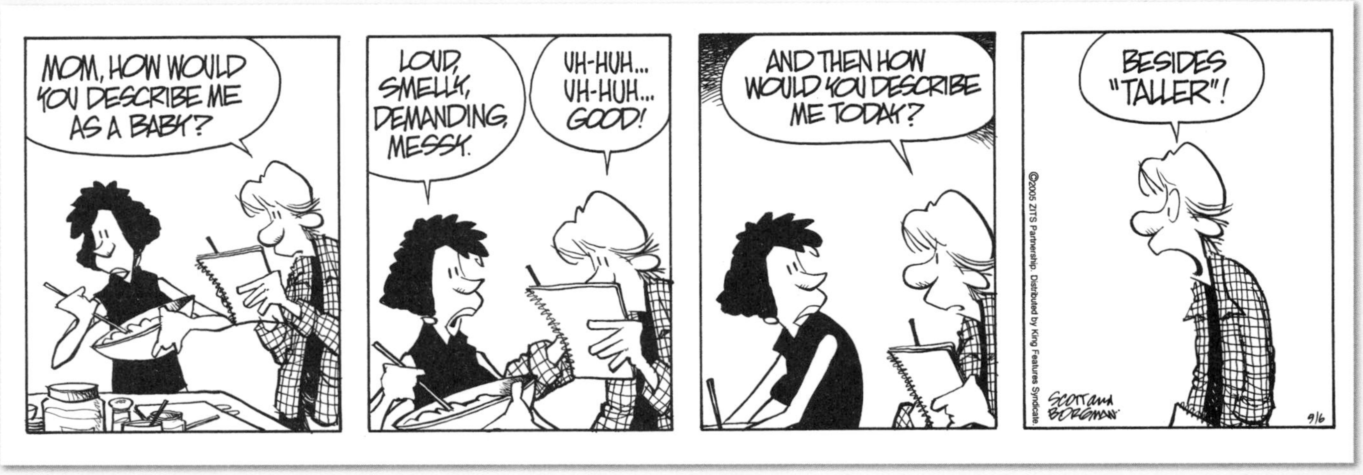
MOM, HOW WOULD YOU DESCRIBE ME AS A BABY?
LOUD, SMELLY, DEMANDING, MESSY.
UH-HUH... UH-HUH... GOOD!
AND THEN HOW WOULD YOU DESCRIBE ME TODAY?
SCOTT and BORGMAN
©2005 ZITS Partnership. Distributed by King Features Syndicate
BESIDES "TALLER"!

October 31, 2005

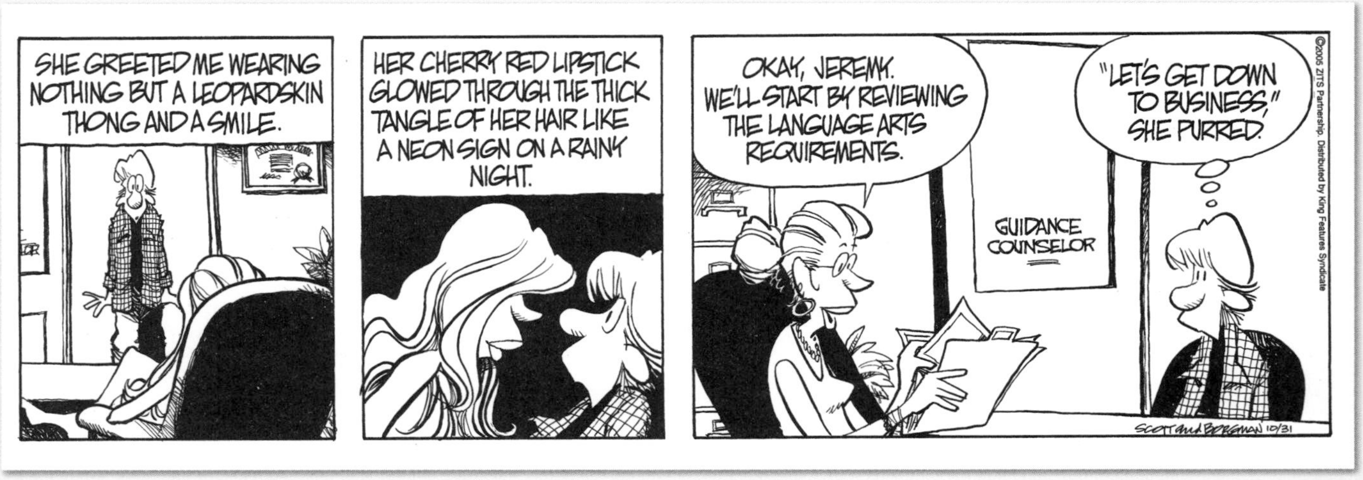
SHE GREETED ME WEARING NOTHING BUT A LEOPARDSKIN THONG AND A SMILE.
HER CHERRY RED LIPSTICK GLOWED THROUGH THE THICK TANGLE OF HER HAIR LIKE A NEON SIGN ON A RAINY NIGHT.
OKAY, JEREMY. WE'LL START BY REVIEWING THE LANGUAGE ARTS REQUIREMENTS.
GUIDANCE COUNSELOR
"LET'S GET DOWN TO BUSINESS," SHE PURRED.
©2005 ZITS Partnership. Distributed by King Features Syndicate
SCOTT and BORGMAN

November 29, 2005

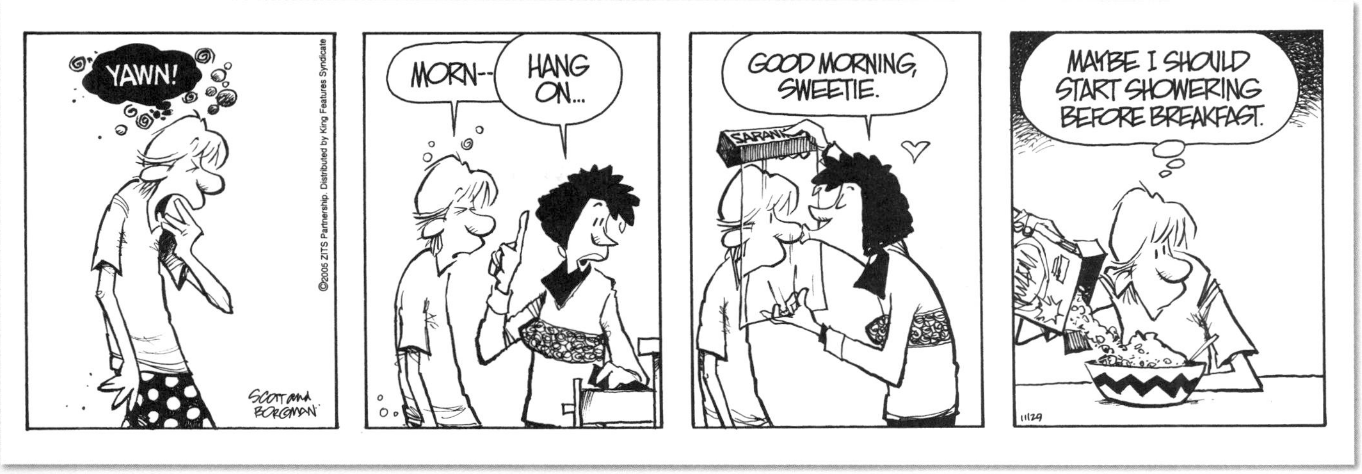
YAWN!
©2005 ZITS Partnership. Distributed by King Features Syndicate
MORN--
HANG ON...
GOOD MORNING, SWEETIE.
MAYBE I SHOULD START SHOWERING BEFORE BREAKFAST.

December 7, 2005

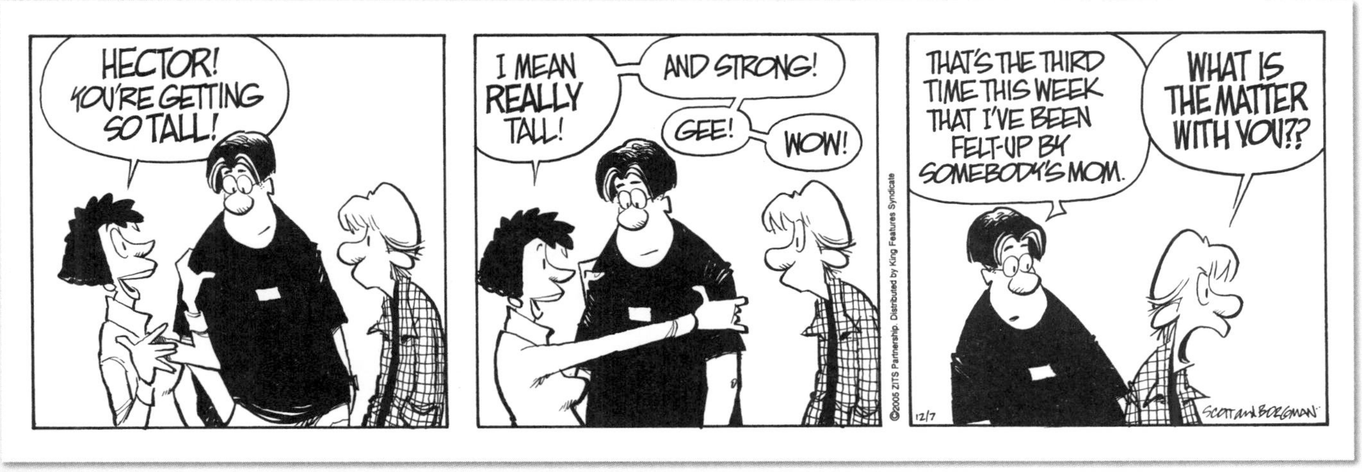
HECTOR! YOU'RE GETTING SO TALL!
I MEAN REALLY TALL!
AND STRONG!
GEE!
WOW!
©2005 ZITS Partnership. Distributed by King Features Syndicate
THAT'S THE THIRD TIME THIS WEEK THAT I'VE BEEN FELT-UP BY SOMEBODY'S MOM.
WHAT IS THE MATTER WITH YOU??

December 12, 2005

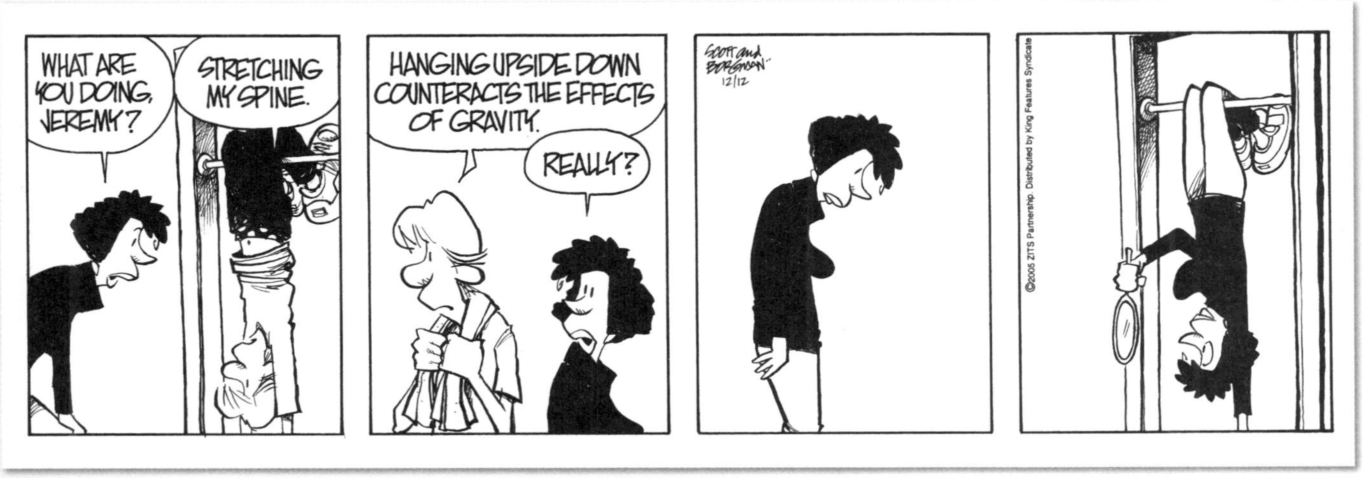
WHAT ARE YOU DOING, JEREMY?
STRETCHING MY SPINE.
HANGING UPSIDE DOWN COUNTERACTS THE EFFECTS OF GRAVITY.
REALLY?
©2005 ZITS Partnership. Distributed by King Features Syndicate

CAROL and the MONKEES

Jim Borgman

The hardest part about moving to a new neighborhood when I was in seventh grade was finding my place in a new group of kids. By the time I worked up the courage to join their game of kick the can, identities had long ago been assigned among them: Mike and Johnny were the athletes, Wayne was the comedian, Joe knew cars, Steve had a swimming pool, and Larry could talk to girls. The only thing that distinguished me was that I had outlined my sixth-grade history textbook the summer after fifth grade, and that wasn't going to help me make friends or meet girls, that was for sure.

Besides, everyone in the new neighborhood went to St. Dominic School, and my parents had worked it out that I would continue on at my old school. I didn't understand any of these guys' references to crazy teachers, the creepy school janitor, or skanky girls in class. Their jokes were codes from childhood that I couldn't crack. I was doomed to a life on the periphery of the group until I could find my hook.

One afternoon Wayne was telling a story about a classmate who threw a cheese sandwich at another kid in the cafeteria at lunchtime. I started idly drawing the scene in a notebook, but in my version a full-scale riot proceeded to break out, and a SWAT team dropped out of helicopters to break it up. Wayne looked at it and sort of guffawed, so I drew airplanes strafing the schoolyard with Cheez Whiz and then a giant nun swatting the planes out of the sky like King Kong. Now all the guys were crowding around, and I drew panel after panel using the kids' names I'd heard them mention from their school, all screaming, farting, bursting into flames. They wouldn't let me stop.

I'd found my place. I was the kid who could draw.

Wayne's sister Carol was boy crazy and would flirt with us until he chased her away. I was Carol crazy and looked for any opportunity to catch a glimpse of her. She had chestnut hair, freckles, and a sexy overbite that said, "Come hither." Or maybe she was saying "corn fritter"; I couldn't really tell with the braces. The buttons of her white blouse starred nightly in my dreams. I was smitten. During that summer between seventh and eighth grade, I struggled to distinguish myself from the pack in her eyes.

One day she let it drop that she had a crush on Davy Jones of The Monkees.

The Monkees were a made-for-TV band cynically concocted to take advantage of the spillover hormones from Beatlemania. There was Micky Dolenz, the zany drummer; Peter Tork, the lovable clown; Mike Nesmith, the cerebral one with the hat; and Davy Jones, the dreamy lead singer with the British accent and perfect hair. I knew all of this because my older sisters subscribed to *16* magazine, and The Monkees soaked up all the ink between its covers.

One night I slipped a few of the magazines out of my sisters' room, locked my bedroom door, and spread them out on my desk. Working from a swoony centerfold of Davy Jones, I began making a pencil portrait, complete with shadows and highlights and all the artistic flourishes that drive girls crazy. It was a risky jiujitsu move, using the force of my opponent's charm to propel Carol into my arms. By midnight the drawing was finished, and I tucked it into the back of my three-ring binder and waited for the right moment.

Carol and her friends hung out every afternoon on the Sparks' lawn at the end of Sunburst Lane. I could spy the cluster from my bedroom window and watched one day until a few girls said goodbye and peeled away. Hurrying down to the spot with my binder, I caught up to Carol just as she was the last to leave.

"Hey," I said.

"Hey," she smiled. She crinkled her nose, and I almost fainted.

"I heard you say once that you like The Monkees," I said. "I had this drawing lying around that I thought you might, you know, like to have 'cause I don't need it or anything." I handed it to her.

Carol looked at the drawing. For a while she had no reaction as she studied it. My heart fluttered, shuddered, sank, crashed, burned to ashes, blew away in the wind, was inhaled by demons who excreted—

"IT'S DAVY JONES! I LOVE THIS! WHERE DID YOU GET IT?" she shrieked.

"I drew it," I said. "I draw The Monkees all the time. It's no big deal."

"Can I keep it?" she asked, holding it to her chest and jumping up and down.

"Sure," I shrugged. "I mean, it's for you."

That autumn I spent every night drawing The Monkees. Sometimes it was Davy Jones, of course, gazing romantically from a field of sunflowers or gooning with the other Monkees in cowboy hats. But other nights I drew Micky playing drums, Peter wearing love beads, or, once, an ambitious pose featuring the whole band in paisley shirts and bell-bottoms. I was training my eye to work with my hand, teaching myself to smudge and smear graphite and lift highlights from eyes with a kneaded eraser. I was learning the joy of drawing late into the night when the house had gone to sleep, with only the AM radio DJ, the chill night air, and the chirping crickets outside my window as companions. But mostly I was winning the heart of Carol, who I would meet the next day at the corner in order to thrill her with my latest gift.

Our romance ended abruptly that winter when her dad got a promotion to branch manager of a men's clothing store and moved the family to a suburb far north of town. When the snows finally melted in April, I packed a lunch and launched out early one Saturday on my bike determined to pedal to her house, all the while negotiating sketchy neighborhoods, roaring highways, and treacherous intersections. By dusk I was out of time and only halfway there. I knew Carol would be crushed. I called to gently tell her the news. Her mom said she was at a dance. My dad picked me up at a Marathon station, annoyed to have been dragged away from a Knights of Columbus meeting, and stuck my bike in the trunk of our LTD.

Before long, word got back to the neighborhood that Carol's dad had been promoted again and moved the family to Indianapolis.

My office phone rang one afternoon at the *Cincinnati Enquirer*. I'd just returned from the conference room where the managing editor had thrown a little bash for those of us celebrating twenty-five years in the newsroom. I'd already finished drawing my cartoon for the day and had sent it off to the syndicate. Setting down my paper plate of cake crumbs, I took the call. The voice was a woman's, her name unfamiliar, probably about my age.

"This is a strange call, I know," she began. "You don't know me, but I live in Delhi."

"My old neighborhood," I said. "What's on your mind?"

"Well, I have this pencil drawing of one of The Monkees, you know, the band—I've had it for ages—that I think you may have drawn. I just came across it in a scrapbook and noticed your signature on it. I know it sounds crazy, but . . . is there any chance you actually drew this?"

I paused, reeling through the years. "Yes," I said. "Yes, I think I probably did. I used to draw The Monkees from photos in my sisters' boy band magazines when I was a teenager. Ha. What do you know. But you and I have never met, and I can't imagine how you would have come to own one of them."

"Oh," she said, "when I went to St. Dominic School, there was a girl who used to sell them on the playground for a quarter."

January 3, 2006

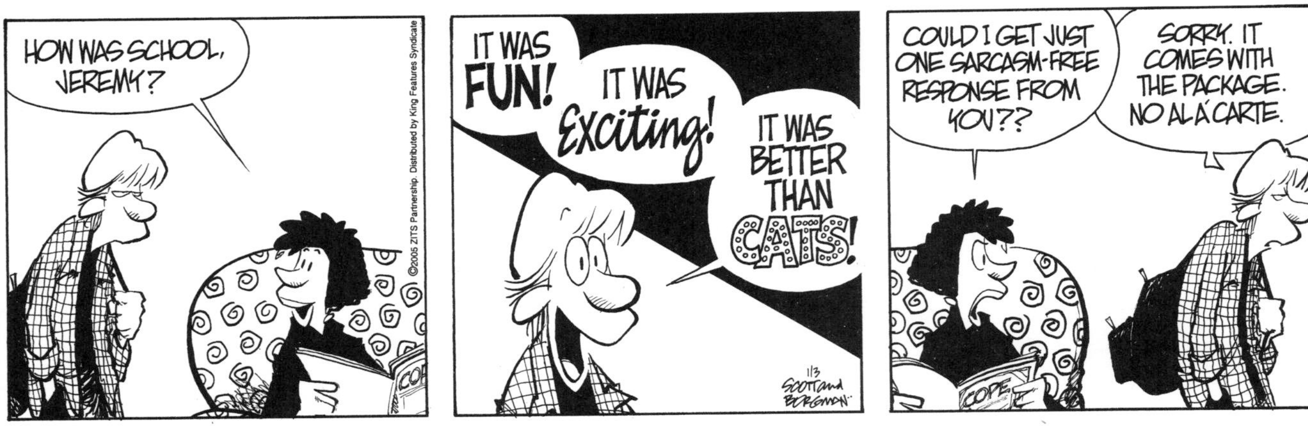
HOW WAS SCHOOL, JEREMY?
©2005 ZITS Partnership. Distributed by King Features Syndicate
IT WAS FUN!
IT WAS Exciting!
IT WAS BETTER THAN CATS!
1/3 SCOTT and BORGMAN
COULD I GET JUST ONE SARCASM-FREE RESPONSE FROM YOU??
SORRY. IT COMES WITH THE PACKAGE. NO AL-A-CARTE.
COPE

February 4, 2006

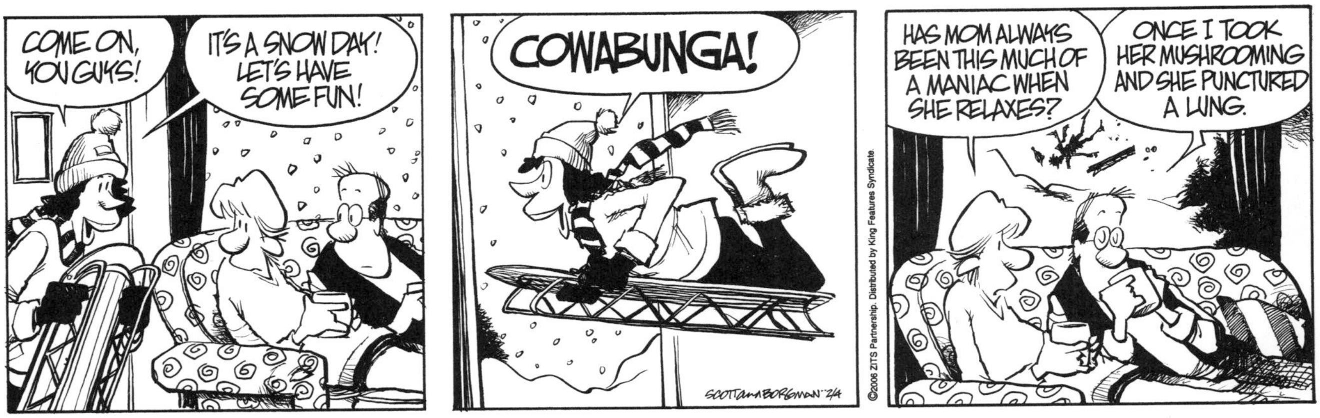
COME ON, YOU GUYS!
IT'S A SNOW DAY! LET'S HAVE SOME FUN!
COWABUNGA!
SCOTT and BORGMAN 2/4
©2006 ZITS Partnership. Distributed by King Features Syndicate.
HAS MOM ALWAYS BEEN THIS MUCH OF A MANIAC WHEN SHE RELAXES?
ONCE I TOOK HER MUSHROOMING AND SHE PUNCTURED A LUNG.

February 6, 2006

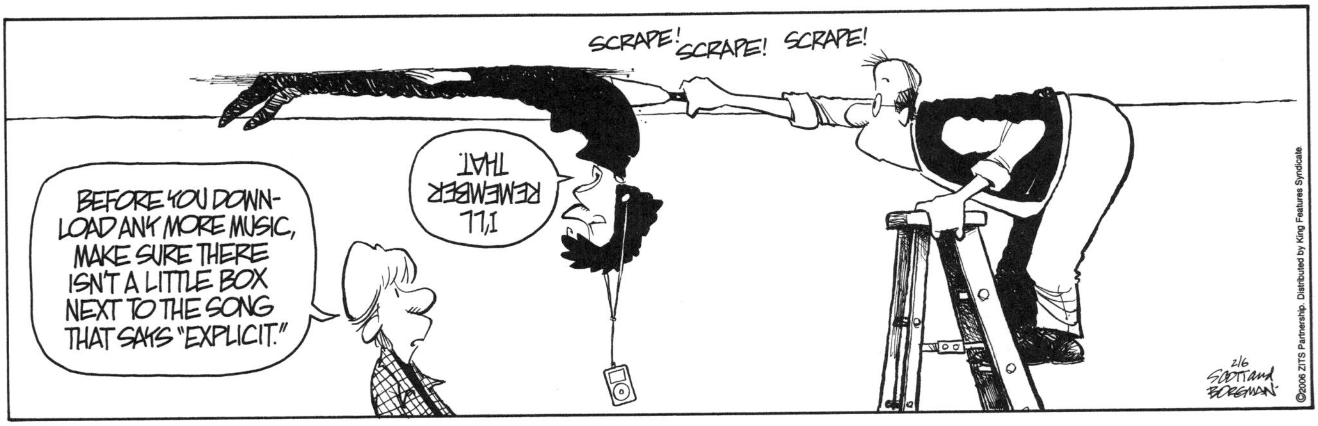
SCRAPE! SCRAPE! SCRAPE! SCRAPE!
I'LL REMEMBER THAT.
BEFORE YOU DOWN-LOAD ANY MORE MUSIC, MAKE SURE THERE ISN'T A LITTLE BOX NEXT TO THE SONG THAT SAYS "EXPLICIT."
2/6 SCOTT and BORGMAN
©2006 ZITS Partnership. Distributed by King Features Syndicate.

February 9, 2006

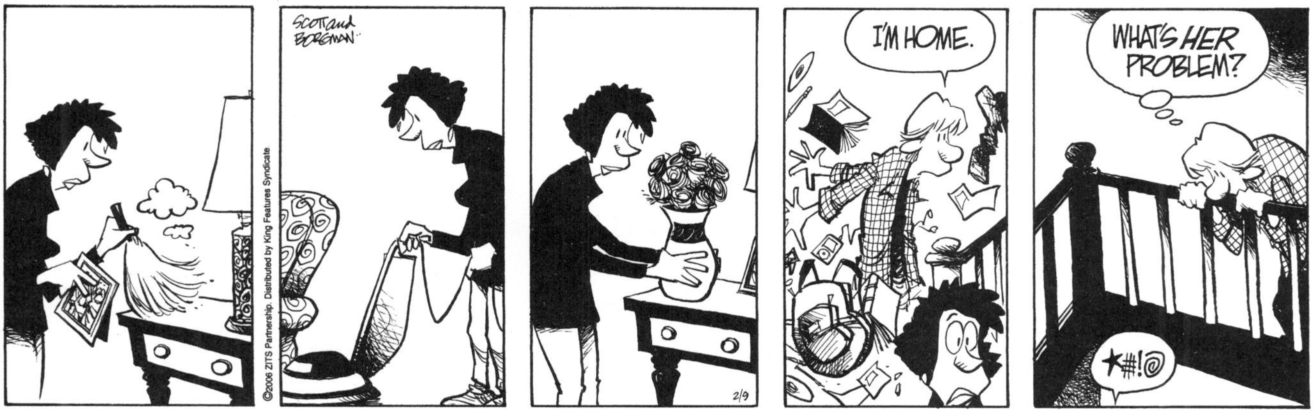
SCOTT and BORGMAN
©2006 ZITS Partnership. Distributed by King Features Syndicate
2/9
I'M HOME.
WHAT'S HER PROBLEM?
*#!@

February 10, 2006

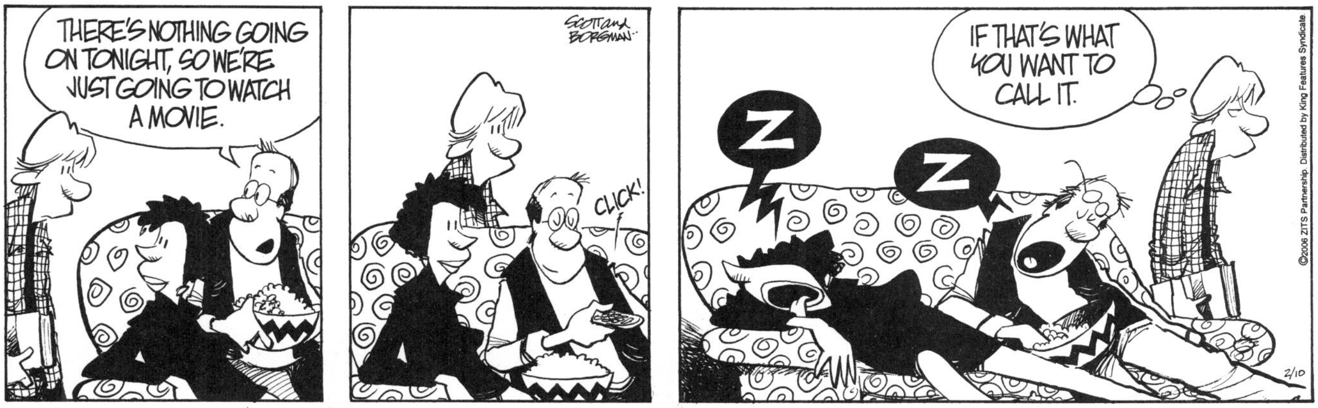
THERE'S NOTHING GOING ON TONIGHT, SO WE'RE JUST GOING TO WATCH A MOVIE.
SCOTT and BORGMAN
CLICK!
Z
Z
IF THAT'S WHAT YOU WANT TO CALL IT.
©2006 ZITS Partnership. Distributed by King Features Syndicate
2/10

February 24, 2006

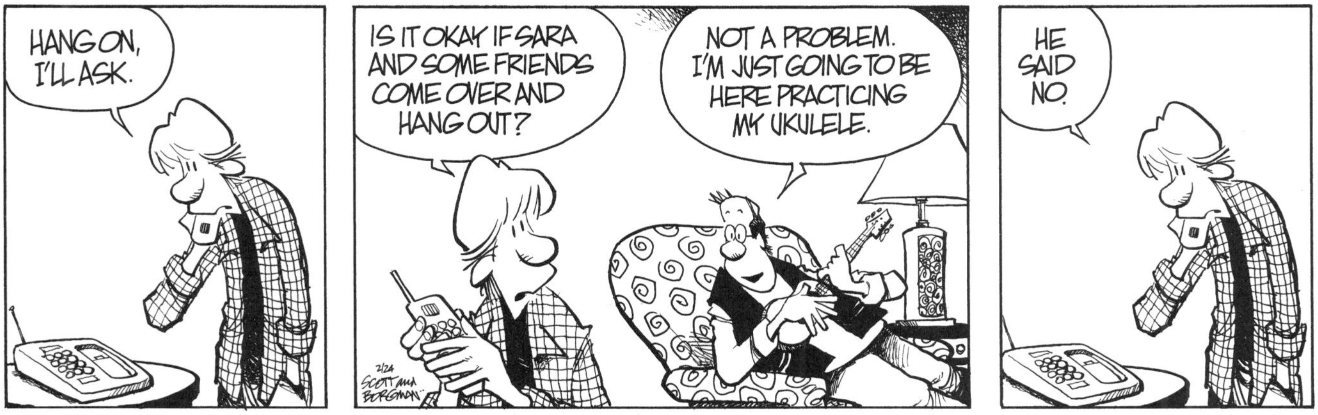
HANG ON, I'LL ASK.
IS IT OKAY IF SARA AND SOME FRIENDS COME OVER AND HANG OUT?
NOT A PROBLEM. I'M JUST GOING TO BE HERE PRACTICING MY UKULELE.
2/24 SCOTT and BORGMAN
HE SAID NO.

February 28, 2006

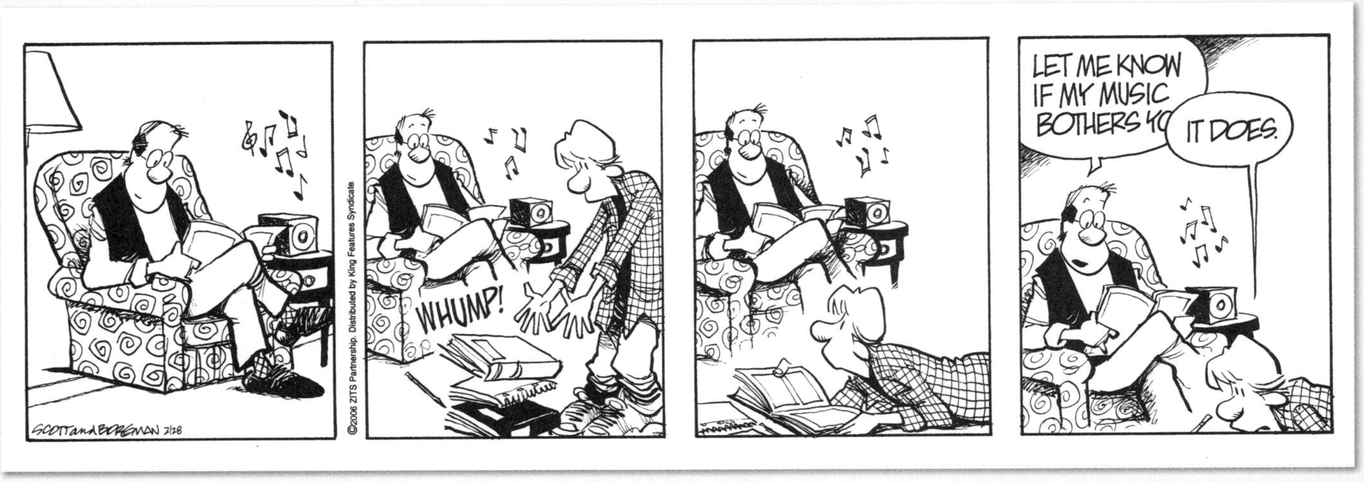

WHUMP!
LET ME KNOW IF MY MUSIC BOTHERS YO
IT DOES.
SCOTT and BORGMAN 2/28
©2006 ZITS Partnership. Distributed by King Features Syndicate

March 13, 2006

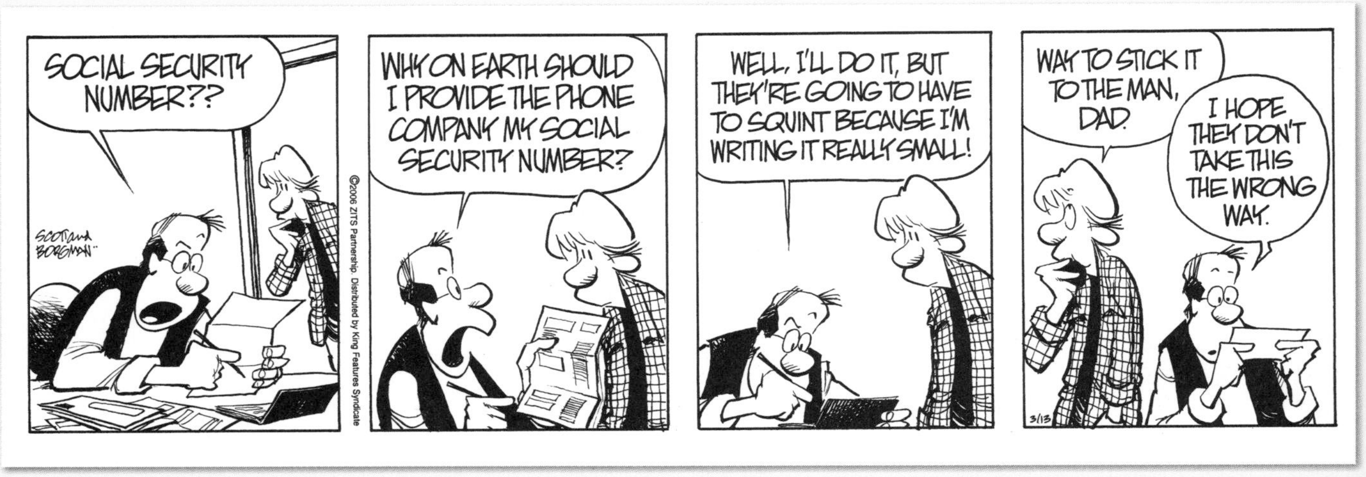

SOCIAL SECURITY NUMBER??
WHY ON EARTH SHOULD I PROVIDE THE PHONE COMPANY MY SOCIAL SECURITY NUMBER?
WELL, I'LL DO IT, BUT THEY'RE GOING TO HAVE TO SQUINT BECAUSE I'M WRITING IT REALLY SMALL!
WAY TO STICK IT TO THE MAN, DAD.
I HOPE THEY DON'T TAKE THIS THE WRONG WAY.
SCOTT and BORGMAN
3/13
©2006 ZITS Partnership. Distributed by King Features Syndicate

April 24, 2006

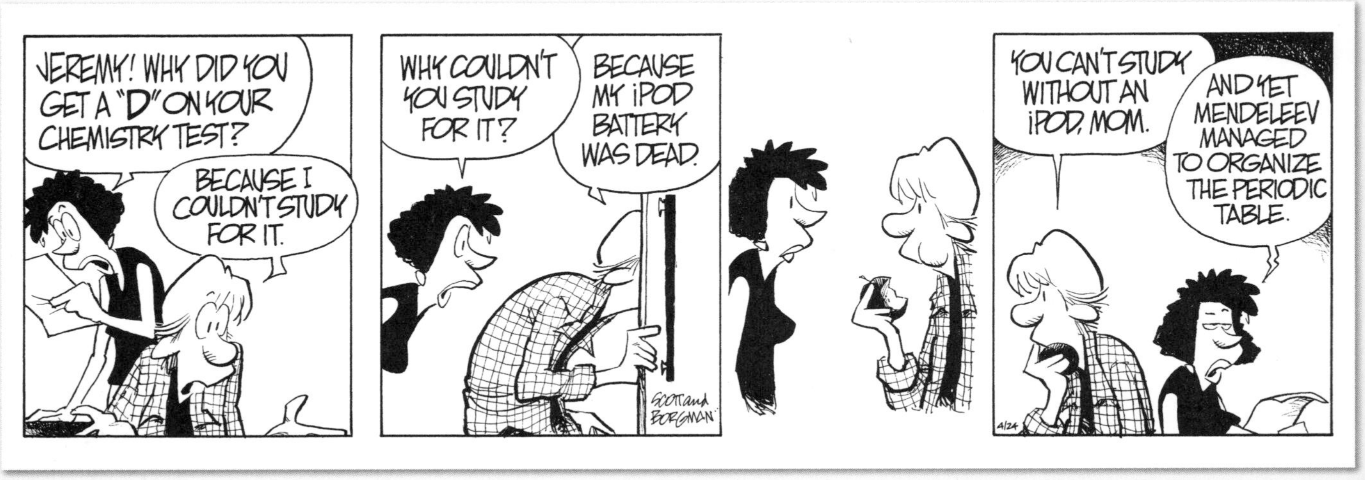

JEREMY! WHY DID YOU GET A "D" ON YOUR CHEMISTRY TEST?
BECAUSE I COULDN'T STUDY FOR IT.
WHY COULDN'T YOU STUDY FOR IT?
BECAUSE MY iPOD BATTERY WAS DEAD.
YOU CAN'T STUDY WITHOUT AN iPOD, MOM.
AND YET MENDELEEV MANAGED TO ORGANIZE THE PERIODIC TABLE.
SCOTT and BORGMAN
4/24

June 13, 2006

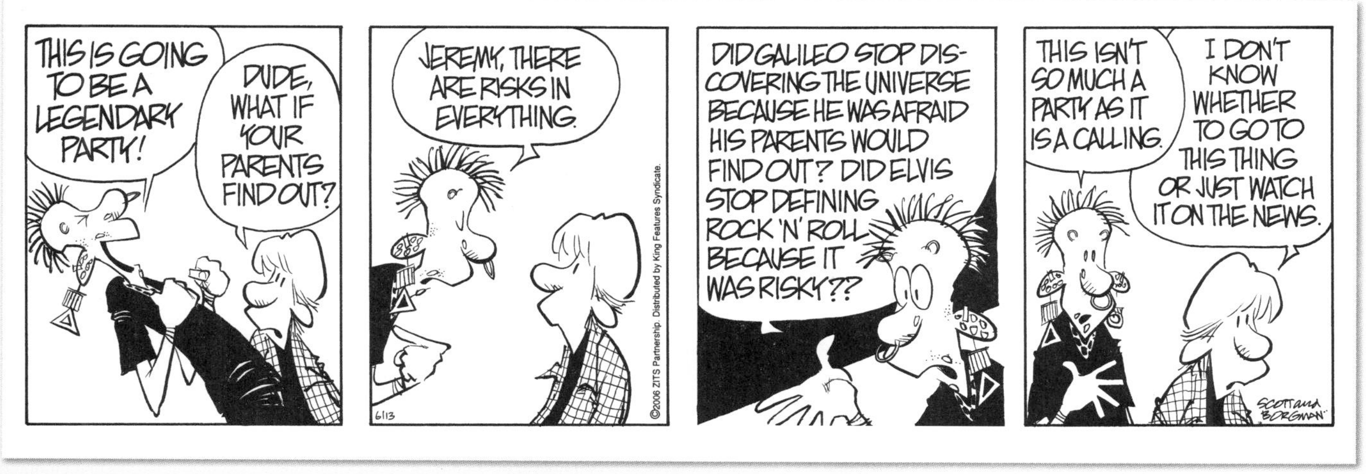

THIS IS GOING TO BE A LEGENDARY PARTY!
DUDE, WHAT IF YOUR PARENTS FIND OUT?
JEREMY, THERE ARE RISKS IN EVERYTHING.
DID GALILEO STOP DISCOVERING THE UNIVERSE BECAUSE HE WAS AFRAID HIS PARENTS WOULD FIND OUT? DID ELVIS STOP DEFINING ROCK 'N' ROLL BECAUSE IT WAS RISKY??
THIS ISN'T SO MUCH A PARTY AS IT IS A CALLING.
I DON'T KNOW WHETHER TO GO TO THIS THING OR JUST WATCH IT ON THE NEWS.
©2006 ZITS Partnership. Distributed by King Features Syndicate.
SCOTT and BORGMAN

June 17, 2006

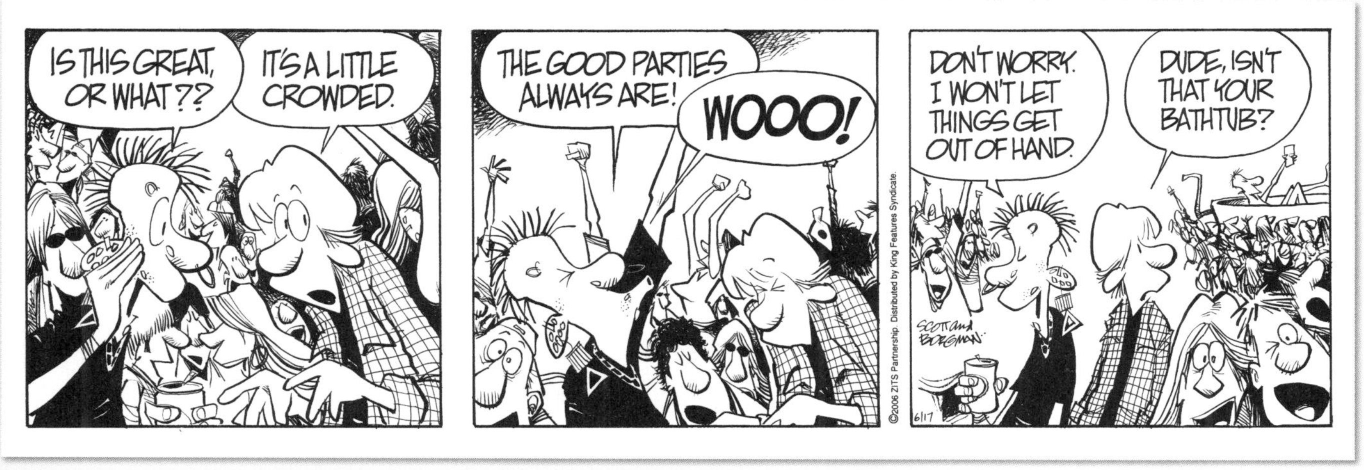

IS THIS GREAT, OR WHAT??
IT'S A LITTLE CROWDED.
THE GOOD PARTIES ALWAYS ARE!
WOOO!
DON'T WORRY. I WON'T LET THINGS GET OUT OF HAND.
DUDE, ISN'T THAT YOUR BATHTUB?
©2006 ZITS Partnership. Distributed by King Features Syndicate.
SCOTT and BORGMAN

June 20, 2006

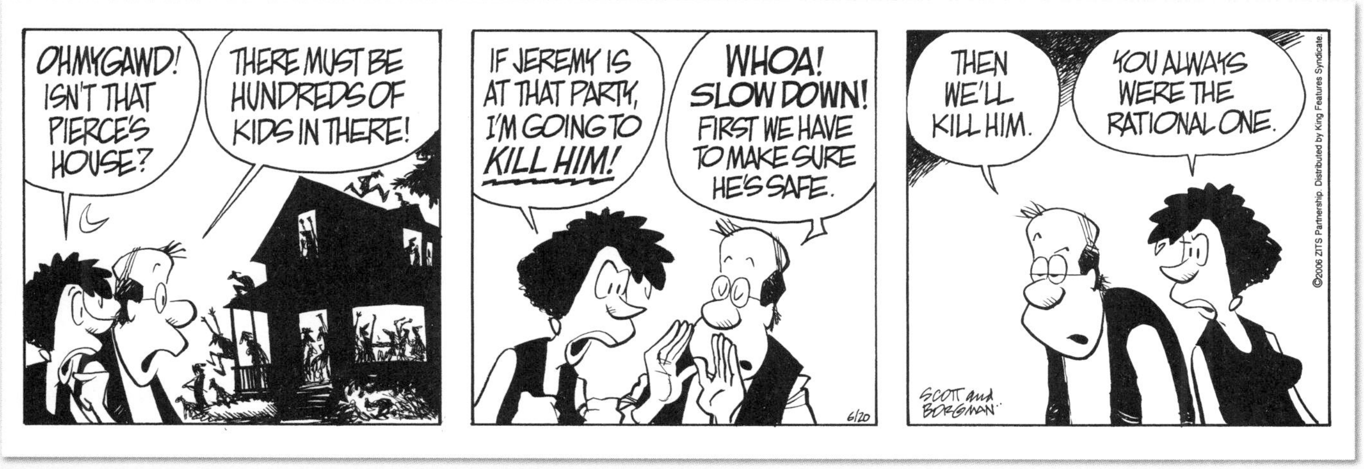

OHMYGAWD! ISN'T THAT PIERCE'S HOUSE?
THERE MUST BE HUNDREDS OF KIDS IN THERE!
IF JEREMY IS AT THAT PARTY, I'M GOING TO KILL HIM!
WHOA! SLOW DOWN! FIRST WE HAVE TO MAKE SURE HE'S SAFE.
THEN WE'LL KILL HIM.
YOU ALWAYS WERE THE RATIONAL ONE.
©2006 ZITS Partnership. Distributed by King Features Syndicate.
SCOTT and BORGMAN

June 23, 2006

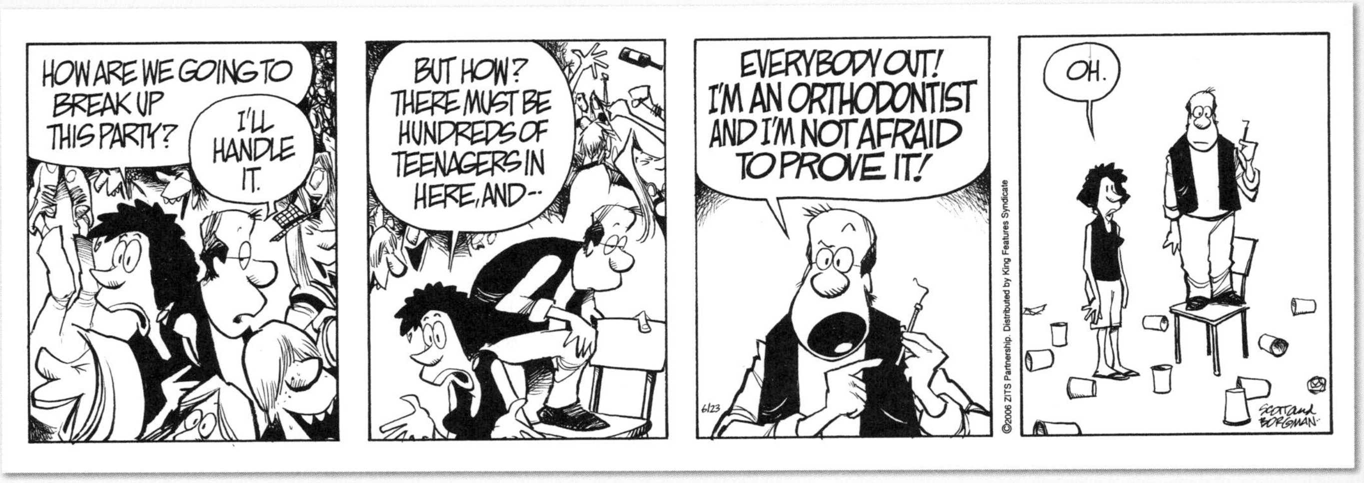

HOW ARE WE GOING TO BREAK UP THIS PARTY?
I'LL HANDLE IT.
BUT HOW? THERE MUST BE HUNDREDS OF TEENAGERS IN HERE, AND--
EVERYBODY OUT! I'M AN ORTHODONTIST AND I'M NOT AFRAID TO PROVE IT!
OH.

July 25, 2006

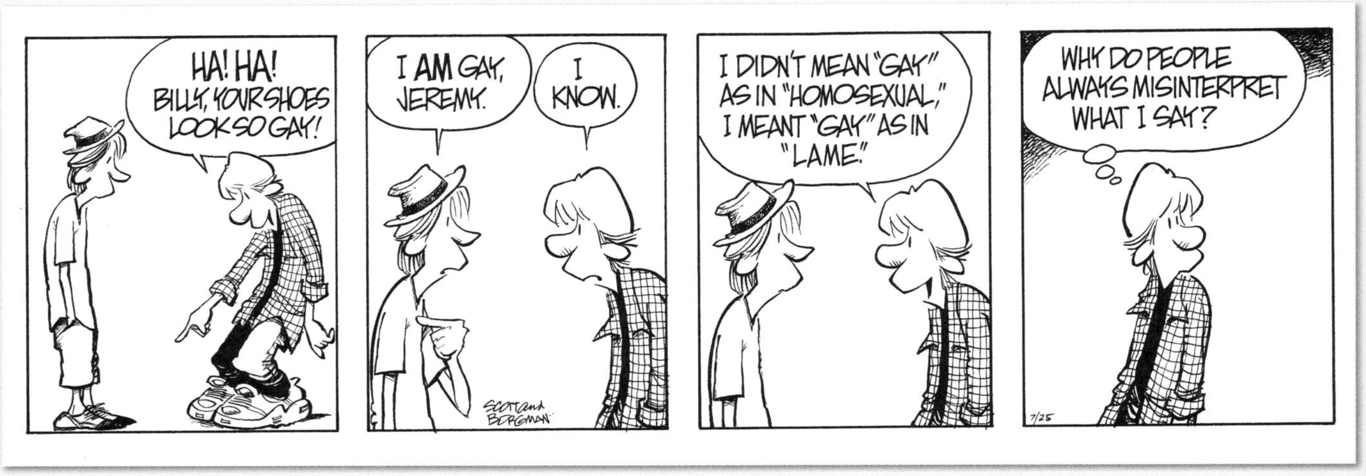

HA! HA! BILLY, YOUR SHOES LOOK SO GAY!
I AM GAY, JEREMY.
I KNOW.
I DIDN'T MEAN "GAY" AS IN "HOMOSEXUAL," I MEANT "GAY" AS IN "LAME."
WHY DO PEOPLE ALWAYS MISINTERPRET WHAT I SAY?

August 2, 2006

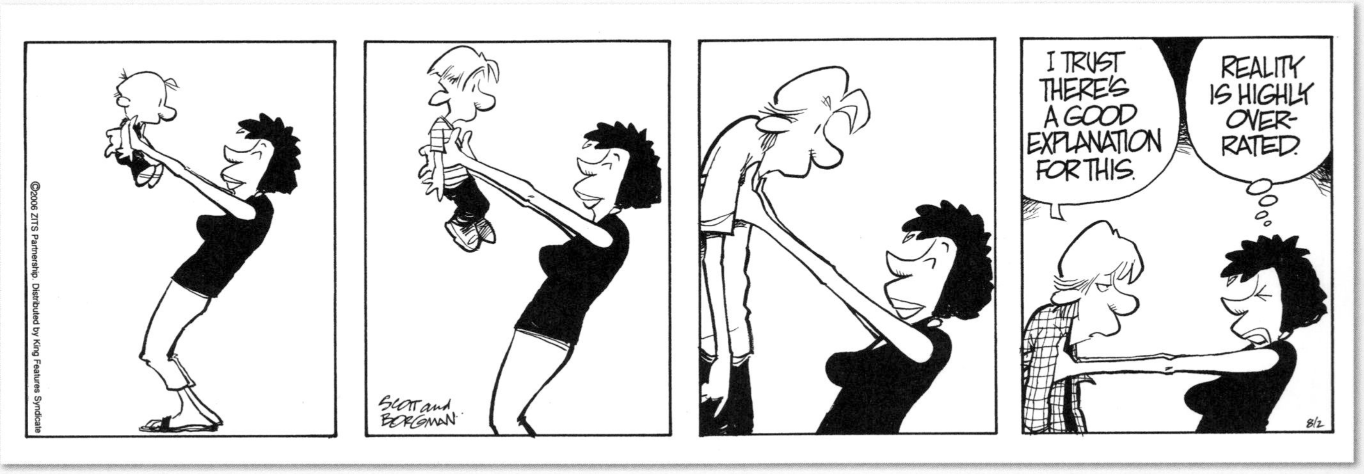

I TRUST THERE'S A GOOD EXPLANATION FOR THIS.
REALITY IS HIGHLY OVER-RATED.

January 1, 2006

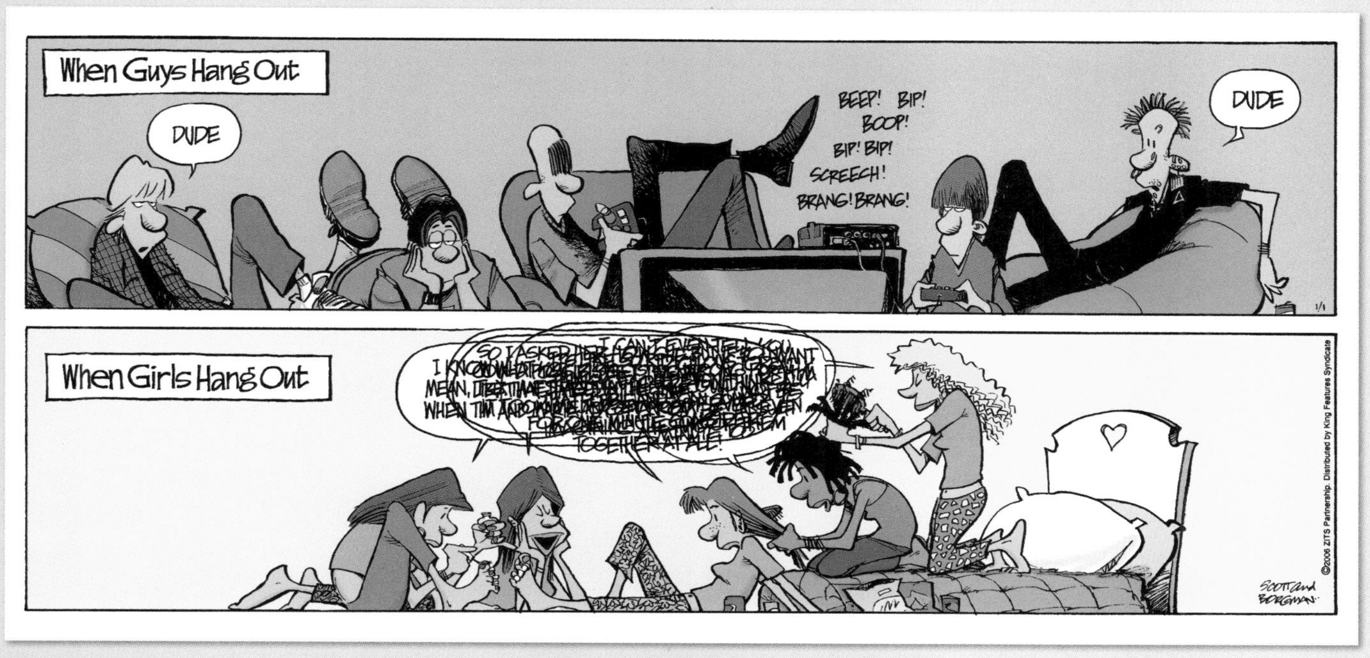

When Guys Hang Out
DUDE
BEEP! BIP! BOOP! BIP! BIP! SCREECH! BRANG! BRANG!
DUDE
1/1
When Girls Hang Out
©2006 ZITS Partnership. Distributed by King Features Syndicate
SCOTT and BORGMAN

June 18, 2006

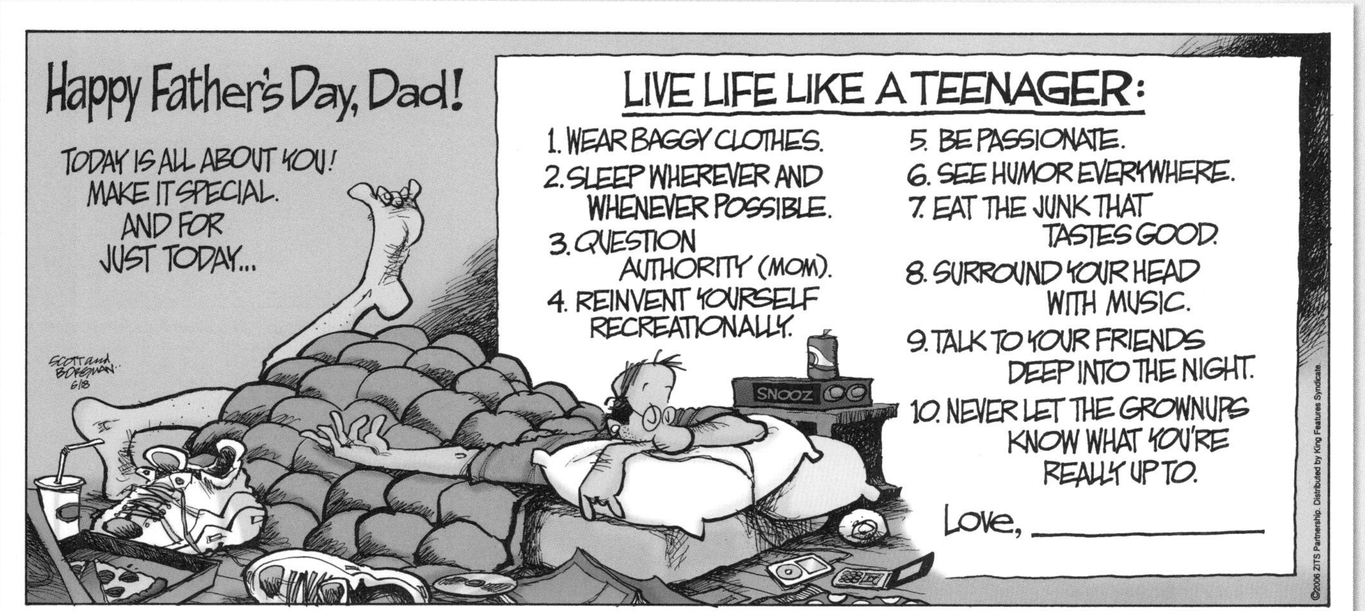

Happy Father's Day, Dad!
TODAY IS ALL ABOUT YOU! MAKE IT SPECIAL. AND FOR JUST TODAY...
LIVE LIFE LIKE A TEENAGER:
1. WEAR BAGGY CLOTHES.
2. SLEEP WHEREVER AND WHENEVER POSSIBLE.
3. QUESTION AUTHORITY (MOM).
4. REINVENT YOURSELF RECREATIONALLY.
5. BE PASSIONATE.
6. SEE HUMOR EVERYWHERE.
7. EAT THE JUNK THAT TASTES GOOD.
8. SURROUND YOUR HEAD WITH MUSIC.
9. TALK TO YOUR FRIENDS DEEP INTO THE NIGHT.
10. NEVER LET THE GROWNUPS KNOW WHAT YOU'RE REALLY UP TO.
Love, ____________
SNOOZ
SCOTT and BORGMAN 6/18
©2006 ZITS Partnership. Distributed by King Features Syndicate.

August 20, 2006

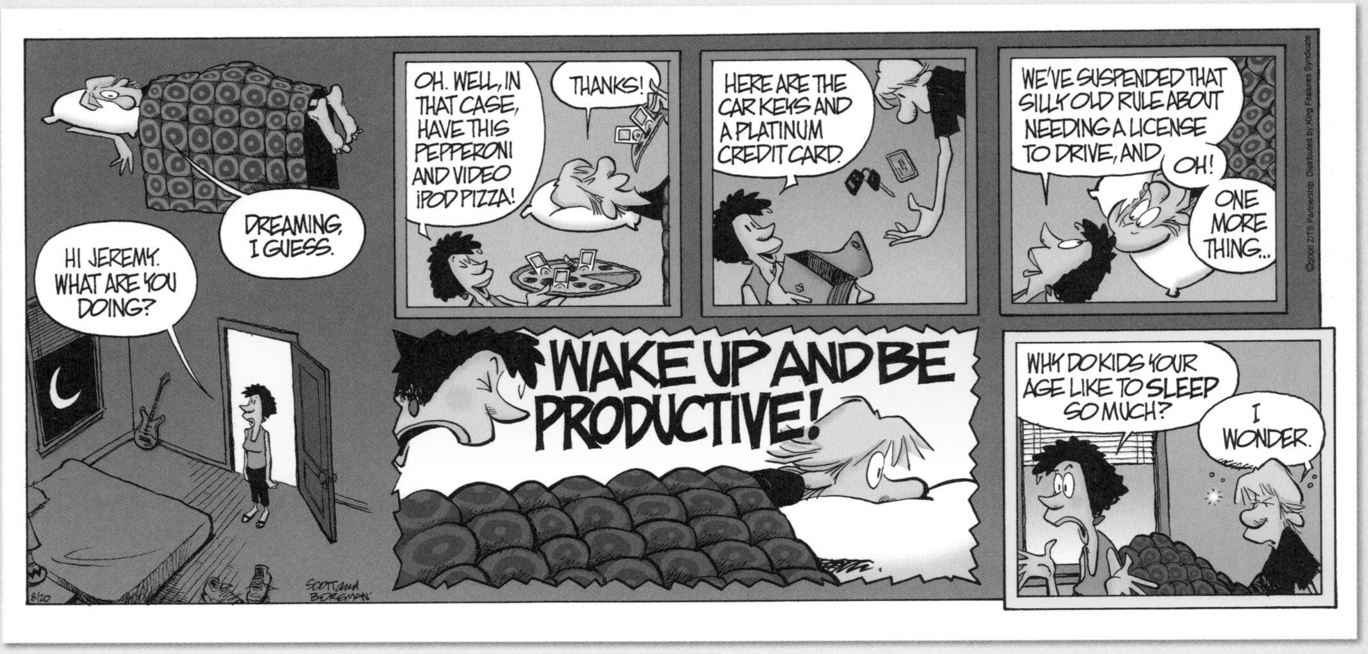

HI JEREMY. WHAT ARE YOU DOING?
DREAMING, I GUESS.
OH. WELL, IN THAT CASE, HAVE THIS PEPPERONI AND VIDEO iPOD PIZZA!
THANKS!
HERE ARE THE CAR KEYS AND A PLATINUM CREDIT CARD.
WE'VE SUSPENDED THAT SILLY OLD RULE ABOUT NEEDING A LICENSE TO DRIVE, AND
OH!
ONE MORE THING...
WAKE UP AND BE PRODUCTIVE!
WHY DO KIDS YOUR AGE LIKE TO SLEEP SO MUCH?
I WONDER.
©2006 ZITS Partnership. Distributed by King Features Syndicate

September 3, 2006

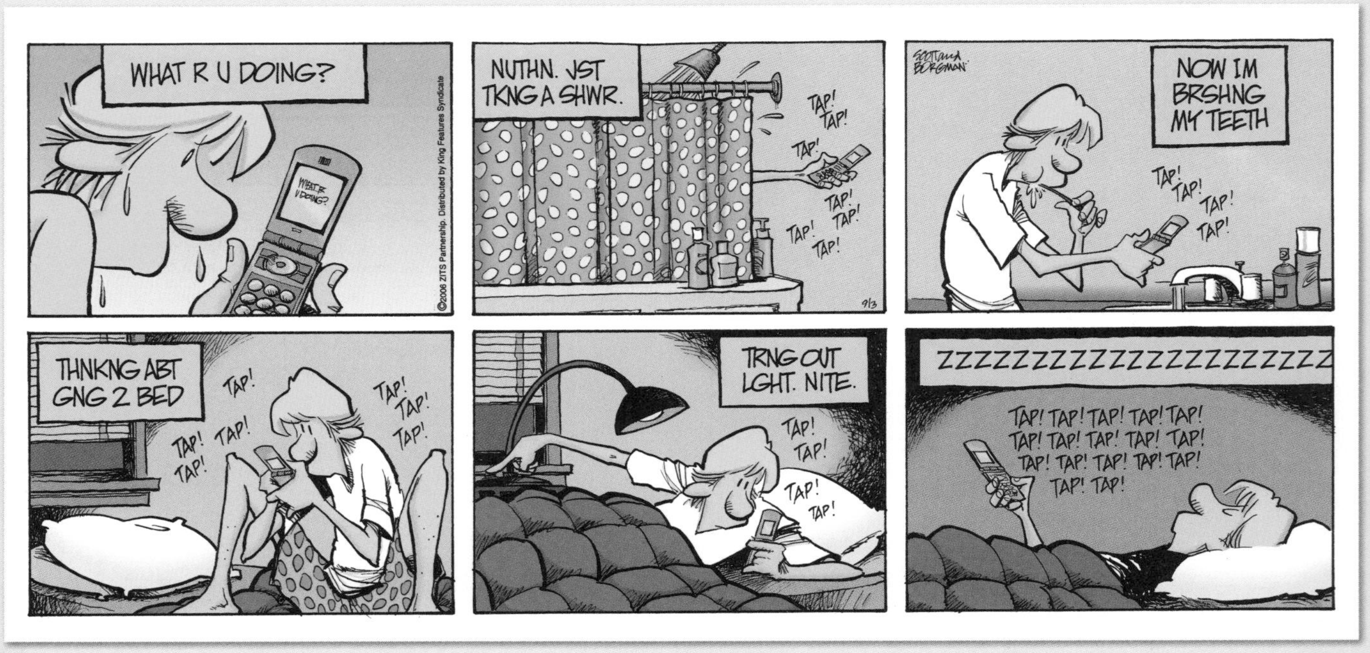

WHAT R U DOING?
WHAT R U DOING?
©2006 ZITS Partnership. Distributed by King Features Syndicate
NUTHN. JST TKNG A SHWR.
TAP! TAP! TAP! TAP! TAP! TAP! TAP!
NOW IM BRSHNG MY TEETH
TAP! TAP! TAP! TAP!
THNKNG ABT GNG 2 BED
TAP! TAP! TAP! TAP! TAP! TAP!
TRNG OUT LGHT. NITE.
TAP! TAP! TAP! TAP!
ZZZZZZZZZZZZZZZZZZZZZ
TAP! TAP! TAP! TAP! TAP! TAP! TAP! TAP! TAP! TAP! TAP! TAP! TAP! TAP! TAP! TAP! TAP!

September 7, 2006

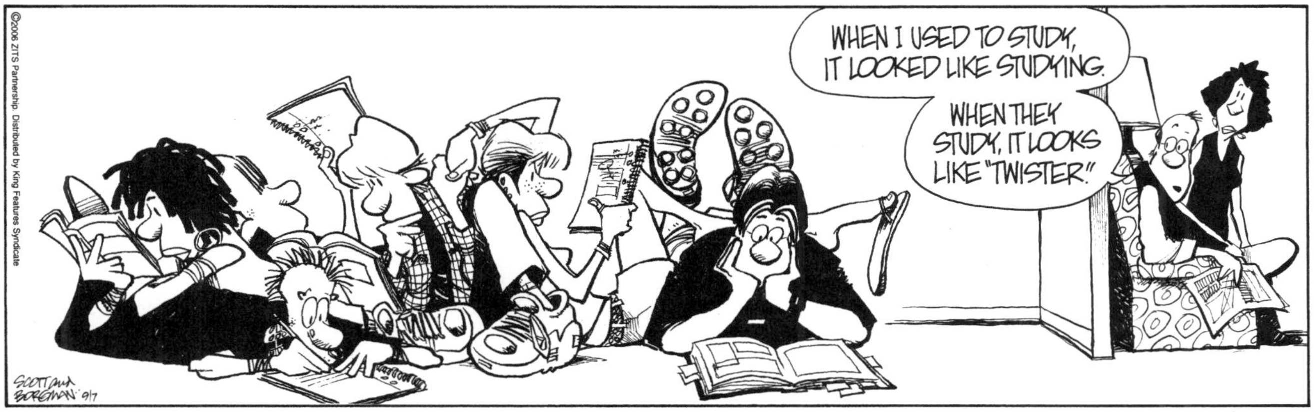

©2006 ZITS Partnership. Distributed by King Features Syndicate.
WHEN I USED TO STUDY, IT LOOKED LIKE STUDYING.
WHEN THEY STUDY, IT LOOKS LIKE "TWISTER."
SCOTT and BORGMAN 9/7

September 16, 2006

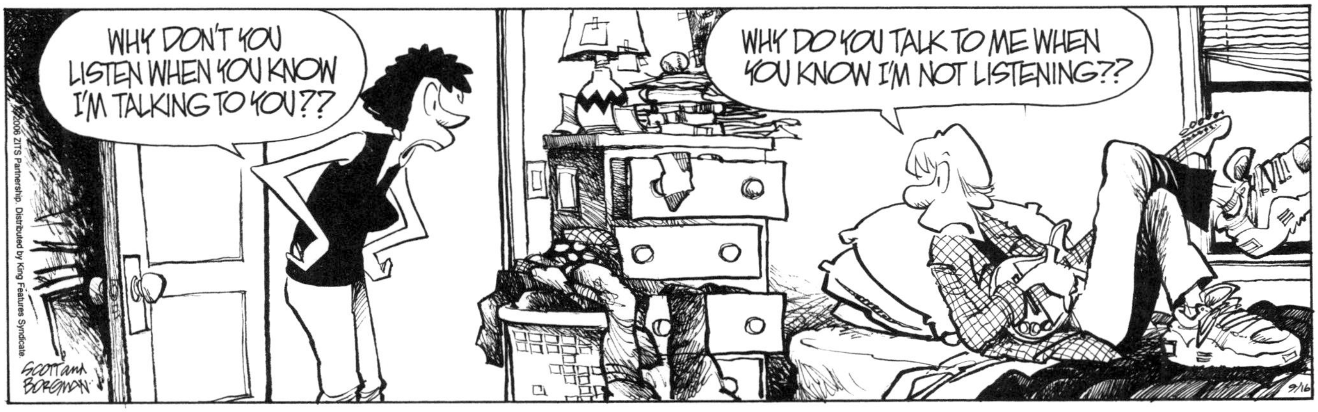

WHY DON'T YOU LISTEN WHEN YOU KNOW I'M TALKING TO YOU??
©2006 ZITS Partnership. Distributed by King Features Syndicate.
WHY DO YOU TALK TO ME WHEN YOU KNOW I'M NOT LISTENING??
SCOTT and BORGMAN 9/16

September 26, 2006

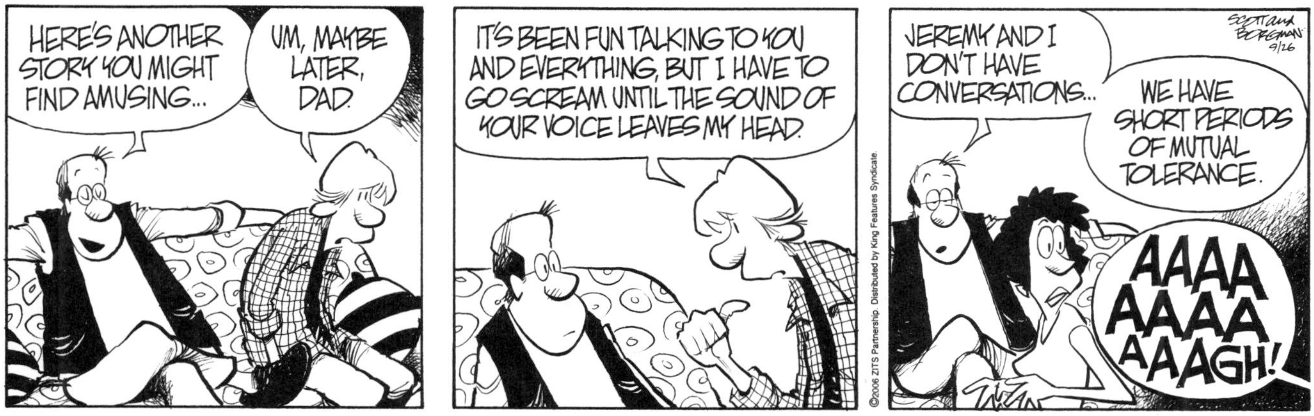

HERE'S ANOTHER STORY YOU MIGHT FIND AMUSING...
UM, MAYBE LATER, DAD.
IT'S BEEN FUN TALKING TO YOU AND EVERYTHING, BUT I HAVE TO GO SCREAM UNTIL THE SOUND OF YOUR VOICE LEAVES MY HEAD.
©2006 ZITS Partnership. Distributed by King Features Syndicate.
SCOTT and BORGMAN 9/26
JEREMY AND I DON'T HAVE CONVERSATIONS...
WE HAVE SHORT PERIODS OF MUTUAL TOLERANCE.
AAAA AAAA AAAGH!

October 13, 2006

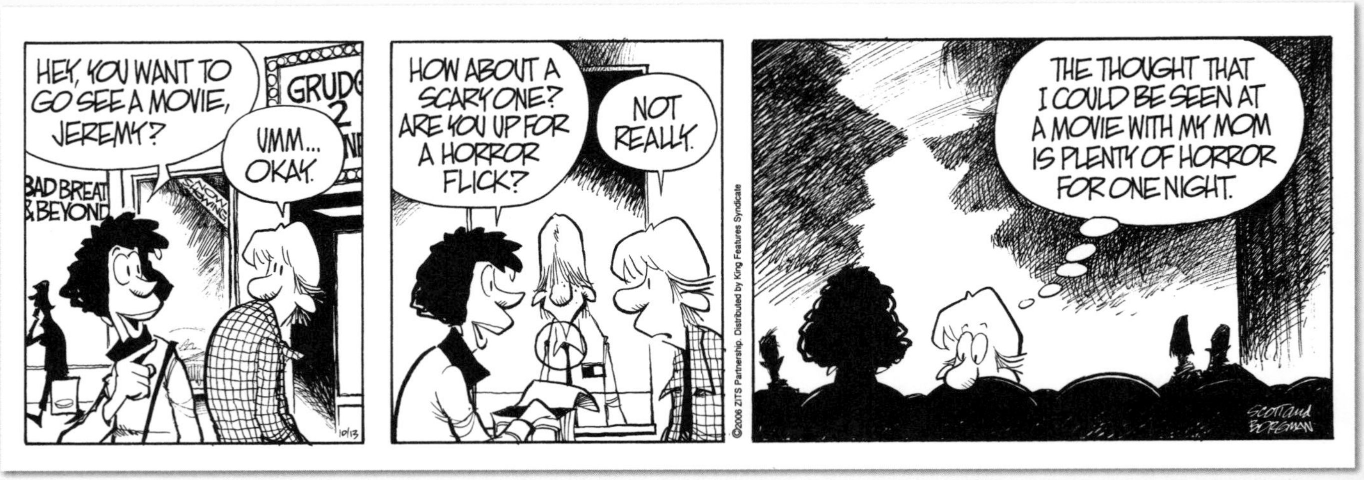
HEY, YOU WANT TO GO SEE A MOVIE, JEREMY?
UMM... OKAY.
GRUDG 2
BAD BREATH & BEYOND
HOW ABOUT A SCARY ONE? ARE YOU UP FOR A HORROR FLICK?
NOT REALLY.
©2006 ZITS Partnership. Distributed by King Features Syndicate
THE THOUGHT THAT I COULD BE SEEN AT A MOVIE WITH MY MOM IS PLENTY OF HORROR FOR ONE NIGHT.
SCOTT and BORGMAN

October 16, 2006

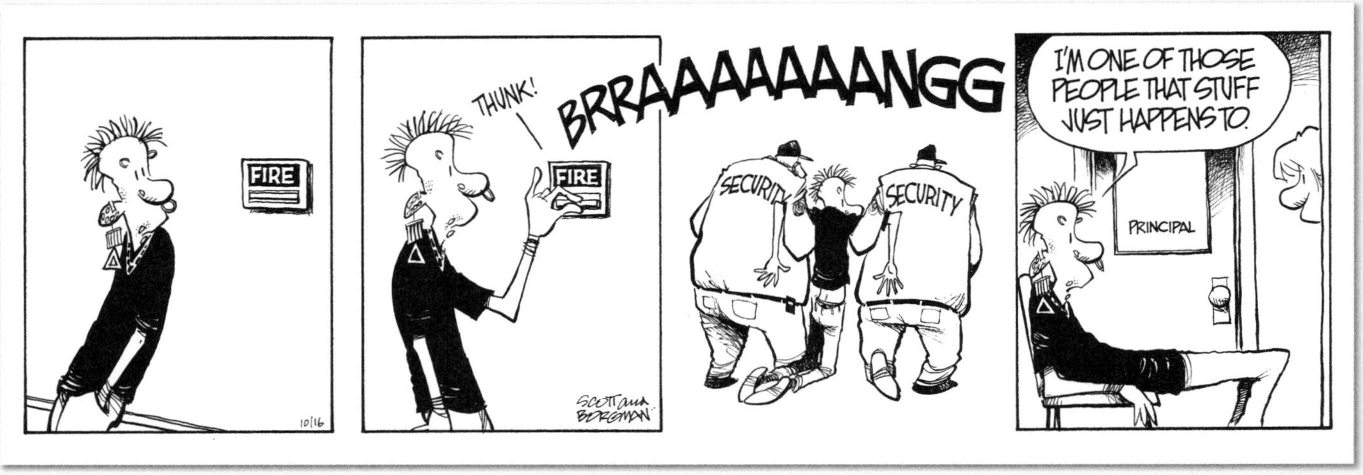
FIRE
THUNK!
FIRE
SCOTT and BORGMAN
BRRAAAAAAAANGG
SECURITY
SECURITY
I'M ONE OF THOSE PEOPLE THAT STUFF JUST HAPPENS TO.
PRINCIPAL

October 23, 2006

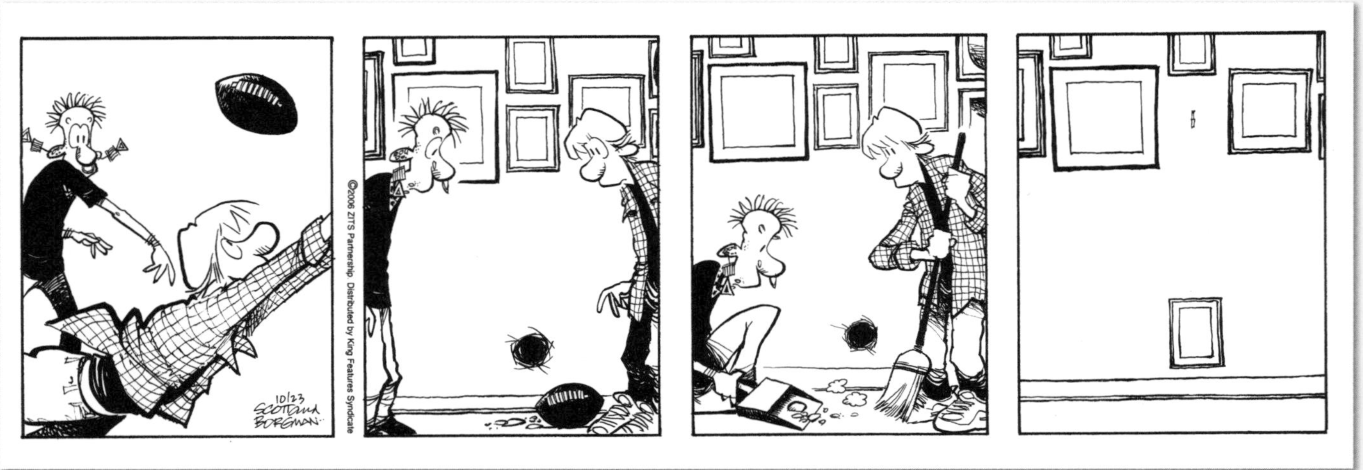
SCOTT and BORGMAN
©2006 ZITS Partnership. Distributed by King Features Syndicate

October 27, 2006

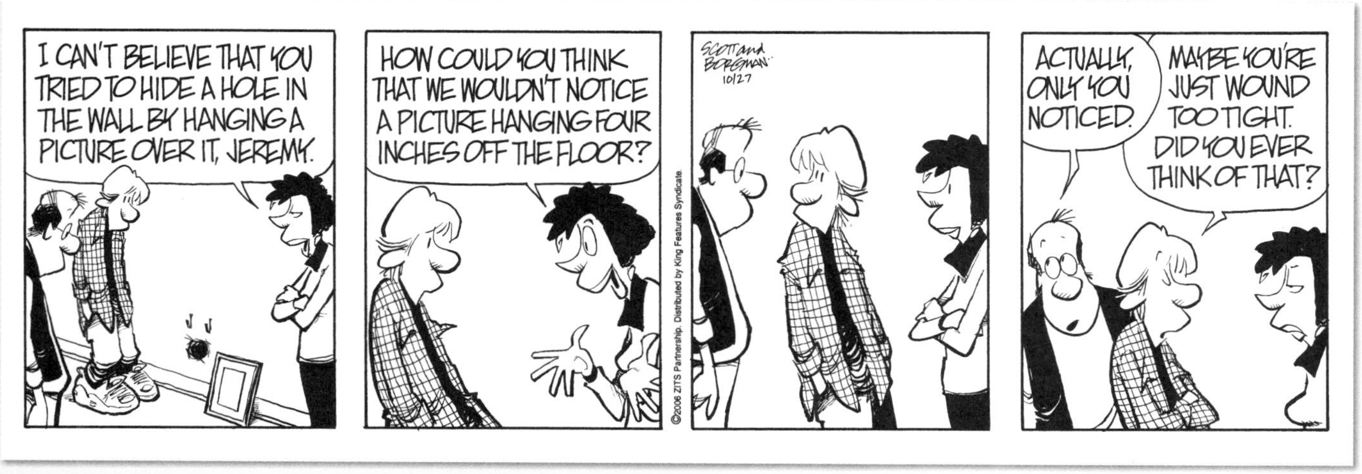
I CAN'T BELIEVE THAT YOU TRIED TO HIDE A HOLE IN THE WALL BY HANGING A PICTURE OVER IT, JEREMY.
HOW COULD YOU THINK THAT WE WOULDN'T NOTICE A PICTURE HANGING FOUR INCHES OFF THE FLOOR?
SCOTT AND BORGMAN 10/27
©2006 ZITS Partnership. Distributed by King Features Syndicate.
ACTUALLY, ONLY YOU NOTICED.
MAYBE YOU'RE JUST WOUND TOO TIGHT. DID YOU EVER THINK OF THAT?

December 11, 2006

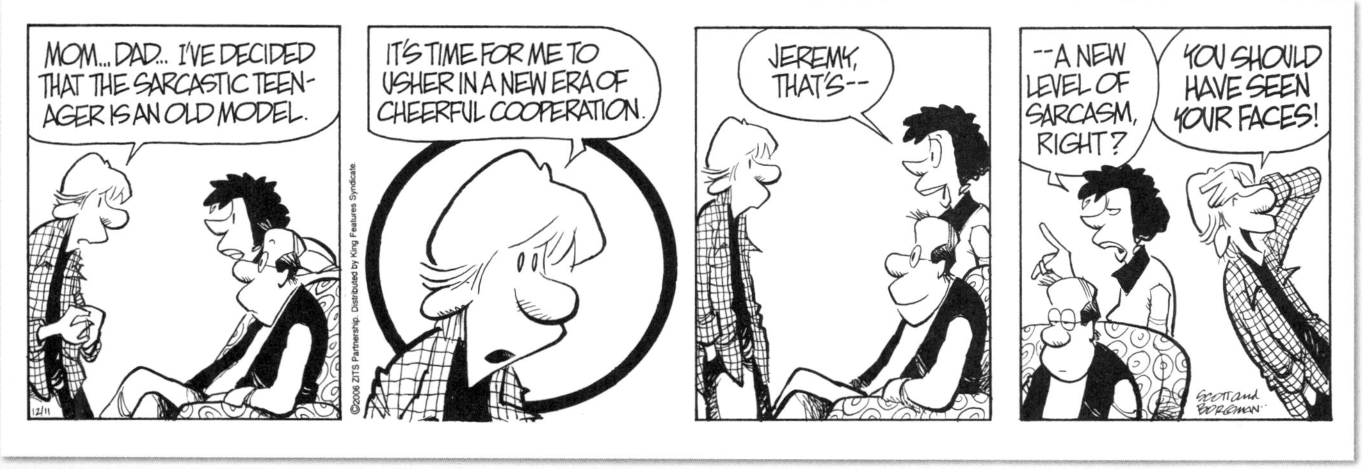
MOM... DAD... I'VE DECIDED THAT THE SARCASTIC TEEN-AGER IS AN OLD MODEL.
12/11
©2006 ZITS Partnership. Distributed by King Features Syndicate
IT'S TIME FOR ME TO USHER IN A NEW ERA OF CHEERFUL COOPERATION.
JEREMY, THAT'S--
--A NEW LEVEL OF SARCASM, RIGHT?
YOU SHOULD HAVE SEEN YOUR FACES!
SCOTT AND BORGMAN

December 20, 2006

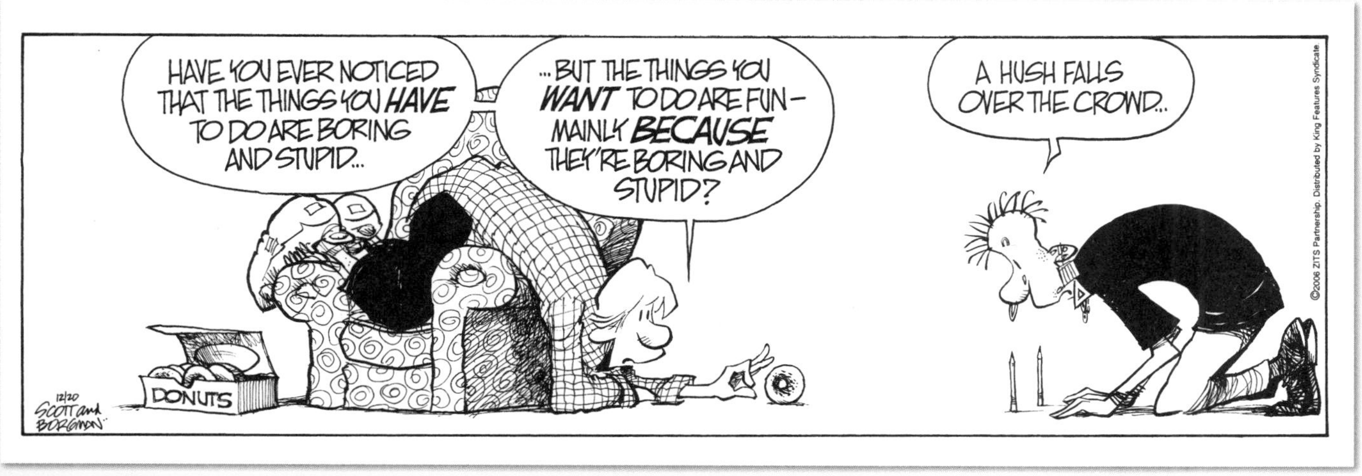
HAVE YOU EVER NOTICED THAT THE THINGS YOU HAVE TO DO ARE BORING AND STUPID...
...BUT THE THINGS YOU WANT TO DO ARE FUN-MAINLY BECAUSE THEY'RE BORING AND STUPID?
A HUSH FALLS OVER THE CROWD...
DONUTS
12/20 SCOTT AND BORGMAN
©2006 ZITS Partnership. Distributed by King Features Syndicate

November 5, 2006

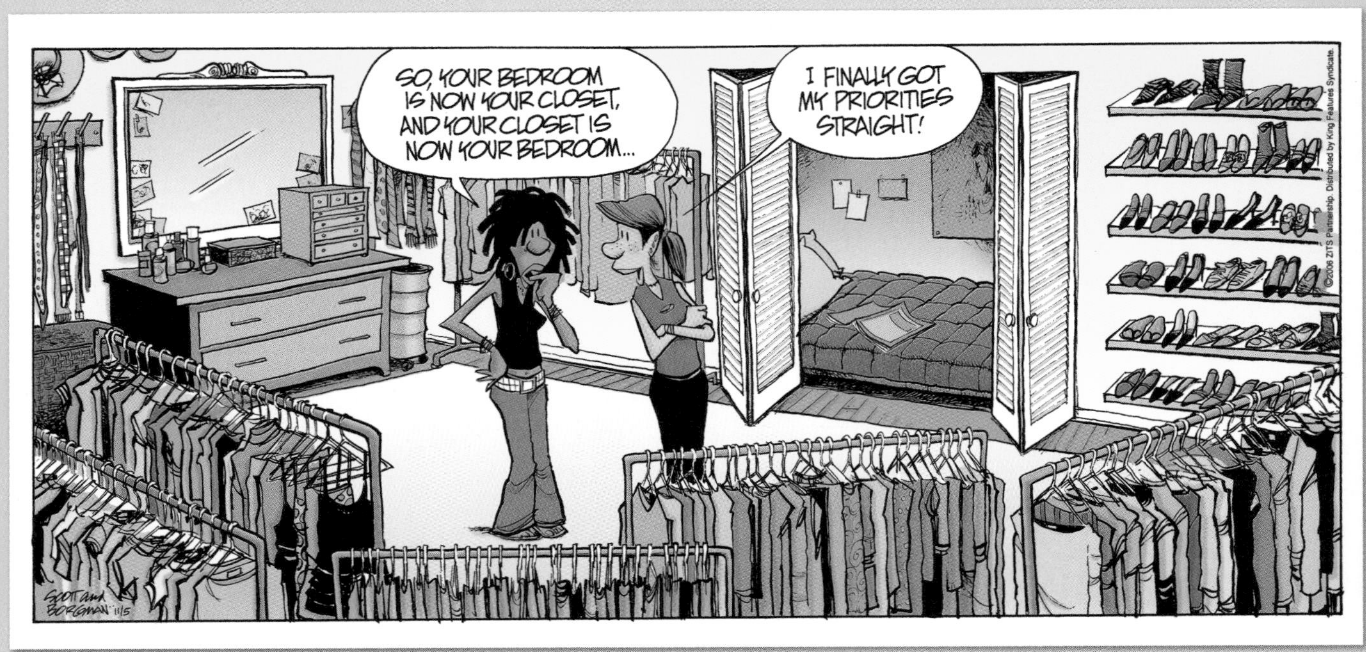

SO, YOUR BEDROOM IS NOW YOUR CLOSET, AND YOUR CLOSET IS NOW YOUR BEDROOM...
I FINALLY GOT MY PRIORITIES STRAIGHT!
©2006 ZITS Partnership. Distributed by King Features Syndicate.

December 18, 2006

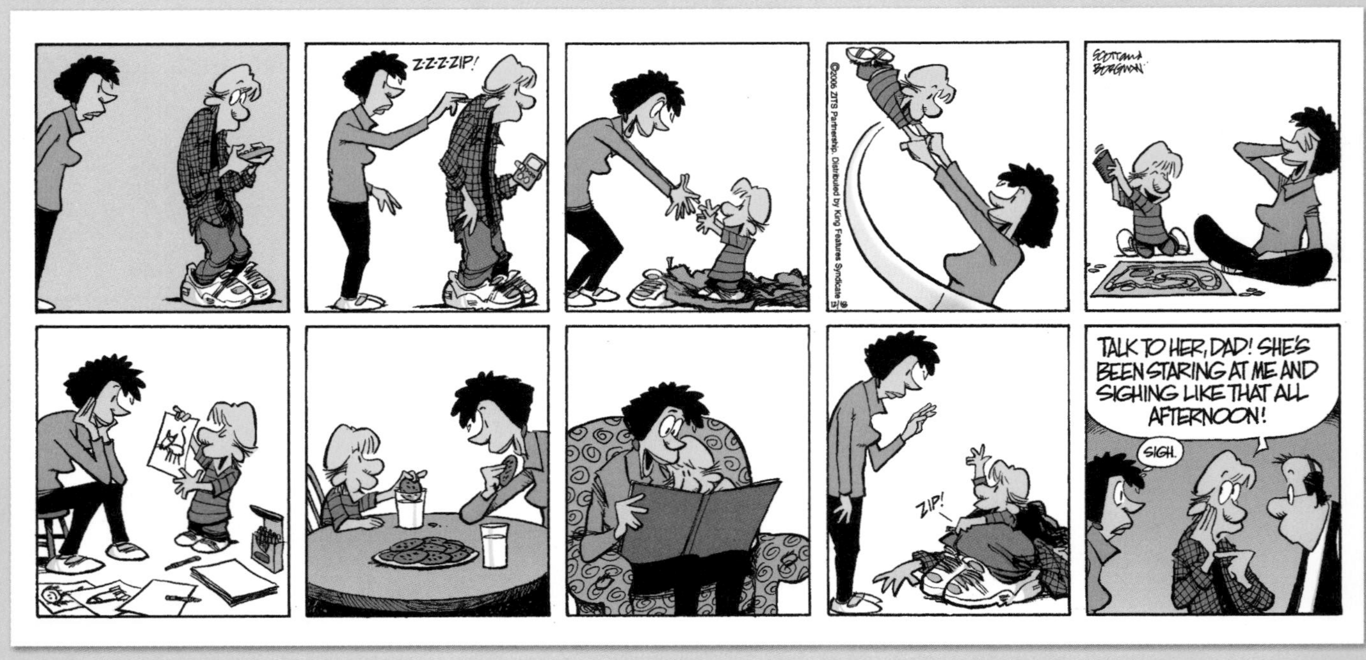

Z-Z-Z-ZIP!
ZIP!
TALK TO HER, DAD! SHE'S BEEN STARING AT ME AND SIGHING LIKE THAT ALL AFTERNOON!
SIGH.

July 30, 2006

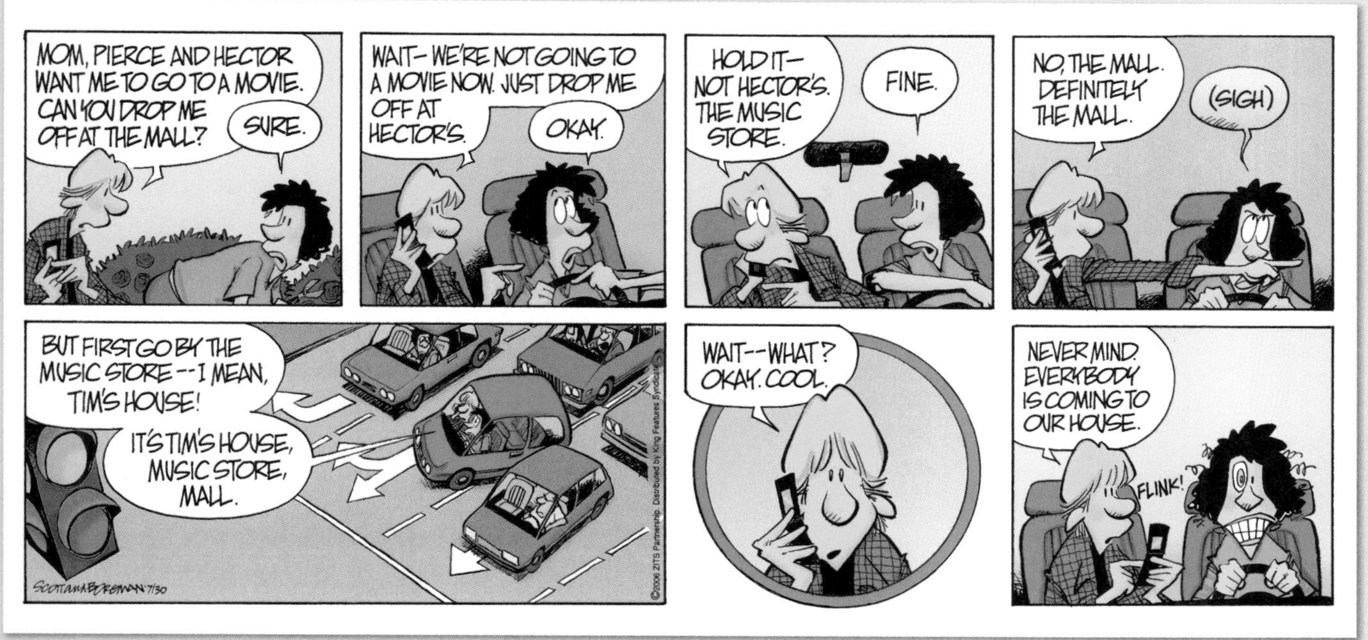
MOM, PIERCE AND HECTOR WANT ME TO GO TO A MOVIE. CAN YOU DROP ME OFF AT THE MALL?
SURE.
WAIT– WE'RE NOT GOING TO A MOVIE NOW. JUST DROP ME OFF AT HECTOR'S.
OKAY.
HOLD IT– NOT HECTOR'S. THE MUSIC STORE.
FINE.
NO, THE MALL. DEFINITELY THE MALL.
(SIGH)
BUT FIRST GO BY THE MUSIC STORE --I MEAN, TIM'S HOUSE!
IT'S TIM'S HOUSE, MUSIC STORE, MALL.
WAIT--WHAT? OKAY. COOL.
NEVER MIND. EVERYBODY IS COMING TO OUR HOUSE.
FLINK!
©2006 ZITS Partnership. Distributed by King Features Syndicate
SCOTTANDBORGMAN 7/30

December 24, 2006

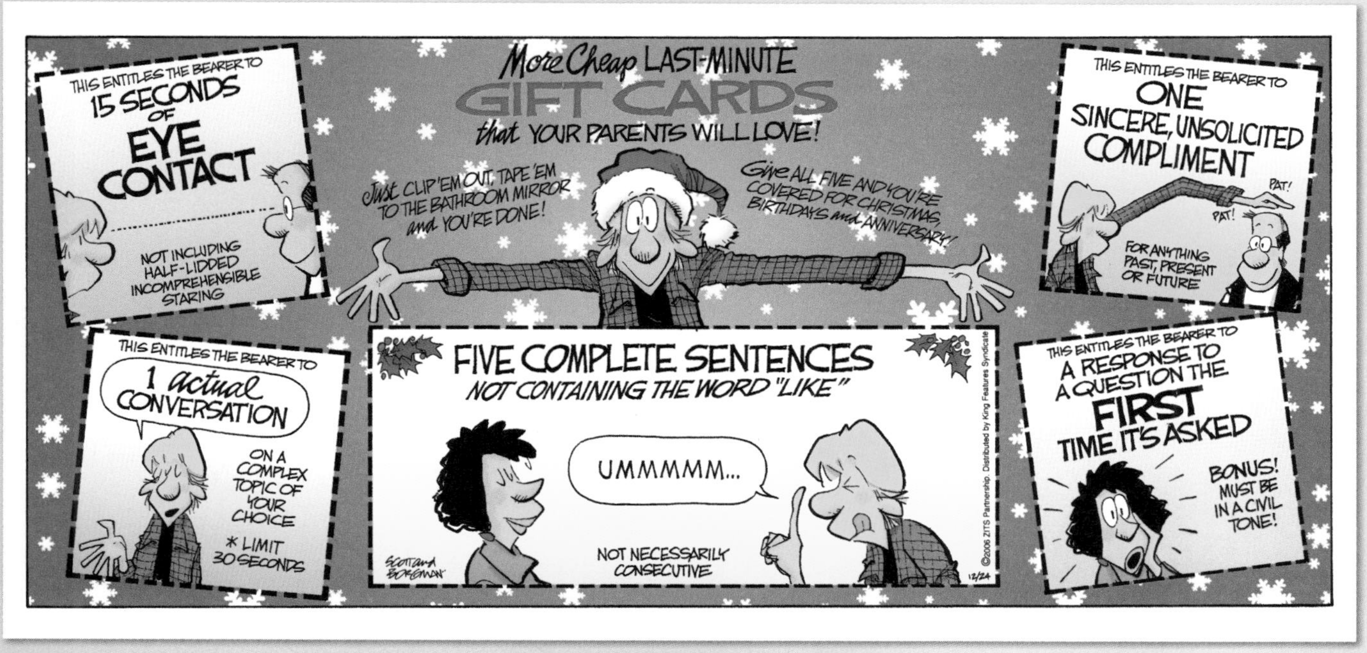
More Cheap LAST-MINUTE GIFT CARDS that YOUR PARENTS WILL LOVE!
Just CLIP 'EM OUT, TAPE 'EM TO THE BATHROOM MIRROR and YOU'RE DONE!
Give ALL FIVE AND YOU'RE COVERED FOR CHRISTMAS, BIRTHDAYS and ANNIVERSARY!
THIS ENTITLES THE BEARER TO 15 SECONDS OF EYE CONTACT
NOT INCLUDING HALF-LIDDED INCOMPREHENSIBLE STARING
THIS ENTITLES THE BEARER TO ONE SINCERE, UNSOLICITED COMPLIMENT
PAT! PAT!
FOR ANYTHING PAST, PRESENT OR FUTURE
THIS ENTITLES THE BEARER TO 1 actual CONVERSATION
ON A COMPLEX TOPIC OF YOUR CHOICE
* LIMIT 30 SECONDS
FIVE COMPLETE SENTENCES NOT CONTAINING THE WORD "LIKE"
UMMMMM...
NOT NECESSARILY CONSECUTIVE
THIS ENTITLES THE BEARER TO A RESPONSE TO A QUESTION THE FIRST TIME IT'S ASKED
BONUS! MUST BE IN A CIVIL TONE!
©2006 ZITS Partnership. Distributed by King Features Syndicate
SCOTTANDBORGMAN 12/24

Six Bricks

Jim Borgman

Jerry and I work in weeklong batches of dailies, "six bricks to a load," as we say. In our quirky division of labor, it has evolved that I assign dates to the dailies before filing them.

When we're telling a story, the chronology of the strips is obvious. Otherwise, day and date selection is arbitrary, and I find myself wondering whether there should be any rhyme or reason to choosing certain strips for certain days.

I used to hear that the weakest strip in a week's batch should run on Saturday. That seems upside-down to me—Saturday is the one day besides Sunday when a reader would seem more likely to linger an extra moment. I usually schedule one of our best for that day.

Sometimes subject matter suggests placement. We don't run a strip that's happening in school on a Saturday. Likewise, a strip about sleeping till the crack of noon probably won't run on a Monday. I don't know whether readers make these literal connections, but I like the sense of being in loose rhythm with their lives.

There's a wonderful comic strip editor we'd see in Sweden whenever we did book tours through Scandinavia—Alf Thörsen is his name, give or take an umlaut. Alf had a philosophy about the weekly pacing of a comic strip that he would narrate with great affection for readers.

"On Monday, the working man must rise and face the week—you must give him your most hopeful and funniest strip. On Tuesday, he has begun to find his energy—try to sustain his sense of purpose. On Wednesday, his spirits have begun to fade—you must . . ."

It was quaint and charming, and you wanted to hug the guy. Comic strip reading now seems so much more random and sporadic. Does anybody have a new philosophy for the age of DailyINK, iPads, and binge reading?

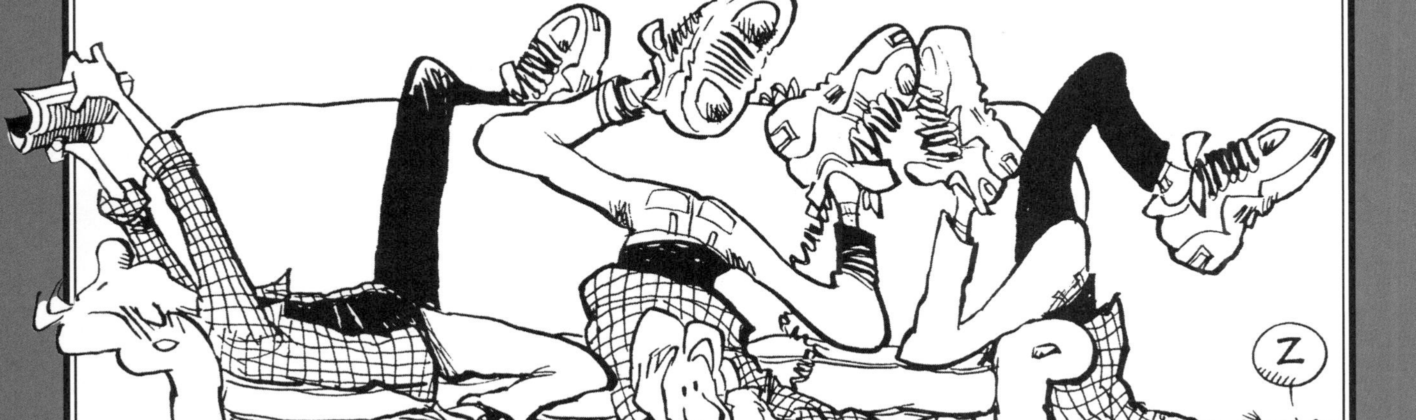
Z

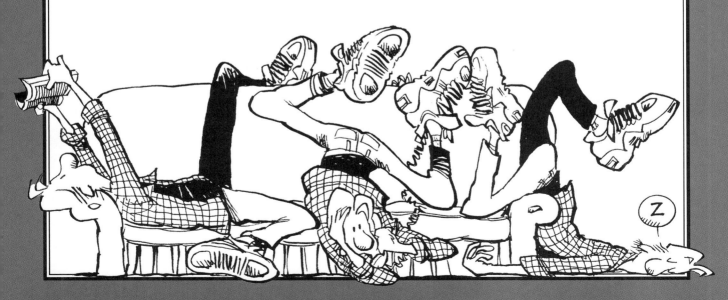

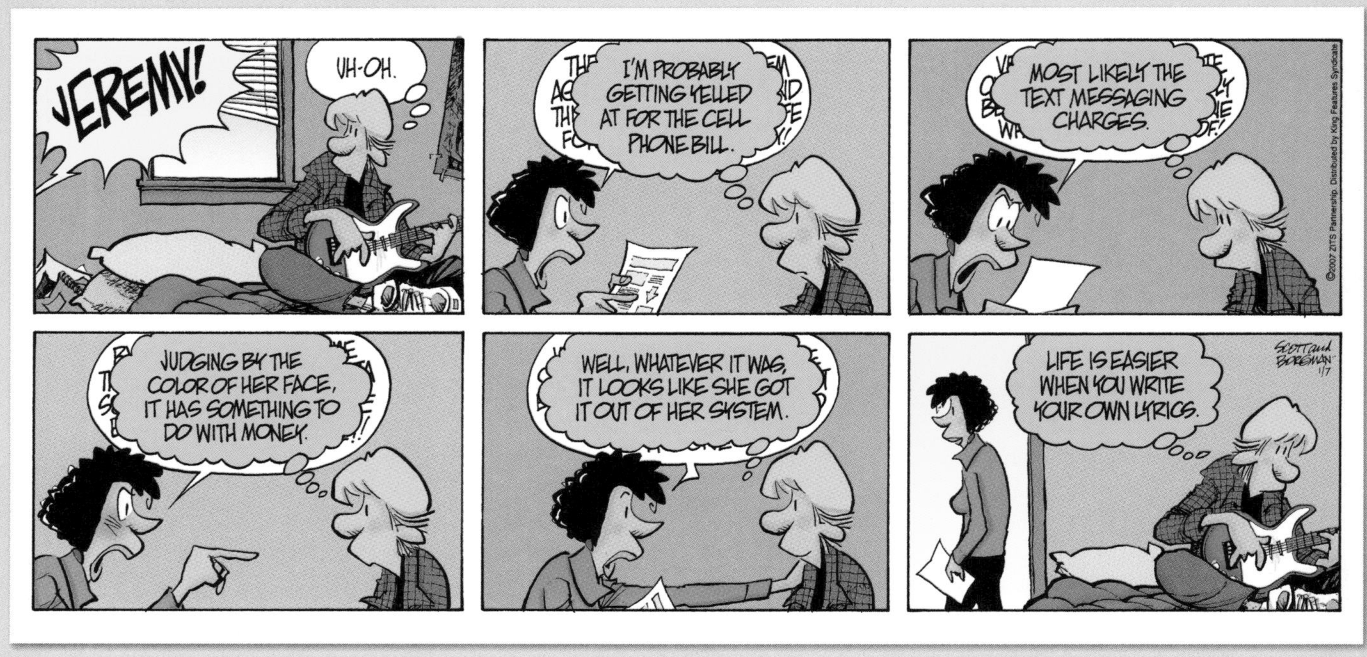
JEREMY!
UH-OH.
I'M PROBABLY GETTING YELLED AT FOR THE CELL PHONE BILL.
MOST LIKELY THE TEXT MESSAGING CHARGES.
JUDGING BY THE COLOR OF HER FACE, IT HAS SOMETHING TO DO WITH MONEY.
WELL, WHATEVER IT WAS, IT LOOKS LIKE SHE GOT IT OUT OF HER SYSTEM.
LIFE IS EASIER WHEN YOU WRITE YOUR OWN LYRICS.
SCOTT and BORGMAN 1/7
©2007 ZITS Partnership. Distributed by King Features Syndicate

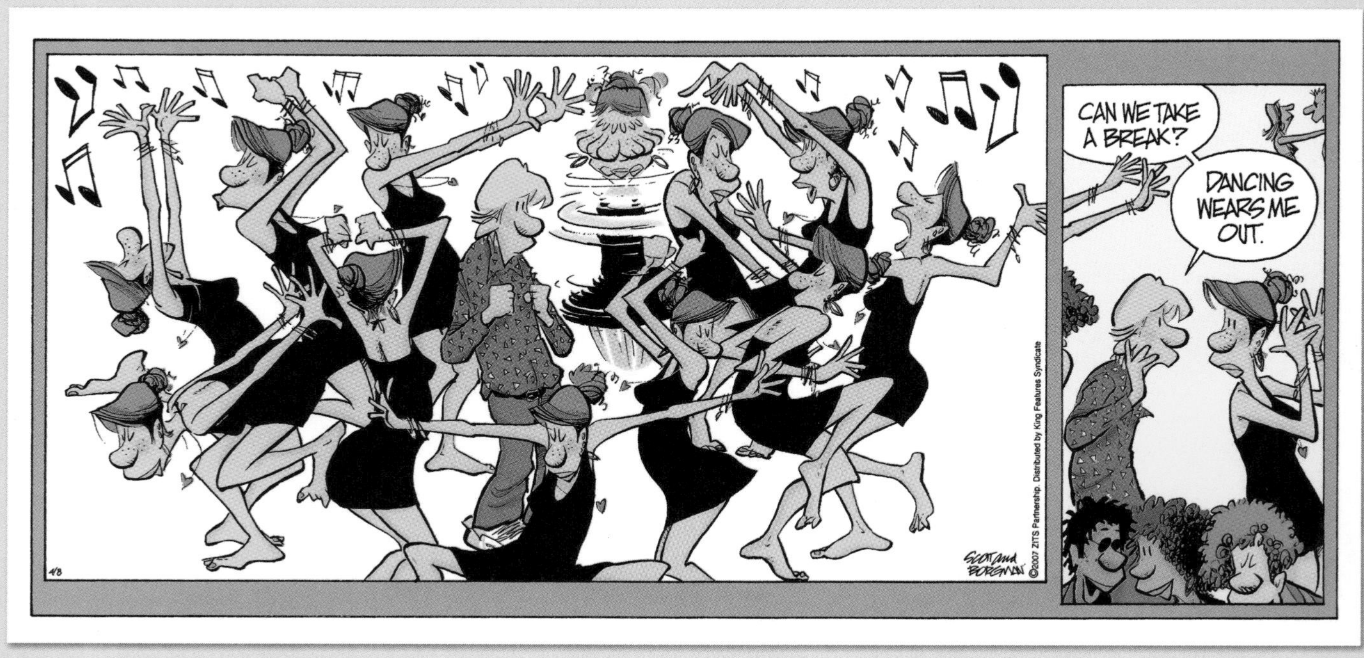
CAN WE TAKE A BREAK?
DANCING WEARS ME OUT.
4/8
SCOTT and BORGMAN
©2007 ZITS Partnership. Distributed by King Features Syndicate

January 16, 2007

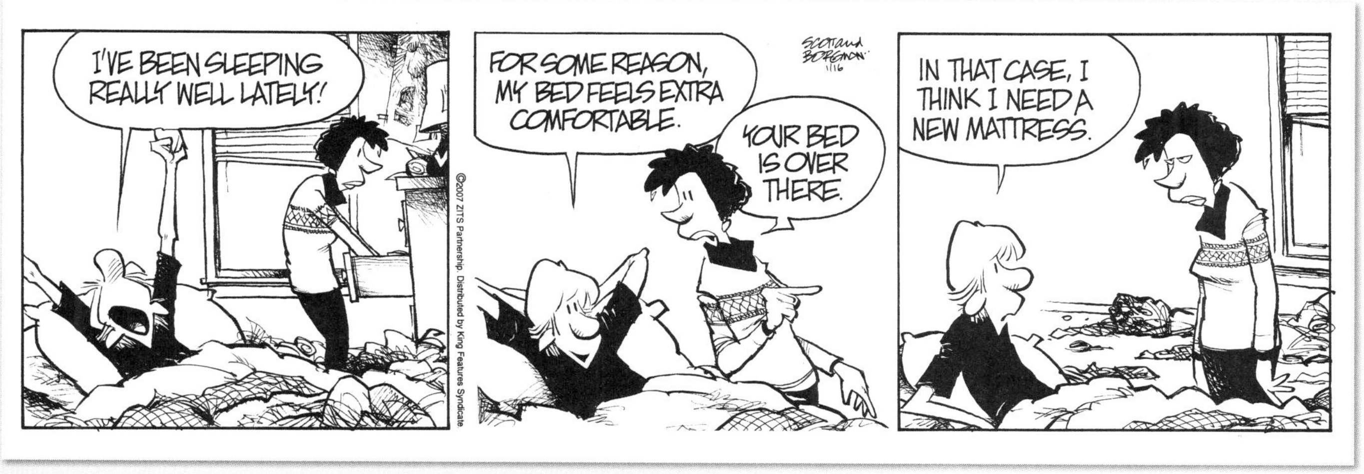
I'VE BEEN SLEEPING REALLY WELL LATELY!
FOR SOME REASON, MY BED FEELS EXTRA COMFORTABLE.
YOUR BED IS OVER THERE.
IN THAT CASE, I THINK I NEED A NEW MATTRESS.
SCOTT and BORGMAN 1/16
©2007 ZITS Partnership. Distributed by King Features Syndicate

February 12, 2007

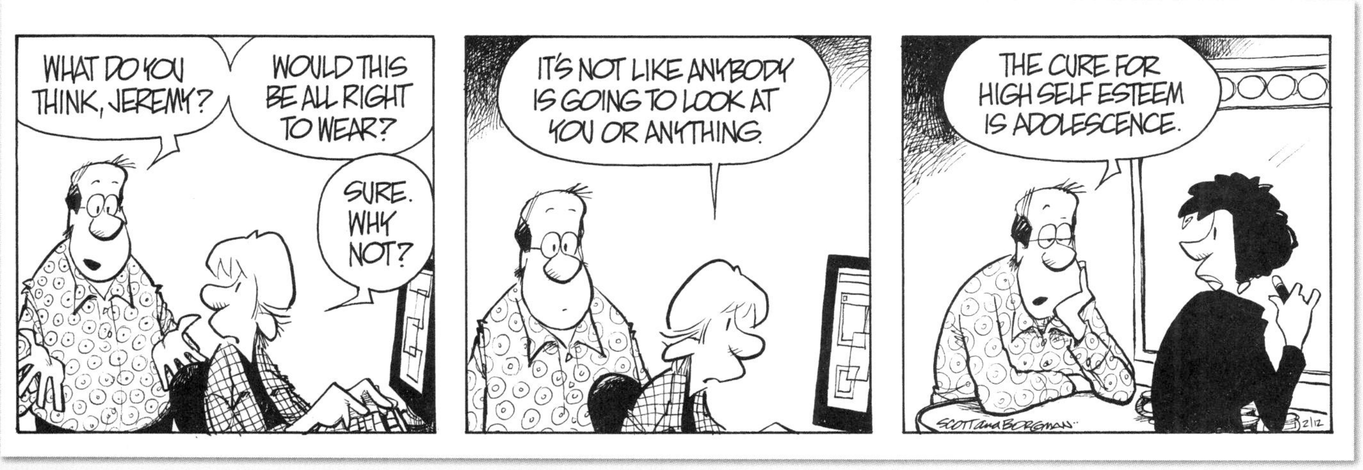
WHAT DO YOU THINK, JEREMY?
WOULD THIS BE ALL RIGHT TO WEAR?
SURE. WHY NOT?
IT'S NOT LIKE ANYBODY IS GOING TO LOOK AT YOU OR ANYTHING.
THE CURE FOR HIGH SELF ESTEEM IS ADOLESCENCE.
SCOTT and BORGMAN 2/12

March 5, 2007

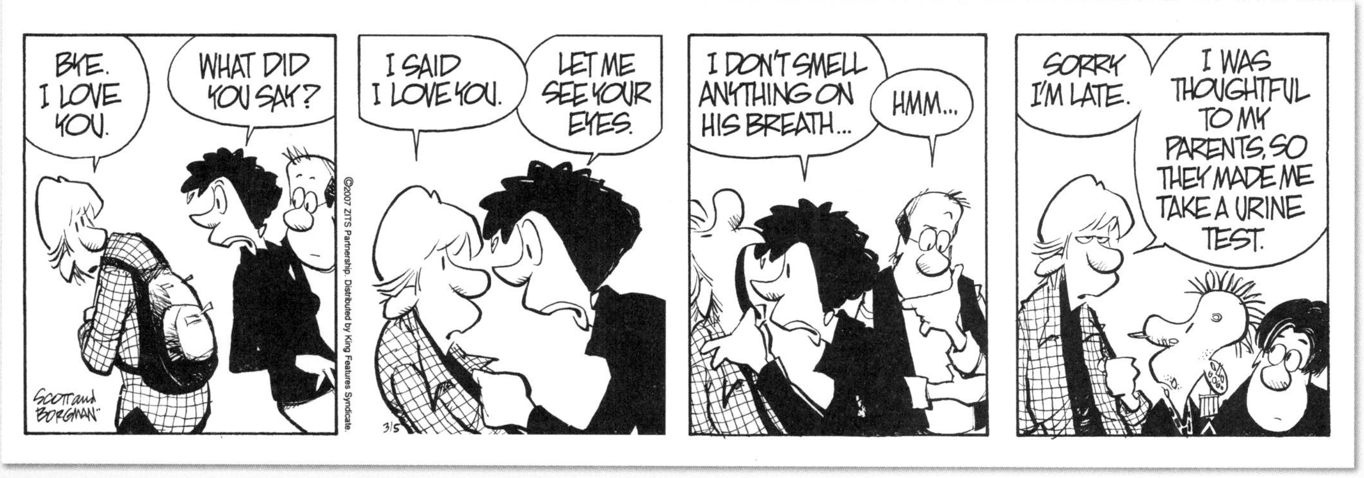
BYE. I LOVE YOU.
WHAT DID YOU SAY?
I SAID I LOVE YOU.
LET ME SEE YOUR EYES.
I DON'T SMELL ANYTHING ON HIS BREATH...
HMM...
SORRY I'M LATE.
I WAS THOUGHTFUL TO MY PARENTS, SO THEY MADE ME TAKE A URINE TEST.
SCOTT and BORGMAN 3/5
©2007 ZITS Partnership. Distributed by King Features Syndicate

May 18, 2007

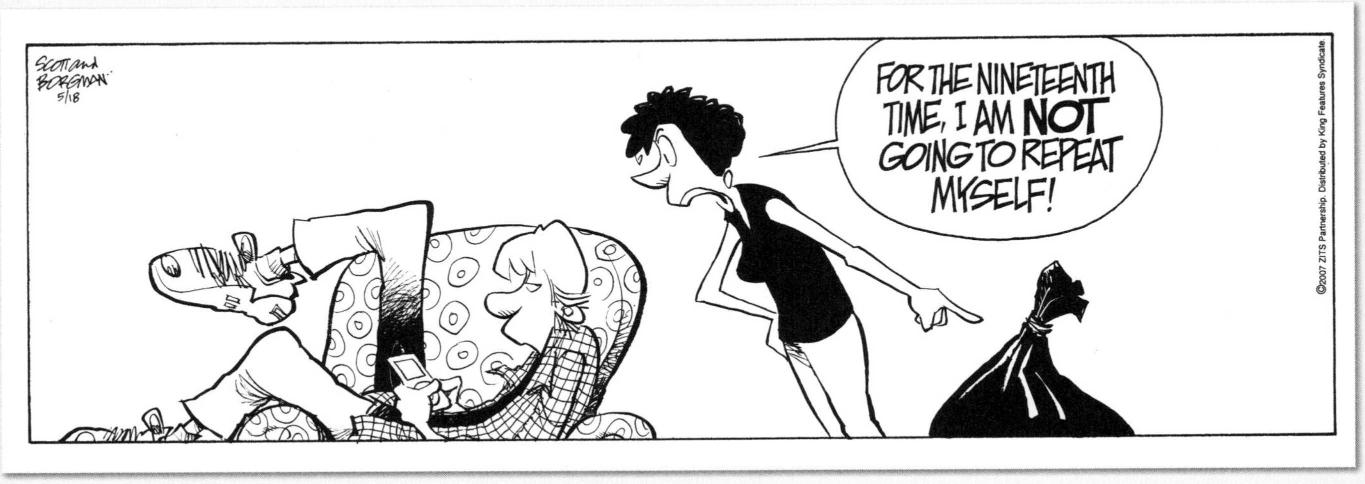
SCOTT and BORGMAN 5/18
FOR THE NINETEENTH TIME, I AM NOT GOING TO REPEAT MYSELF!
©2007 ZITS Partnership. Distributed by King Features Syndicate

June 18, 2007

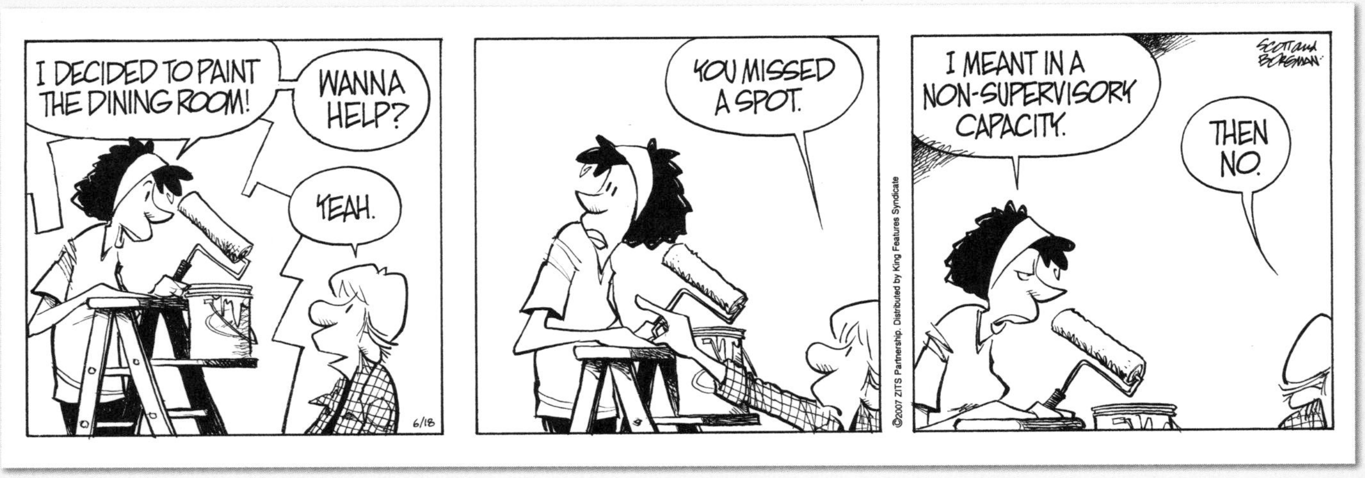
I DECIDED TO PAINT THE DINING ROOM!
WANNA HELP?
YEAH.
6/18
YOU MISSED A SPOT.
©2007 ZITS Partnership. Distributed by King Features Syndicate
SCOTT and BORGMAN
I MEANT IN A NON-SUPERVISORY CAPACITY.
THEN NO.

July 18, 2007

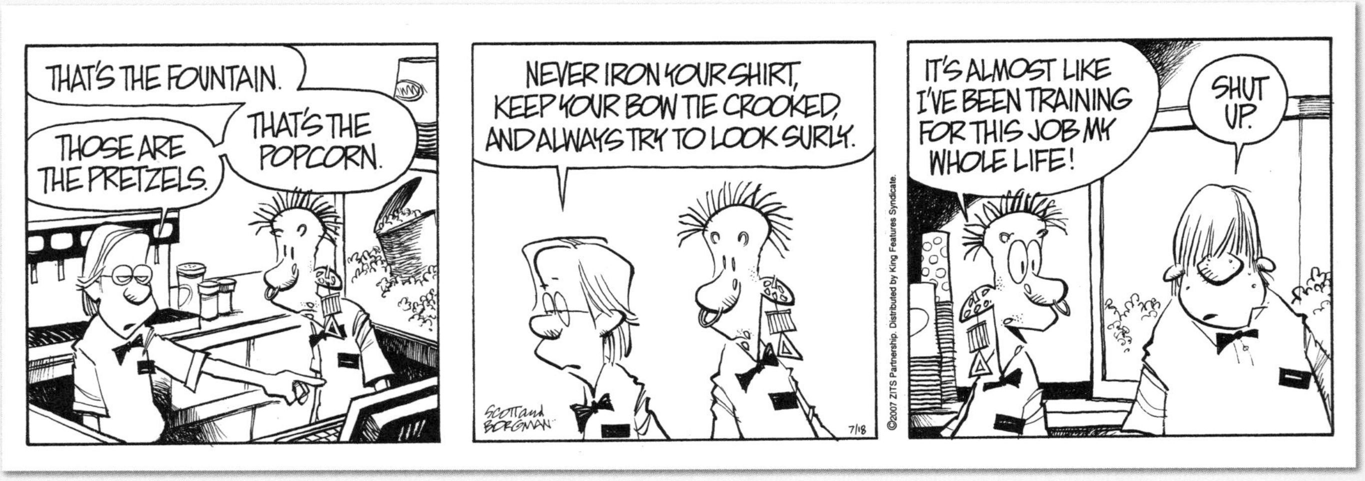
THAT'S THE FOUNTAIN.
THOSE ARE THE PRETZELS.
THAT'S THE POPCORN.
NEVER IRON YOUR SHIRT, KEEP YOUR BOW TIE CROOKED, AND ALWAYS TRY TO LOOK SURLY.
SCOTT and BORGMAN
7/18
©2007 ZITS Partnership. Distributed by King Features Syndicate.
IT'S ALMOST LIKE I'VE BEEN TRAINING FOR THIS JOB MY WHOLE LIFE!
SHUT UP.

June 3, 2007

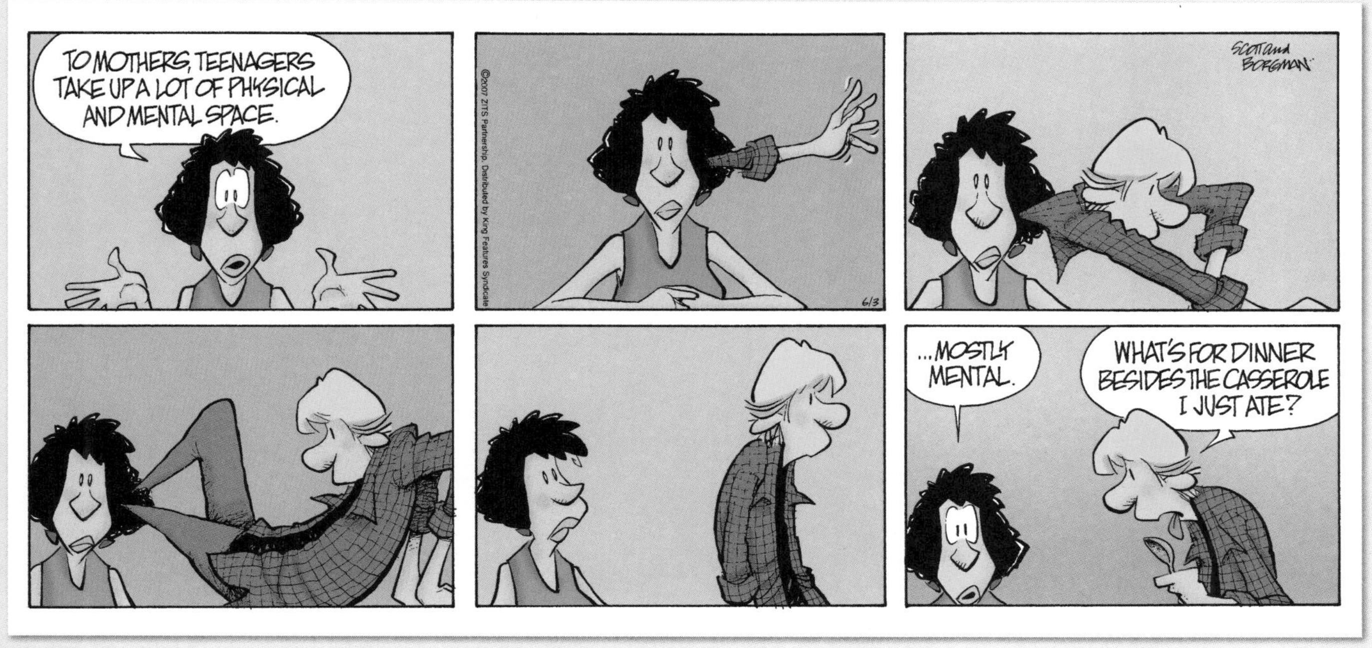
TO MOTHERS, TEENAGERS TAKE UP A LOT OF PHYSICAL AND MENTAL SPACE.
©2007 ZITS Partnership. Distributed by King Features Syndicate
SCOTT and BORGMAN
...MOSTLY MENTAL.
WHAT'S FOR DINNER BESIDES THE CASSEROLE I JUST ATE?

July 1, 2007

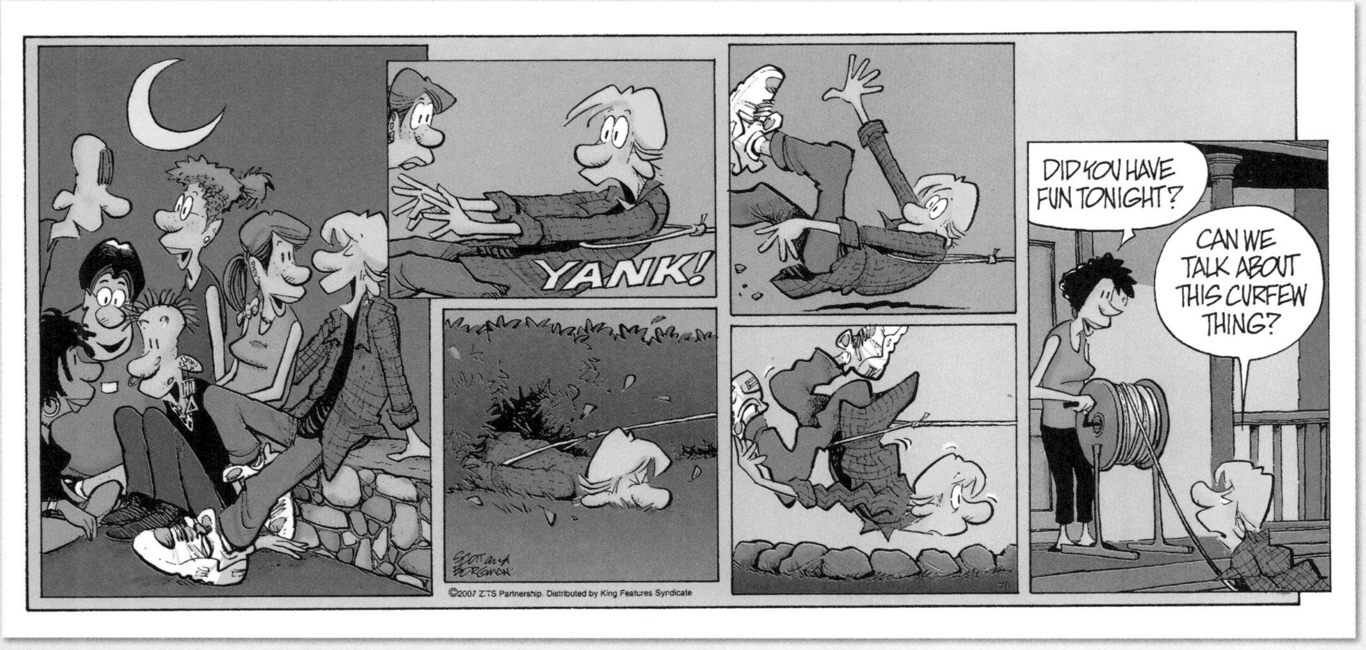
YANK!
SCOTT and BORGMAN
©2007 ZITS Partnership. Distributed by King Features Syndicate
DID YOU HAVE FUN TONIGHT?
CAN WE TALK ABOUT THIS CURFEW THING?

September 14, 2007

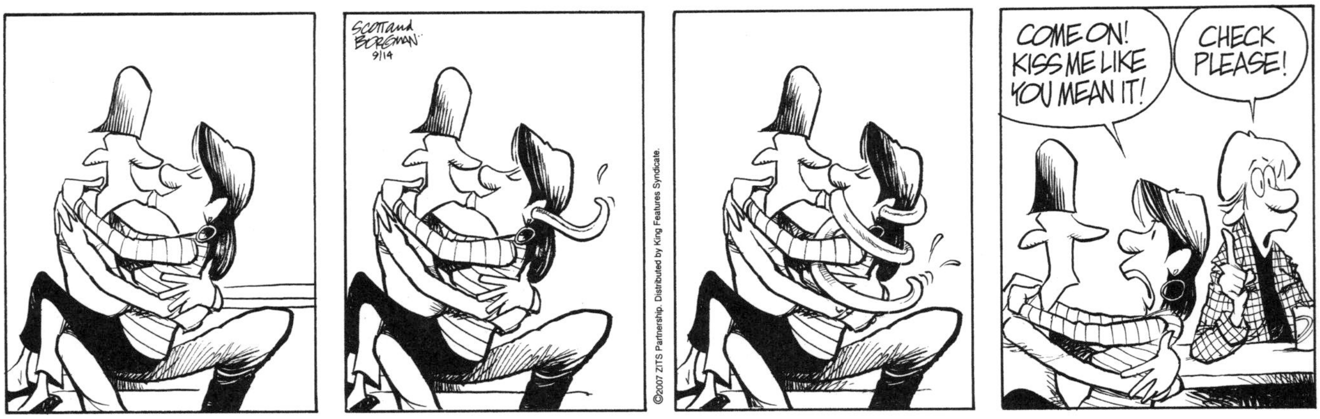
SCOTT and BORGMAN 9/14
©2007 ZITS Partnership. Distributed by King Features Syndicate.
COME ON! KISS ME LIKE YOU MEAN IT!
CHECK PLEASE!

September 18, 2007

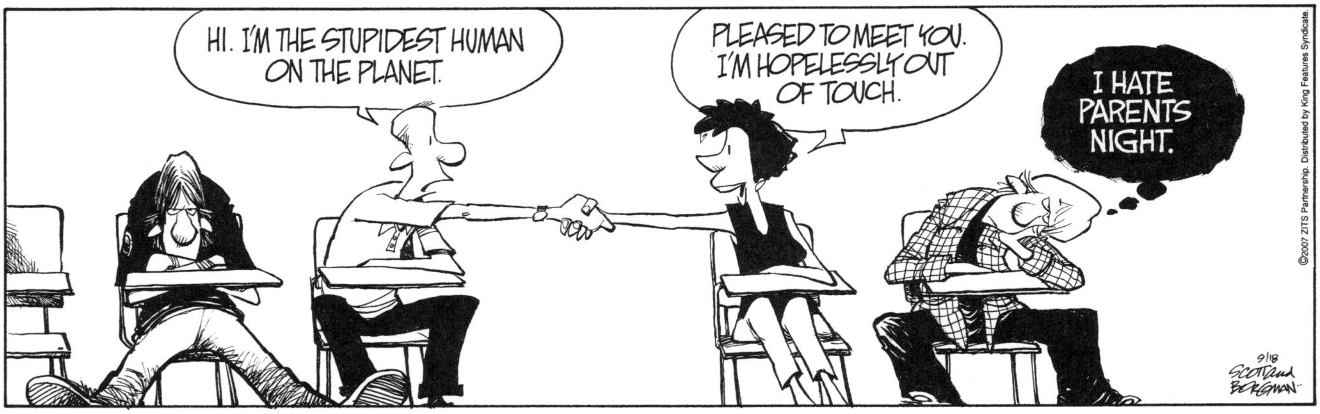
HI. I'M THE STUPIDEST HUMAN ON THE PLANET.
PLEASED TO MEET YOU. I'M HOPELESSLY OUT OF TOUCH.
I HATE PARENTS NIGHT.
©2007 ZITS Partnership. Distributed by King Features Syndicate.
9/18 SCOTT and BORGMAN

December 7, 2007

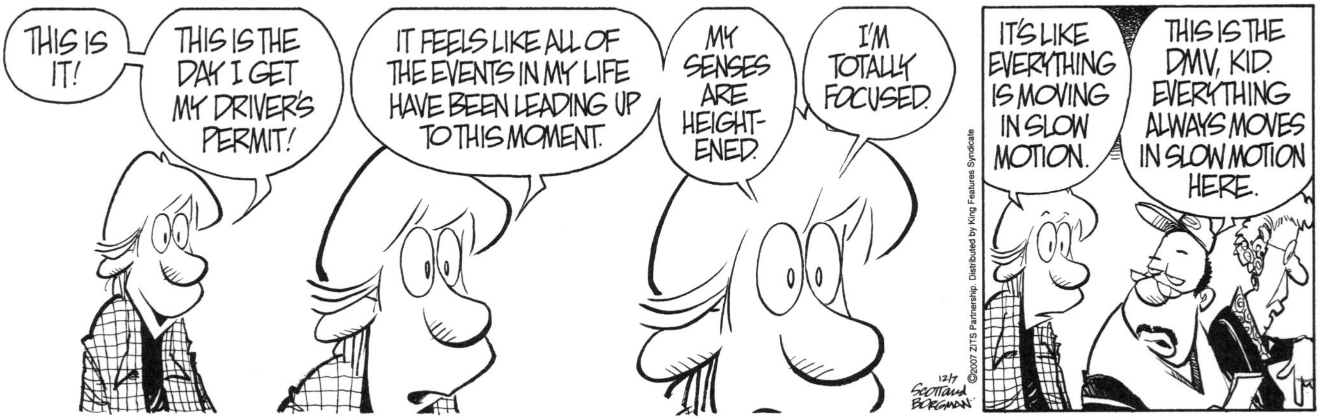
THIS IS IT!
THIS IS THE DAY I GET MY DRIVER'S PERMIT!
IT FEELS LIKE ALL OF THE EVENTS IN MY LIFE HAVE BEEN LEADING UP TO THIS MOMENT.
MY SENSES ARE HEIGHT-ENED.
I'M TOTALLY FOCUSED.
©2007 ZITS Partnership. Distributed by King Features Syndicate
12/7 SCOTT and BORGMAN
IT'S LIKE EVERYTHING IS MOVING IN SLOW MOTION.
THIS IS THE DMV, KID. EVERYTHING ALWAYS MOVES IN SLOW MOTION HERE.

August 5, 2007

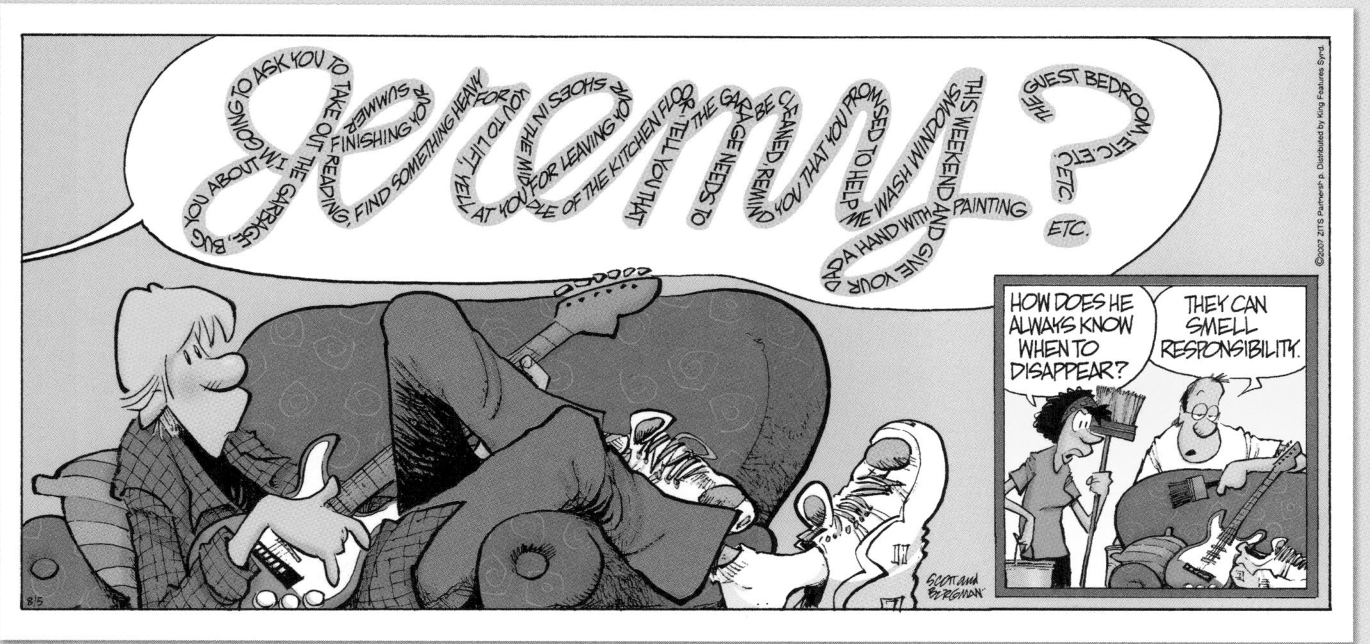
JEREMY? I'M GOING TO ASK YOU TO TAKE OUT THE GARBAGE, BUG YOU ABOUT FINISHING YOUR SUMMER READING, FIND SOMETHING HEAVY FOR YOU TO LIFT, YELL AT YOU FOR LEAVING YOUR SHOES IN THE MIDDLE OF THE KITCHEN FLOOR, TELL YOU THAT THE GARAGE NEEDS TO BE CLEANED, REMIND YOU THAT YOU PROMISED TO HELP ME WASH WINDOWS THIS WEEKEND AND GIVE YOUR DAD A HAND WITH PAINTING THE GUEST BEDROOM, ETC. ETC. ETC.
HOW DOES HE ALWAYS KNOW WHEN TO DISAPPEAR?
THEY CAN SMELL RESPONSIBILITY.
©2007 ZITS Partnership. Distributed by King Features Synd.
SCOTT AND BORGMAN
8/5

August 26, 2007

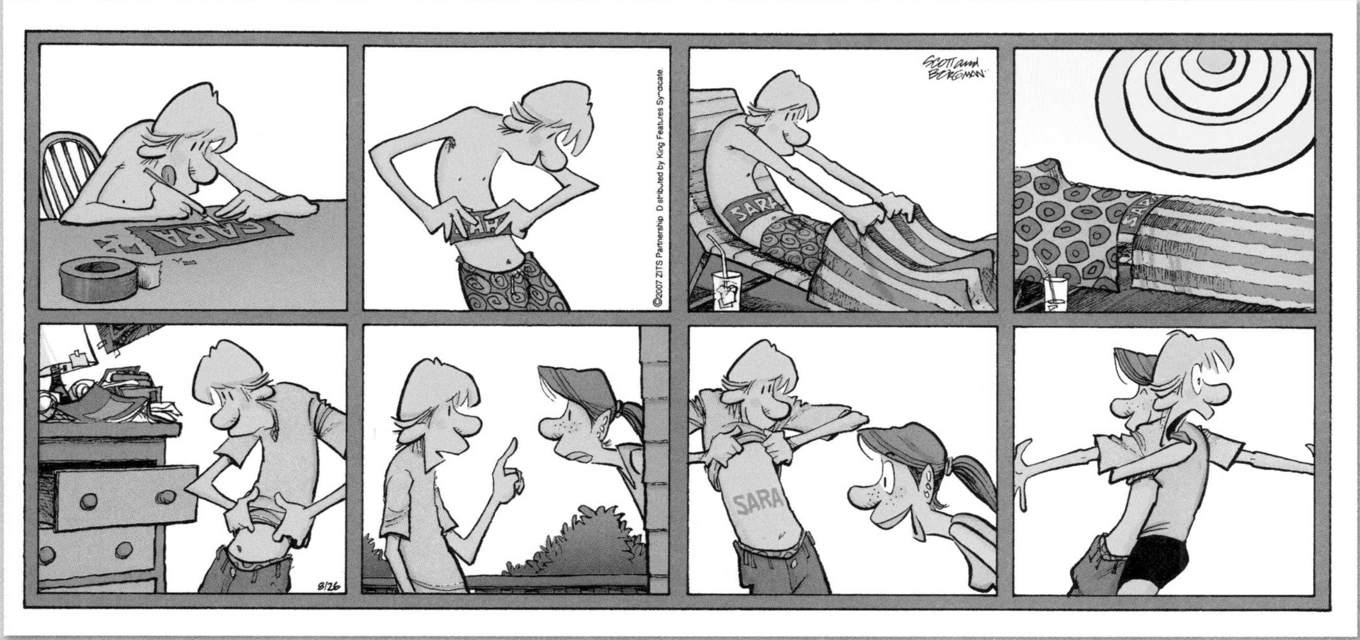
SARA
©2007 ZITS Partnership. Distributed by King Features Syndicate.
SCOTT AND BORGMAN
8/26

ZITS AROUND the WORLD

Jim Borgman

They tell us *Zits* appears in forty-five countries and fifteen different languages, which we try not to think about. If I start wondering what would make an Estonian teenager laugh, or for that matter, his parents, I roll up into a tight little ball and wet myself. It's best to just draw and write for the people we know. Somehow it translates.

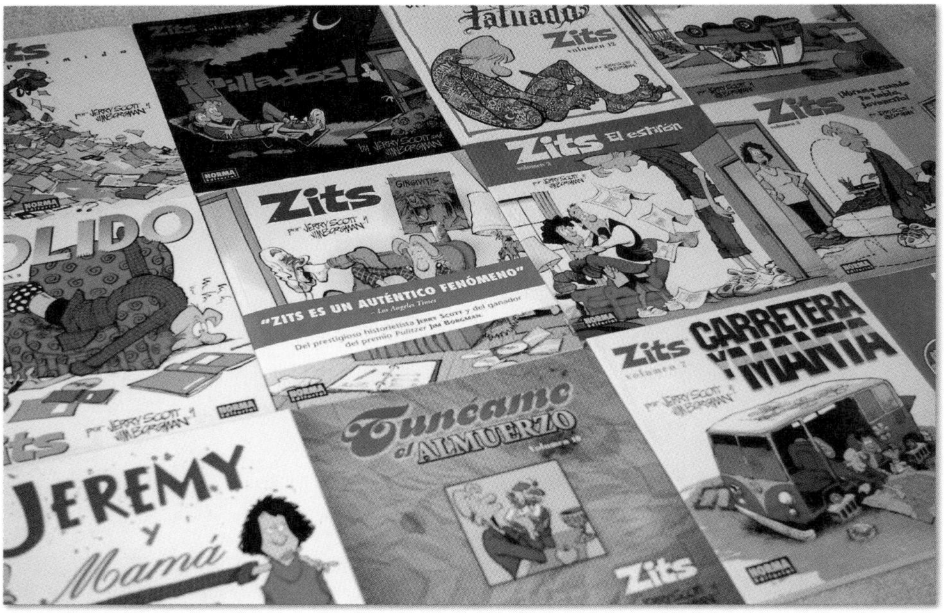
Zits
Zits El estirón
Zits
"ZITS ES UN AUTÉNTICO FENÓMENO"
Zits CARRETERA
JEREMY
Y
Mamá
Zits

The *Zits* foreign book publishing program has always been a bit of a mystery to me. But from time to time I receive books in the mail with familiar drawings and foreign words where I'm quite sure I lettered English ones. How this is all accomplished I really don't know. Translators and calligraphers must be involved, of course, but there must also be foreign editors in charge of random changes.

For example, who names these things? This book was published in the US as *Zits Supersized*.

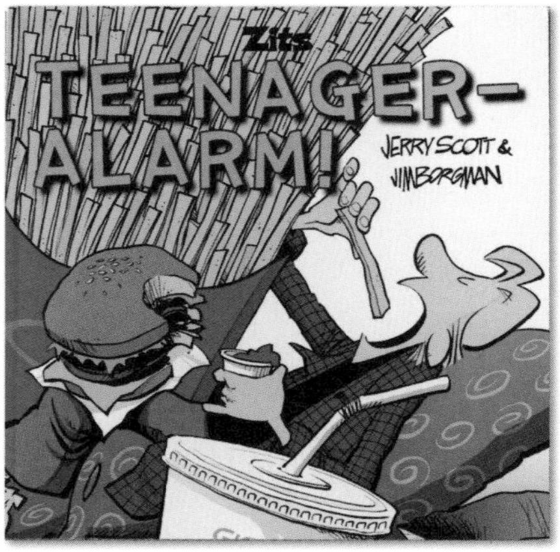
Zits
TEENAGER-ALARM!
JERRY SCOTT & JIM BORGMAN

In Sweden, our strip was renamed *Jere*. For years, we learned later, the Swedish syndicate was having all of our strips re-colored for newspapers and making Jeremy's hair red and his shirt green. Do purple shirts mean something subversive in Scandinavia? And surely the Swedes are familiar with blondes.

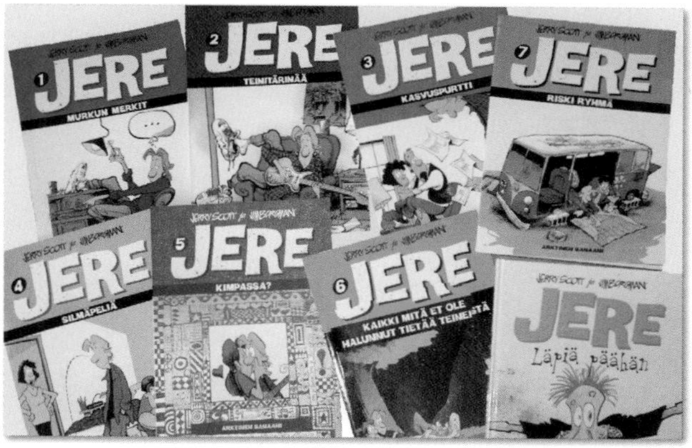
JERE
MURKUN MERKIT
TEINITÄRIMÄÄ
KASVUSPURTTI
RISKI RYHMÄ
SILMÄPELIÄ
KIMPASSA?
Läpiä päähän

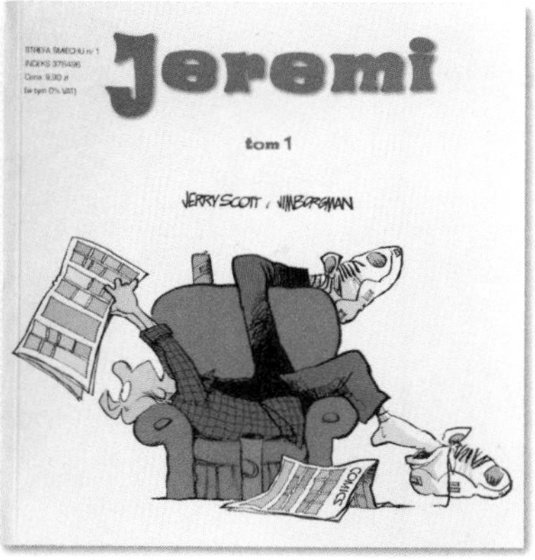
Jeromi
tom 1
JERRY SCOTT i JIM BORGMAN

Our friends at Gradiva put out some very handsome books in Portuguese, we think. Which leads to the question, do all of these jokes make sense in Portuguese? We once asked a publishing agent what they do when a strip relies on a cultural reference that wouldn't make sense in another language. "We make something up," he shrugged. Okay then.

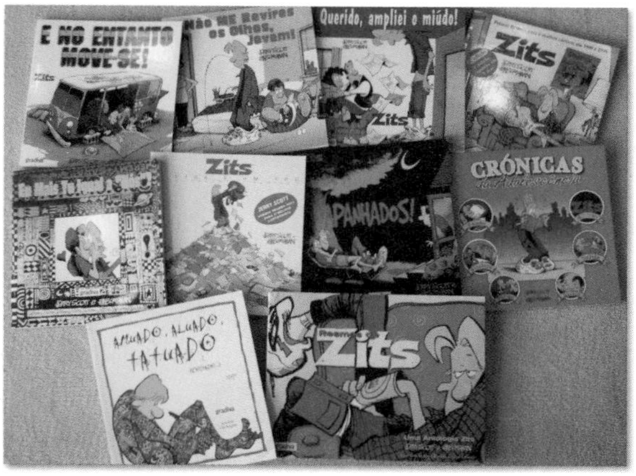
E NO ENTANTO MOVE-SE!
Não me Revires os Olhos, Jovem!
Querido, ampliei o miúdo!
Zits
CRÓNICAS
APANHADOS!
AMUADO, ALUADO, TATUADO

If you happen to be snowshoeing through Oslo or Bergen, you can pick up a copy of our monthly comic book. The Norwegians prefer to get their comics in comic book compilations every few weeks, so a bunch of strips are gathered together under one of the titles and stapled together just like we bought *Little Lulu* and *Richie Rich* off drugstore racks back in the 1960s. *Zits* used to run in the *Beetle Bailey* comic book there, which the editor in charge of random changes retitled *Billy*. You heard me right—*Beetle Bailey* is called *Billy* in Scandinavia. And when Mort Walker goes to Goteborg to sign books, they have to shut down streets to handle the crowds. All of this is true.

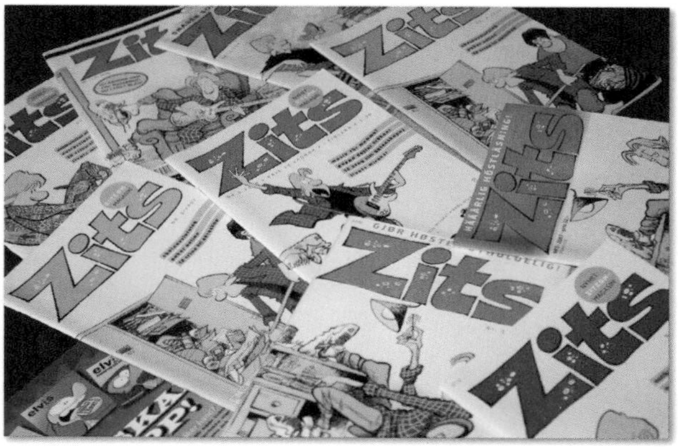
Zits

And it always cracks me up to see how *Zits* translates in Finnish.

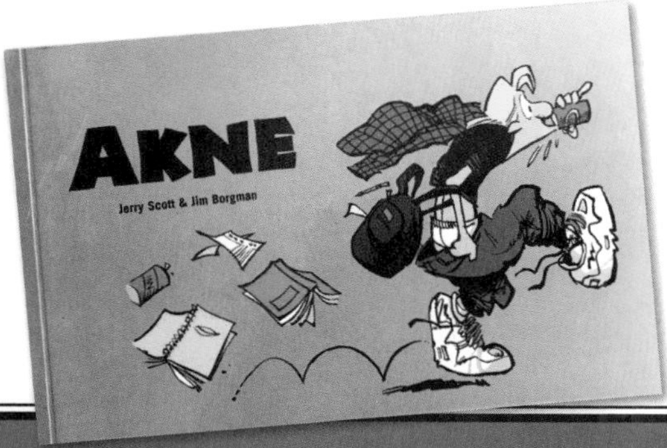
AKNE
Jerry Scott & Jim Borgman

March 16, 2008

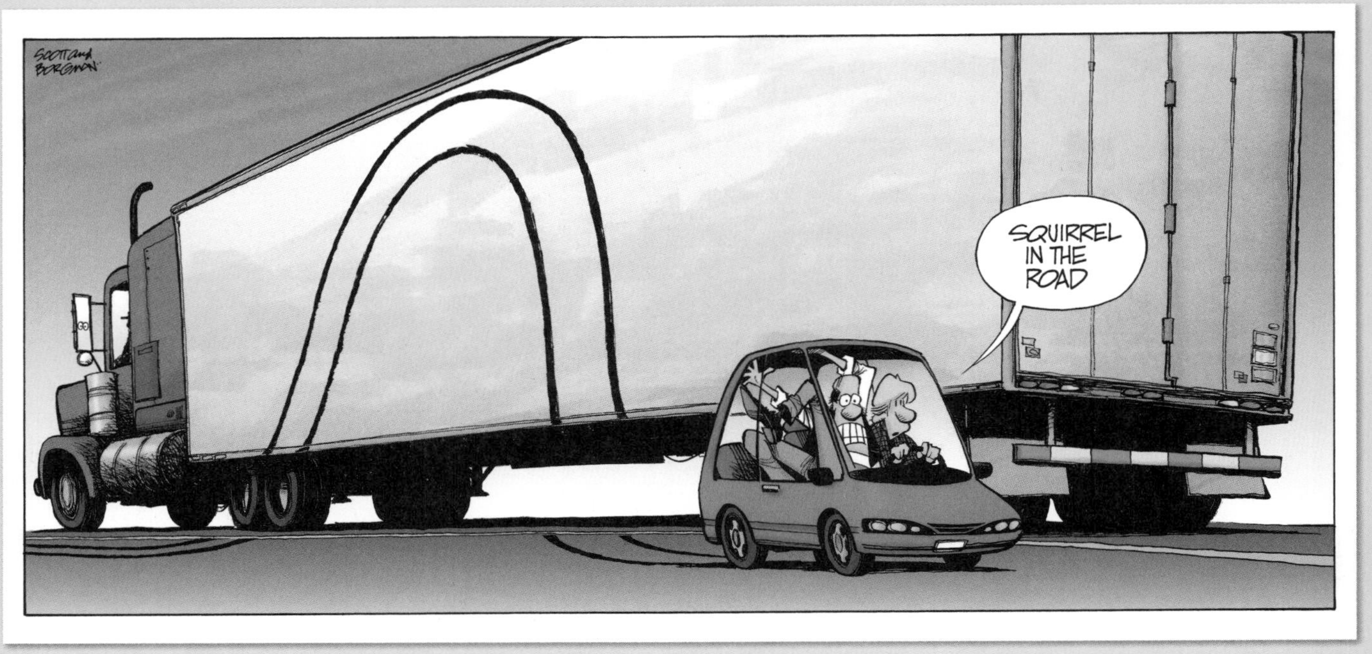
SCOTT AND BORGMAN
SQUIRREL IN THE ROAD

March 23, 2008

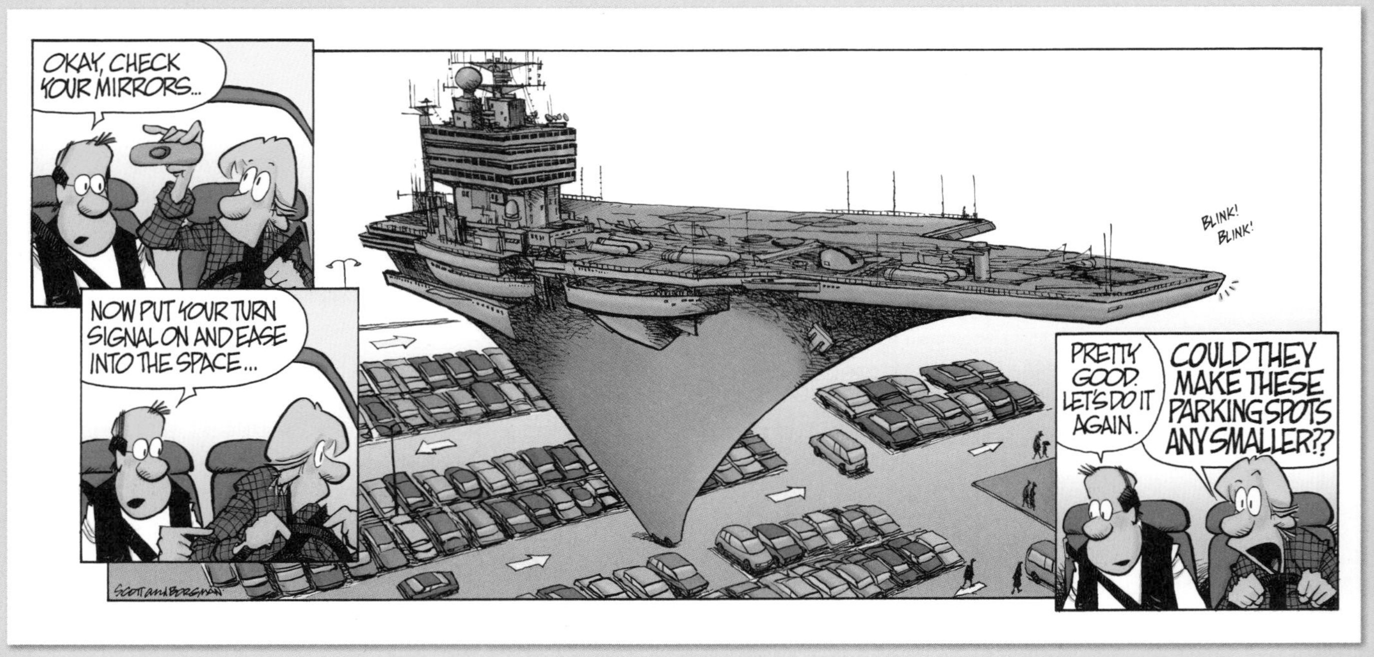
OKAY, CHECK YOUR MIRRORS...
NOW PUT YOUR TURN SIGNAL ON AND EASE INTO THE SPACE...
BLINK! BLINK!
PRETTY GOOD. LET'S DO IT AGAIN.
COULD THEY MAKE THESE PARKING SPOTS ANY SMALLER??
SCOTT AND BORGMAN

April 7, 2008

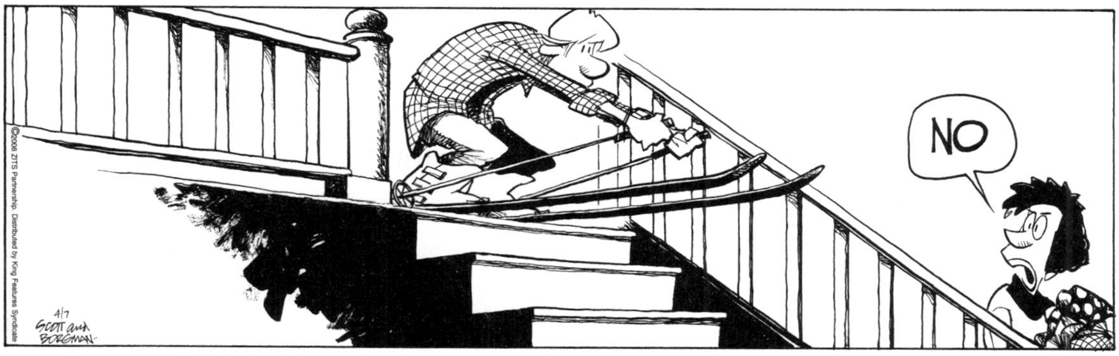
NO
4/7 SCOTT and BORGMAN
©2008 ZITS Partnership. Distributed by King Features Syndicate

April 8, 2008

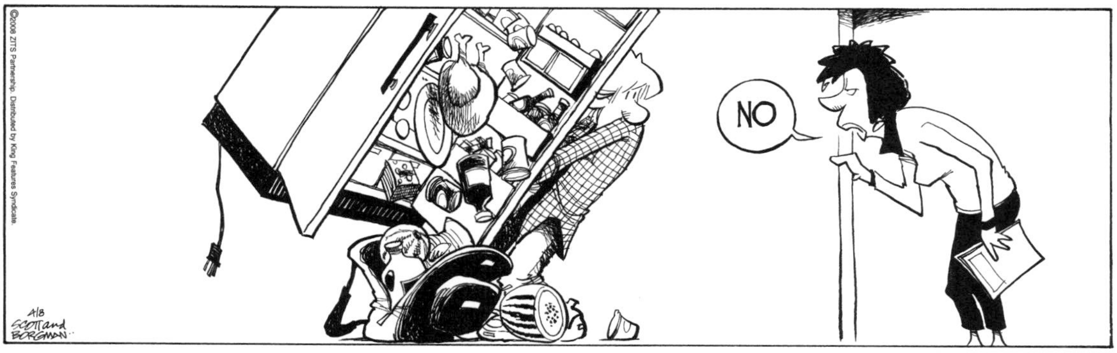
NO
4/8 SCOTT and BORGMAN
©2008 ZITS Partnership. Distributed by King Features Syndicate

April 9, 2008

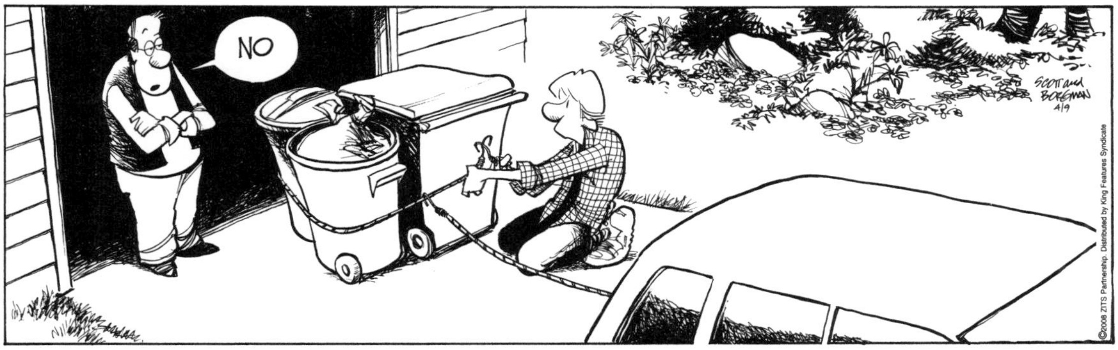
NO
SCOTT and BORGMAN 4/9
©2008 ZITS Partnership. Distributed by King Features Syndicate

April 10, 2008

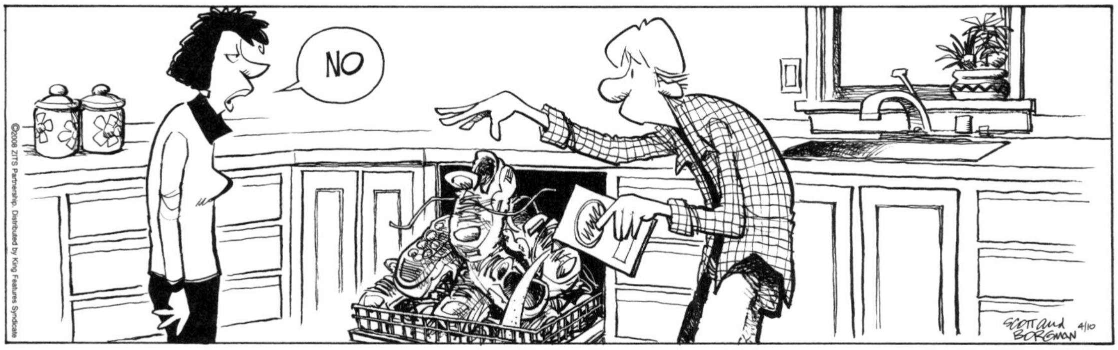
NO
SCOTT and BORGMAN 4/10
©2008 ZITS Partnership. Distributed by King Features Syndicate

January 1, 2008

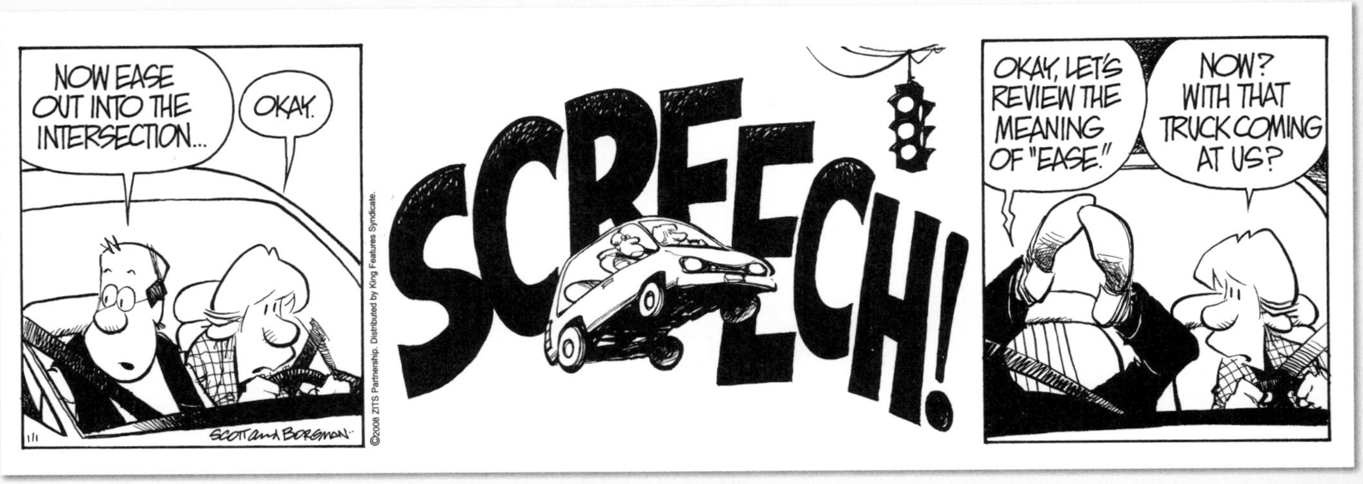
NOW EASE OUT INTO THE INTERSECTION...
OKAY.
1/1
SCOTT and BORGMAN
©2008 ZITS Partnership. Distributed by King Features Syndicate.
SCREECH!
OKAY, LET'S REVIEW THE MEANING OF "EASE."
NOW? WITH THAT TRUCK COMING AT US?

April 21, 2008

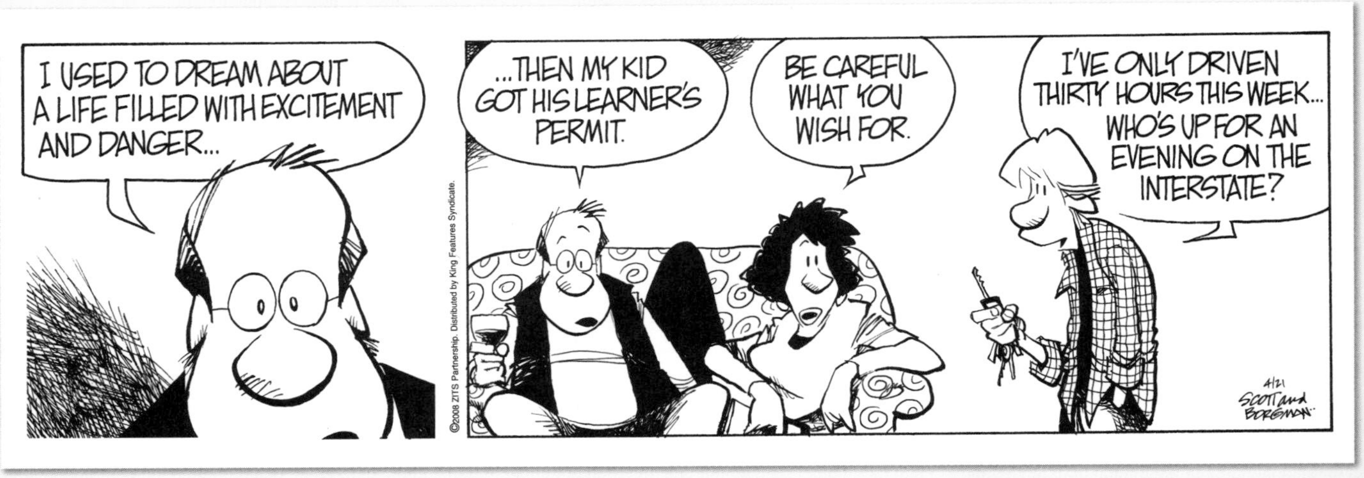
I USED TO DREAM ABOUT A LIFE FILLED WITH EXCITEMENT AND DANGER...
©2008 ZITS Partnership. Distributed by King Features Syndicate.
...THEN MY KID GOT HIS LEARNER'S PERMIT.
BE CAREFUL WHAT YOU WISH FOR.
I'VE ONLY DRIVEN THIRTY HOURS THIS WEEK... WHO'S UP FOR AN EVENING ON THE INTERSTATE?
4/21
SCOTT and BORGMAN

May 15, 2008

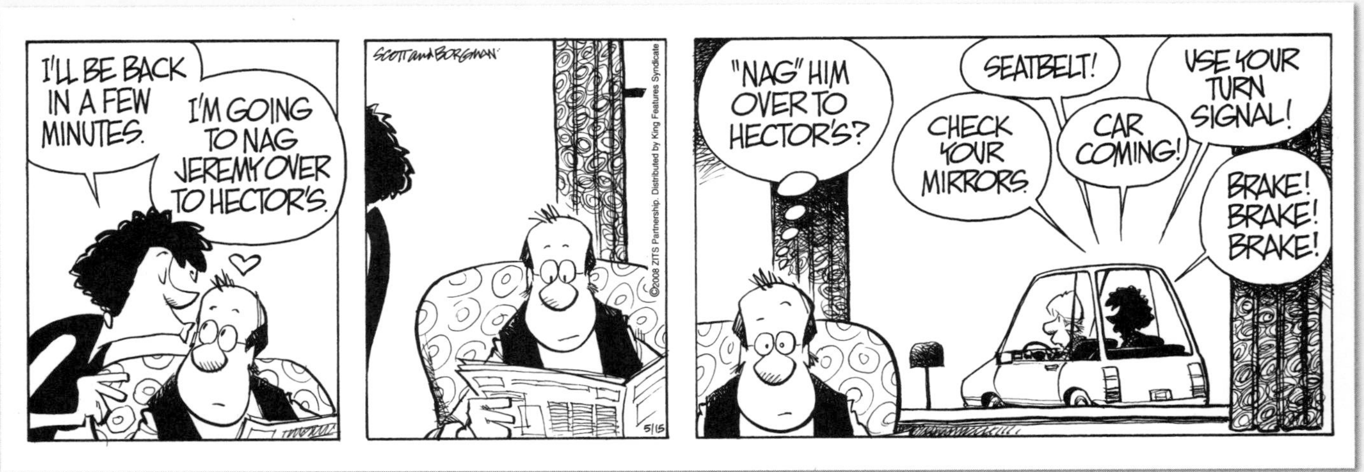
I'LL BE BACK IN A FEW MINUTES.
I'M GOING TO NAG JEREMY OVER TO HECTOR'S.
SCOTT and BORGMAN
©2008 ZITS Partnership. Distributed by King Features Syndicate.
5/15
"NAG" HIM OVER TO HECTOR'S?
CHECK YOUR MIRRORS.
SEATBELT!
CAR COMING!
USE YOUR TURN SIGNAL!
BRAKE! BRAKE! BRAKE!

May 12, 2008

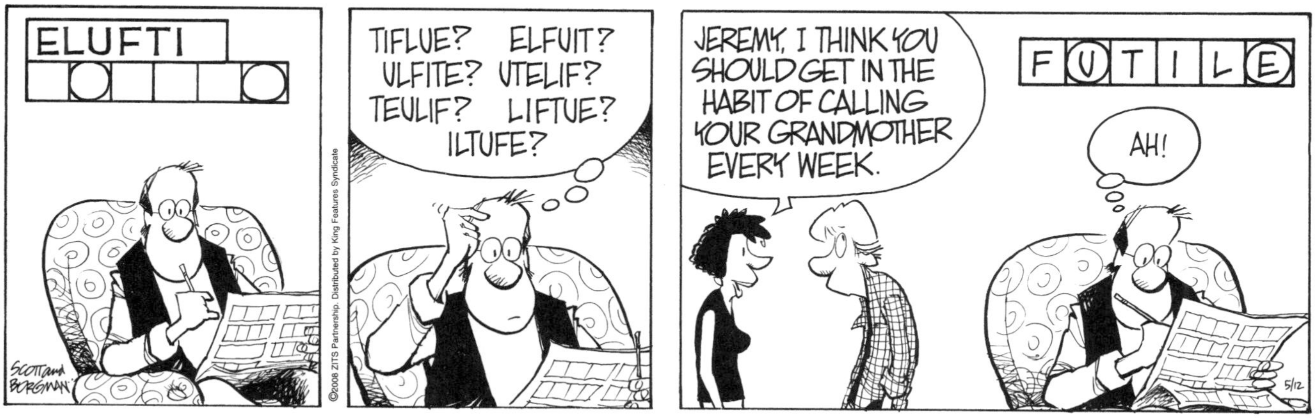
ELUFTI
TIFLUE? ELFUIT? ULFITE? UTELIF? TEULIF? LIFTUE? ILTUFE?
JEREMY, I THINK YOU SHOULD GET IN THE HABIT OF CALLING YOUR GRANDMOTHER EVERY WEEK.
FUTILE
AH!
©2008 ZITS Partnership. Distributed by King Features Syndicate
SCOTT and BORGMAN
5/12

May 13, 2008

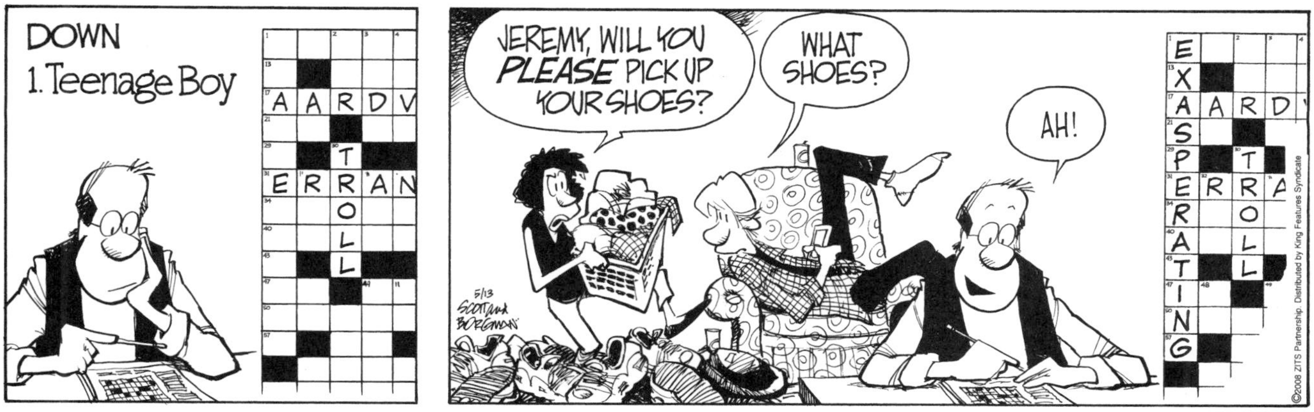
DOWN
1. Teenage Boy
JEREMY, WILL YOU PLEASE PICK UP YOUR SHOES?
WHAT SHOES?
AH!
EXASPERATING
©2008 ZITS Partnership. Distributed by King Features Syndicate
5/13 SCOTT and BORGMAN

May 14, 2008

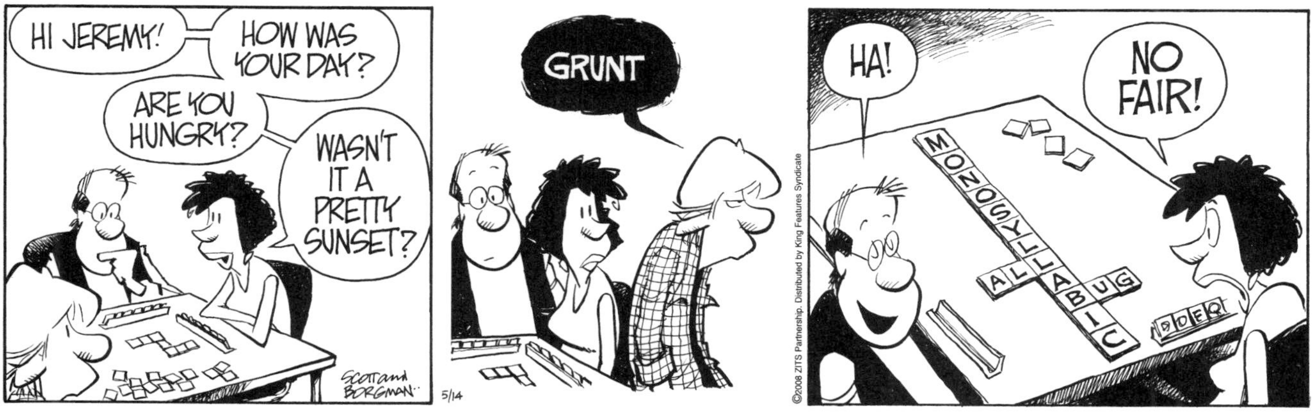
HI JEREMY!
HOW WAS YOUR DAY?
ARE YOU HUNGRY?
WASN'T IT A PRETTY SUNSET?
GRUNT
HA!
NO FAIR!
MONOSYLLABIC
©2008 ZITS Partnership. Distributed by King Features Syndicate
SCOTT and BORGMAN
5/14

May 23, 2008

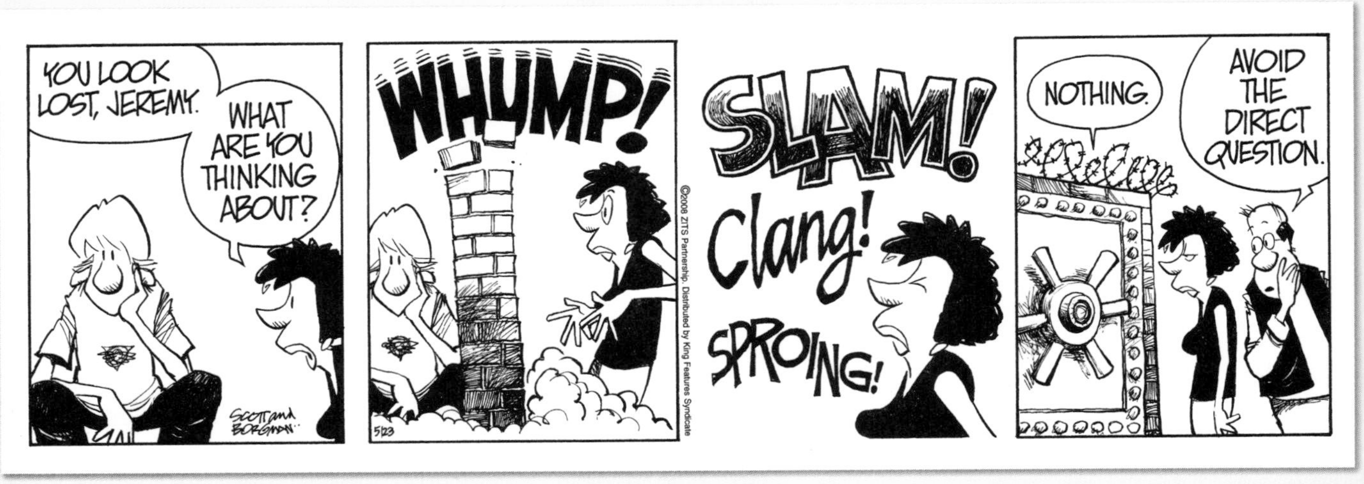
YOU LOOK LOST, JEREMY.
WHAT ARE YOU THINKING ABOUT?
WHUMP!
SLAM!
Clang!
SPROING!
NOTHING.
AVOID THE DIRECT QUESTION.
©2008 ZITS Partnership. Distributed by King Features Syndicate
SCOTT and BORGMAN

May 31, 2008

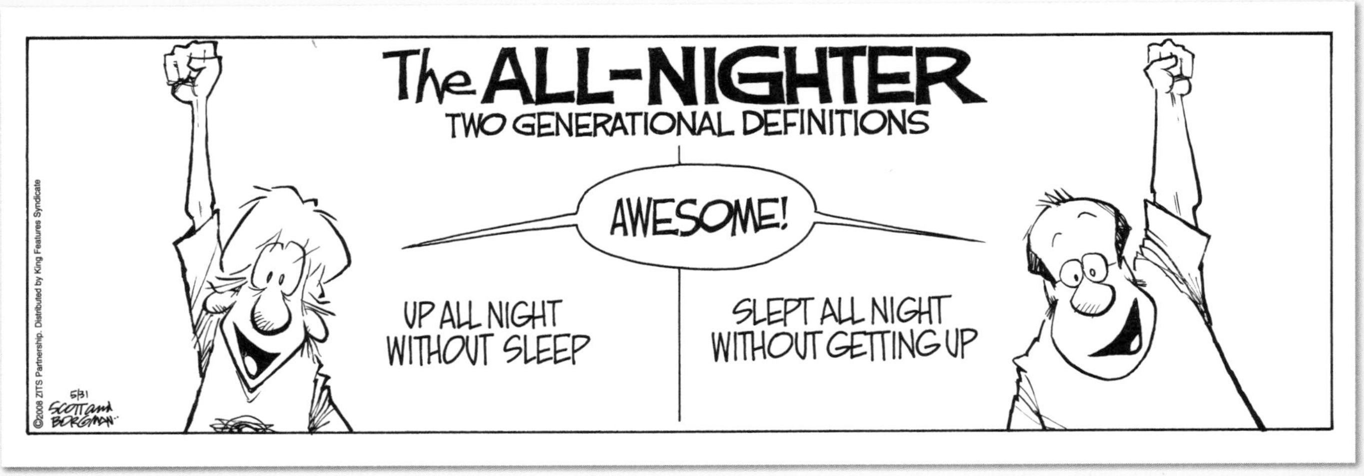
The ALL-NIGHTER
TWO GENERATIONAL DEFINITIONS
AWESOME!
UP ALL NIGHT WITHOUT SLEEP
SLEPT ALL NIGHT WITHOUT GETTING UP
©2008 ZITS Partnership. Distributed by King Features Syndicate
SCOTT and BORGMAN

November 17, 2008

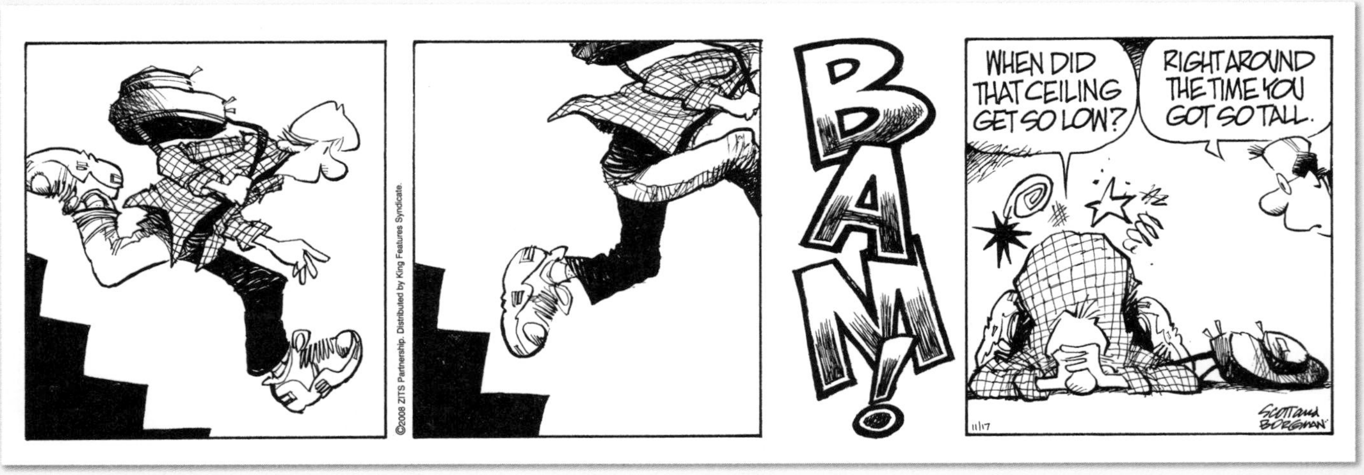
BAM!
WHEN DID THAT CEILING GET SO LOW?
RIGHT AROUND THE TIME YOU GOT SO TALL.
©2008 ZITS Partnership. Distributed by King Features Syndicate.
SCOTT and BORGMAN

June 11, 2008

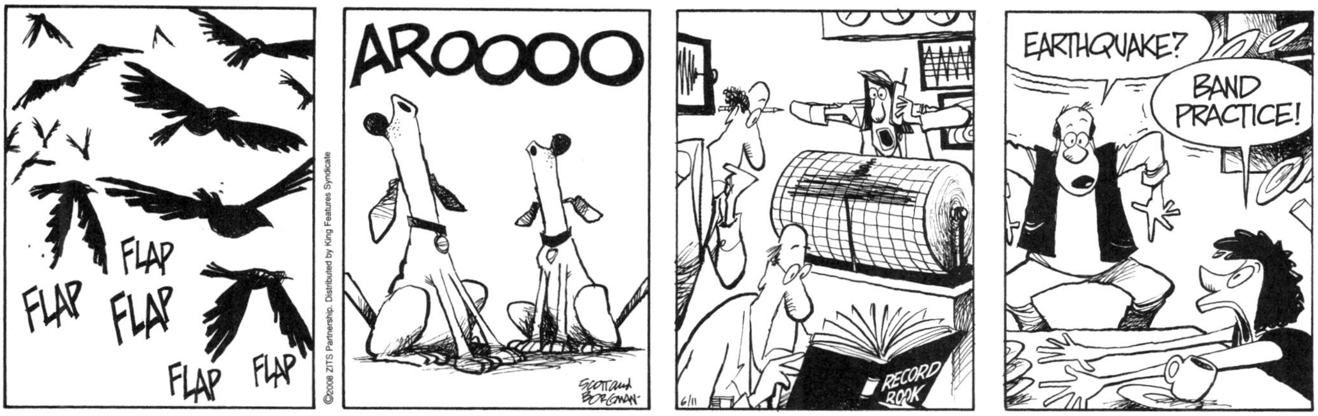
FLAP
FLAP
FLAP
FLAP
FLAP
©2008 ZITS Partnership. Distributed by King Features Syndicate
AROOOO
SCOTT and BORGMAN
6/11
RECORD BOOK
EARTHQUAKE?
BAND PRACTICE!

June 16, 2008

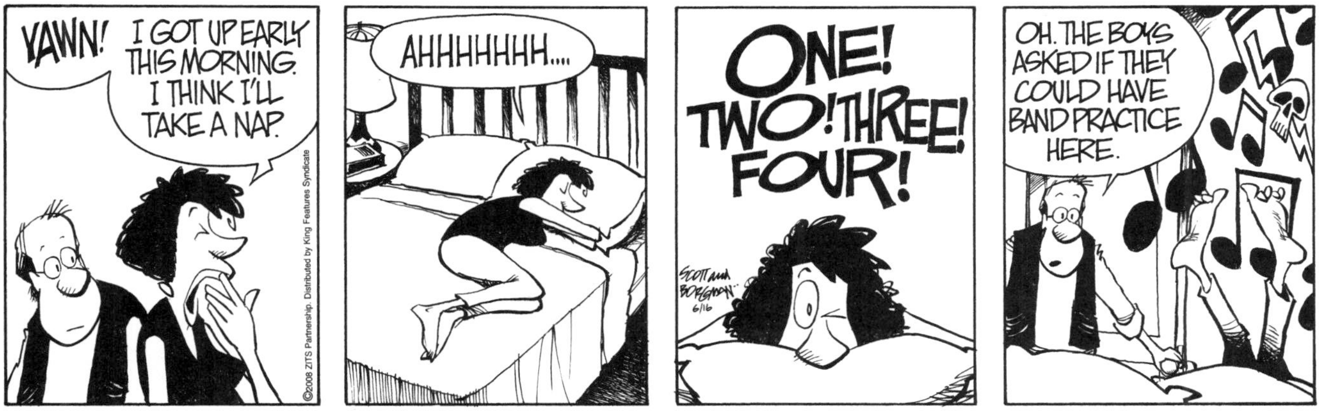
YAWN!
I GOT UP EARLY THIS MORNING. I THINK I'LL TAKE A NAP.
©2008 ZITS Partnership. Distributed by King Features Syndicate
AHHHHHHH....
ONE! TWO! THREE! FOUR!
SCOTT and BORGMAN 6/16
OH. THE BOYS ASKED IF THEY COULD HAVE BAND PRACTICE HERE.

June 20, 2008

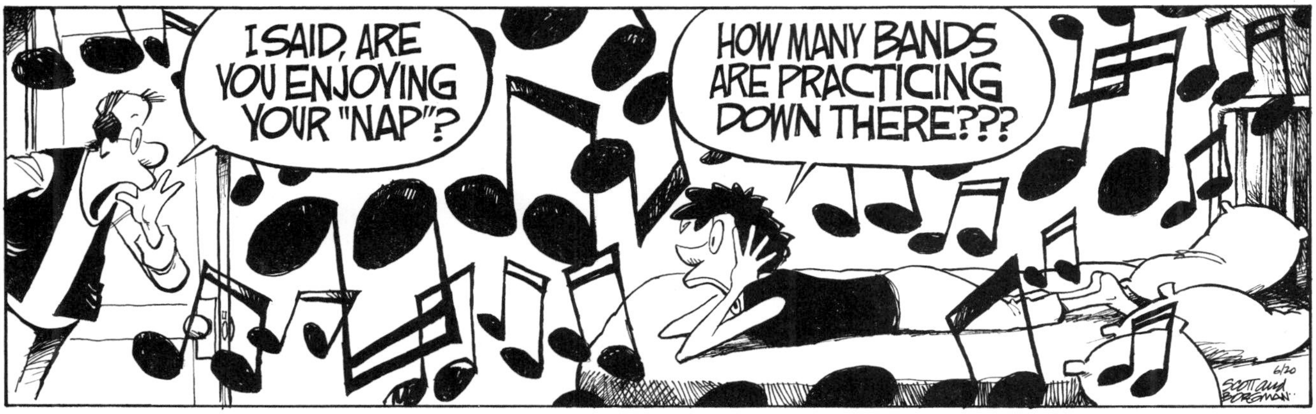
I SAID, ARE YOU ENJOYING YOUR "NAP"?
HOW MANY BANDS ARE PRACTICING DOWN THERE???
6/20
SCOTT and BORGMAN

July 14, 2008

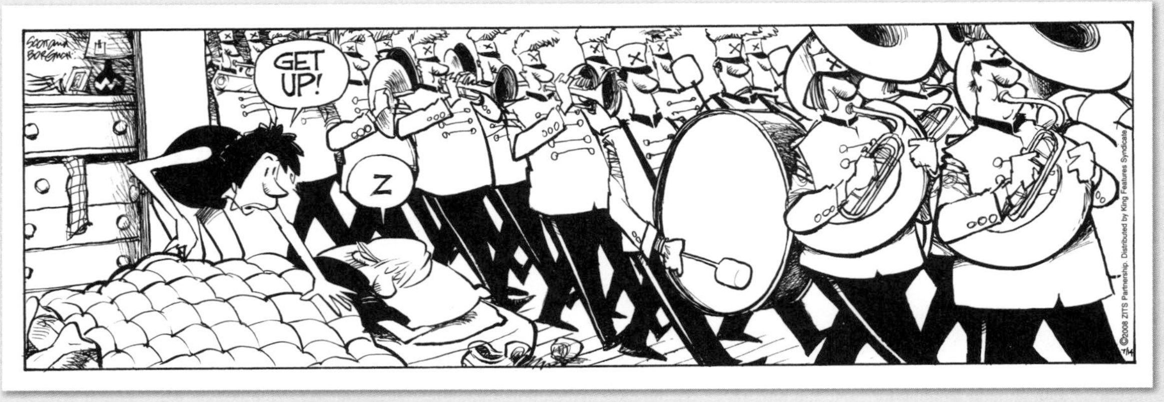
GET UP!
Z
©2008 ZITS Partnership. Distributed by King Features Syndicate.

July 15, 2008

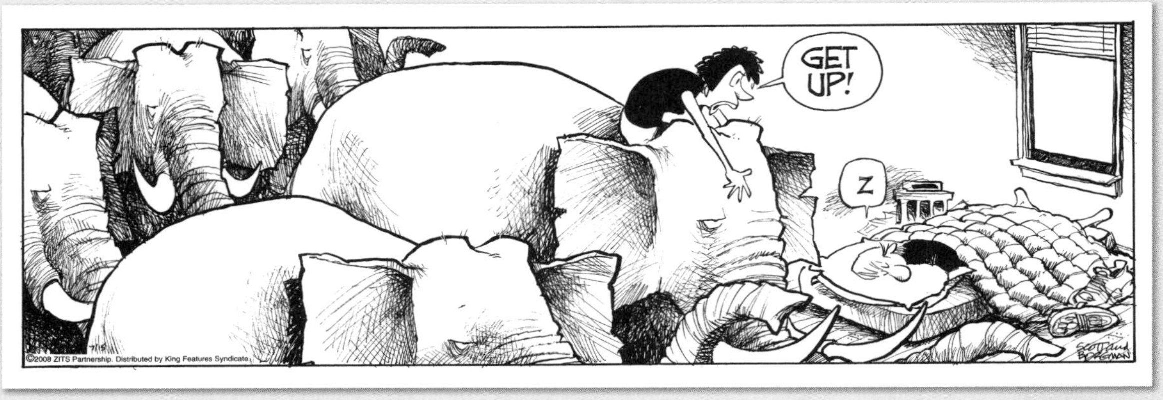
GET UP!
Z
©2008 ZITS Partnership. Distributed by King Features Syndicate.

July 16, 2008

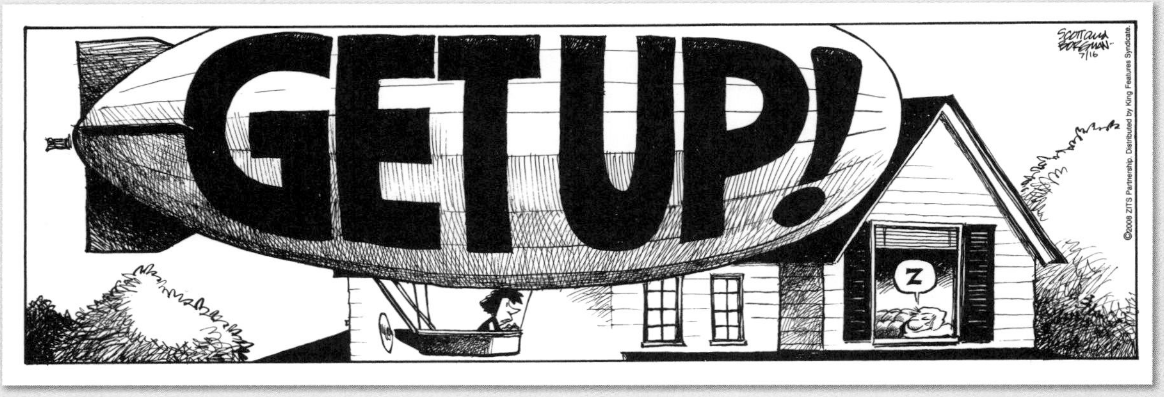
GET UP!
Z
©2008 ZITS Partnership. Distributed by King Features Syndicate.

July 19, 2008

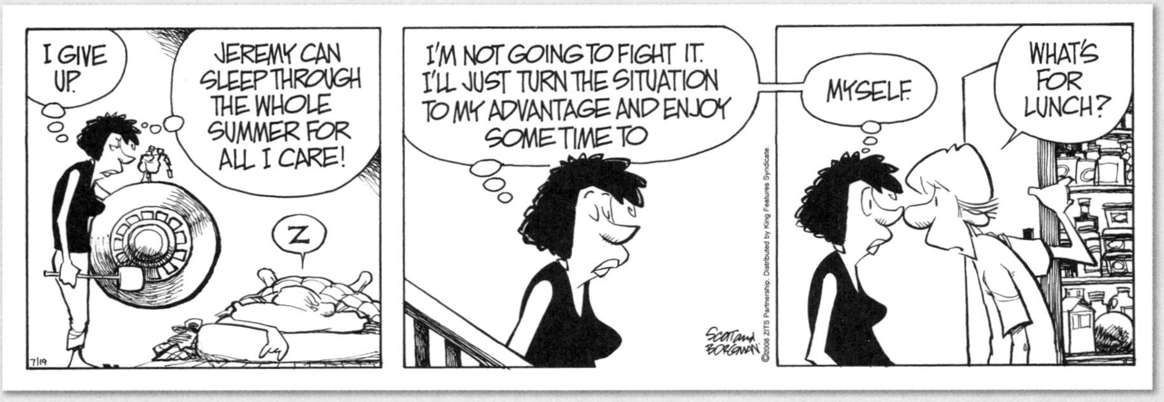
I GIVE UP.
JEREMY CAN SLEEP THROUGH THE WHOLE SUMMER FOR ALL I CARE!
Z
I'M NOT GOING TO FIGHT IT. I'LL JUST TURN THE SITUATION TO MY ADVANTAGE AND ENJOY SOME TIME TO
MYSELF.
WHAT'S FOR LUNCH?
©2008 ZITS Partnership. Distributed by King Features Syndicate.

June 8, 2008

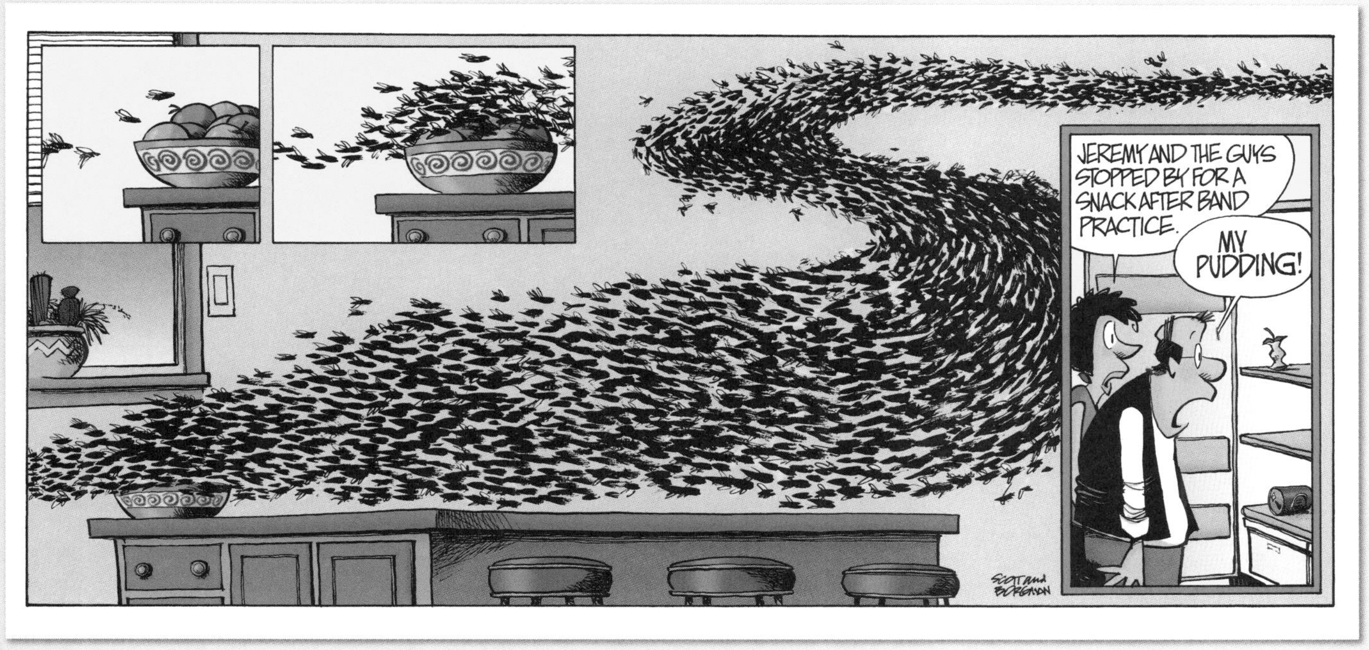

JEREMY AND THE GUYS STOPPED BY FOR A SNACK AFTER BAND PRACTICE.
MY PUDDING!
SCOTT and BORGMAN

July 6, 2008

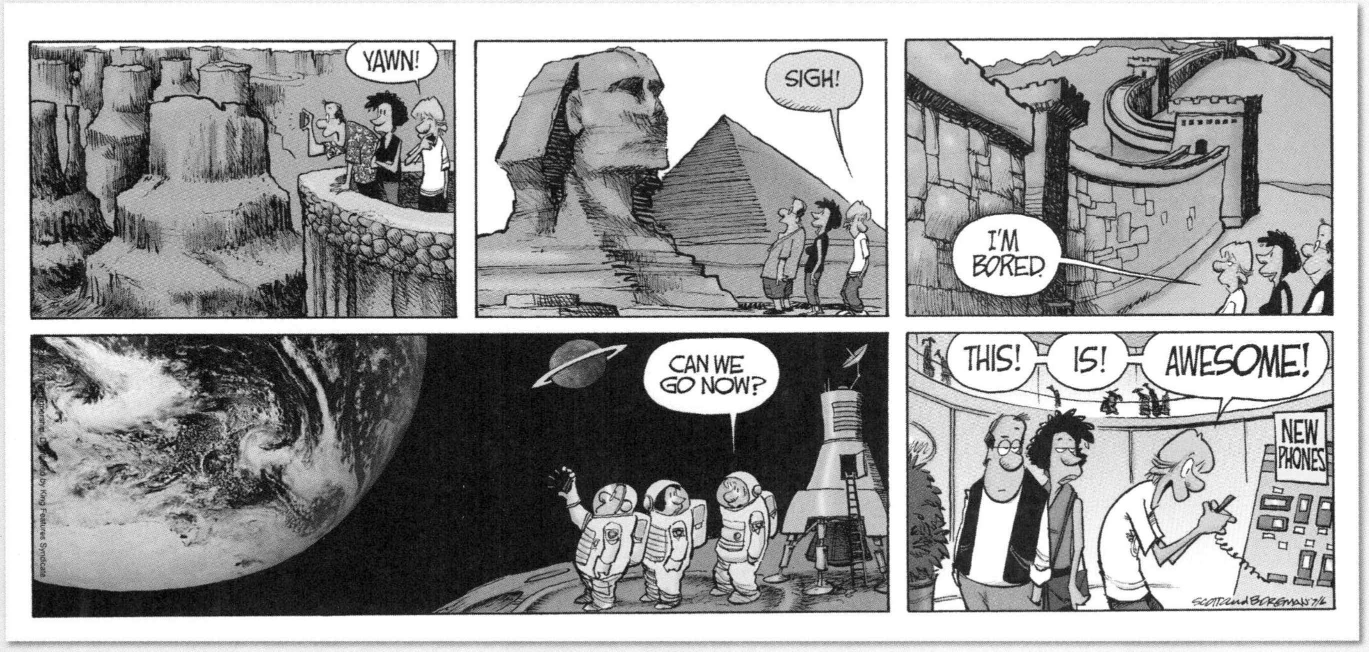

YAWN!
SIGH!
I'M BORED.
CAN WE GO NOW?
THIS!
IS!
AWESOME!
NEW PHONES

August 4, 2008

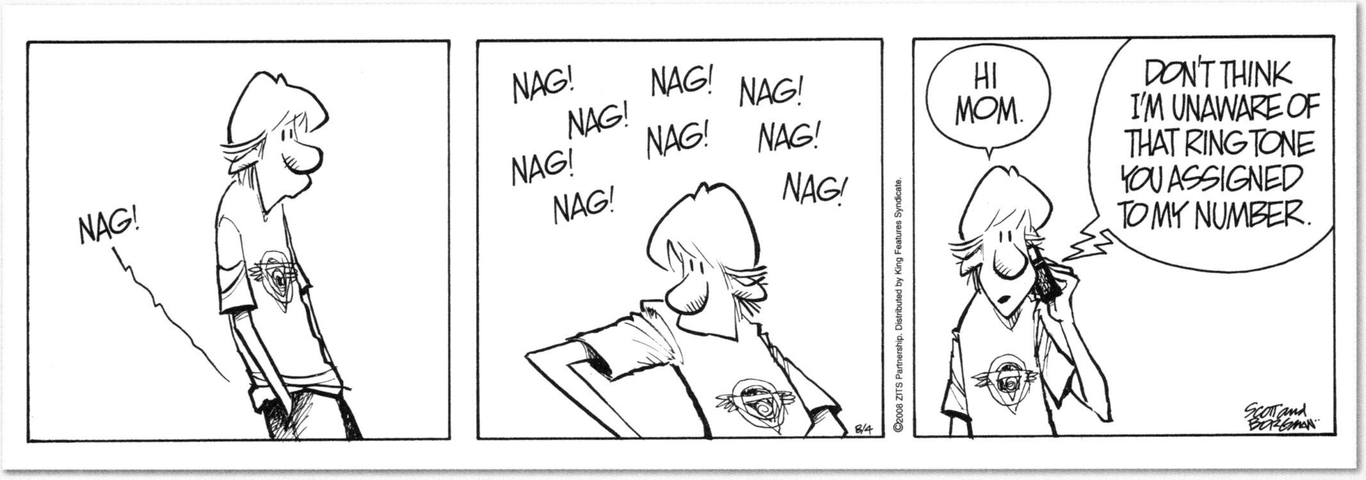
NAG!
NAG! NAG! NAG! NAG! NAG! NAG! NAG! NAG!
HI MOM.
DON'T THINK I'M UNAWARE OF THAT RINGTONE YOU ASSIGNED TO MY NUMBER.
©2008 ZITS Partnership. Distributed by King Features Syndicate.
8/4
SCOTT and BORGMAN

November 10, 2008

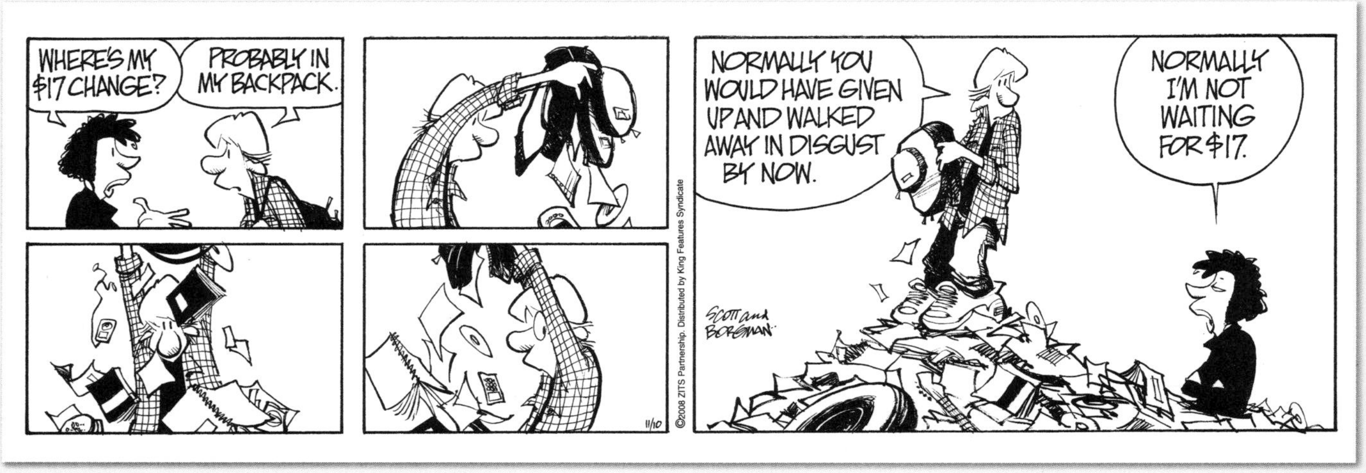
WHERE'S MY $17 CHANGE?
PROBABLY IN MY BACKPACK.
NORMALLY YOU WOULD HAVE GIVEN UP AND WALKED AWAY IN DISGUST BY NOW.
NORMALLY I'M NOT WAITING FOR $17.
©2008 ZITS Partnership. Distributed by King Features Syndicate
11/10
SCOTT and BORGMAN

September 1, 2008

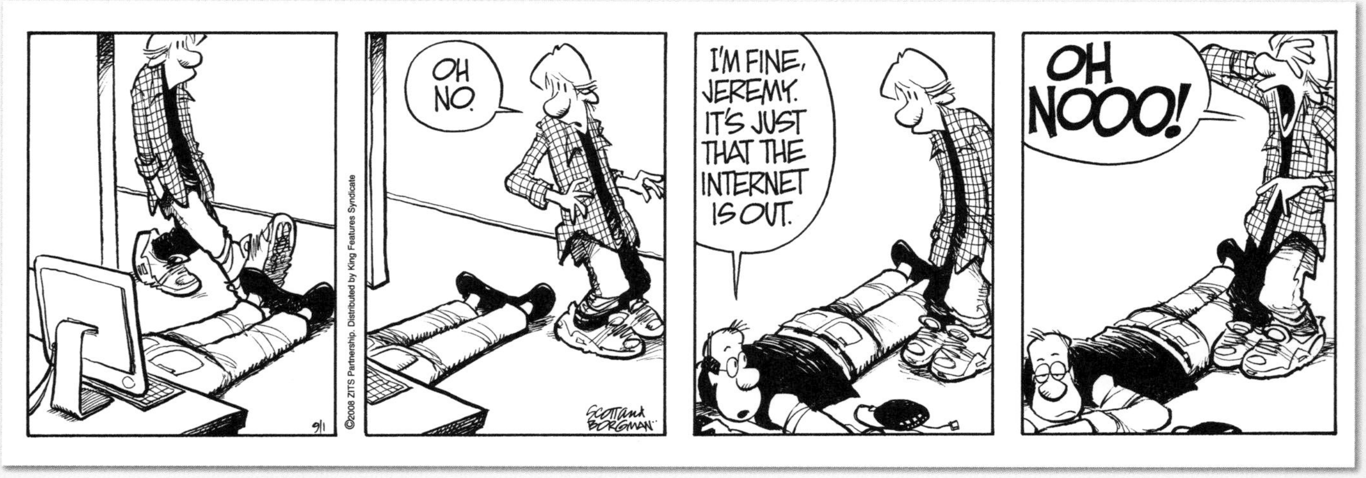
OH NO.
I'M FINE, JEREMY. IT'S JUST THAT THE INTERNET IS OUT.
OH NOOO!
©2008 ZITS Partnership. Distributed by King Features Syndicate
9/1
SCOTT and BORGMAN

September 15, 2008

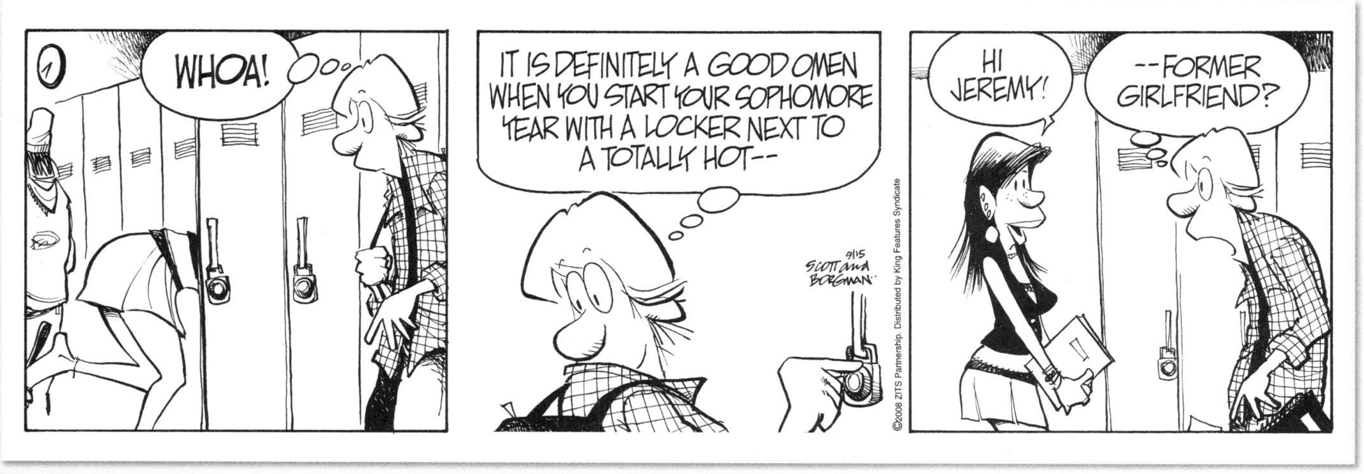
WHOA!
IT IS DEFINITELY A GOOD OMEN WHEN YOU START YOUR SOPHOMORE YEAR WITH A LOCKER NEXT TO A TOTALLY HOT--
SCOTT AND BORGMAN
©2008 ZITS Partnership. Distributed by King Features Syndicate
HI JEREMY!
--FORMER GIRLFRIEND?

September 26, 2008

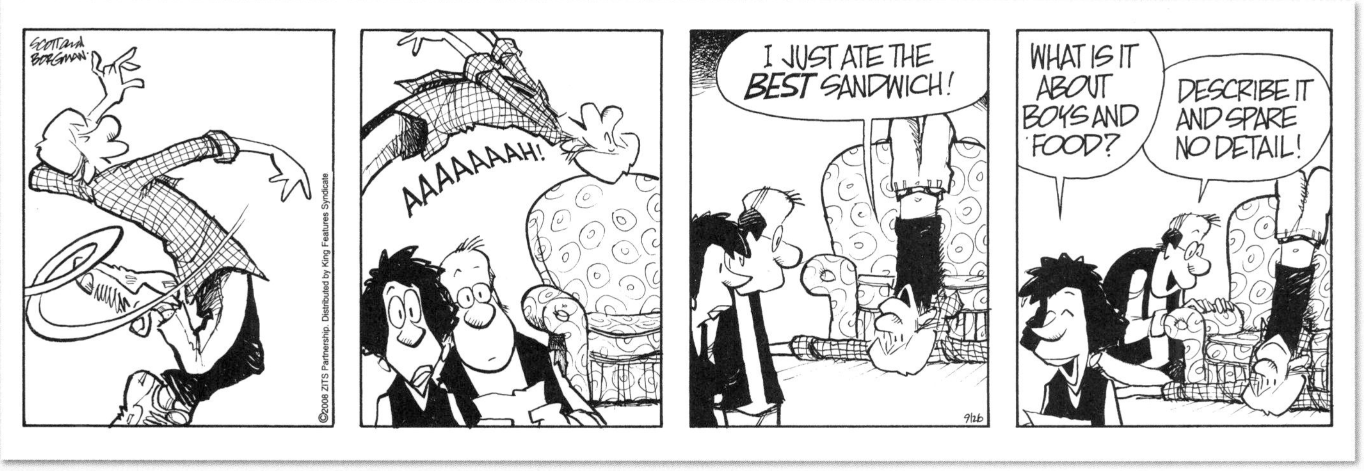
SCOTT AND BORGMAN
©2008 ZITS Partnership. Distributed by King Features Syndicate
AAAAAAAH!
I JUST ATE THE BEST SANDWICH!
WHAT IS IT ABOUT BOYS AND FOOD?
DESCRIBE IT AND SPARE NO DETAIL!

October 17, 2008

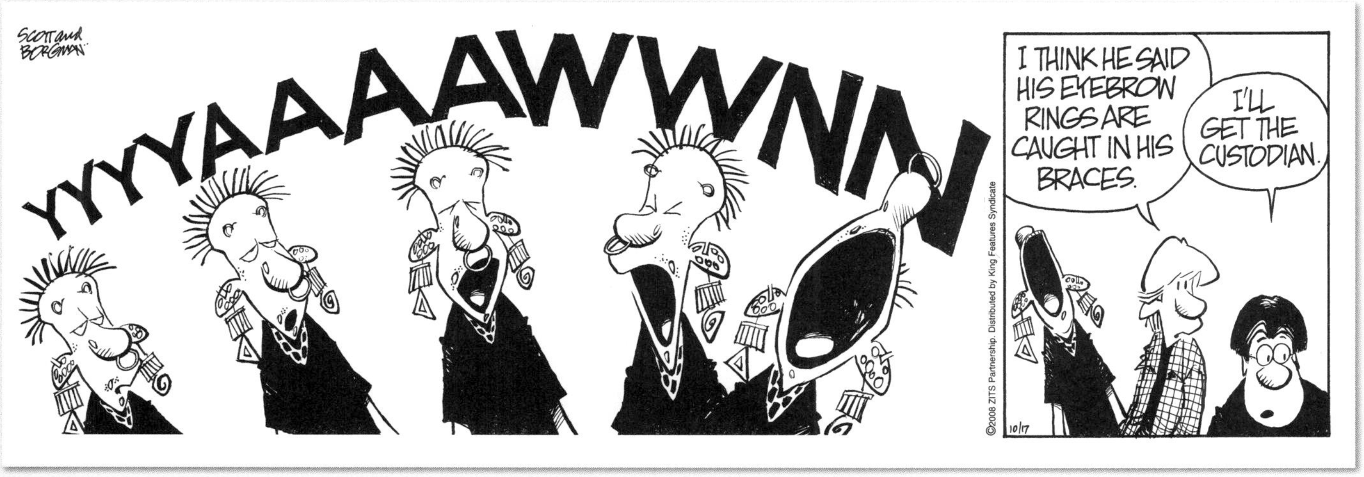
SCOTT AND BORGMAN
YYYYAAAAAWWNN
©2008 ZITS Partnership. Distributed by King Features Syndicate
I THINK HE SAID HIS EYEBROW RINGS ARE CAUGHT IN HIS BRACES.
I'LL GET THE CUSTODIAN.

August 17, 2008

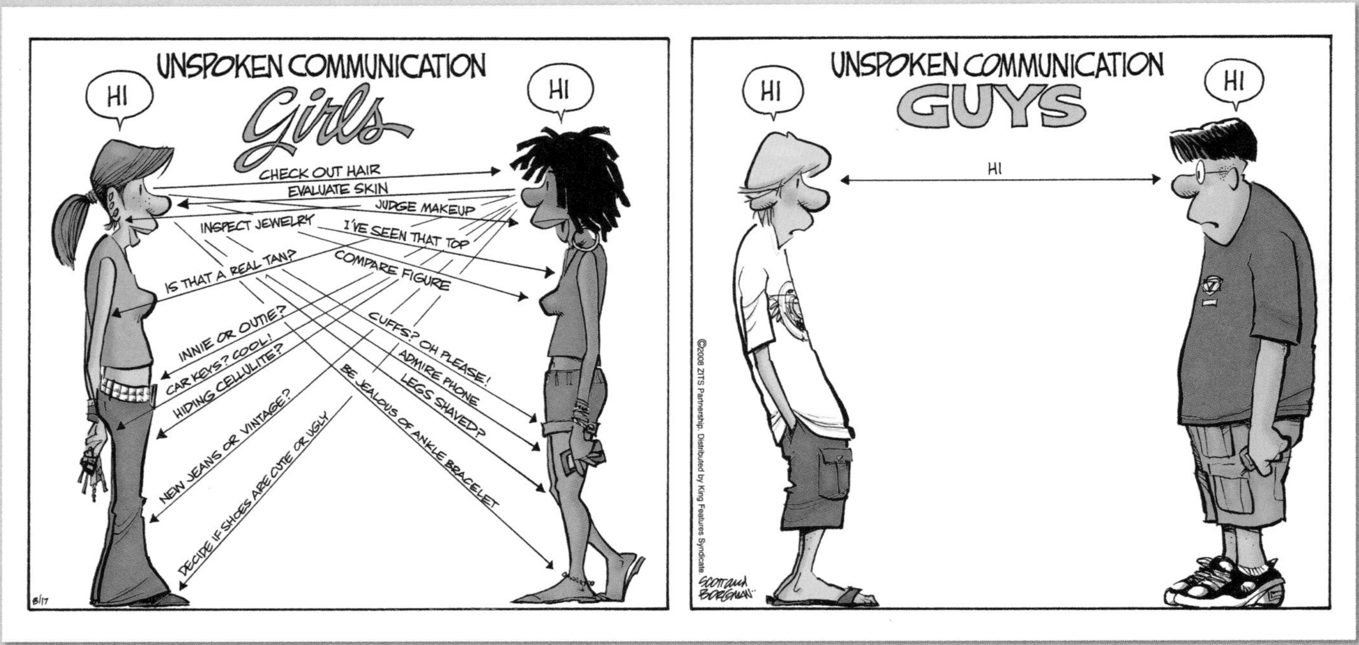
UNSPOKEN COMMUNICATION
Girls
HI
HI
CHECK OUT HAIR
EVALUATE SKIN
JUDGE MAKEUP
INSPECT JEWELRY
I'VE SEEN THAT TOP
IS THAT A REAL TAN?
COMPARE FIGURE
INNIE OR OUTIE?
CAR KEYS? COOL!
HIDING CELLULITE?
NEW JEANS OR VINTAGE?
DECIDE IF SHOES ARE CUTE OR UGLY
CUFFS? OH PLEASE!
ADMIRE PHONE
LEGS SHAVED?
BE JEALOUS OF ANKLE BRACELET
UNSPOKEN COMMUNICATION
GUYS
HI
HI
HI
©2008 ZITS Partnership. Distributed by King Features Syndicate
SCOTT AND BORGMAN

November 9, 2008

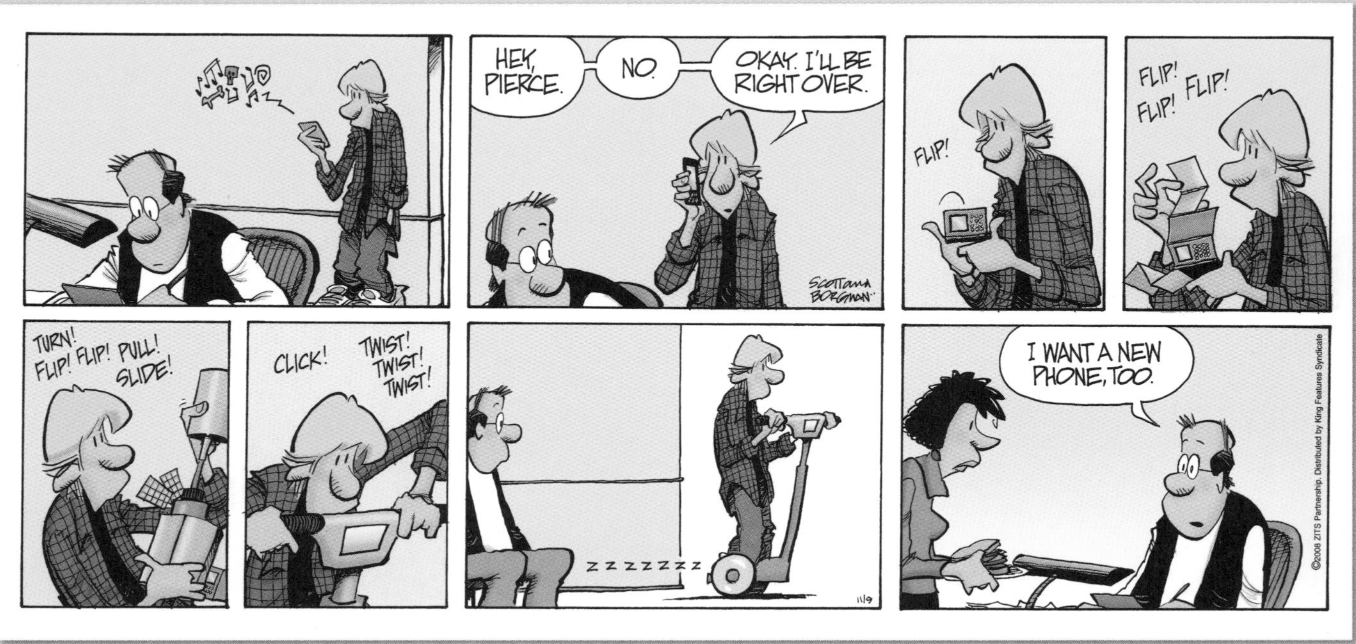
HEY, PIERCE.
NO.
OKAY. I'LL BE RIGHT OVER.
SCOTT AND BORGMAN
FLIP!
FLIP! FLIP! FLIP!
TURN! FLIP! FLIP! PULL! SLIDE!
CLICK!
TWIST! TWIST! TWIST!
ZZZZZZZ
I WANT A NEW PHONE, TOO.
©2008 ZITS Partnership. Distributed by King Features Syndicate

That Kid Reminds me of my Son!

Jim Borgman

I was waiting for an elevator in the newspaper building where I used to work, heading home for the night, when an older gentleman joined me. He must have spotted the half-finished drawings tucked under my arm.

"Do you draw that comic strip about the teenager?" he asked.

"Yes, I draw *Zits*," I said.

"That kid reminds me of my son!" he said.

We boarded the elevator, and as we rode down, I snuck a glance at his white hair and stooped posture.

"If you don't mind me asking, sir," I said, "how old is your son?"

"He's sixty-five!" he snorted. "He's retiring next week!"

January 4, 2009

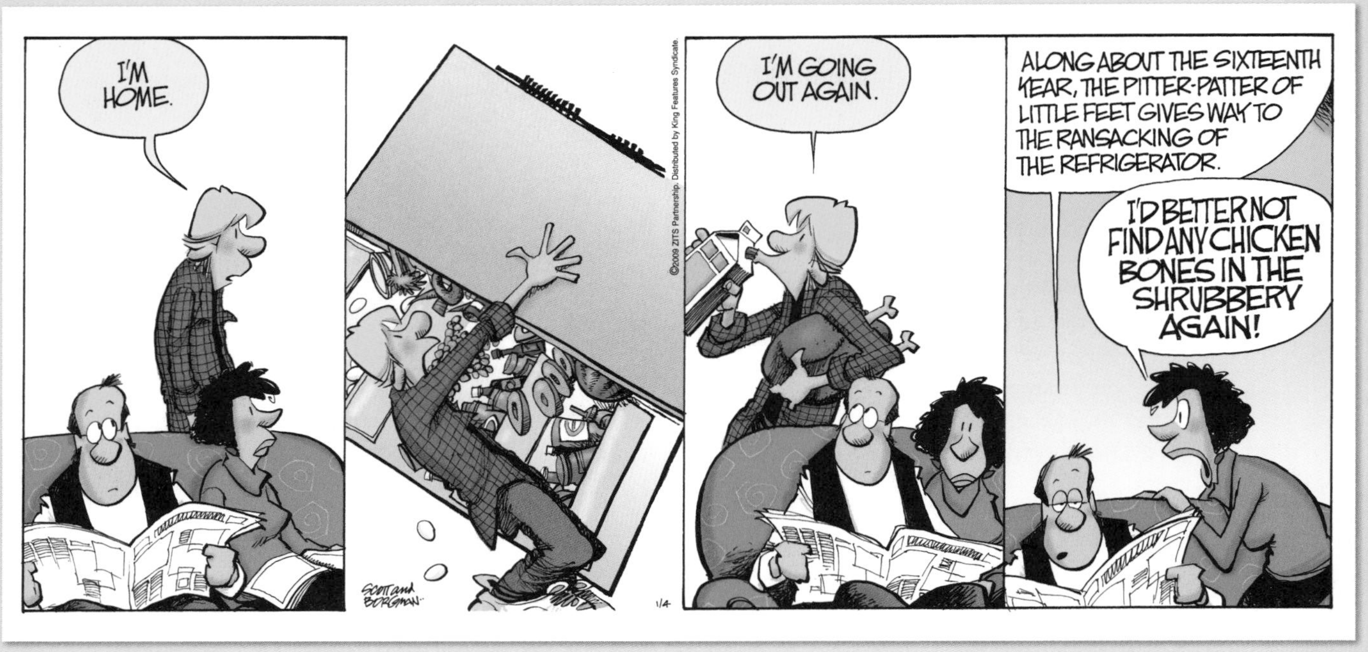

I'M HOME.
©2009 ZITS Partnership. Distributed by King Features Syndicate.
SCOTT AND BORGMAN
1/4
I'M GOING OUT AGAIN.
ALONG ABOUT THE SIXTEENTH YEAR, THE PITTER-PATTER OF LITTLE FEET GIVES WAY TO THE RANSACKING OF THE REFRIGERATOR.
I'D BETTER NOT FIND ANY CHICKEN BONES IN THE SHRUBBERY AGAIN!

January 18, 2009

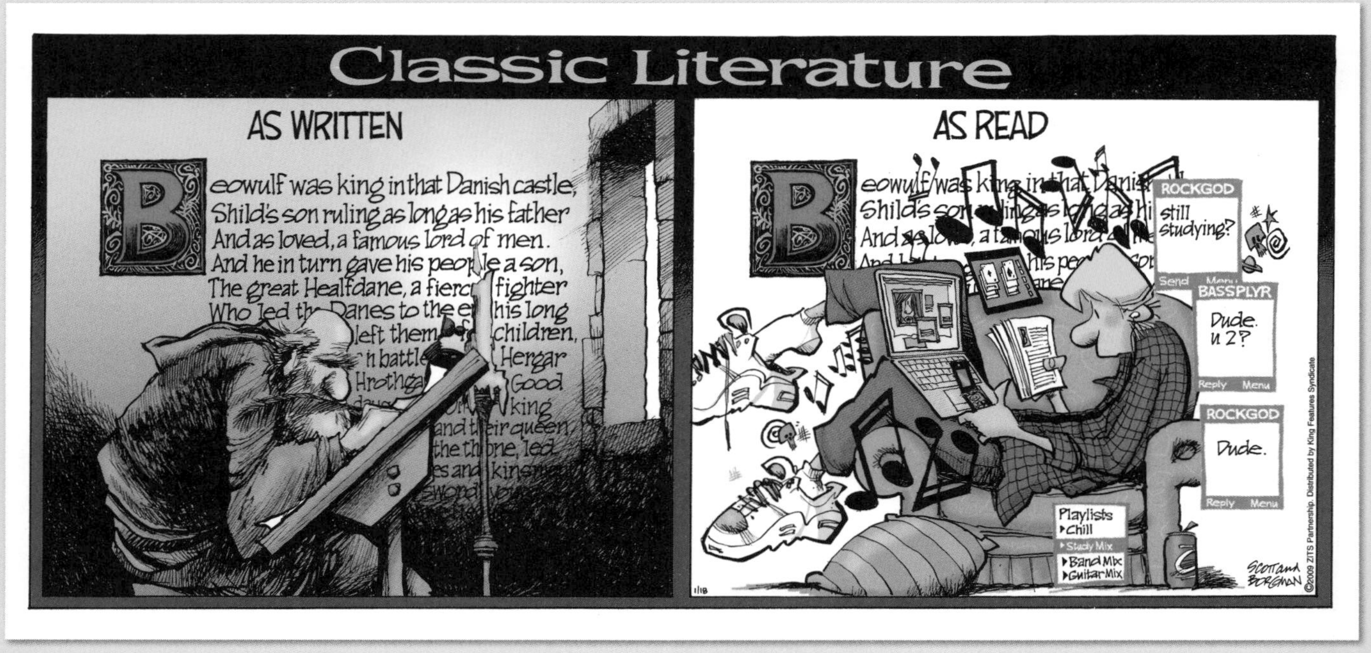

Classic Literature
AS WRITTEN
Beowulf was king in that Danish castle,
Shild's son ruling as long as his father
And as loved, a famous lord of men.
And he in turn gave his people a son,
1/18
AS READ
ROCKGOD
still studying?
BASSPLYR
Dude. u 2?
ROCKGOD
Dude.
Playlists
▸Chill
▸Study Mix
▸Band Mix
▸Guitar Mix
SCOTT AND BORGMAN
©2009 ZITS Partnership. Distributed by King Features Syndicate

January 26, 2009

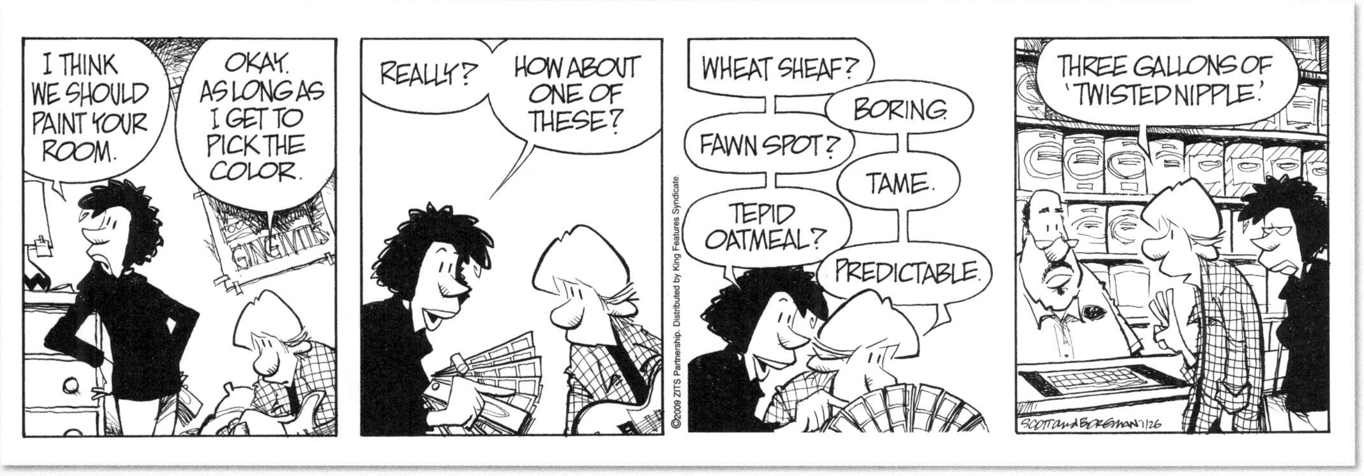
I THINK WE SHOULD PAINT YOUR ROOM.
OKAY. AS LONG AS I GET TO PICK THE COLOR.
GINGIVITIS
REALLY?
HOW ABOUT ONE OF THESE?
WHEAT SHEAF?
BORING.
FAWN SPOT?
TAME.
TEPID OATMEAL?
PREDICTABLE.
THREE GALLONS OF 'TWISTED NIPPLE.'
©2009 ZITS Partnership. Distributed by King Features Syndicate
SCOTT and BORGMAN 1/26

February 23, 2009

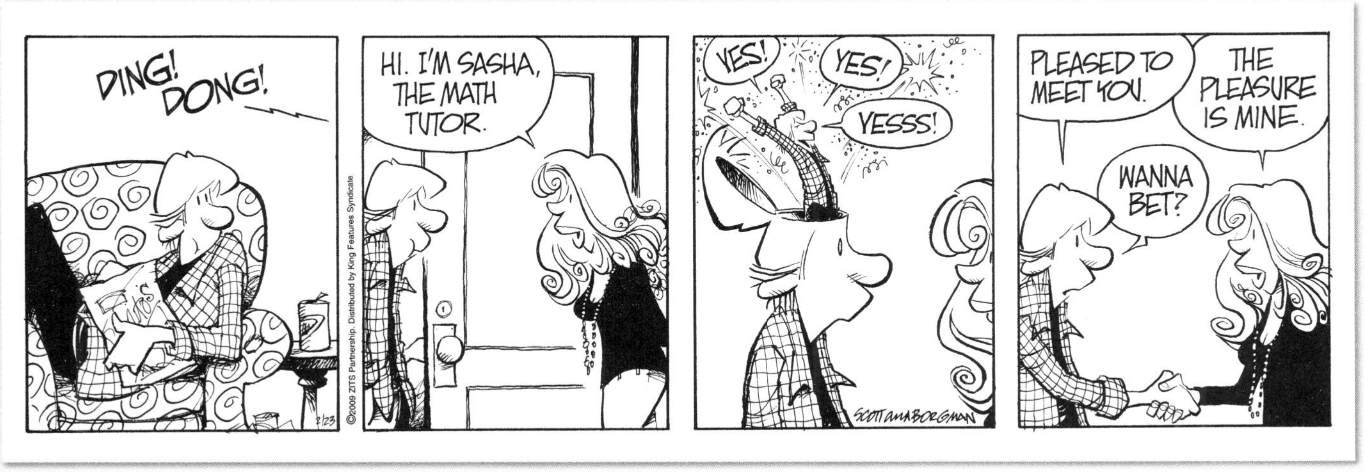
DING! DONG!
HI. I'M SASHA, THE MATH TUTOR.
YES!
YES!
YESSS!
PLEASED TO MEET YOU.
THE PLEASURE IS MINE.
WANNA BET?
©2009 ZITS Partnership. Distributed by King Features Syndicate
SCOTT and BORGMAN

February 24, 2009

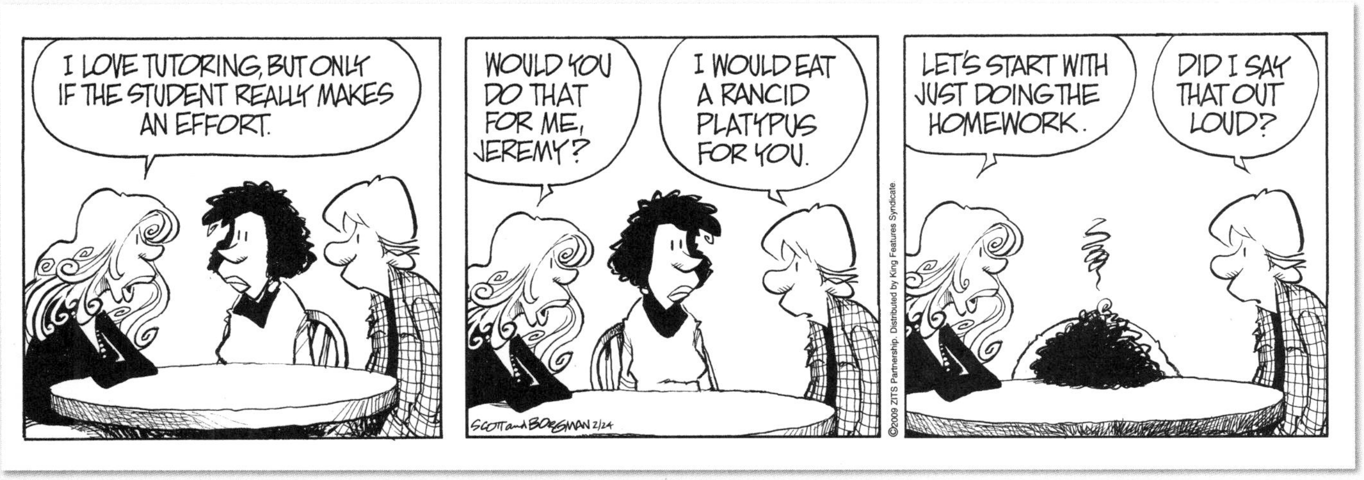
I LOVE TUTORING, BUT ONLY IF THE STUDENT REALLY MAKES AN EFFORT.
WOULD YOU DO THAT FOR ME, JEREMY?
I WOULD EAT A RANCID PLATYPUS FOR YOU.
LET'S START WITH JUST DOING THE HOMEWORK.
DID I SAY THAT OUT LOUD?
©2009 ZITS Partnership. Distributed by King Features Syndicate
SCOTT and BORGMAN 2/24

March 3, 2009

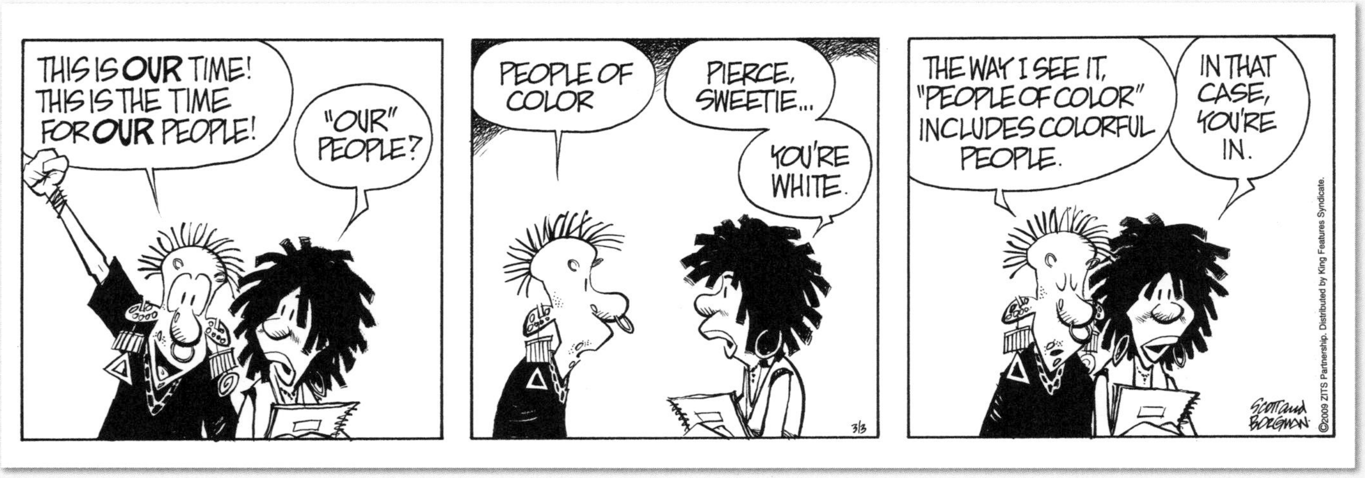
THIS IS OUR TIME! THIS IS THE TIME FOR OUR PEOPLE!
"OUR" PEOPLE?
PEOPLE OF COLOR
PIERCE, SWEETIE...
YOU'RE WHITE.
THE WAY I SEE IT, "PEOPLE OF COLOR" INCLUDES COLORFUL PEOPLE.
IN THAT CASE, YOU'RE IN.
3/3
SCOTT and BORGMAN
©2009 ZITS Partnership. Distributed by King Features Syndicate.

March 13, 2009

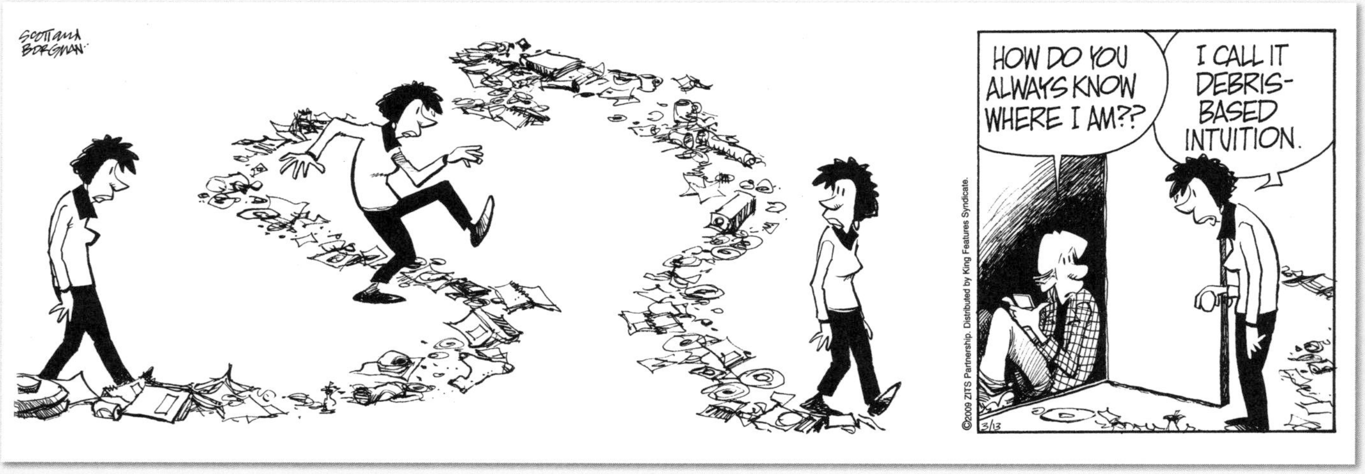
SCOTT and BORGMAN
©2009 ZITS Partnership. Distributed by King Features Syndicate.
HOW DO YOU ALWAYS KNOW WHERE I AM??
I CALL IT DEBRIS-BASED INTUITION.
3/13

March 31, 2009

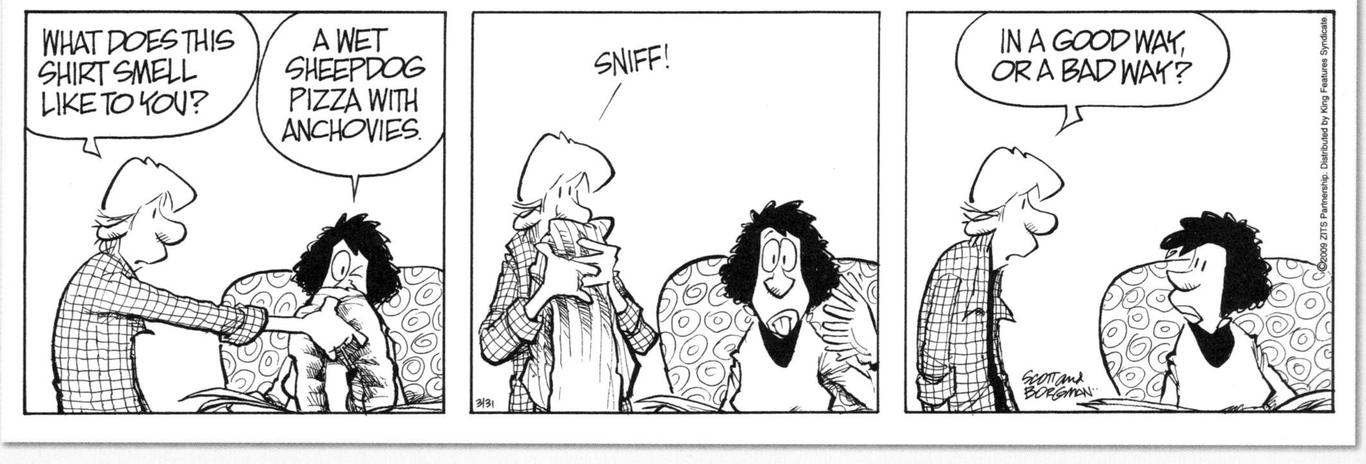
WHAT DOES THIS SHIRT SMELL LIKE TO YOU?
A WET SHEEPDOG PIZZA WITH ANCHOVIES.
SNIFF!
3/31
IN A GOOD WAY, OR A BAD WAY?
SCOTT and BORGMAN
©2009 ZITS Partnership. Distributed by King Features Syndicate.

February 1, 2009

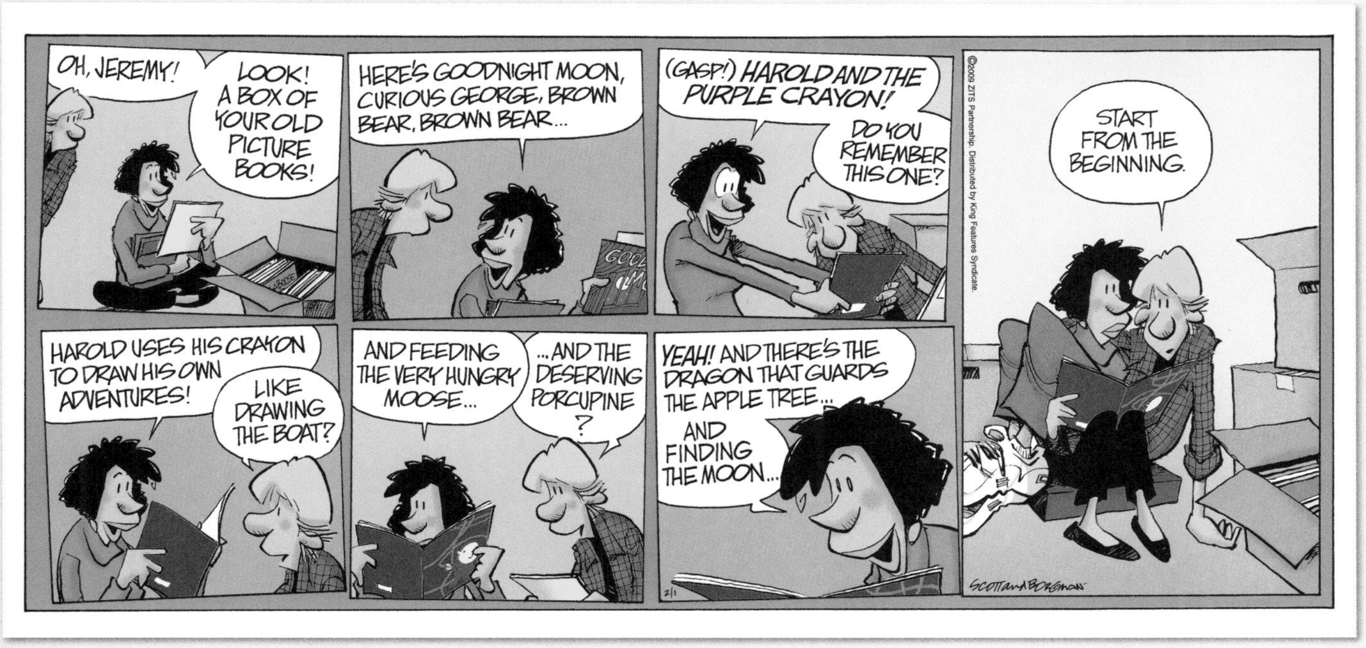
OH, JEREMY!
LOOK! A BOX OF YOUR OLD PICTURE BOOKS!
HERE'S GOODNIGHT MOON, CURIOUS GEORGE, BROWN BEAR, BROWN BEAR...
(GASP!) HAROLD AND THE PURPLE CRAYON!
DO YOU REMEMBER THIS ONE?
START FROM THE BEGINNING.
HAROLD USES HIS CRAYON TO DRAW HIS OWN ADVENTURES!
LIKE DRAWING THE BOAT?
AND FEEDING THE VERY HUNGRY MOOSE...
...AND THE DESERVING PORCUPINE?
YEAH! AND THERE'S THE DRAGON THAT GUARDS THE APPLE TREE...
AND FINDING THE MOON...
©2009 ZITS Partnership. Distributed by King Features Syndicate.
SCOTT AND BORGMAN

April 12, 2009

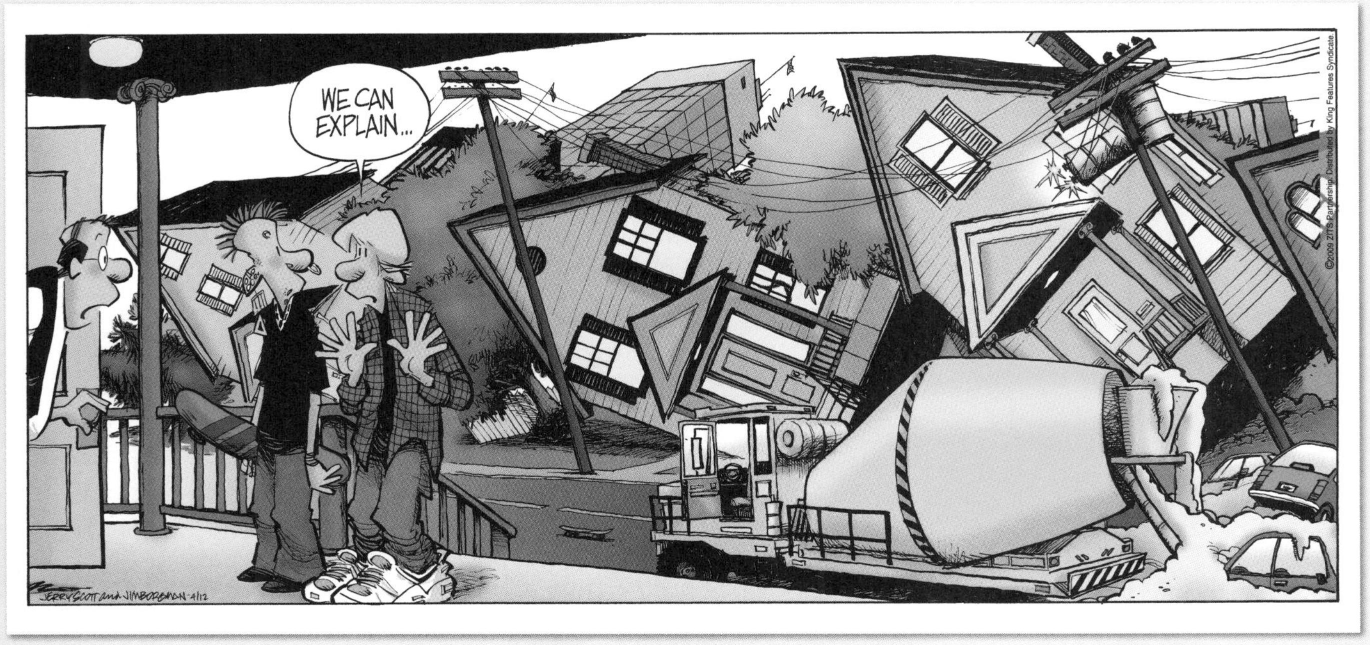
WE CAN EXPLAIN...
©2009 ZITS Partnership. Distributed by King Features Syndicate
JERRY SCOTT AND JIM BORGMAN 4/12

April 22, 2009

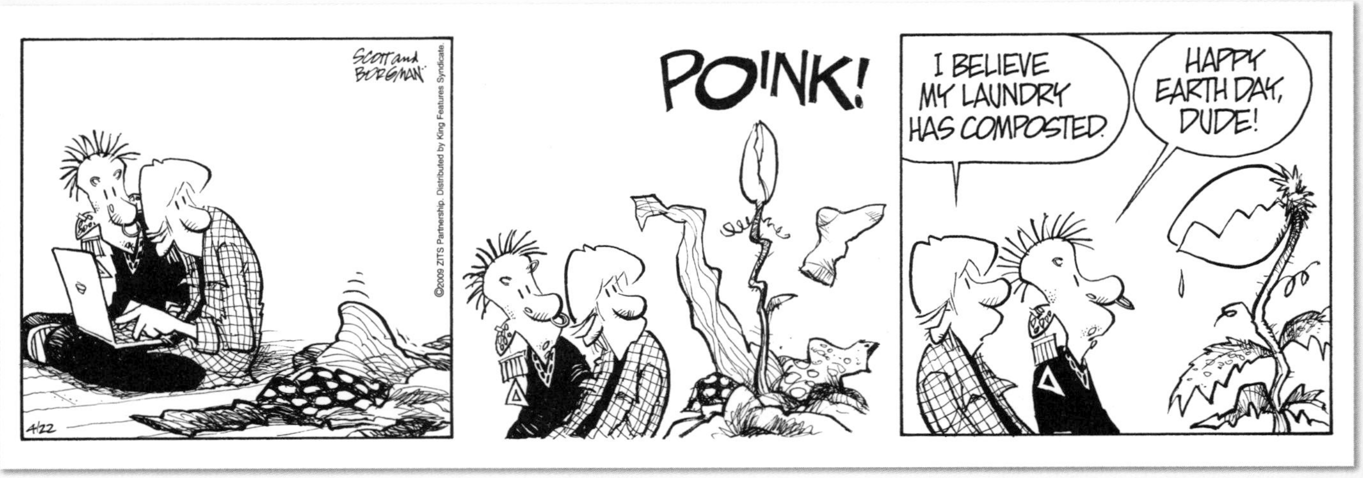

SCOTT and BORGMAN
©2009 ZITS Partnership. Distributed by King Features Syndicate.
4/22
POINK!
I BELIEVE MY LAUNDRY HAS COMPOSTED.
HAPPY EARTH DAY, DUDE!

April 30, 2009

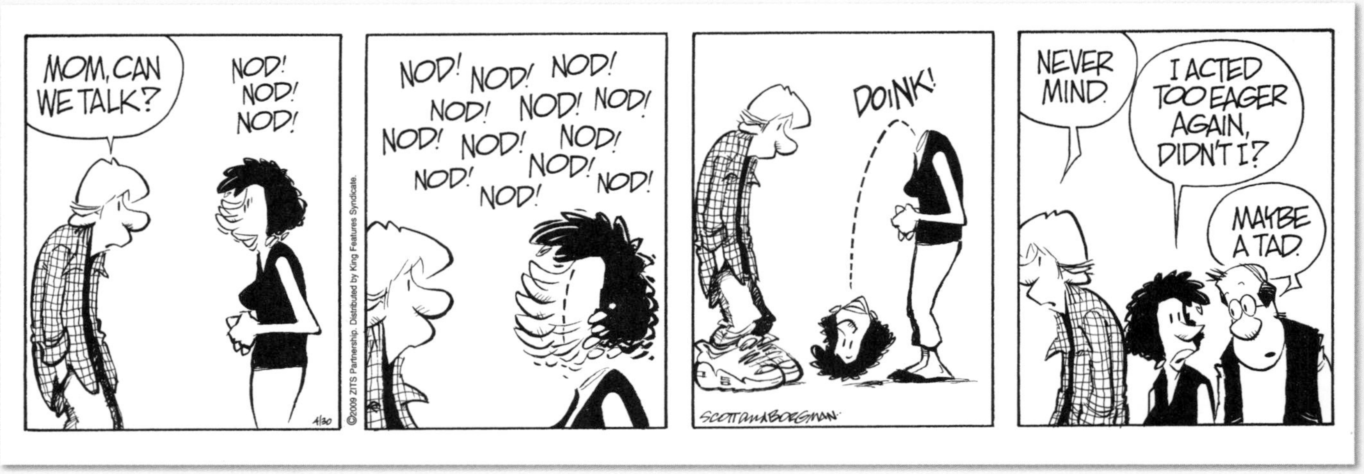

MOM, CAN WE TALK?
NOD! NOD! NOD!
4/30
©2009 ZITS Partnership. Distributed by King Features Syndicate.
NOD! NOD! NOD! NOD! NOD! NOD! NOD! NOD! NOD! NOD! NOD! NOD! NOD!
DOINK!
SCOTT and BORGMAN
NEVER MIND.
I ACTED TOO EAGER AGAIN, DIDN'T I?
MAYBE A TAD.

May 1, 2009

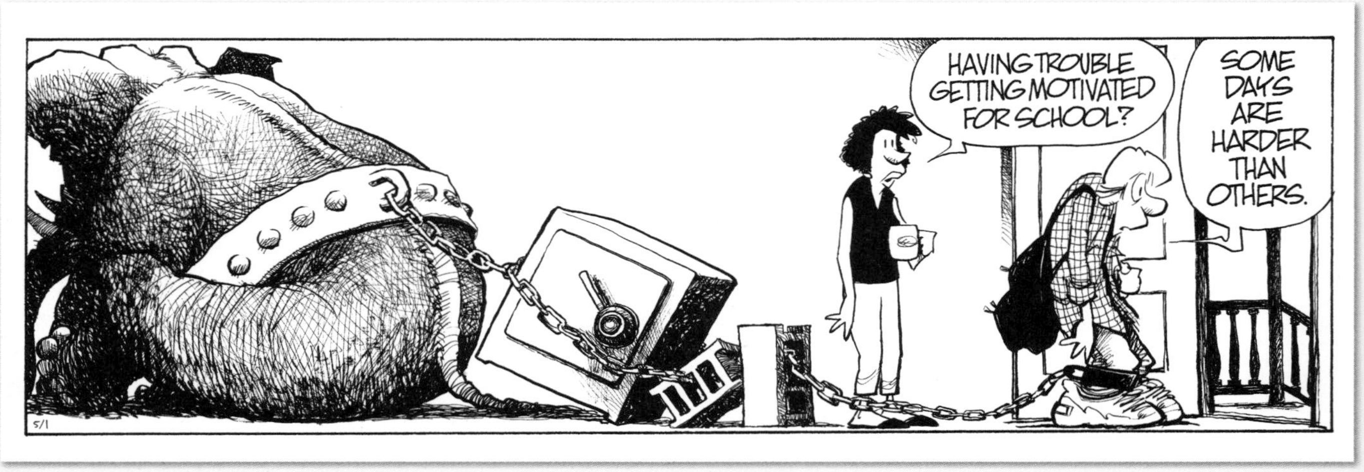

5/1
HAVING TROUBLE GETTING MOTIVATED FOR SCHOOL?
SOME DAYS ARE HARDER THAN OTHERS.

June 18, 2009

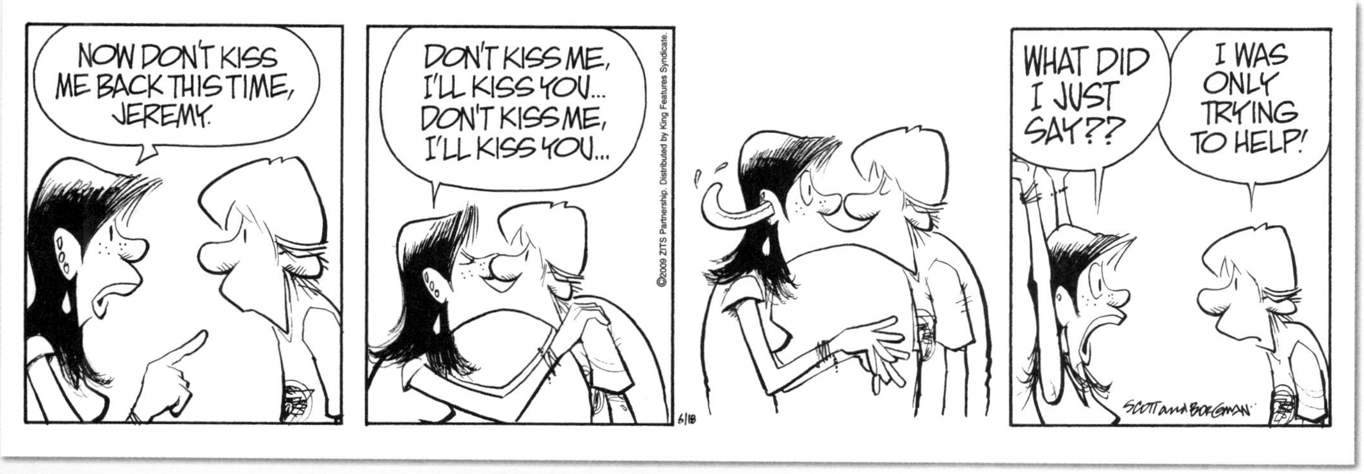
NOW DON'T KISS ME BACK THIS TIME, JEREMY.
DON'T KISS ME, I'LL KISS YOU... DON'T KISS ME, I'LL KISS YOU...
WHAT DID I JUST SAY??
I WAS ONLY TRYING TO HELP!
©2009 ZITS Partnership. Distributed by King Features Syndicate.
6/18
SCOTT and BORGMAN

June 22, 2009

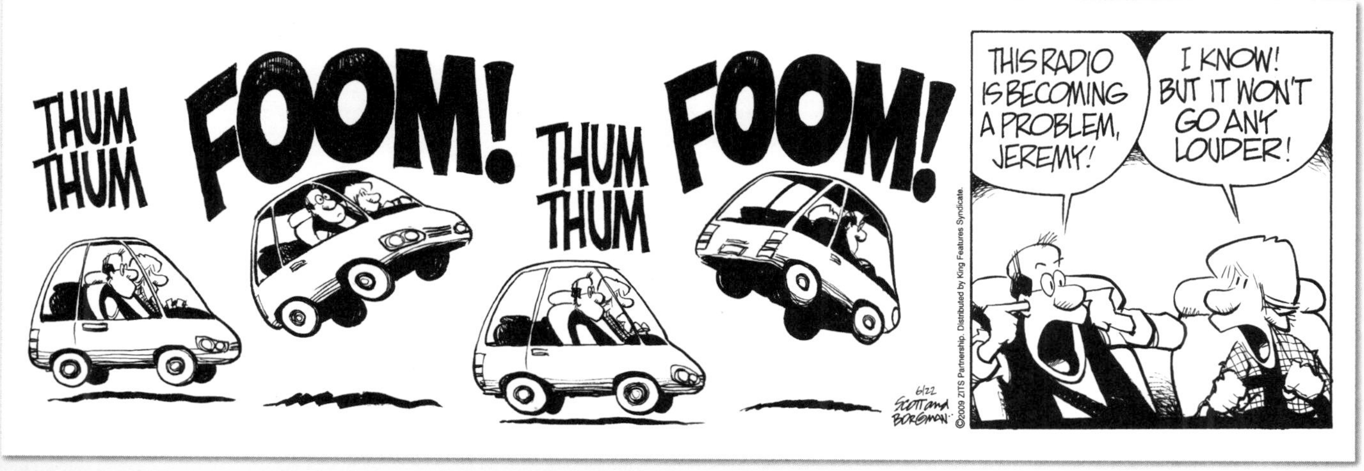
THUM THUM
FOOM!
THUM THUM
FOOM!
THIS RADIO IS BECOMING A PROBLEM, JEREMY!
I KNOW! BUT IT WON'T GO ANY LOUDER!
©2009 ZITS Partnership. Distributed by King Features Syndicate.
6/22
SCOTT and BORGMAN

June 23, 2009

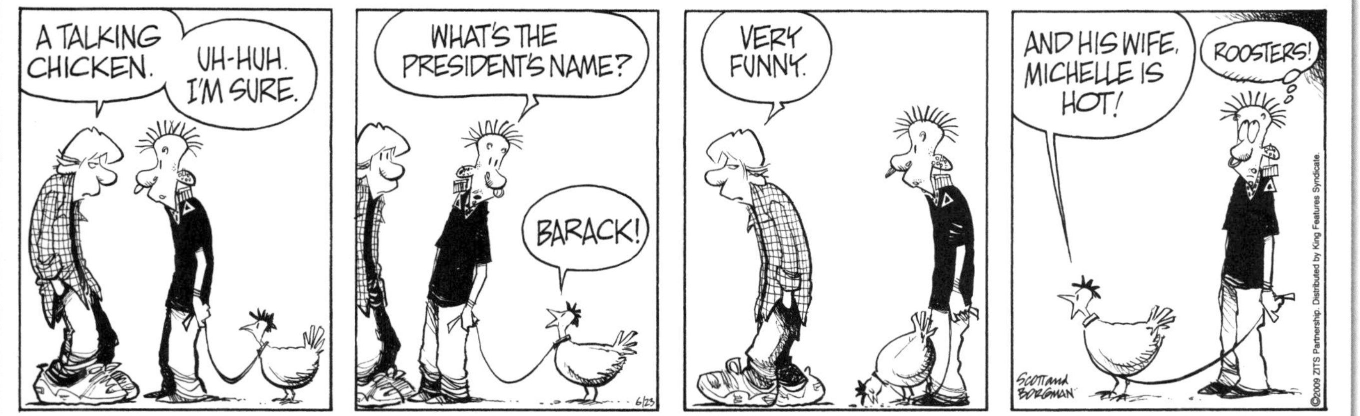
A TALKING CHICKEN.
UH-HUH. I'M SURE.
WHAT'S THE PRESIDENT'S NAME?
BARACK!
VERY FUNNY.
AND HIS WIFE, MICHELLE IS HOT!
ROOSTERS!
6/23
SCOTT and BORGMAN
©2009 ZITS Partnership. Distributed by King Features Syndicate.

April 19, 2009

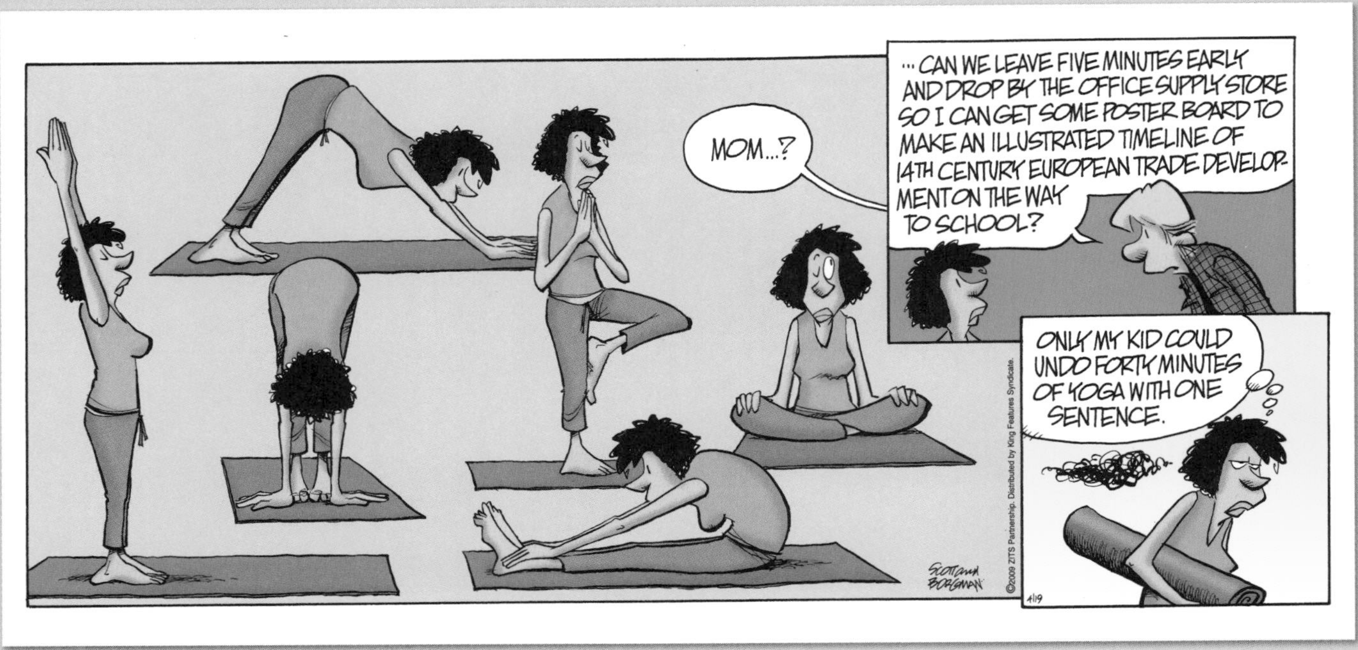
MOM...?
...CAN WE LEAVE FIVE MINUTES EARLY AND DROP BY THE OFFICE SUPPLY STORE SO I CAN GET SOME POSTER BOARD TO MAKE AN ILLUSTRATED TIMELINE OF 14TH CENTURY EUROPEAN TRADE DEVELOP-MENT ON THE WAY TO SCHOOL?
ONLY MY KID COULD UNDO FORTY MINUTES OF YOGA WITH ONE SENTENCE.
©2009 ZITS Partnership. Distributed by King Features Syndicate.
SCOTT and BORGMAN
4/19

June 28, 2009

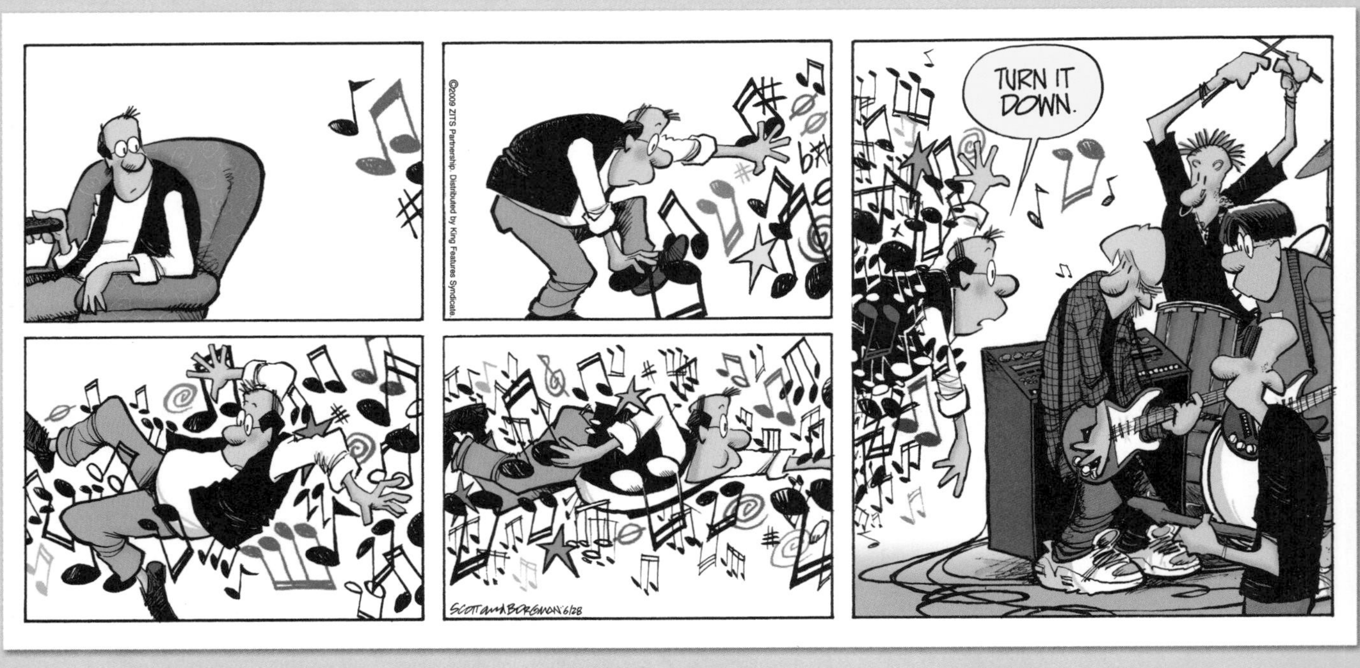
©2009 ZITS Partnership. Distributed by King Features Syndicate.
SCOTT and BORGMAN 6/28
TURN IT DOWN.

July 7, 2009

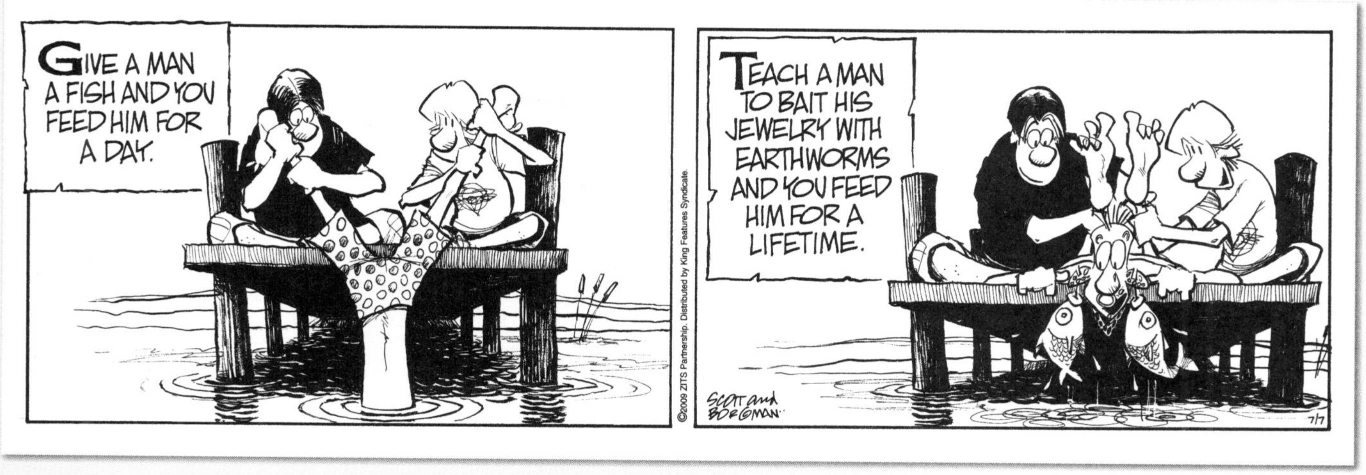
GIVE A MAN A FISH AND YOU FEED HIM FOR A DAY.
TEACH A MAN TO BAIT HIS JEWELRY WITH EARTHWORMS AND YOU FEED HIM FOR A LIFETIME.
©2009 ZITS Partnership. Distributed by King Features Syndicate.
SCOTT and BORGMAN
7/7

August 7, 2009

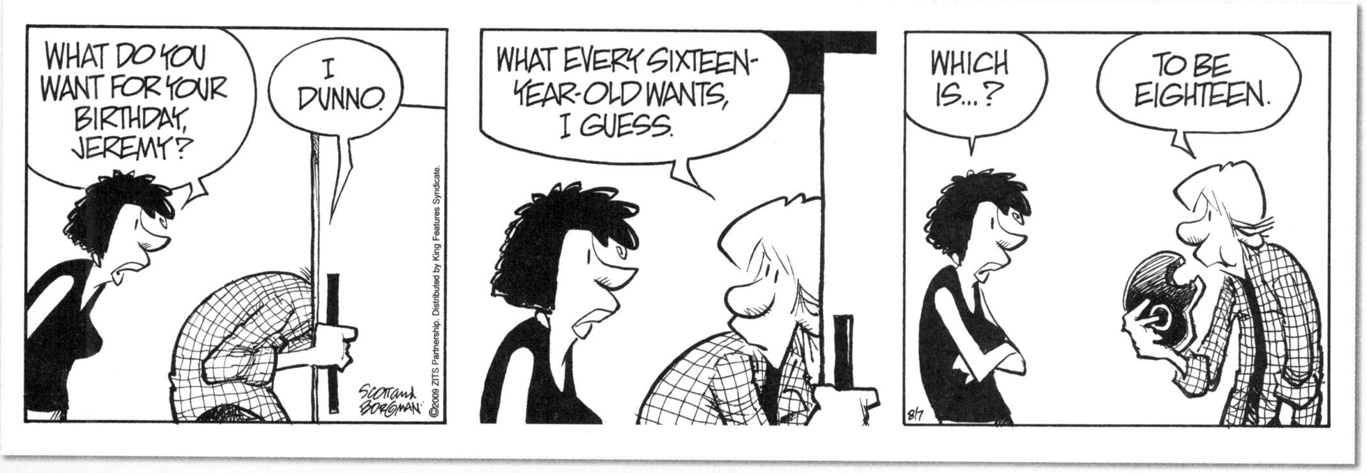
WHAT DO YOU WANT FOR YOUR BIRTHDAY, JEREMY?
I DUNNO.
©2009 ZITS Partnership. Distributed by King Features Syndicate.
SCOTT and BORGMAN
WHAT EVERY SIXTEEN-YEAR-OLD WANTS, I GUESS.
WHICH IS...?
TO BE EIGHTEEN.
8/7

August 10, 2009

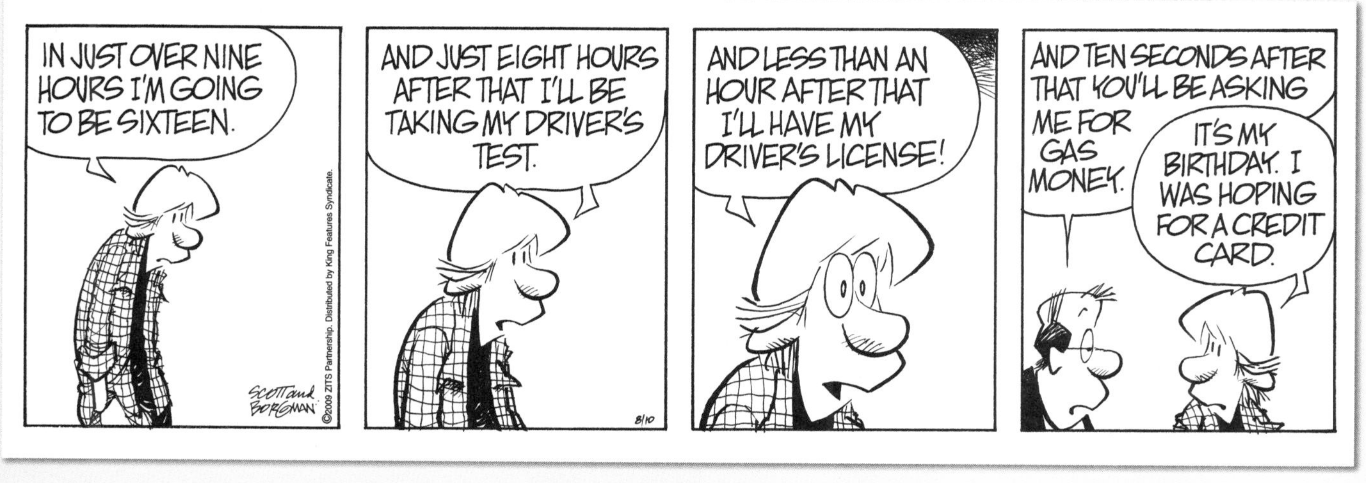
IN JUST OVER NINE HOURS I'M GOING TO BE SIXTEEN.
©2009 ZITS Partnership. Distributed by King Features Syndicate.
SCOTT and BORGMAN
AND JUST EIGHT HOURS AFTER THAT I'LL BE TAKING MY DRIVER'S TEST.
8/10
AND LESS THAN AN HOUR AFTER THAT I'LL HAVE MY DRIVER'S LICENSE!
AND TEN SECONDS AFTER THAT YOU'LL BE ASKING ME FOR GAS MONEY.
IT'S MY BIRTHDAY. I WAS HOPING FOR A CREDIT CARD.

August 12, 2009

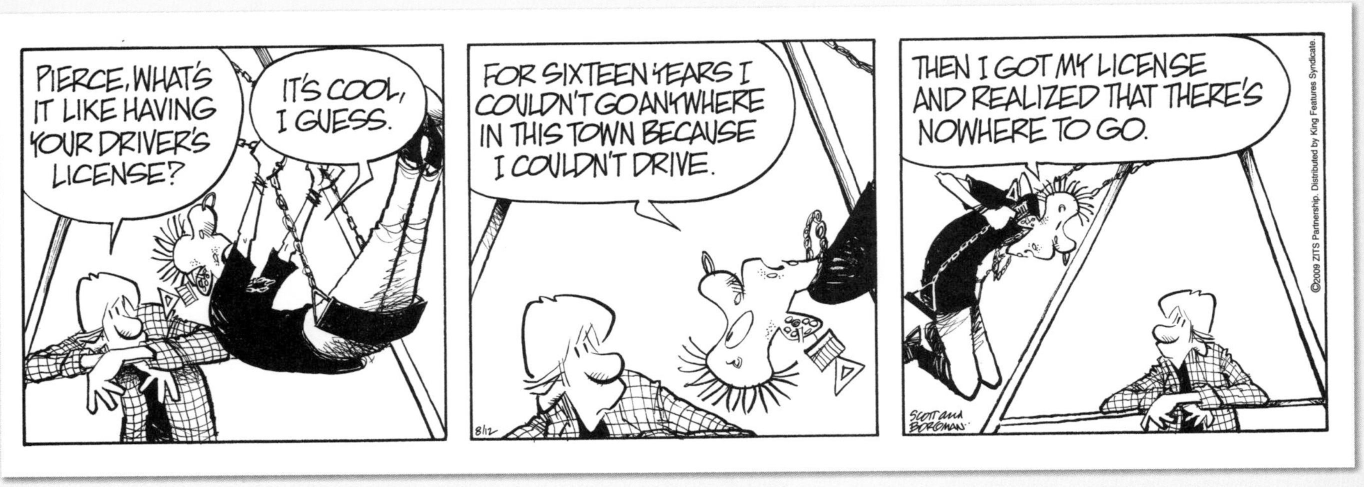
PIERCE, WHAT'S IT LIKE HAVING YOUR DRIVER'S LICENSE?
IT'S COOL, I GUESS.
FOR SIXTEEN YEARS I COULDN'T GO ANYWHERE IN THIS TOWN BECAUSE I COULDN'T DRIVE.
THEN I GOT MY LICENSE AND REALIZED THAT THERE'S NOWHERE TO GO.
©2009 ZITS Partnership. Distributed by King Features Syndicate.
SCOTT AND BORGMAN

August 17, 2009

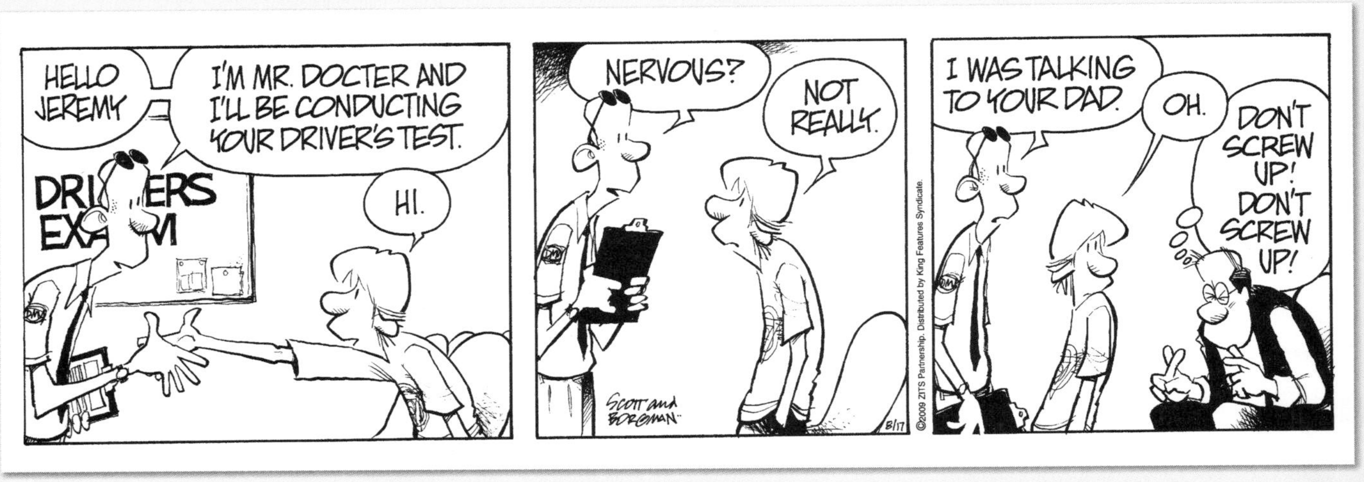
HELLO JEREMY
I'M MR. DOCTER AND I'LL BE CONDUCTING YOUR DRIVER'S TEST.
HI.
NERVOUS?
NOT REALLY.
I WAS TALKING TO YOUR DAD.
OH.
DON'T SCREW UP! DON'T SCREW UP!
©2009 ZITS Partnership. Distributed by King Features Syndicate.
SCOTT AND BORGMAN

August 23, 2009

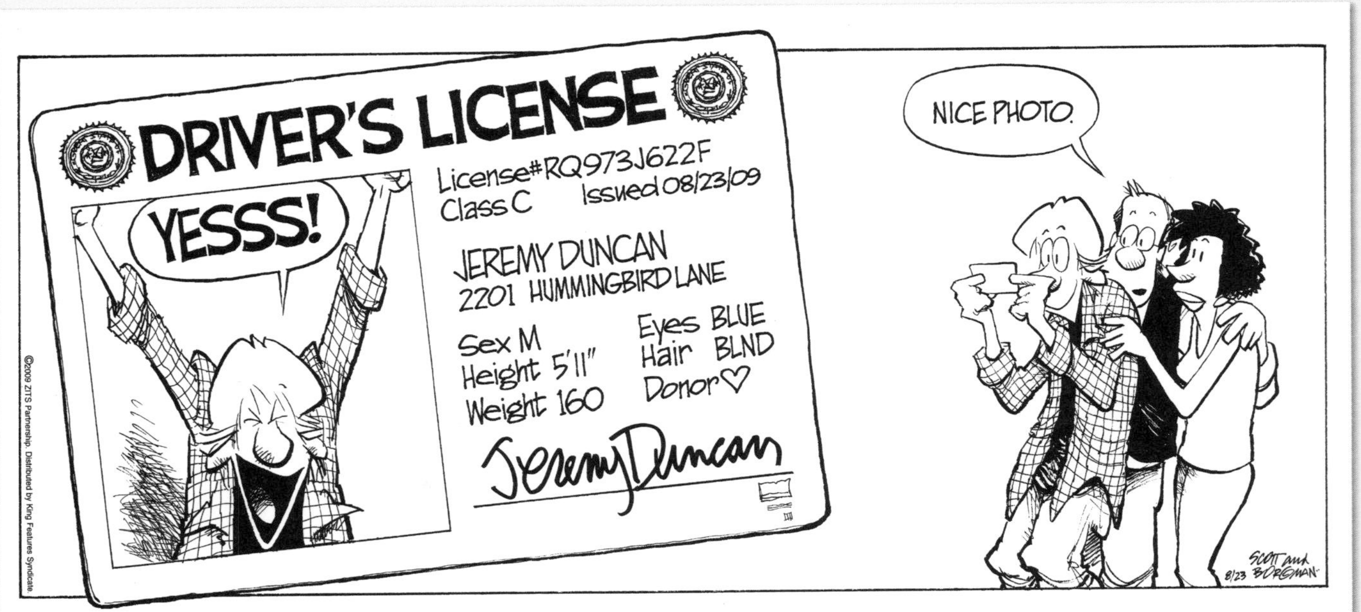
DRIVER'S LICENSE
YESSS!
License#RQ973J622F
Class C Issued 08/23/09
JEREMY DUNCAN
2201 HUMMINGBIRD LANE
Sex M
Height 5'11"
Weight 160
Eyes BLUE
Hair BLND
Donor♡
Jeremy Duncan
NICE PHOTO.
©2009 ZITS Partnership. Distributed by King Features Syndicate.
SCOTT AND BORGMAN

August 9, 2009

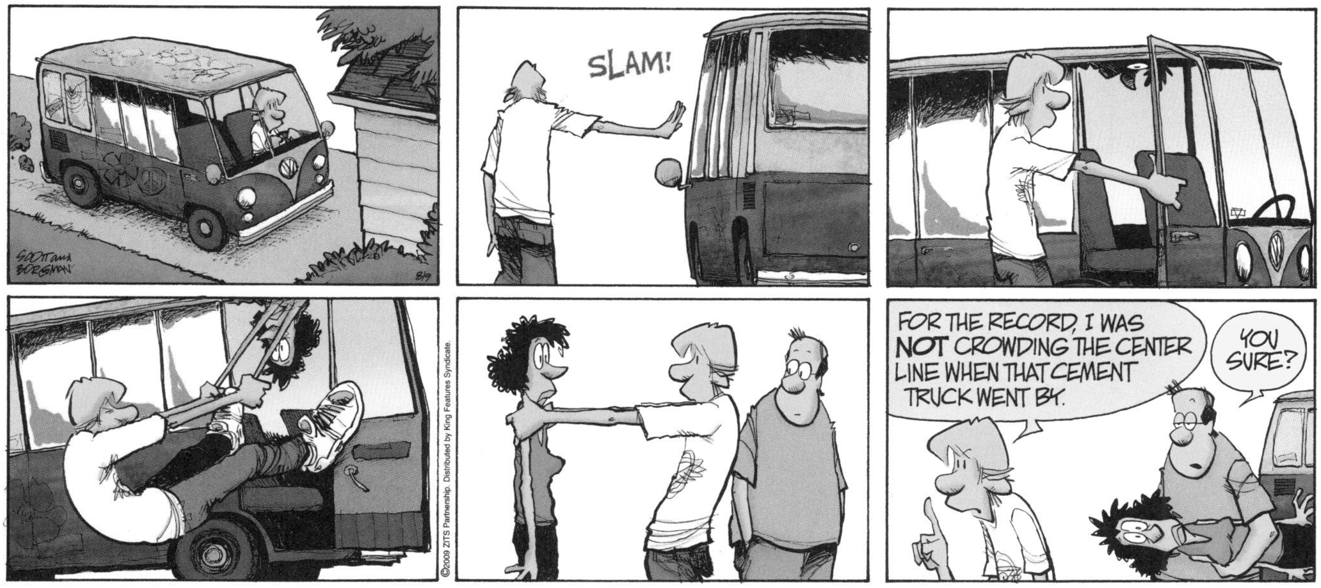
SCOTT and BORGMAN
8/9
SLAM!
©2009 ZITS Partnership. Distributed by King Features Syndicate.
FOR THE RECORD, I WAS NOT CROWDING THE CENTER LINE WHEN THAT CEMENT TRUCK WENT BY.
YOU SURE?

August 16, 2009

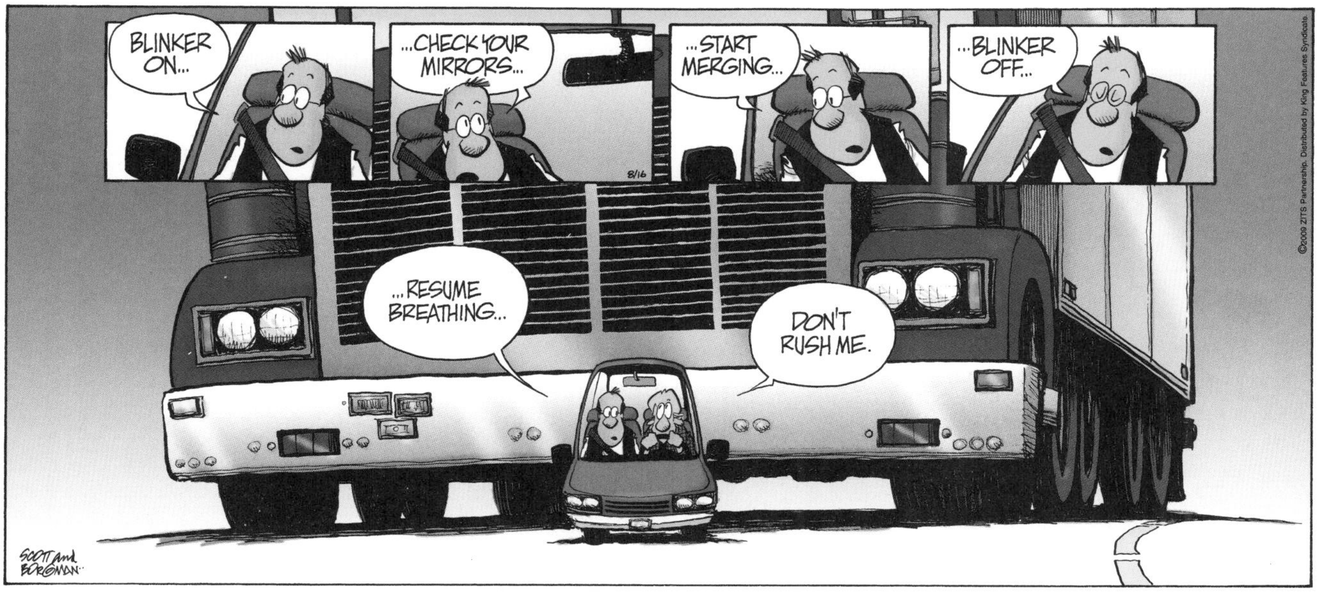
BLINKER ON...
...CHECK YOUR MIRRORS...
...START MERGING...
...BLINKER OFF...
8/16
©2009 ZITS Partnership. Distributed by King Features Syndicate.
...RESUME BREATHING...
DON'T RUSH ME.
SCOTT and BORGMAN

August 27, 2009

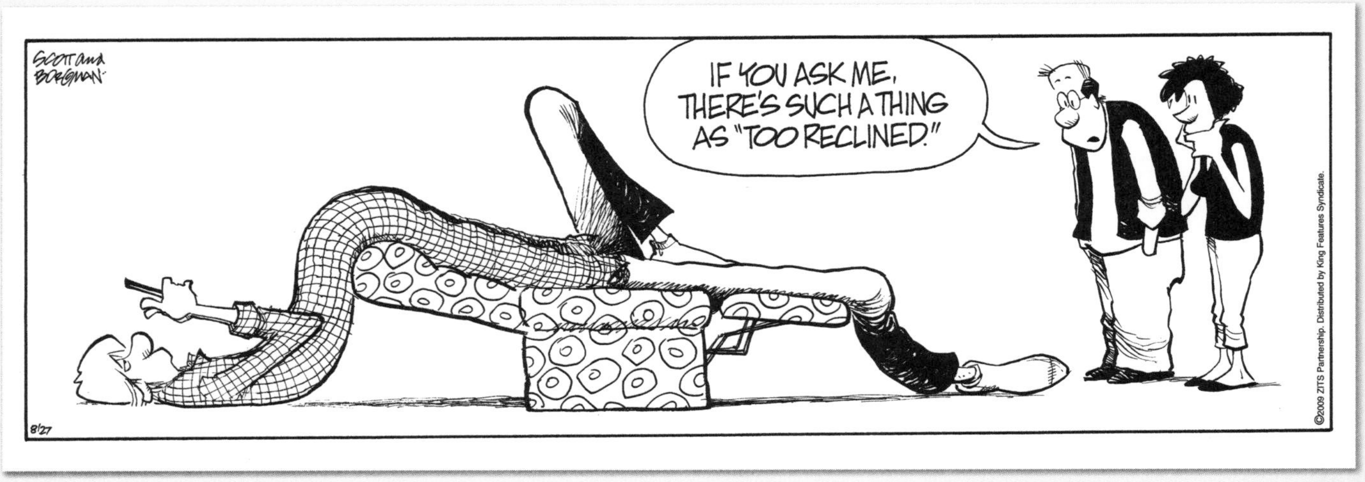
SCOTT and BORGMAN
IF YOU ASK ME, THERE'S SUCH A THING AS "TOO RECLINED."
8/27
©2009 ZITS Partnership. Distributed by King Features Syndicate.

September 24, 2009

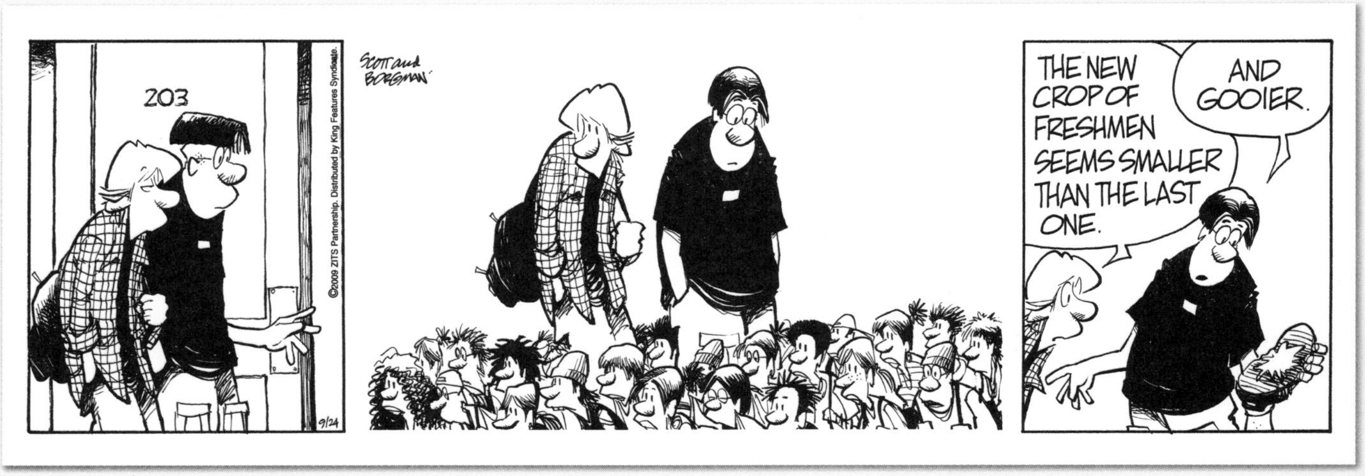
203
©2009 ZITS Partnership. Distributed by King Features Syndicate.
9/24
SCOTT and BORGMAN
THE NEW CROP OF FRESHMEN SEEMS SMALLER THAN THE LAST ONE.
AND GOOIER.

November 4, 2009

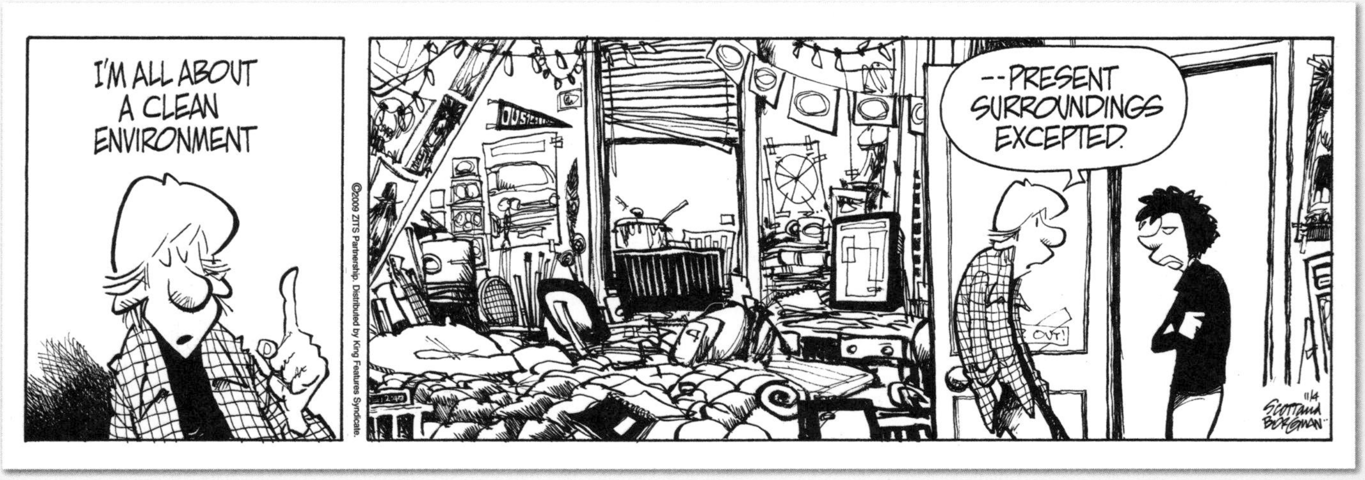
I'M ALL ABOUT A CLEAN ENVIRONMENT
©2009 ZITS Partnership. Distributed by King Features Syndicate.
--PRESENT SURROUNDINGS EXCEPTED.
OUT!
11/4
SCOTT and BORGMAN

September 13, 2009

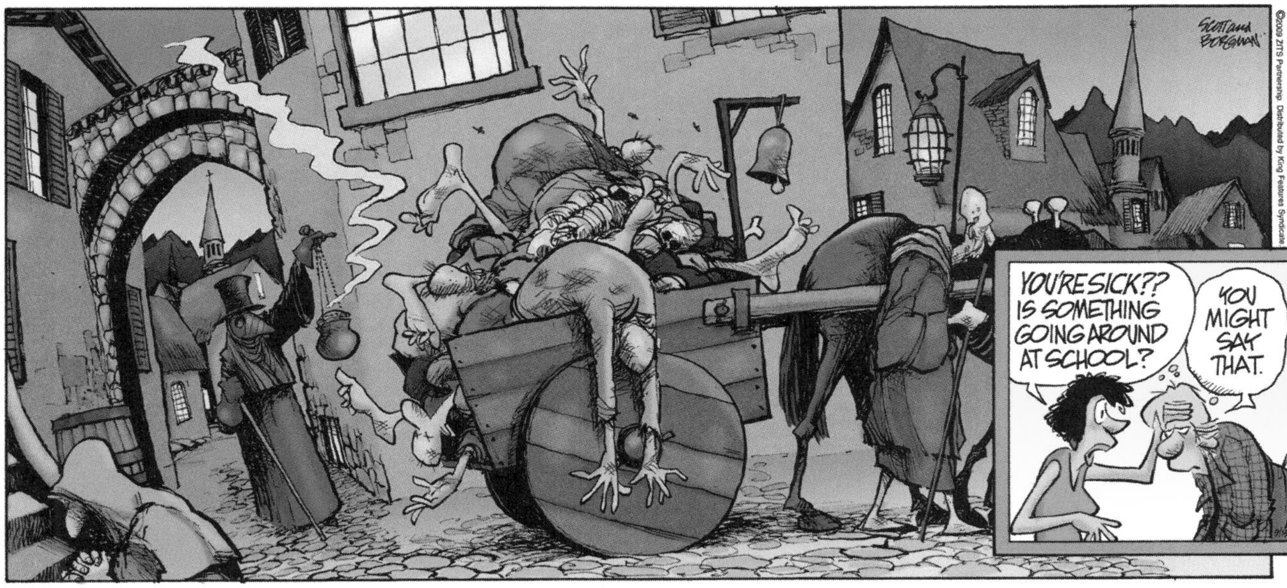
YOU'RE SICK?? IS SOMETHING GOING AROUND AT SCHOOL?
YOU MIGHT SAY THAT.
©2009 ZITS Partnership. Distributed by King Features Syndicate
SCOTT and BORGMAN

October 4, 2009

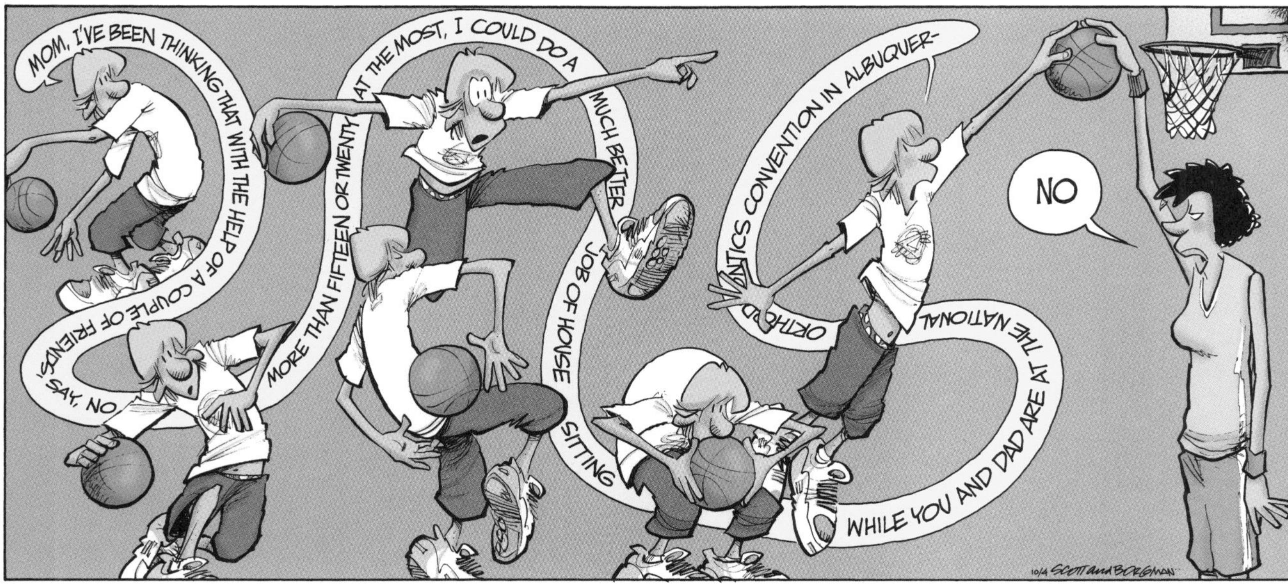
MOM, I'VE BEEN THINKING THAT WITH THE HELP OF A COUPLE OF FRIENDS, SAY, NO MORE THAN FIFTEEN OR TWENTY AT THE MOST, I COULD DO A MUCH BETTER JOB OF HOUSE SITTING WHILE YOU AND DAD ARE AT THE NATIONAL ORTHODONTICS CONVENTION IN ALBUQUER-
NO
©2009 ZITS Partnership. Distributed by King Features Syndicate
10/4 SCOTT and BORGMAN

December 8, 2009

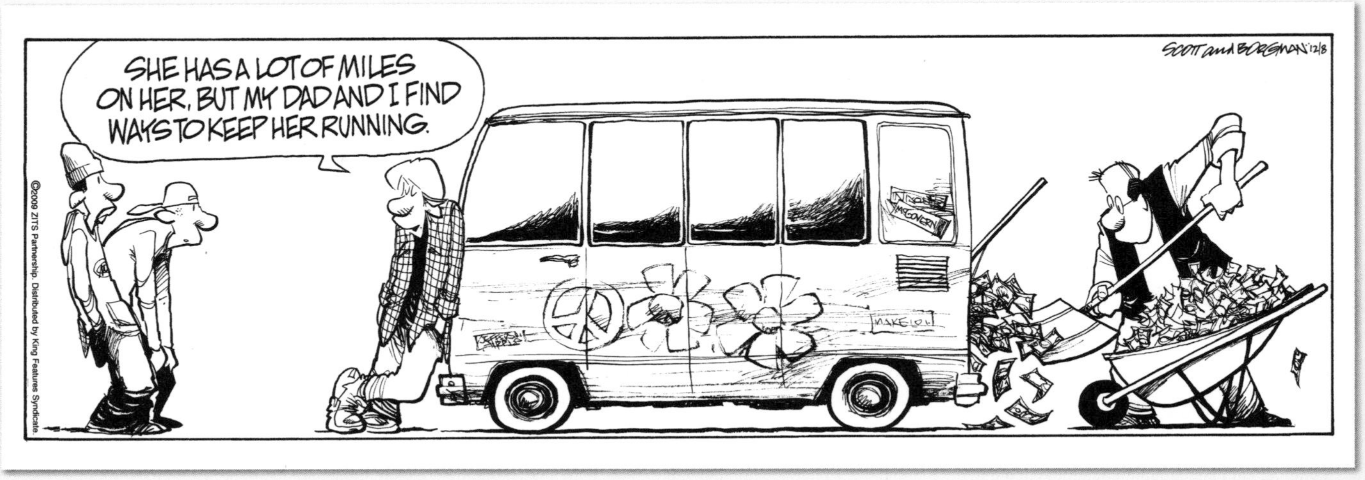
SHE HAS A LOT OF MILES ON HER, BUT MY DAD AND I FIND WAYS TO KEEP HER RUNNING.
©2009 ZITS Partnership. Distributed by King Features Syndicate.

December 29, 2009

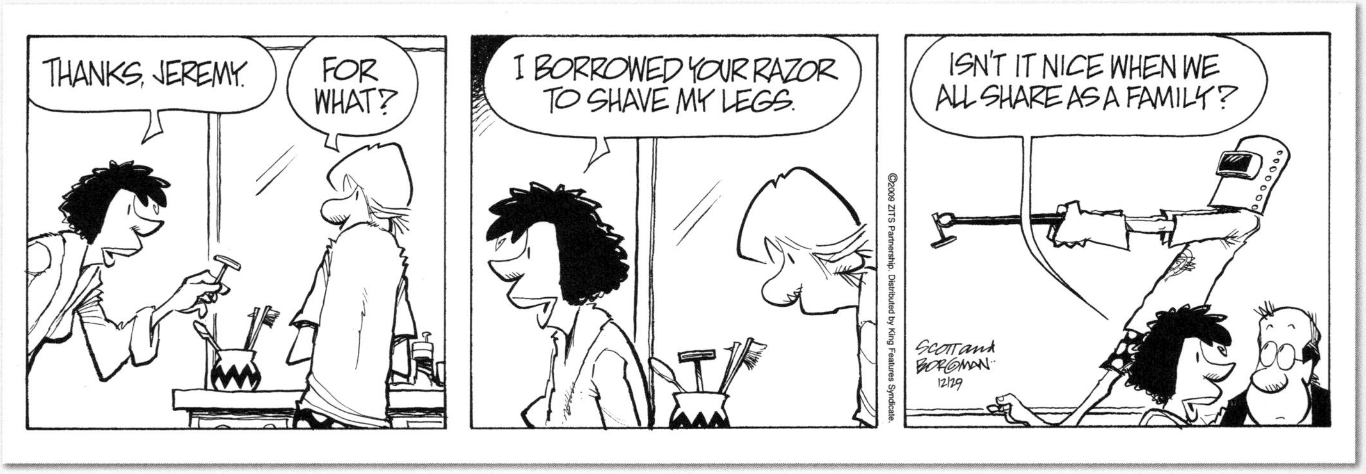
THANKS, JEREMY.
FOR WHAT?
I BORROWED YOUR RAZOR TO SHAVE MY LEGS.
ISN'T IT NICE WHEN WE ALL SHARE AS A FAMILY?
©2009 ZITS Partnership. Distributed by King Features Syndicate.

May 6, 2009

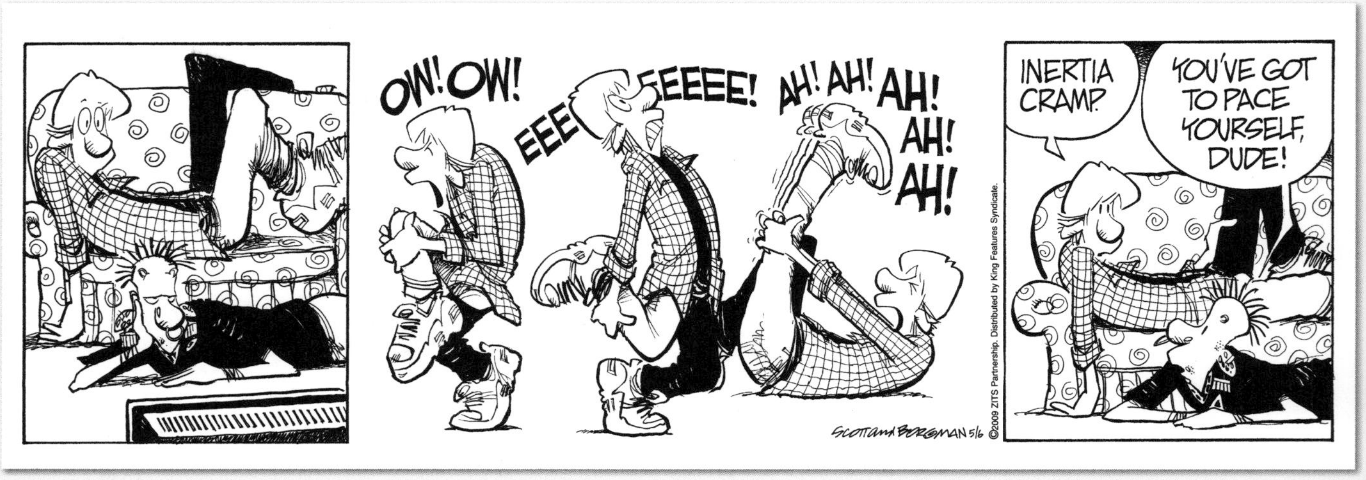
OW! OW!
EEEEEEEE!
AH! AH! AH! AH! AH!
INERTIA CRAMP.
YOU'VE GOT TO PACE YOURSELF, DUDE!
©2009 ZITS Partnership. Distributed by King Features Syndicate.

May 24, 2009

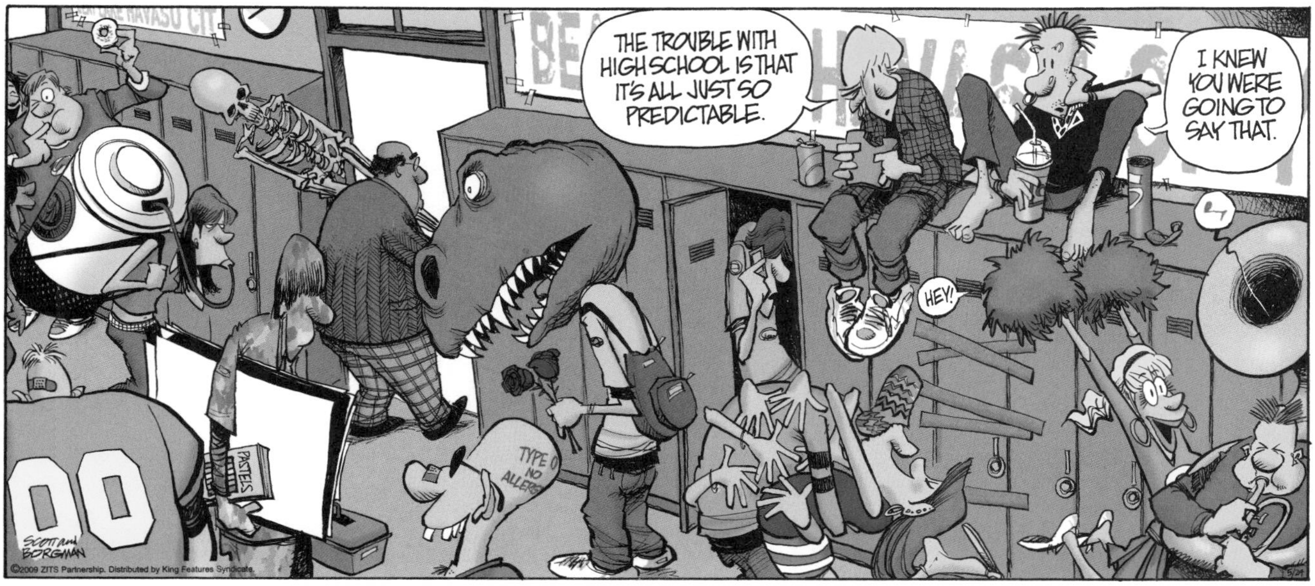

THE TROUBLE WITH HIGH SCHOOL IS THAT IT'S ALL JUST SO PREDICTABLE.
I KNEW YOU WERE GOING TO SAY THAT.
HEY!
PASTELS
TYPE O NO ALLERG
00
SCOTT AND BORGMAN
©2009 ZITS Partnership. Distributed by King Features Syndicate.

November 1, 2009

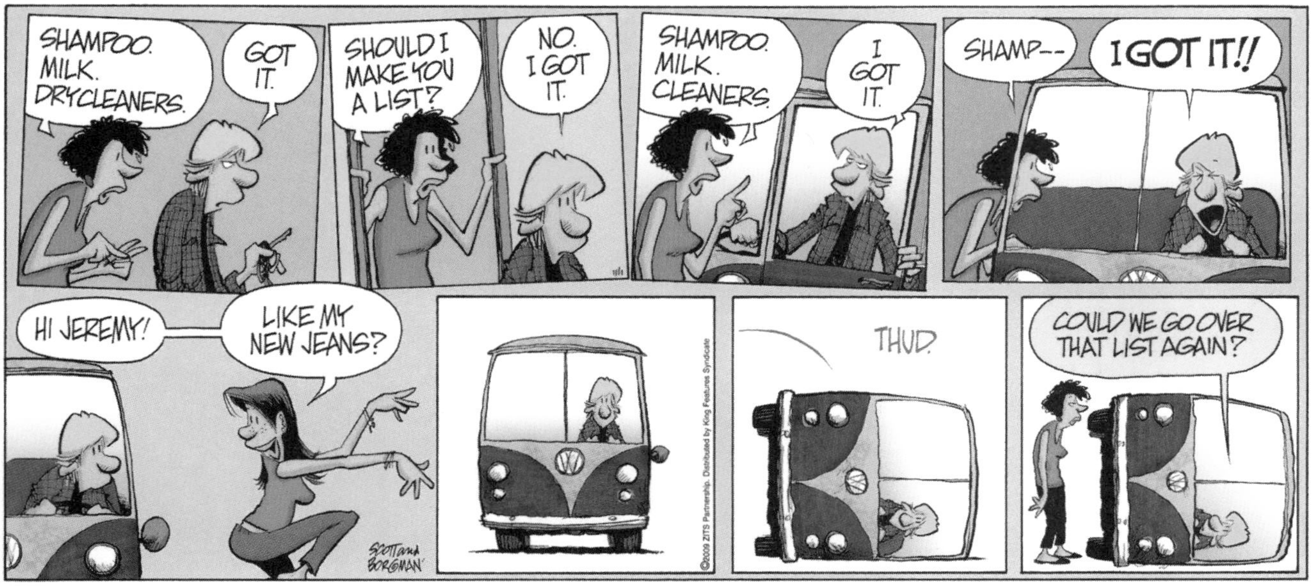

SHAMPOO. MILK. DRYCLEANERS.
GOT IT.
SHOULD I MAKE YOU A LIST?
NO. I GOT IT.
SHAMPOO. MILK. CLEANERS.
I GOT IT.
SHAMP--
I GOT IT!!
HI JEREMY!
LIKE MY NEW JEANS?
SCOTT AND BORGMAN
©2009 ZITS Partnership. Distributed by King Features Syndicate.
THUD
COULD WE GO OVER THAT LIST AGAIN?

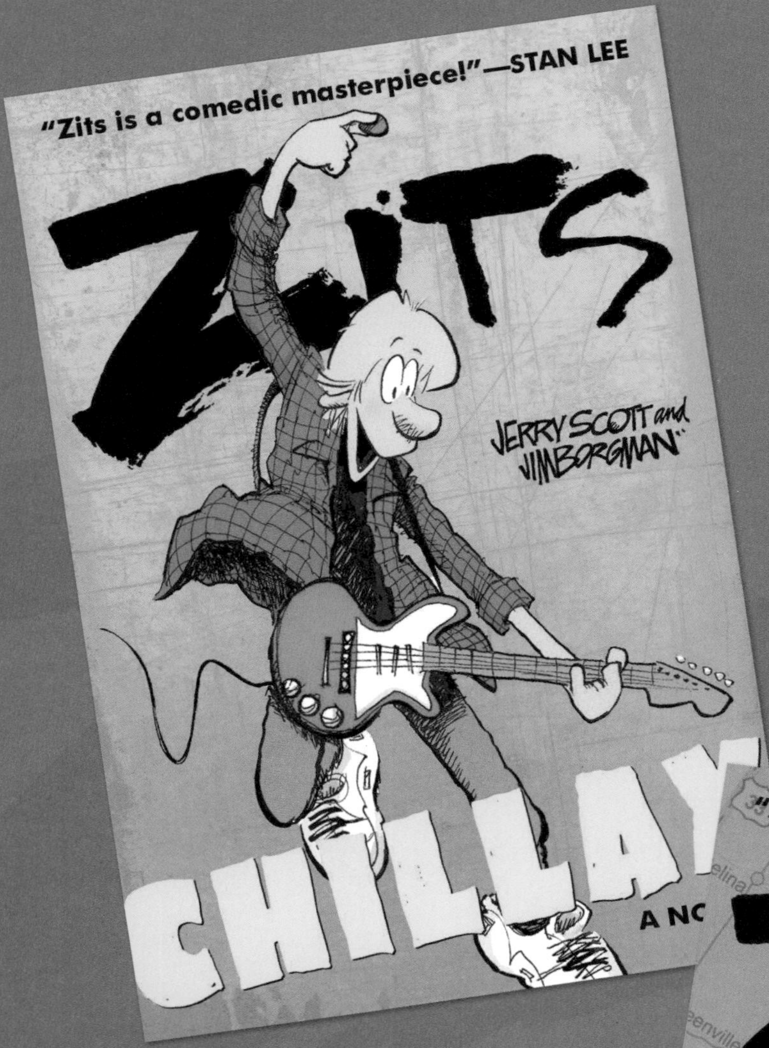
"Zits is a comedic masterpiece!"—STAN LEE
ZITS
JERRY SCOTT and JIM BORGMAN

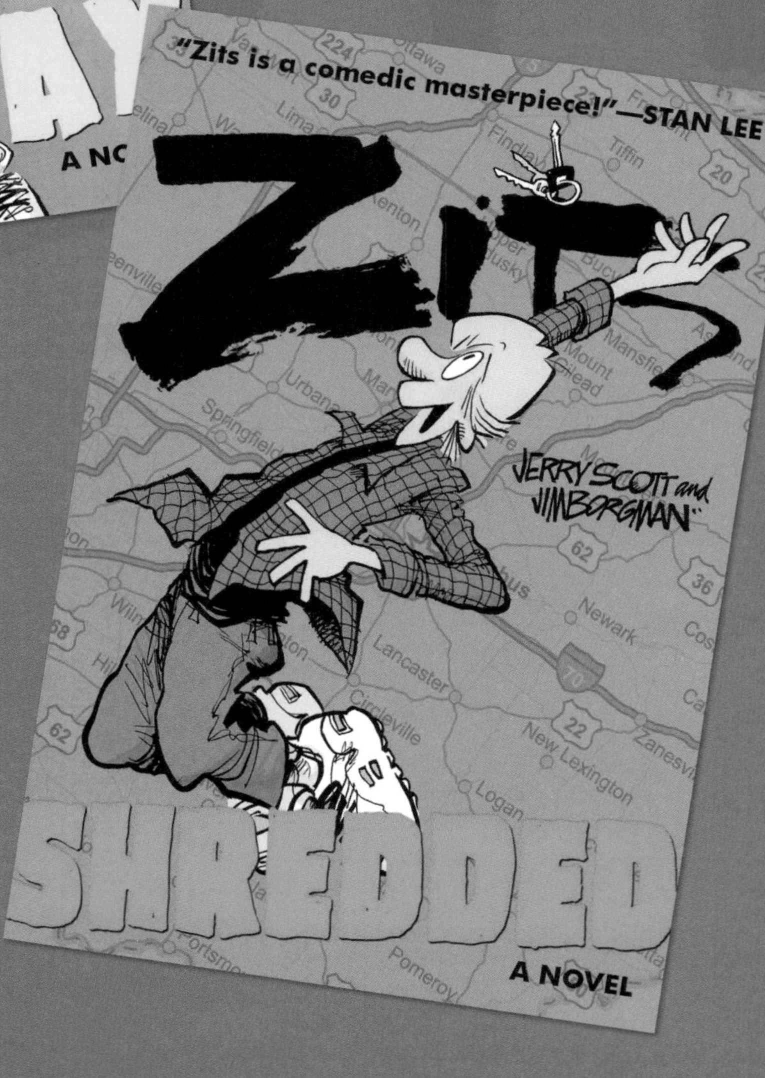
"Zits is a comedic masterpiece!"—STAN LEE
ZITS
JERRY SCOTT and JIM BORGMAN
SHREDDED
A NOVEL

CHILLAX and SHREDDED

Jim Borgman

As a kid I was what would now be called a "reluctant reader." At the time I just knew that books looked hopelessly thick, gray, and impenetrable. Maybe that's why I was so happy to discover comic books full of pictures, and later, novels with occasional illustrations. Even today, the first thing I check in a new book is the number at the bottom of the last page before deciding whether to plunge in.

With HarperCollins as our publisher, we created a couple of heavily illustrated novels aimed at young teenagers starring our cast of characters from *Zits*. Writing long-form stories was a chance to use new muscles. It was a blast. And it felt good to know we might be keeping some kids from abandoning books for a bit longer, maybe until a strong breeze or a talented teacher could lift them into the land of great literature.

MOM, I DON'T WANT TO SPEND MY SUMMER READING SOME BORING BOOK!
WHAT ABOUT THIS ONE?
WELL?
YOUNG ADU FICTION
SHH!
©2013 ZITS Partnership. Dist. by King Features
SCOTT and BORGMAN
zitscomics.com
7/31

I GUESS I'LL GET THIS ONE.
"ZITS: CHILLAX." WHAT'S IT ABOUT?
*DUDE, IT'S REAL! LOOK IT UP!
TWO GUYS MY AGE WHO GO TO A CONCERT.
THAT SOUNDS LIKE YOU ALL OVER!
WHO'S IT BY?
NOBODY I'VE EVER HEARD OF.
zitscomics.com
©2013 ZITS Partnership. Dist. by King Features
SCOTT and BORGMAN

I'M SO GLAD YOU FOUND A BOOK TO BUY, JEREMY.
YEAH. I'M KIND OF STOKED, TOO.
WHAT MADE YOU CHOOSE IT? THE THEME? THE STORY? THE CHARACTERS?
YEAH, THAT...
...PLUS, IT'S GREEN AND HAS PICTURES.
zitscomics.com
8/12
SCOTT and BORGMAN
©2013 ZITS Partnership. Dist. by King Features

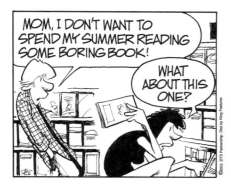

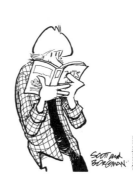

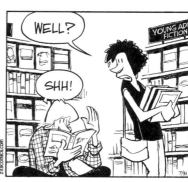

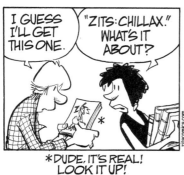

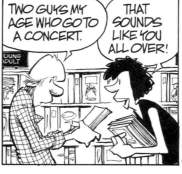

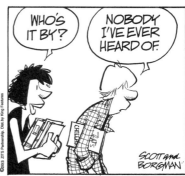

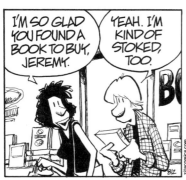

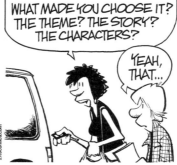

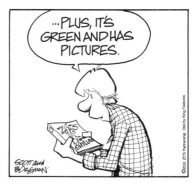

January 24, 2010

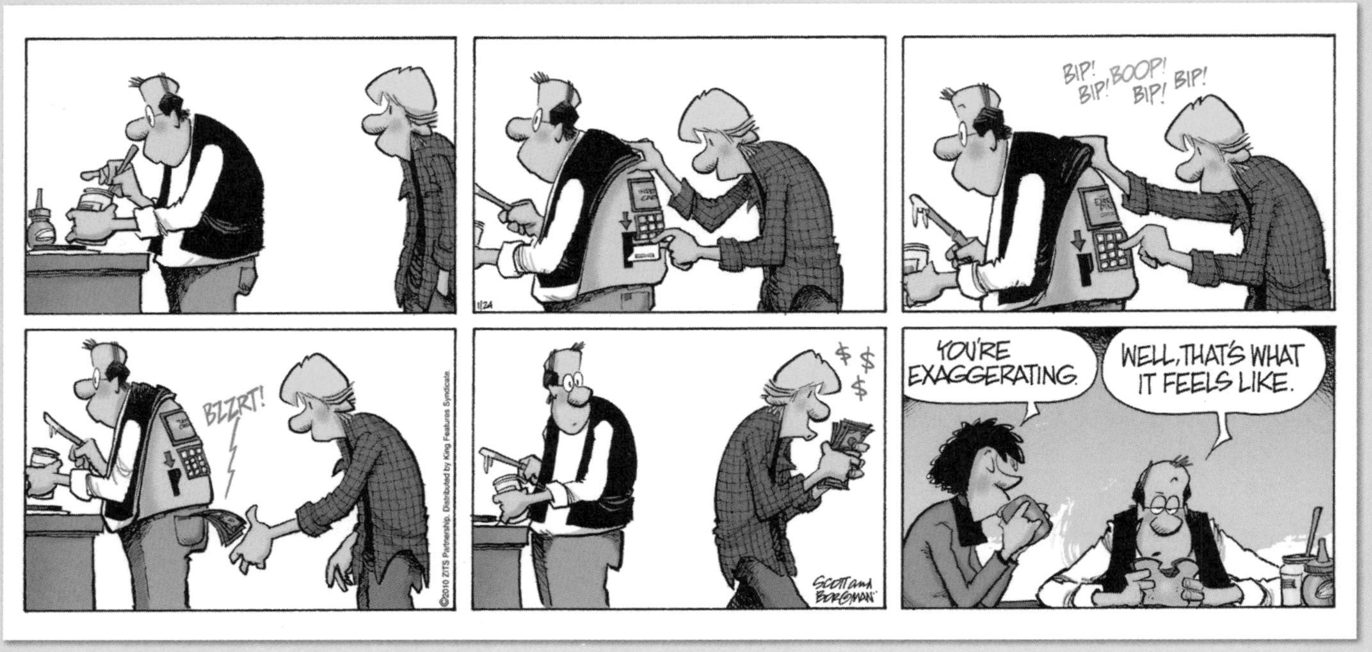

April 11, 2010

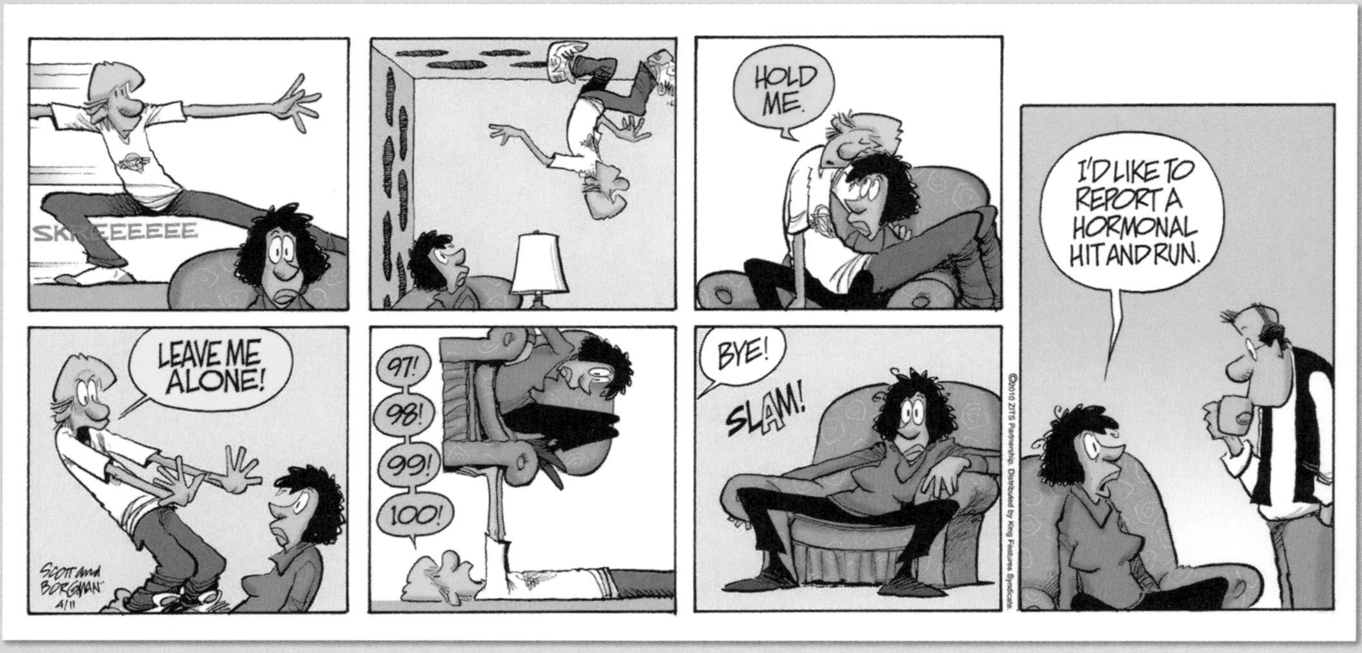

February 10, 2010

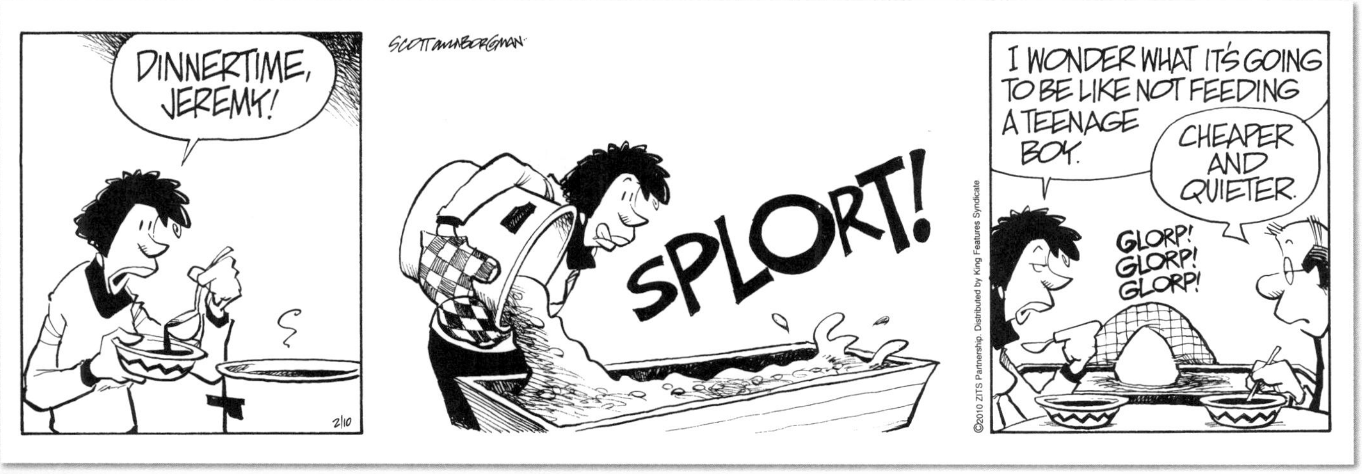

DINNERTIME, JEREMY!
SCOTT and BORGMAN
SPLORT!
2/10
©2010 ZITS Partnership. Distributed by King Features Syndicate
I WONDER WHAT IT'S GOING TO BE LIKE NOT FEEDING A TEENAGE BOY.
CHEAPER AND QUIETER.
GLORP! GLORP! GLORP!

February 27, 2010

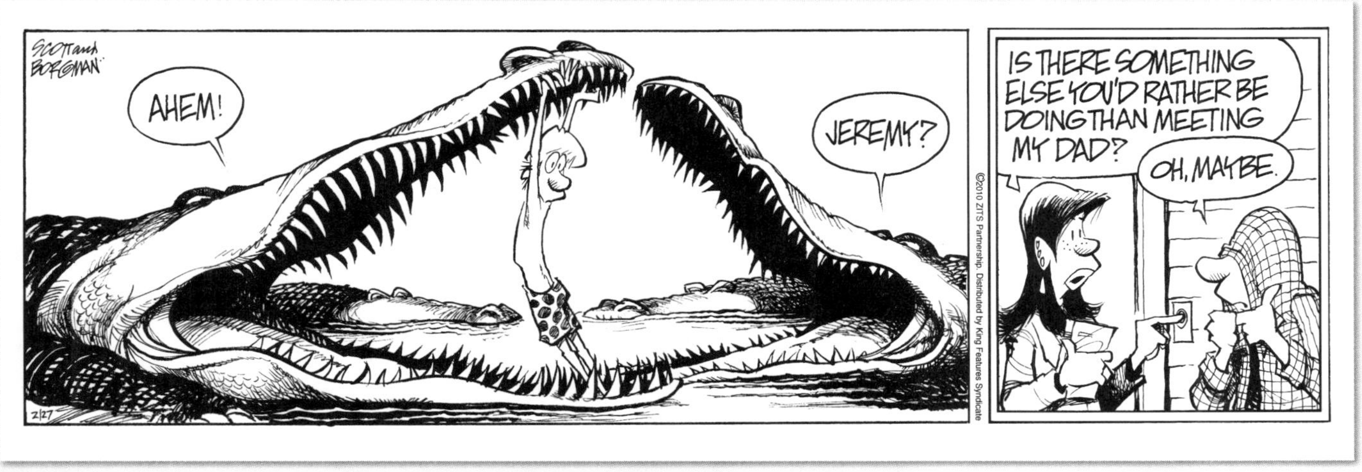

SCOTT and BORGMAN
AHEM!
JEREMY?
2/27
©2010 ZITS Partnership. Distributed by King Features Syndicate
IS THERE SOMETHING ELSE YOU'D RATHER BE DOING THAN MEETING MY DAD?
OH, MAYBE.

April 13, 2010

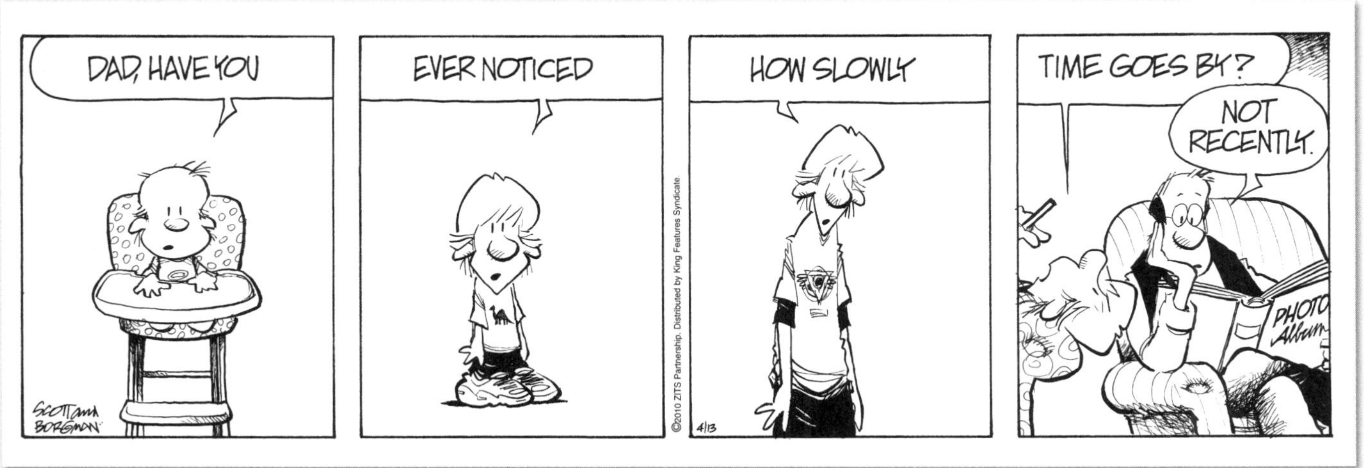

DAD, HAVE YOU
SCOTT and BORGMAN
EVER NOTICED
©2010 ZITS Partnership. Distributed by King Features Syndicate
HOW SLOWLY
4/13
TIME GOES BY?
NOT RECENTLY.
PHOTO Album

April 19, 2010

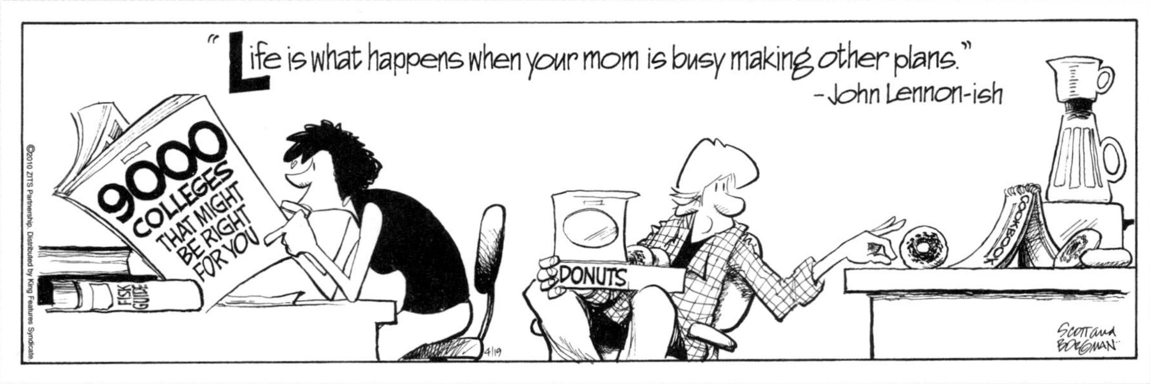

"Life is what happens when your mom is busy making other plans."
-John Lennon-ish
9000 COLLEGES THAT MIGHT BE RIGHT FOR YOU
FISK 2010
DONUTS
COOKBOOK
SCOTT and BORGMAN
©2010 ZITS Partnership. Distributed by King Features Syndicate
4/19

April 20, 2010

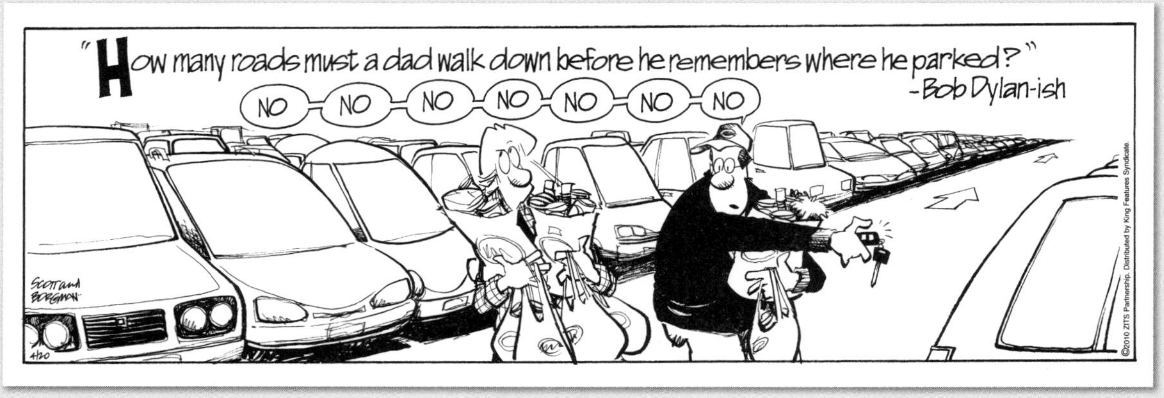

"How many roads must a dad walk down before he remembers where he parked?"
-Bob Dylan-ish
NO
NO
NO
NO
NO
NO
NO
SCOTT and BORGMAN
4/20
©2010 ZITS Partnership. Distributed by King Features Syndicate

April 21, 2010

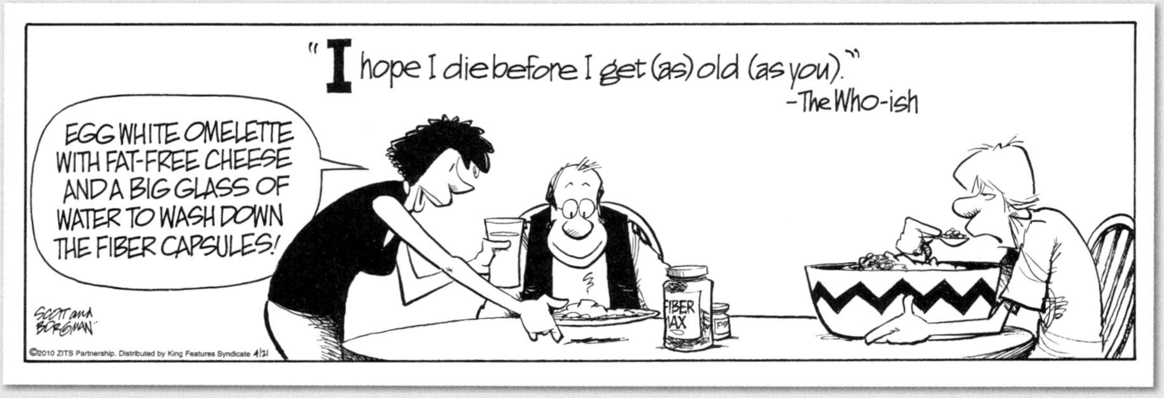

"I hope I die before I get (as) old (as you)."
-The Who-ish
EGG WHITE OMELETTE WITH FAT-FREE CHEESE AND A BIG GLASS OF WATER TO WASH DOWN THE FIBER CAPSULES!
FIBER MAX
SCOTT and BORGMAN
©2010 ZITS Partnership. Distributed by King Features Syndicate 4/21

April 23, 2010

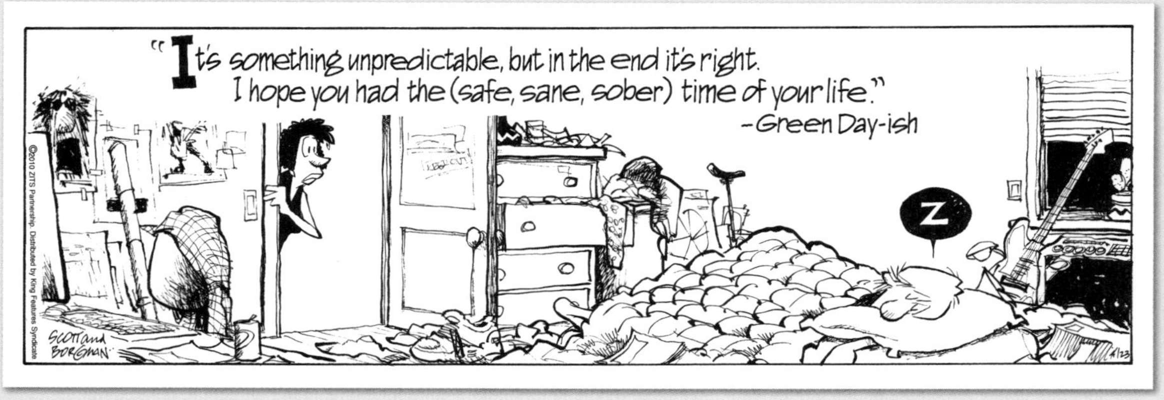

"It's something unpredictable, but in the end it's right. I hope you had the (safe, sane, sober) time of your life."
-Green Day-ish
Z
SCOTT and BORGMAN
©2010 ZITS Partnership. Distributed by King Features Syndicate
4/23

April 29, 2010

JEREMY, I JUST LEARNED SOMETHING REALLY INTERESTING ABOUT COLLEGE APPLICATIONS!
HM. I WONDER IF I SHOULD LISTEN IN.
NOPE.
SCOTT and BORGMAN
4/29
©2010 ZITS Partnership. Distributed by King Features Syndicate.

May 11, 2010

JEREMY, DO YOU HAVE A MIN--
WHY DO YOU GET THAT APPROACHING-A-WATERFALL-IN-A-CANOE LOOK ON YOUR FACE WHENEVER I WANT TO TALK TO YOU?
SORRY.
SCOTT and BORGMAN
5/11
©2010 ZITS Partnership. Distributed by King Features Syndicate.
ANYWAY, I FOUND THIS ARTICLE ON BIRTH CONTROL THAT I WANTED TO SHARE...

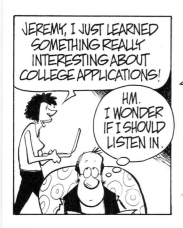

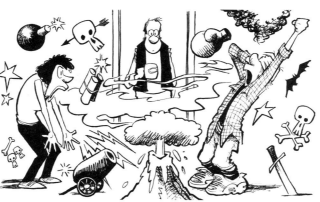

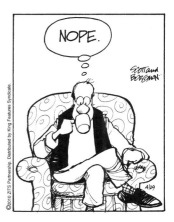

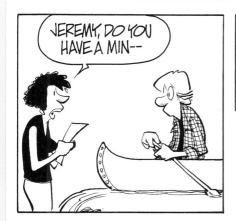

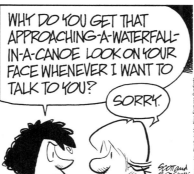

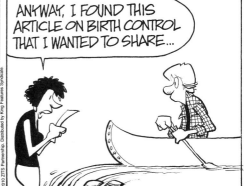

May 26, 2010

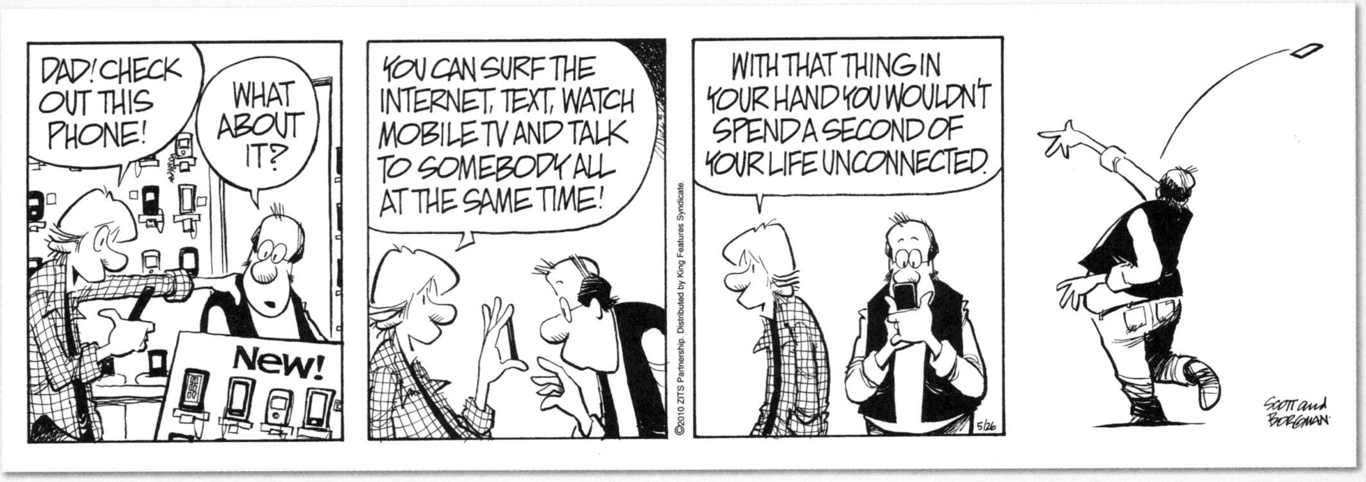
DAD! CHECK OUT THIS PHONE!
WHAT ABOUT IT?
New!
YOU CAN SURF THE INTERNET, TEXT, WATCH MOBILE TV AND TALK TO SOMEBODY ALL AT THE SAME TIME!
©2010 ZITS Partnership. Distributed by King Features Syndicate.
WITH THAT THING IN YOUR HAND YOU WOULDN'T SPEND A SECOND OF YOUR LIFE UNCONNECTED.
5/26
SCOTT and BORGMAN

June 4, 2010

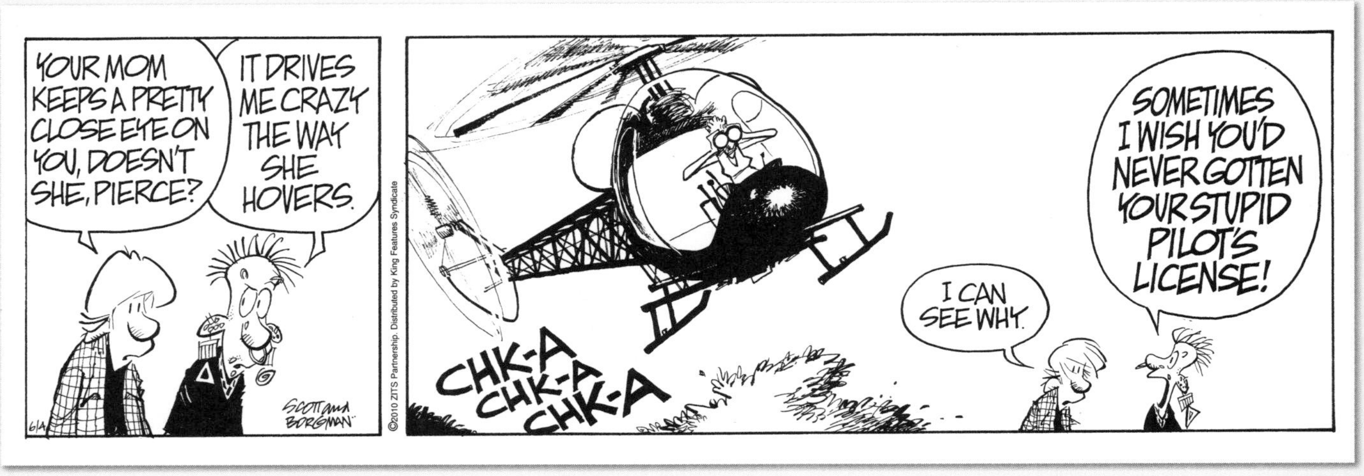
YOUR MOM KEEPS A PRETTY CLOSE EYE ON YOU, DOESN'T SHE, PIERCE?
IT DRIVES ME CRAZY THE WAY SHE HOVERS.
6/4
SCOTT and BORGMAN
©2010 ZITS Partnership. Distributed by King Features Syndicate
CHK-A CHK-A CHK-A
I CAN SEE WHY.
SOMETIMES I WISH YOU'D NEVER GOTTEN YOUR STUPID PILOT'S LICENSE!

June 23, 2010

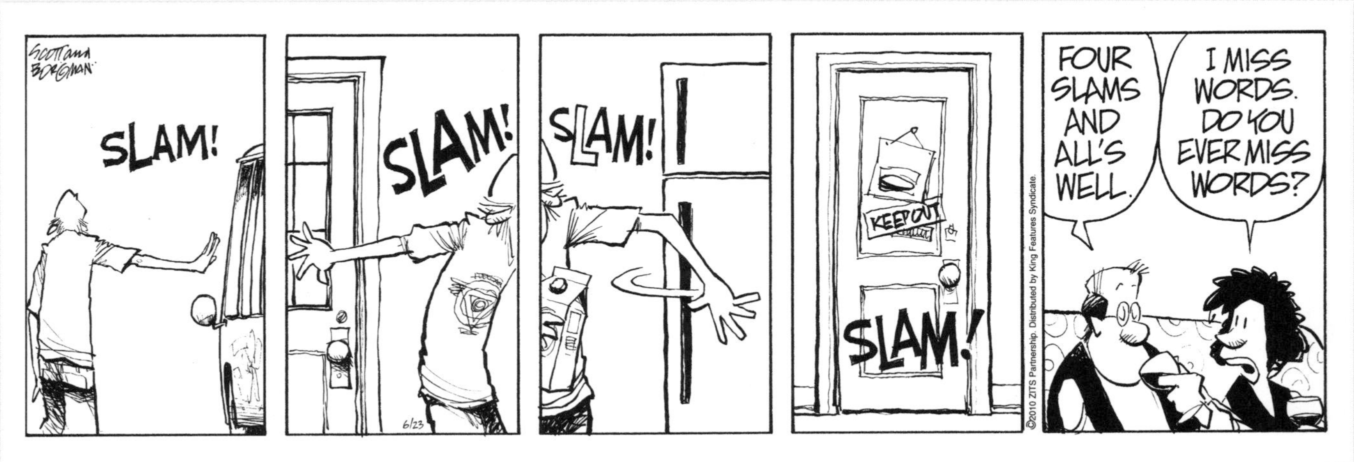
SCOTT and BORGMAN
SLAM!
SLAM!
6/23
SLAM!
KEEP OUT
SLAM!
©2010 ZITS Partnership. Distributed by King Features Syndicate.
FOUR SLAMS AND ALL'S WELL.
I MISS WORDS. DO YOU EVER MISS WORDS?

June 24, 2010

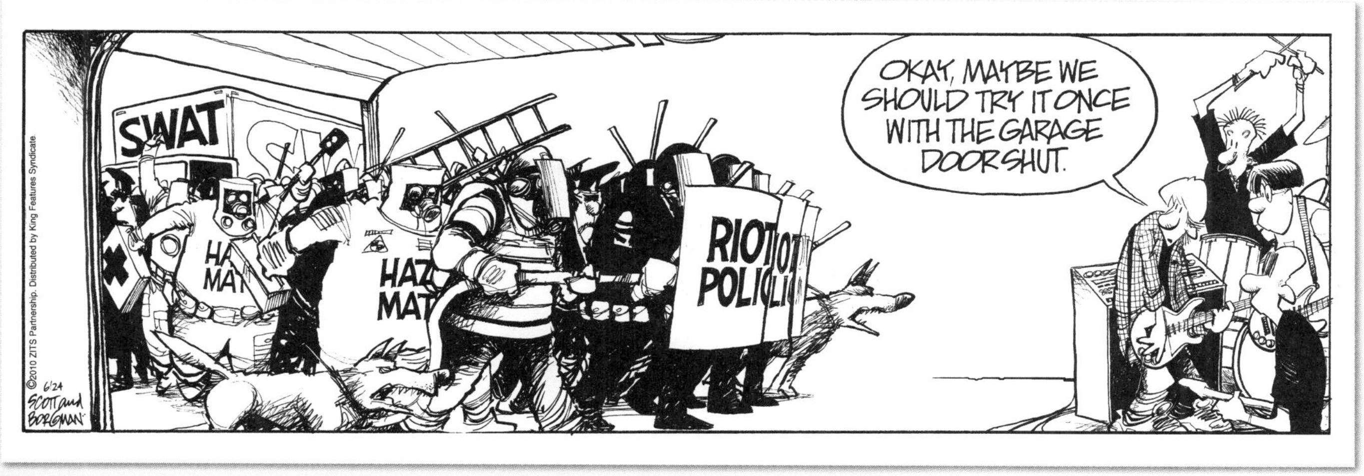
SWAT
HAZ MAT
HAZ MAT
RIOT POLICE
OKAY, MAYBE WE SHOULD TRY IT ONCE WITH THE GARAGE DOOR SHUT.
©2010 ZITS Partnership. Distributed by King Features Syndicate
6/24 SCOTT and BORGMAN

July 24, 2010

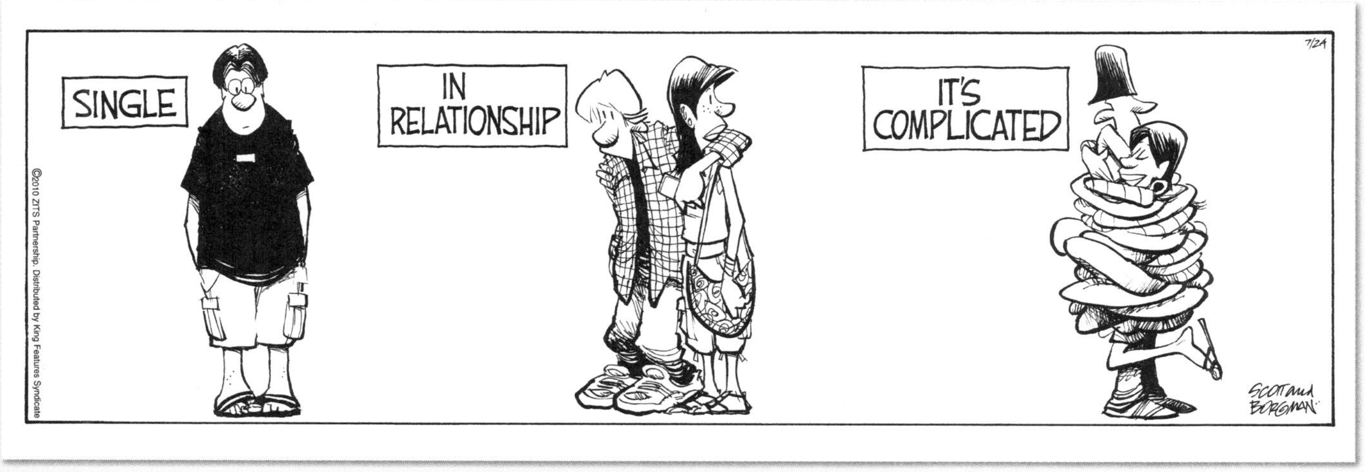
SINGLE
IN RELATIONSHIP
IT'S COMPLICATED
©2010 ZITS Partnership. Distributed by King Features Syndicate
7/24
SCOTT and BORGMAN

July 28, 2010

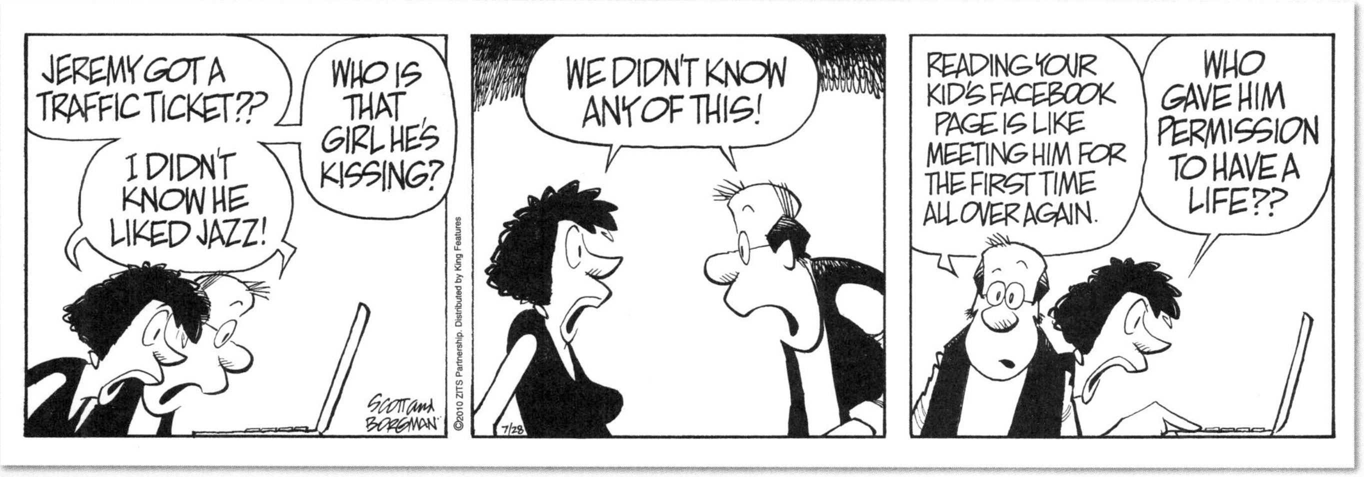
JEREMY GOT A TRAFFIC TICKET??
WHO IS THAT GIRL HE'S KISSING?
I DIDN'T KNOW HE LIKED JAZZ!
SCOTT and BORGMAN
©2010 ZITS Partnership. Distributed by King Features
WE DIDN'T KNOW ANY OF THIS!
7/28
READING YOUR KID'S FACEBOOK PAGE IS LIKE MEETING HIM FOR THE FIRST TIME ALL OVER AGAIN.
WHO GAVE HIM PERMISSION TO HAVE A LIFE??

August 7, 2010

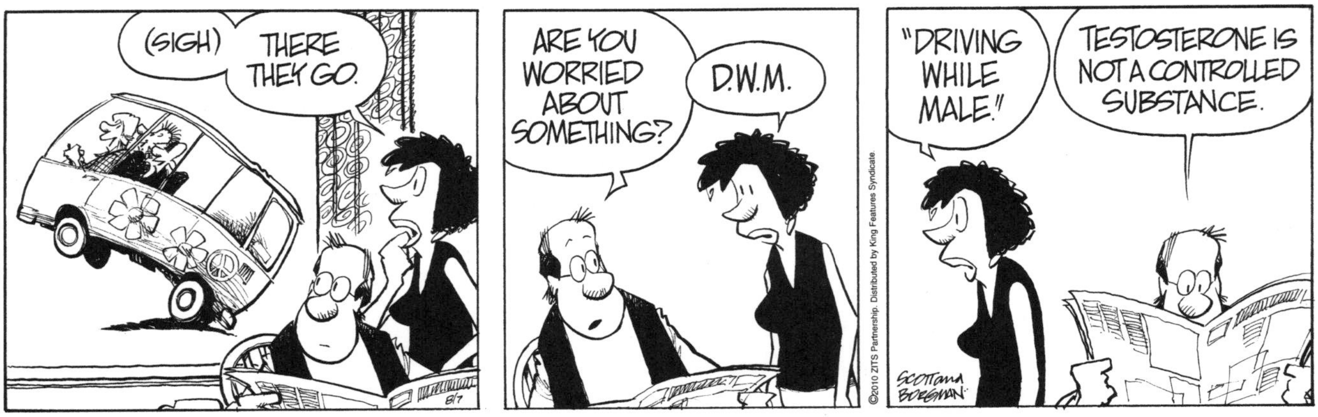
(SIGH)
THERE THEY GO.
ARE YOU WORRIED ABOUT SOMETHING?
D.W.M.
"DRIVING WHILE MALE."
TESTOSTERONE IS NOT A CONTROLLED SUBSTANCE.
8/7
©2010 ZITS Partnership. Distributed by King Features Syndicate.
SCOTT and BORGMAN

August 14, 2010

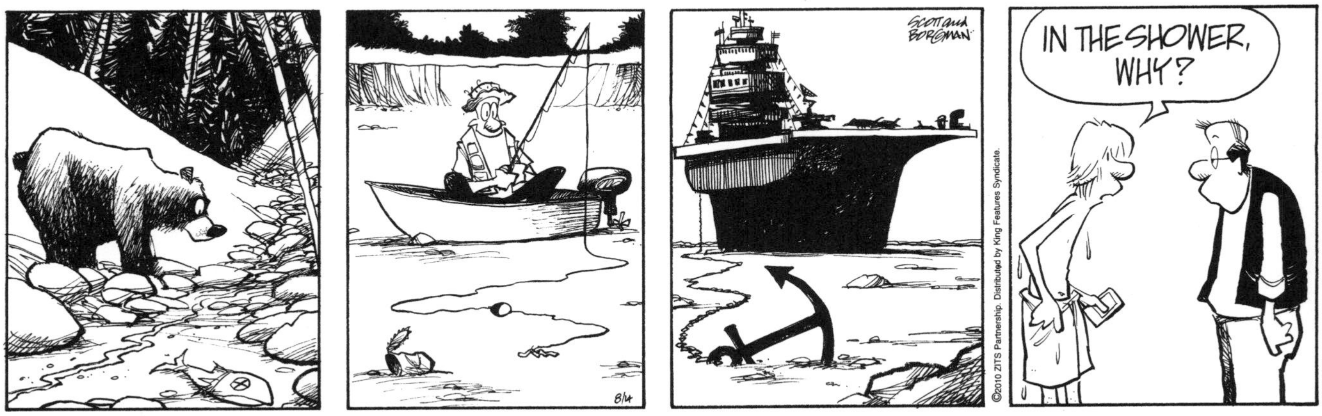
8/14
SCOTT and BORGMAN
©2010 ZITS Partnership. Distributed by King Features Syndicate.
IN THE SHOWER, WHY?

August 17, 2010

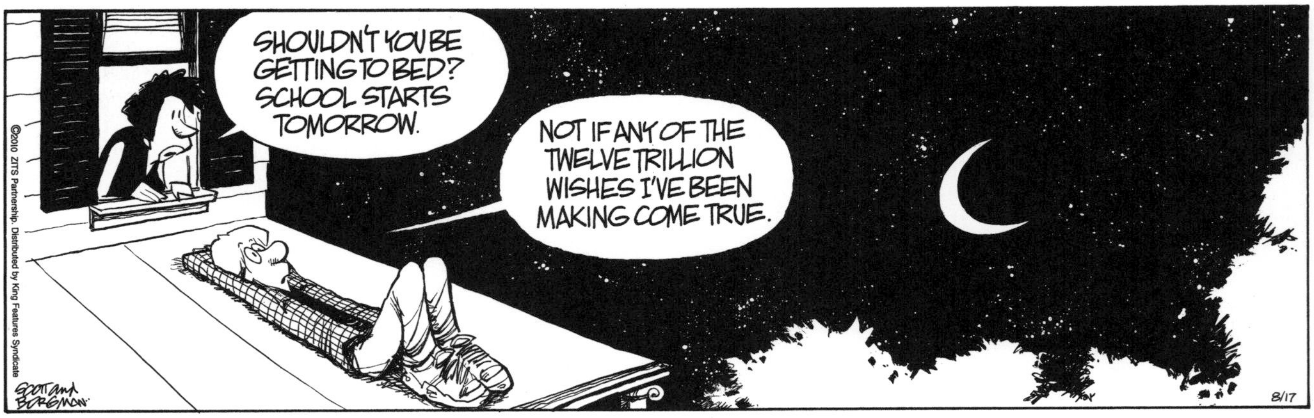
SHOULDN'T YOU BE GETTING TO BED? SCHOOL STARTS TOMORROW.
NOT IF ANY OF THE TWELVE TRILLION WISHES I'VE BEEN MAKING COME TRUE.
©2010 ZITS Partnership. Distributed by King Features Syndicate
SCOTT and BORGMAN
8/17

August 29, 2010

I'M THINKING ABOUT PAINTING MY ROOM THIS WEEK.
OUT!
IT WENT FASTER THAN I THOUGHT!
©2010 ZITS Partnership. Distributed by King Features Syndicate
SCOTT and BORGMAN
8/29

September 5, 2010

9/5
©2010 ZITS Partnership. Distributed by King Features Syndicate
ISN'T IT WEIRD THAT IT'S CALLED "SEEING EACH OTHER" EVEN THOUGH OUR EYES ARE ALMOST NEVER OPEN WHEN WE'RE TOGETHER?
SCOTT and BORGMAN

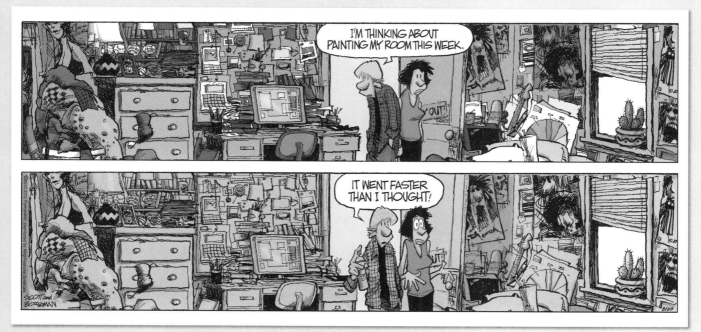

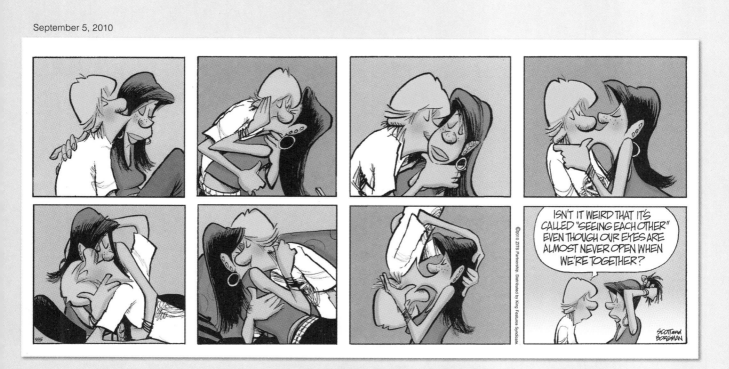

August 24, 2010

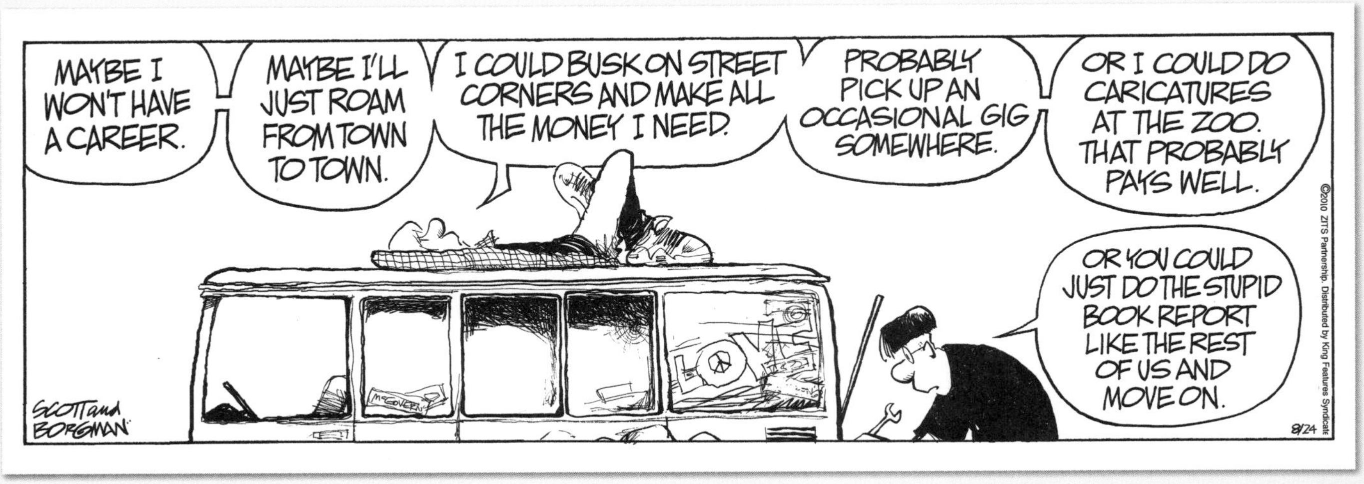
MAYBE I WON'T HAVE A CAREER.
MAYBE I'LL JUST ROAM FROM TOWN TO TOWN.
I COULD BUSK ON STREET CORNERS AND MAKE ALL THE MONEY I NEED.
PROBABLY PICK UP AN OCCASIONAL GIG SOMEWHERE.
OR I COULD DO CARICATURES AT THE ZOO. THAT PROBABLY PAYS WELL.
OR YOU COULD JUST DO THE STUPID BOOK REPORT LIKE THE REST OF US AND MOVE ON.
LOVE
SCOTT and BORGMAN
8/24
©2010 ZITS Partnership. Distributed by King Features Syndicate

October 6, 2010

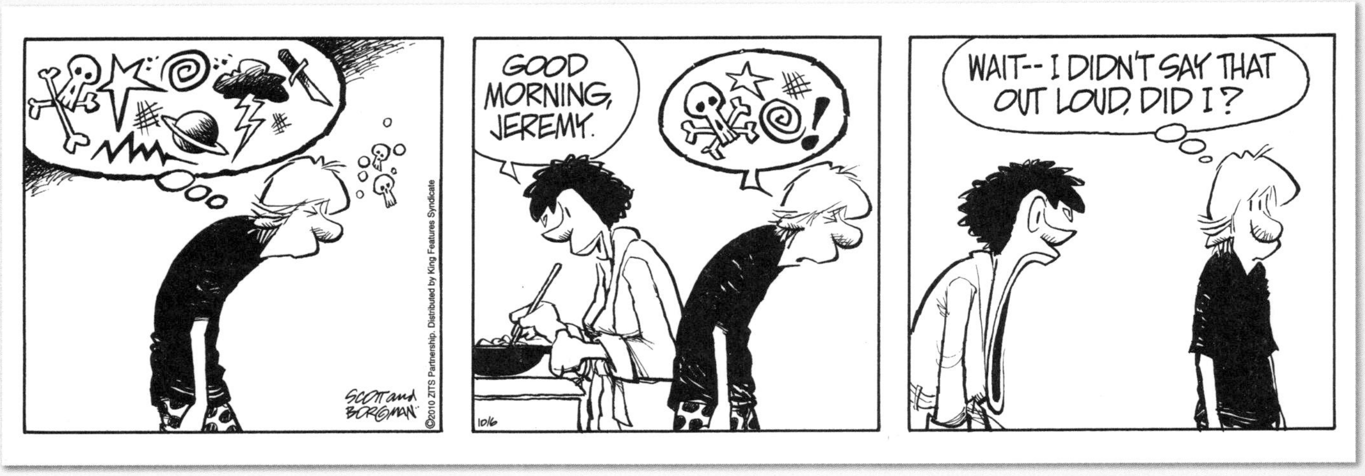
SCOTT and BORGMAN
©2010 ZITS Partnership. Distributed by King Features Syndicate
GOOD MORNING, JEREMY.
10/6
WAIT-- I DIDN'T SAY THAT OUT LOUD, DID I?

November 27, 2010

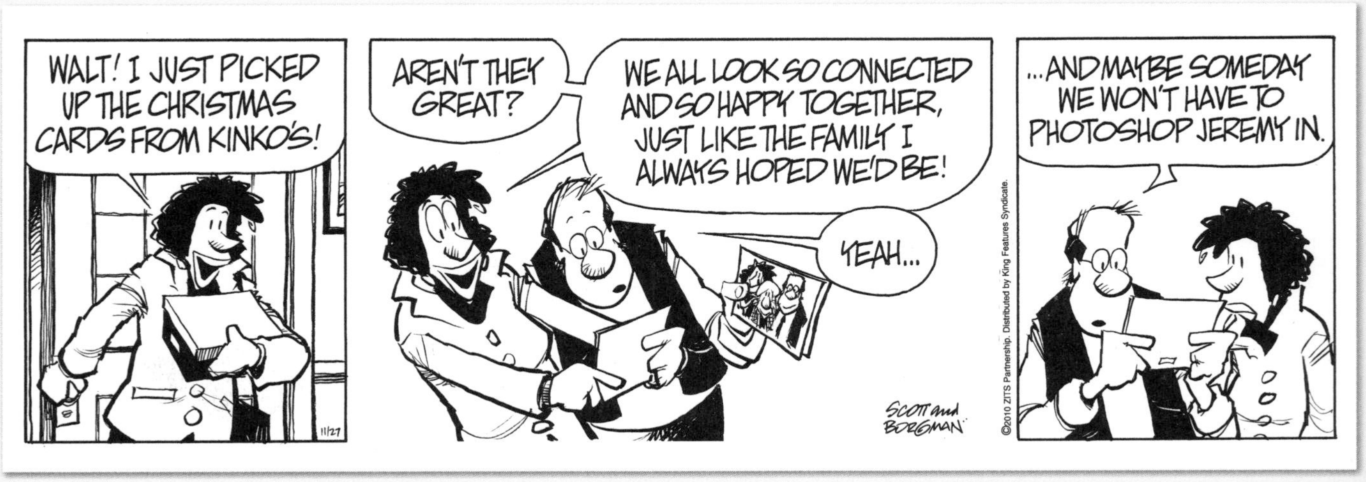
WALT! I JUST PICKED UP THE CHRISTMAS CARDS FROM KINKO'S!
11/27
AREN'T THEY GREAT?
WE ALL LOOK SO CONNECTED AND SO HAPPY TOGETHER, JUST LIKE THE FAMILY I ALWAYS HOPED WE'D BE!
YEAH...
SCOTT and BORGMAN
©2010 ZITS Partnership. Distributed by King Features Syndicate.
...AND MAYBE SOMEDAY WE WON'T HAVE TO PHOTOSHOP JEREMY IN.

October 25, 2010

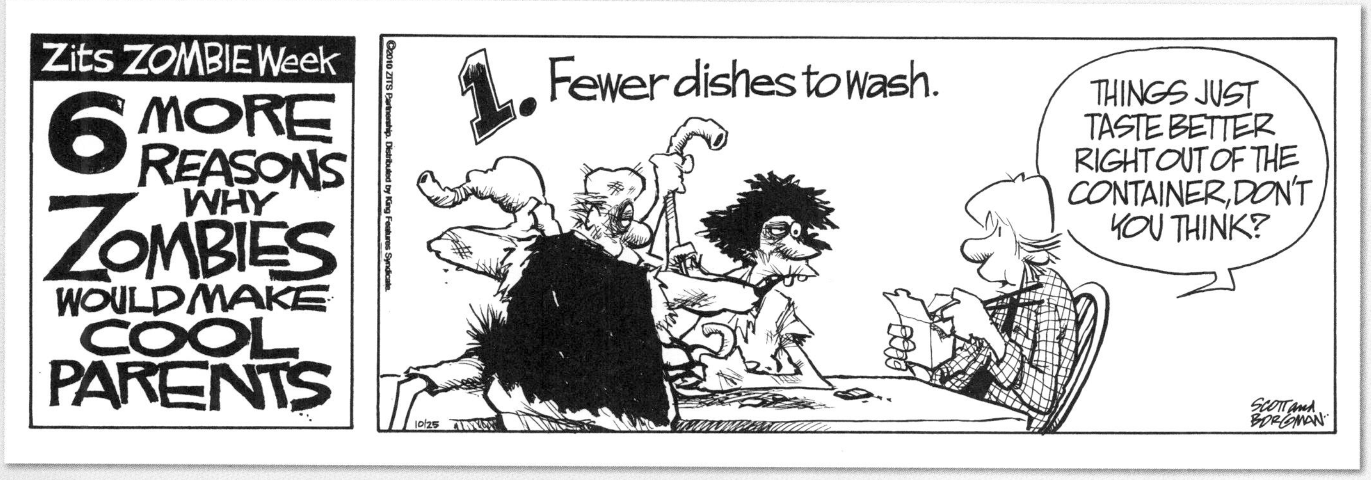

Zits ZOMBIE Week
6 MORE REASONS WHY ZOMBIES WOULD MAKE COOL PARENTS
©2010 ZITS Partnership. Distributed by King Features Syndicate.
1. Fewer dishes to wash.
THINGS JUST TASTE BETTER RIGHT OUT OF THE CONTAINER, DON'T YOU THINK?
10/25
SCOTT and BORGMAN

October 26, 2010

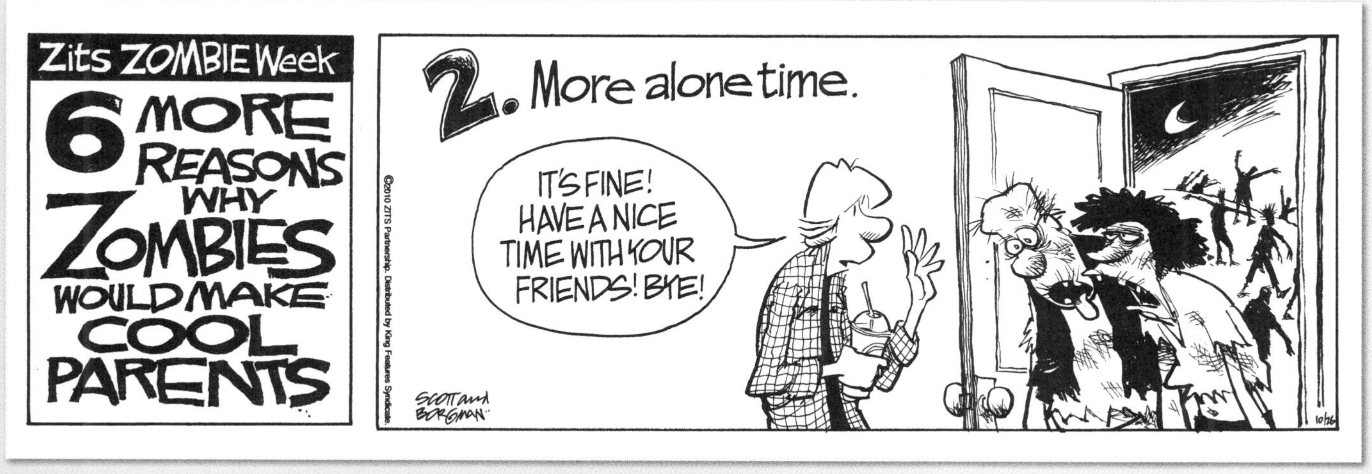

Zits ZOMBIE Week
6 MORE REASONS WHY ZOMBIES WOULD MAKE COOL PARENTS
©2010 ZITS Partnership. Distributed by King Features Syndicate.
2. More alone time.
IT'S FINE! HAVE A NICE TIME WITH YOUR FRIENDS! BYE!
SCOTT and BORGMAN
10/26

October 27, 2010

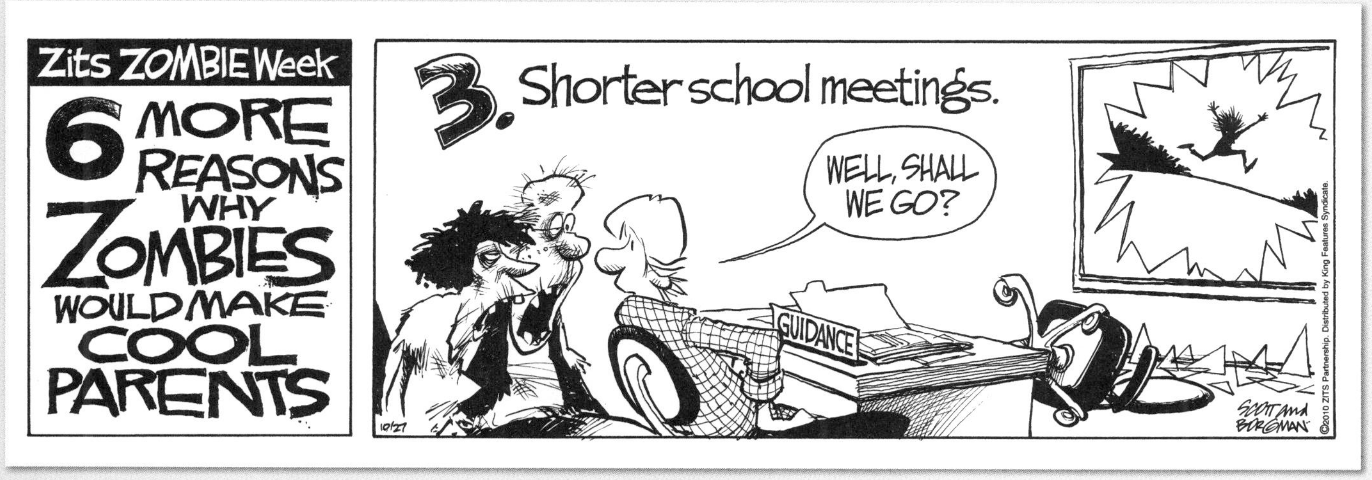

Zits ZOMBIE Week
6 MORE REASONS WHY ZOMBIES WOULD MAKE COOL PARENTS
3. Shorter school meetings.
WELL, SHALL WE GO?
GUIDANCE
10/27
SCOTT and BORGMAN
©2010 ZITS Partnership. Distributed by King Features Syndicate.

FROM the WAYBACK Machine

Jim Borgman

Look what I found in the attic while doing a bit of spring-cleaning. These are some of the original faxes (yes, I said faxes) Jerry and I sent back and forth to each other in 1996 when we were developing *Zits*.

A lot has changed (check out that phone!), but it's all kinda there-ish. Even those weird rooster-comb hairdos I thought were the bomb.

I'd forgotten how we struggled for a title for the strip. Cowboy was going to have been Mom's nickname for Jeremy when he was tracking as a much younger teenager in our minds.

I think that's the Generation Gap between them; get it? Oh man, how close we came to disaster.

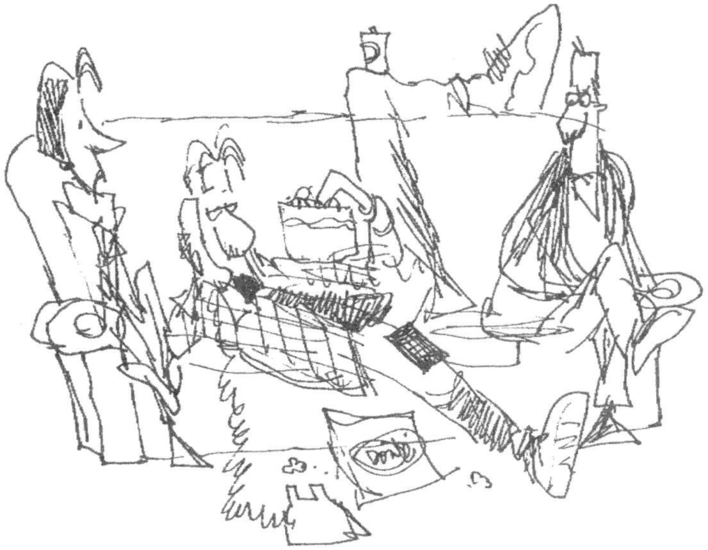

Other rejected titles for the strip:

Grounded for Life
Work in Progress
Yo
Why Me?
Stuff about Me
As If
Chad and Jeremy

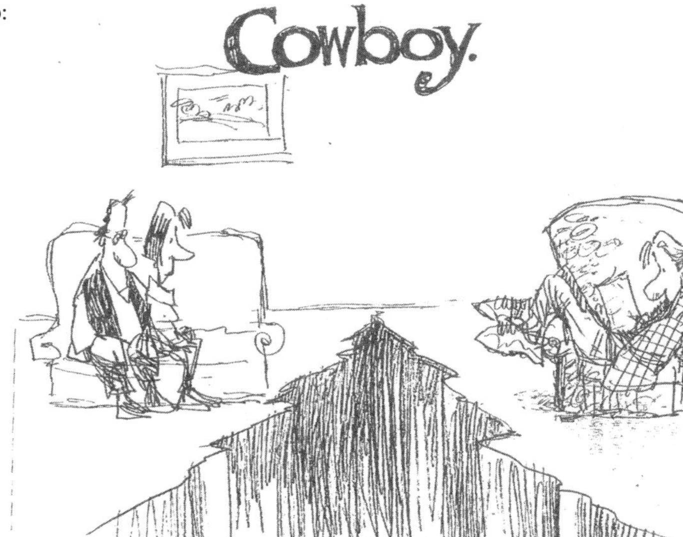
Cowboy.

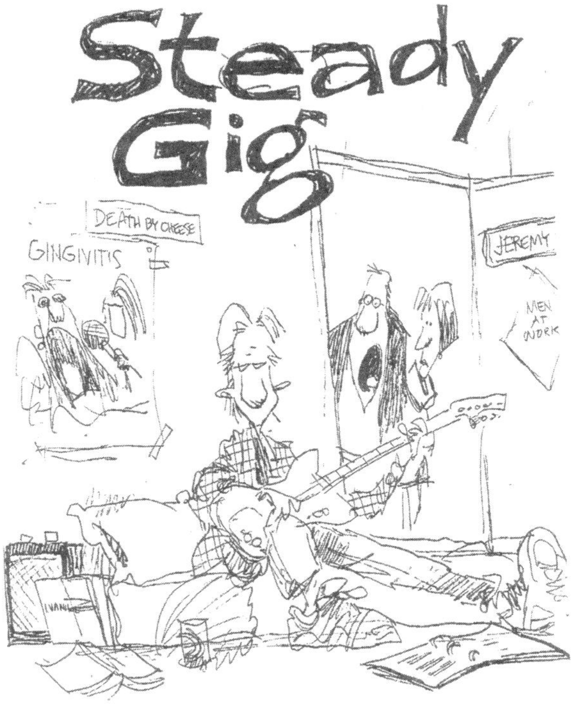
Steady Gig
DEATH BY CHEESE
GINGIVITIS
JEREMY
MEN AT WORK

Yes, that's how close we came to a complete dumpster-fire launch, friends.

You see, we were searching for a title that succinctly conveyed what we hoped the strip would be about: a gritty look at life with a teenager in the house.

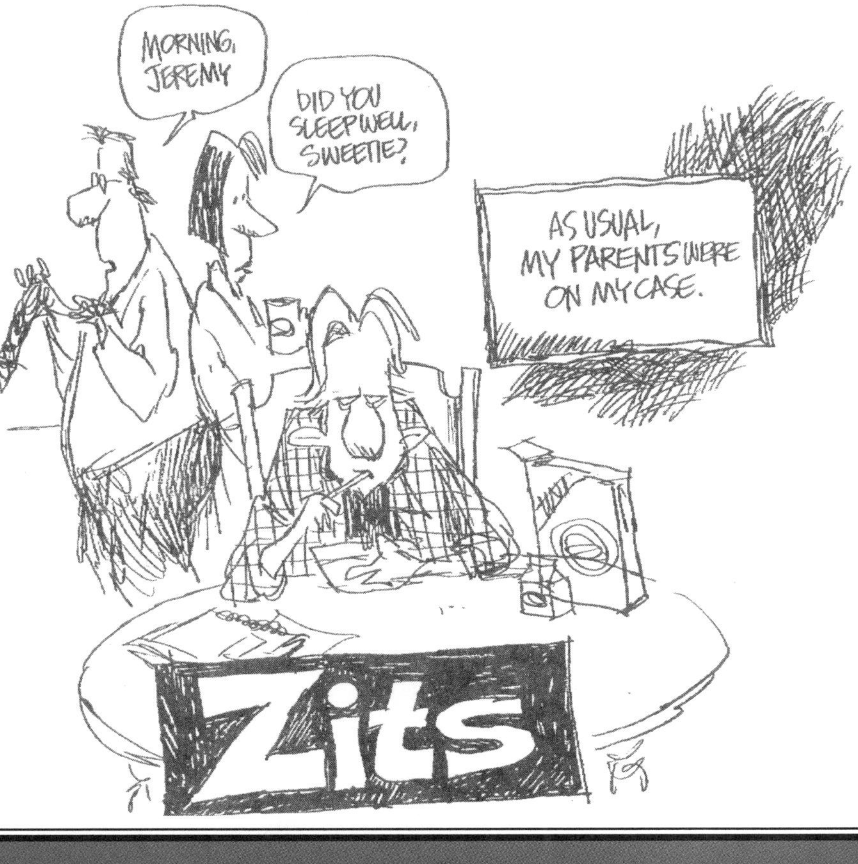
MORNING, JEREMY
DID YOU SLEEP WELL, SWEETIE?
AS USUAL, MY PARENTS WERE ON MY CASE.
Zits

January 8, 2011

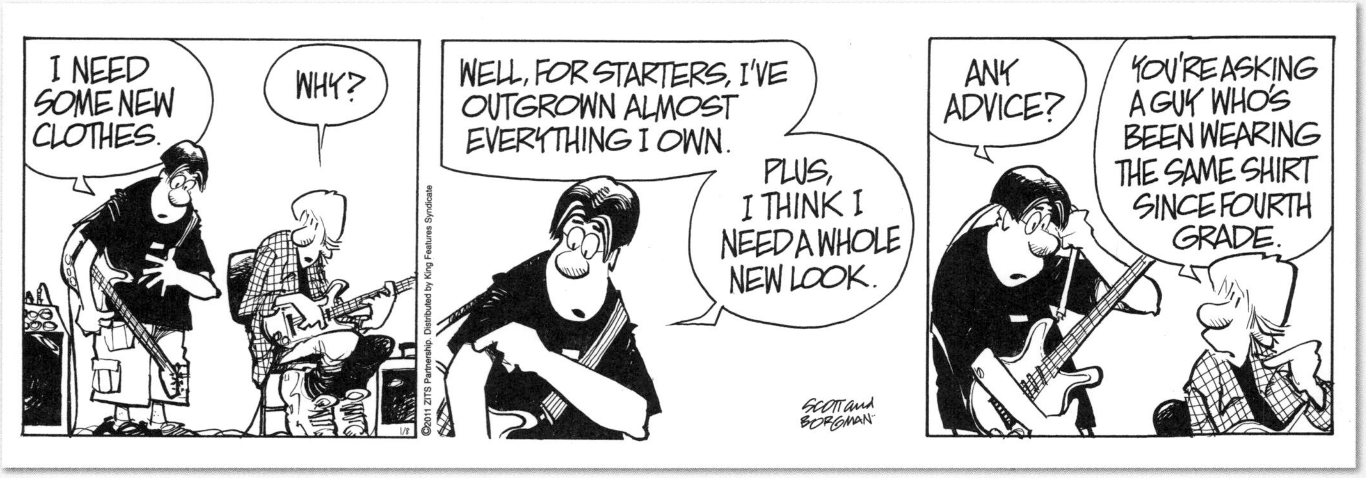
I NEED SOME NEW CLOTHES.
WHY?
WELL, FOR STARTERS, I'VE OUTGROWN ALMOST EVERYTHING I OWN.
PLUS, I THINK I NEED A WHOLE NEW LOOK.
ANY ADVICE?
YOU'RE ASKING A GUY WHO'S BEEN WEARING THE SAME SHIRT SINCE FOURTH GRADE.
©2011 ZITS Partnership. Distributed by King Features Syndicate
SCOTT and BORGMAN

January 10, 2011

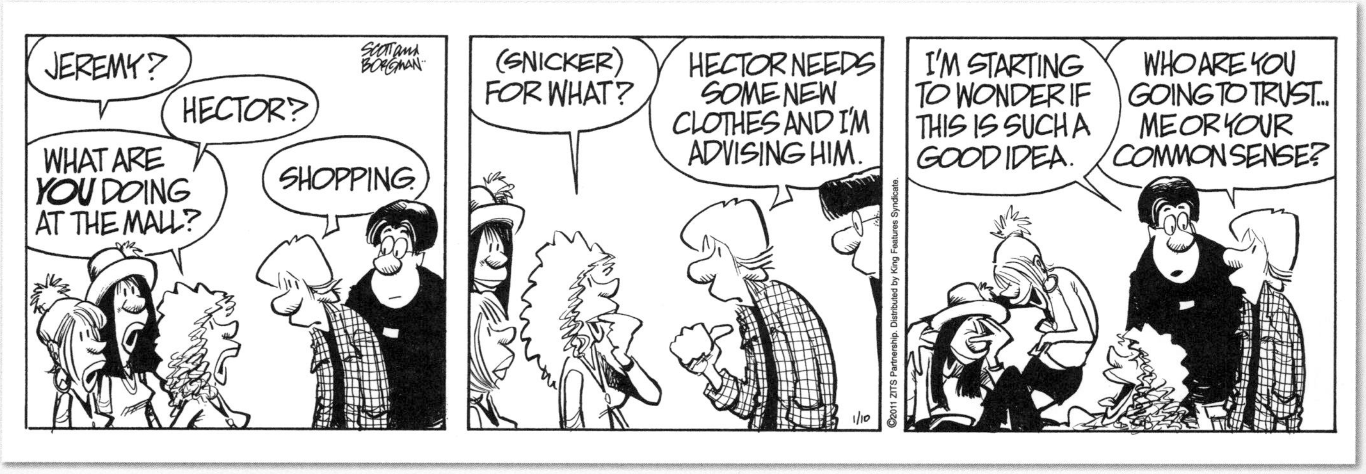
JEREMY?
HECTOR?
WHAT ARE **YOU** DOING AT THE MALL?
SHOPPING.
(SNICKER) FOR WHAT?
HECTOR NEEDS SOME NEW CLOTHES AND I'M ADVISING HIM.
I'M STARTING TO WONDER IF THIS IS SUCH A GOOD IDEA.
WHO ARE YOU GOING TO TRUST... ME OR YOUR COMMON SENSE?
SCOTT and BORGMAN
©2011 ZITS Partnership. Distributed by King Features Syndicate.

January 12, 2011

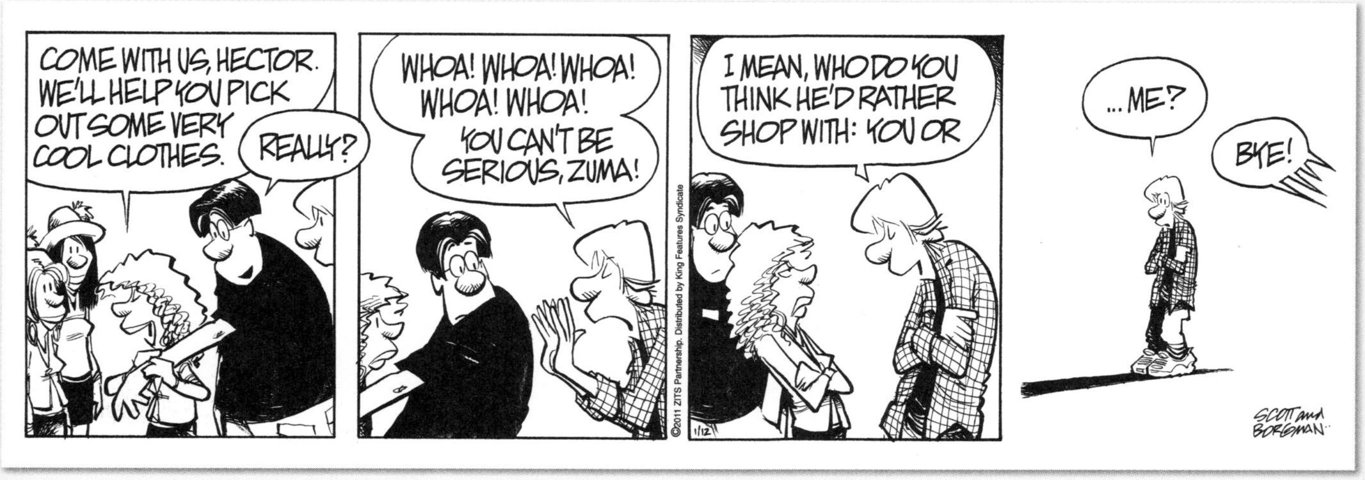
COME WITH US, HECTOR. WE'LL HELP YOU PICK OUT SOME VERY COOL CLOTHES.
REALLY?
WHOA! WHOA! WHOA! WHOA! WHOA! YOU CAN'T BE SERIOUS, ZUMA!
I MEAN, WHO DO YOU THINK HE'D RATHER SHOP WITH: YOU OR
... ME?
BYE!
©2011 ZITS Partnership. Distributed by King Features Syndicate
SCOTT and BORGMAN

January 13, 2011

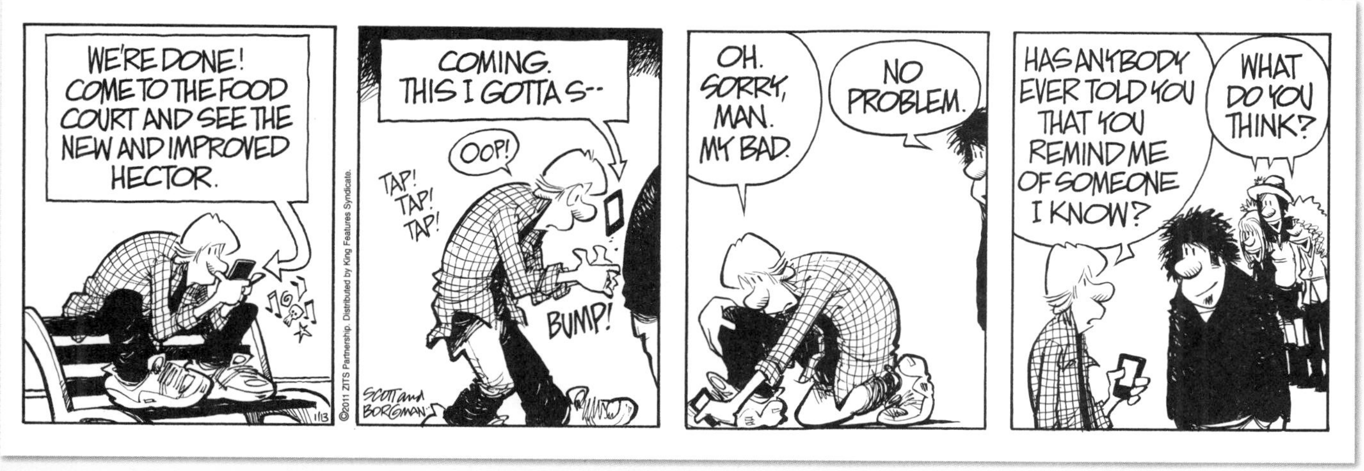

WE'RE DONE! COME TO THE FOOD COURT AND SEE THE NEW AND IMPROVED HECTOR.
COMING. THIS I GOTTA S--
OOP!
TAP! TAP! TAP!
BUMP!
OH. SORRY, MAN. MY BAD.
NO PROBLEM.
HAS ANYBODY EVER TOLD YOU THAT YOU REMIND ME OF SOMEONE I KNOW?
WHAT DO YOU THINK?
©2011 ZITS Partnership. Distributed by King Features Syndicate.
SCOTT and BORGMAN

January 15, 2011

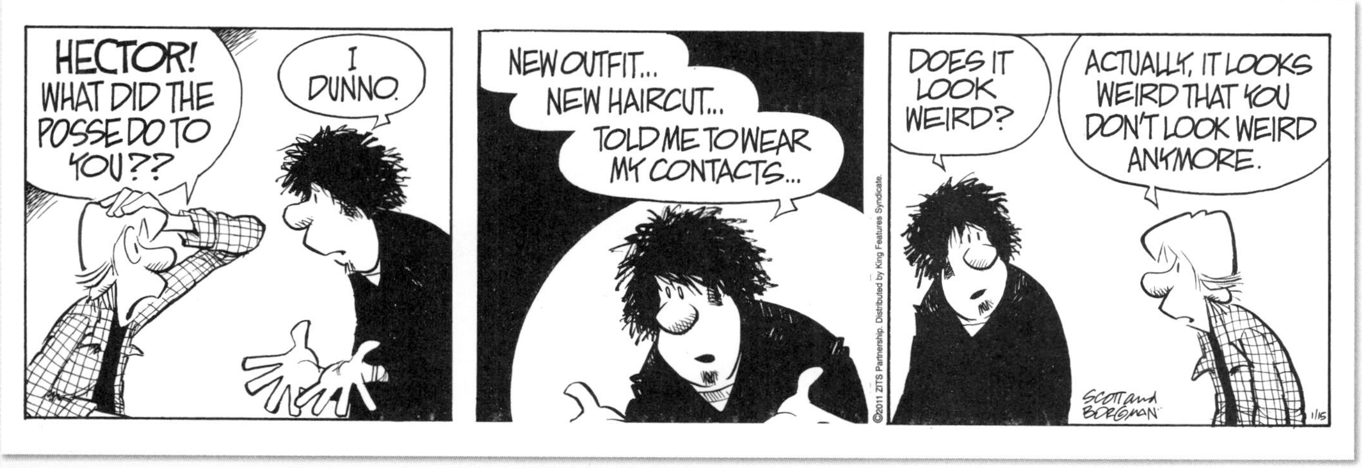

HECTOR! WHAT DID THE POSSE DO TO YOU??
I DUNNO.
NEW OUTFIT... NEW HAIRCUT...
TOLD ME TO WEAR MY CONTACTS...
©2011 ZITS Partnership. Distributed by King Features Syndicate.
DOES IT LOOK WEIRD?
ACTUALLY, IT LOOKS WEIRD THAT YOU DON'T LOOK WEIRD ANYMORE.
SCOTT and BORGMAN

February 2, 2011

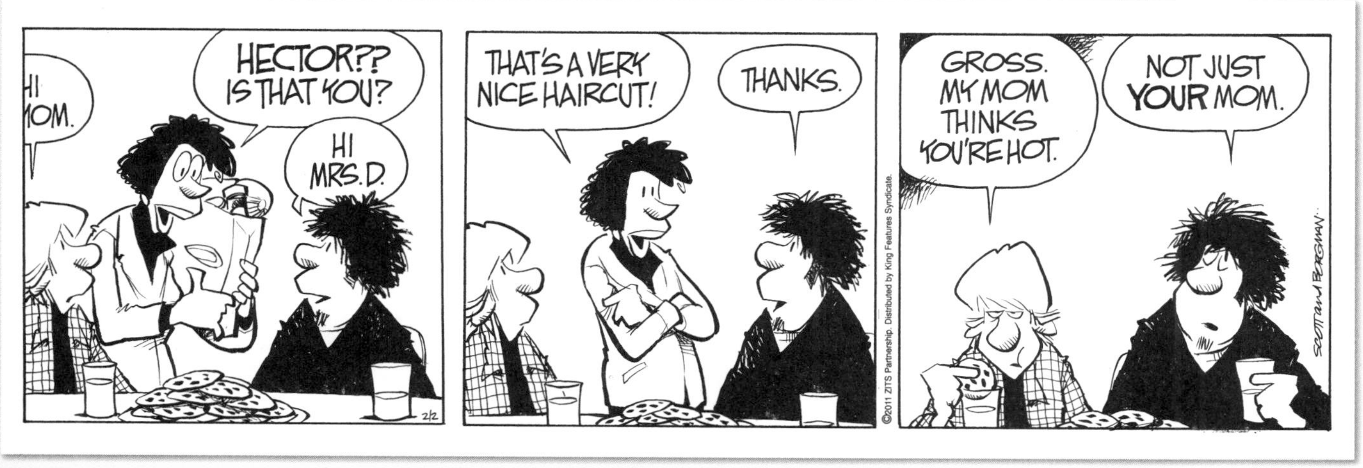

HI MOM.
HECTOR?? IS THAT YOU?
HI MRS. D.
THAT'S A VERY NICE HAIRCUT!
THANKS.
©2011 ZITS Partnership. Distributed by King Features Syndicate.
GROSS. MY MOM THINKS YOU'RE HOT.
NOT JUST **YOUR** MOM.
SCOTT and BORGMAN

January 5, 2011

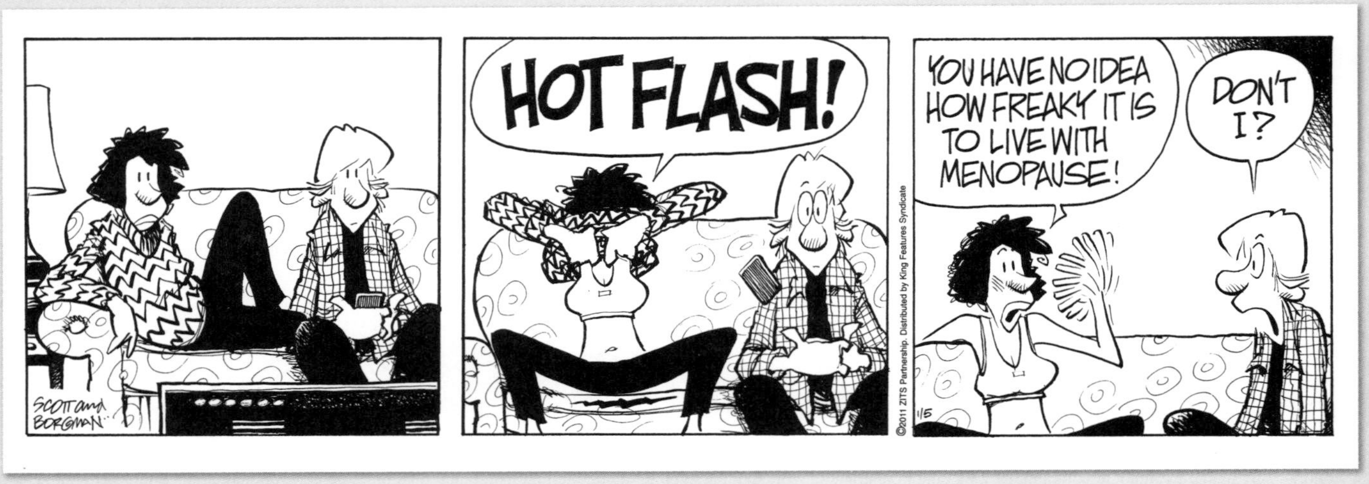
SCOTT and BORGMAN
HOT FLASH!
©2011 ZITS Partnership. Distributed by King Features Syndicate
1/5
YOU HAVE NO IDEA HOW FREAKY IT IS TO LIVE WITH MENOPAUSE!
DON'T I?

January 6, 2011

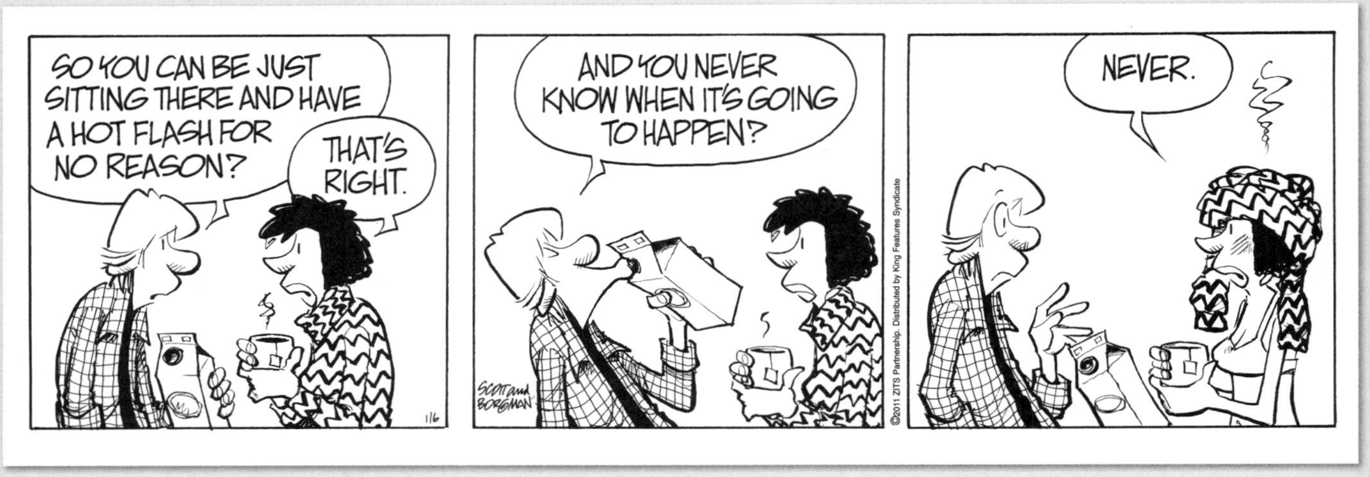
SO YOU CAN BE JUST SITTING THERE AND HAVE A HOT FLASH FOR NO REASON?
THAT'S RIGHT.
1/6
AND YOU NEVER KNOW WHEN IT'S GOING TO HAPPEN?
SCOTT and BORGMAN
©2011 ZITS Partnership. Distributed by King Features Syndicate
NEVER.

February 14, 2011

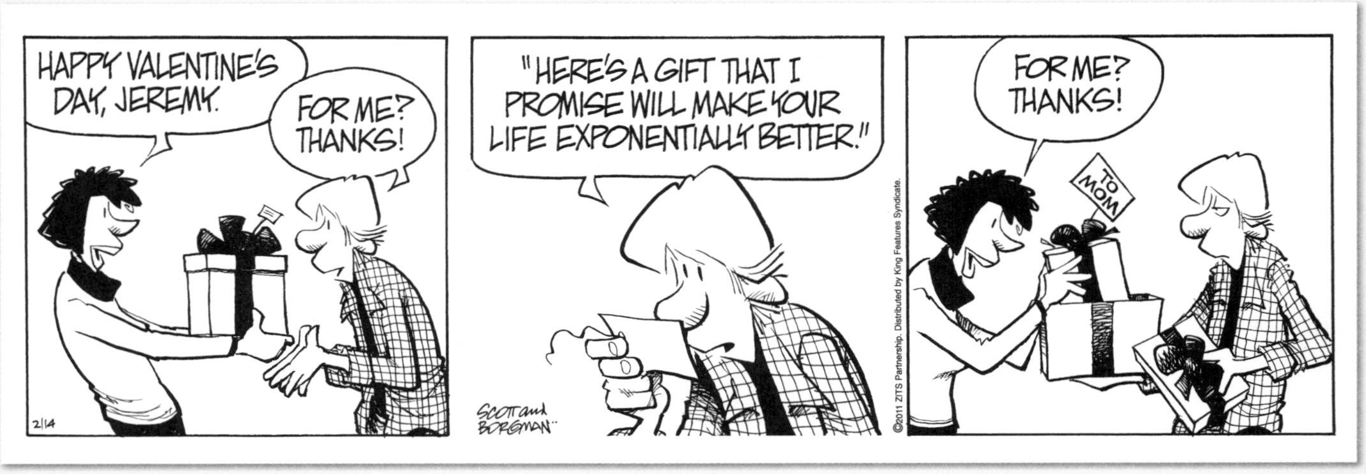
HAPPY VALENTINE'S DAY, JEREMY.
FOR ME? THANKS!
2/14
"HERE'S A GIFT THAT I PROMISE WILL MAKE YOUR LIFE EXPONENTIALLY BETTER."
SCOTT and BORGMAN
©2011 ZITS Partnership. Distributed by King Features Syndicate.
FOR ME? THANKS!
TO MOM

February 19, 2011

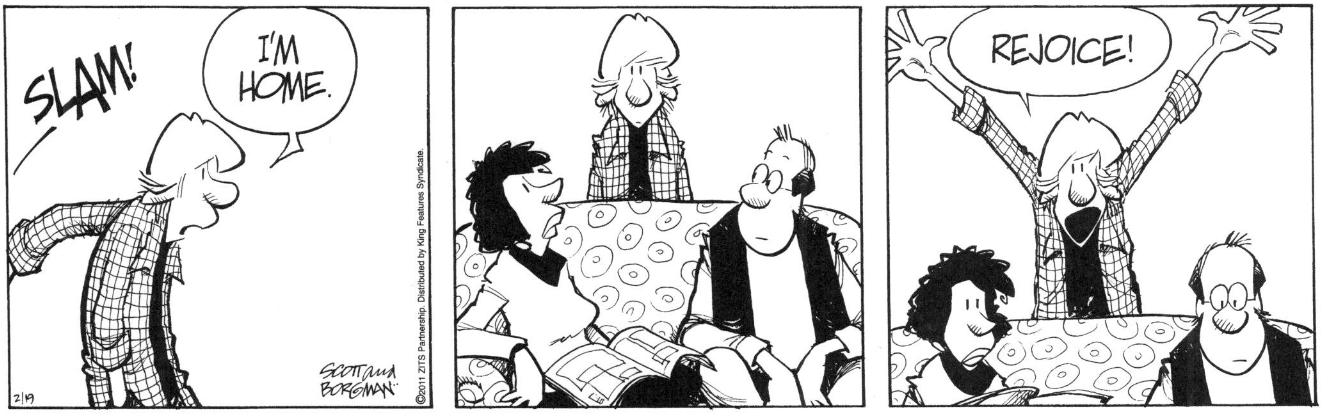
SLAM!
I'M HOME.
REJOICE!
2/19
SCOTT and BORGMAN
©2011 ZITS Partnership. Distributed by King Features Syndicate.

February 22, 2011

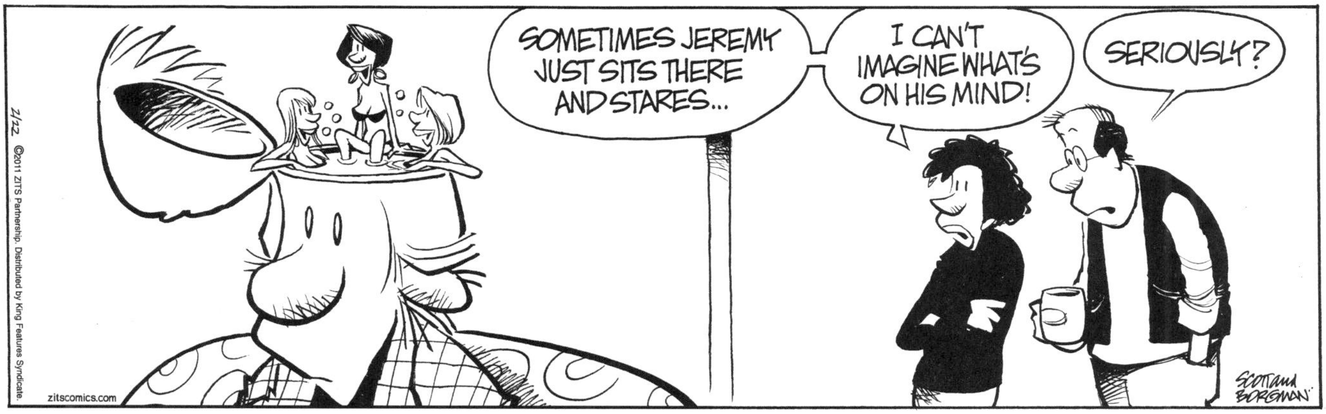
SOMETIMES JEREMY JUST SITS THERE AND STARES...
I CAN'T IMAGINE WHAT'S ON HIS MIND!
SERIOUSLY?
2/22
©2011 ZITS Partnership. Distributed by King Features Syndicate.
zitscomics.com
SCOTT and BORGMAN

March 3, 2011

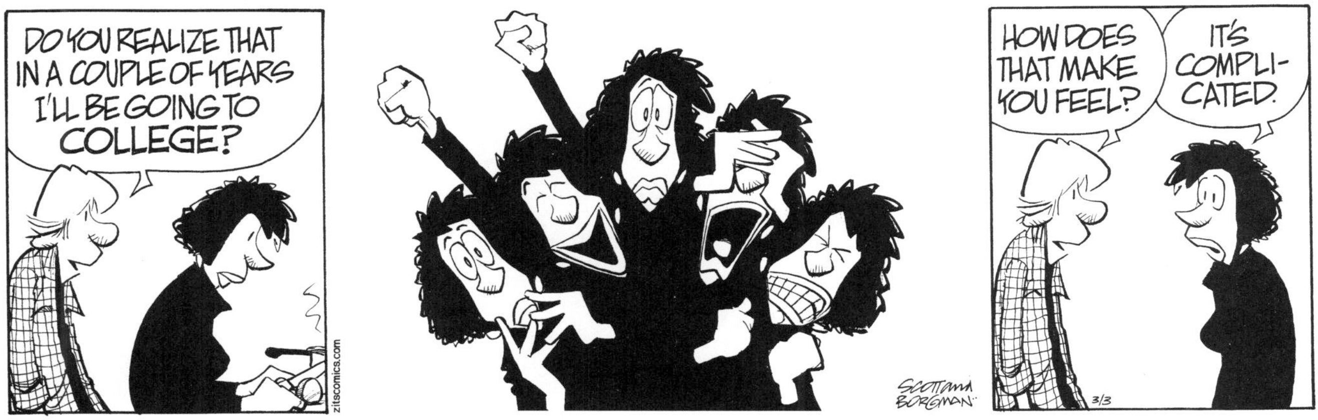
DO YOU REALIZE THAT IN A COUPLE OF YEARS I'LL BE GOING TO COLLEGE?
zitscomics.com
SCOTT and BORGMAN
HOW DOES THAT MAKE YOU FEEL?
IT'S COMPLI-CATED.
3/3

February 20, 2011

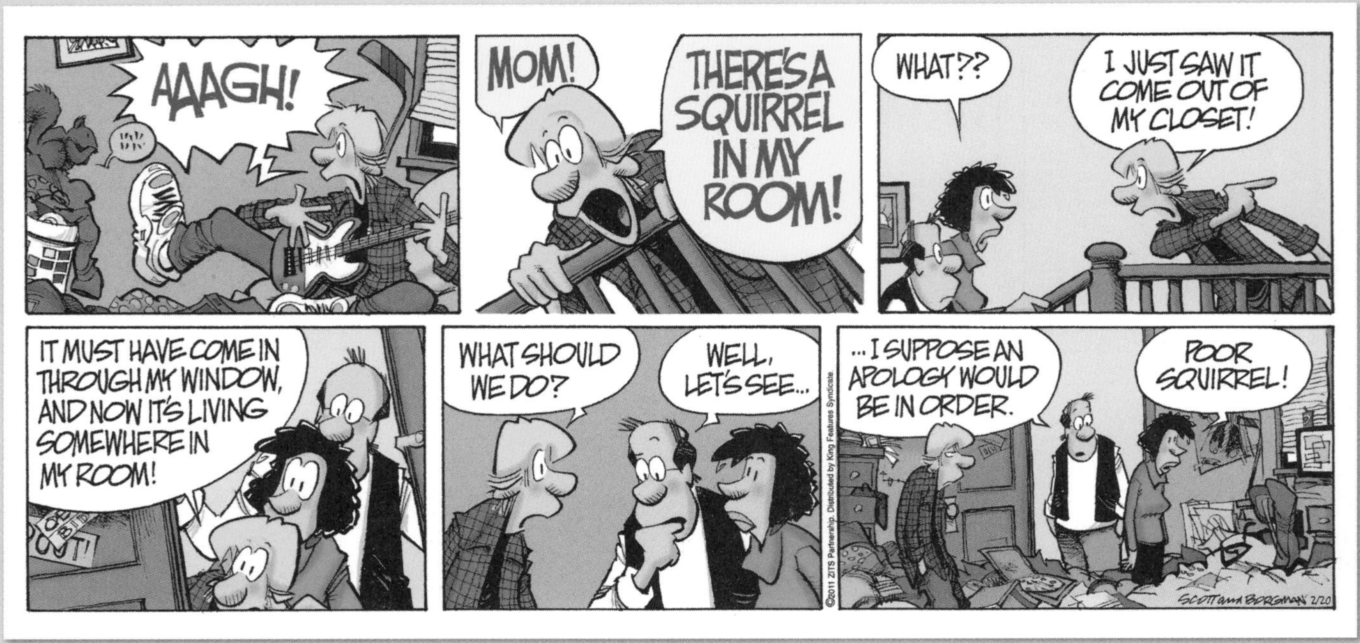
AAAGH!
MOM!
THERE'S A SQUIRREL IN MY ROOM!
WHAT??
I JUST SAW IT COME OUT OF MY CLOSET!
IT MUST HAVE COME IN THROUGH MY WINDOW, AND NOW IT'S LIVING SOMEWHERE IN MY ROOM!
WHAT SHOULD WE DO?
WELL, LET'S SEE...
...I SUPPOSE AN APOLOGY WOULD BE IN ORDER.
POOR SQUIRREL!
©2011 ZITS Partnership. Distributed by King Features Syndicate.
SCOTT and BORGMAN 2/20

February 13, 2011

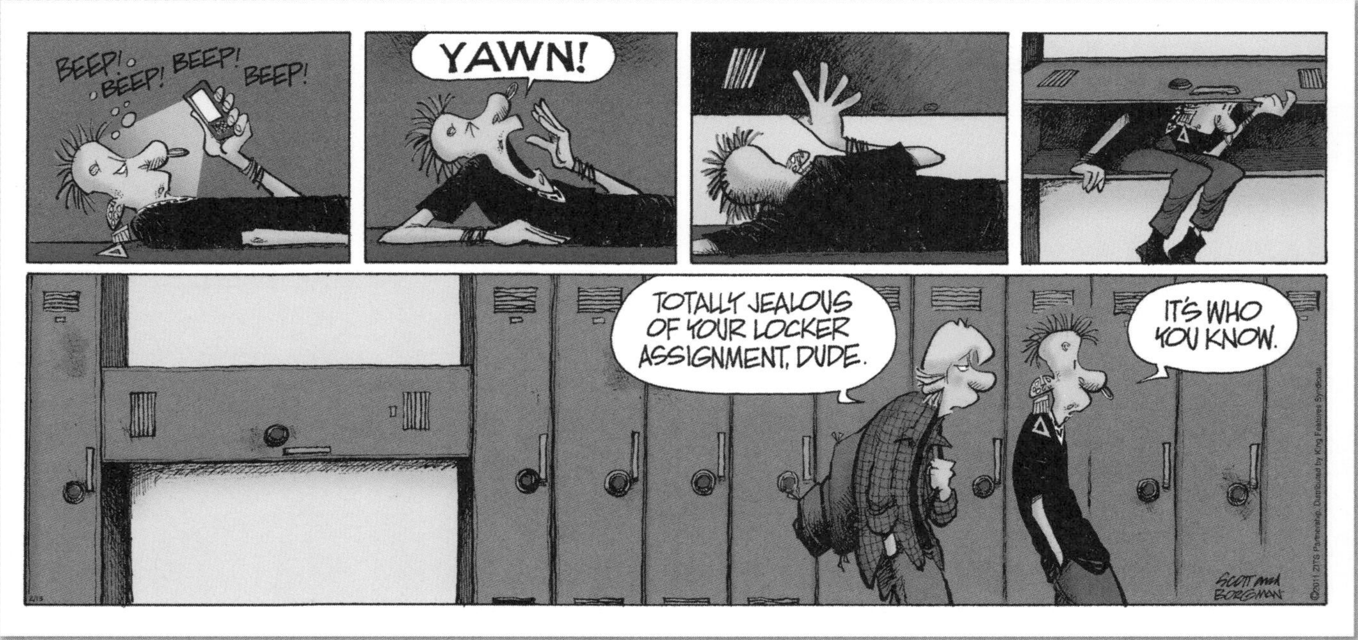
BEEP! BEEP! BEEP! BEEP!
YAWN!
TOTALLY JEALOUS OF YOUR LOCKER ASSIGNMENT, DUDE.
IT'S WHO YOU KNOW.
SCOTT and BORGMAN

March 21, 2011

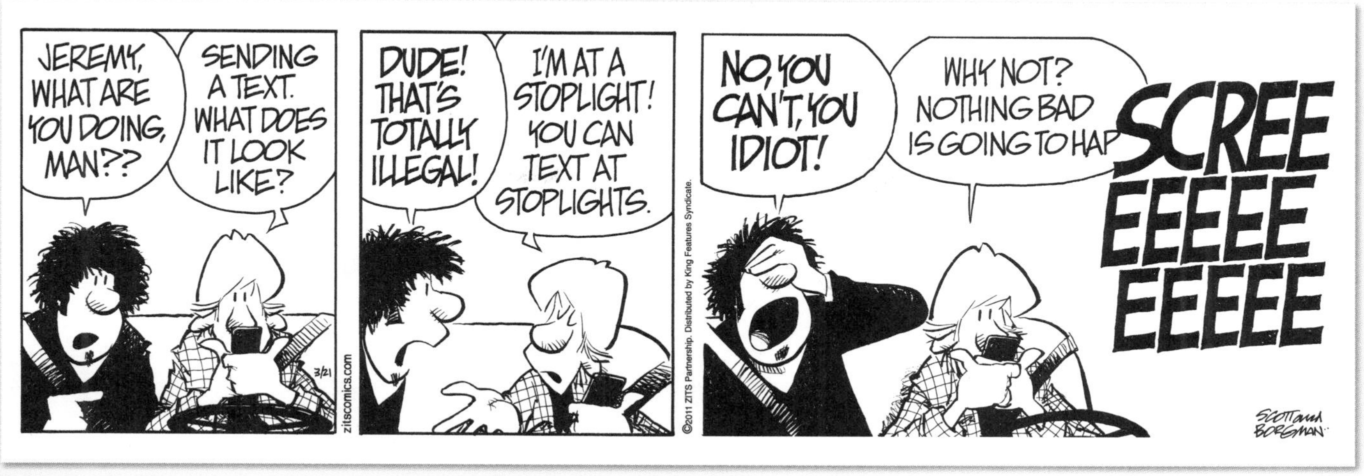
JEREMY, WHAT ARE YOU DOING, MAN??
SENDING A TEXT. WHAT DOES IT LOOK LIKE?
3/21
zitscomics.com
DUDE! THAT'S TOTALLY ILLEGAL!
I'M AT A STOPLIGHT! YOU CAN TEXT AT STOPLIGHTS.
©2011 ZITS Partnership. Distributed by King Features Syndicate.
NO, YOU CAN'T, YOU IDIOT!
WHY NOT? NOTHING BAD IS GOING TO HAP
SCREE EEEEE EEEEE
SCOTT and BORGMAN

March 23, 2011

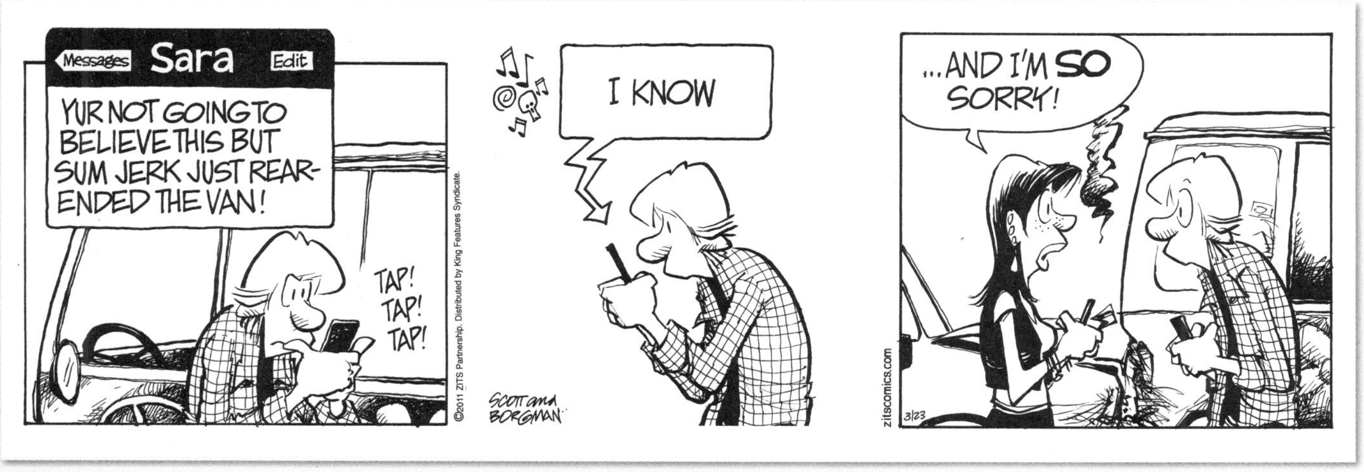
Messages Sara Edit
YUR NOT GOING TO BELIEVE THIS BUT SUM JERK JUST REAR-ENDED THE VAN!
TAP! TAP! TAP!
©2011 ZITS Partnership. Distributed by King Features Syndicate.
I KNOW
SCOTT and BORGMAN
zitscomics.com
...AND I'M SO SORRY!
3/23

March 24, 2011

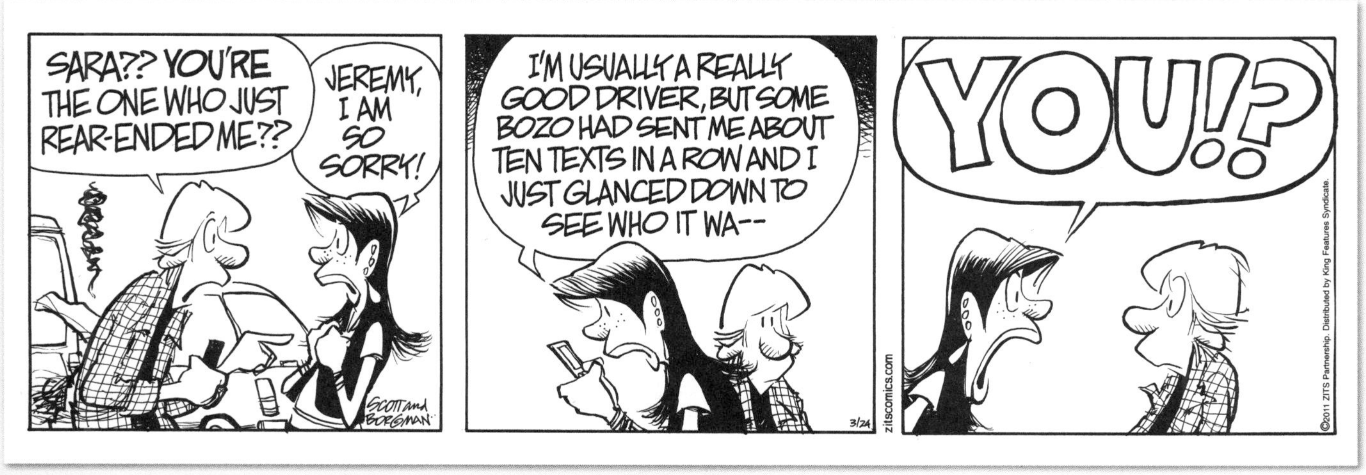
SARA?? YOU'RE THE ONE WHO JUST REAR-ENDED ME??
JEREMY, I AM SO SORRY!
SCOTT and BORGMAN
I'M USUALLY A REALLY GOOD DRIVER, BUT SOME BOZO HAD SENT ME ABOUT TEN TEXTS IN A ROW AND I JUST GLANCED DOWN TO SEE WHO IT WA--
3/24
zitscomics.com
YOU!?
©2011 ZITS Partnership. Distributed by King Features Syndicate.

April 5, 2011

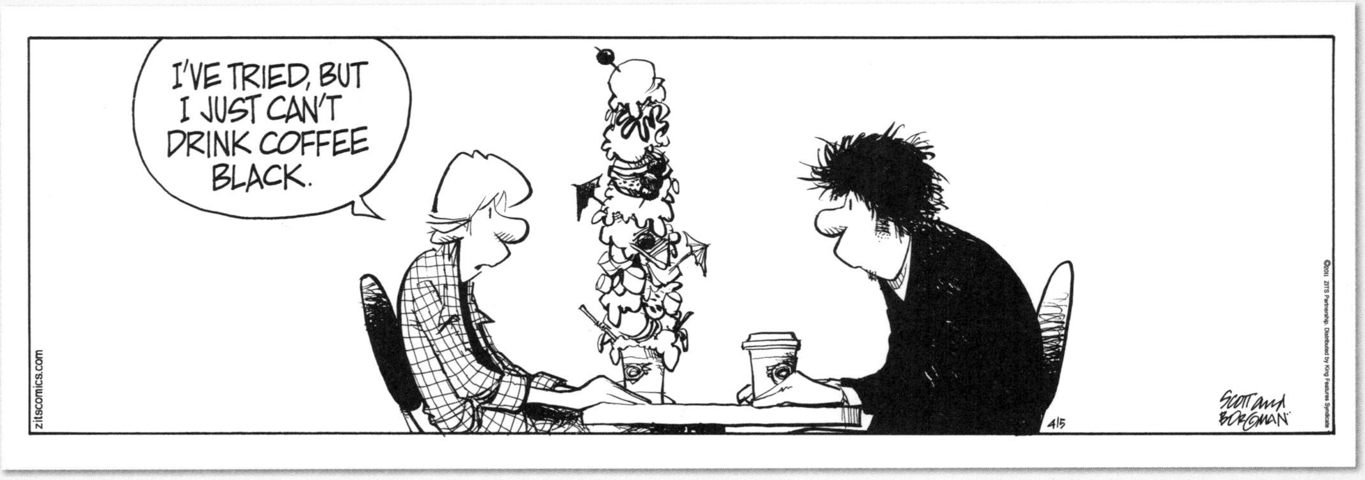
I'VE TRIED, BUT I JUST CAN'T DRINK COFFEE BLACK.
zitscomics.com
©2011 ZITS Partnership. Distributed by King Features Syndicate
SCOTT AND BORGMAN
4/5

April 6, 2011

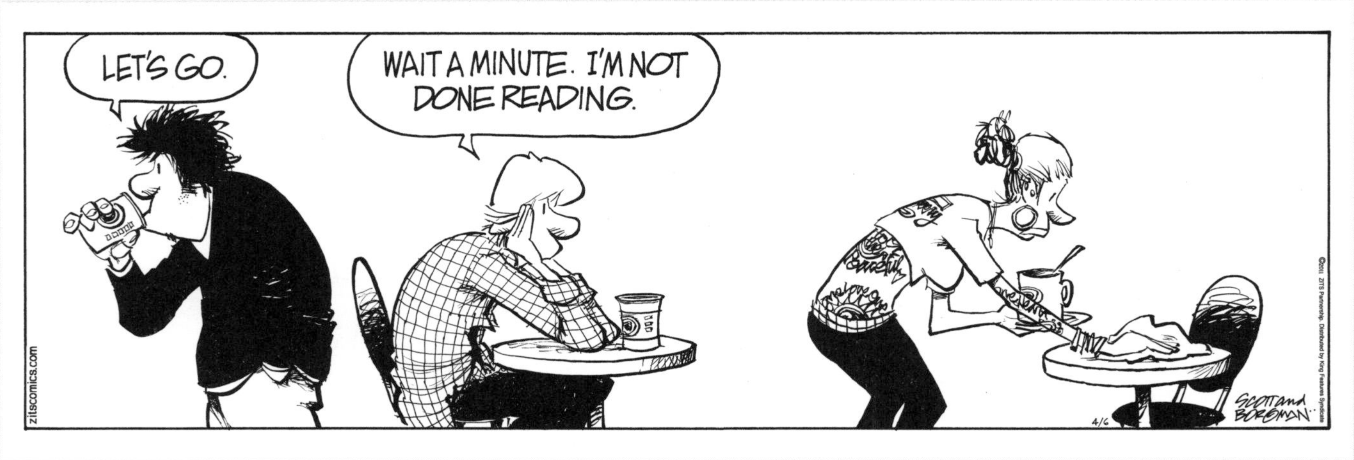
LET'S GO.
WAIT A MINUTE. I'M NOT DONE READING.
zitscomics.com
©2011 ZITS Partnership. Distributed by King Features Syndicate
SCOTT AND BORGMAN
4/6

April 16, 2011

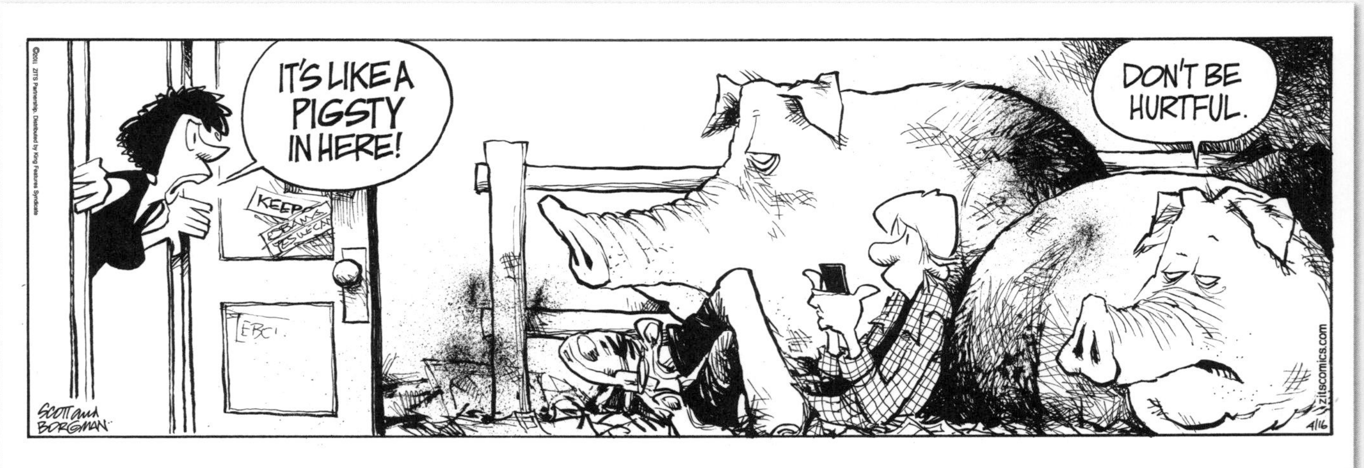
IT'S LIKE A PIGSTY IN HERE!
DON'T BE HURTFUL.
KEEP
zitscomics.com
©2011 ZITS Partnership. Distributed by King Features Syndicate
SCOTT AND BORGMAN
4/16

March 6, 2011

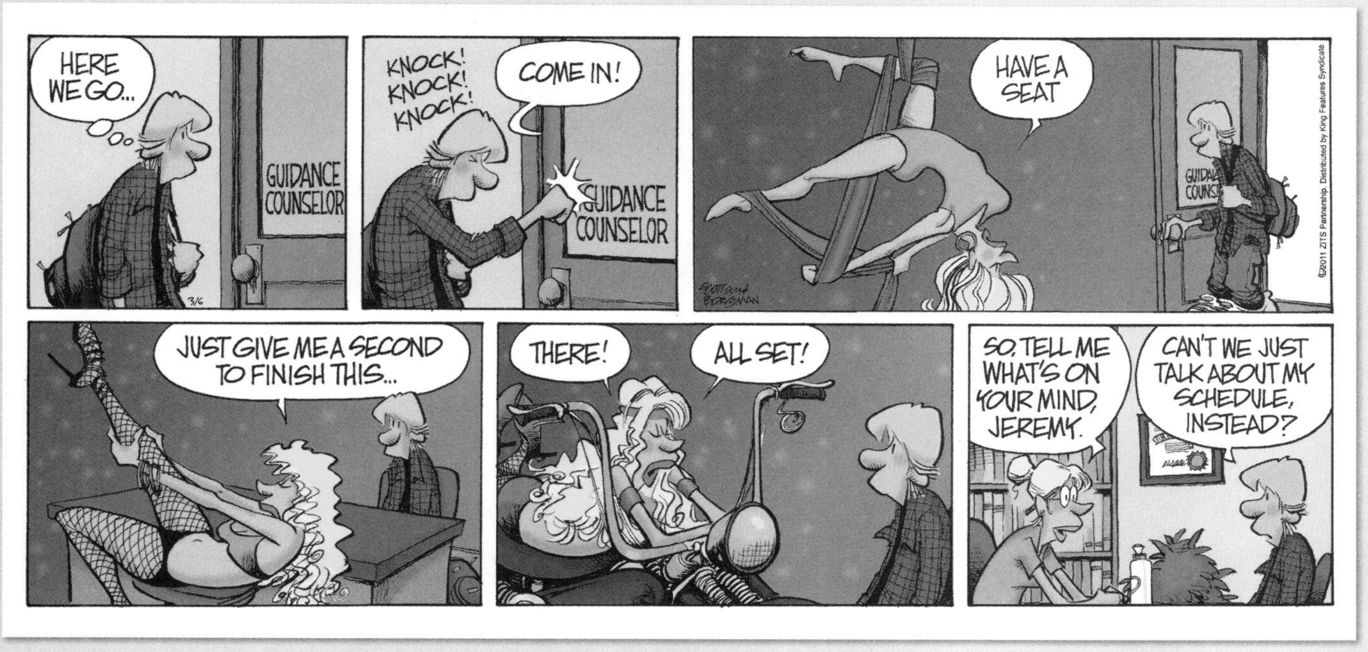
HERE WE GO...
GUIDANCE COUNSELOR
KNOCK! KNOCK! KNOCK!
COME IN!
GUIDANCE COUNSELOR
HAVE A SEAT
©2011 ZITS Partnership. Distributed by King Features Syndicate
JUST GIVE ME A SECOND TO FINISH THIS...
THERE!
ALL SET!
SO, TELL ME WHAT'S ON YOUR MIND, JEREMY.
CAN'T WE JUST TALK ABOUT MY SCHEDULE, INSTEAD?

April 24, 2011

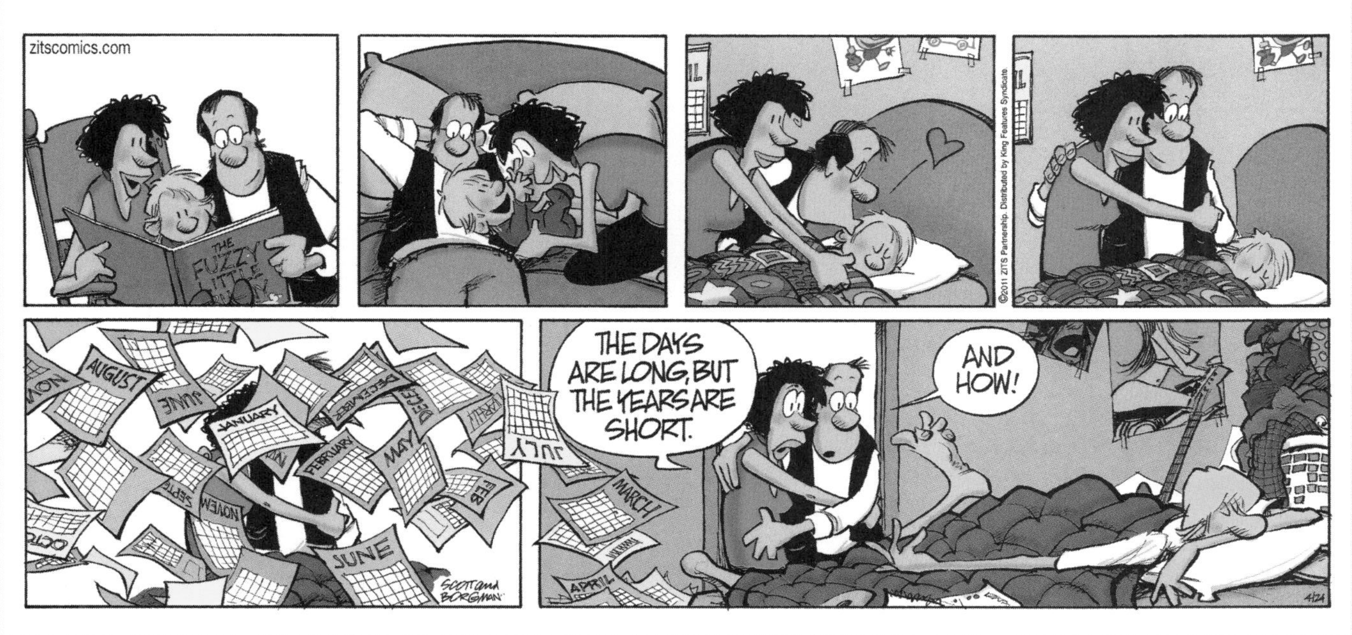
zitscomics.com
THE FUZZY LITTLE
©2011 ZITS Partnership. Distributed by King Features Syndicate
AUGUST
JUNE
JANUARY
FEBRUARY
MAY
JULY
FEB
JUNE
MARCH
APRIL
THE DAYS ARE LONG, BUT THE YEARS ARE SHORT.
AND HOW!

April 28, 2011

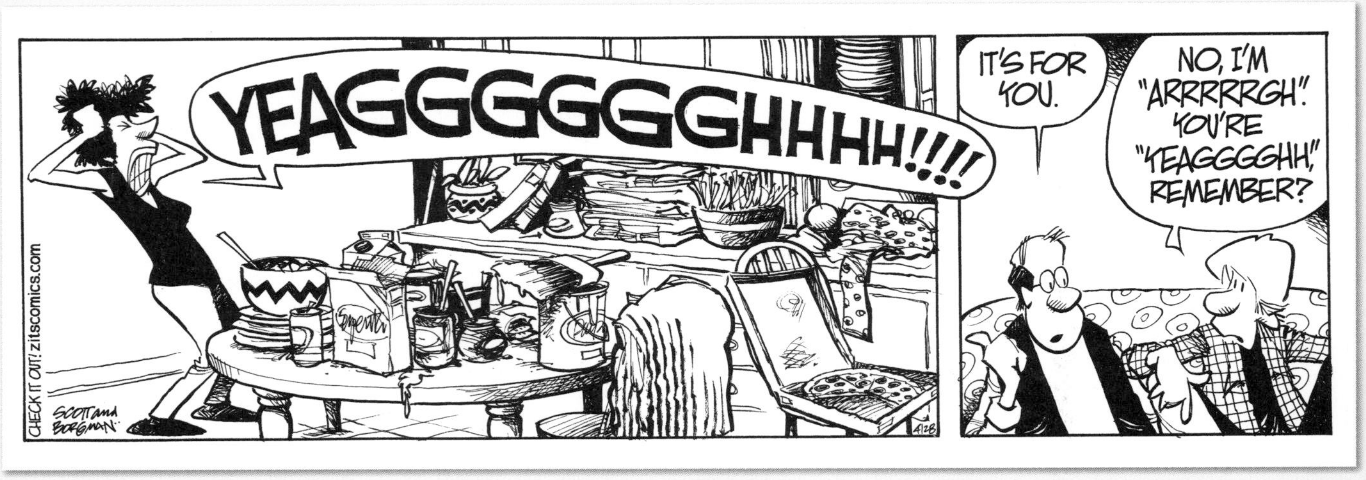
YEAGGGGGGGHHHH!!!!
IT'S FOR YOU.
NO, I'M "ARRRRRGH". YOU'RE "YEAGGGGHH," REMEMBER?
CHECK IT OUT! zitscomics.com
SCOTT and BORGMAN

April 29, 2011

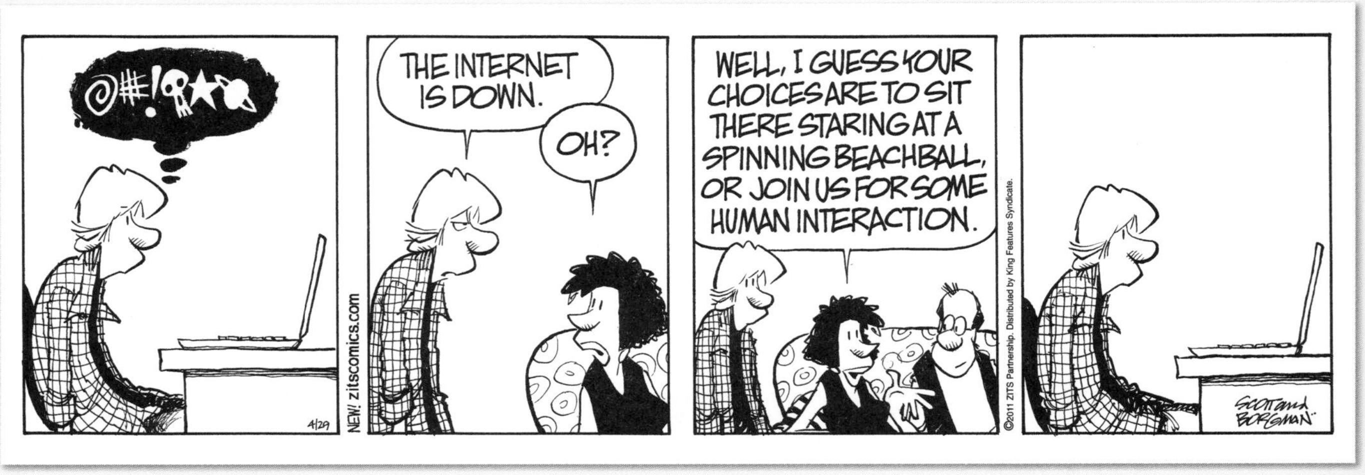
THE INTERNET IS DOWN.
OH?
WELL, I GUESS YOUR CHOICES ARE TO SIT THERE STARING AT A SPINNING BEACHBALL, OR JOIN US FOR SOME HUMAN INTERACTION.
NEW! zitscomics.com
©2011 ZITS Partnership. Distributed by King Features Syndicate.
SCOTT and BORGMAN

May 19, 2011

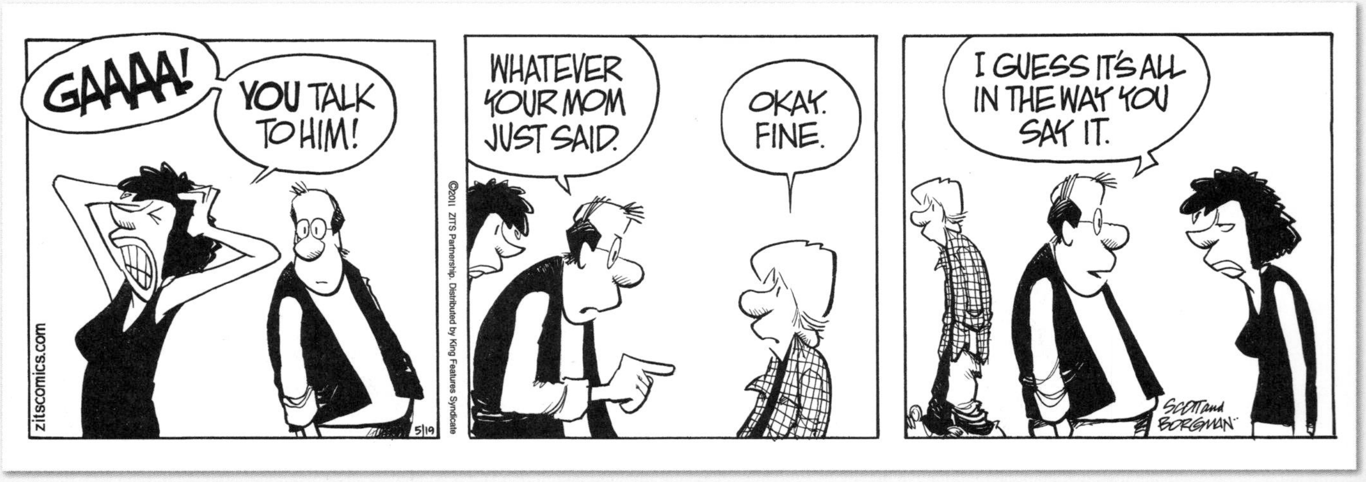
GAAAA!
YOU TALK TO HIM!
WHATEVER YOUR MOM JUST SAID.
OKAY. FINE.
I GUESS IT'S ALL IN THE WAY YOU SAY IT.
zitscomics.com
©2011 ZITS Partnership. Distributed by King Features Syndicate
SCOTT and BORGMAN

May 21, 2011

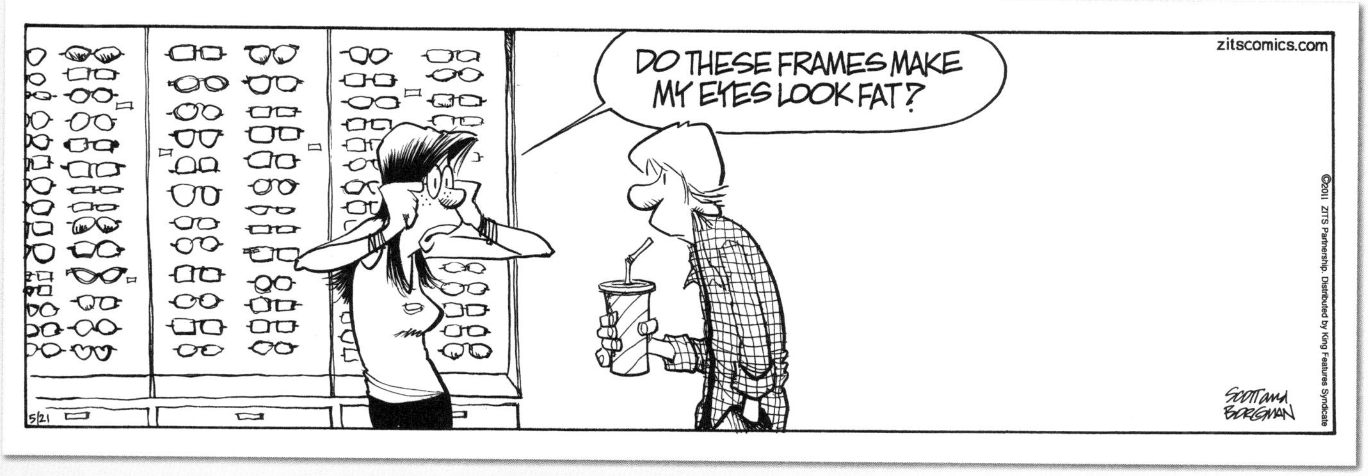
DO THESE FRAMES MAKE MY EYES LOOK FAT?
zitscomics.com
©2011 ZITS Partnership. Distributed by King Features Syndicate
SCOTT and BORGMAN

May 24, 2011

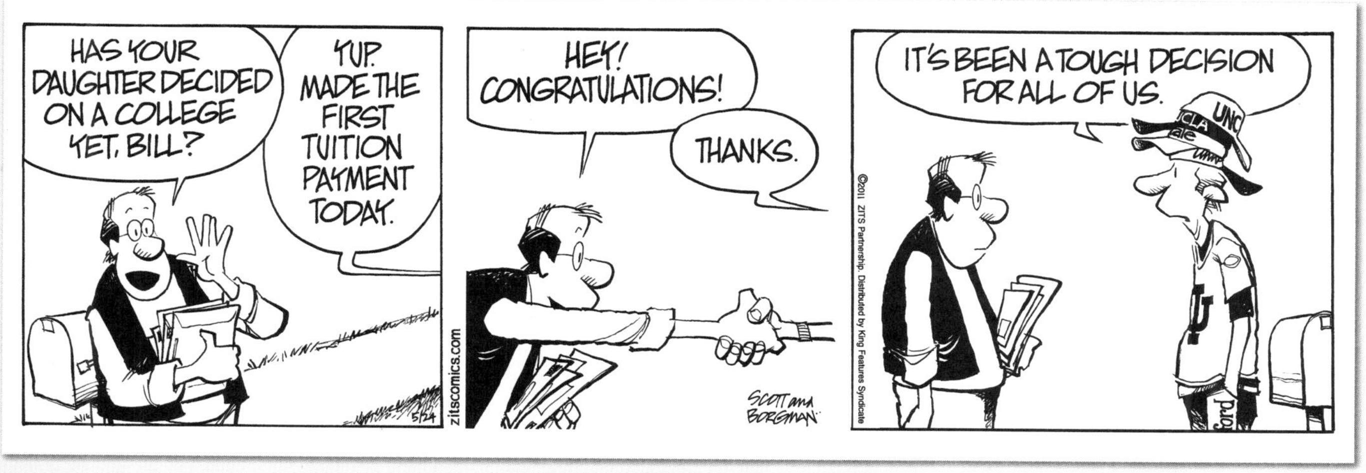
HAS YOUR DAUGHTER DECIDED ON A COLLEGE YET, BILL?
YUP. MADE THE FIRST TUITION PAYMENT TODAY.
HEY! CONGRATULATIONS!
THANKS.
IT'S BEEN A TOUGH DECISION FOR ALL OF US.
zitscomics.com
©2011 ZITS Partnership. Distributed by King Features Syndicate
SCOTT and BORGMAN

June 3, 2011

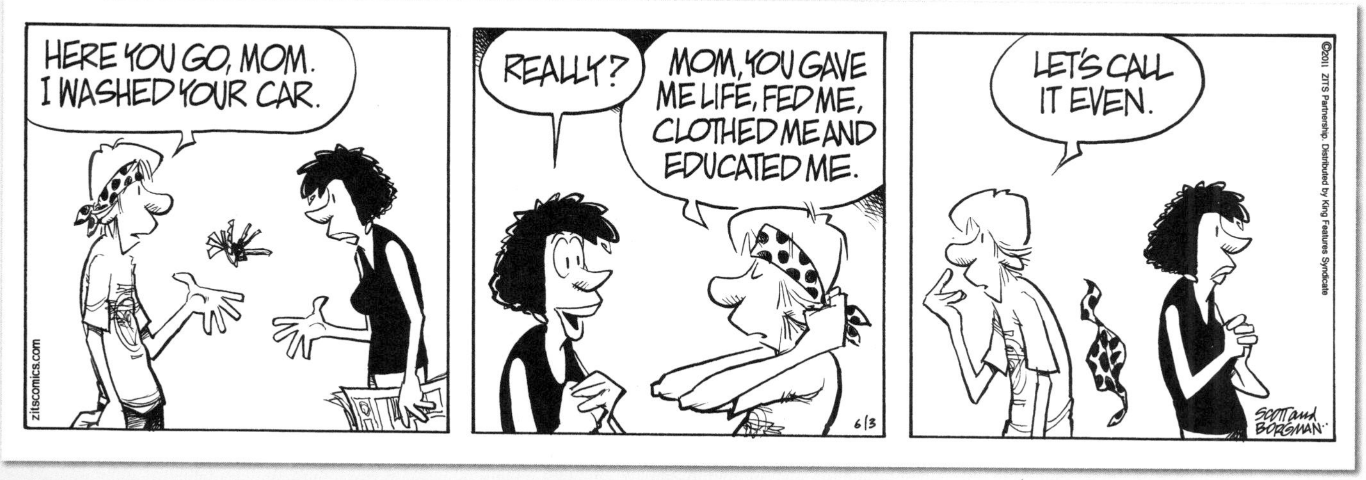
HERE YOU GO, MOM. I WASHED YOUR CAR.
REALLY?
MOM, YOU GAVE ME LIFE, FED ME, CLOTHED ME AND EDUCATED ME.
LET'S CALL IT EVEN.
zitscomics.com
©2011 ZITS Partnership. Distributed by King Features Syndicate
SCOTT and BORGMAN

June 9, 2011

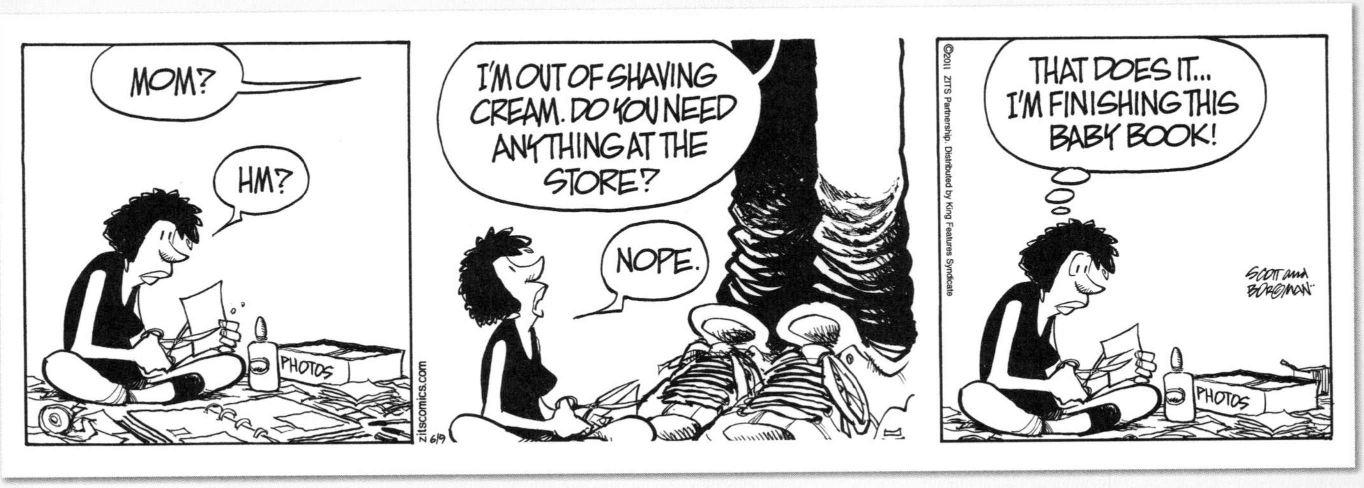
MOM?
HM?
I'M OUT OF SHAVING CREAM. DO YOU NEED ANYTHING AT THE STORE?
NOPE.
THAT DOES IT... I'M FINISHING THIS BABY BOOK!
PHOTOS
zitscomics.com
6/9
©2011 ZITS Partnership. Distributed by King Features Syndicate
SCOTT AND BORGMAN

June 23, 2011

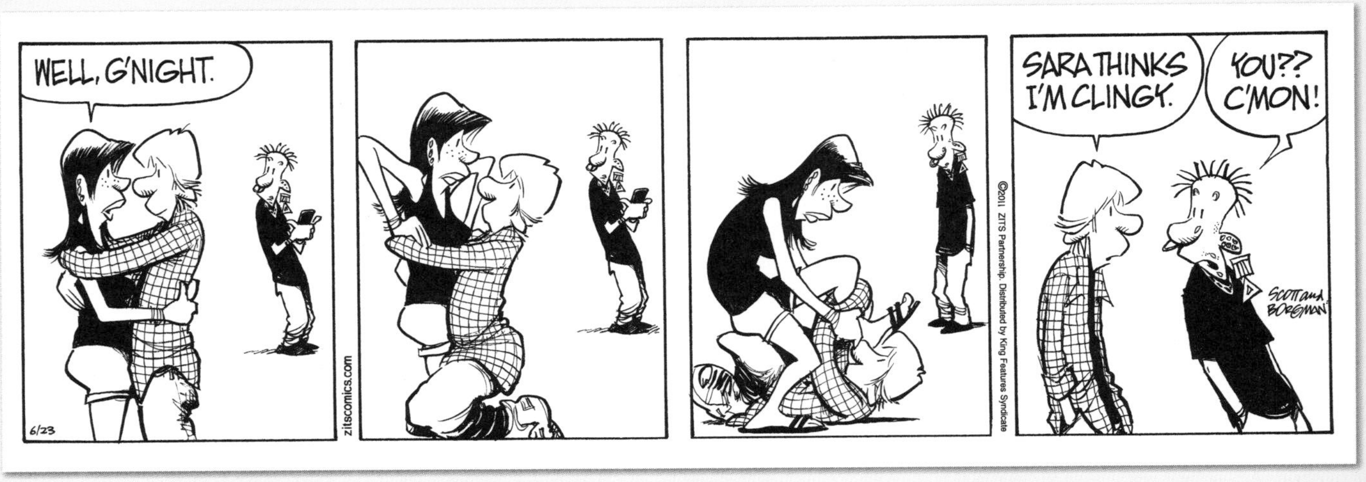
WELL, G'NIGHT.
SARA THINKS I'M CLINGY.
YOU?? C'MON!
6/23
zitscomics.com
©2011 ZITS Partnership. Distributed by King Features Syndicate
SCOTT AND BORGMAN

June 24, 2011

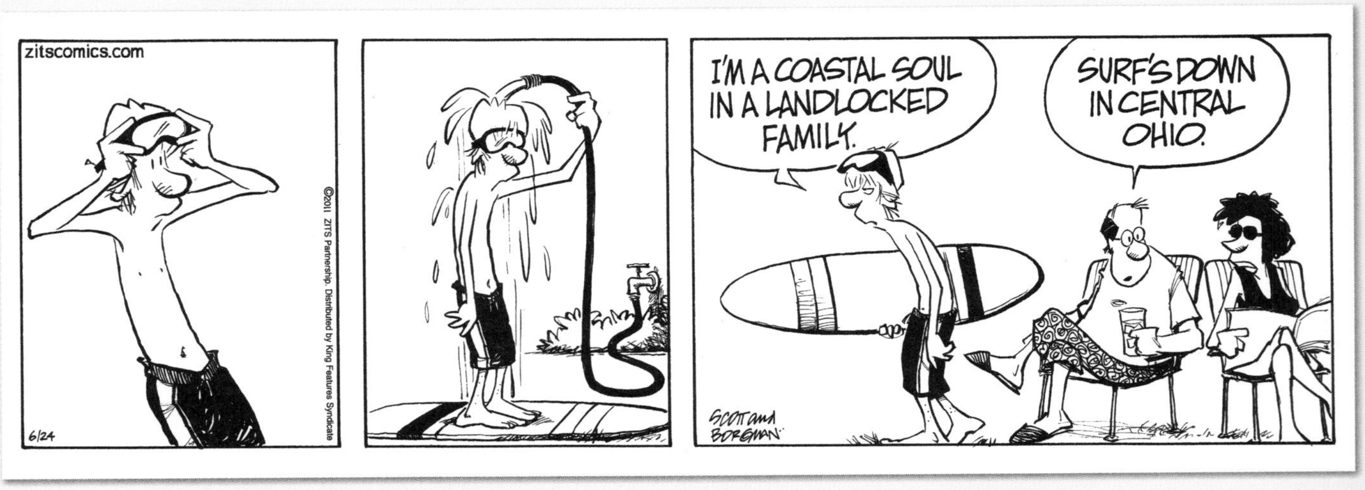
zitscomics.com
6/24
©2011 ZITS Partnership. Distributed by King Features Syndicate
I'M A COASTAL SOUL IN A LANDLOCKED FAMILY.
SURF'S DOWN IN CENTRAL OHIO.
SCOTT AND BORGMAN

July 18, 2011

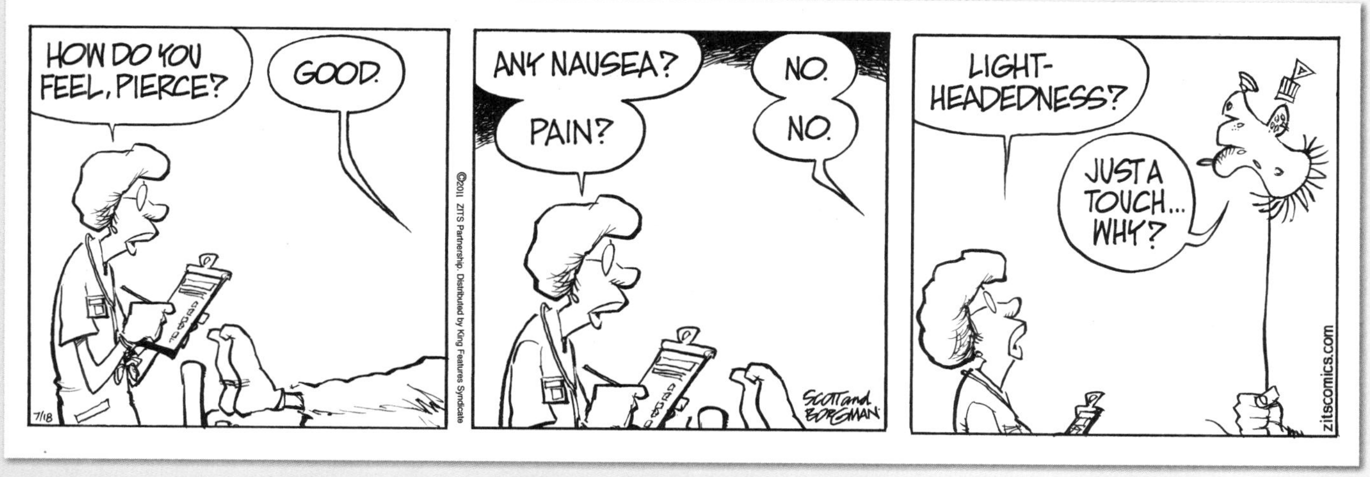
HOW DO YOU FEEL, PIERCE?
GOOD.
ANY NAUSEA?
NO.
PAIN?
NO.
LIGHT-HEADEDNESS?
JUST A TOUCH... WHY?
©2011 ZITS Partnership. Distributed by King Features Syndicate
SCOTT and BORGMAN
zitscomics.com

July 20, 2011

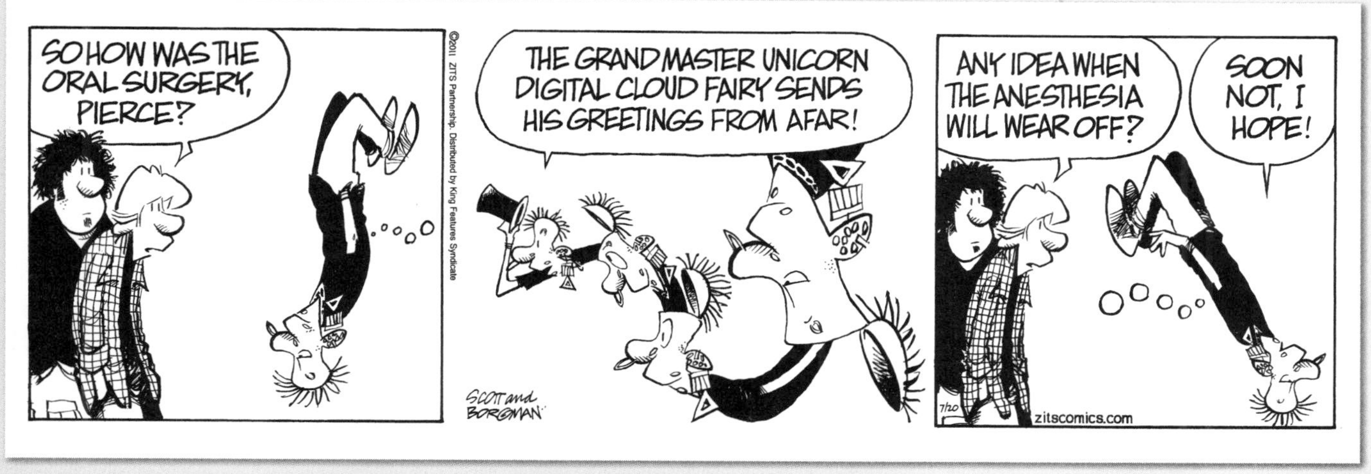
SO HOW WAS THE ORAL SURGERY, PIERCE?
THE GRAND MASTER UNICORN DIGITAL CLOUD FAIRY SENDS HIS GREETINGS FROM AFAR!
ANY IDEA WHEN THE ANESTHESIA WILL WEAR OFF?
SOON NOT, I HOPE!
©2011 ZITS Partnership. Distributed by King Features Syndicate
SCOTT and BORGMAN
zitscomics.com

July 21, 2011

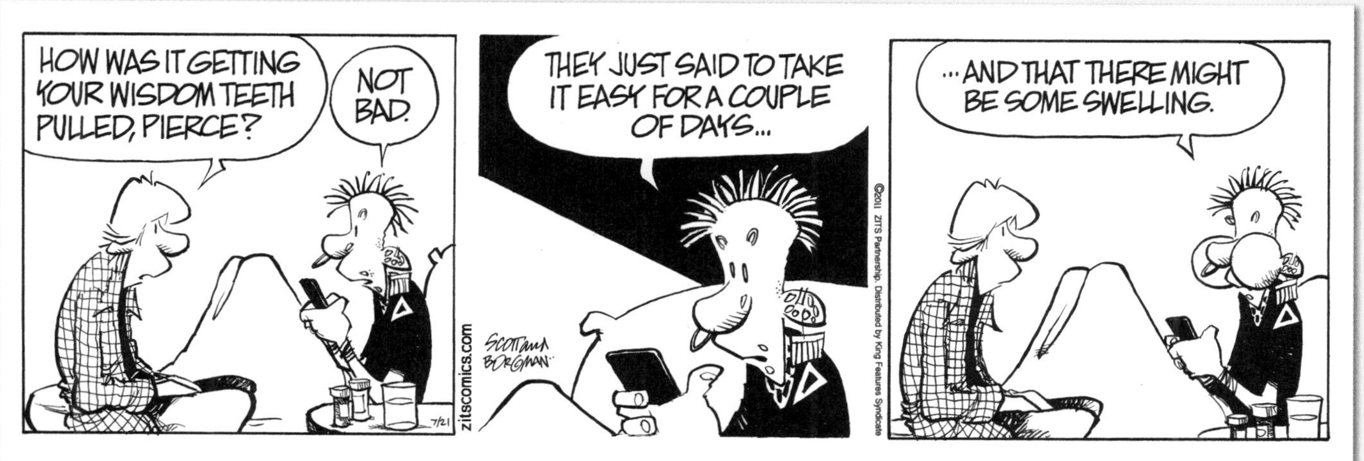
HOW WAS IT GETTING YOUR WISDOM TEETH PULLED, PIERCE?
NOT BAD.
THEY JUST SAID TO TAKE IT EASY FOR A COUPLE OF DAYS...
...AND THAT THERE MIGHT BE SOME SWELLING.
©2011 ZITS Partnership. Distributed by King Features Syndicate
SCOTT and BORGMAN
zitscomics.com

June 26, 2011

SCOTT and BORGMAN
DUDE, WHAT UP?
NOTHING. MOWING THE STUPID YARD.
TAP! TAP! TAP!
SO BORING.
TAP! TAP! TAP!
I COULD DO THIS STUPID JOB WITH MY EYES CLOSED.
TAP! TAP! TAP!
©2011 ZITS Partnership. Distributed by King Features
6/26
I SHOULD GO.
zitscomics.com

July 31, 2011

©2011 ZITS Partnership. Distributed by King Features
SCOTT and BORGMAN
zitscomics.com
7/31
DID YOU AND JEREMY HAVE ANOTHER ONE OF YOUR BLOW-UPS?

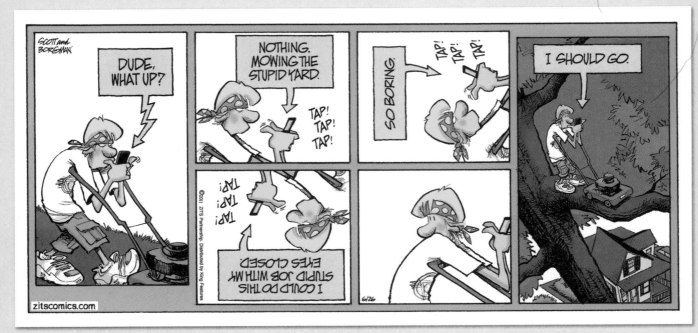

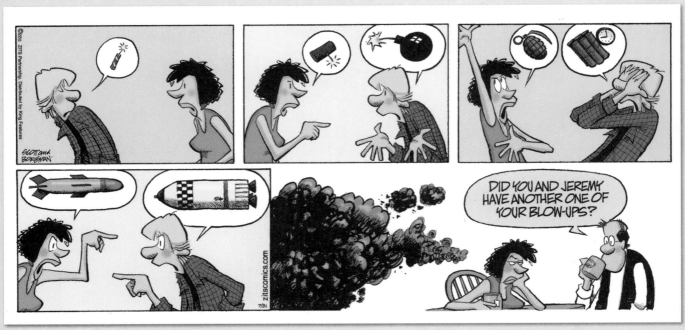

August 3, 2011

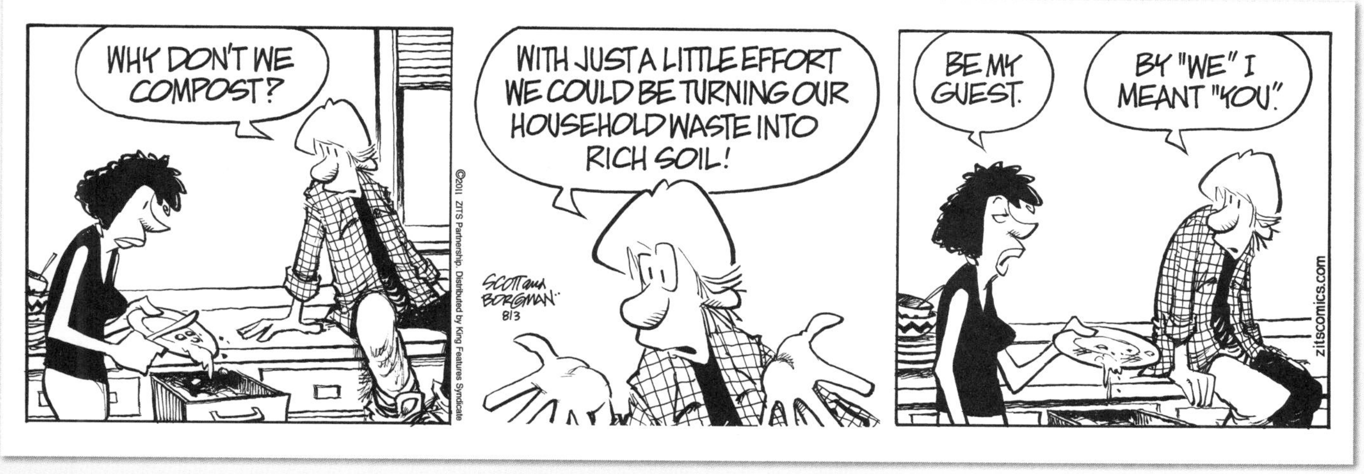
WHY DON'T WE COMPOST?
WITH JUST A LITTLE EFFORT WE COULD BE TURNING OUR HOUSEHOLD WASTE INTO RICH SOIL!
BE MY GUEST.
BY "WE" I MEANT "YOU".
©2011 ZITS Partnership. Distributed by King Features Syndicate
SCOTT and BORGMAN
8/3
zitscomics.com

August 5, 2011

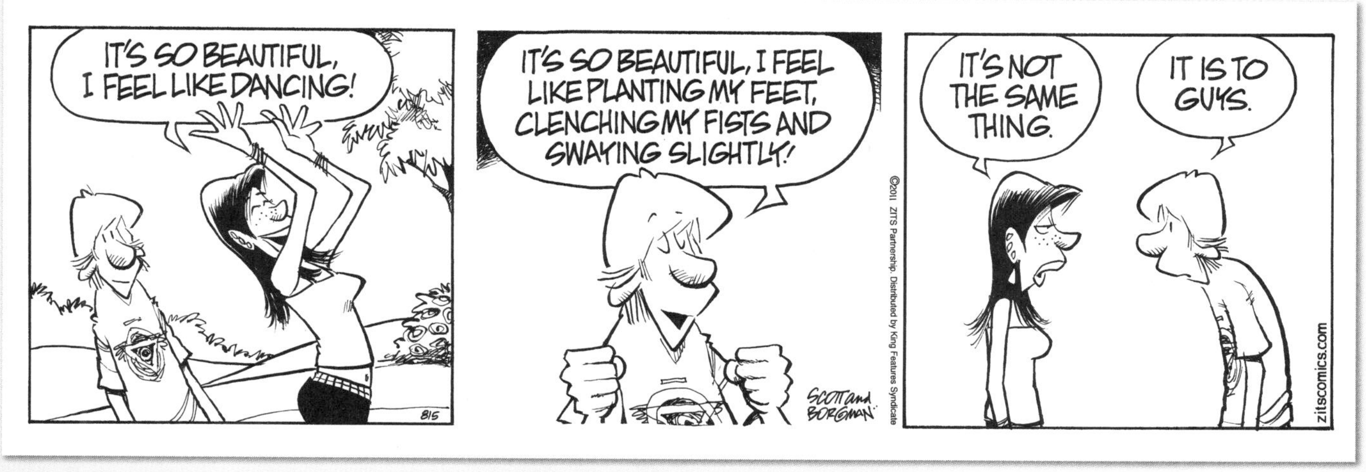
IT'S SO BEAUTIFUL, I FEEL LIKE DANCING!
IT'S SO BEAUTIFUL, I FEEL LIKE PLANTING MY FEET, CLENCHING MY FISTS AND SWAYING SLIGHTLY!
IT'S NOT THE SAME THING.
IT IS TO GUYS.
8/5
SCOTT and BORGMAN
©2011 ZITS Partnership. Distributed by King Features Syndicate
zitscomics.com

August 19, 2011

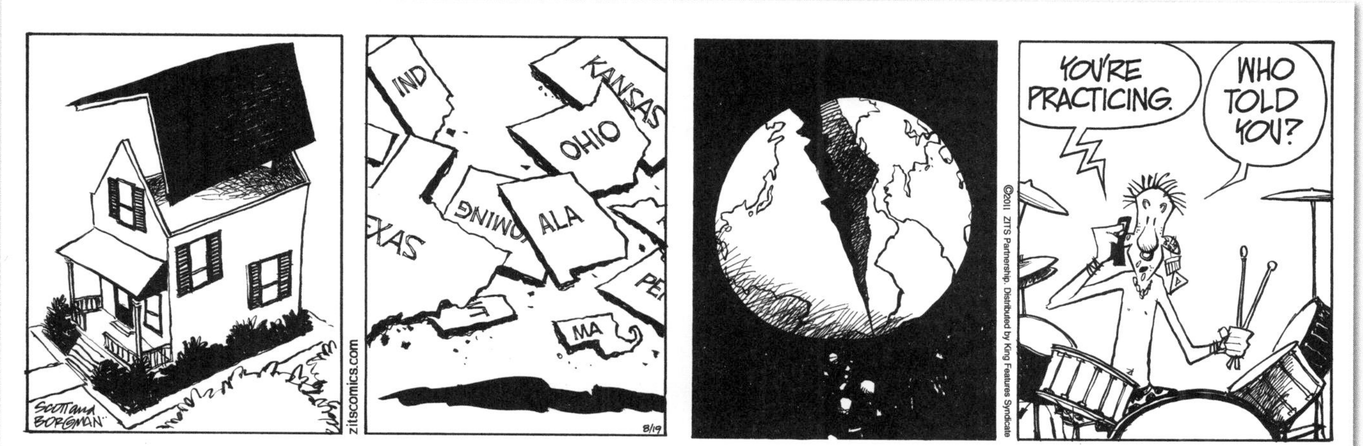
SCOTT and BORGMAN
zitscomics.com
IND
KANSAS
OHIO
ALA
MA
8/19
YOU'RE PRACTICING.
WHO TOLD YOU?
©2011 ZITS Partnership. Distributed by King Features Syndicate

October 9, 2011

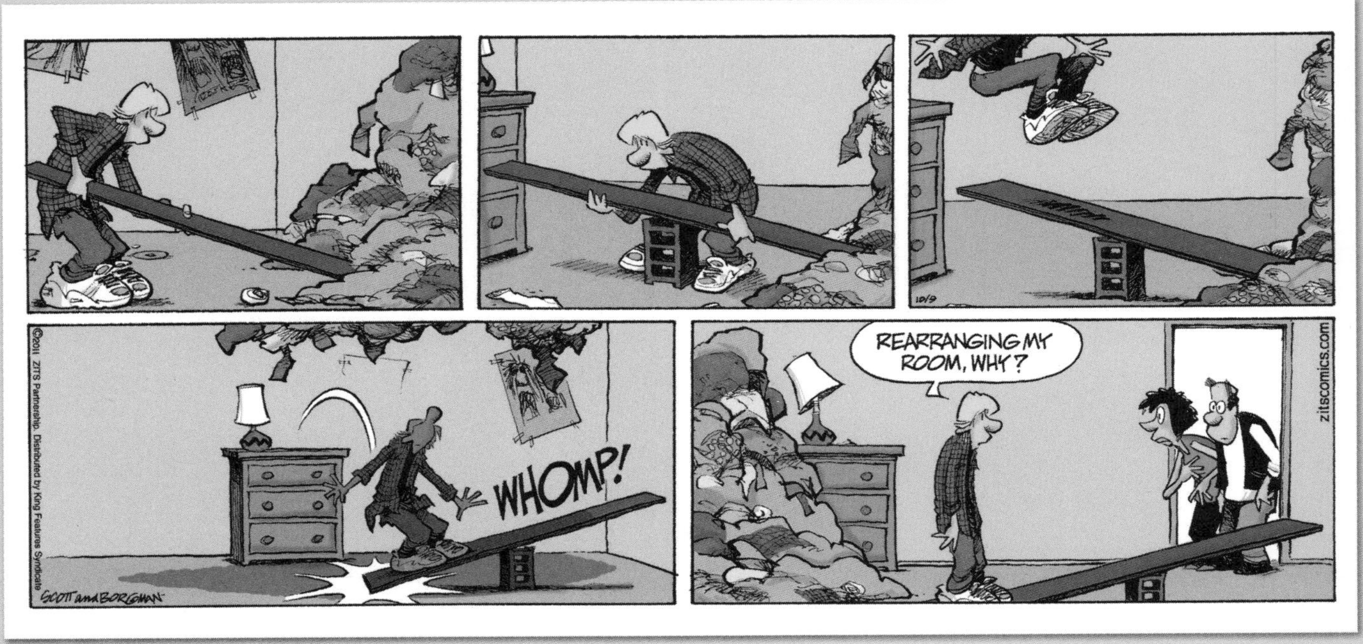

10/9
©2011 ZITS Partnership. Distributed by King Features Syndicate
SCOTT and BORGMAN
WHOMP!
REARRANGING MY ROOM, WHY?
zitscomics.com

November 27, 2011

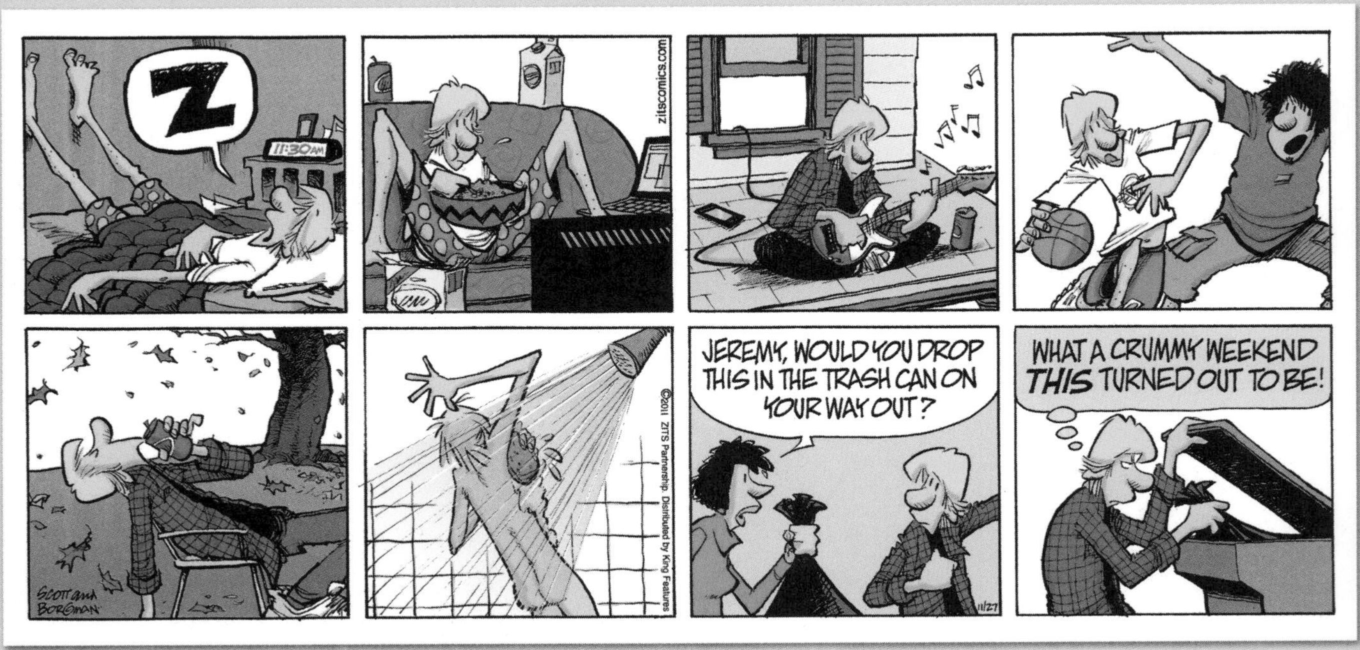

Z
11:30 AM
zitscomics.com
SCOTT and BORGMAN
©2011 ZITS Partnership. Distributed by King Features
JEREMY, WOULD YOU DROP THIS IN THE TRASH CAN ON YOUR WAY OUT?
11/27
WHAT A CRUMMY WEEKEND **THIS** TURNED OUT TO BE!

October 22, 2011

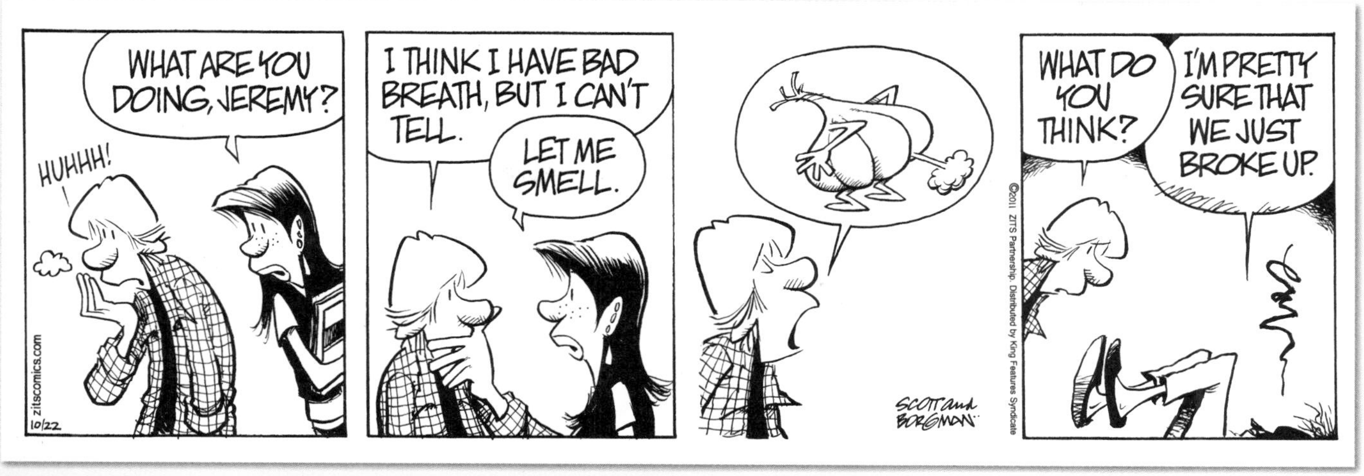
WHAT ARE YOU DOING, JEREMY?
HUHHH!
I THINK I HAVE BAD BREATH, BUT I CAN'T TELL.
LET ME SMELL.
WHAT DO YOU THINK?
I'M PRETTY SURE THAT WE JUST BROKE UP.
zitscomics.com
10/22
SCOTT and BORGMAN
©2011 ZITS Partnership. Distributed by King Features Syndicate

November 3, 2011

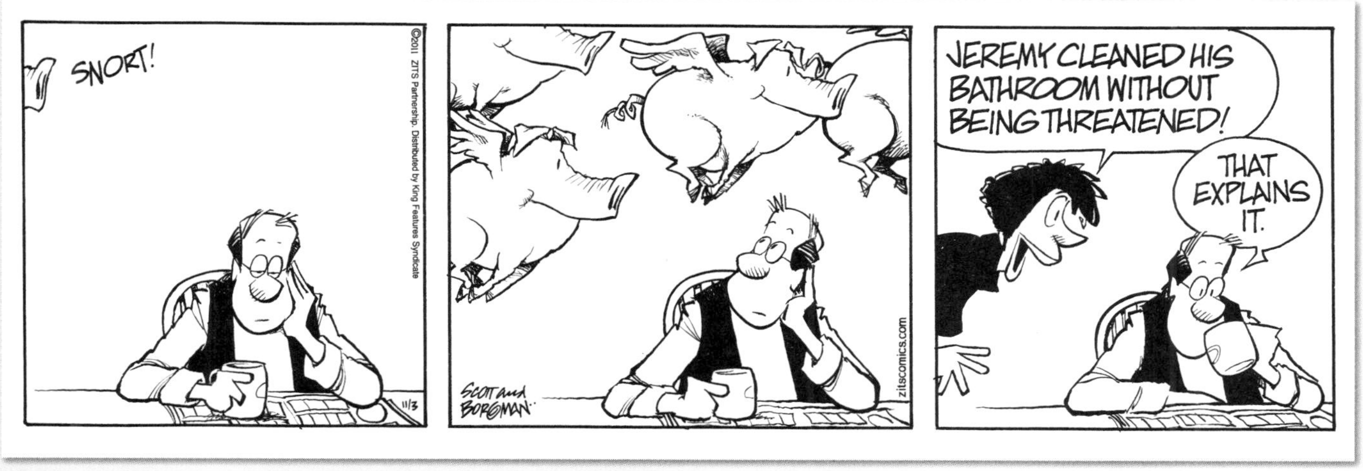
SNORT!
©2011 ZITS Partnership. Distributed by King Features Syndicate
11/3
SCOTT and BORGMAN
zitscomics.com
JEREMY CLEANED HIS BATHROOM WITHOUT BEING THREATENED!
THAT EXPLAINS IT.

November 14, 2011

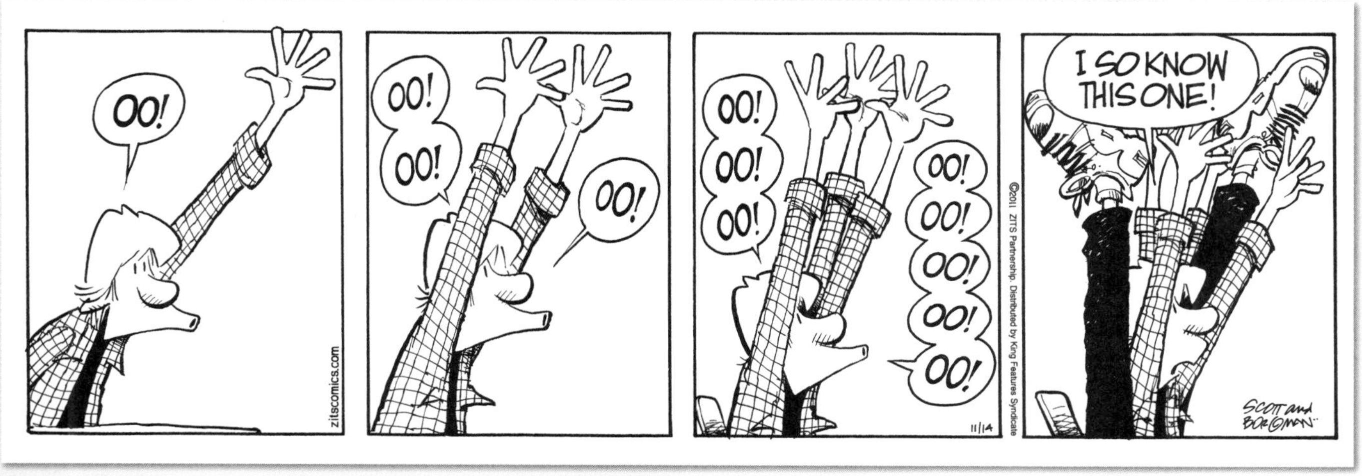
OO!
zitscomics.com
OO!
OO!
OO!
OO!
OO!
OO!
OO!
OO!
OO!
OO!
OO!
11/14
©2011 ZITS Partnership. Distributed by King Features Syndicate
I SO KNOW THIS ONE!
SCOTT and BORGMAN

November 22, 2011

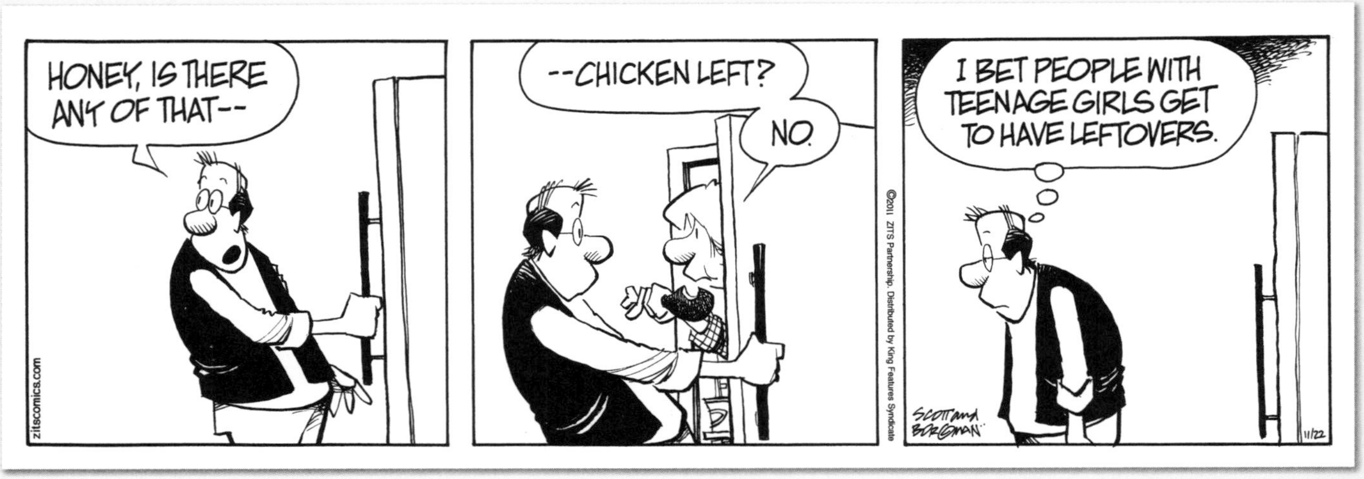
HONEY, IS THERE ANY OF THAT--
--CHICKEN LEFT?
NO.
I BET PEOPLE WITH TEENAGE GIRLS GET TO HAVE LEFTOVERS.
©2011 ZITS Partnership. Distributed by King Features Syndicate
zitscomics.com
SCOTT and BORGMAN 11/22

December 4, 2011

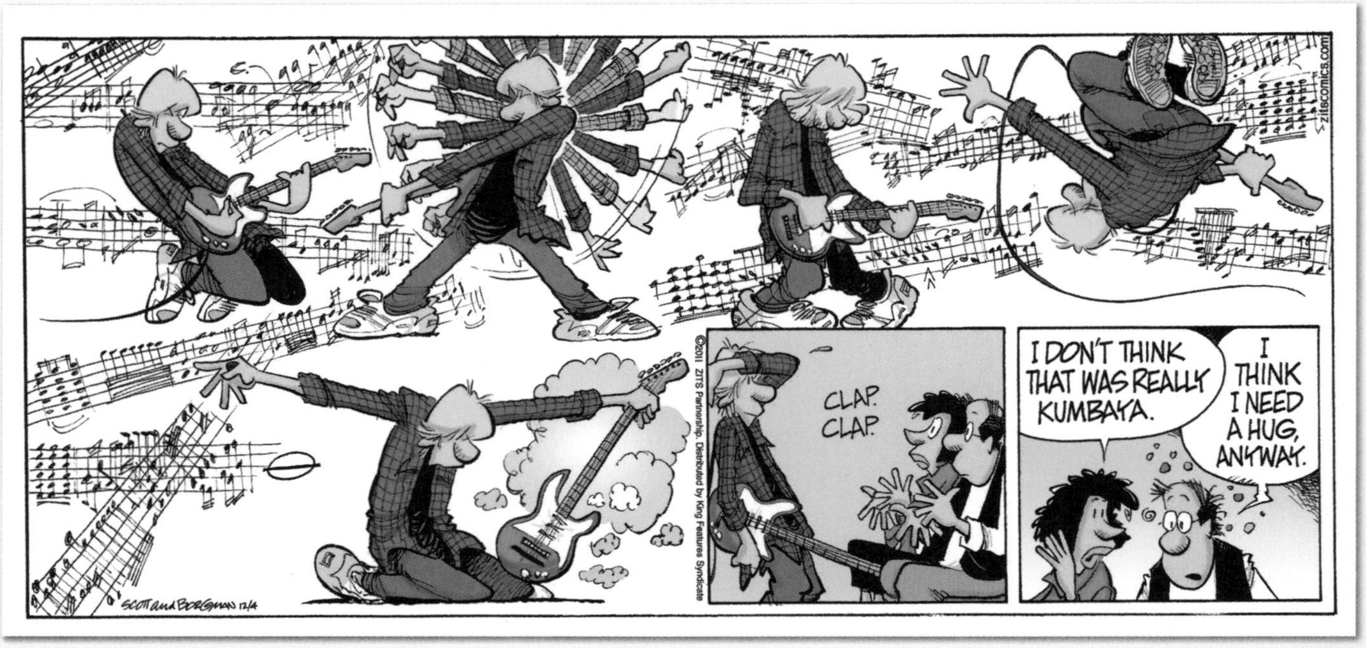
zitscomics.com
©2011 ZITS Partnership. Distributed by King Features Syndicate
SCOTT and BORGMAN 12/4
CLAP. CLAP.
I DON'T THINK THAT WAS REALLY KUMBAYA.
I THINK I NEED A HUG, ANYWAY.

Paris in Pajamas

Jim Borgman

It was our first visit to Europe to meet our fans, and we had wheedled first-class airline tickets out of our syndicate through much whining and groveling. Never having flown first class, we happily accepted every sumptuous thing the flight attendants offered us at dinnertime—champagne, gourmet entrées, French pastries, Swiss chocolates—and, when dinner was over and the cabin lights dimmed, eye masks, earplugs, slippers, and, unexpectedly, lightweight loose-fitting gray pajamas to sleep in. Ha! When in Rome, do as the Romans do.

Maybe it was the Ambien or possibly the bubbly, but we later agreed that neither of us had ever slept so deeply on a plane, because suddenly we were jarred from our dreams by the bump of the plane wheels on the runway. It was light outside, empty breakfast trays were being cleared, and passengers were filing off the plane. Groggily, we grabbed our overhead bags, forced our legs to move, and found ourselves blinking in the bright sunlight on the airport tarmac, stepping forward to meet our host committee while wearing slippers and our matching pajamas.

It's been twenty years since we began creating *Zits*, and we could never have imagined Jeremy would be oversleeping and rolling his eyes in forty-five countries and fifteen languages. Jerry and I just compare notes on raising our own teenagers, remember our own trials at that age, and try to make each other laugh as we toss ideas and sketches back and forth from our homes in California and Colorado. It still astonishes us when someone from, say, Estonia tells us, "You must have a camera in my house!"

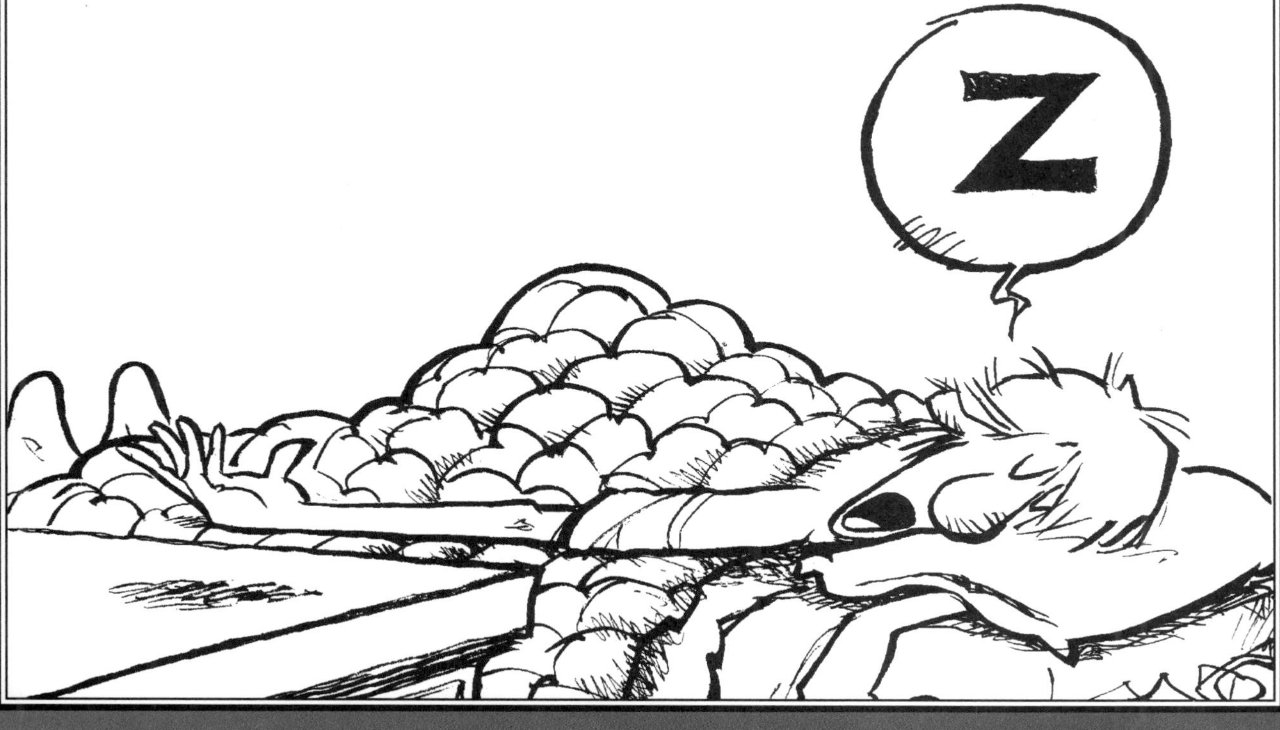
Z

January 10, 2012

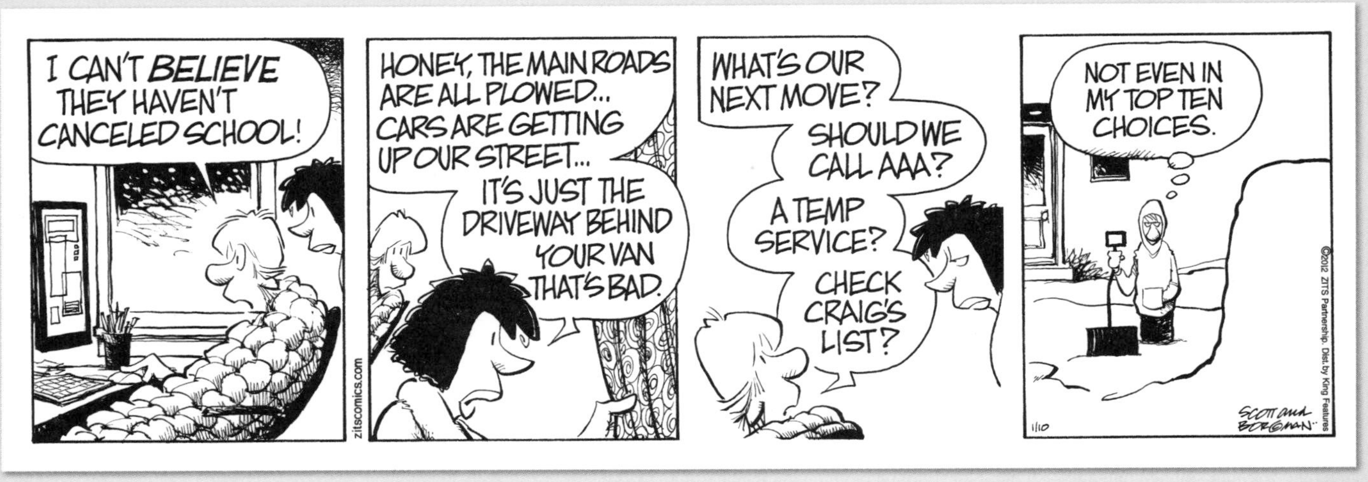
I CAN'T BELIEVE THEY HAVEN'T CANCELED SCHOOL!
HONEY, THE MAIN ROADS ARE ALL PLOWED... CARS ARE GETTING UP OUR STREET...
IT'S JUST THE DRIVEWAY BEHIND YOUR VAN THAT'S BAD.
zitscomics.com
WHAT'S OUR NEXT MOVE?
SHOULD WE CALL AAA?
A TEMP SERVICE?
CHECK CRAIG'S LIST?
NOT EVEN IN MY TOP TEN CHOICES.
©2012 ZITS Partnership. Dist. by King Features
SCOTT and BORGMAN
1/10

January 11, 2012

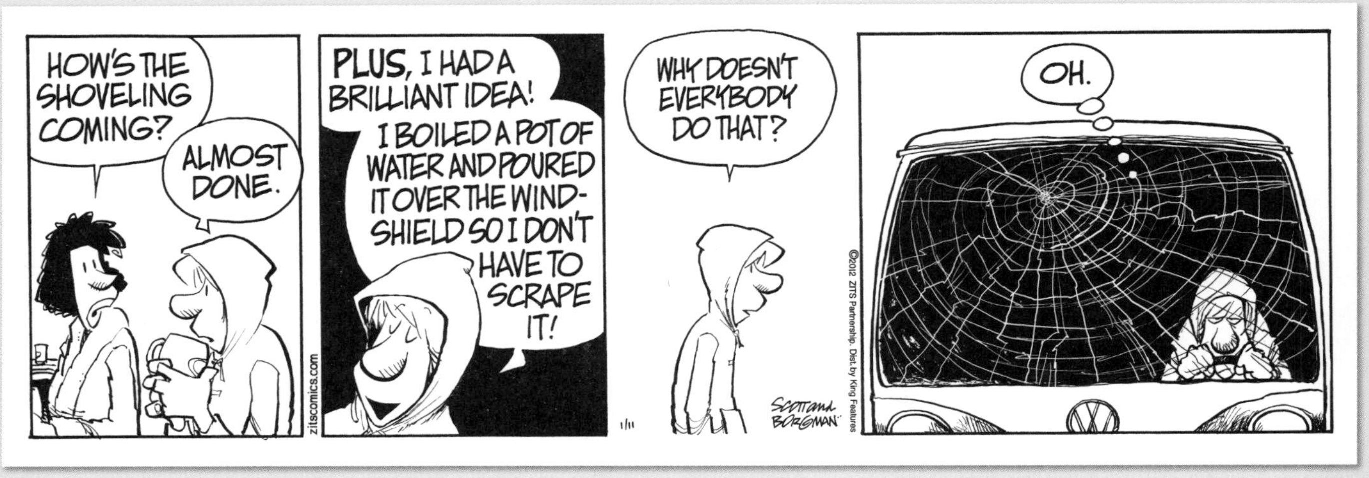
HOW'S THE SHOVELING COMING?
ALMOST DONE.
zitscomics.com
PLUS, I HAD A BRILLIANT IDEA!
I BOILED A POT OF WATER AND POURED IT OVER THE WIND-SHIELD SO I DON'T HAVE TO SCRAPE IT!
WHY DOESN'T EVERYBODY DO THAT?
1/11
SCOTT and BORGMAN
©2012 ZITS Partnership. Dist. by King Features
OH.

January 12, 2012

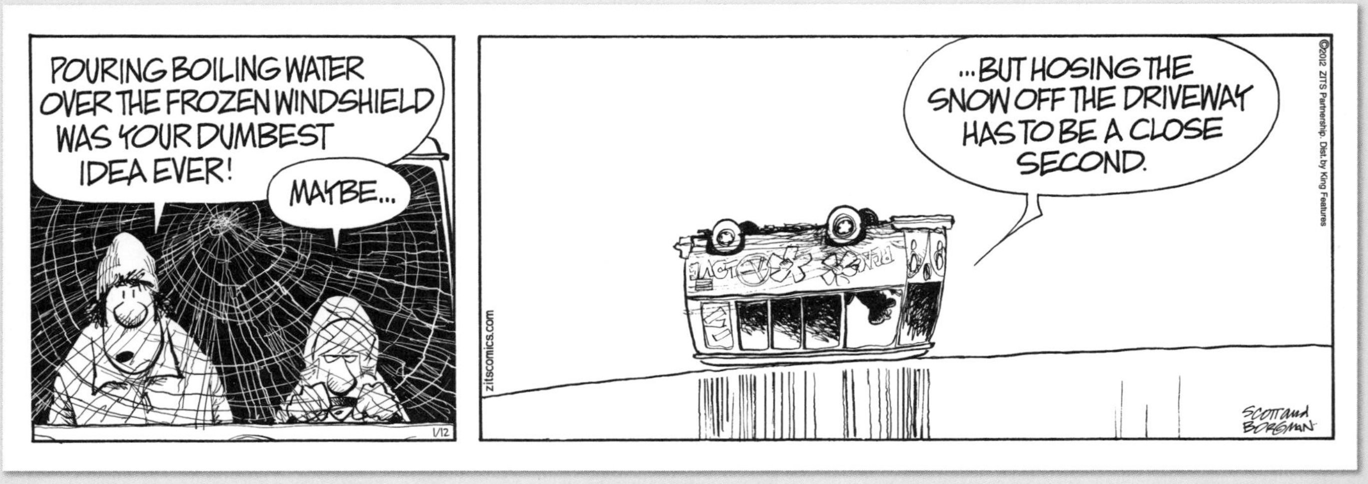
POURING BOILING WATER OVER THE FROZEN WINDSHIELD WAS YOUR DUMBEST IDEA EVER!
MAYBE...
1/12
zitscomics.com
...BUT HOSING THE SNOW OFF THE DRIVEWAY HAS TO BE A CLOSE SECOND.
©2012 ZITS Partnership. Dist. by King Features
SCOTT and BORGMAN

January 16, 2012

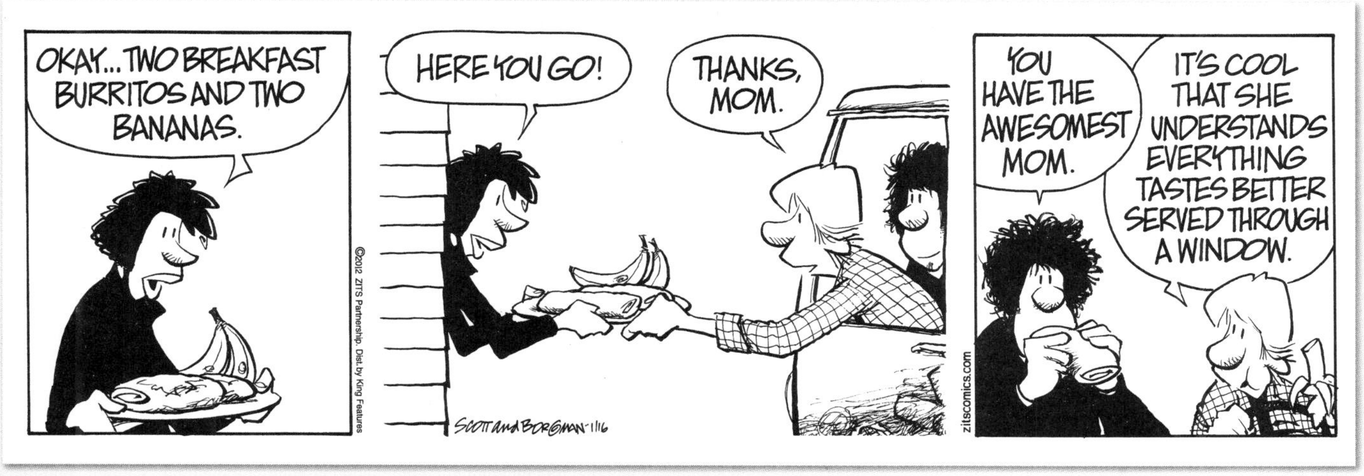

OKAY... TWO BREAKFAST BURRITOS AND TWO BANANAS.
HERE YOU GO!
THANKS, MOM.
YOU HAVE THE AWESOMEST MOM.
IT'S COOL THAT SHE UNDERSTANDS EVERYTHING TASTES BETTER SERVED THROUGH A WINDOW.
©2012 ZITS Partnership. Dist. by King Features
SCOTT and BORGMAN 1/16
zitscomics.com

February 29, 2012

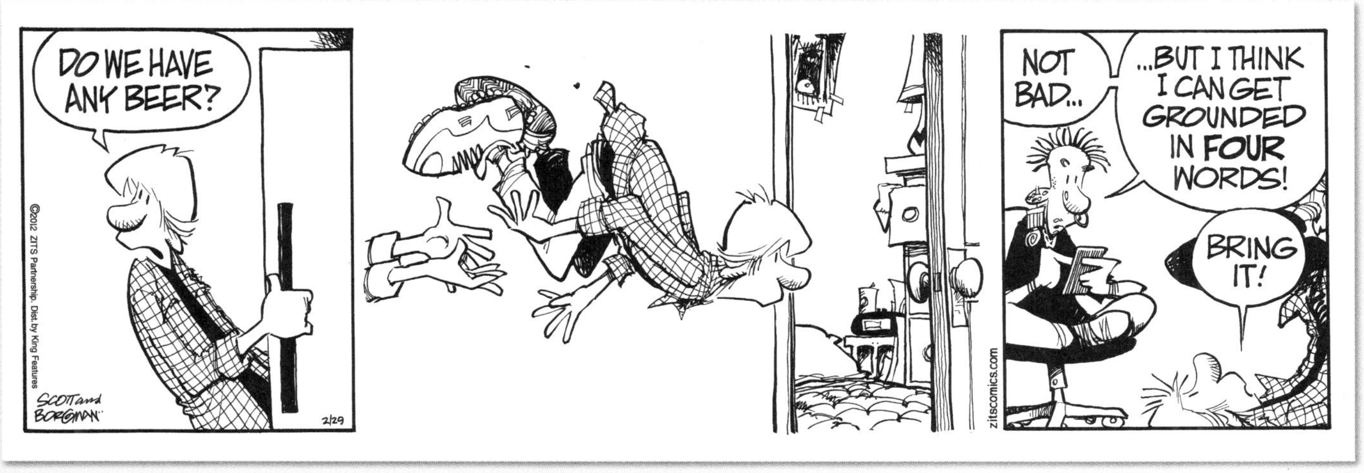

DO WE HAVE ANY BEER?
©2012 ZITS Partnership. Dist. by King Features
SCOTT and BORGMAN
2/29
NOT BAD...
...BUT I THINK I CAN GET GROUNDED IN **FOUR** WORDS!
BRING IT!
zitscomics.com

March 12, 2012

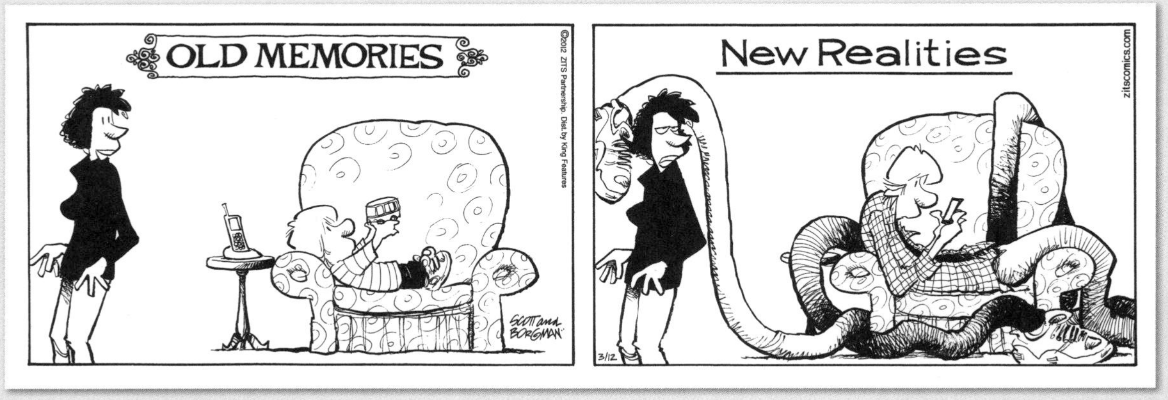

OLD MEMORIES
New Realities
©2012 ZITS Partnership. Dist. by King Features
zitscomics.com
SCOTT and BORGMAN
3/12

March 13, 2012

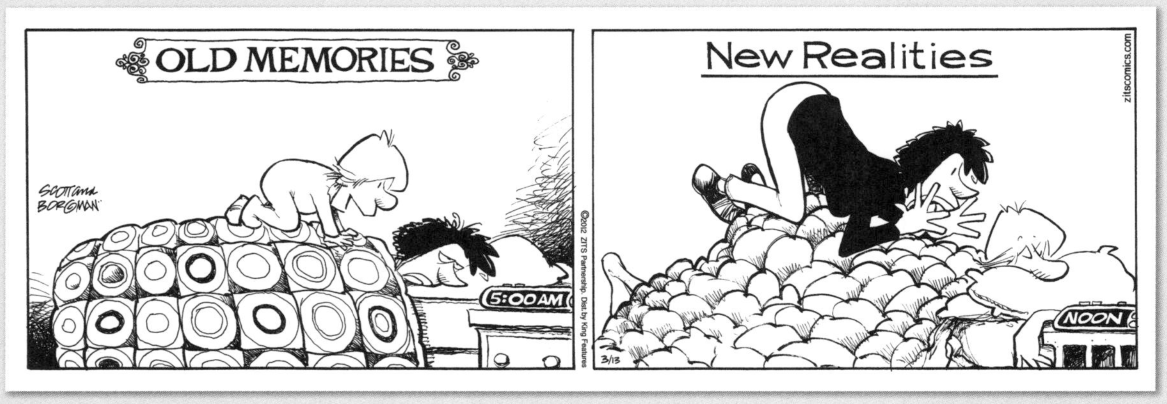

OLD MEMORIES
New Realities
SCOTT and BORGMAN
5:00 AM
©2012 ZITS Partnership. Dist. by King Features
NOON
zitscomics.com
3/13

March 14, 2012

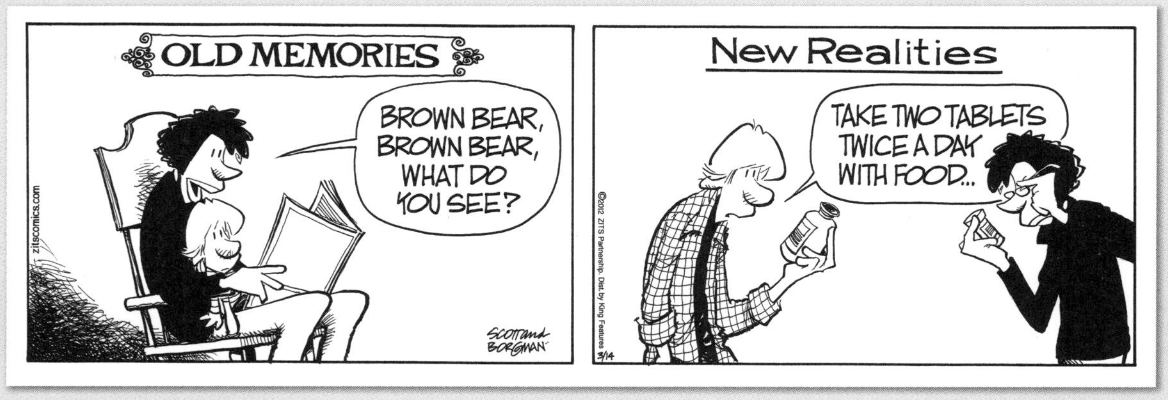

OLD MEMORIES
New Realities
BROWN BEAR, BROWN BEAR, WHAT DO YOU SEE?
TAKE TWO TABLETS TWICE A DAY WITH FOOD...
zitscomics.com
©2012 ZITS Partnership. Dist. by King Features
SCOTT and BORGMAN
3/14

March 15, 2012

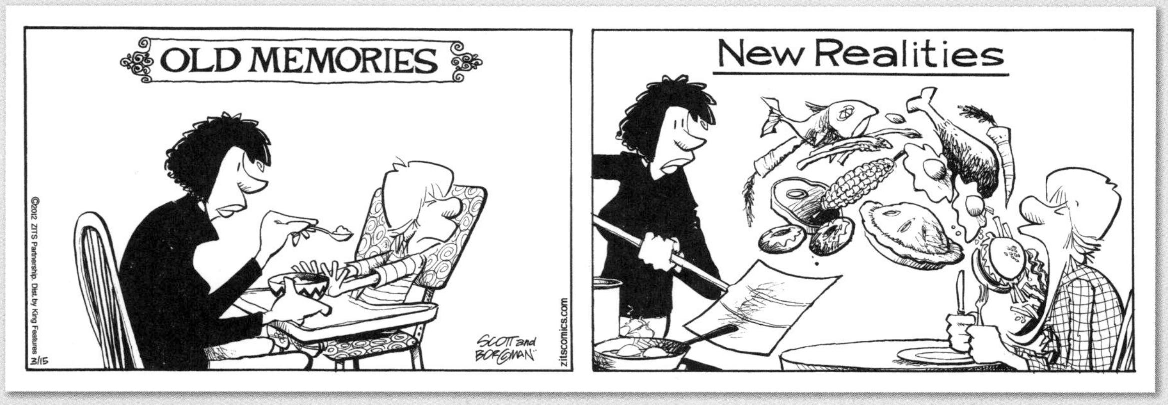

OLD MEMORIES
New Realities
©2012 ZITS Partnership. Dist. by King Features
3/15
SCOTT and BORGMAN
zitscomics.com

March 26, 2012

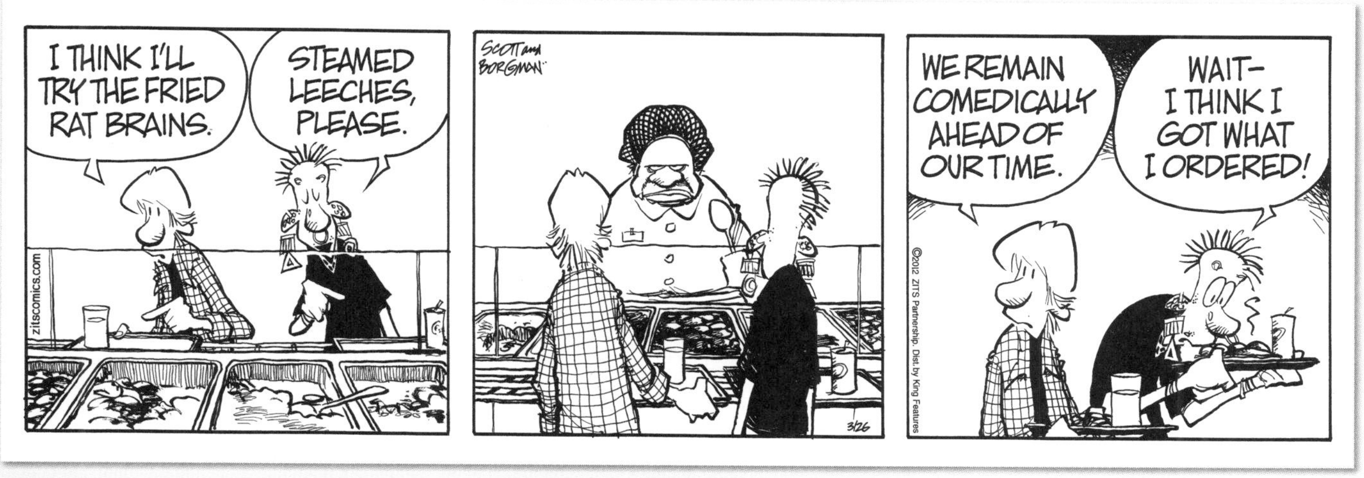
I THINK I'LL TRY THE FRIED RAT BRAINS.
STEAMED LEECHES, PLEASE.
SCOTT AND BORGMAN
WE REMAIN COMEDICALLY AHEAD OF OUR TIME.
WAIT- I THINK I GOT WHAT I ORDERED!
zitscomics.com
©2012 ZITS Partnership. Dist. by King Features
3/26

April 23, 2012

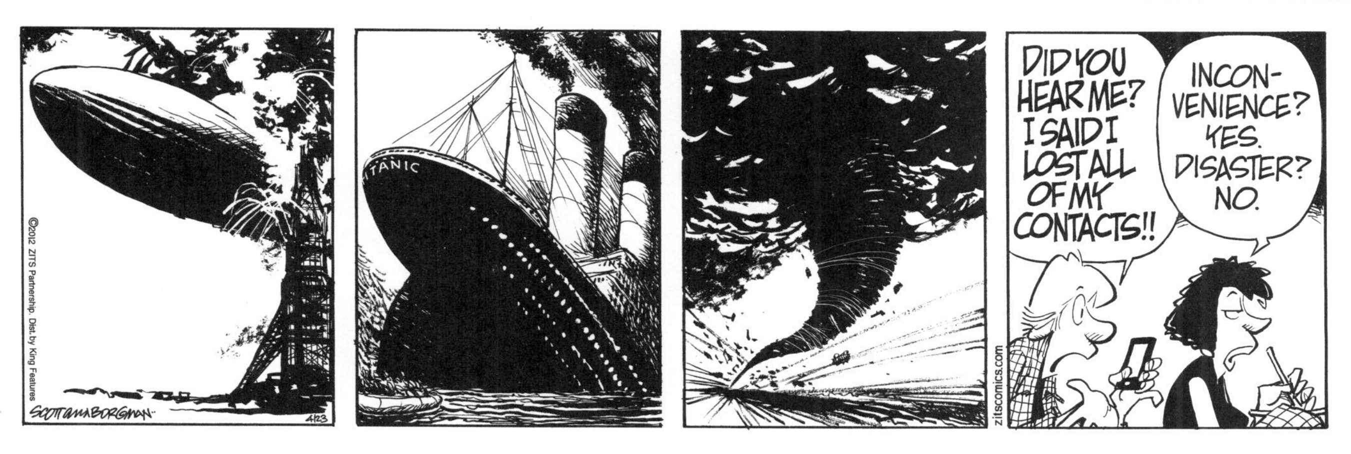
TANIC
DID YOU HEAR ME? I SAID I LOST ALL OF MY CONTACTS!!
INCON-VENIENCE? YES. DISASTER? NO.
SCOTT AND BORGMAN
©2012 ZITS Partnership. Dist. by King Features
zitscomics.com
4/23

April 26, 2012

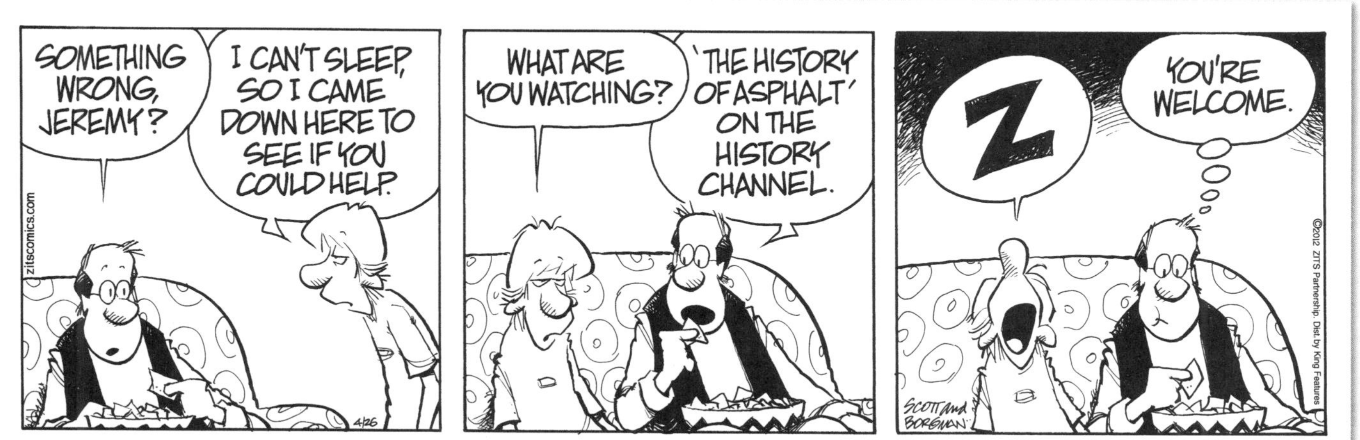
SOMETHING WRONG, JEREMY?
I CAN'T SLEEP, SO I CAME DOWN HERE TO SEE IF YOU COULD HELP.
WHAT ARE YOU WATCHING?
'THE HISTORY OF ASPHALT' ON THE HISTORY CHANNEL.
Z
YOU'RE WELCOME.
SCOTT AND BORGMAN
zitscomics.com
©2012 ZITS Partnership. Dist. by King Features
4/26

May 18, 2012

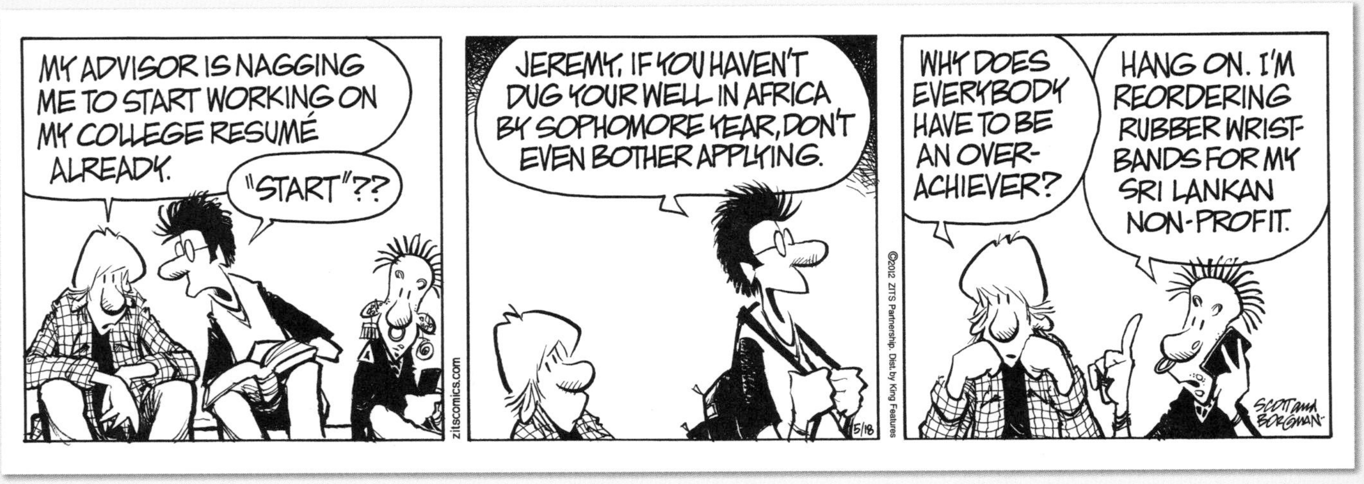
MY ADVISOR IS NAGGING ME TO START WORKING ON MY COLLEGE RESUMÉ ALREADY.
"START"??
zitscomics.com
JEREMY, IF YOU HAVEN'T DUG YOUR WELL IN AFRICA BY SOPHOMORE YEAR, DON'T EVEN BOTHER APPLYING.
5/18
©2012 ZITS Partnership. Dist. by King Features
WHY DOES EVERYBODY HAVE TO BE AN OVER-ACHIEVER?
HANG ON. I'M REORDERING RUBBER WRIST-BANDS FOR MY SRI LANKAN NON-PROFIT.
SCOTT and BORGMAN

May 29, 2012

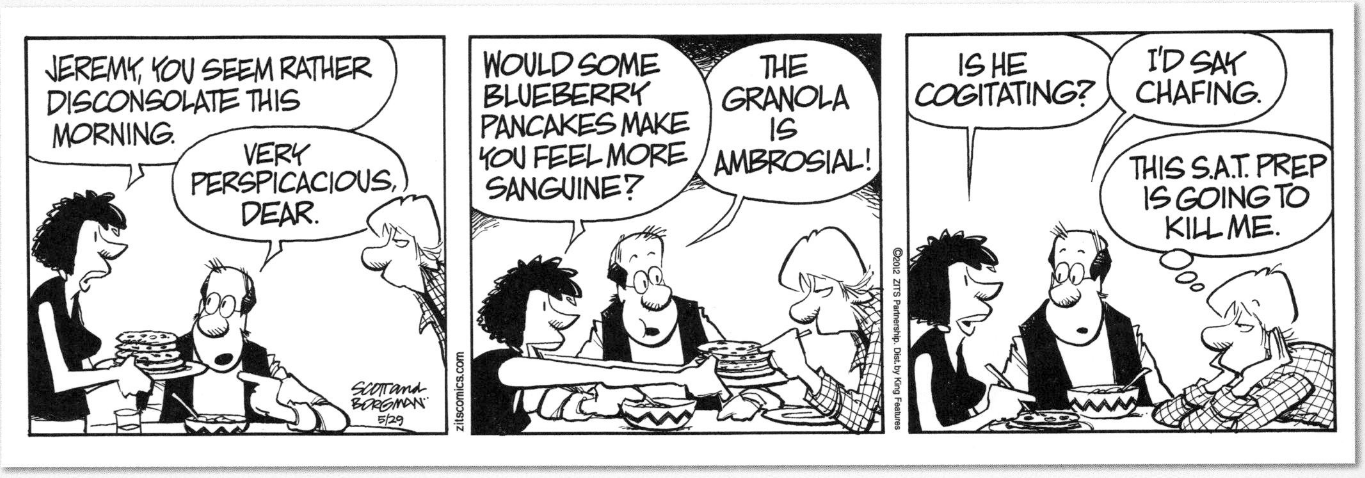
JEREMY, YOU SEEM RATHER DISCONSOLATE THIS MORNING.
VERY PERSPICACIOUS, DEAR.
SCOTT and BORGMAN
5/29
zitscomics.com
WOULD SOME BLUEBERRY PANCAKES MAKE YOU FEEL MORE SANGUINE?
THE GRANOLA IS AMBROSIAL!
©2012 ZITS Partnership. Dist. by King Features
IS HE COGITATING?
I'D SAY CHAFING.
THIS S.A.T. PREP IS GOING TO KILL ME.

June 1, 2012

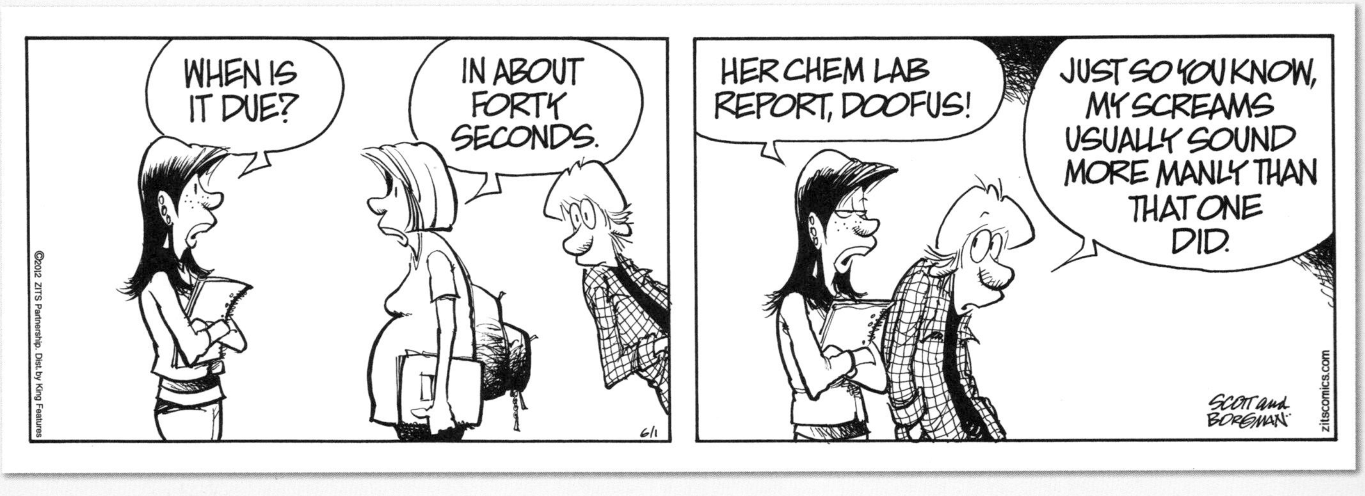
©2012 ZITS Partnership. Dist. by King Features
WHEN IS IT DUE?
IN ABOUT FORTY SECONDS.
6/1
HER CHEM LAB REPORT, DOOFUS!
JUST SO YOU KNOW, MY SCREAMS USUALLY SOUND MORE MANLY THAN THAT ONE DID.
SCOTT and BORGMAN
zitscomics.com

April 29, 2012

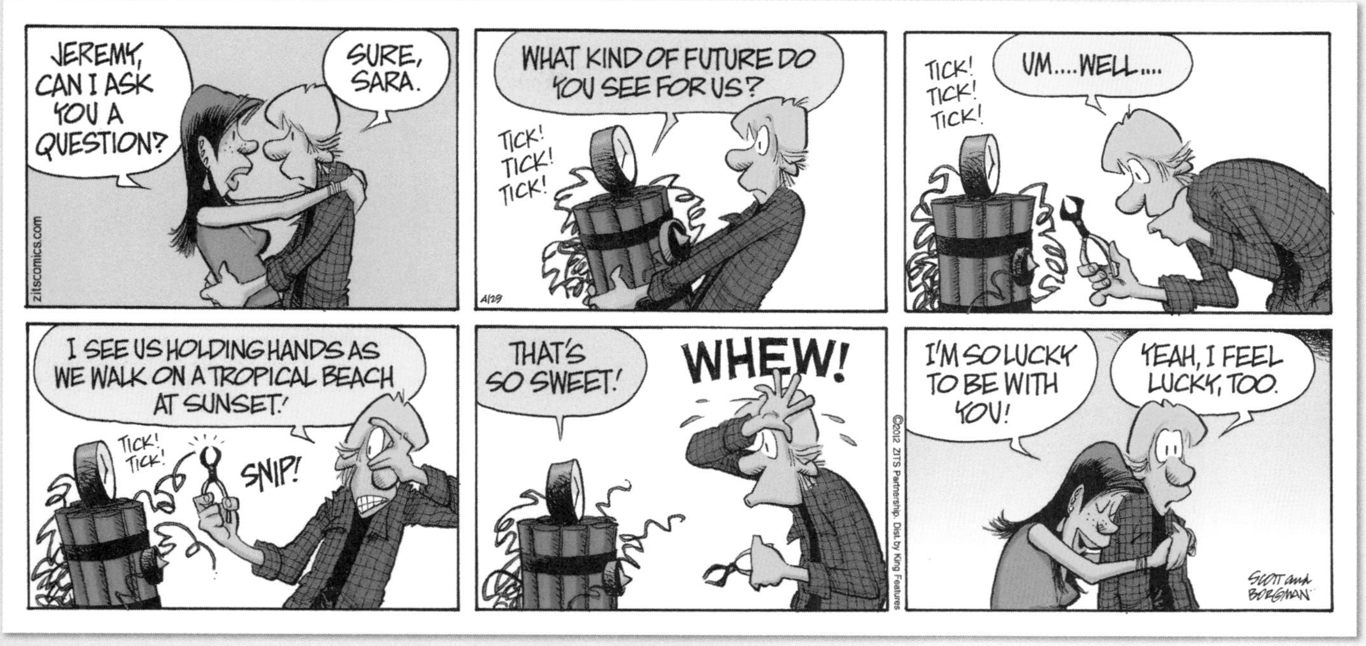

JEREMY, CAN I ASK YOU A QUESTION?
SURE, SARA.
WHAT KIND OF FUTURE DO YOU SEE FOR US?
TICK! TICK! TICK!
TICK! TICK! TICK!
UM....WELL....
I SEE US HOLDING HANDS AS WE WALK ON A TROPICAL BEACH AT SUNSET!
TICK! TICK!
SNIP!
THAT'S SO SWEET!
WHEW!
I'M SO LUCKY TO BE WITH YOU!
YEAH, I FEEL LUCKY, TOO.
zitscomics.com
©2012 ZITS Partnership. Dist. by King Features
SCOTT and BORGMAN

June 3, 2012

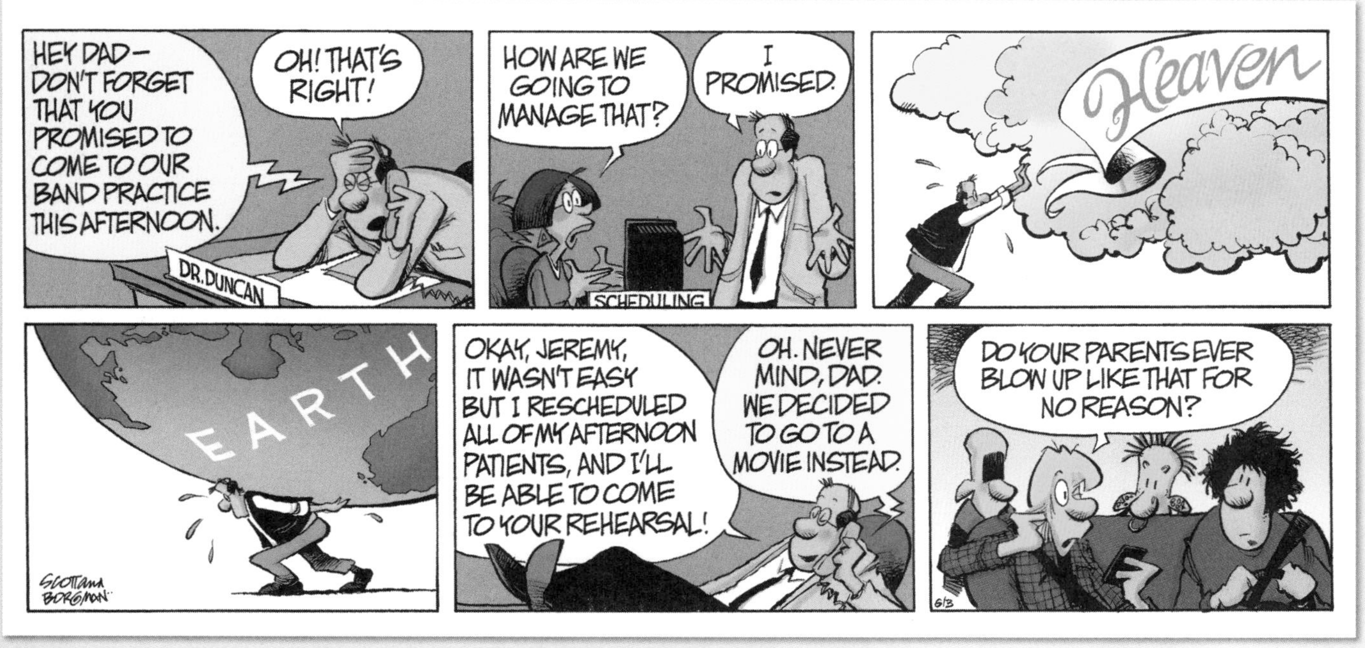

HEY DAD— DON'T FORGET THAT YOU PROMISED TO COME TO OUR BAND PRACTICE THIS AFTERNOON.
OH! THAT'S RIGHT!
DR. DUNCAN
HOW ARE WE GOING TO MANAGE THAT?
I PROMISED.
SCHEDULING
Heaven
EARTH
SCOTT and BORGMAN
OKAY, JEREMY, IT WASN'T EASY BUT I RESCHEDULED ALL OF MY AFTERNOON PATIENTS, AND I'LL BE ABLE TO COME TO YOUR REHEARSAL!
OH. NEVER MIND, DAD. WE DECIDED TO GO TO A MOVIE INSTEAD.
DO YOUR PARENTS EVER BLOW UP LIKE THAT FOR NO REASON?

June 8, 2012

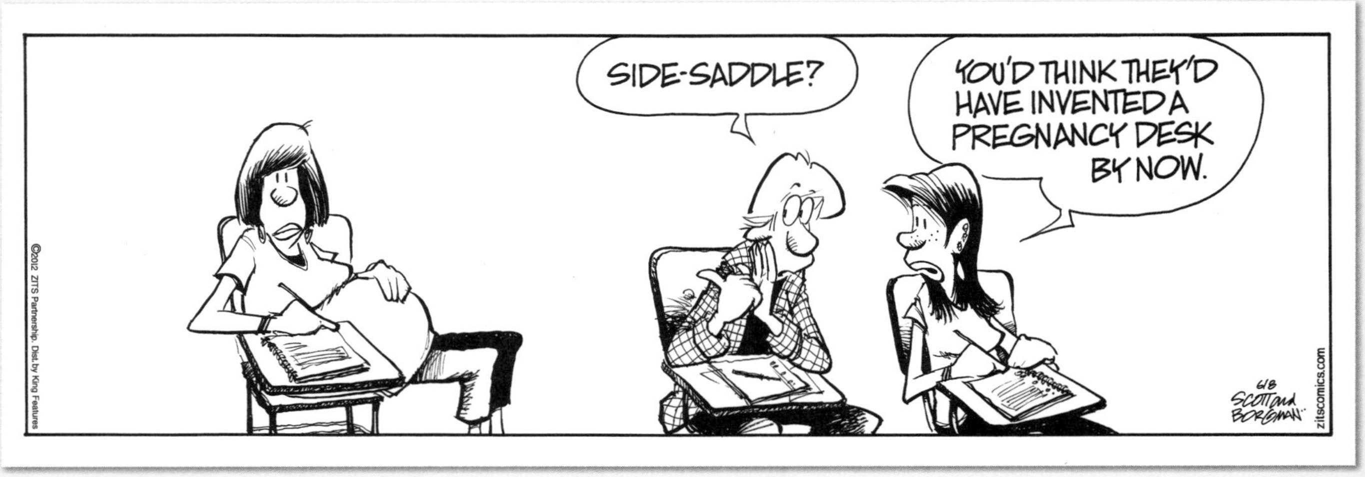
SIDE-SADDLE?
YOU'D THINK THEY'D HAVE INVENTED A PREGNANCY DESK BY NOW.
©2012 ZITS Partnership. Dist. by King Features
zitscomics.com
6/8 SCOTT and BORGMAN

June 11, 2012

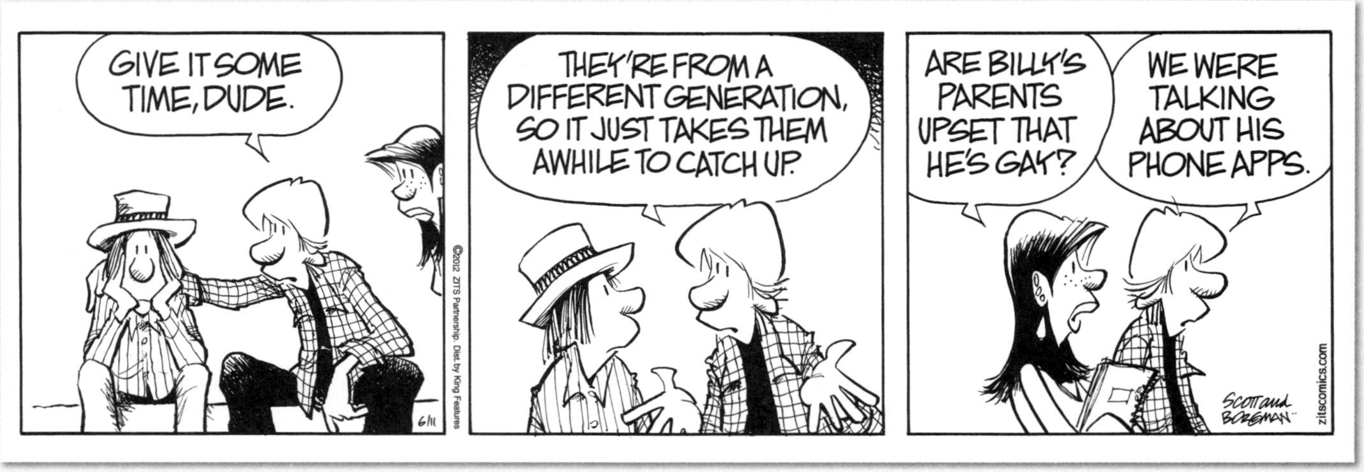
GIVE IT SOME TIME, DUDE.
THEY'RE FROM A DIFFERENT GENERATION, SO IT JUST TAKES THEM AWHILE TO CATCH UP.
ARE BILLY'S PARENTS UPSET THAT HE'S GAY?
WE WERE TALKING ABOUT HIS PHONE APPS.
©2012 ZITS Partnership. Dist. by King Features
zitscomics.com
6/11 SCOTT and BORGMAN

June 12, 2012

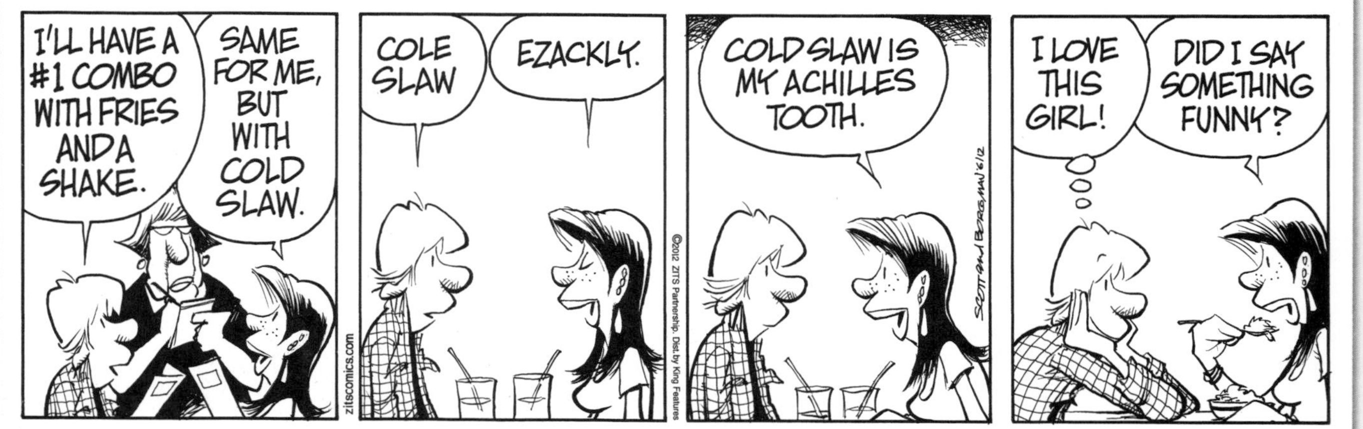
I'LL HAVE A #1 COMBO WITH FRIES AND A SHAKE.
SAME FOR ME, BUT WITH COLD SLAW.
COLE SLAW
EZACKLY.
COLD SLAW IS MY ACHILLES TOOTH.
I LOVE THIS GIRL!
DID I SAY SOMETHING FUNNY?
zitscomics.com
©2012 ZITS Partnership. Dist. by King Features
SCOTT and BORGMAN 6/12

June 23, 2012

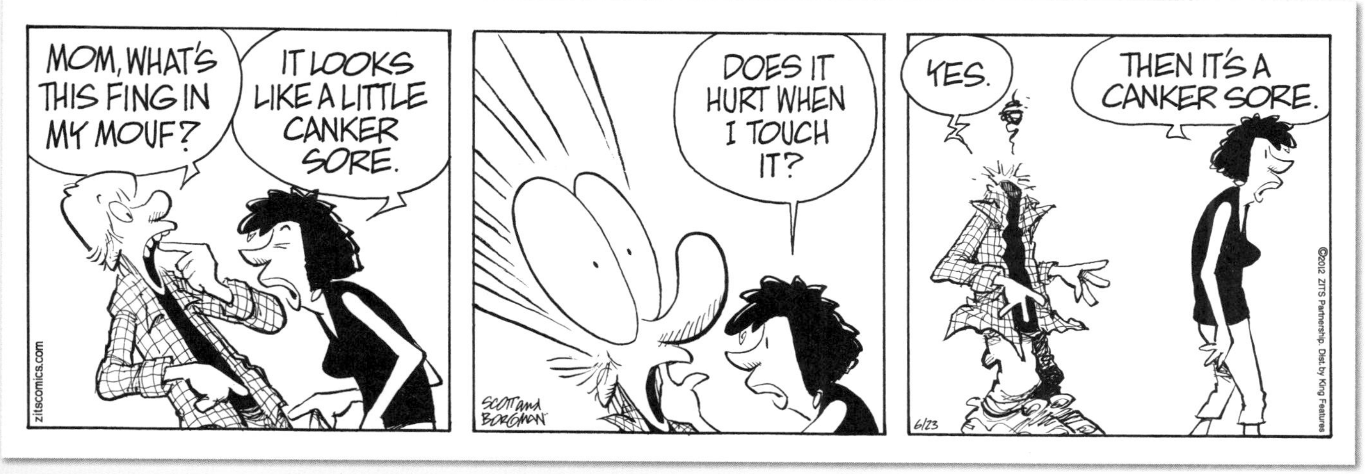
MOM, WHAT'S THIS FING IN MY MOUF?
IT LOOKS LIKE A LITTLE CANKER SORE.
DOES IT HURT WHEN I TOUCH IT?
YES.
THEN IT'S A CANKER SORE.
zitscomics.com
SCOTT and BORGMAN
6/23
©2012 ZITS Partnership. Dist. by King Features

August 9, 2012

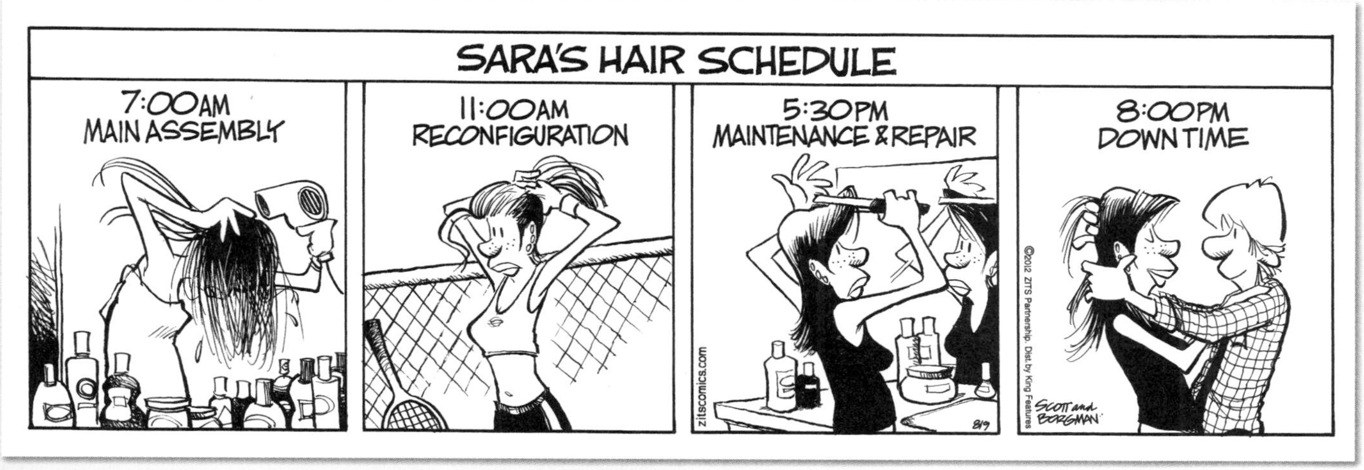
SARA'S HAIR SCHEDULE
7:00AM MAIN ASSEMBLY
11:00AM RECONFIGURATION
5:30PM MAINTENANCE & REPAIR
8:00PM DOWN TIME
zitscomics.com
8/9
©2012 ZITS Partnership. Dist. by King Features
SCOTT and BORGMAN

October 2, 2012

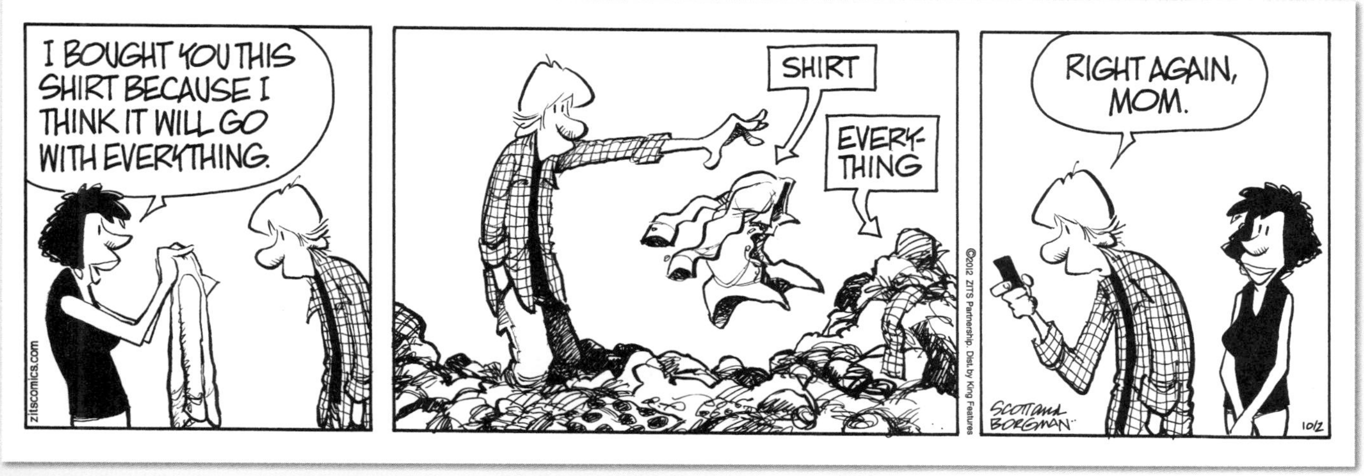
I BOUGHT YOU THIS SHIRT BECAUSE I THINK IT WILL GO WITH EVERYTHING.
SHIRT
EVERY-THING
RIGHT AGAIN, MOM.
zitscomics.com
©2012 ZITS Partnership. Dist. by King Features
SCOTT and BORGMAN
10/2

October 8, 2012

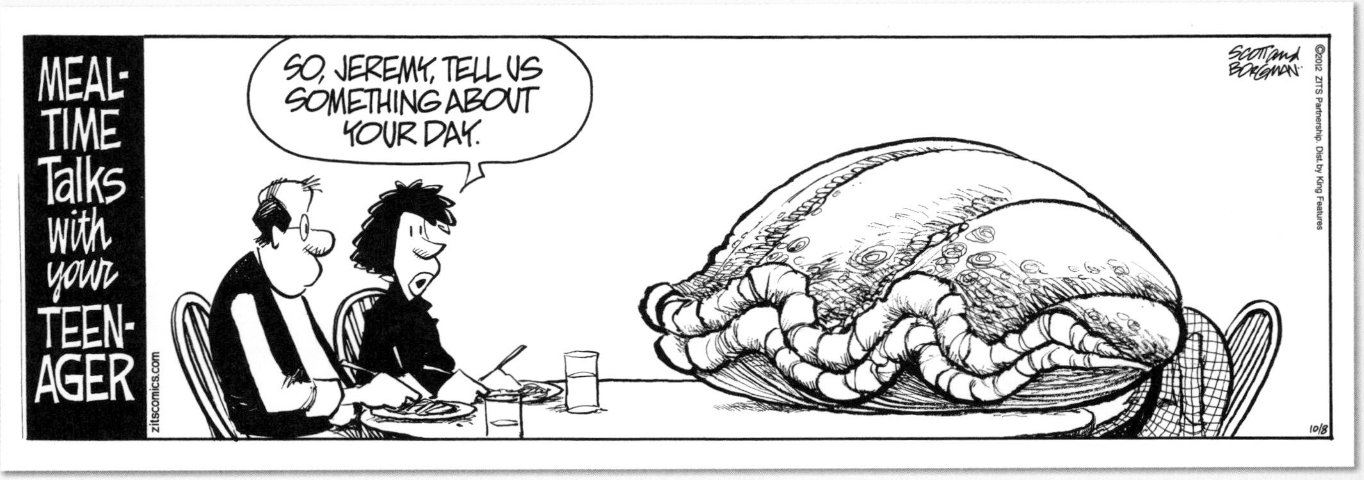
MEAL-TIME Talks with your TEEN-AGER
SO, JEREMY, TELL US SOMETHING ABOUT YOUR DAY.
SCOTT and BORGMAN
©2012 ZITS Partnership. Dist. by King Features
zitscomics.com
10/8

October 10, 2012

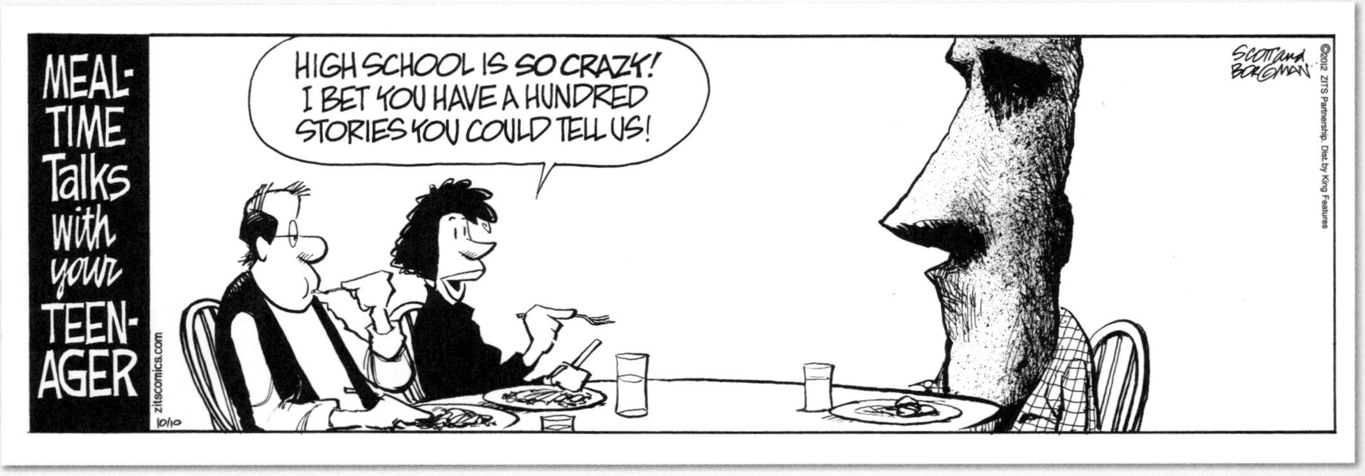
MEAL-TIME Talks with your TEEN-AGER
HIGH SCHOOL IS SO CRAZY! I BET YOU HAVE A HUNDRED STORIES YOU COULD TELL US!
SCOTT and BORGMAN
©2012 ZITS Partnership. Dist. by King Features
zitscomics.com
10/10

October 11, 2012

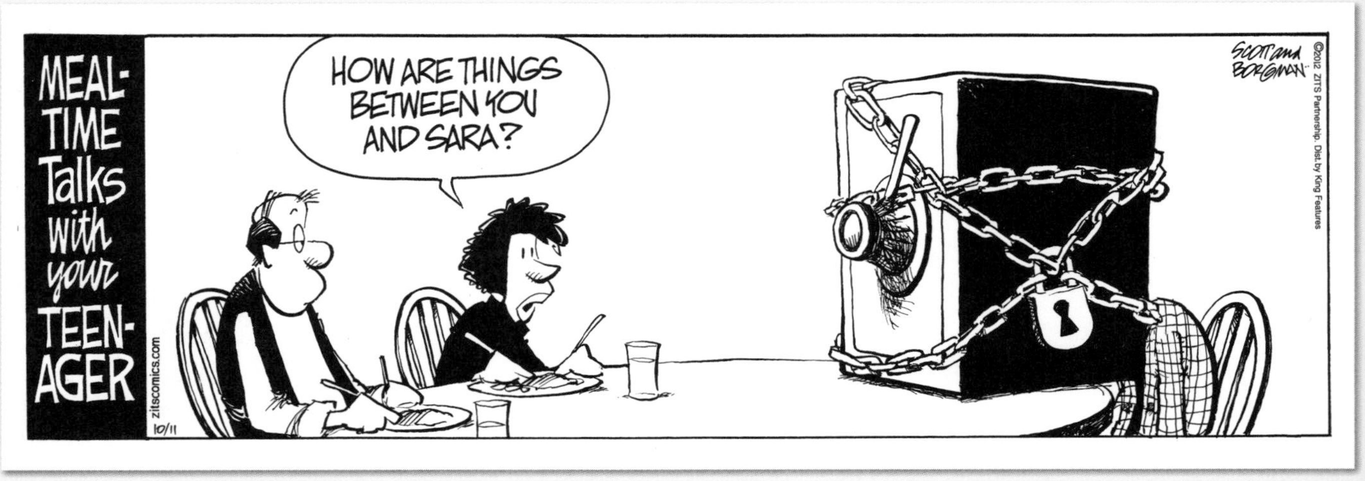
MEAL-TIME Talks with your TEEN-AGER
HOW ARE THINGS BETWEEN YOU AND SARA?
SCOTT and BORGMAN
©2012 ZITS Partnership. Dist. by King Features
zitscomics.com
10/11

October 26, 2012

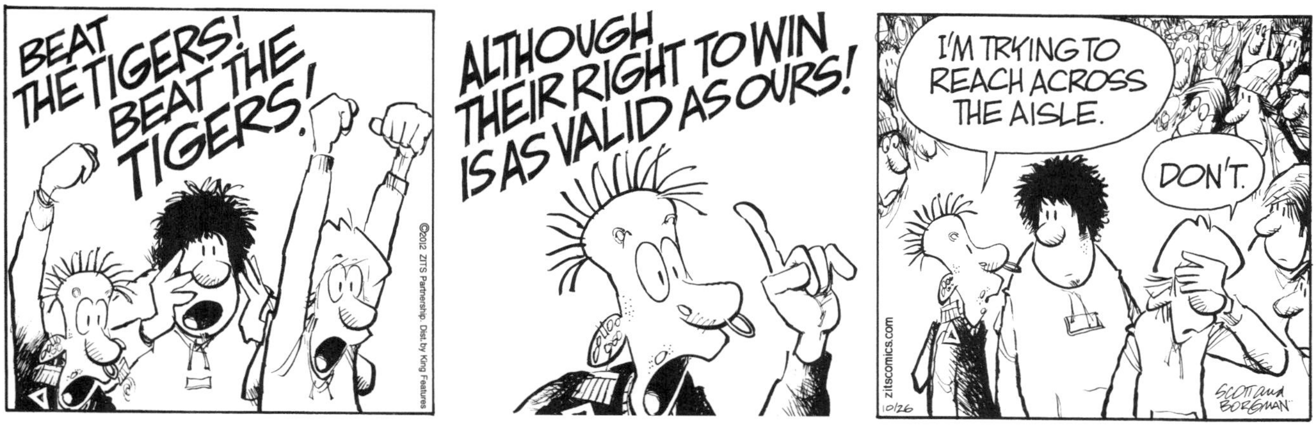
BEAT THE TIGERS! BEAT THE TIGERS!
©2012 ZITS Partnership. Dist. by King Features
ALTHOUGH THEIR RIGHT TO WIN IS AS VALID AS OURS!
zitscomics.com
10/26
I'M TRYING TO REACH ACROSS THE AISLE.
DON'T.
SCOTT and BORGMAN

November 26, 2012

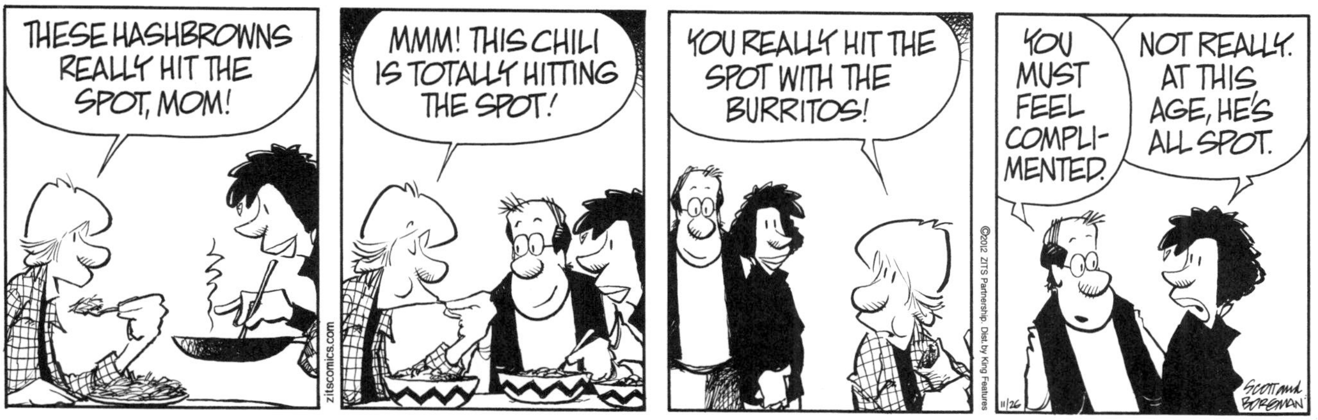
THESE HASHBROWNS REALLY HIT THE SPOT, MOM!
zitscomics.com
MMM! THIS CHILI IS TOTALLY HITTING THE SPOT!
YOU REALLY HIT THE SPOT WITH THE BURRITOS!
©2012 ZITS Partnership. Dist. by King Features
11/26
YOU MUST FEEL COMPLI-MENTED.
NOT REALLY. AT THIS AGE, HE'S ALL SPOT.
SCOTT and BORGMAN

December 17, 2012

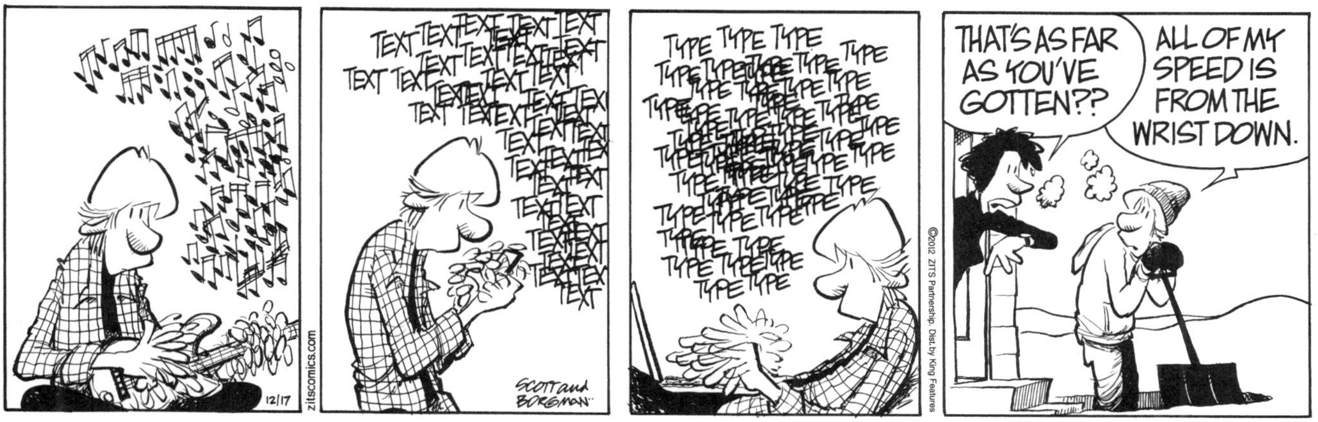
12/17
zitscomics.com
TEXT TEXT TEXT TEXT TEXT
SCOTT and BORGMAN
TYPE TYPE TYPE
©2012 ZITS Partnership. Dist. by King Features
THAT'S AS FAR AS YOU'VE GOTTEN??
ALL OF MY SPEED IS FROM THE WRIST DOWN.

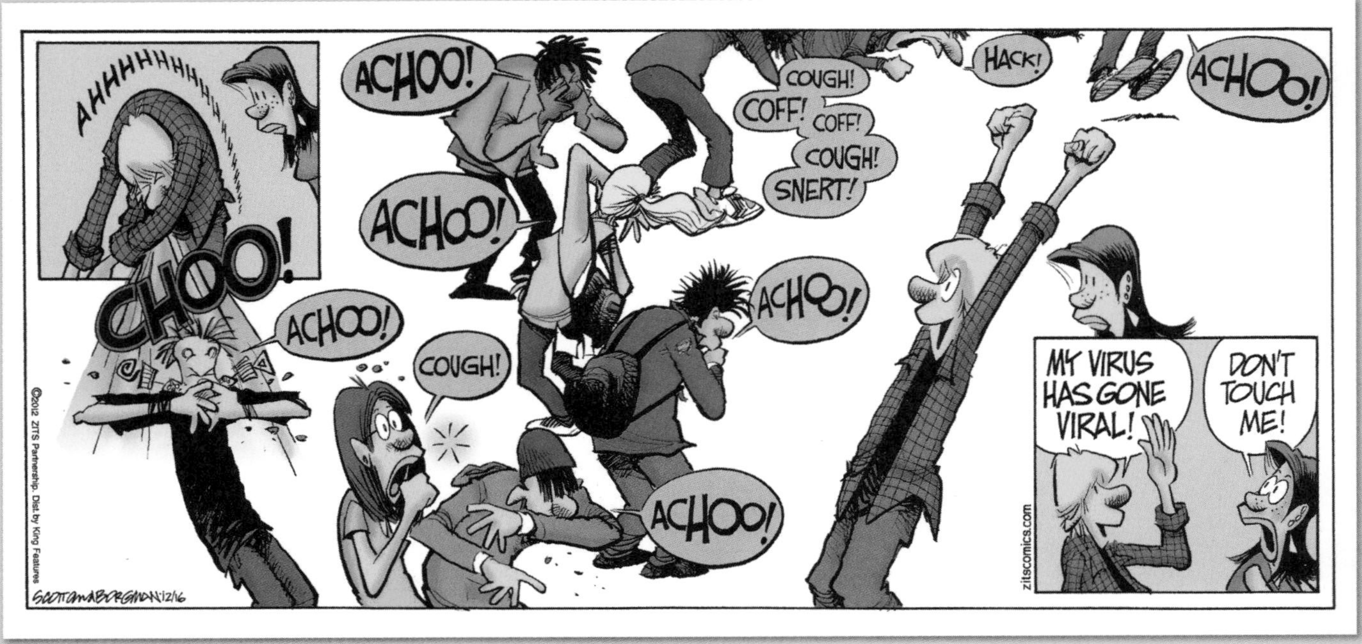
AHHHHHHHHHHHHHHHH
CHOO!
ACHOO!
©2012 ZITS Partnership. Dist. by King Features
SCOTTandBORGMAN 12/16
ACHOO!
ACHOO!
COUGH!
COUGH!
COFF!
COFF!
COUGH!
SNERT!
HACK!
ACHOO!
ACHOO!
ACHOO!
MY VIRUS HAS GONE VIRAL!
DON'T TOUCH ME!
zitscomics.com

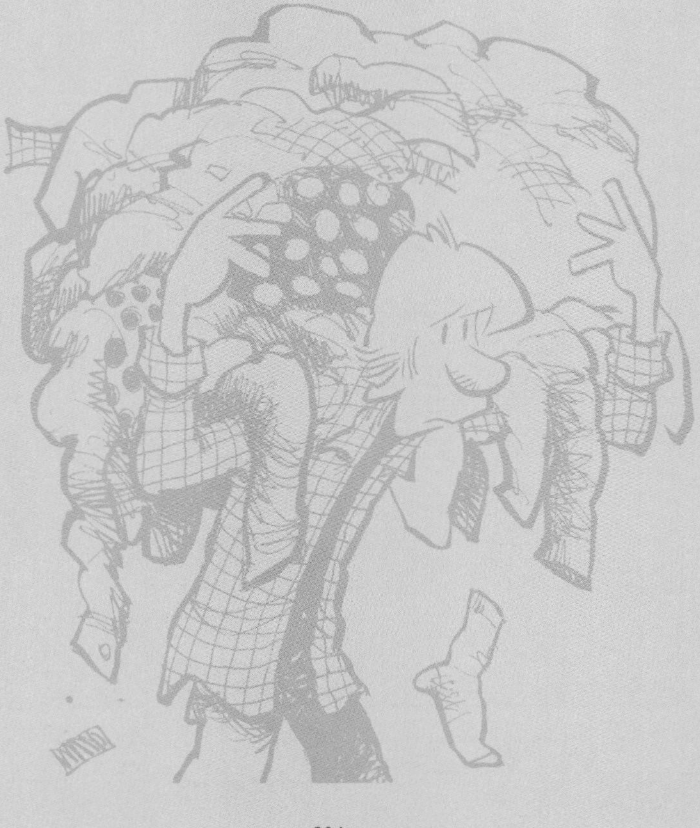

MAILBAG

Most of our correspondence comes from parents who wonder, "where'd you hide the camera in our house?!" Stop looking—we use drones. Now and then we get a gem like this from a kid living in the belly of the teenage beast. Don't you just want to hug her?

Hi,

So, when I was younger, I used to read *Zits* and think, "So this is definitely not what high school will be like, but you tried." Of course, my childhood delusions also included thinking that my future car would be a pink limo with a hot tub in the back and that Disney would cast me in *High School Musical*, so I think we can all guess how wrong I was. As a high school sophomore, I relate more and more to Jeremy. Every. Freaking. Day. And while I may have relatively clear skin (except for that one damn pimple on my nose), I feel like a comic strip about me would be called *Zits* because I am a teenager, going through four years of living a life equivalent to that of a zit.

Anyway, though I'm sure you know this, your comic strip is amazing, and I read it in the bubble bath while I cry about finals and avoid doing my laundry (it's been two weeks and counting). I have three *Zits* treasuries, but I hope to acquire more because I do so much stressing in the bubble bath that I've read them all at least ten times. I only have ten dollars right now, and I guess I could save it, but do you KNOW how much candy corn I could buy with that much money? (Six bags at Kroger right now.)

So yes, keep doing what you do, otherwise I would have to read *Baby Blues* in the bath, which is much less relatable. If you'll excuse me, I'm going to go check my Instagram—oops, I meant write that essay and get tears all over my 150 precious German flashcards. I hope you enjoy not being in high school.

Jordan
CEO of B Average Nerds & Co.

PS: What was the point of this email?

January 24, 2013

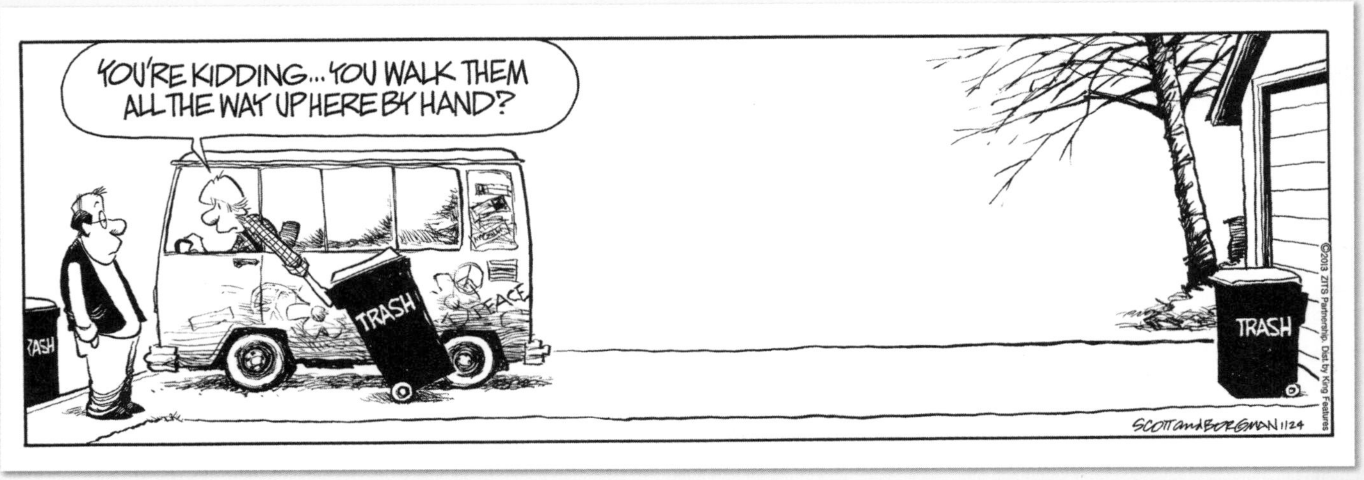
YOU'RE KIDDING... YOU WALK THEM ALL THE WAY UP HERE BY HAND?
TRASH
PEACE
TRASH
©2013 ZITS Partnership. Dist. by King Features
SCOTT and BORGMAN 1/24

February 15, 2013

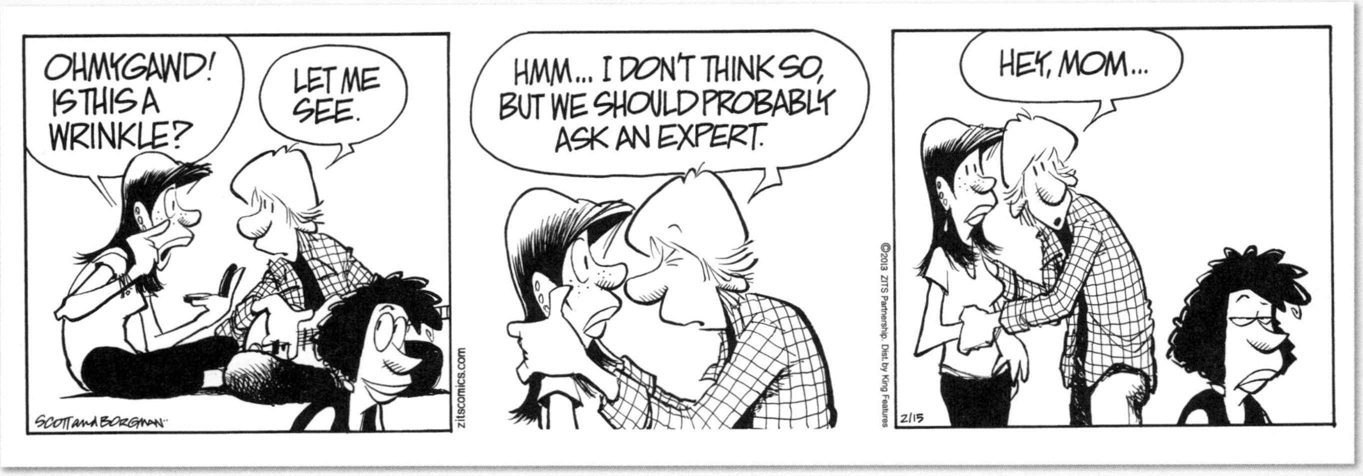
OHMYGAWD! IS THIS A WRINKLE?
LET ME SEE.
SCOTT and BORGMAN
zitscomics.com
HMM... I DON'T THINK SO, BUT WE SHOULD PROBABLY ASK AN EXPERT.
©2013 ZITS Partnership. Dist. by King Features
HEY, MOM...
2/15

March 5, 2013

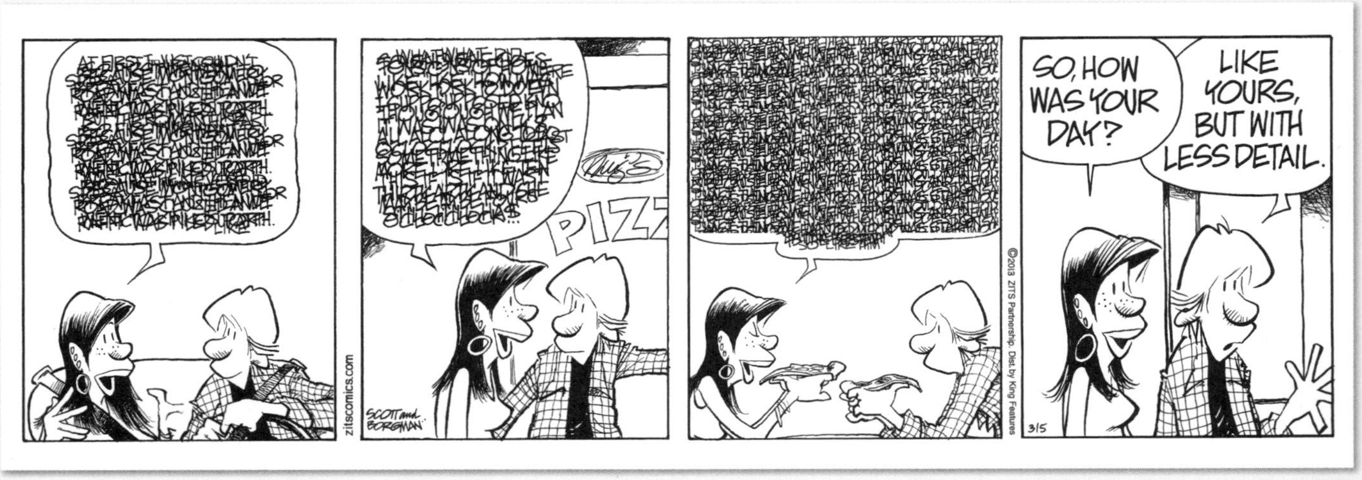
zitscomics.com
PIZZ
SCOTT and BORGMAN
©2013 ZITS Partnership. Dist. by King Features
SO, HOW WAS YOUR DAY?
LIKE YOURS, BUT WITH LESS DETAIL.
3/5

April 12, 2013

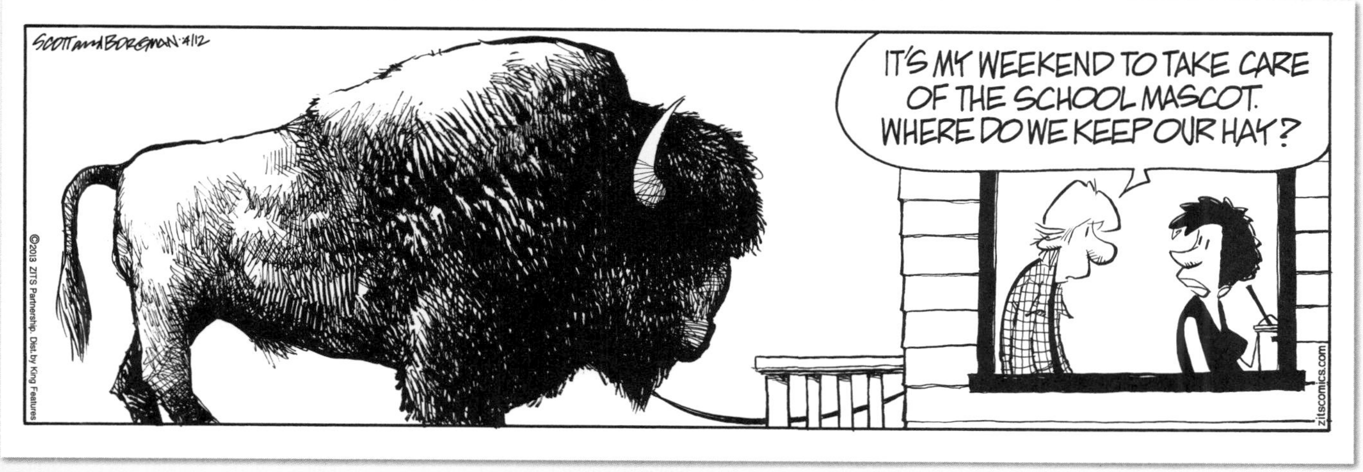
SCOTT AND BORGMAN 4/12
IT'S MY WEEKEND TO TAKE CARE OF THE SCHOOL MASCOT. WHERE DO WE KEEP OUR HAY?
©2013 ZITS Partnership. Dist. by King Features
zitscomics.com

May 8, 2013

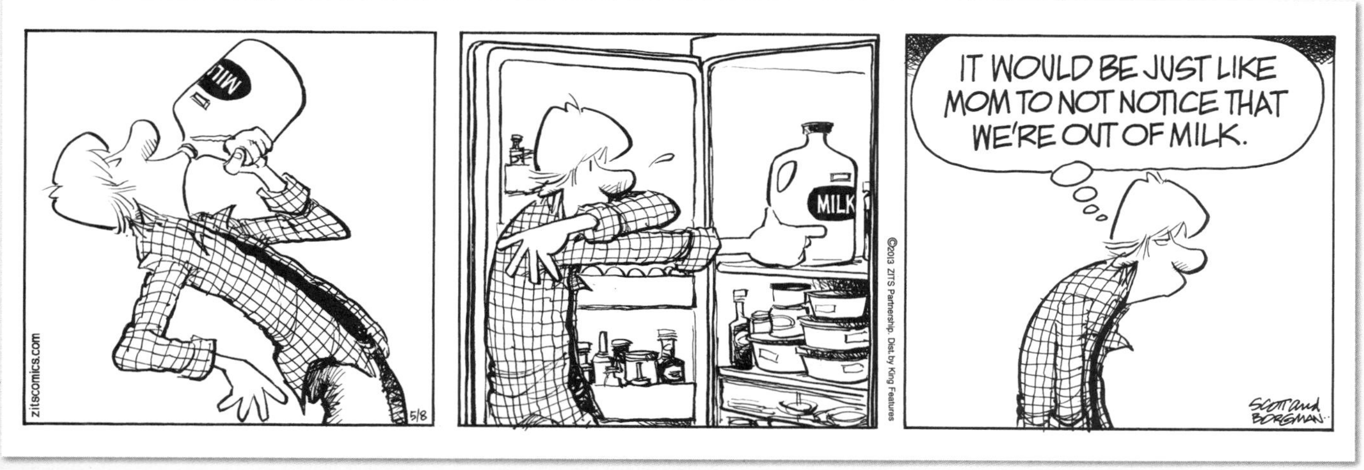
MILK
zitscomics.com
5/8
MILK
©2013 ZITS Partnership. Dist. by King Features
IT WOULD BE JUST LIKE MOM TO NOT NOTICE THAT WE'RE OUT OF MILK.
SCOTT AND BORGMAN

June 24, 2013

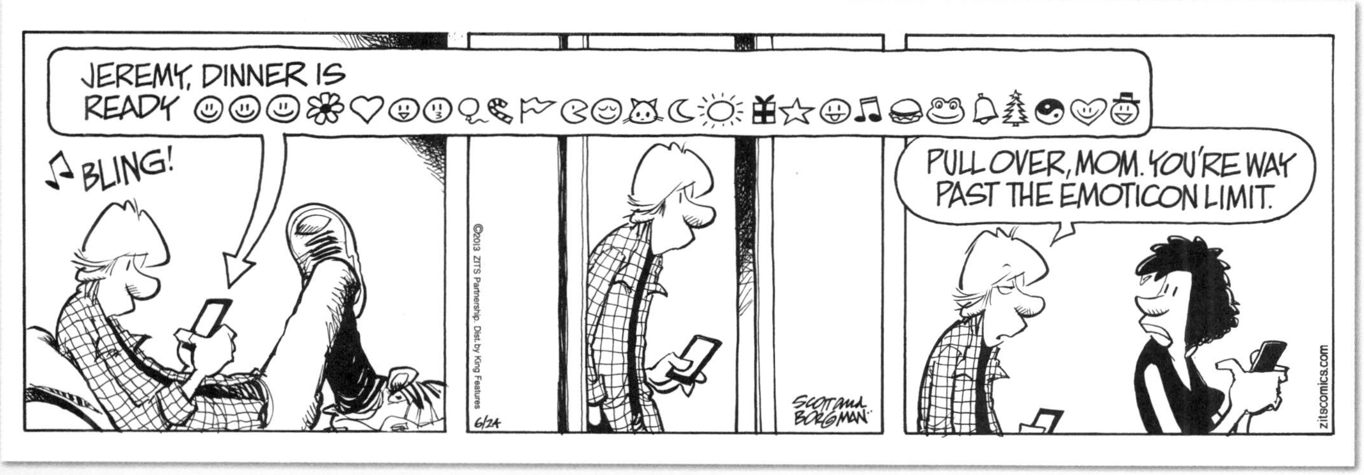
JEREMY, DINNER IS READY
BLING!
©2013 ZITS Partnership. Dist. by King Features
6/24
SCOTT AND BORGMAN
PULL OVER, MOM. YOU'RE WAY PAST THE EMOTICON LIMIT.
zitscomics.com

May 13, 2013

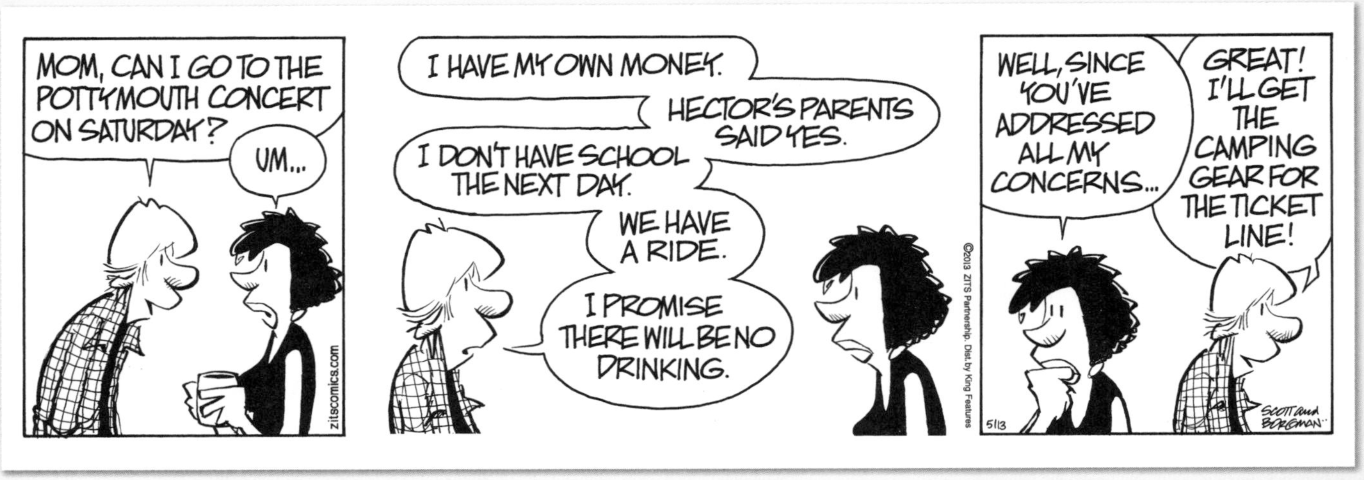
MOM, CAN I GO TO THE POTTYMOUTH CONCERT ON SATURDAY?
UM...
zitscomics.com
I HAVE MY OWN MONEY.
HECTOR'S PARENTS SAID YES.
I DON'T HAVE SCHOOL THE NEXT DAY.
WE HAVE A RIDE.
I PROMISE THERE WILL BE NO DRINKING.
©2013 ZITS Partnership. Dist. by King Features
WELL, SINCE YOU'VE ADDRESSED ALL MY CONCERNS...
GREAT! I'LL GET THE CAMPING GEAR FOR THE TICKET LINE!
5/13
SCOTT and BORGMAN

May 14, 2013

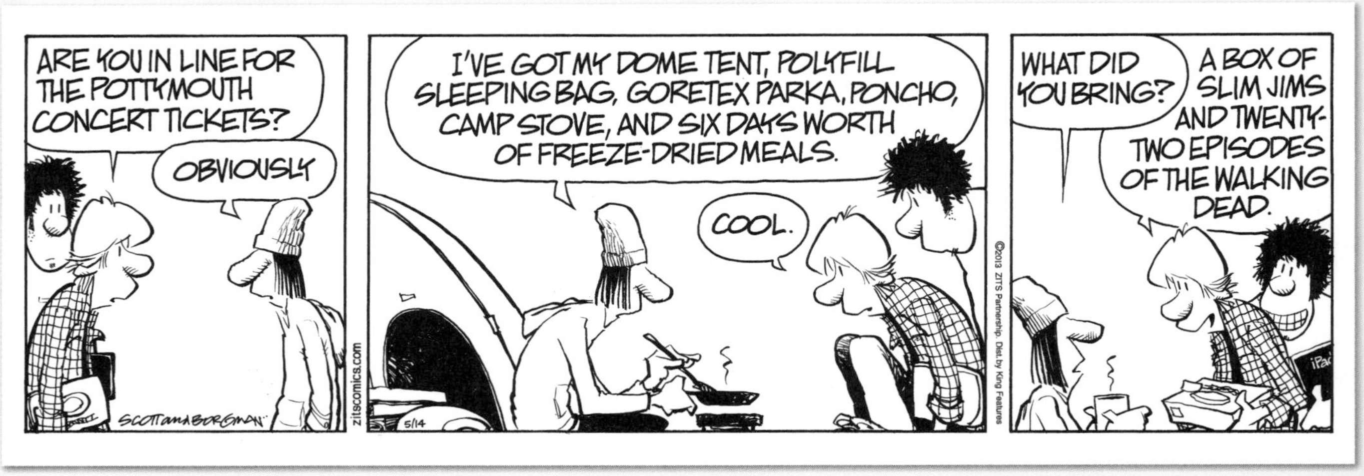
ARE YOU IN LINE FOR THE POTTYMOUTH CONCERT TICKETS?
OBVIOUSLY
SCOTT and BORGMAN
zitscomics.com
I'VE GOT MY DOME TENT, POLYFILL SLEEPING BAG, GORETEX PARKA, PONCHO, CAMP STOVE, AND SIX DAYS WORTH OF FREEZE-DRIED MEALS.
COOL.
5/14
©2013 ZITS Partnership. Dist. by King Features
WHAT DID YOU BRING?
A BOX OF SLIM JIMS AND TWENTY-TWO EPISODES OF THE WALKING DEAD.

May 15, 2013

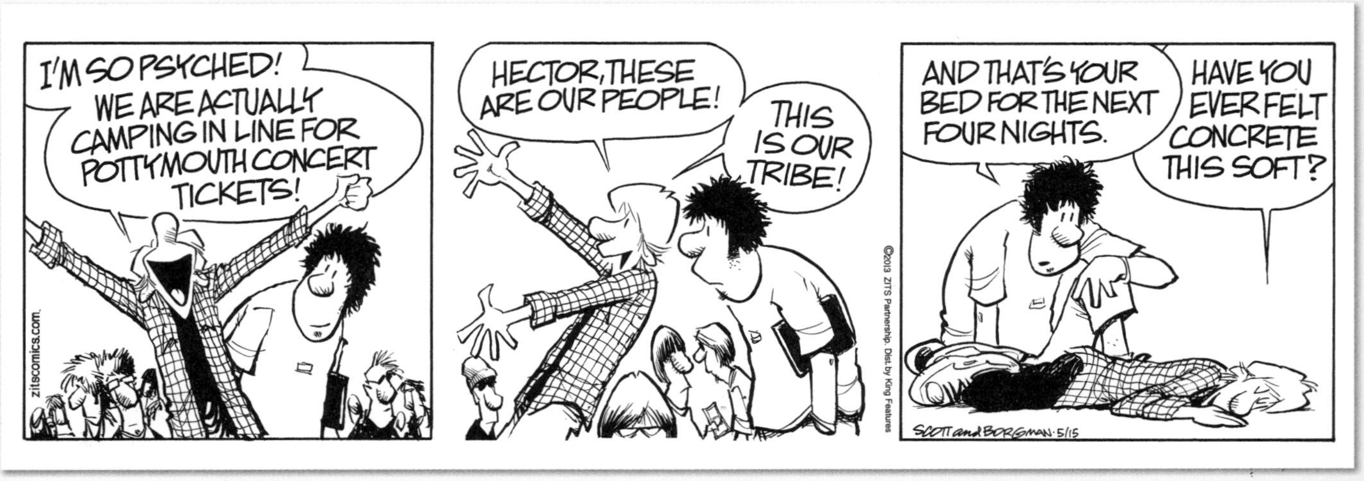
I'M SO PSYCHED! WE ARE ACTUALLY CAMPING IN LINE FOR POTTYMOUTH CONCERT TICKETS!
zitscomics.com
HECTOR, THESE ARE OUR PEOPLE!
THIS IS OUR TRIBE!
©2013 ZITS Partnership. Dist. by King Features
AND THAT'S YOUR BED FOR THE NEXT FOUR NIGHTS.
HAVE YOU EVER FELT CONCRETE THIS SOFT?
SCOTT and BORGMAN 5/15

May 16, 2013

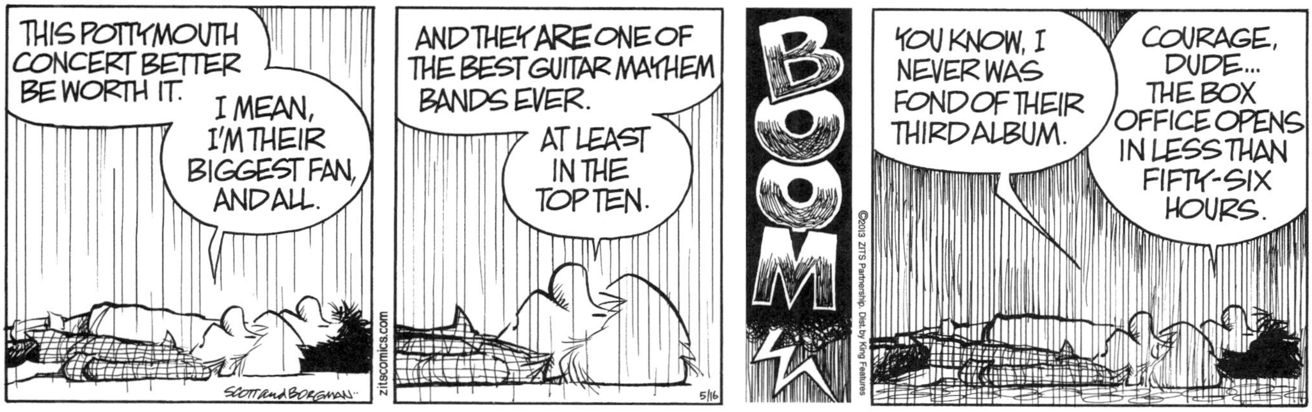
THIS POTTYMOUTH CONCERT BETTER BE WORTH IT.
I MEAN, I'M THEIR BIGGEST FAN, AND ALL.
SCOTT and BORGMAN
zitscomics.com
AND THEY ARE ONE OF THE BEST GUITAR MAYHEM BANDS EVER.
AT LEAST IN THE TOP TEN.
5/16
BOOM
©2013 ZITS Partnership. Dist. by King Features
YOU KNOW, I NEVER WAS FOND OF THEIR THIRD ALBUM.
COURAGE, DUDE... THE BOX OFFICE OPENS IN LESS THAN FIFTY-SIX HOURS.

May 17, 2013

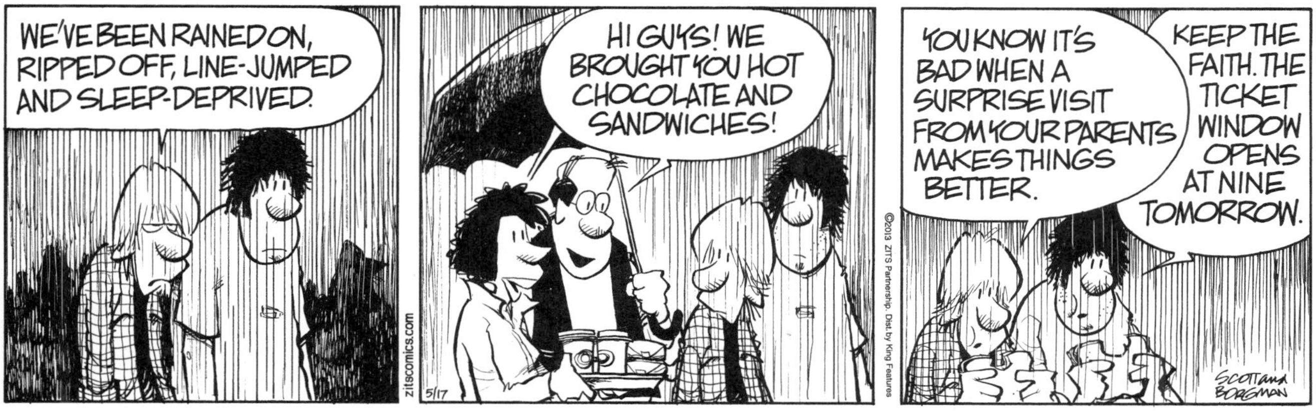
WE'VE BEEN RAINED ON, RIPPED OFF, LINE-JUMPED AND SLEEP-DEPRIVED.
zitscomics.com
5/17
HI GUYS! WE BROUGHT YOU HOT CHOCOLATE AND SANDWICHES!
©2013 ZITS Partnership. Dist. by King Features
YOU KNOW IT'S BAD WHEN A SURPRISE VISIT FROM YOUR PARENTS MAKES THINGS BETTER.
KEEP THE FAITH. THE TICKET WINDOW OPENS AT NINE TOMORROW.
SCOTT and BORGMAN

May 18, 2013

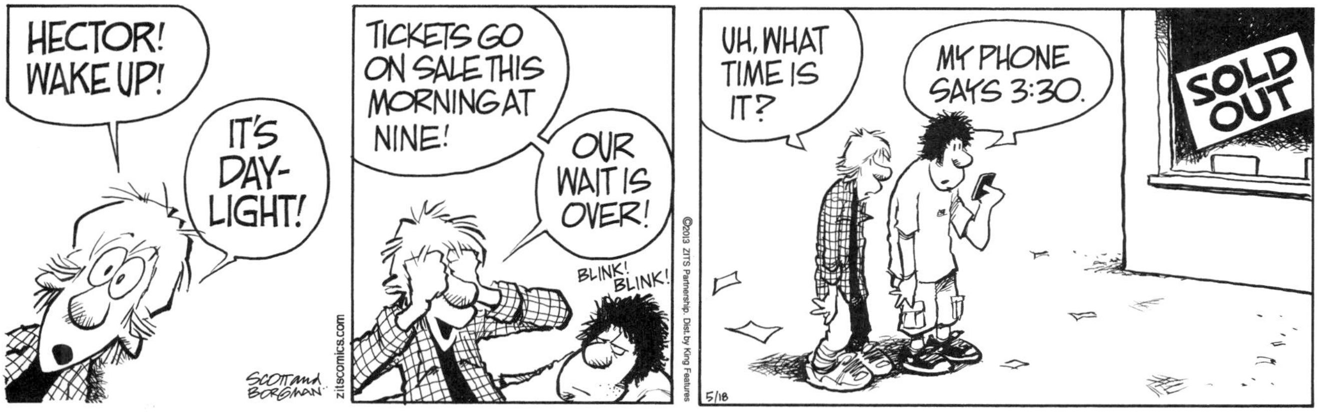
HECTOR! WAKE UP!
IT'S DAY-LIGHT!
SCOTT and BORGMAN
zitscomics.com
TICKETS GO ON SALE THIS MORNING AT NINE!
OUR WAIT IS OVER!
BLINK! BLINK!
©2013 ZITS Partnership. Dist. by King Features
5/18
UH, WHAT TIME IS IT?
MY PHONE SAYS 3:30.
SOLD OUT

April 7, 2013

YAWN!
THIS SIDE UP
GLAD I CHECKED.
JERRY SCOTT and JIM BORGMAN 4/7
zitscomics.com
©2013 ZITS Partnership. Dist. by King Features

June 16, 2013

MOBY GRAPE
FLAMING LIPS
ELECTRIC PRUNES
6/16
BLACK KEYS
zitscomics.com
LED ZEPPELIN
LED ZEPPELIN
©2013 ZITS Partnership. Dist. by King Features
SCOTT and BORGMAN
?

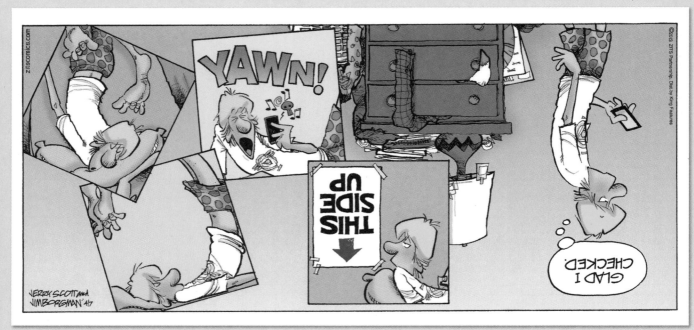

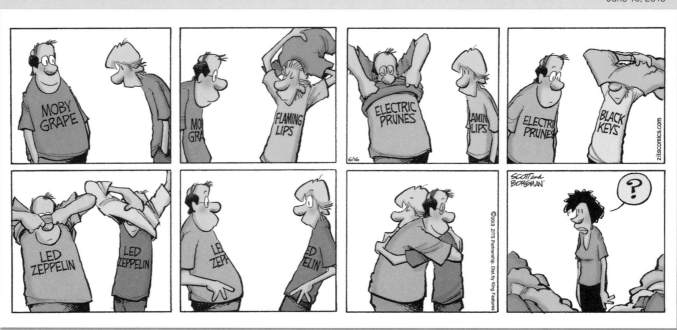

July 16, 2013

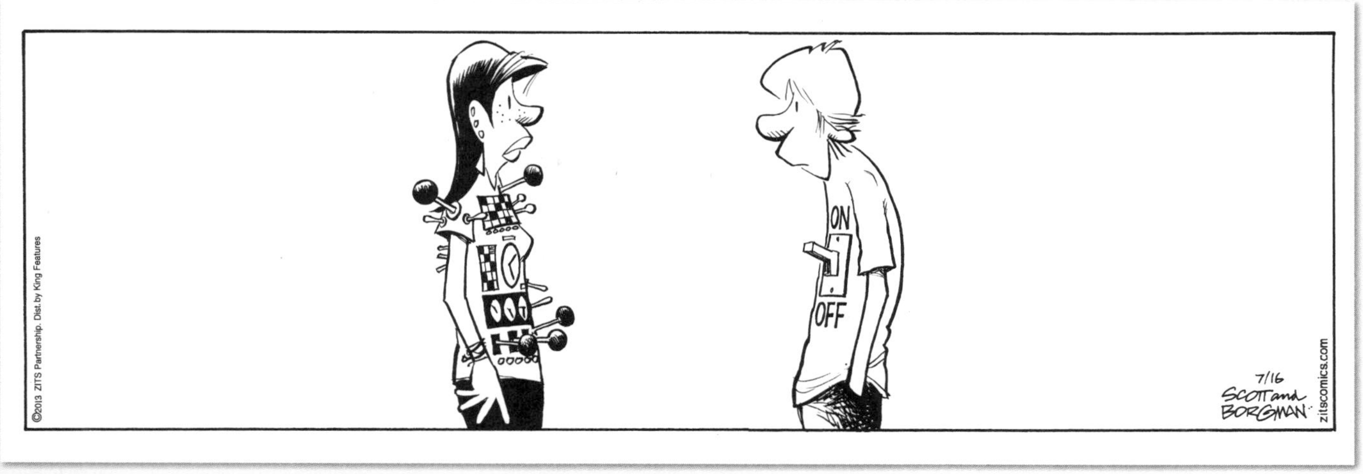
ON
OFF
7/16 SCOTT and BORGMAN
©2013 ZITS Partnership. Dist. by King Features
zitscomics.com

July 19, 2013

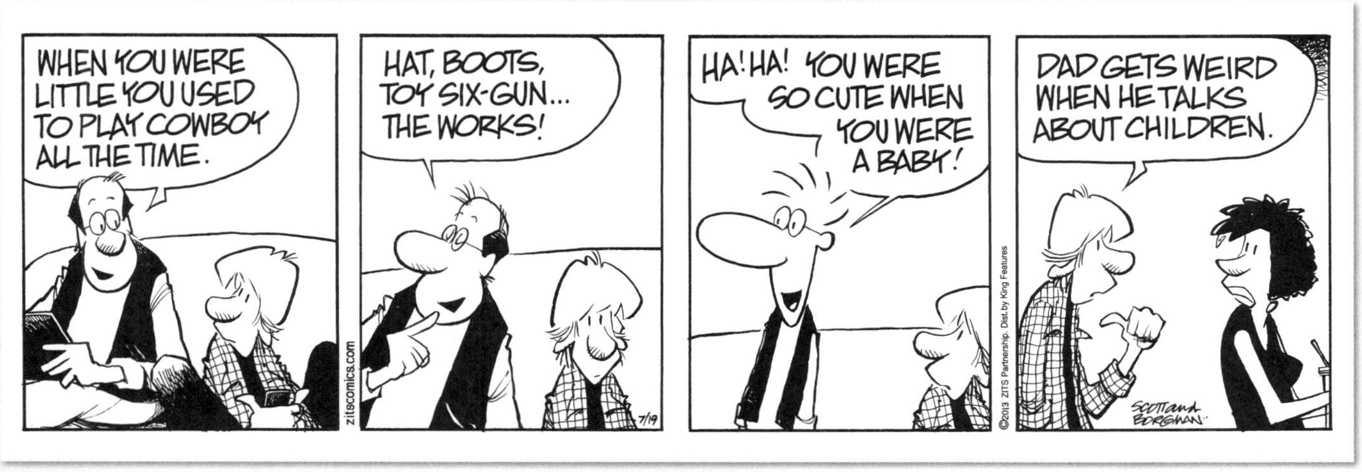
WHEN YOU WERE LITTLE YOU USED TO PLAY COWBOY ALL THE TIME.
HAT, BOOTS, TOY SIX-GUN... THE WORKS!
HA! HA! YOU WERE SO CUTE WHEN YOU WERE A BABY!
DAD GETS WEIRD WHEN HE TALKS ABOUT CHILDREN.
zitscomics.com
7/19
©2013 ZITS Partnership. Dist. by King Features
SCOTT and BORGMAN

August 9, 2013

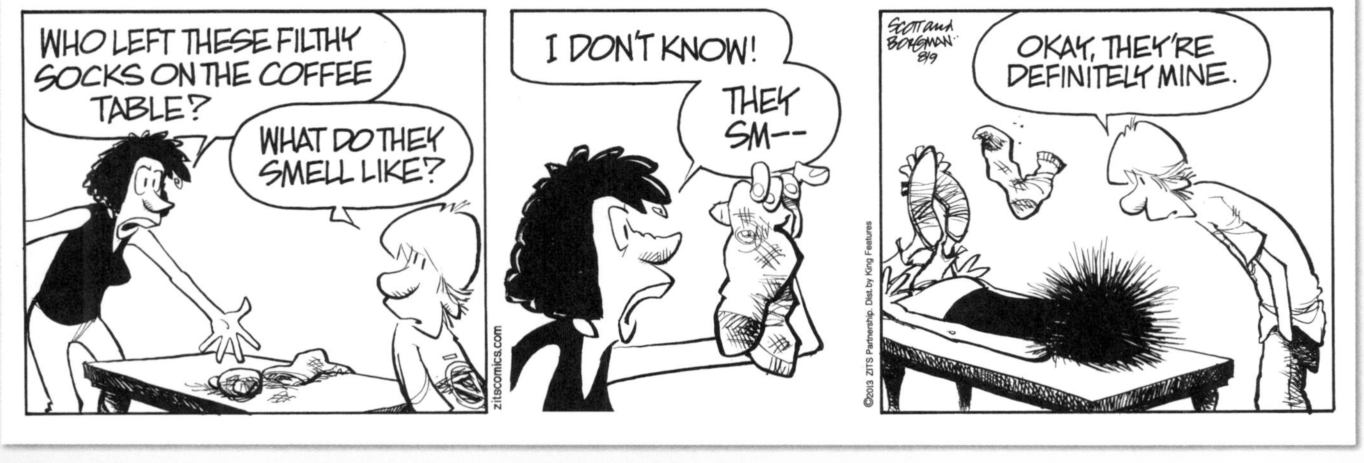
WHO LEFT THESE FILTHY SOCKS ON THE COFFEE TABLE?
WHAT DO THEY SMELL LIKE?
I DON'T KNOW!
THEY SM--
SCOTT and BORGMAN 8/9
OKAY, THEY'RE DEFINITELY MINE.
zitscomics.com
©2013 ZITS Partnership. Dist. by King Features

September 1, 2013

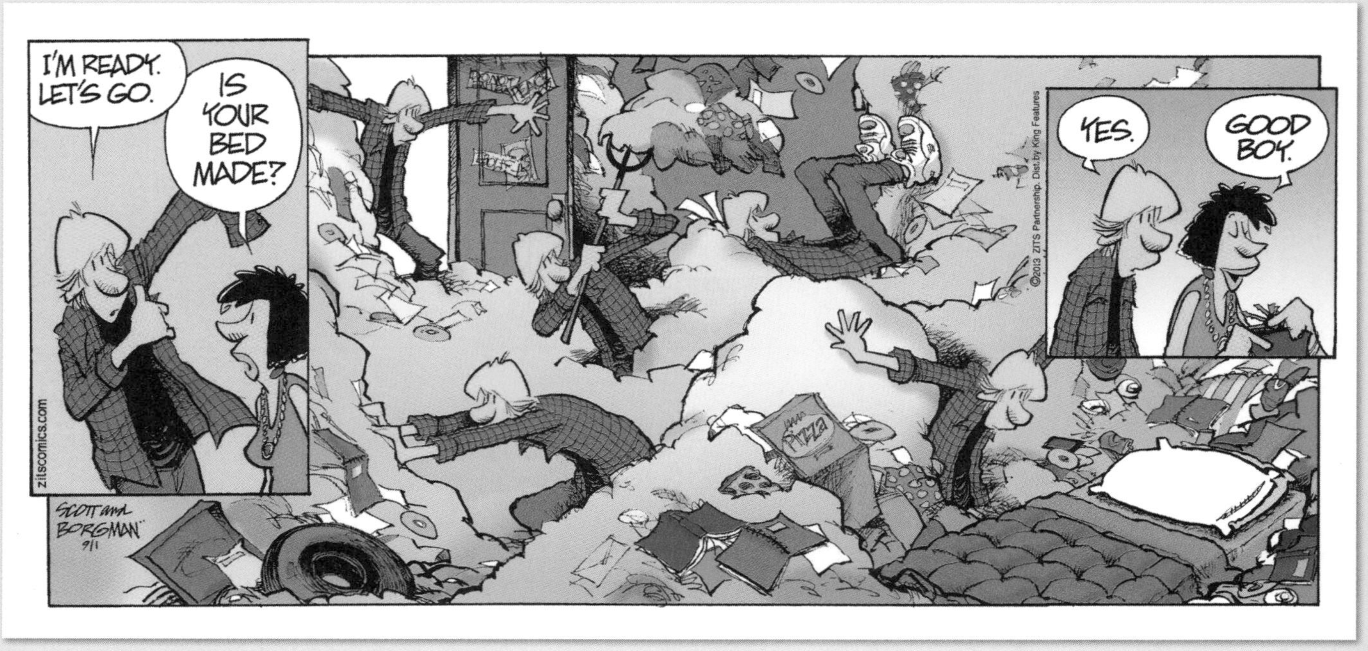
I'M READY. LET'S GO.
IS YOUR BED MADE?
YES.
GOOD BOY.
SCOTT AND BORGMAN 9/1
zitscomics.com
©2013 ZITS Partnership. Dist. by King Features
PIZZA

October 13, 2013

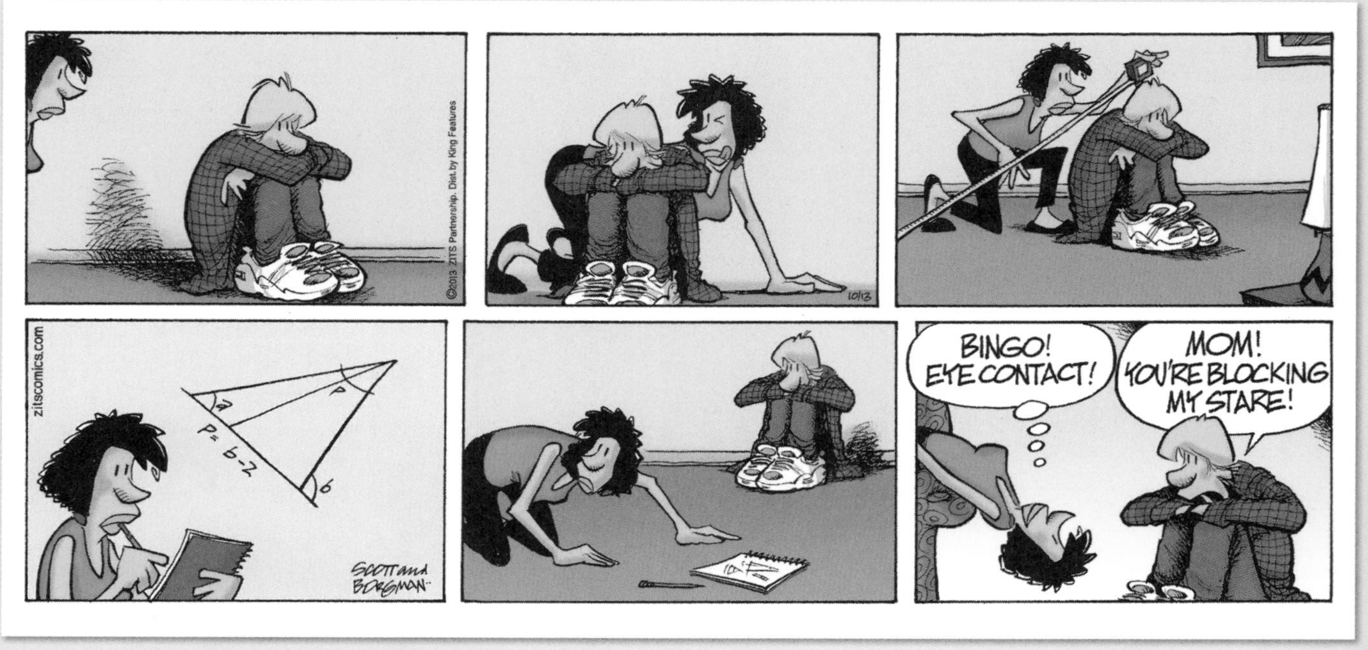
©2013 ZITS Partnership. Dist. by King Features
zitscomics.com
p = b-2
SCOTT AND BORGMAN
BINGO! EYE CONTACT!
MOM! YOU'RE BLOCKING MY STARE!

September 20, 2013

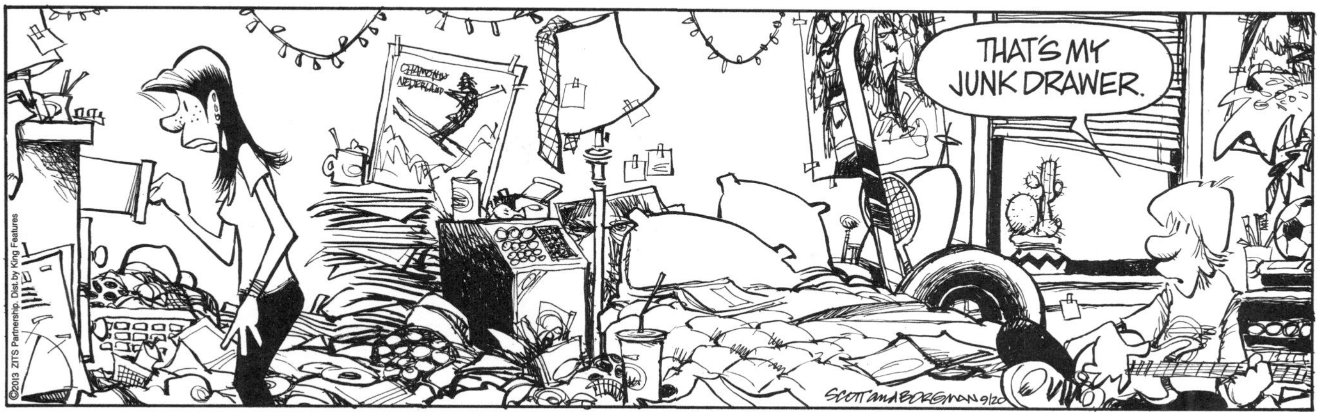
THAT'S MY JUNK DRAWER.
©2013 ZITS Partnership. Dist. by King Features
SCOTT and BORGMAN 9/20

October 19, 2013

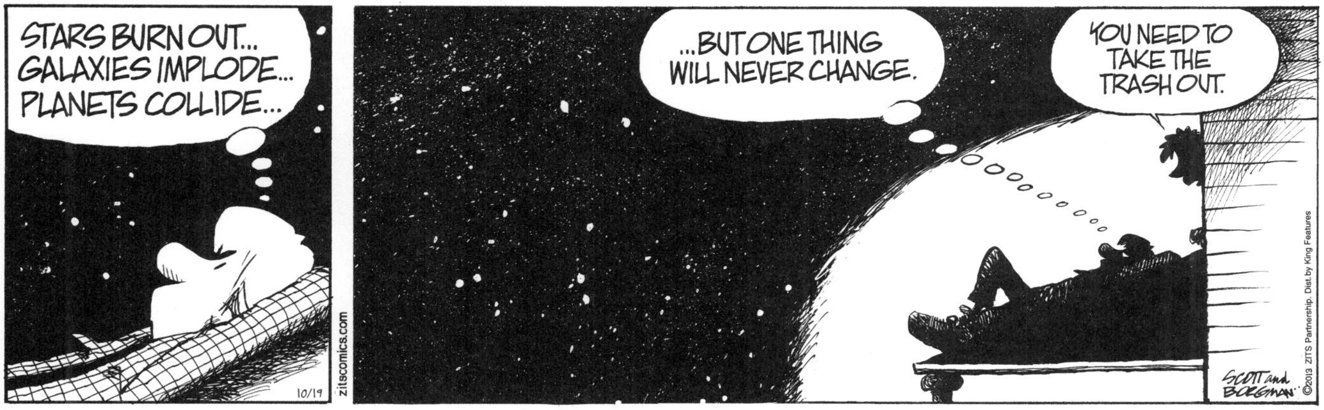
STARS BURN OUT... GALAXIES IMPLODE... PLANETS COLLIDE...
...BUT ONE THING WILL NEVER CHANGE.
YOU NEED TO TAKE THE TRASH OUT.
10/19
zitscomics.com
©2013 ZITS Partnership. Dist. by King Features
SCOTT and BORGMAN

November 12, 2013

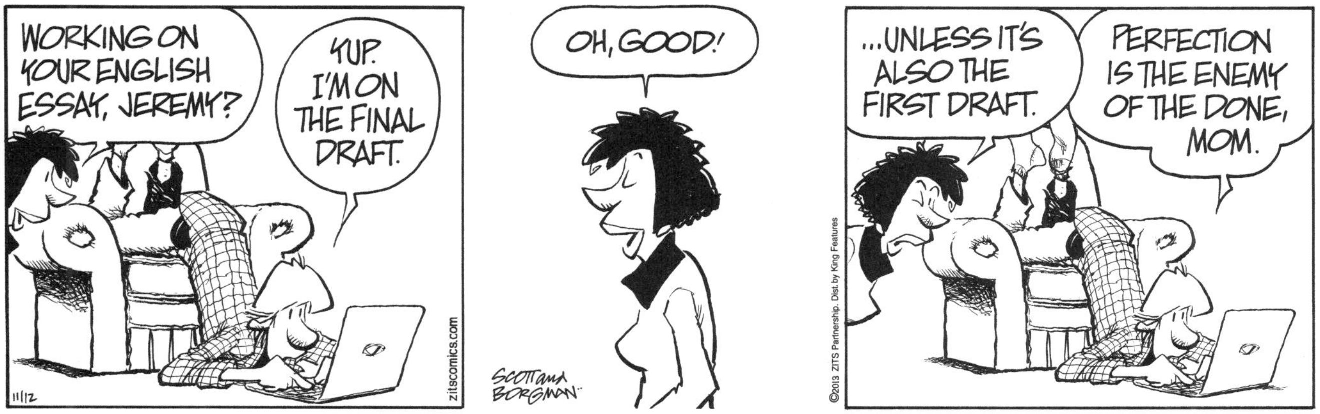
WORKING ON YOUR ENGLISH ESSAY, JEREMY?
YUP. I'M ON THE FINAL DRAFT.
OH, GOOD!
...UNLESS IT'S ALSO THE FIRST DRAFT.
PERFECTION IS THE ENEMY OF THE DONE, MOM.
11/12
zitscomics.com
SCOTT and BORGMAN
©2013 ZITS Partnership. Dist. by King Features

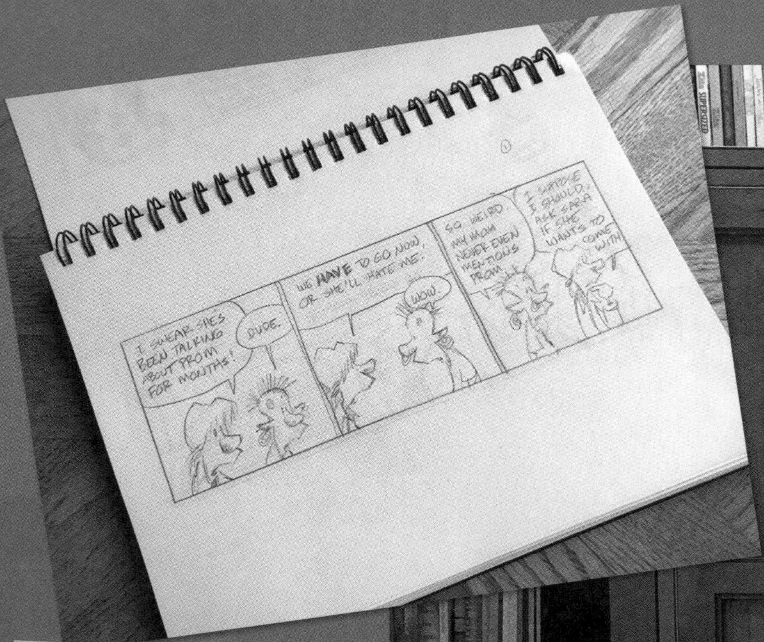
I SWEAR SHE'S BEEN TALKING ABOUT PROM FOR MONTHS!
DUDE.
WE HAVE TO GO NOW, OR SHE'LL HATE ME.
WOW.
SO WEIRD. MY MOM NEVER EVEN MENTIONS PROM.
I SUPPOSE I SHOULD ASK SARA IF SHE WANTS TO COME WITH.

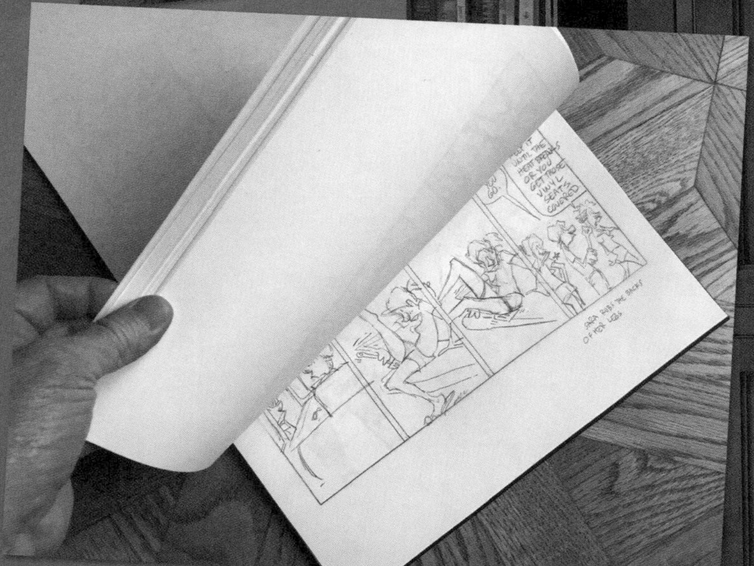

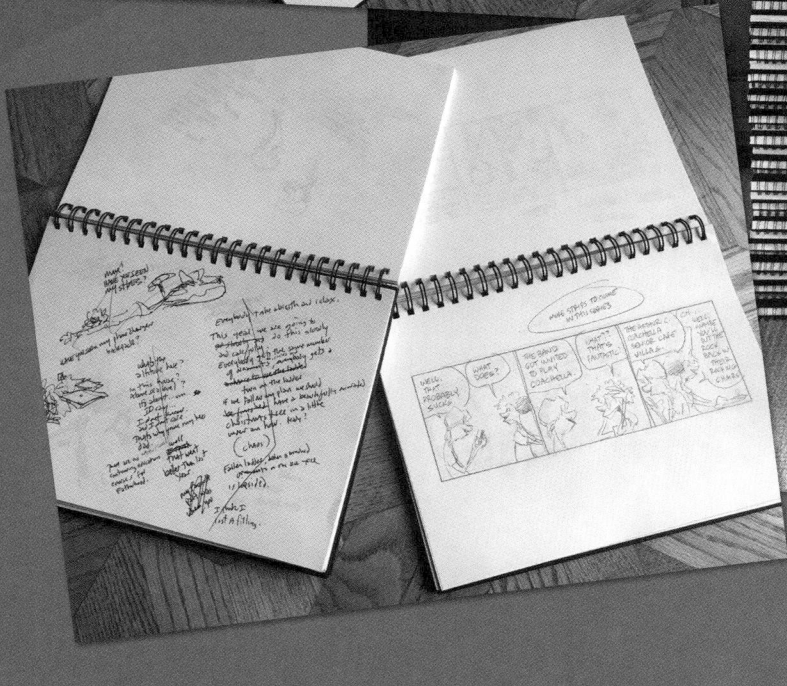

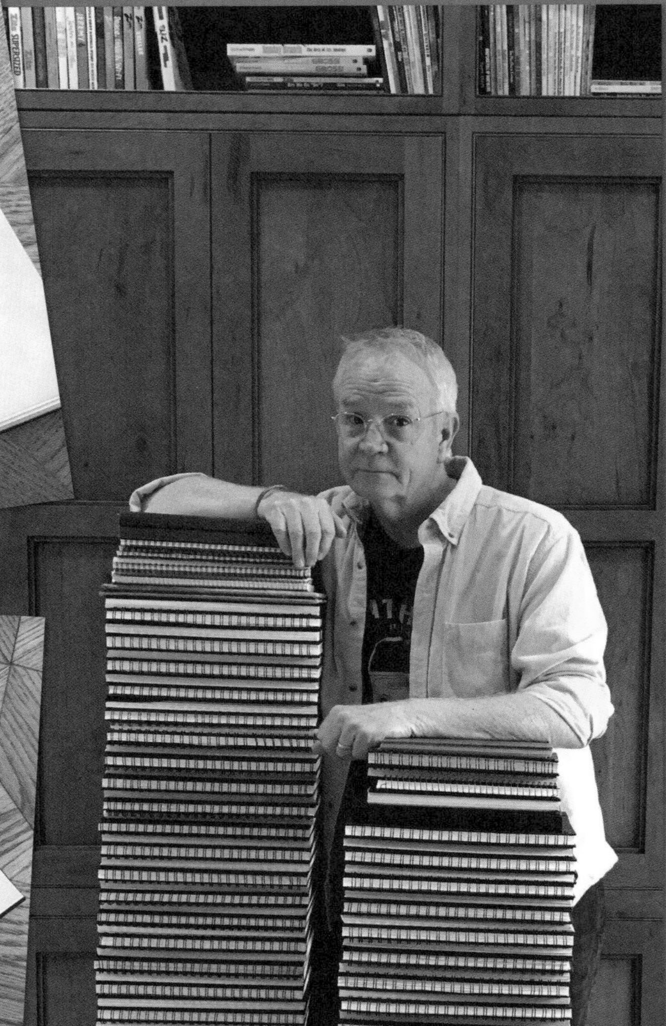

Twenty years of Jerry's sketchbooks, neatly stacked and organized for the first time. Ever.

da Vinciphobia

Jerry Scott and Jim Borgman

Leonardo da Vinci scared a lot of young artists away from carrying a sketchbook, myself included. Too much genius to the page—who can handle the pressure? In the Louvre, a da Vinci notebook is enclosed in a glass case, and one page is turned each day. People line up for hours to catch a glimpse. Bill Gates bought another one, the Codex Leicester, for $30.8 million.

I got over my fear of sketchbooks when my wife told me about a book she'd read called *The New Diary*. The book suggests using a journal or sketchbook loosely and creatively, filling it with dreams, to-do lists, phone messages, doodles, clippings, drawings, whatever. I never read the book, but I got the point. It was what I needed to cure my da Vinciphobia.

I probably have thirty or forty filled sketchbooks piled up here and there, and I flip through them sometimes as a way of prompting new ideas or odd connections. Their randomness is their beauty. My sketchbooks contain a million seeds of ideas. In the dark, the ideas grow at different rates, but I almost always find something worth harvesting when I go looking.

Likewise, a lot of the drawing in *Zits* begins in my sketchbooks when I'm just killing time. My advice to kids who want to be cartoonists is to always carry a sketchbook and draw what's in front of you, even if it's just the backs of people's heads on the school bus ride home. Most stuff in sketchbooks isn't profound, but it's where your hand does its calisthenics. When I was a young cartoonist trying to find my authentic voice, it was by looking through my sketchbooks that I found how I drew when I wasn't concerned with others seeing it. My sketchbooks were a clue to how I naturally expressed myself.

I still try to bring a sketchbook with me when I go to performances. Sometimes drawing what's in front of me keeps me engaged when my mind wanders. Other times, I like letting my mind wander and recording some of the connections that come to me.

Mostly, a sketchbook is a way of keeping a lot of good thoughts from evaporating into thin air. When I look through my old sketchbooks, I usually have no memory of having had these thoughts, as if they were someone else's entirely. Some make me laugh, like a joke I'm hearing for the first time. Sometimes I suddenly realize the small new element that would make an idea work, as if a blacksmith in the back of my brain has been hammering away at the problem all this time. Sometimes the sketches are like gifts from my former self to my current self, saved for a rainy day. There's all kinds of stuff in there.

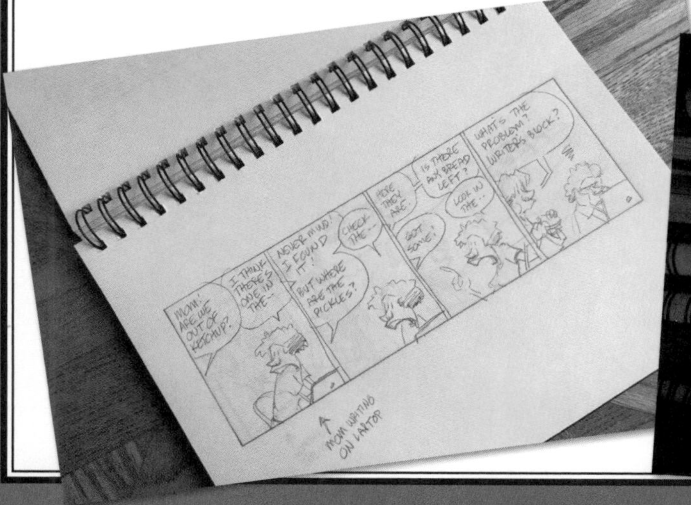

MOM! ARE WE OUT OF KETCHUP?
I THINK THERE'S ONE IN THE--
NEVER MIND! I FOUND IT!
BUT WHERE ARE THE PICKLES?
CHECK THE--
HERE THEY ARE.
IS THERE ANY BREAD LEFT?
LOOK IN THE--
GOT SOME!
WHAT'S THE PROBLEM? WRITER'S BLOCK?
MOM WRITING ON LAPTOP

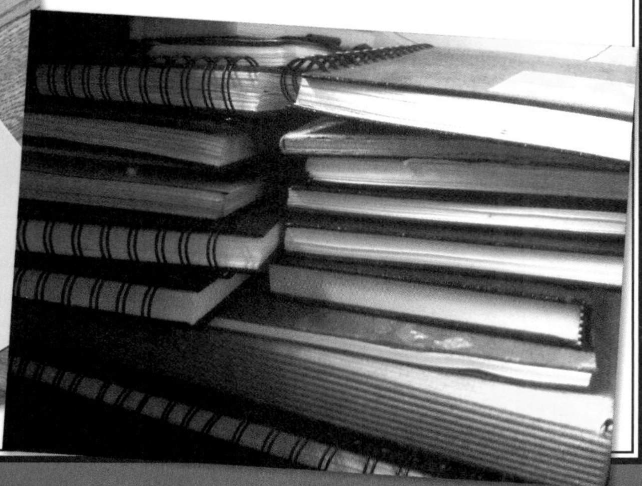

January 30, 2014

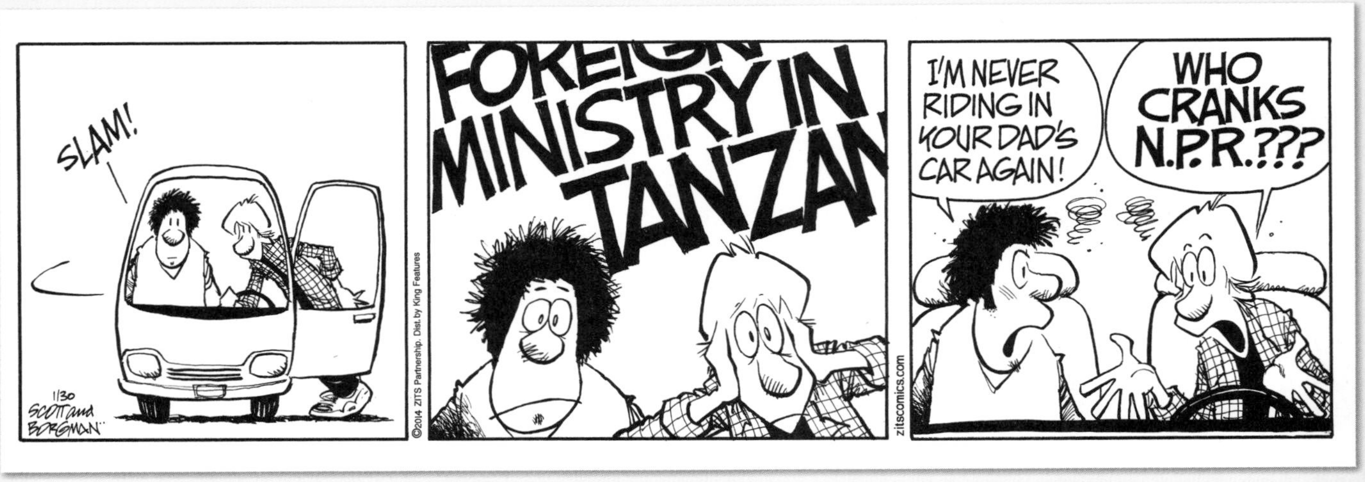
SLAM!
1/30 SCOTT and BORGMAN
©2014 ZITS Partnership. Dist. by King Features
FOREIGN MINISTRY IN TANZAN
zitscomics.com
I'M NEVER RIDING IN YOUR DAD'S CAR AGAIN!
WHO CRANKS N.P.R.???

March 5, 2014

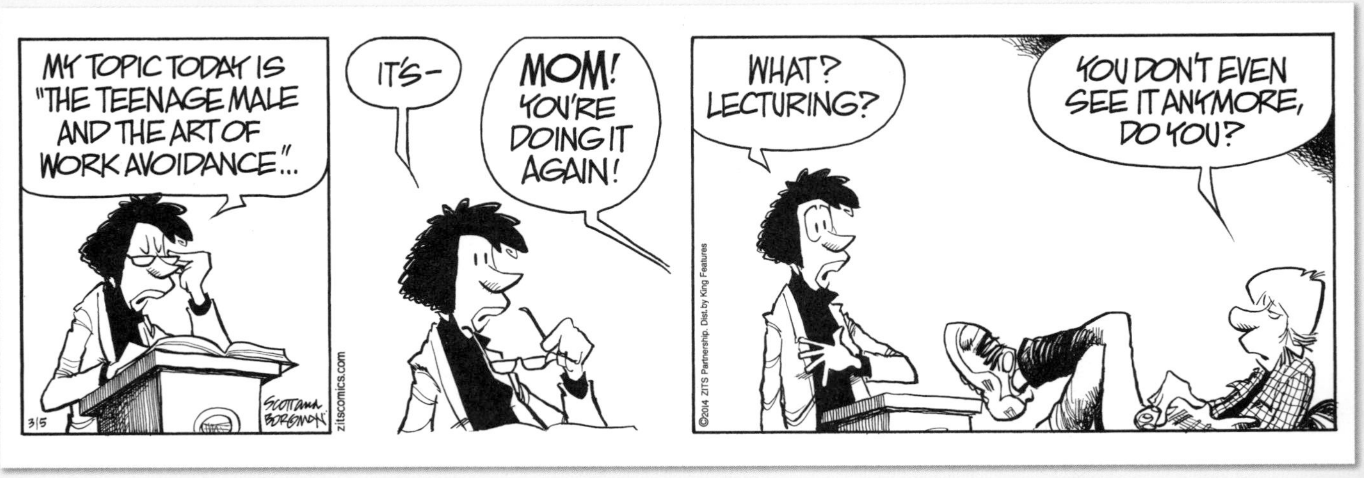
MY TOPIC TODAY IS "THE TEENAGE MALE AND THE ART OF WORK AVOIDANCE"...
3/5 SCOTT and BORGMAN
zitscomics.com
IT'S-
MOM! YOU'RE DOING IT AGAIN!
©2014 ZITS Partnership. Dist. by King Features
WHAT? LECTURING?
YOU DON'T EVEN SEE IT ANYMORE, DO YOU?

March 19, 2014

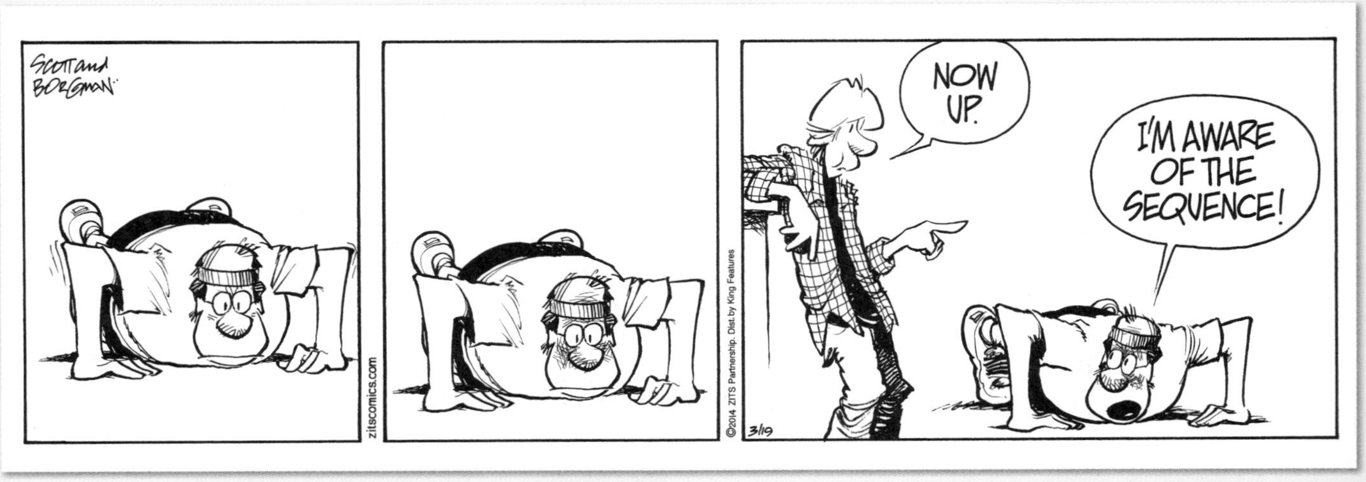
SCOTT and BORGMAN
zitscomics.com
©2014 ZITS Partnership. Dist. by King Features
3/19
NOW UP.
I'M AWARE OF THE SEQUENCE!

April 10, 2014

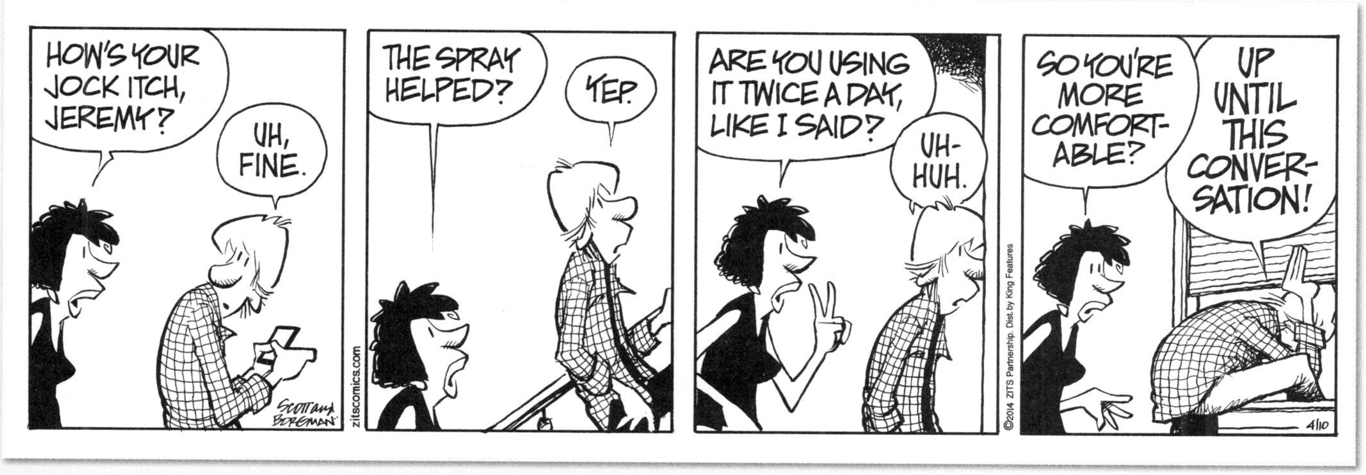
HOW'S YOUR JOCK ITCH, JEREMY?
UH, FINE.
SCOTT and BORGMAN
zitscomics.com
THE SPRAY HELPED?
YEP.
ARE YOU USING IT TWICE A DAY, LIKE I SAID?
UH-HUH.
©2014 ZITS Partnership. Dist. by King Features
SO YOU'RE MORE COMFORTABLE?
UP UNTIL THIS CONVERSATION!
4/10

April 30, 2014

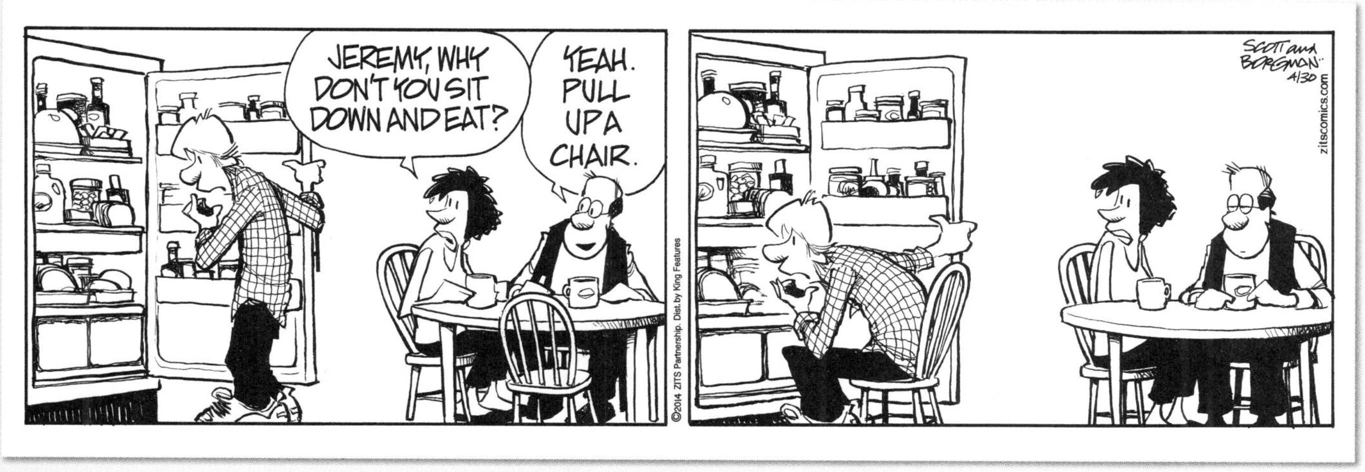
JEREMY, WHY DON'T YOU SIT DOWN AND EAT?
YEAH. PULL UP A CHAIR.
©2014 ZITS Partnership. Dist. by King Features
SCOTT and BORGMAN 4/30
zitscomics.com

May 16, 2014

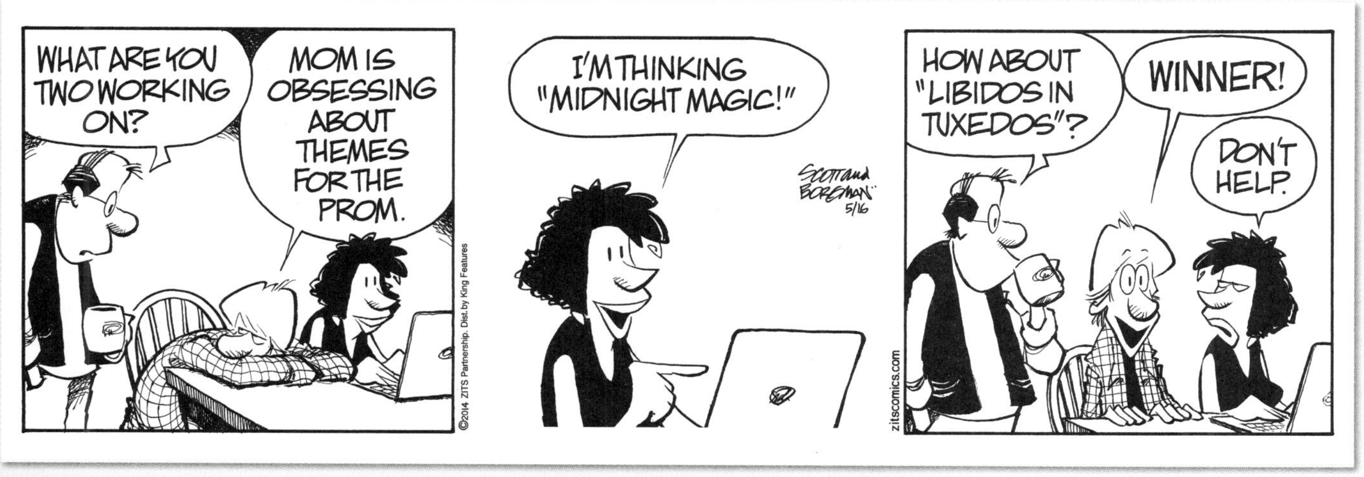
WHAT ARE YOU TWO WORKING ON?
MOM IS OBSESSING ABOUT THEMES FOR THE PROM.
©2014 ZITS Partnership. Dist. by King Features
I'M THINKING "MIDNIGHT MAGIC!"
SCOTT and BORGMAN 5/16
zitscomics.com
HOW ABOUT "LIBIDOS IN TUXEDOS"?
WINNER!
DON'T HELP.

April 13, 2014

JEREMY, SOMETHING IS BOTHERING YOU, I CAN TELL.
YEAH.
DO YOU WANT TO TALK ABOUT IT?
THAT WON'T HELP.
BUT YOU LOOK LIKE YOU'RE IN PAIN!
YEAH. IT'S PRETTY BAD.
OH, HONEY!
IS IT GRADES? GIRLS? PLEASE TELL ME WHAT IT IS!
I THINK I'M LYING ON MY KEYS.
zitscomics.com
©2014 ZITS Partnership. Dist. by King Features
SCOTT AND BORGMAN

April 20, 2014

7:59 AM
7:58 AM
PUNCTUAL AS USUAL.
IGNORING THE SPACE/TIME CONTINUUM HELPED.
zitscomics.com
©2014 ZITS Partnership. Dist. by King Features
SCOTT AND BORGMAN

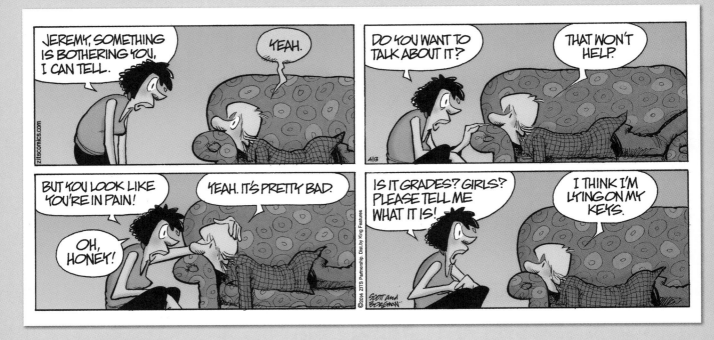

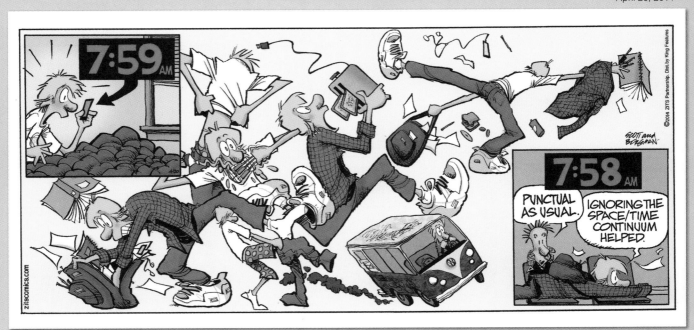

May 20, 2014

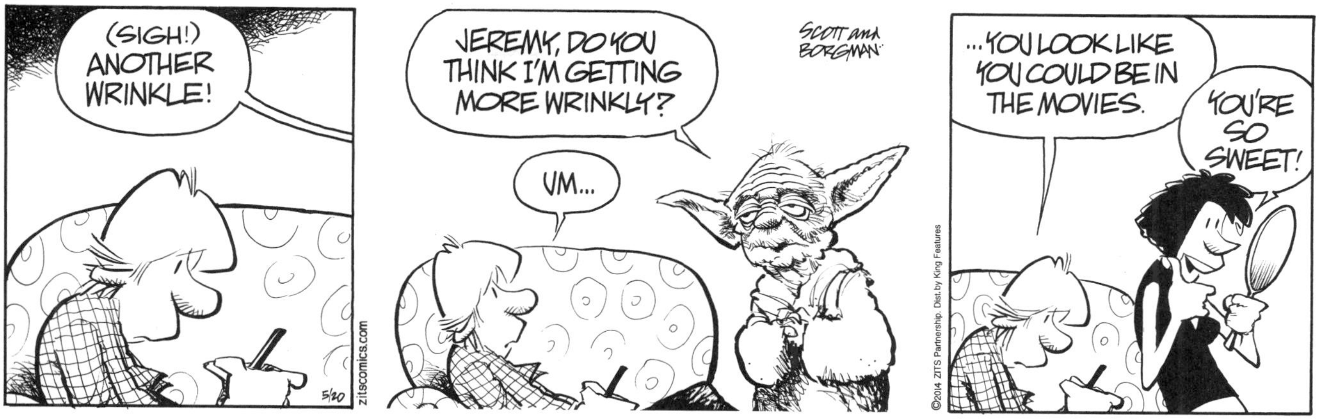
(SIGH!) ANOTHER WRINKLE!
5/20
zitscomics.com
JEREMY, DO YOU THINK I'M GETTING MORE WRINKLY?
UM...
SCOTT AND BORGMAN
...YOU LOOK LIKE YOU COULD BE IN THE MOVIES.
YOU'RE SO SWEET!
©2014 ZITS Partnership. Dist. by King Features

May 28, 2014

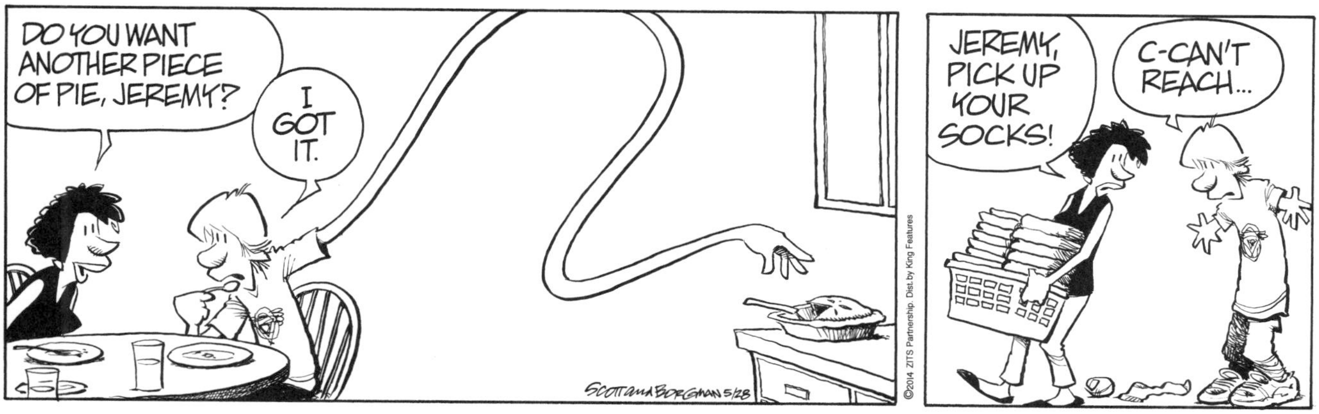
DO YOU WANT ANOTHER PIECE OF PIE, JEREMY?
I GOT IT.
SCOTT AND BORGMAN 5/28
JEREMY, PICK UP YOUR SOCKS!
C-CAN'T REACH...
©2014 ZITS Partnership. Dist. by King Features

May 31, 2014

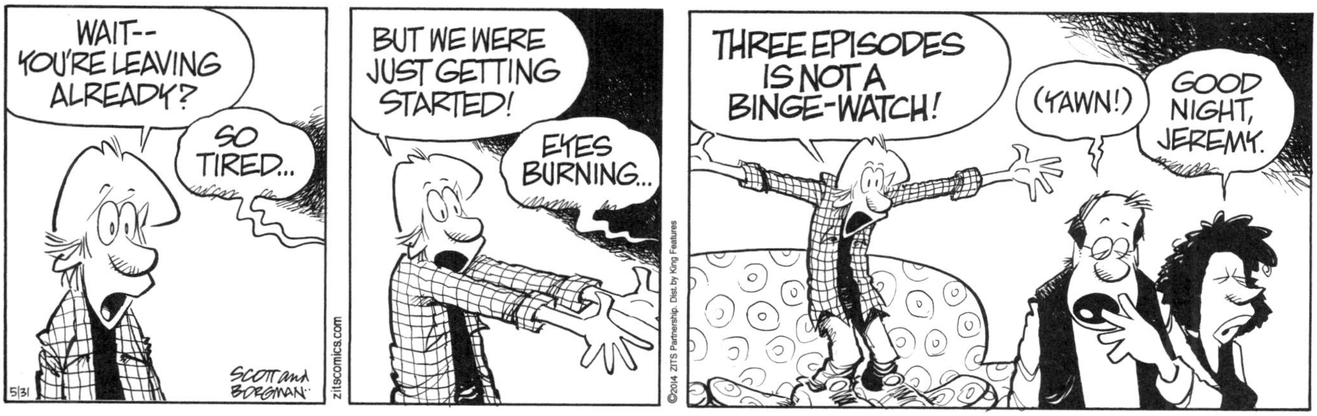
WAIT-- YOU'RE LEAVING ALREADY?
SO TIRED...
5/31
SCOTT AND BORGMAN
zitscomics.com
BUT WE WERE JUST GETTING STARTED!
EYES BURNING...
©2014 ZITS Partnership. Dist. by King Features
THREE EPISODES IS NOT A BINGE-WATCH!
(YAWN!)
GOOD NIGHT, JEREMY.

July 6, 2014

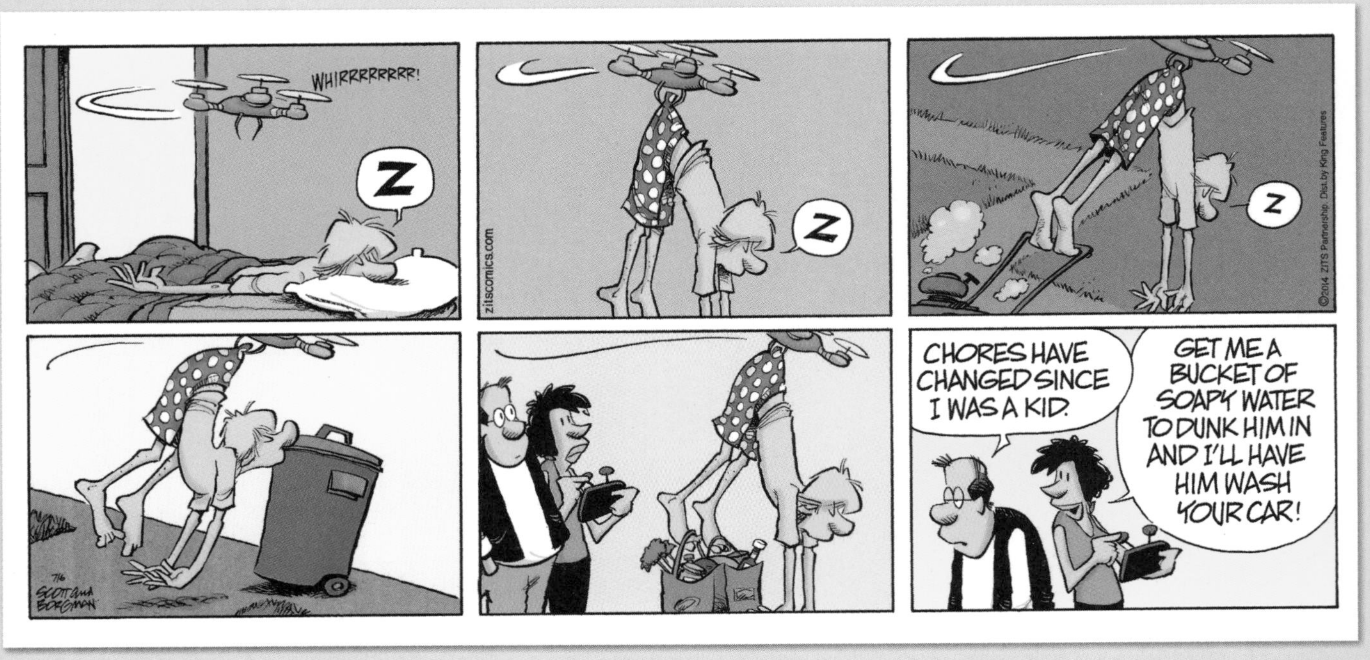
WHIRRRRRRRR!
Z
zitscomics.com
Z
©2014 ZITS Partnership. Dist. by King Features
Z
CHORES HAVE CHANGED SINCE I WAS A KID.
GET ME A BUCKET OF SOAPY WATER TO DUNK HIM IN AND I'LL HAVE HIM WASH YOUR CAR!

August 10, 2014

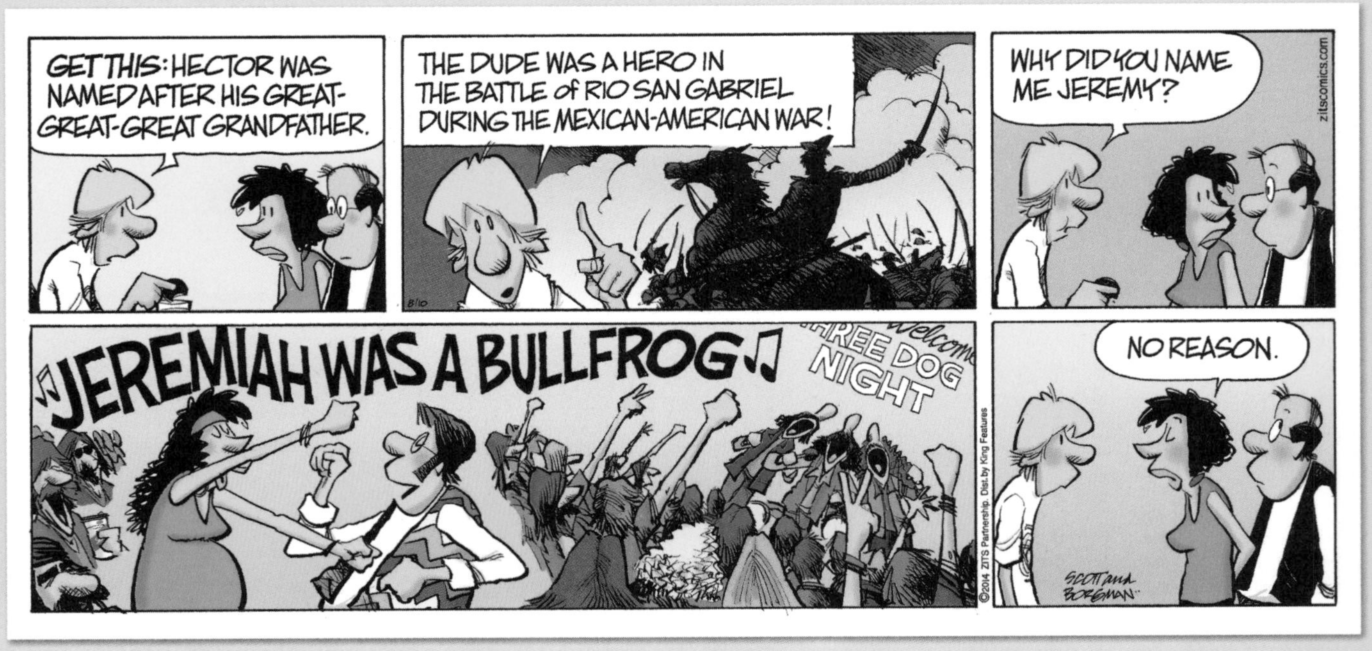
GET THIS: HECTOR WAS NAMED AFTER HIS GREAT-GREAT-GREAT GRANDFATHER.
THE DUDE WAS A HERO IN THE BATTLE of RIO SAN GABRIEL DURING THE MEXICAN-AMERICAN WAR!
WHY DID YOU NAME ME JEREMY?
zitscomics.com
JEREMIAH WAS A BULLFROG
THREE DOG NIGHT
©2014 ZITS Partnership. Dist. by King Features
NO REASON.

August 11, 2014

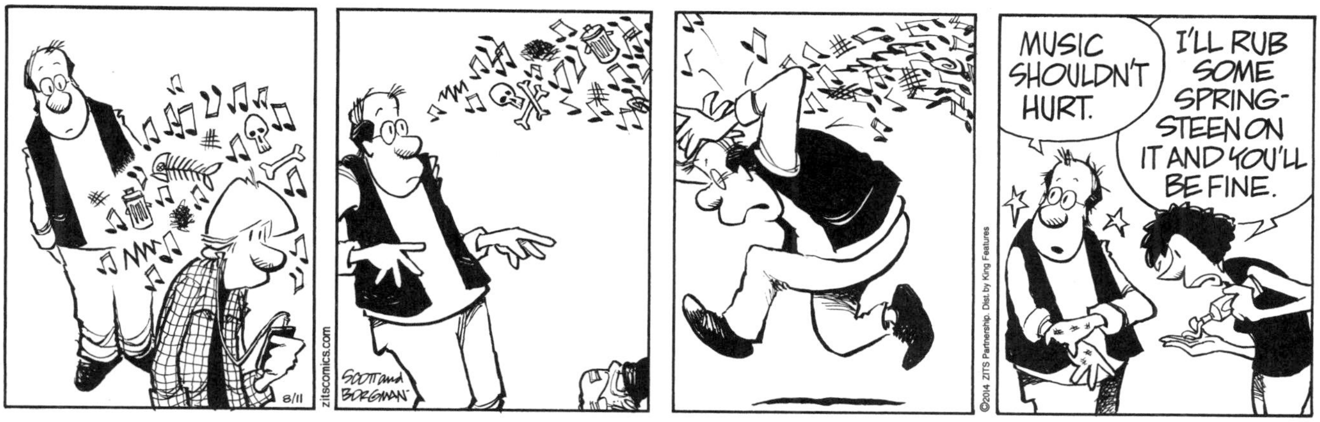
zitscomics.com
8/11
SCOTT and BORGMAN
MUSIC SHOULDN'T HURT.
I'LL RUB SOME SPRING-STEEN ON IT AND YOU'LL BE FINE.
©2014 ZITS Partnership. Dist. by King Features

August 19, 2014

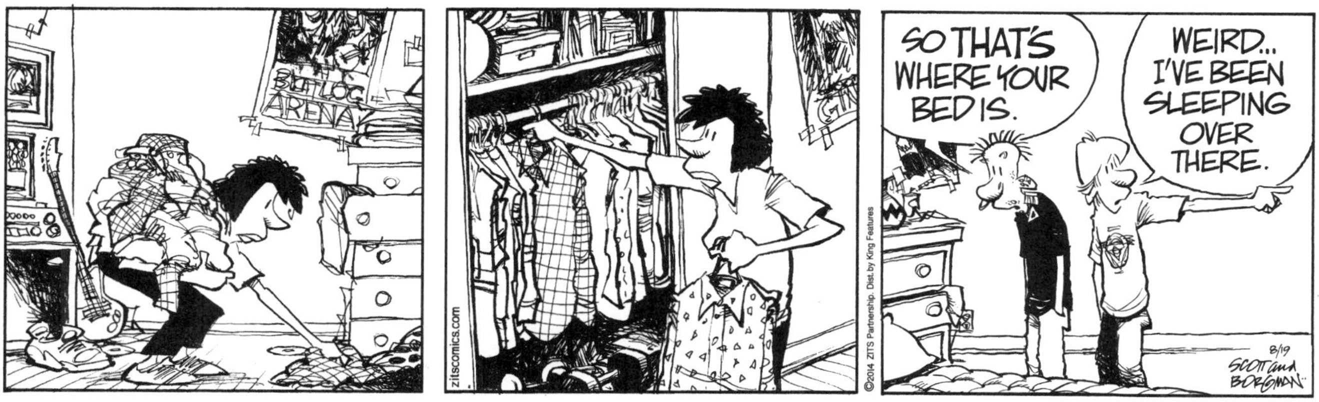
zitscomics.com
©2014 ZITS Partnership. Dist. by King Features
SO THAT'S WHERE YOUR BED IS.
WEIRD... I'VE BEEN SLEEPING OVER THERE.
8/19
SCOTT and BORGMAN

September 4, 2014

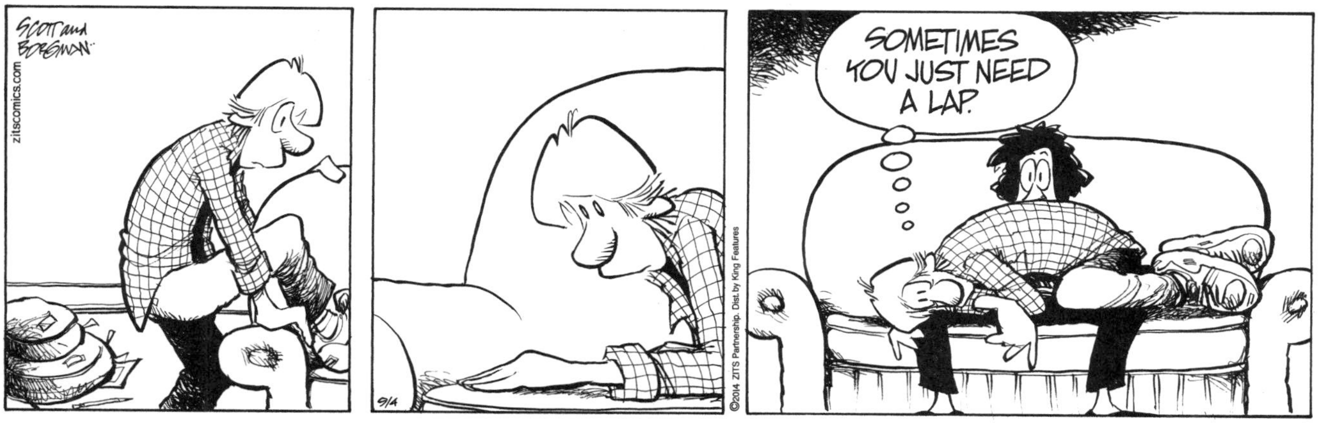
SCOTT and BORGMAN
zitscomics.com
9/4
©2014 ZITS Partnership. Dist. by King Features
SOMETIMES YOU JUST NEED A LAP.

September 15, 2014

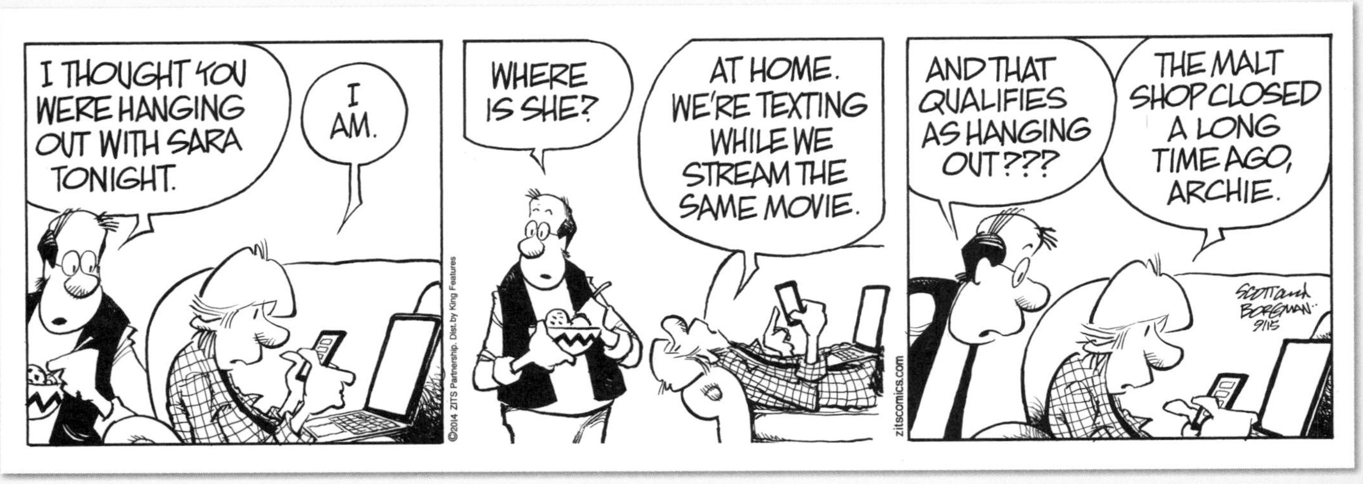
I THOUGHT YOU WERE HANGING OUT WITH SARA TONIGHT.
I AM.
WHERE IS SHE?
AT HOME. WE'RE TEXTING WHILE WE STREAM THE SAME MOVIE.
AND THAT QUALIFIES AS HANGING OUT???
THE MALT SHOP CLOSED A LONG TIME AGO, ARCHIE.
SCOTT and BORGMAN 9/15
©2014 ZITS Partnership. Dist. by King Features
zitscomics.com

September 17, 2014

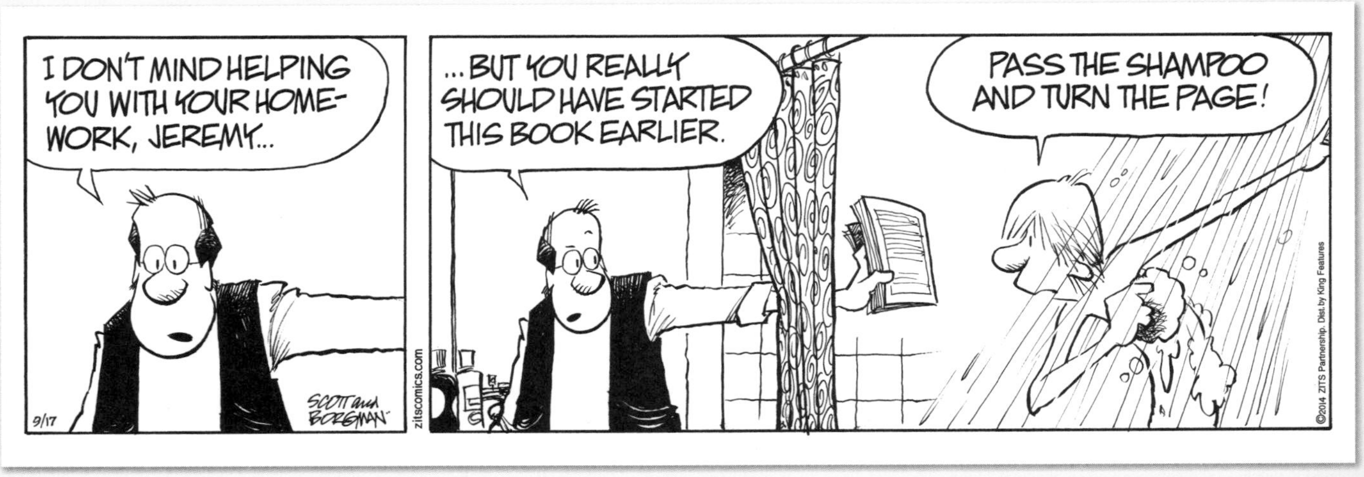
I DON'T MIND HELPING YOU WITH YOUR HOMEWORK, JEREMY...
...BUT YOU REALLY SHOULD HAVE STARTED THIS BOOK EARLIER.
PASS THE SHAMPOO AND TURN THE PAGE!
9/17
SCOTT and BORGMAN
zitscomics.com
©2014 ZITS Partnership. Dist. by King Features

October 20, 2014

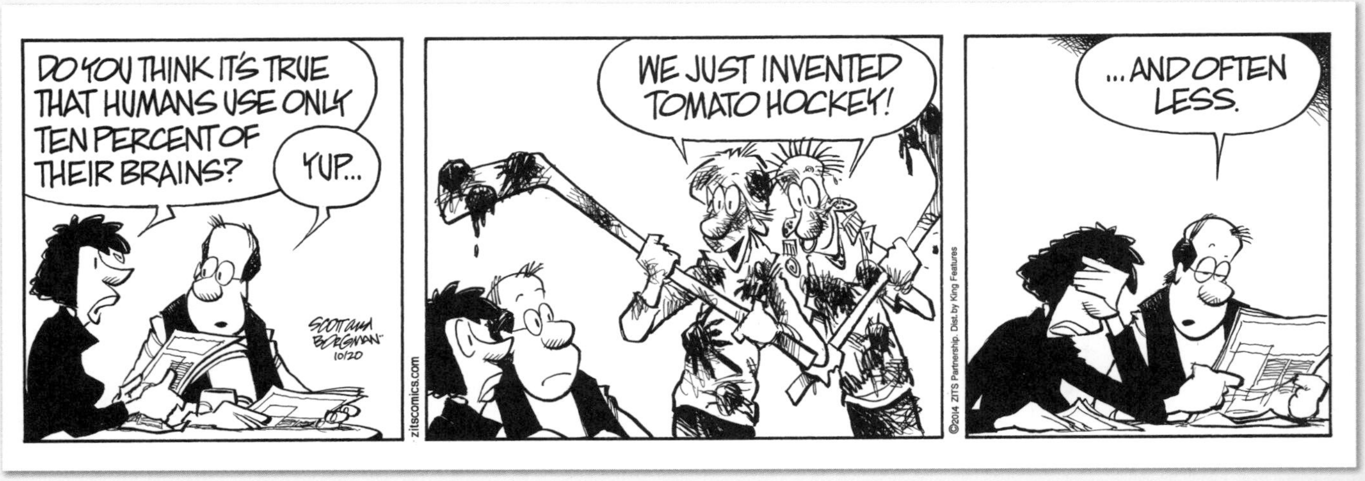
DO YOU THINK IT'S TRUE THAT HUMANS USE ONLY TEN PERCENT OF THEIR BRAINS?
YUP...
WE JUST INVENTED TOMATO HOCKEY!
...AND OFTEN LESS.
SCOTT and BORGMAN 10/20
zitscomics.com
©2014 ZITS Partnership. Dist. by King Features

November 11, 2014

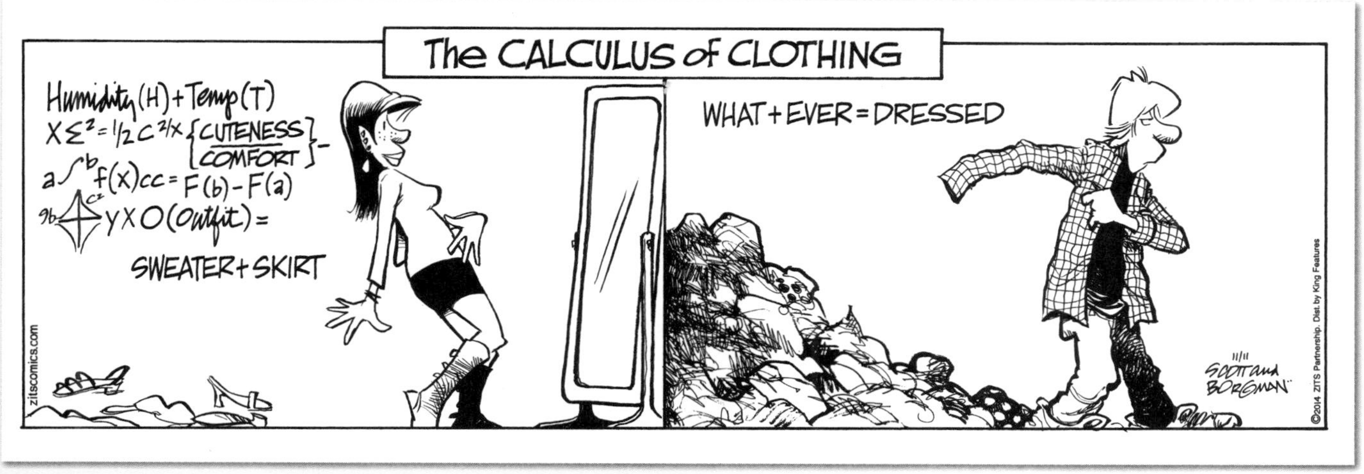
The CALCULUS of CLOTHING
Humidity (H) + Temp (T)
X Σ² = 1/2 C ²/x {CUTENESS / COMFORT} −
a∫b f(x)cc = F(b) − F(a)
YXO (Outfit) =
SWEATER + SKIRT
WHAT + EVER = DRESSED
SCOTT and BORGMAN
zitscomics.com
©2014 ZITS Partnership. Dist. by King Features

November 24, 2014

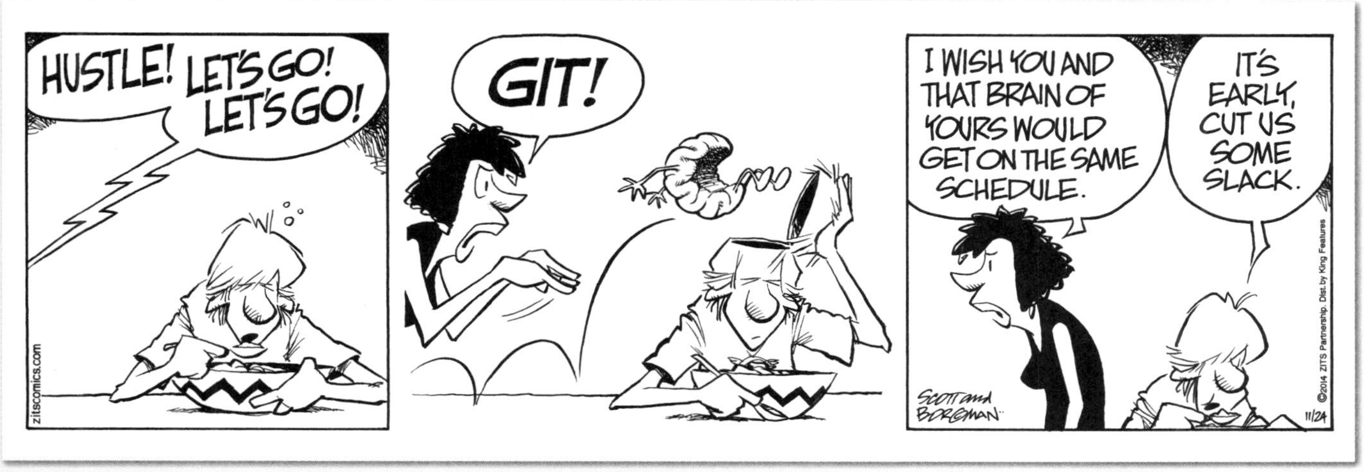
HUSTLE!
LET'S GO! LET'S GO!
GIT!
I WISH YOU AND THAT BRAIN OF YOURS WOULD GET ON THE SAME SCHEDULE.
IT'S EARLY, CUT US SOME SLACK.
SCOTT and BORGMAN
zitscomics.com
©2014 ZITS Partnership. Dist. by King Features

December 26, 2014

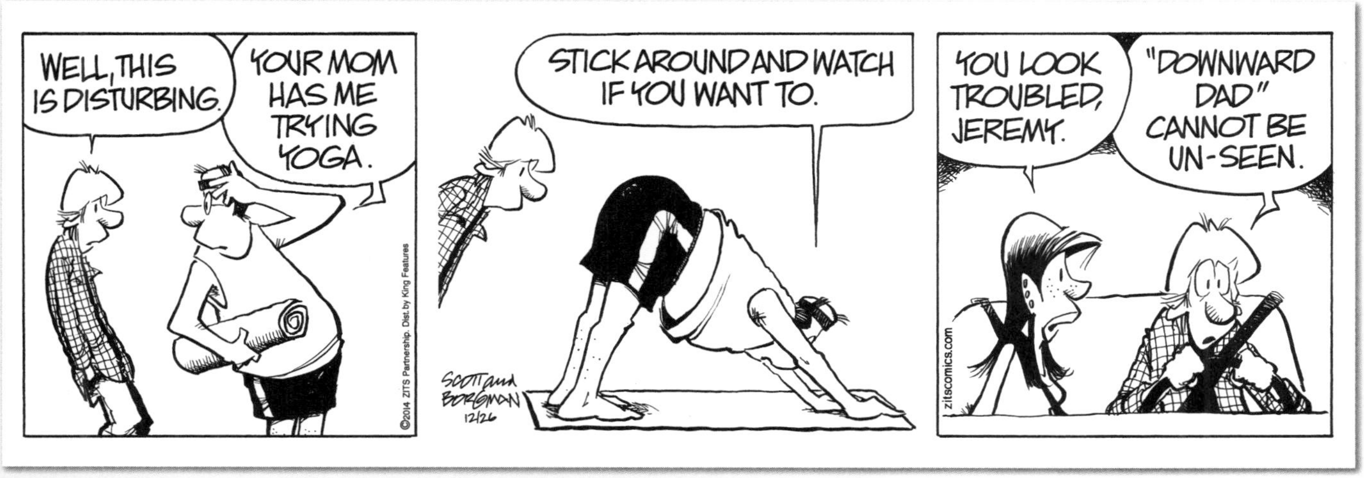
WELL, THIS IS DISTURBING.
YOUR MOM HAS ME TRYING YOGA.
STICK AROUND AND WATCH IF YOU WANT TO.
YOU LOOK TROUBLED, JEREMY.
"DOWNWARD DAD" CANNOT BE UN-SEEN.
SCOTT and BORGMAN
zitscomics.com
©2014 ZITS Partnership. Dist. by King Features

December 4, 2014

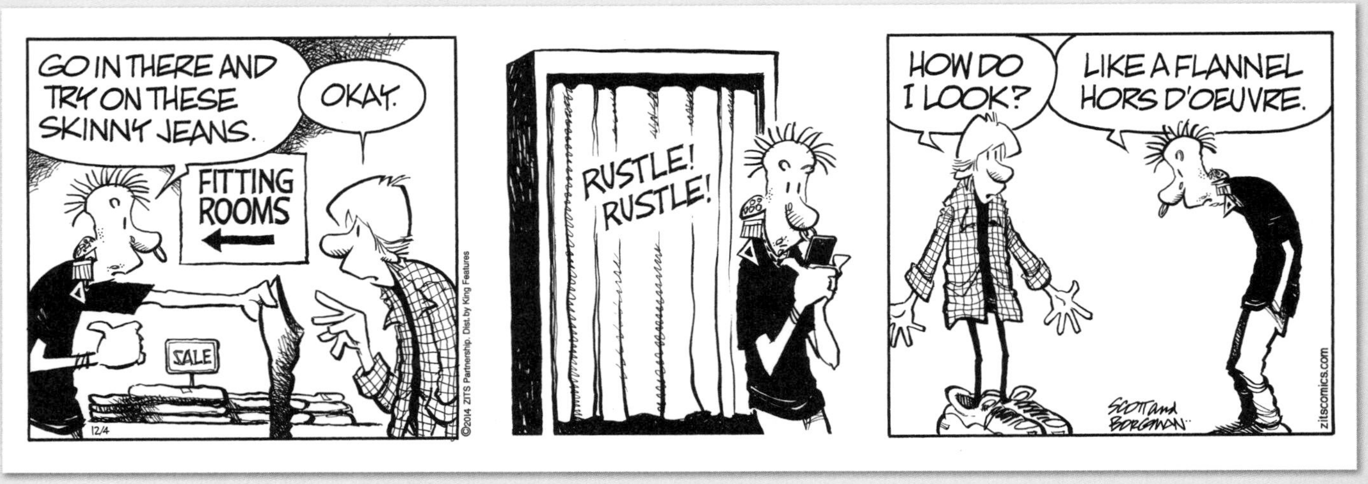
GO IN THERE AND TRY ON THESE SKINNY JEANS.
OKAY.
FITTING ROOMS
SALE
12/4
©2014 ZITS Partnership. Dist. by King Features
RUSTLE! RUSTLE!
HOW DO I LOOK?
LIKE A FLANNEL HORS D'OEUVRE.
SCOTT and BORGMAN
zitscomics.com

December 6, 2014

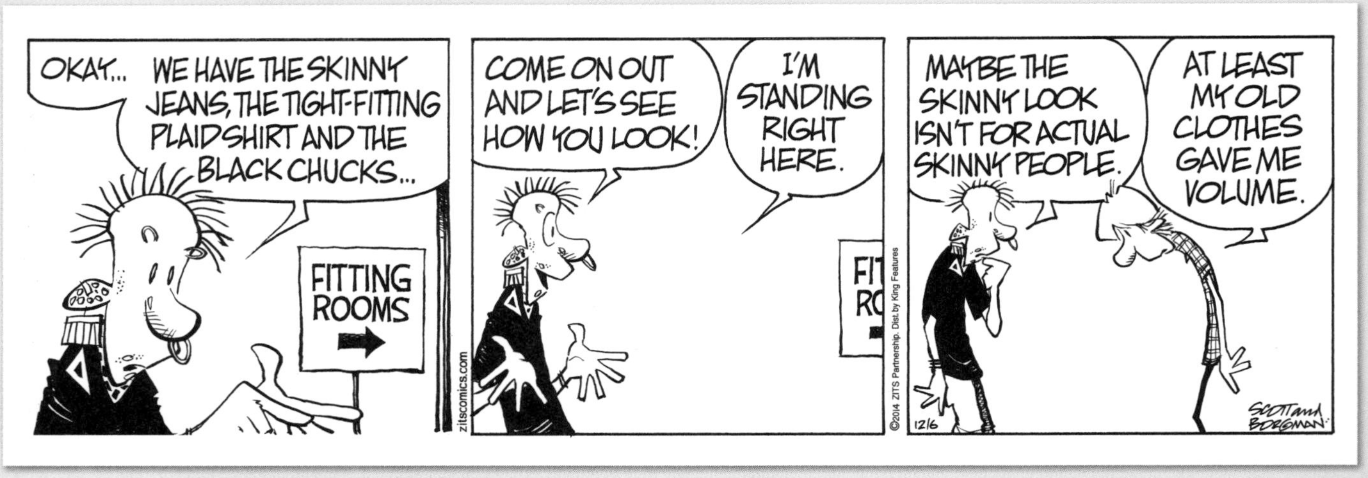
OKAY... WE HAVE THE SKINNY JEANS, THE TIGHT-FITTING PLAID SHIRT AND THE BLACK CHUCKS...
FITTING ROOMS
zitscomics.com
COME ON OUT AND LET'S SEE HOW YOU LOOK!
I'M STANDING RIGHT HERE.
©2014 ZITS Partnership. Dist. by King Features
12/6
MAYBE THE SKINNY LOOK ISN'T FOR ACTUAL SKINNY PEOPLE.
AT LEAST MY OLD CLOTHES GAVE ME VOLUME.
SCOTT and BORGMAN

December 11, 2014

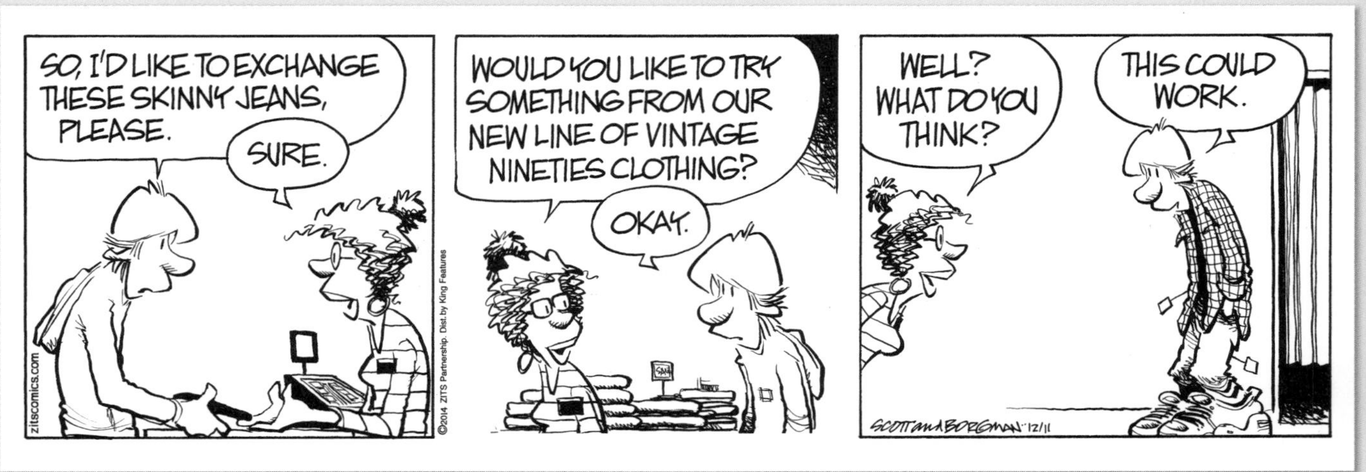
SO, I'D LIKE TO EXCHANGE THESE SKINNY JEANS, PLEASE.
SURE.
zitscomics.com
©2014 ZITS Partnership. Dist. by King Features
WOULD YOU LIKE TO TRY SOMETHING FROM OUR NEW LINE OF VINTAGE NINETIES CLOTHING?
OKAY.
WELL? WHAT DO YOU THINK?
THIS COULD WORK.
SCOTT and BORGMAN 12/11

February 9, 2014

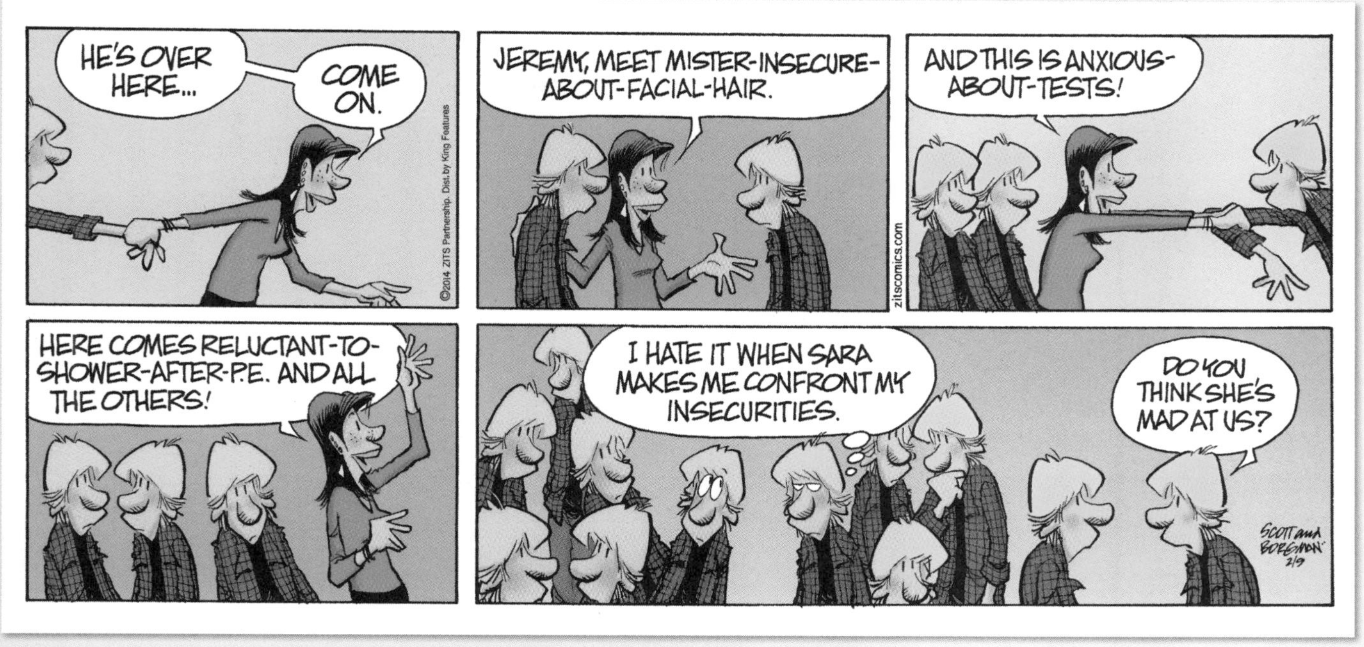
HE'S OVER HERE...
COME ON.
©2014 ZITS Partnership. Dist. by King Features
JEREMY, MEET MISTER-INSECURE-ABOUT-FACIAL-HAIR.
zitscomics.com
AND THIS IS ANXIOUS-ABOUT-TESTS!
HERE COMES RELUCTANT-TO-SHOWER-AFTER-P.E. AND ALL THE OTHERS!
I HATE IT WHEN SARA MAKES ME CONFRONT MY INSECURITIES.
DO YOU THINK SHE'S MAD AT US?
SCOTT AND BORGMAN 2/9

October 19, 2014

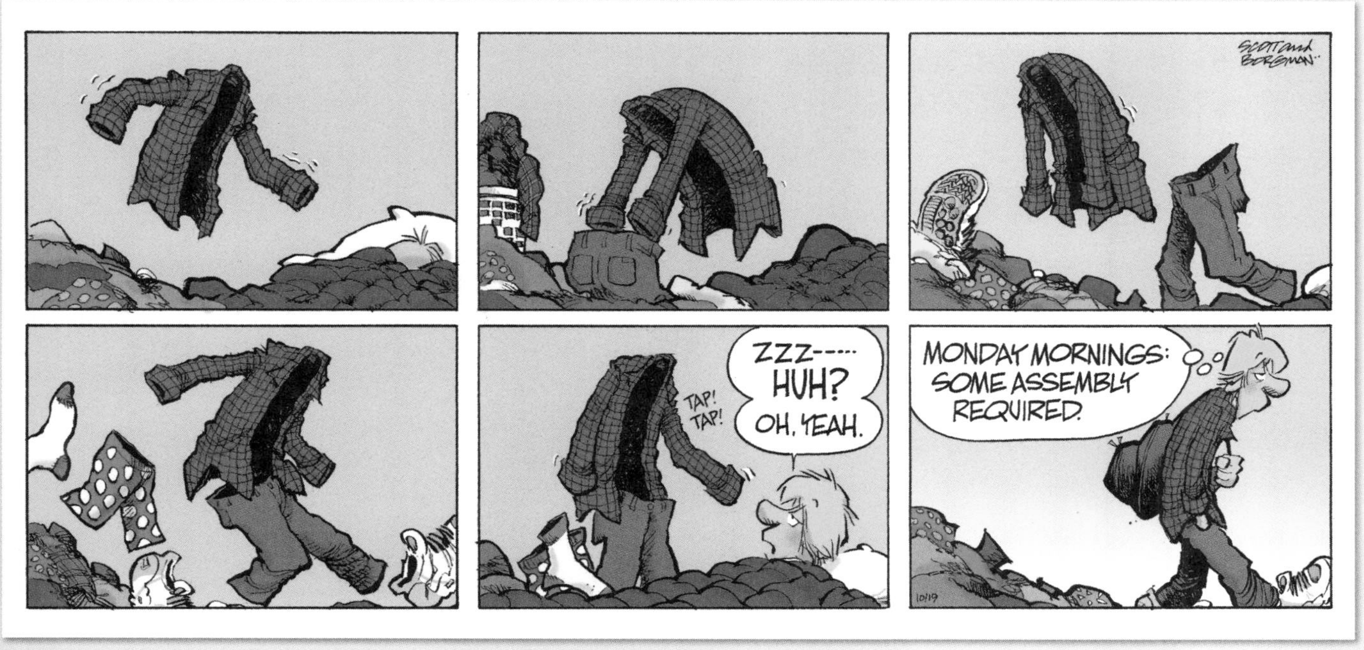
SCOTT AND BORGMAN
TAP! TAP!
ZZZ----- HUH? OH, YEAH.
10/19
MONDAY MORNINGS: SOME ASSEMBLY REQUIRED.

MISHMASH

Jim Borgman

Some years ago I'd sit down to dinner every night with three teenage daughters and brace myself for the onslaught of conversation. This group, when they were in the mood, could spray words with the force of a fire hose. Usually spirited, funny, and lightning fast conversations piled on top of each other like a rugby scrum. It was a force to behold. Their brother Jake and I could hardly fit a grunt in edgewise.

When Jerry sent a strip idea one day in which Sara overwhelms Jeremy with talk, I was ready. I lettered an entire monologue in her voice balloon,

then lettered another one right on top of that. It read the way I heard that dinner talk, with occasional phrases poking through the garble and commotion.

Evelyn Smith, an editor at King Features, bears the burden of making sure nothing inappropriate gets snuck onto the comics page by juvenile cartoonists. These mishmash conversations give her fits. I delight in making her brow furrow and suspect that many of her gray hairs have our names on them.

227

January 19, 2015

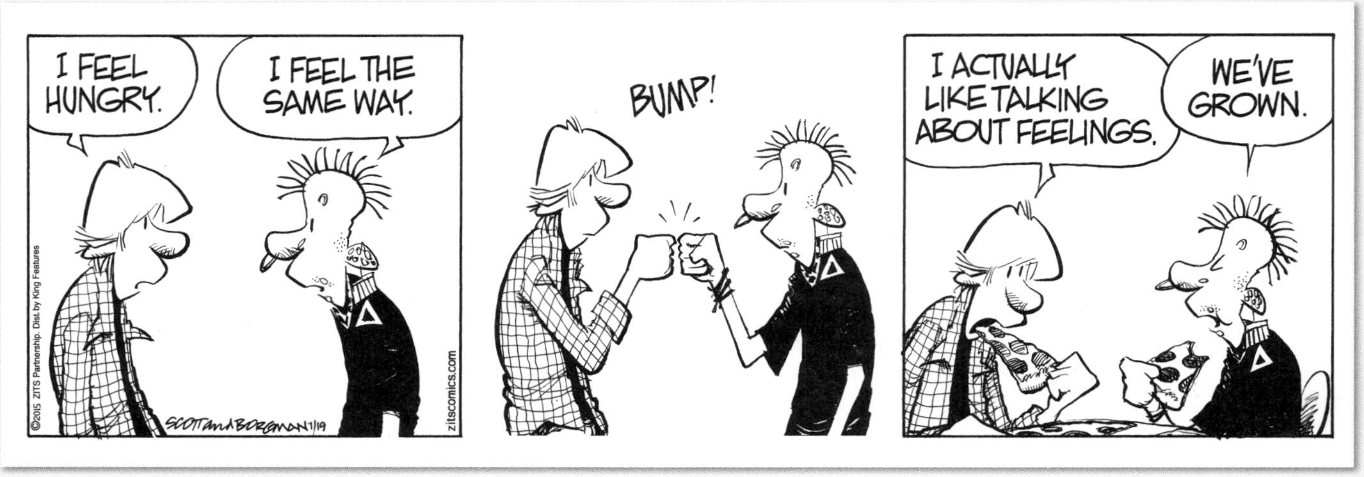
I FEEL HUNGRY.
I FEEL THE SAME WAY.
BUMP!
I ACTUALLY LIKE TALKING ABOUT FEELINGS.
WE'VE GROWN.
©2015 ZITS Partnership. Dist. by King Features
SCOTT and BORGMAN 1/19
zitscomics.com

March 2, 2015

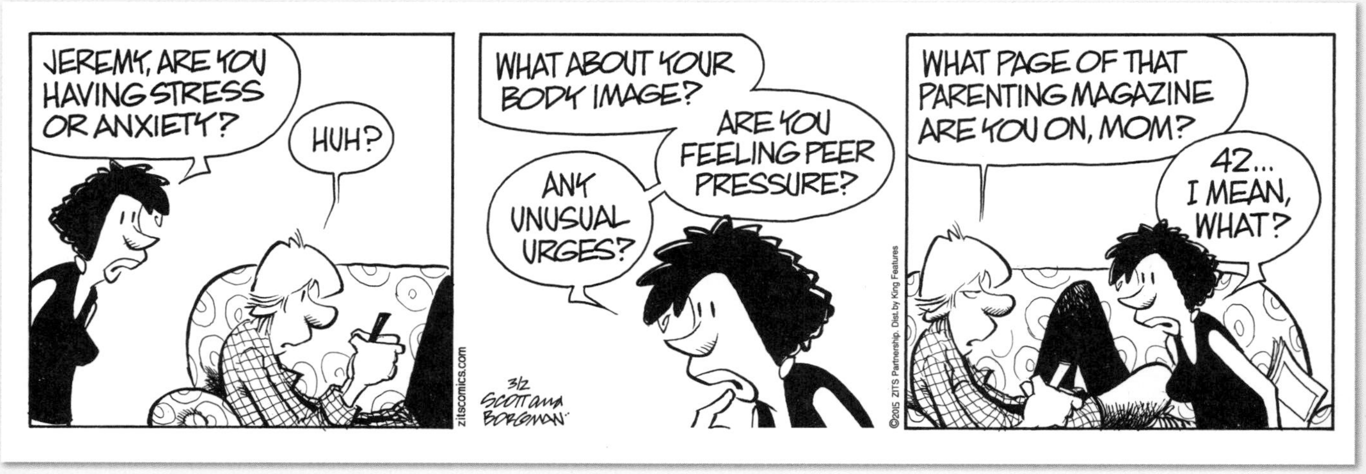
JEREMY, ARE YOU HAVING STRESS OR ANXIETY?
HUH?
WHAT ABOUT YOUR BODY IMAGE?
ARE YOU FEELING PEER PRESSURE?
ANY UNUSUAL URGES?
WHAT PAGE OF THAT PARENTING MAGAZINE ARE YOU ON, MOM?
42... I MEAN, WHAT?
zitscomics.com
3/2 SCOTT and BORGMAN
©2015 ZITS Partnership. Dist. by King Features

March 17, 2015

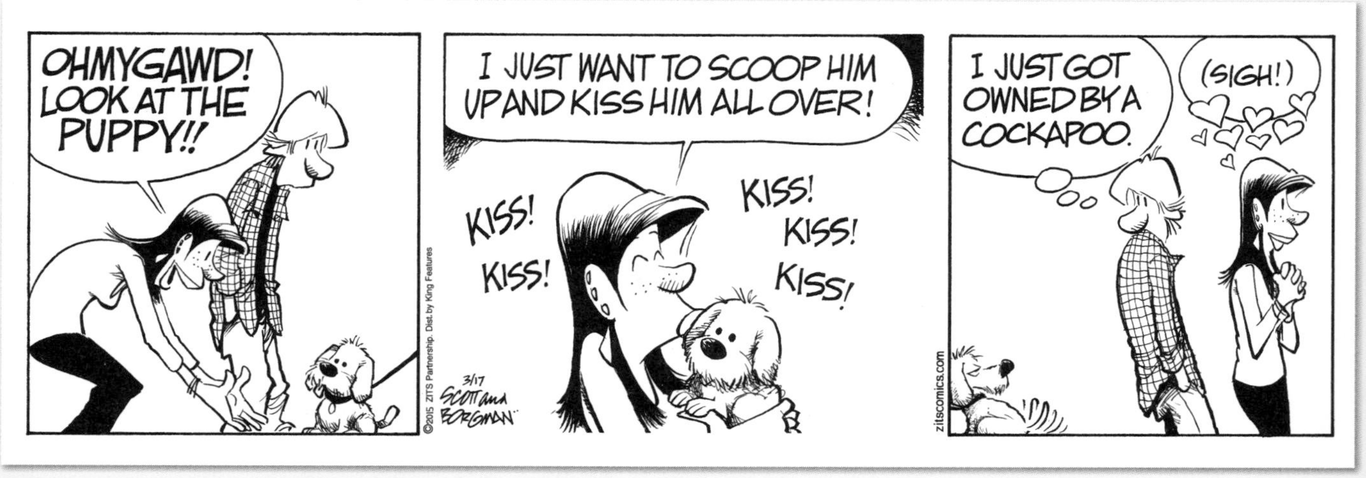
OHMYGAWD! LOOK AT THE PUPPY!!
I JUST WANT TO SCOOP HIM UP AND KISS HIM ALL OVER!
KISS!
KISS!
KISS!
KISS!
KISS!
I JUST GOT OWNED BY A COCKAPOO.
(SIGH!)
©2015 ZITS Partnership. Dist. by King Features
3/17 SCOTT and BORGMAN
zitscomics.com

March 25, 2015

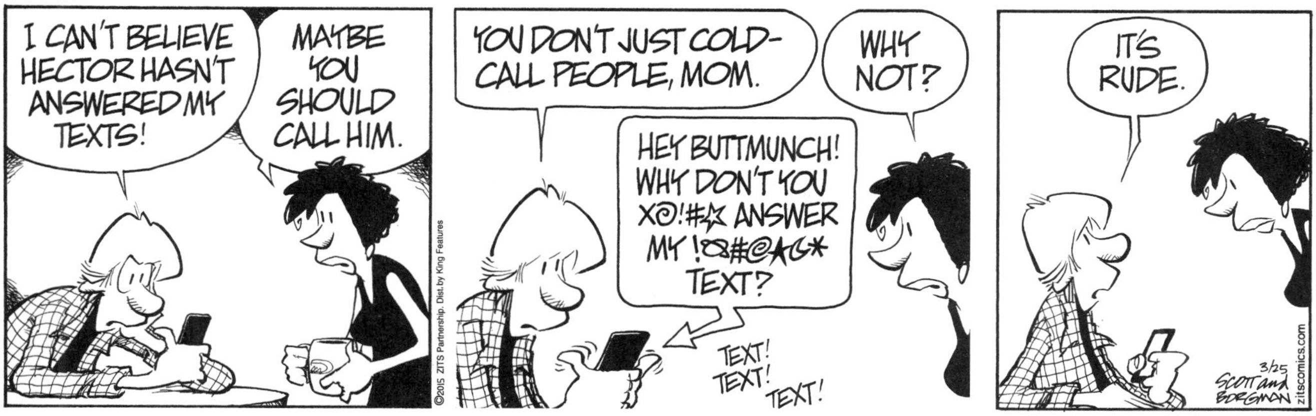
I CAN'T BELIEVE HECTOR HASN'T ANSWERED MY TEXTS!
MAYBE YOU SHOULD CALL HIM.
©2015 ZITS Partnership. Dist. by King Features
YOU DON'T JUST COLD-CALL PEOPLE, MOM.
WHY NOT?
HEY BUTTMUNCH! WHY DON'T YOU X@!#☆ ANSWER MY !&#@★G* TEXT?
TEXT! TEXT! TEXT!
IT'S RUDE.
3/25 SCOTT and BORGMAN
zitscomics.com

April 6, 2015

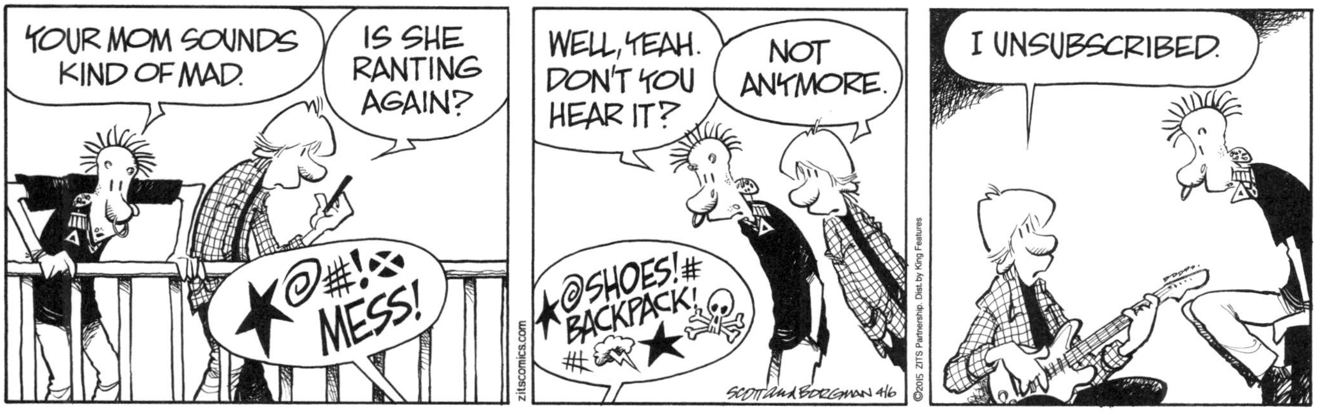
YOUR MOM SOUNDS KIND OF MAD.
IS SHE RANTING AGAIN?
★@#!☒ MESS!
zitscomics.com
WELL, YEAH. DON'T YOU HEAR IT?
NOT ANYMORE.
★@SHOES!# BACKPACK! ★ #
SCOTT and BORGMAN 4/6
©2015 ZITS Partnership. Dist. by King Features
I UNSUBSCRIBED.

April 9, 2015

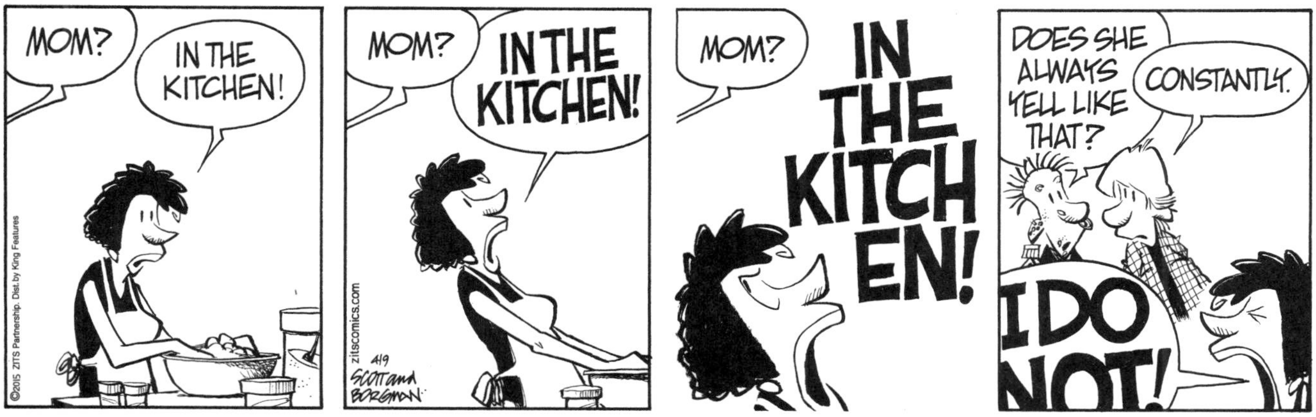
MOM?
IN THE KITCHEN!
©2015 ZITS Partnership. Dist. by King Features
MOM?
IN THE KITCHEN!
zitscomics.com
4/9 SCOTT and BORGMAN
MOM?
IN THE KITCH EN!
DOES SHE ALWAYS YELL LIKE THAT?
CONSTANTLY.
I DO NOT!

April 15, 2015

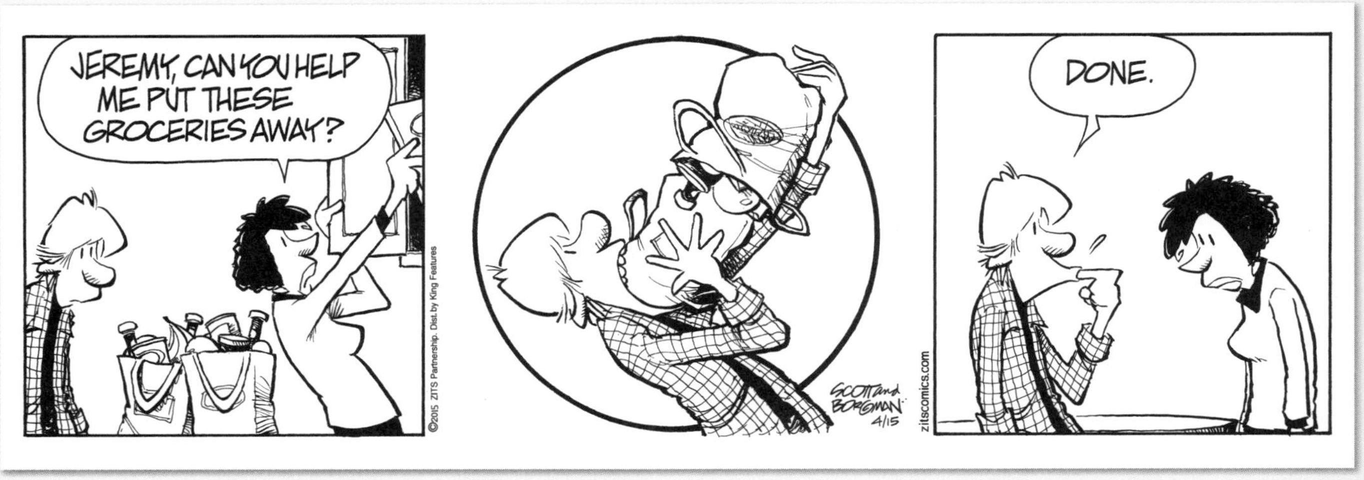
JEREMY, CAN YOU HELP ME PUT THESE GROCERIES AWAY?
DONE.
©2015 ZITS Partnership. Dist. by King Features
SCOTT and BORGMAN 4/15
zitscomics.com

April 20, 2015

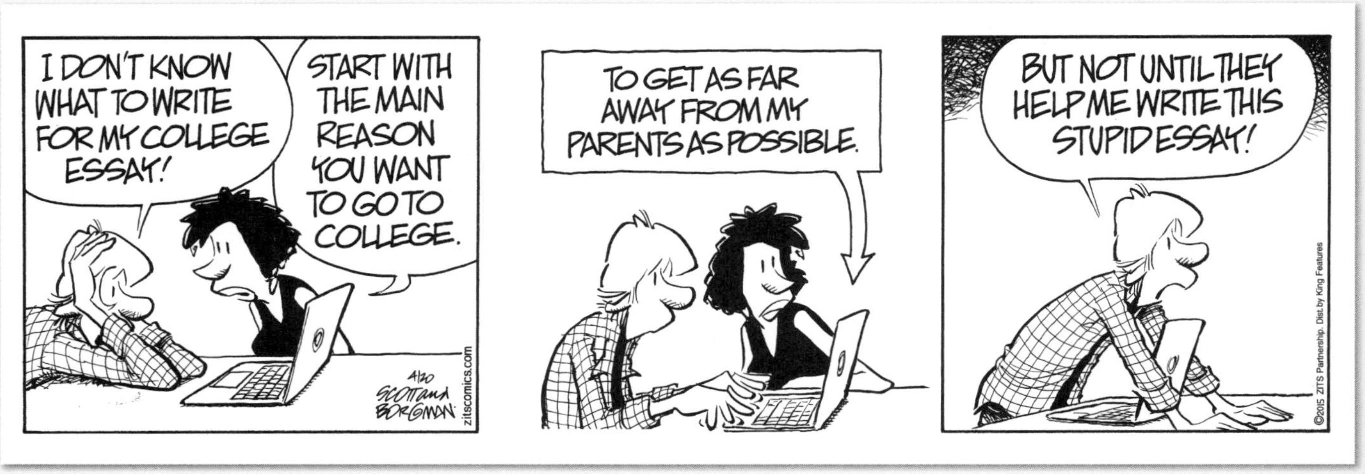
I DON'T KNOW WHAT TO WRITE FOR MY COLLEGE ESSAY!
START WITH THE MAIN REASON YOU WANT TO GO TO COLLEGE.
TO GET AS FAR AWAY FROM MY PARENTS AS POSSIBLE.
BUT NOT UNTIL THEY HELP ME WRITE THIS STUPID ESSAY!
4/20 SCOTT and BORGMAN
zitscomics.com
©2015 ZITS Partnership. Dist. by King Features

April 21, 2015

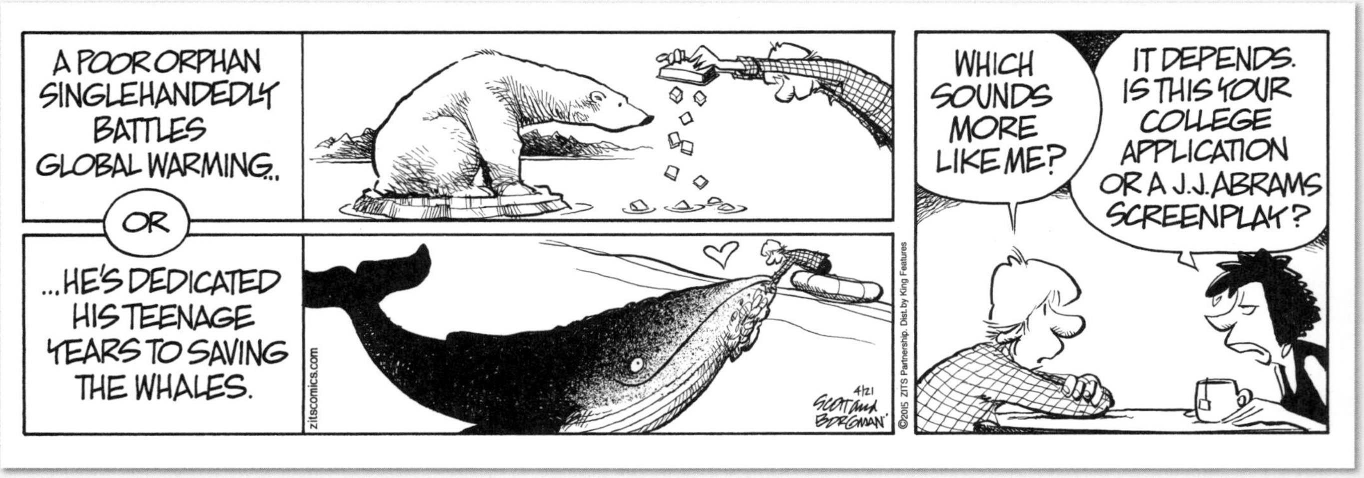
A POOR ORPHAN SINGLEHANDEDLY BATTLES GLOBAL WARMING...
OR
...HE'S DEDICATED HIS TEENAGE YEARS TO SAVING THE WHALES.
WHICH SOUNDS MORE LIKE ME?
IT DEPENDS. IS THIS YOUR COLLEGE APPLICATION OR A J.J. ABRAMS SCREENPLAY?
zitscomics.com
4/21 SCOTT and BORGMAN
©2015 ZITS Partnership. Dist. by King Features

April 29, 2015

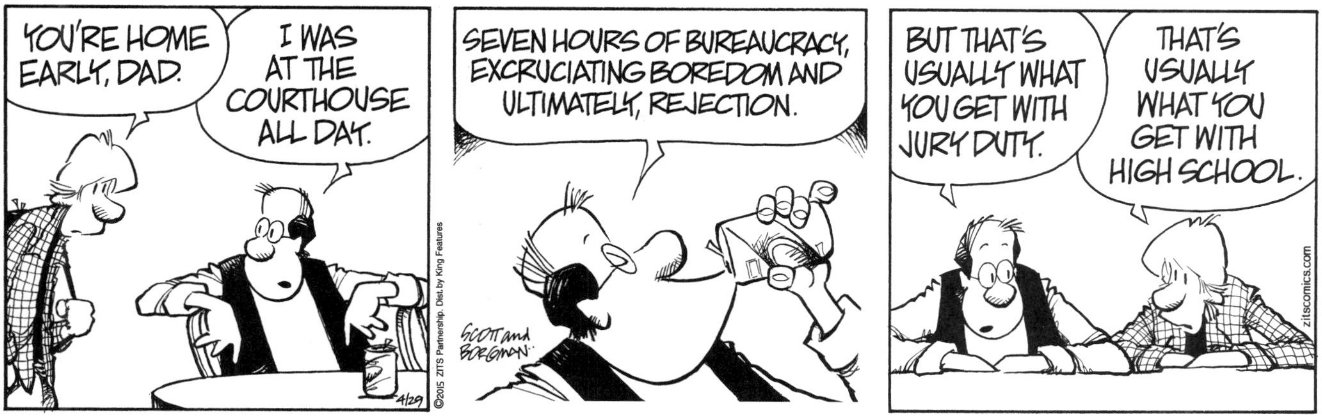

YOU'RE HOME EARLY, DAD.
I WAS AT THE COURTHOUSE ALL DAY.
SEVEN HOURS OF BUREAUCRACY, EXCRUCIATING BOREDOM AND ULTIMATELY, REJECTION.
BUT THAT'S USUALLY WHAT YOU GET WITH JURY DUTY.
THAT'S USUALLY WHAT YOU GET WITH HIGH SCHOOL.
4/29
SCOTT and BORGMAN
©2015 ZITS Partnership. Dist. by King Features
zitscomics.com

May 6, 2015

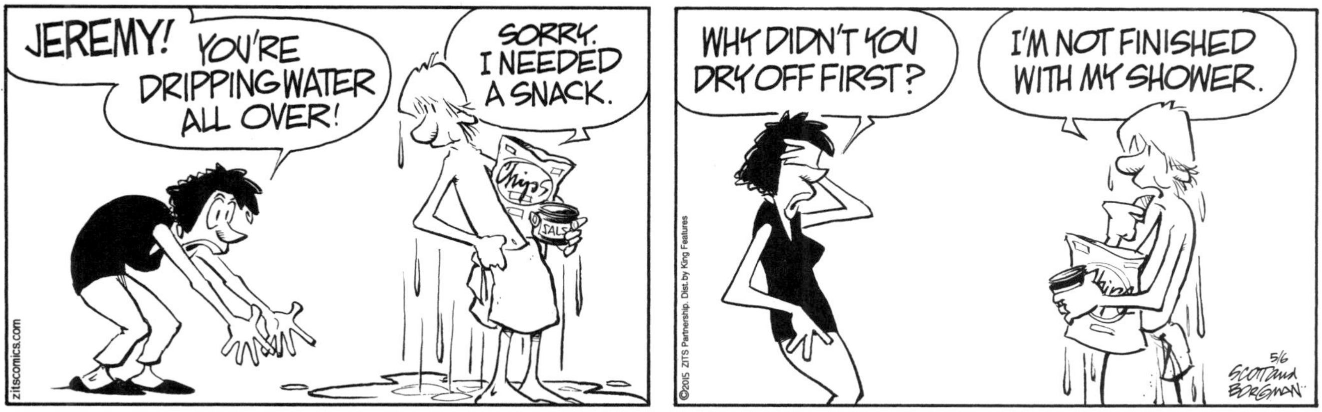

JEREMY!
YOU'RE DRIPPING WATER ALL OVER!
SORRY. I NEEDED A SNACK.
Chips
SALS
WHY DIDN'T YOU DRY OFF FIRST?
I'M NOT FINISHED WITH MY SHOWER.
5/6
SCOTT and BORGMAN
©2015 ZITS Partnership. Dist. by King Features
zitscomics.com

June 19, 2015

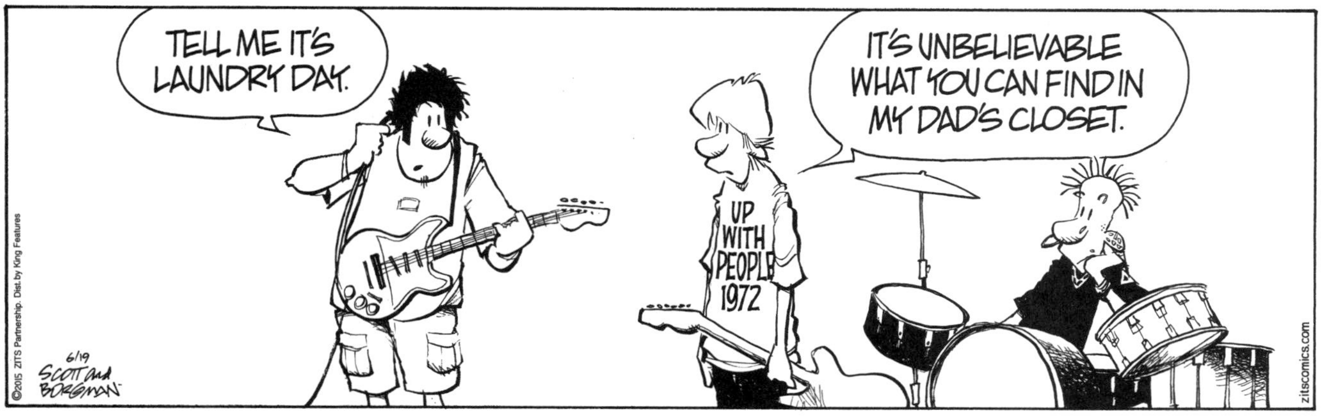

TELL ME IT'S LAUNDRY DAY.
IT'S UNBELIEVABLE WHAT YOU CAN FIND IN MY DAD'S CLOSET.
UP WITH PEOPLE 1972
6/19
SCOTT and BORGMAN
©2015 ZITS Partnership. Dist. by King Features
zitscomics.com

January 4, 2015

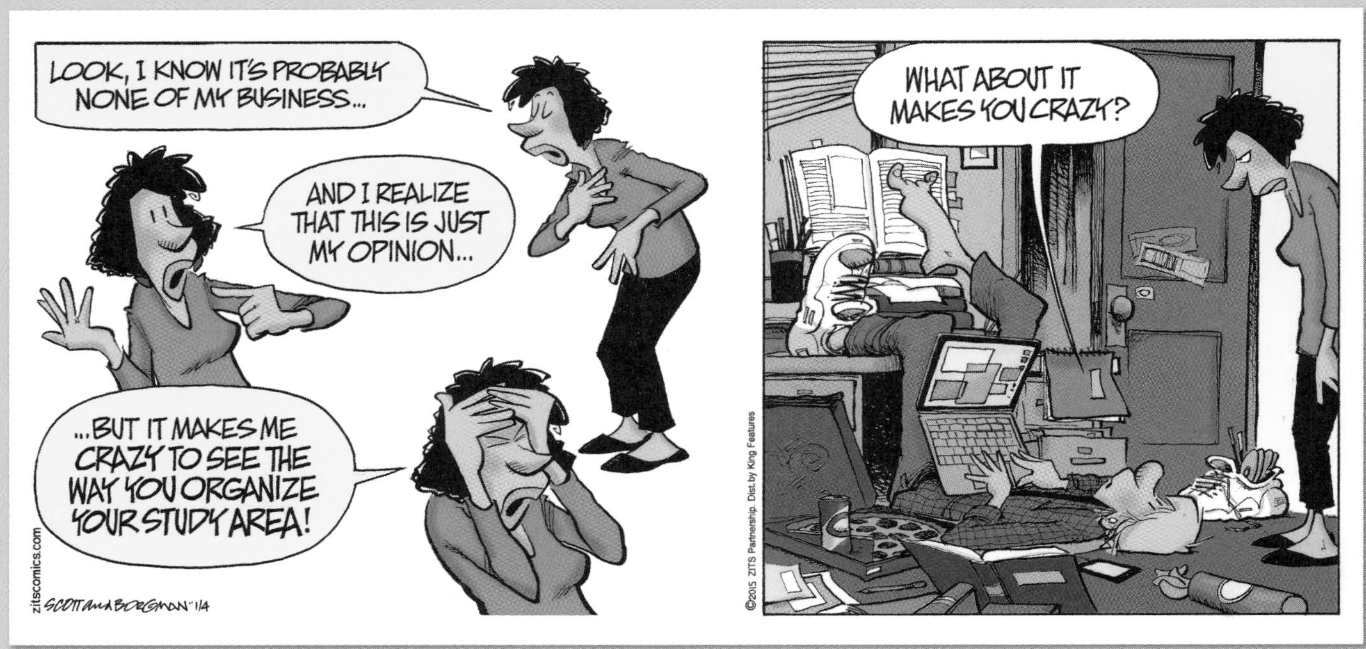
LOOK, I KNOW IT'S PROBABLY NONE OF MY BUSINESS...
AND I REALIZE THAT THIS IS JUST MY OPINION...
...BUT IT MAKES ME CRAZY TO SEE THE WAY YOU ORGANIZE YOUR STUDY AREA!
WHAT ABOUT IT MAKES YOU CRAZY?
zitscomics.com
SCOTT and BORGMAN 1/4
©2015 ZITS Partnership. Dist. by King Features

May 24, 2015

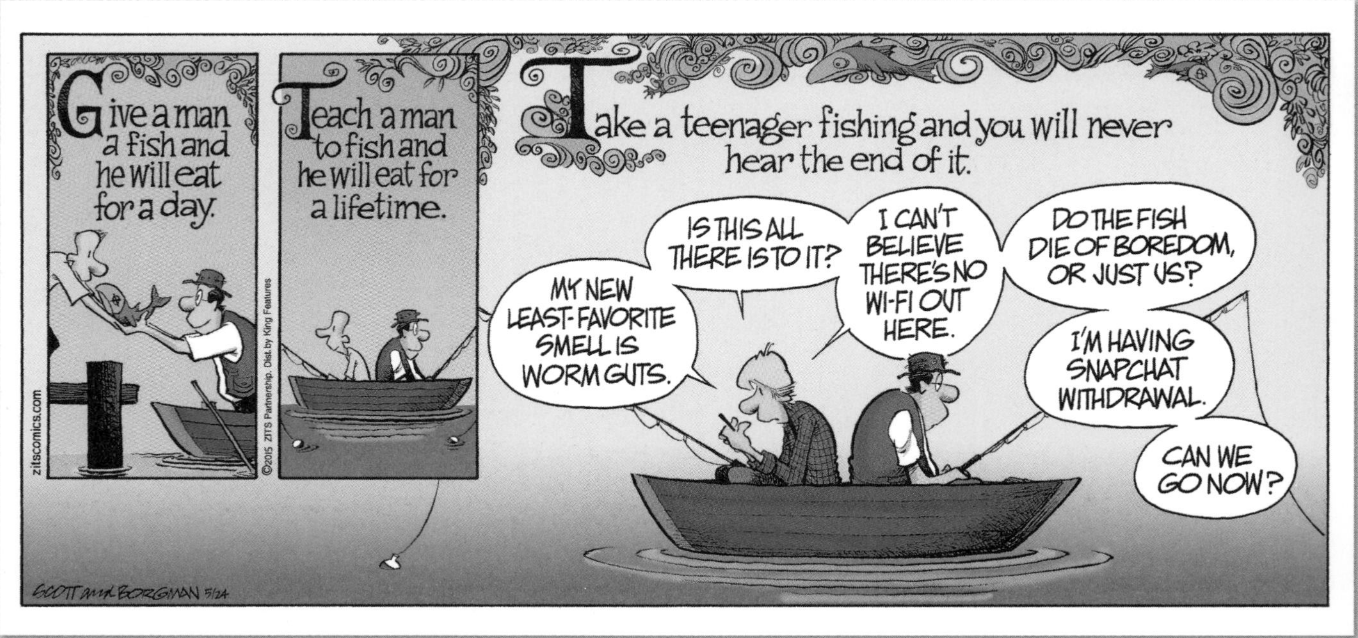
Give a man a fish and he will eat for a day.
Teach a man to fish and he will eat for a lifetime.
Take a teenager fishing and you will never hear the end of it.
MY NEW LEAST-FAVORITE SMELL IS WORM GUTS.
IS THIS ALL THERE IS TO IT?
I CAN'T BELIEVE THERE'S NO WI-FI OUT HERE.
DO THE FISH DIE OF BOREDOM, OR JUST US?
I'M HAVING SNAPCHAT WITHDRAWAL.
CAN WE GO NOW?
zitscomics.com
©2015 ZITS Partnership. Dist. by King Features
SCOTT and BORGMAN 5/24

May 31, 2015

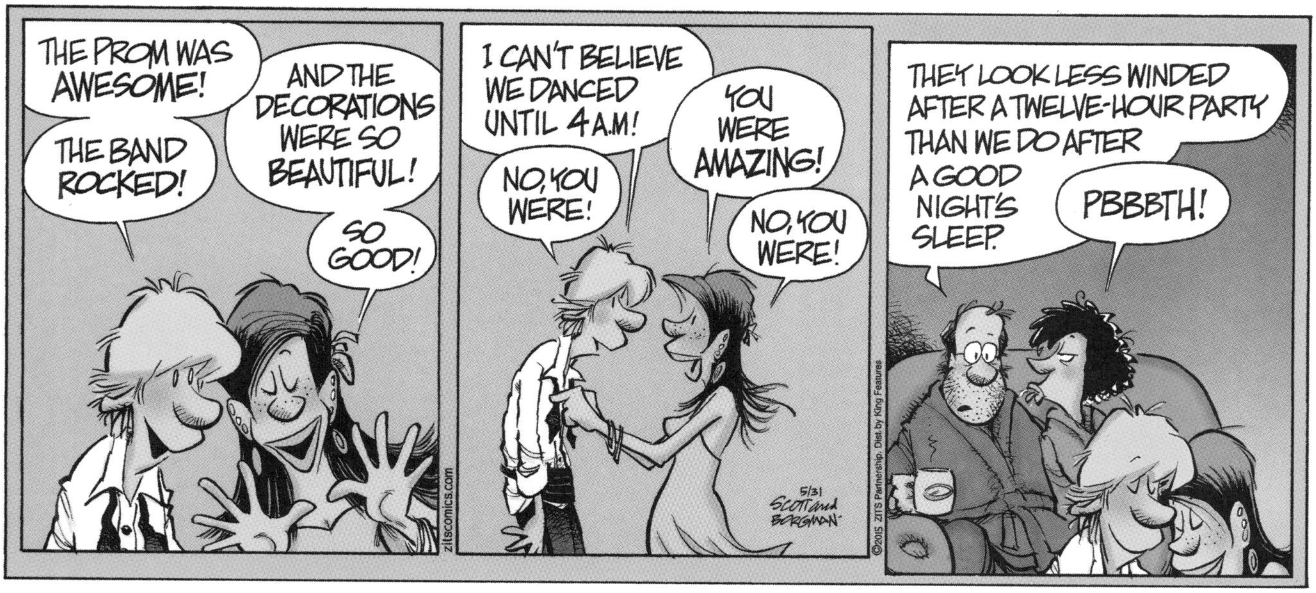
THE PROM WAS AWESOME!
THE BAND ROCKED!
AND THE DECORATIONS WERE SO BEAUTIFUL!
SO GOOD!
I CAN'T BELIEVE WE DANCED UNTIL 4 A.M!
NO, YOU WERE!
YOU WERE AMAZING!
NO, YOU WERE!
THEY LOOK LESS WINDED AFTER A TWELVE-HOUR PARTY THAN WE DO AFTER A GOOD NIGHT'S SLEEP.
PBBBTH!
zitscomics.com
5/31 SCOTT and BORGMAN
©2015 ZITS Partnership. Dist by King Features

July 19, 2015

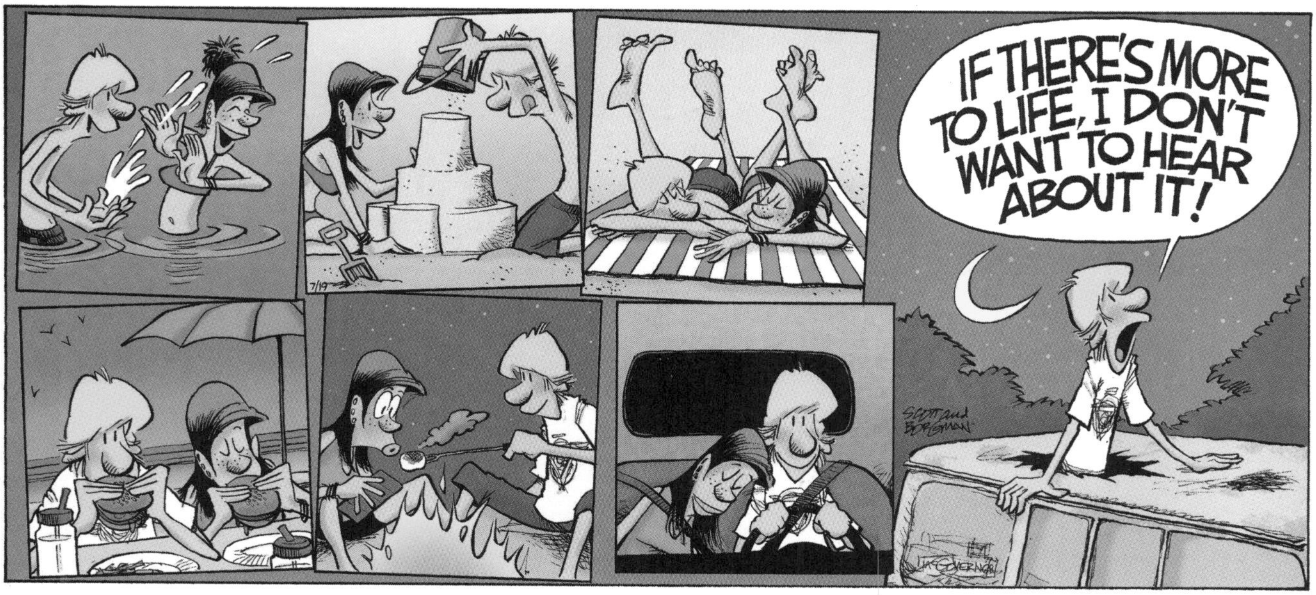
7/19
IF THERE'S MORE TO LIFE, I DON'T WANT TO HEAR ABOUT IT!
SCOTT and BORGMAN

June 29, 2015

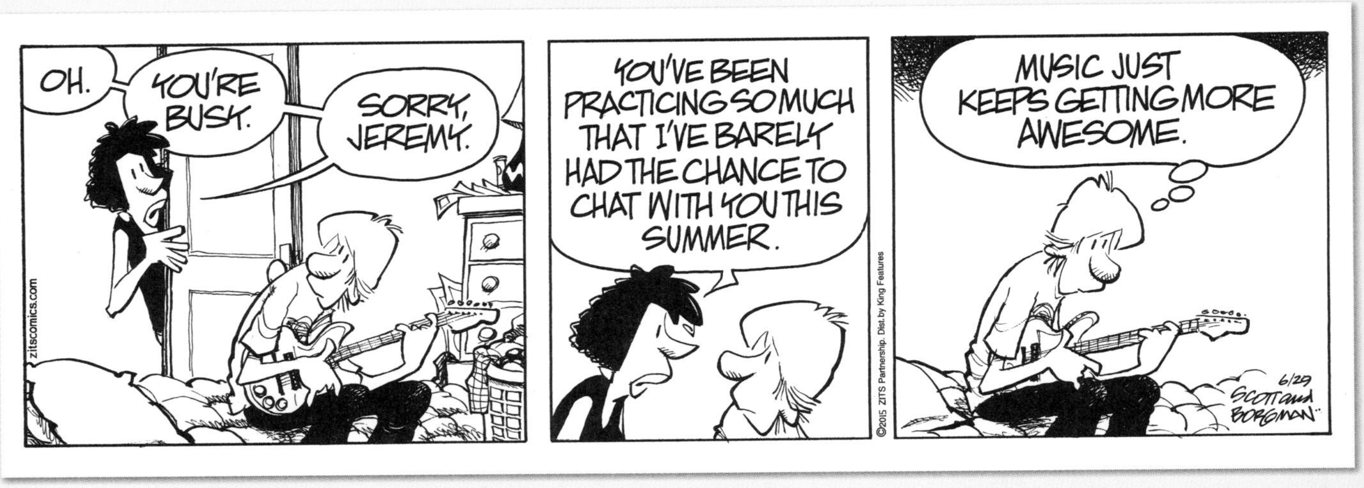
OH.
YOU'RE BUSY.
SORRY, JEREMY.
YOU'VE BEEN PRACTICING SO MUCH THAT I'VE BARELY HAD THE CHANCE TO CHAT WITH YOU THIS SUMMER.
MUSIC JUST KEEPS GETTING MORE AWESOME.
zitscomics.com
©2015 ZITS Partnership. Dist. by King Features
6/29 SCOTT and BORGMAN

July 25, 2015

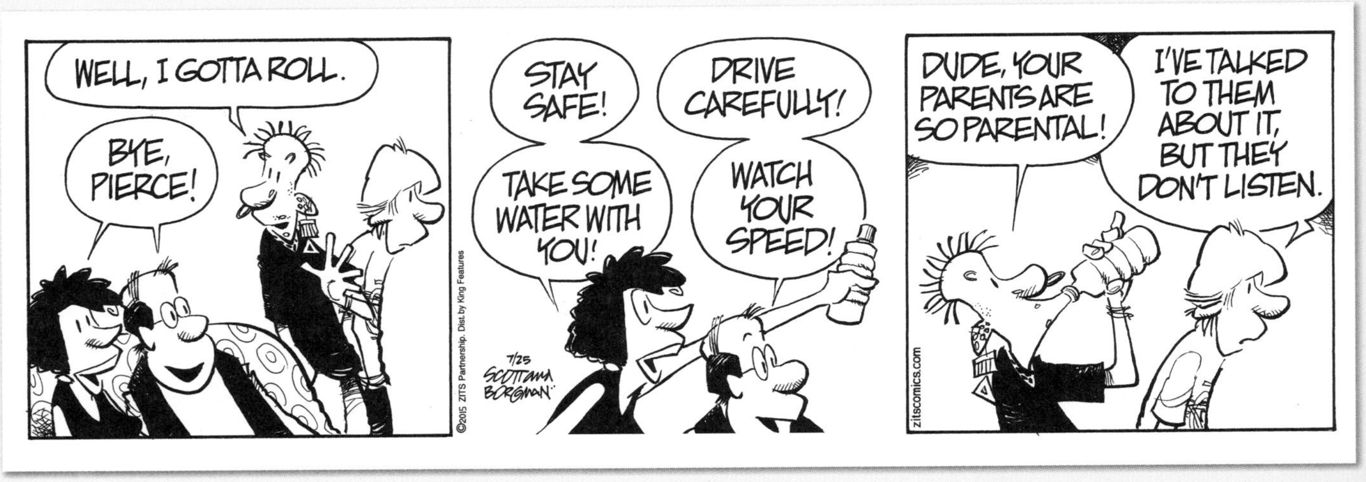
WELL, I GOTTA ROLL.
BYE, PIERCE!
STAY SAFE!
TAKE SOME WATER WITH YOU!
DRIVE CAREFULLY!
WATCH YOUR SPEED!
7/25 SCOTT and BORGMAN
©2015 ZITS Partnership. Dist. by King Features
DUDE, YOUR PARENTS ARE SO PARENTAL!
I'VE TALKED TO THEM ABOUT IT, BUT THEY DON'T LISTEN.
zitscomics.com

August 6, 2015

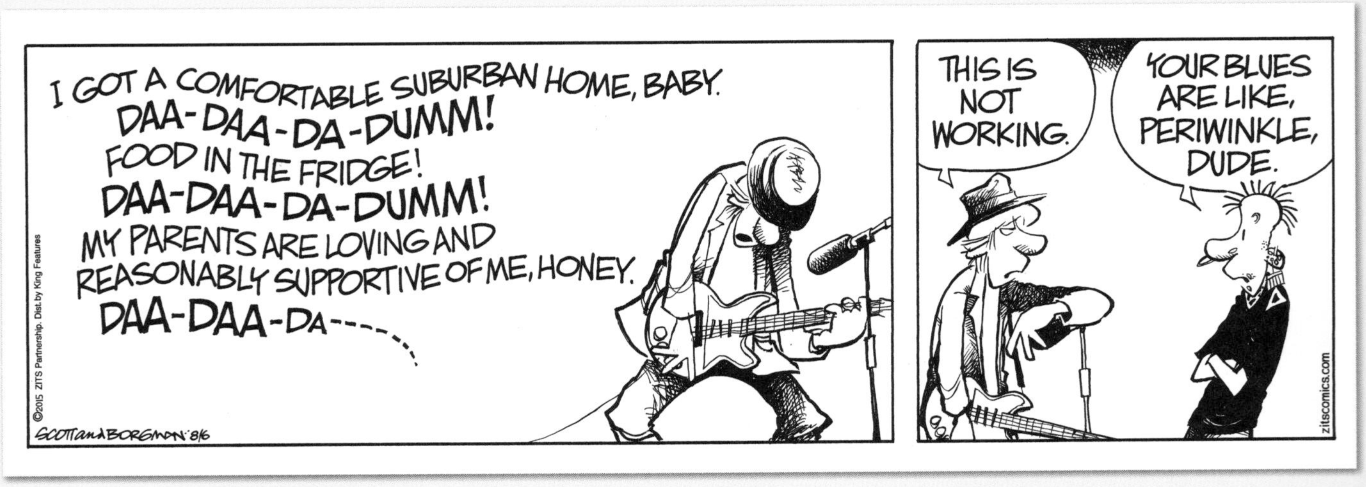
I GOT A COMFORTABLE SUBURBAN HOME, BABY.
DAA-DAA-DA-DUMM!
FOOD IN THE FRIDGE!
DAA-DAA-DA-DUMM!
MY PARENTS ARE LOVING AND REASONABLY SUPPORTIVE OF ME, HONEY.
DAA-DAA-DA-----
©2015 ZITS Partnership. Dist. by King Features
SCOTT and BORGMAN 8/6
THIS IS NOT WORKING.
YOUR BLUES ARE LIKE, PERIWINKLE, DUDE.
zitscomics.com

July 30, 2015

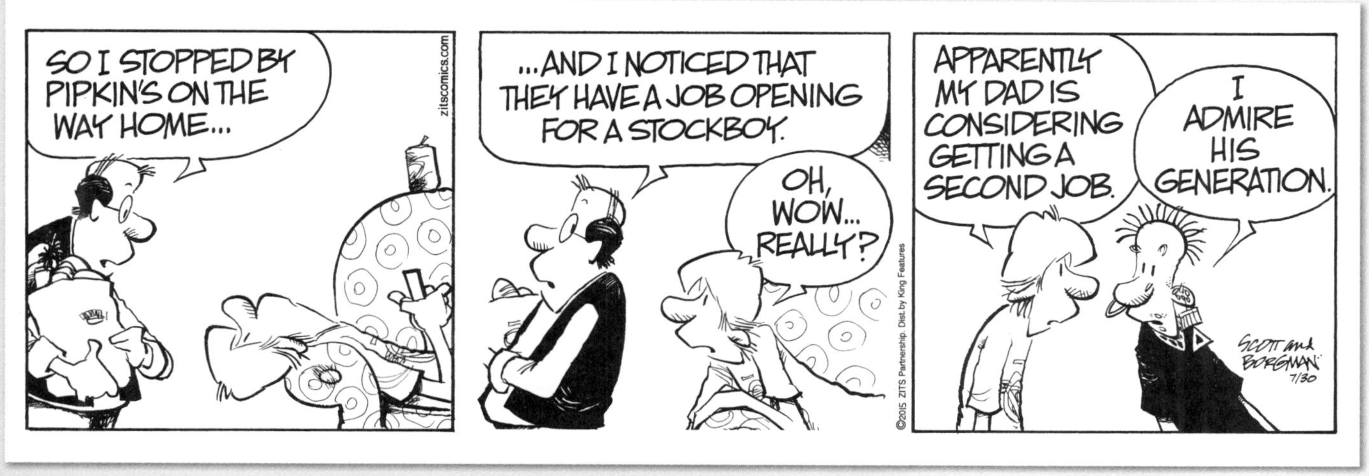
SO I STOPPED BY PIPKIN'S ON THE WAY HOME...
zitscomics.com
...AND I NOTICED THAT THEY HAVE A JOB OPENING FOR A STOCKBOY.
OH, WOW... REALLY?
©2015 ZITS Partnership. Dist. by King Features
APPARENTLY MY DAD IS CONSIDERING GETTING A SECOND JOB.
I ADMIRE HIS GENERATION.
SCOTT and BORGMAN 7/30

July 31, 2015

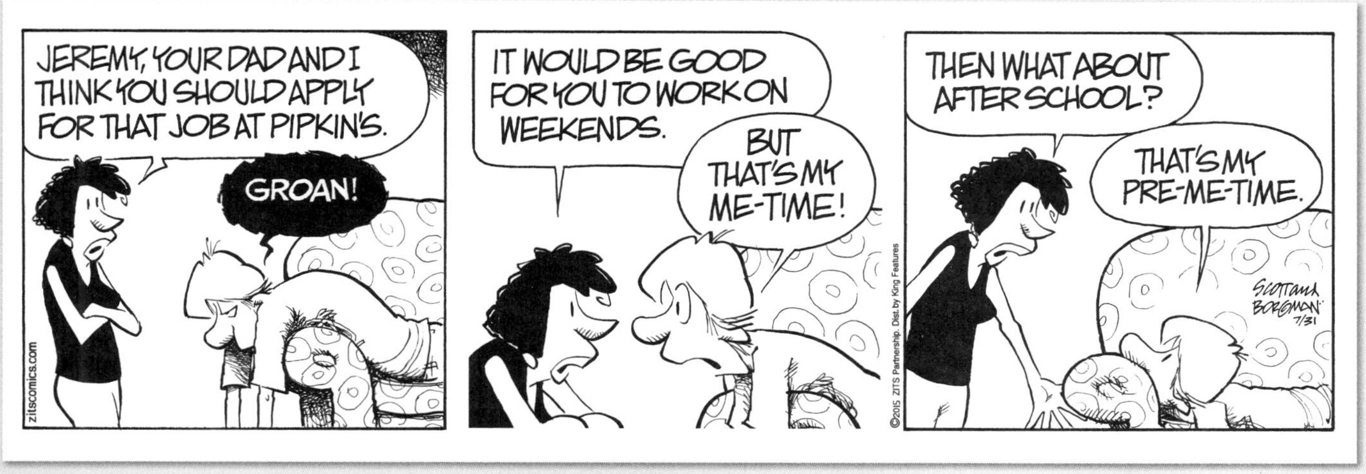
JEREMY, YOUR DAD AND I THINK YOU SHOULD APPLY FOR THAT JOB AT PIPKIN'S.
GROAN!
zitscomics.com
IT WOULD BE GOOD FOR YOU TO WORK ON WEEKENDS.
BUT THAT'S MY ME-TIME!
©2015 ZITS Partnership. Dist. by King Features
THEN WHAT ABOUT AFTER SCHOOL?
THAT'S MY PRE-ME-TIME.
SCOTT and BORGMAN 7/31

August 1, 2015

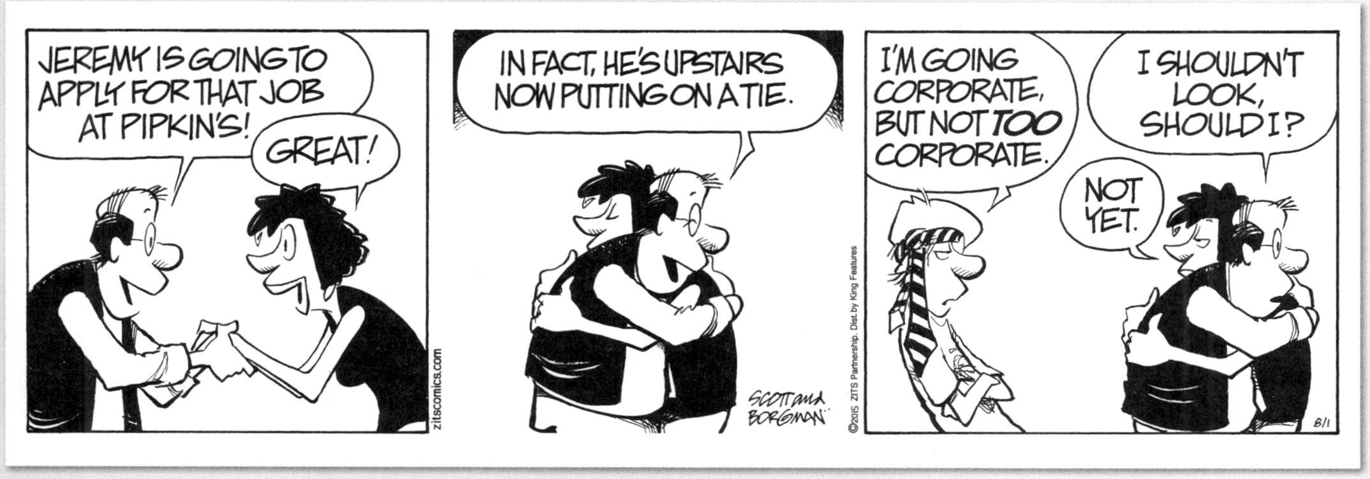
JEREMY IS GOING TO APPLY FOR THAT JOB AT PIPKIN'S!
GREAT!
zitscomics.com
IN FACT, HE'S UPSTAIRS NOW PUTTING ON A TIE.
SCOTT and BORGMAN
©2015 ZITS Partnership. Dist. by King Features
I'M GOING CORPORATE, BUT NOT *TOO* CORPORATE.
I SHOULDN'T LOOK, SHOULD I?
NOT YET.
8/1

August 22, 2015

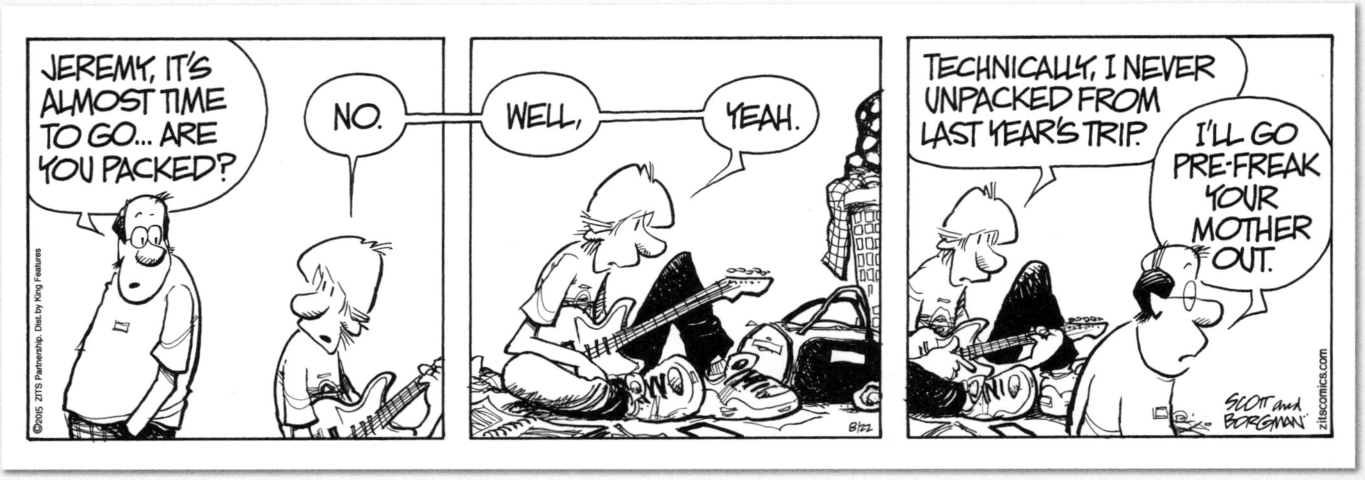
JEREMY, IT'S ALMOST TIME TO GO... ARE YOU PACKED?
NO.
WELL,
YEAH.
TECHNICALLY, I NEVER UNPACKED FROM LAST YEAR'S TRIP.
I'LL GO PRE-FREAK YOUR MOTHER OUT.
©2015 ZITS Partnership. Dist. by King Features
8/22
SCOTT and BORGMAN
zitscomics.com

August 24, 2015

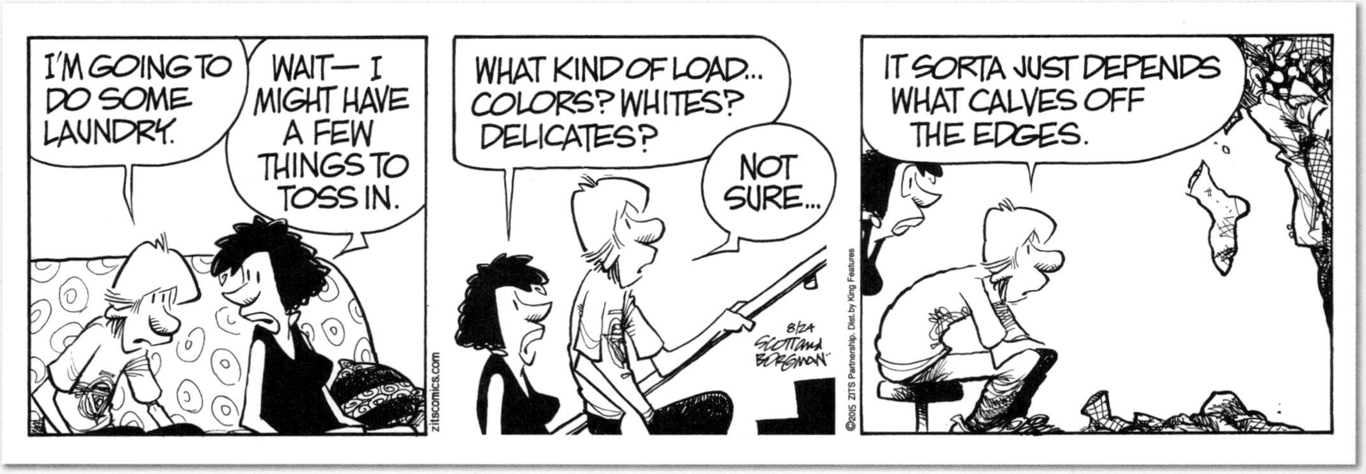
I'M GOING TO DO SOME LAUNDRY.
WAIT— I MIGHT HAVE A FEW THINGS TO TOSS IN.
WHAT KIND OF LOAD... COLORS? WHITES? DELICATES?
NOT SURE...
IT SORTA JUST DEPENDS WHAT CALVES OFF THE EDGES.
zitscomics.com
8/24
SCOTT and BORGMAN
©2015 ZITS Partnership. Dist. by King Features

August 26, 2015

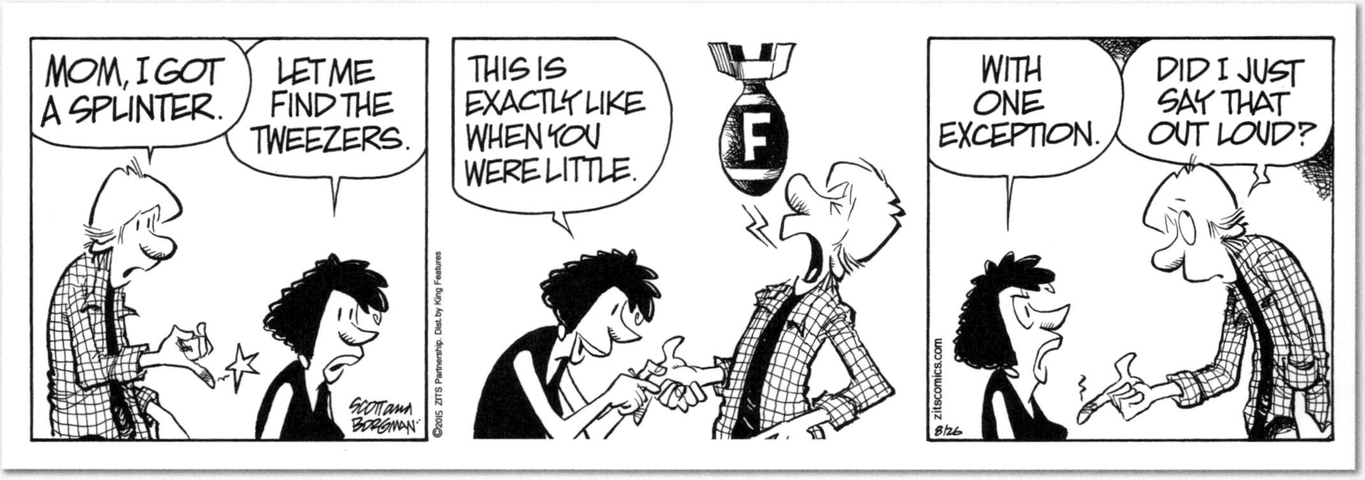
MOM, I GOT A SPLINTER.
LET ME FIND THE TWEEZERS.
SCOTT and BORGMAN
©2015 ZITS Partnership. Dist. by King Features
THIS IS EXACTLY LIKE WHEN YOU WERE LITTLE.
F
WITH ONE EXCEPTION.
DID I JUST SAY THAT OUT LOUD?
zitscomics.com
8/26

August 16, 2015

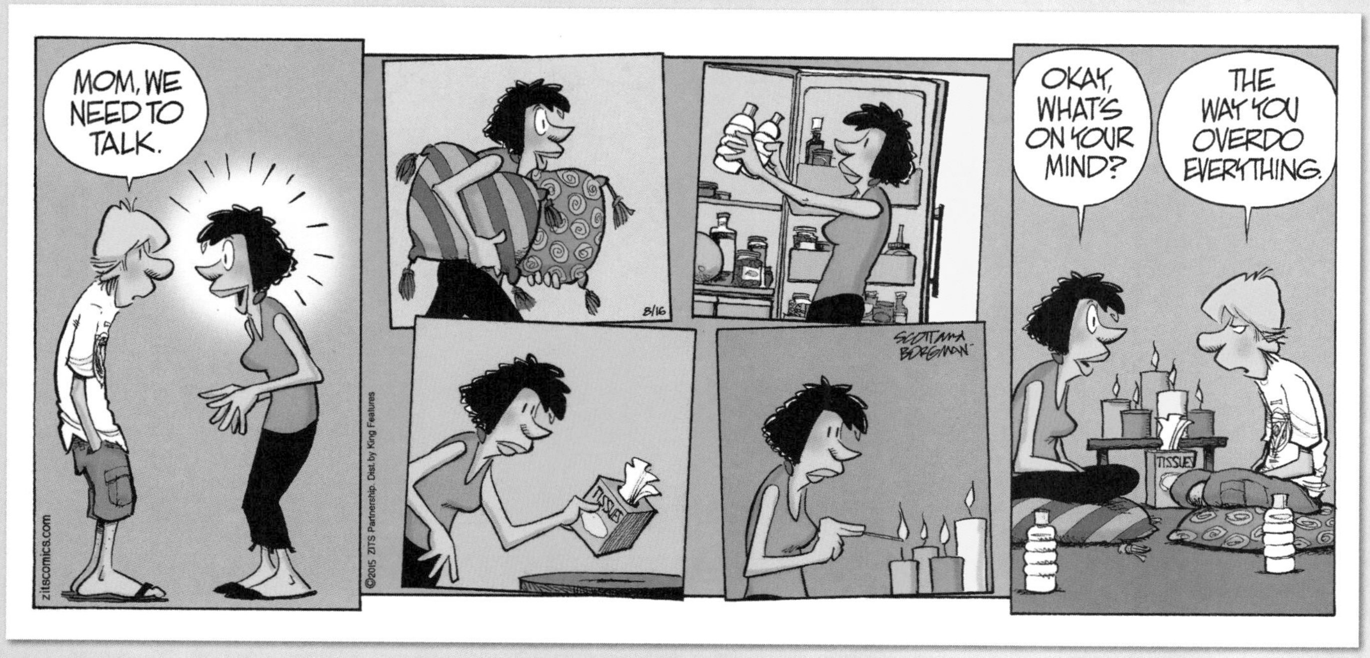
MOM, WE NEED TO TALK.
8/16
SCOTT AND BORGMAN
OKAY, WHAT'S ON YOUR MIND?
THE WAY YOU OVERDO EVERYTHING.
TISSUES
©2015 ZITS Partnership. Dist. by King Features
zitscomics.com

August 30, 2015

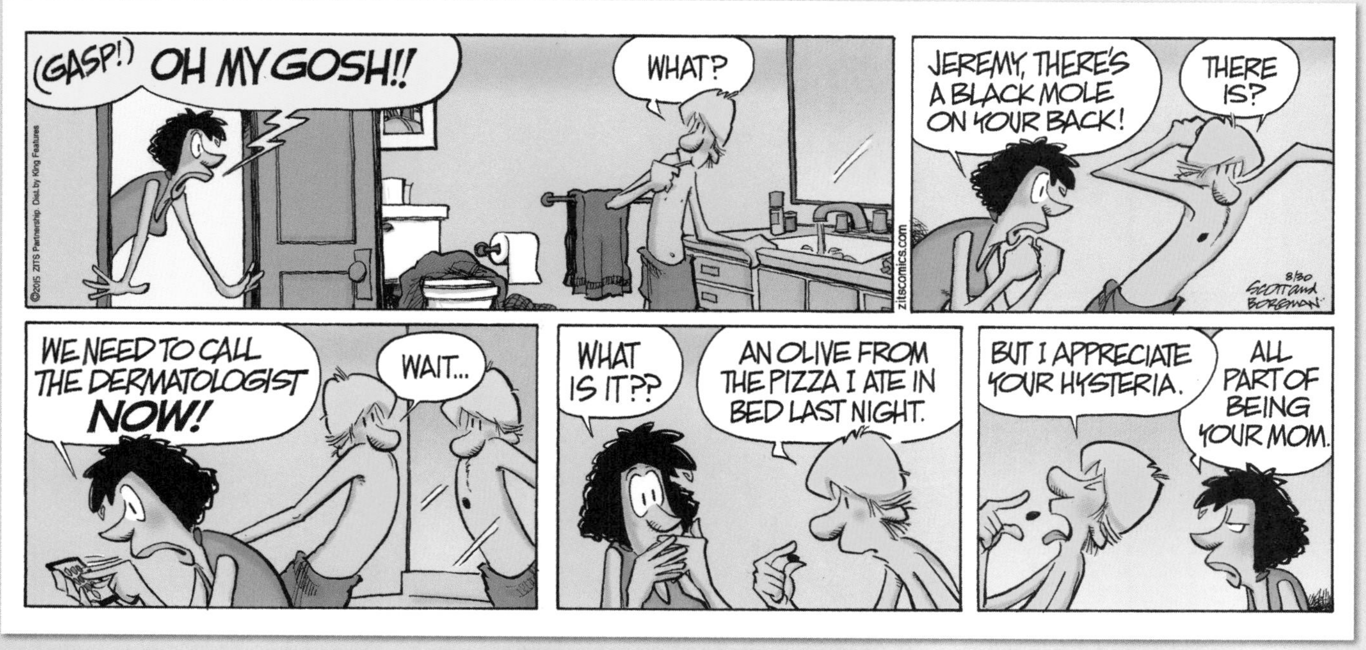
(GASP!) OH MY GOSH!!
WHAT?
©2015 ZITS Partnership. Dist. by King Features
zitscomics.com
JEREMY, THERE'S A BLACK MOLE ON YOUR BACK!
THERE IS?
8/30
SCOTT and BORGMAN
WE NEED TO CALL THE DERMATOLOGIST NOW!
WAIT...
WHAT IS IT??
AN OLIVE FROM THE PIZZA I ATE IN BED LAST NIGHT.
BUT I APPRECIATE YOUR HYSTERIA.
ALL PART OF BEING YOUR MOM.

August 28, 2015

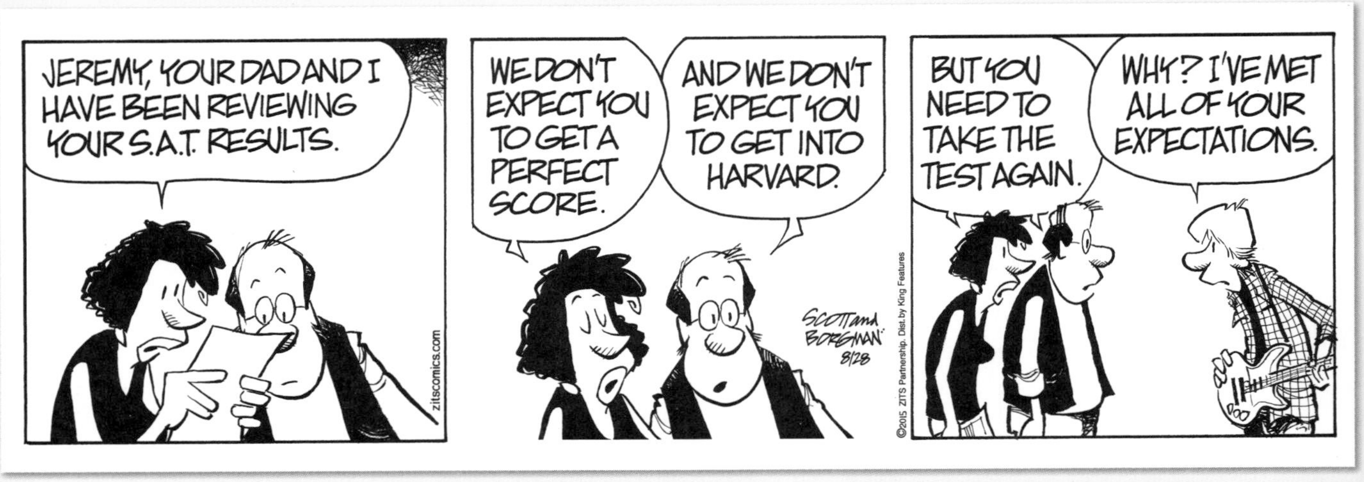
JEREMY, YOUR DAD AND I HAVE BEEN REVIEWING YOUR S.A.T. RESULTS.
WE DON'T EXPECT YOU TO GET A PERFECT SCORE.
AND WE DON'T EXPECT YOU TO GET INTO HARVARD.
BUT YOU NEED TO TAKE THE TEST AGAIN.
WHY? I'VE MET ALL OF YOUR EXPECTATIONS.
zitscomics.com
SCOTT and BORGMAN 8/28
©2015 ZITS Partnership. Dist. by King Features

November 28, 2015

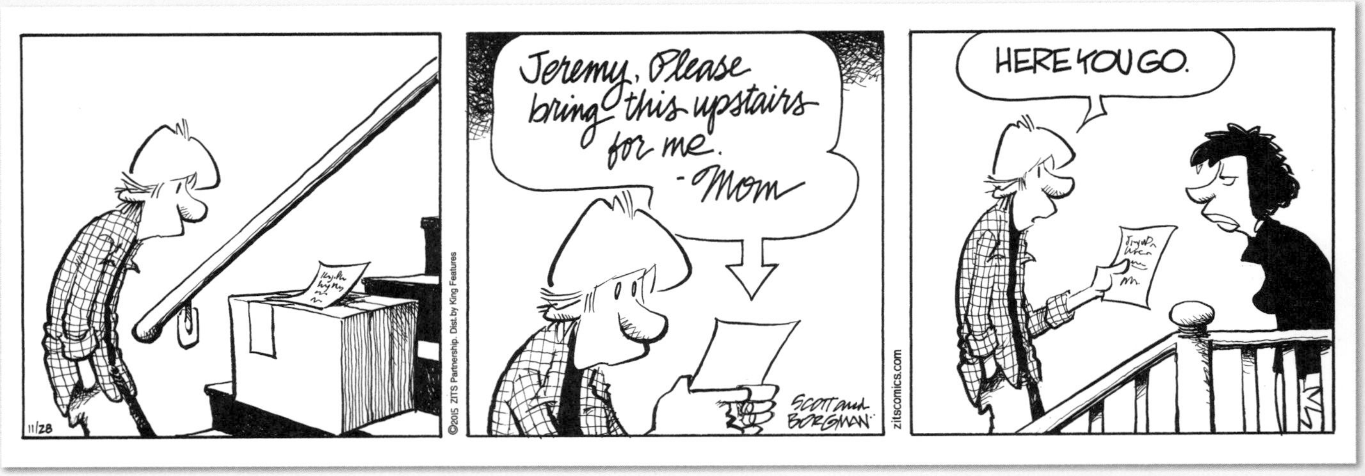
11/28
©2015 ZITS Partnership. Dist. by King Features
Jeremy, Please bring this upstairs for me. - Mom
SCOTT and BORGMAN
zitscomics.com
HERE YOU GO.

December 8, 2015

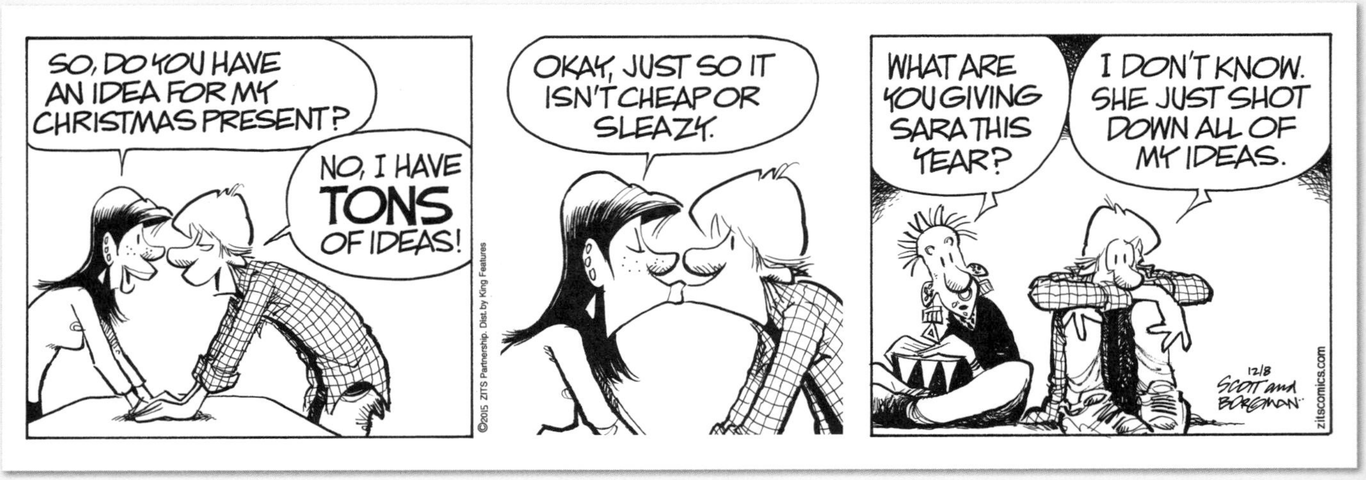
SO, DO YOU HAVE AN IDEA FOR MY CHRISTMAS PRESENT?
NO, I HAVE TONS OF IDEAS!
©2015 ZITS Partnership. Dist. by King Features
OKAY, JUST SO IT ISN'T CHEAP OR SLEAZY.
WHAT ARE YOU GIVING SARA THIS YEAR?
I DON'T KNOW. SHE JUST SHOT DOWN ALL OF MY IDEAS.
12/8 SCOTT and BORGMAN
zitscomics.com

December 9, 2015

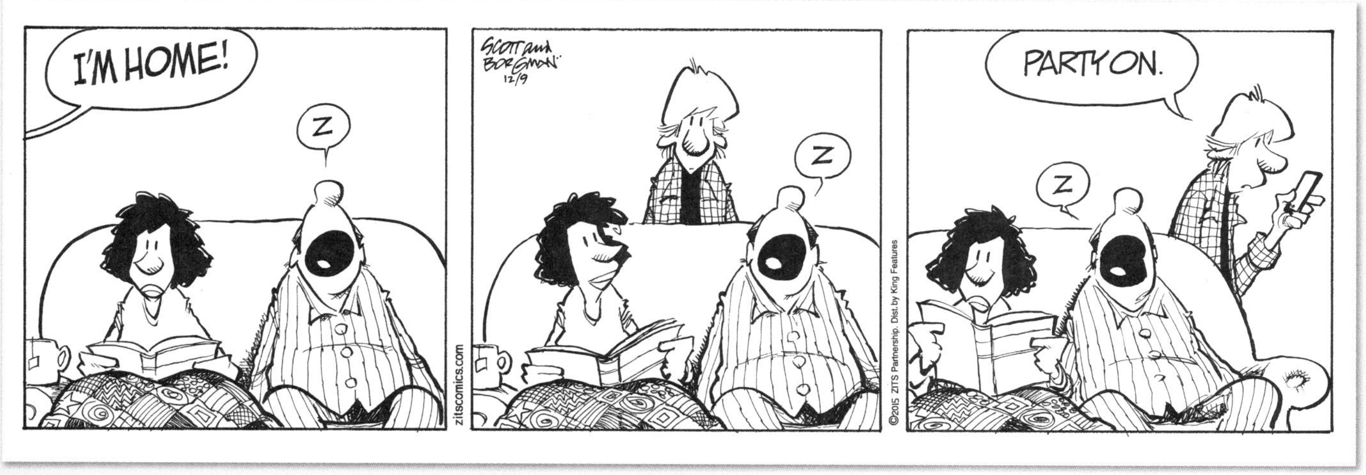
I'M HOME!
Z
SCOTT and BORGMAN 12/9
Z
PARTY ON.
Z
zitscomics.com
©2015 ZITS Partnership. Dist. by King Features

December 12, 2015

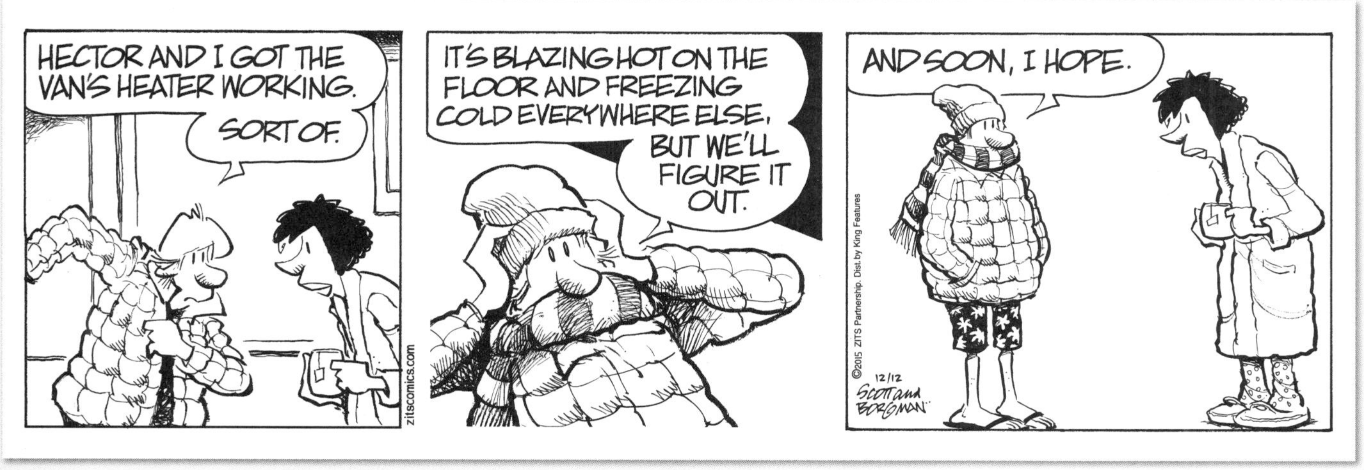
HECTOR AND I GOT THE VAN'S HEATER WORKING.
SORT OF.
IT'S BLAZING HOT ON THE FLOOR AND FREEZING COLD EVERYWHERE ELSE,
BUT WE'LL FIGURE IT OUT.
AND SOON, I HOPE.
zitscomics.com
©2015 ZITS Partnership. Dist. by King Features
12/12 SCOTT and BORGMAN

December 29, 2015

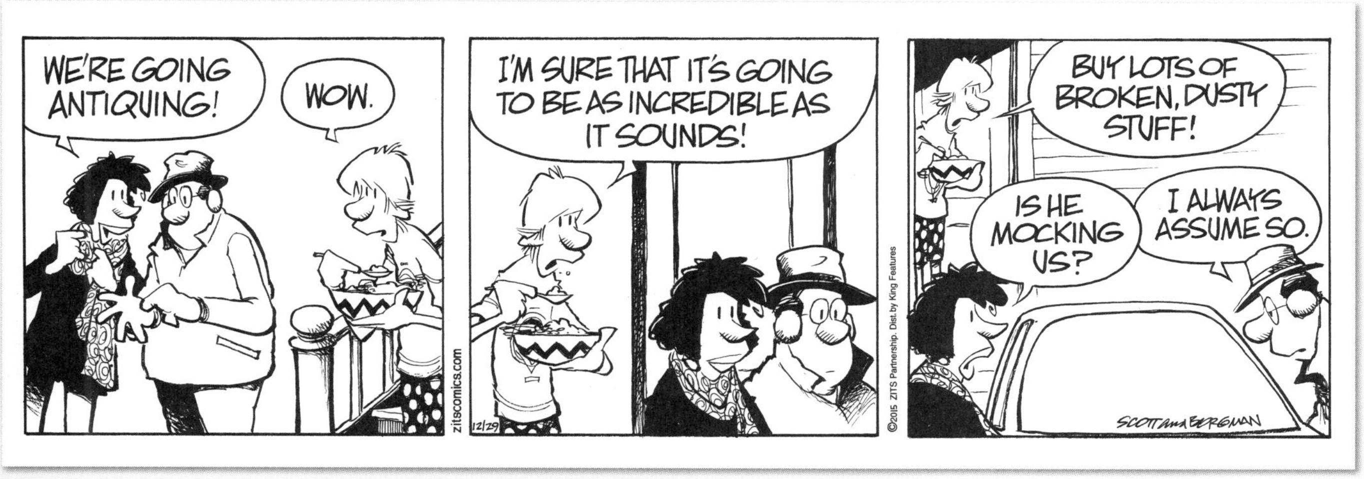
WE'RE GOING ANTIQUING!
WOW.
I'M SURE THAT IT'S GOING TO BE AS INCREDIBLE AS IT SOUNDS!
BUY LOTS OF BROKEN, DUSTY STUFF!
IS HE MOCKING US?
I ALWAYS ASSUME SO.
zitscomics.com
12/29
©2015 ZITS Partnership. Dist. by King Features
SCOTT and BORGMAN

December 13, 2015

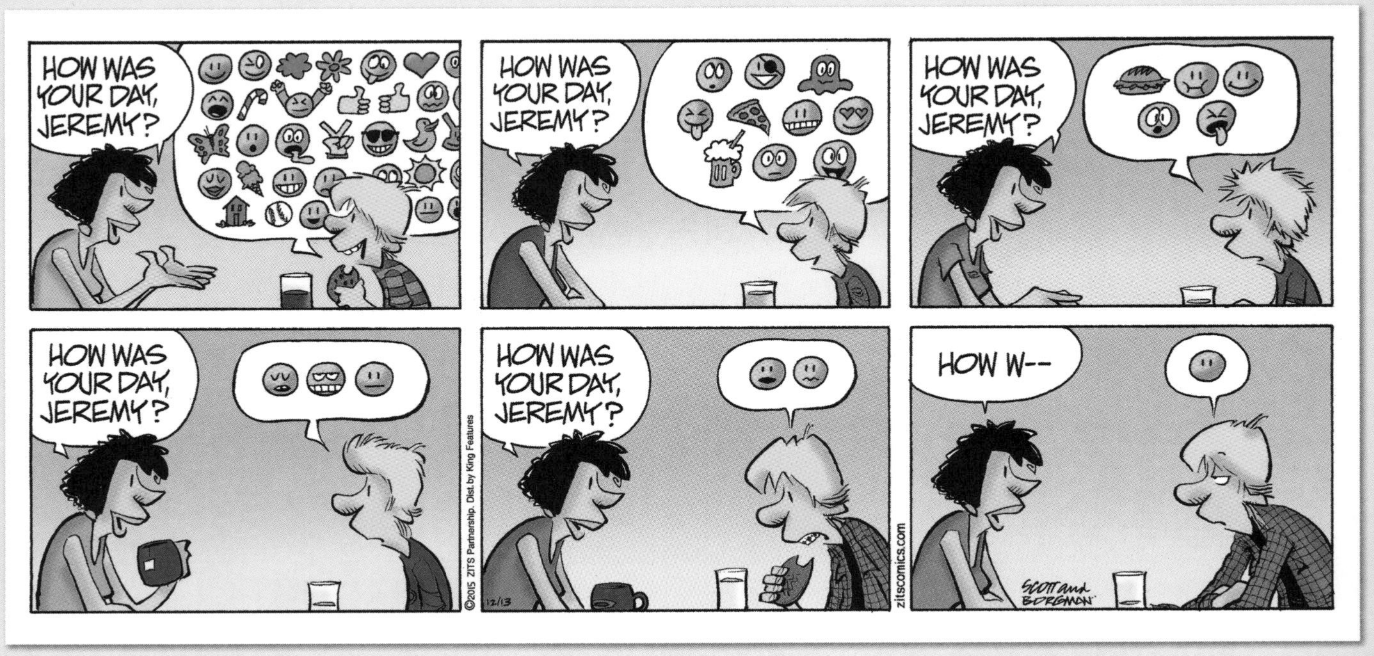
HOW WAS YOUR DAY, JEREMY?
HOW WAS YOUR DAY, JEREMY?
HOW WAS YOUR DAY, JEREMY?
HOW WAS YOUR DAY, JEREMY?
©2015 ZITS Partnership. Dist. by King Features
HOW WAS YOUR DAY, JEREMY?
zitscomics.com
HOW W--
SCOTT and BORGMAN

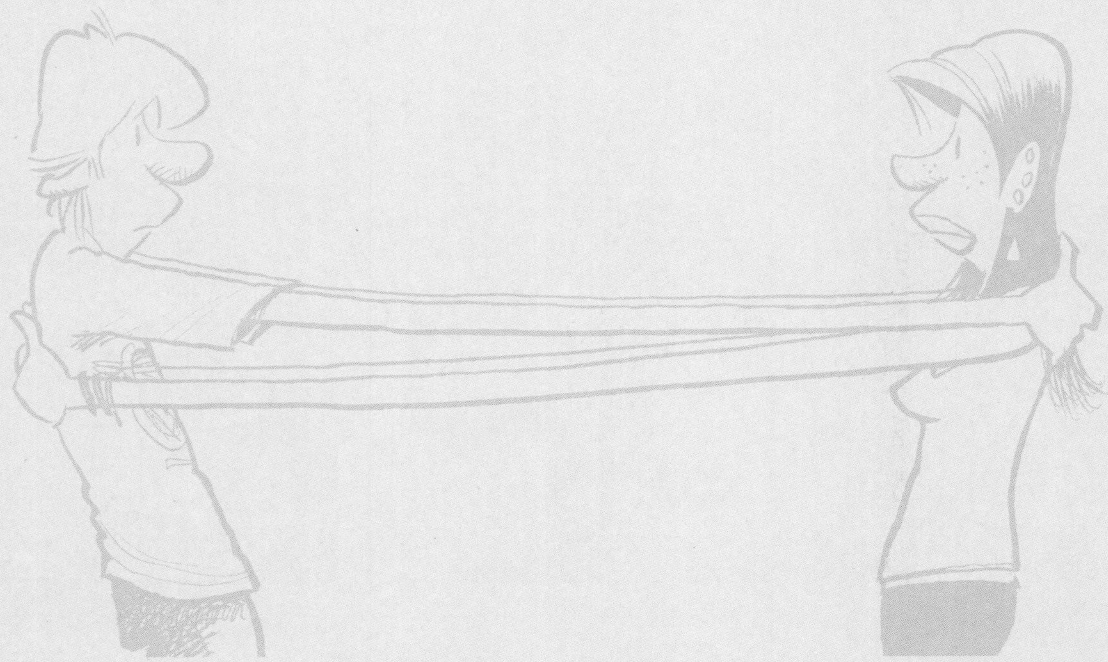

Working Together Apart

Jerry Scott

Zits started out as a partnership between a couple of relative strangers living three time zones and a culture apart. Over the past twenty years, we have developed a long-distance working arrangement and close friendship that suit the two of us pretty well.

In fact, since *Zits* started, we haven't worked on the strip while in the same room more than a handful of times. Collaborating by telephone, e-mail, texts, fax (remember those?), and the occasional letter (remember THOSE??) has become second nature to us. On the rare occasion we have the opportunity to work face-to-face, the rhythm is so wonky that we spend most of the time just staring at blank sketchbooks and swilling coffee.

The last time we tried to brainstorm together was in Boulder, Colorado, several years ago. The New Moon Bakery, a toasty, bricky coffee shop that practically drips with creativity, looked like a likely spot, so we commandeered a table against a sunny wall and got right to work. First hour: nothing. But slowly something started to happen. Gradually, almost imperceptibly, ideas started to take shape as we twisted and scooted in our chairs. About three lattes into the morning when the laughs were finally coming, we realized the secret to our working relationship . . . no eye contact.

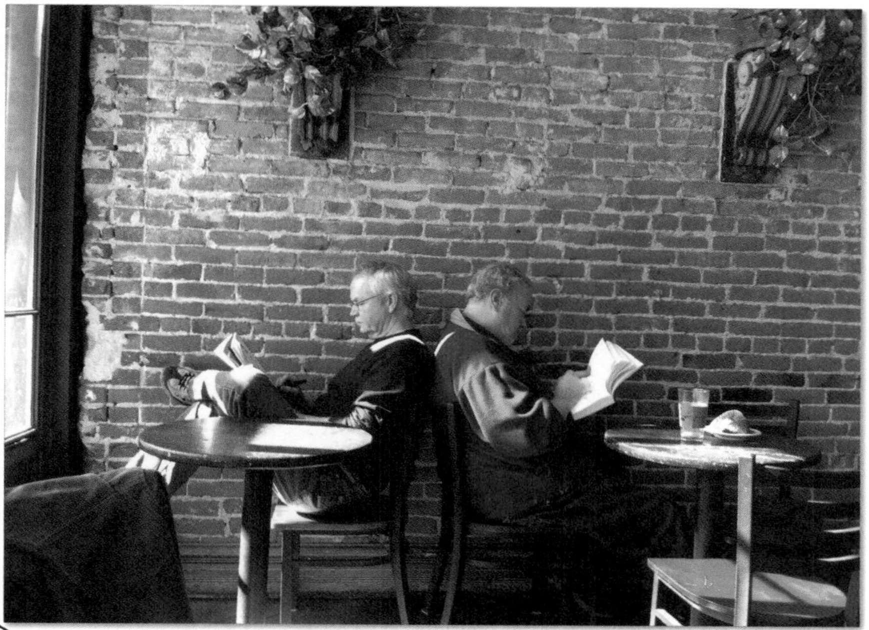

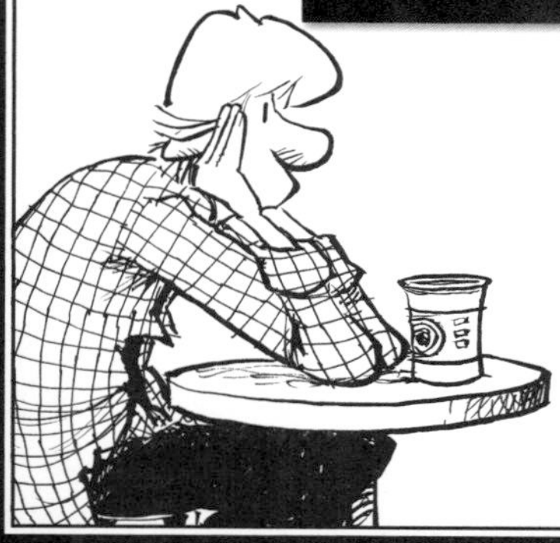

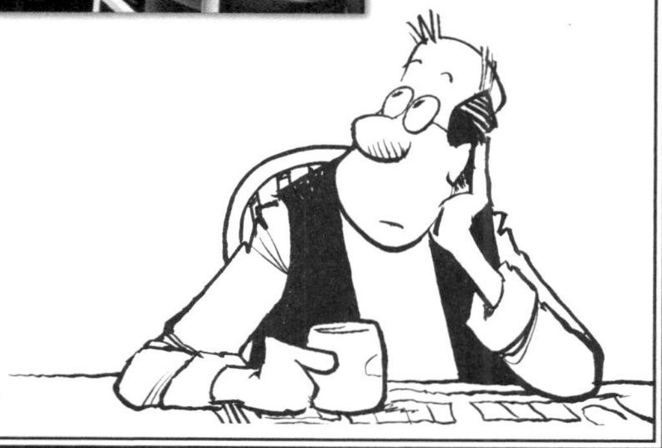

January 11, 2016

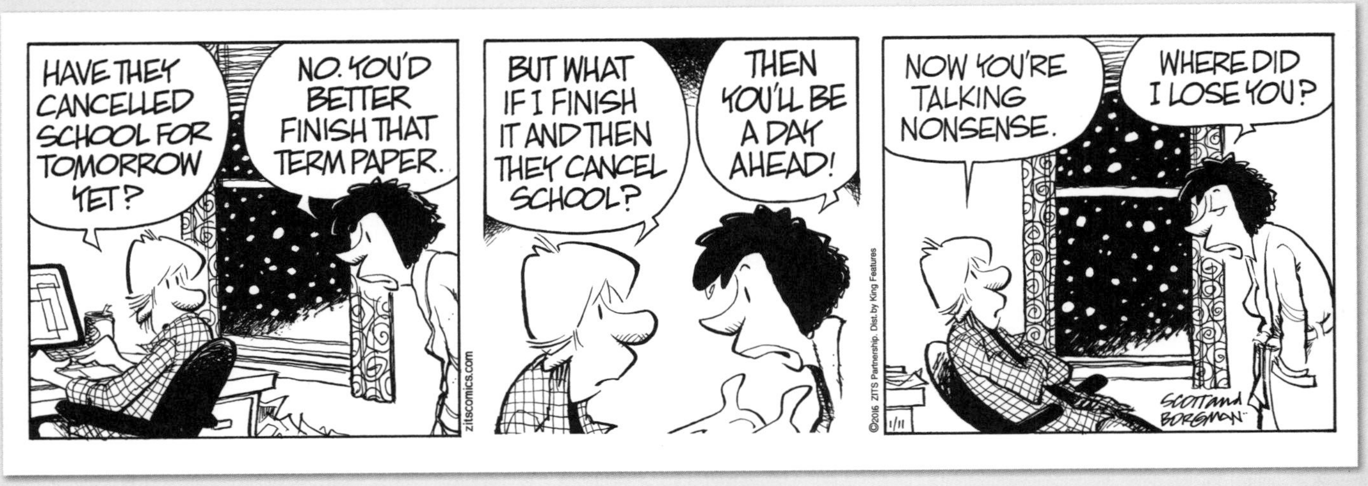

HAVE THEY CANCELLED SCHOOL FOR TOMORROW YET?
NO. YOU'D BETTER FINISH THAT TERM PAPER.
BUT WHAT IF I FINISH IT AND THEN THEY CANCEL SCHOOL?
THEN YOU'LL BE A DAY AHEAD!
NOW YOU'RE TALKING NONSENSE.
WHERE DID I LOSE YOU?
zitscomics.com
©2016 ZITS Partnership. Dist. by King Features
1/11
SCOTT and BORGMAN

January 14, 2016

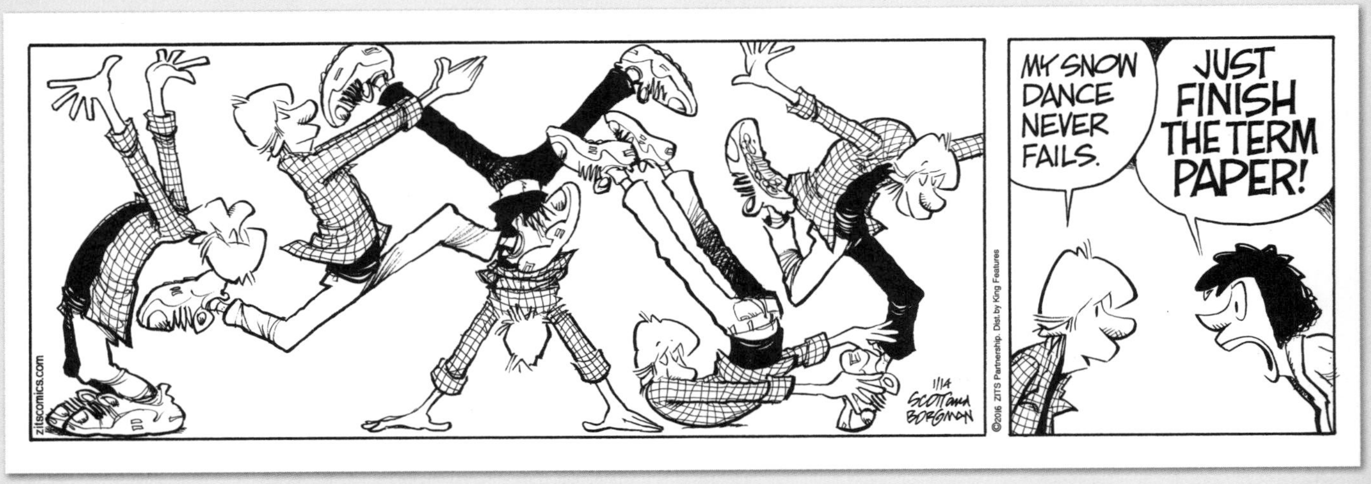

MY SNOW DANCE NEVER FAILS.
JUST FINISH THE TERM PAPER!
zitscomics.com
©2016 ZITS Partnership. Dist. by King Features
1/14
SCOTT and BORGMAN

February 8, 2016

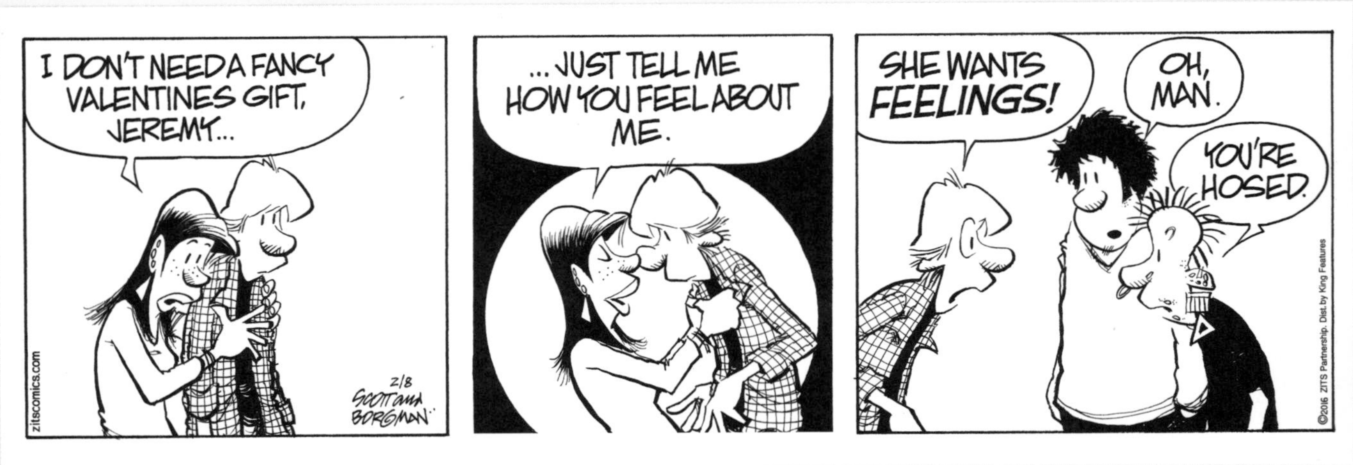

I DON'T NEED A FANCY VALENTINES GIFT, JEREMY...
...JUST TELL ME HOW YOU FEEL ABOUT ME.
SHE WANTS FEELINGS!
OH, MAN.
YOU'RE HOSED.
zitscomics.com
©2016 ZITS Partnership. Dist. by King Features
2/8
SCOTT and BORGMAN

March 10, 2016

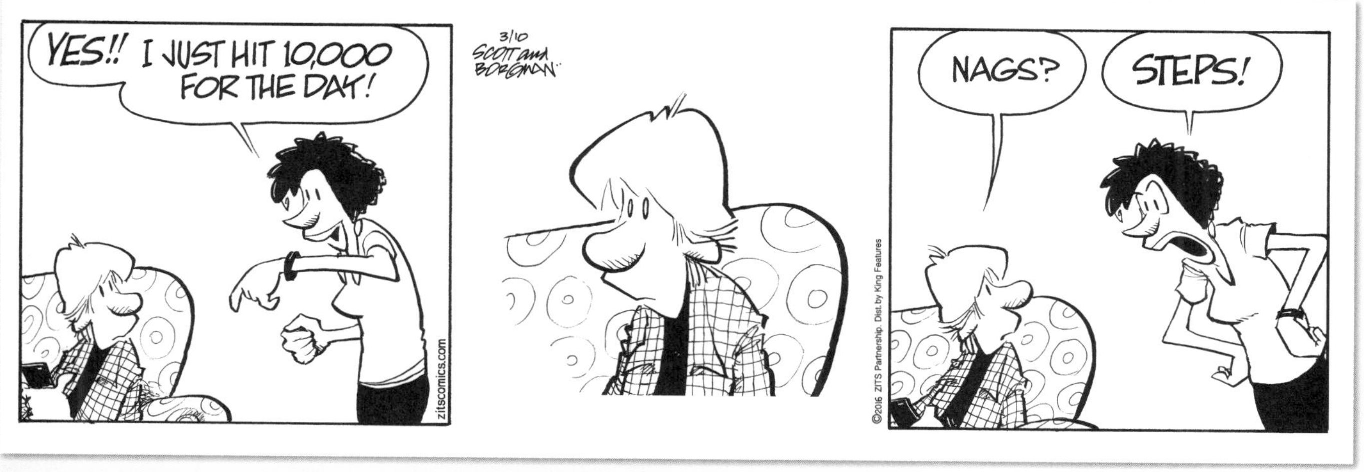
YES!! I JUST HIT 10,000 FOR THE DAY!
3/10 SCOTT and BORGMAN
NAGS?
STEPS!
zitscomics.com
©2016 ZITS Partnership. Dist. by King Features

March 11, 2016

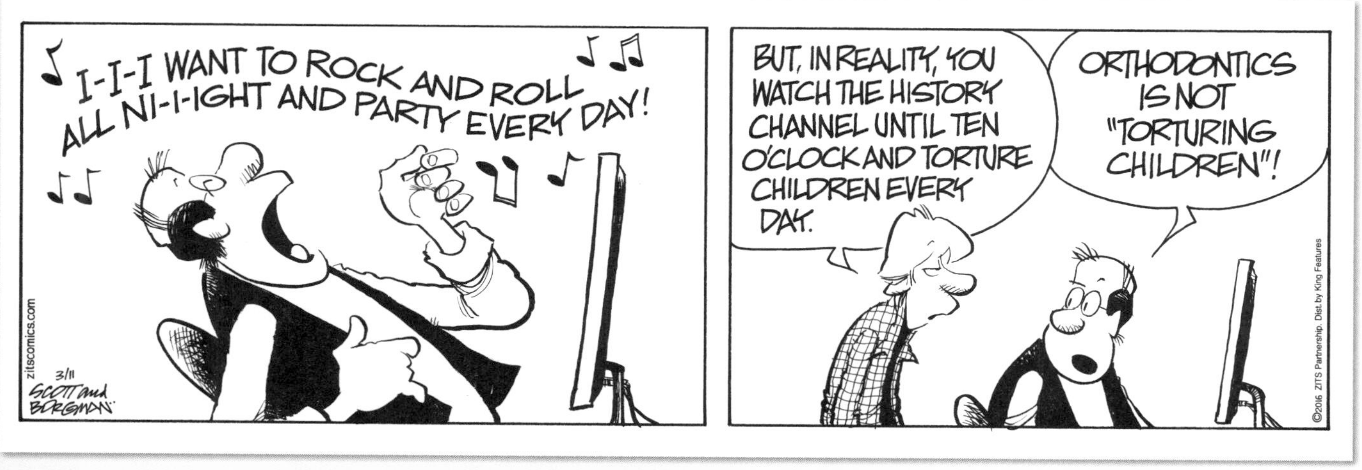
I-I-I WANT TO ROCK AND ROLL ALL NI-I-IGHT AND PARTY EVERY DAY!
3/11 SCOTT and BORGMAN
zitscomics.com
BUT, IN REALITY, YOU WATCH THE HISTORY CHANNEL UNTIL TEN O'CLOCK AND TORTURE CHILDREN EVERY DAY.
ORTHODONTICS IS NOT "TORTURING CHILDREN"!
©2016 ZITS Partnership. Dist. by King Features

March 31, 2016

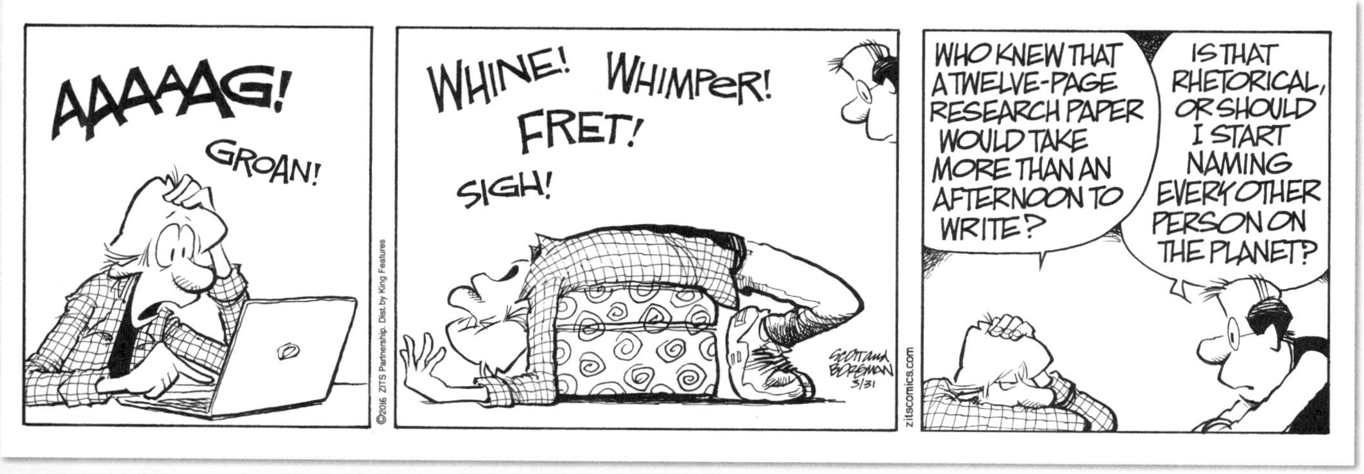
AAAAAG!
GROAN!
©2016 ZITS Partnership. Dist. by King Features
WHINE!
WHIMPER!
FRET!
SIGH!
SCOTT and BORGMAN 3/31
zitscomics.com
WHO KNEW THAT A TWELVE-PAGE RESEARCH PAPER WOULD TAKE MORE THAN AN AFTERNOON TO WRITE?
IS THAT RHETORICAL, OR SHOULD I START NAMING EVERY OTHER PERSON ON THE PLANET?

April 29, 2016

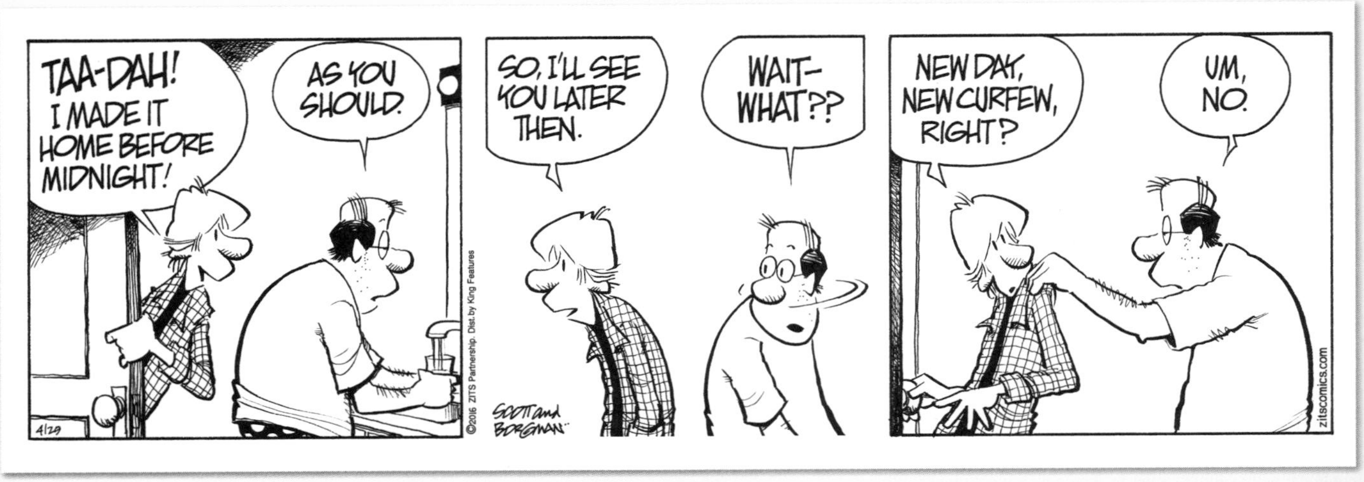
TAA-DAH! I MADE IT HOME BEFORE MIDNIGHT!
AS YOU SHOULD.
SO, I'LL SEE YOU LATER THEN.
WAIT-WHAT??
NEW DAY, NEW CURFEW, RIGHT?
UM, NO.
4/29
SCOTT and BORGMAN
©2016 ZITS Partnership. Dist. by King Features
zitscomics.com

May 5, 2016

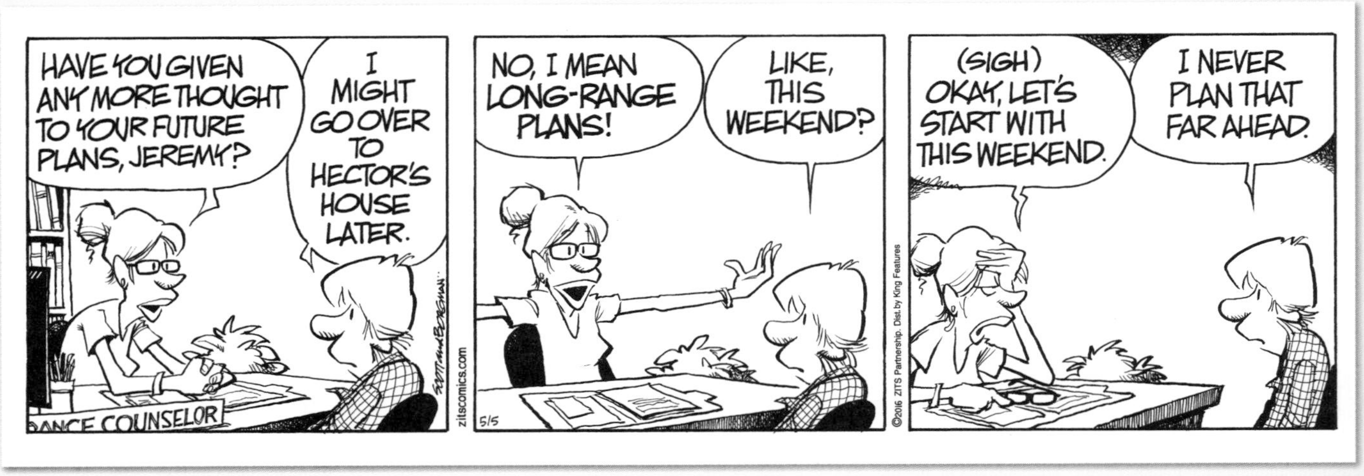
HAVE YOU GIVEN ANY MORE THOUGHT TO YOUR FUTURE PLANS, JEREMY?
I MIGHT GO OVER TO HECTOR'S HOUSE LATER.
NO, I MEAN LONG-RANGE PLANS!
LIKE, THIS WEEKEND?
(SIGH) OKAY, LET'S START WITH THIS WEEKEND.
I NEVER PLAN THAT FAR AHEAD.
ANCE COUNSELOR
SCOTT and BORGMAN
zitscomics.com
5/5
©2016 ZITS Partnership. Dist. by King Features

August 1, 2016

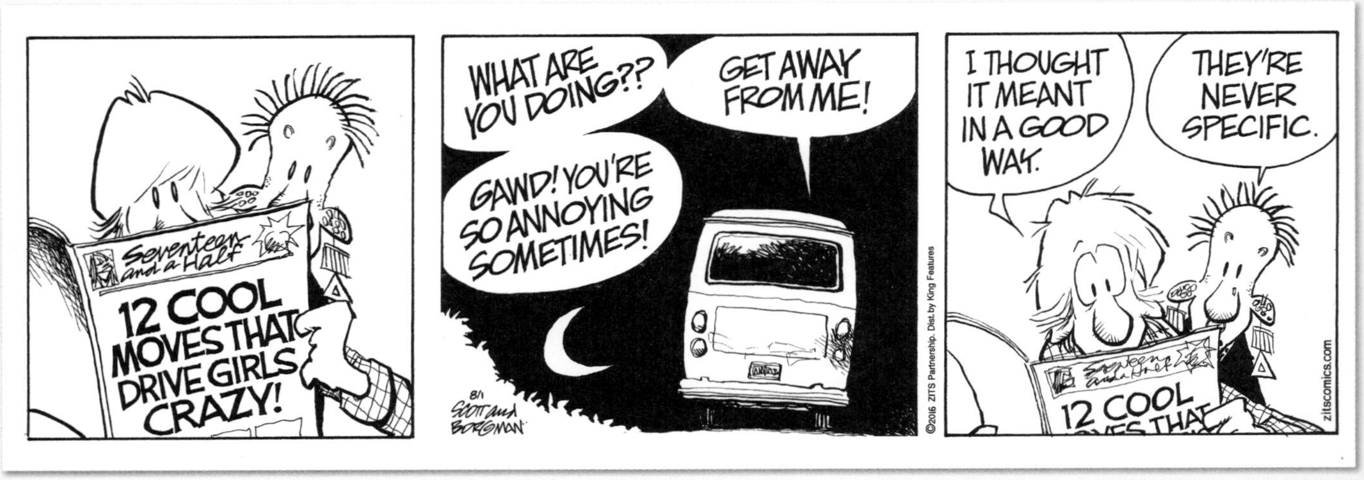
Seventeen and a Half
12 COOL MOVES THAT DRIVE GIRLS CRAZY!
WHAT ARE YOU DOING??
GET AWAY FROM ME!
GAWD! YOU'RE SO ANNOYING SOMETIMES!
8/1
SCOTT and BORGMAN
©2016 ZITS Partnership. Dist. by King Features
I THOUGHT IT MEANT IN A GOOD WAY.
THEY'RE NEVER SPECIFIC.
zitscomics.com

May 27, 2016

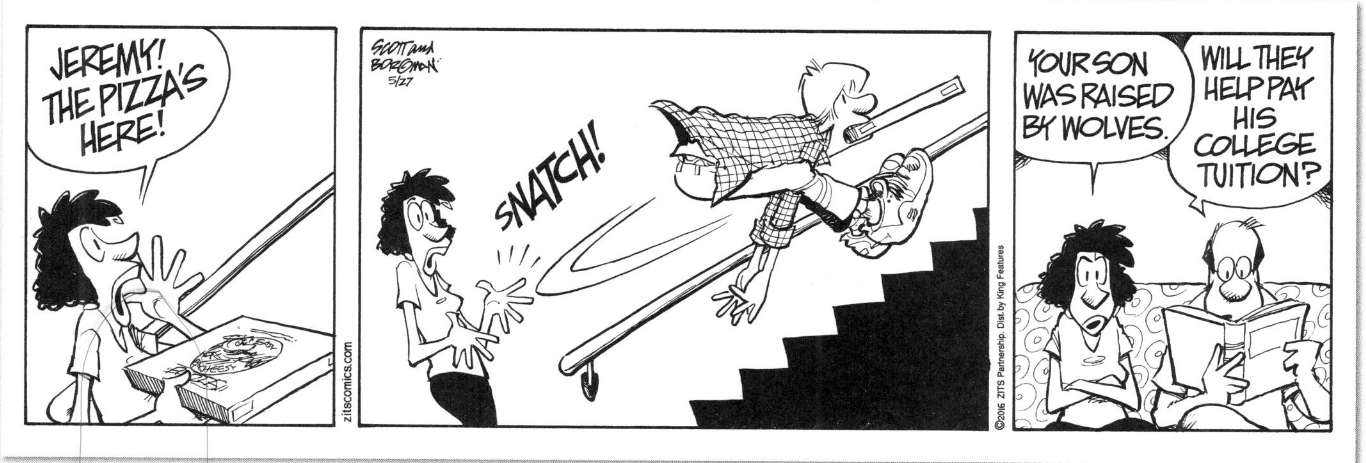
JEREMY! THE PIZZA'S HERE!
SCOTT and BORGMAN 5/27
SNATCH!
zitscomics.com
©2016 ZITS Partnership. Dist. by King Features
YOUR SON WAS RAISED BY WOLVES.
WILL THEY HELP PAY HIS COLLEGE TUITION?

June 25, 2016

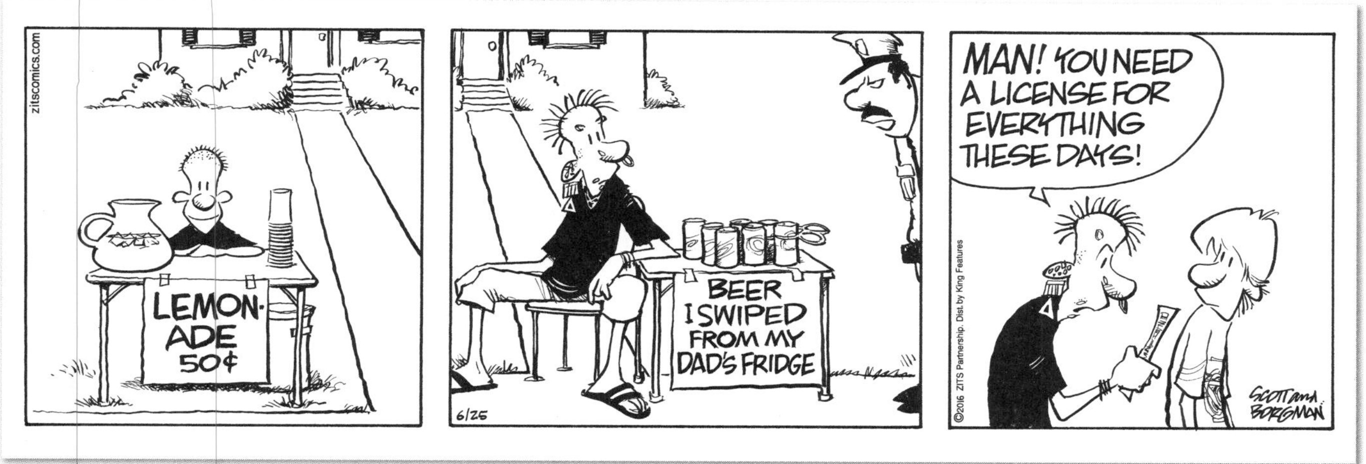
zitscomics.com
LEMON-ADE 50¢
BEER I SWIPED FROM MY DAD'S FRIDGE
6/25
MAN! YOU NEED A LICENSE FOR EVERYTHING THESE DAYS!
©2016 ZITS Partnership. Dist. by King Features
SCOTT and BORGMAN

July 18, 2016

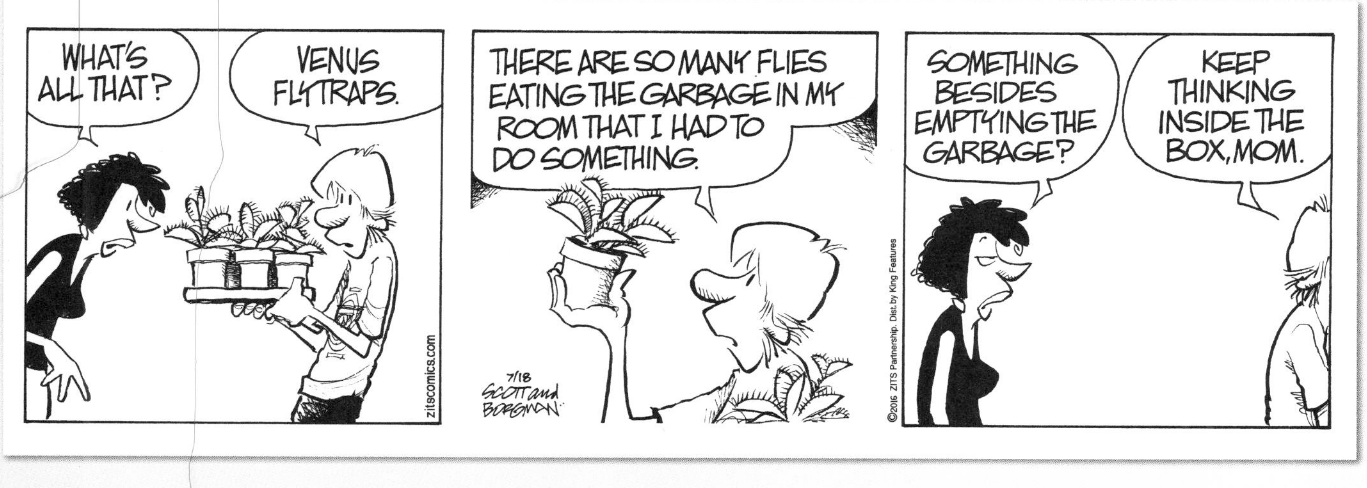
WHAT'S ALL THAT?
VENUS FLYTRAPS.
zitscomics.com
THERE ARE SO MANY FLIES EATING THE GARBAGE IN MY ROOM THAT I HAD TO DO SOMETHING.
7/18 SCOTT and BORGMAN
©2016 ZITS Partnership. Dist. by King Features
SOMETHING BESIDES EMPTYING THE GARBAGE?
KEEP THINKING INSIDE THE BOX, MOM.

May 8, 2016

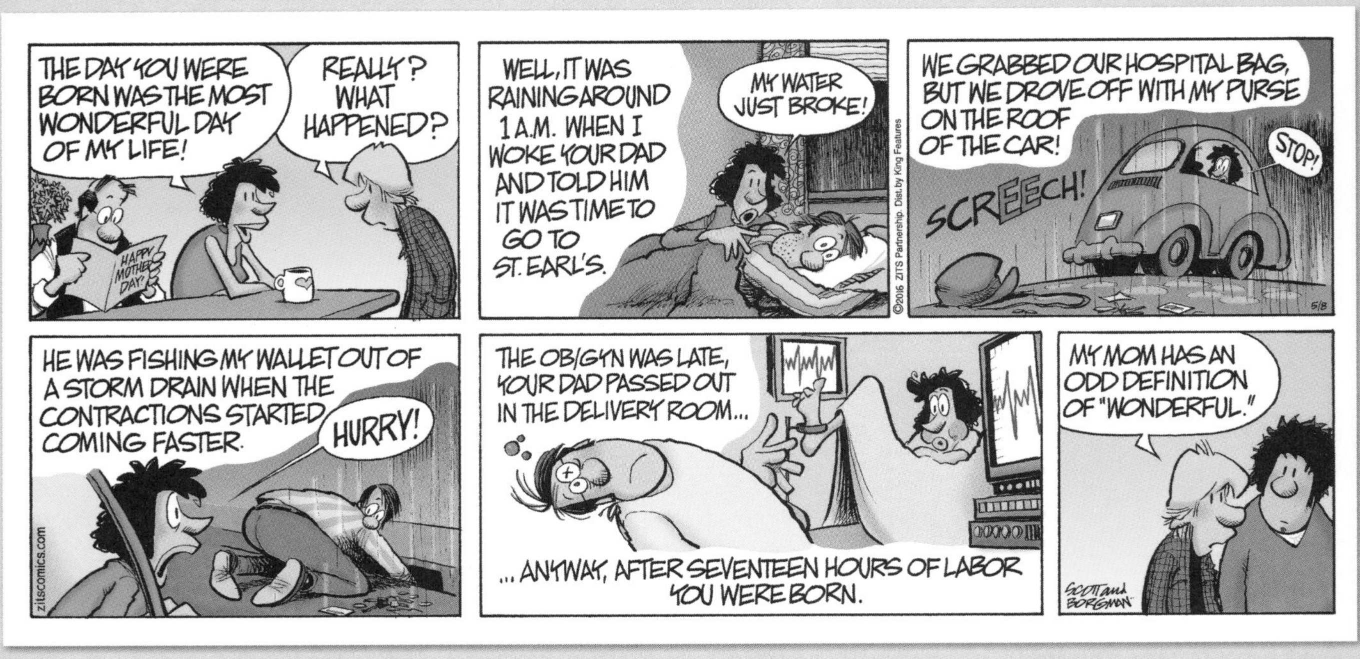
THE DAY YOU WERE BORN WAS THE MOST WONDERFUL DAY OF MY LIFE!
REALLY? WHAT HAPPENED?
HAPPY MOTHER'S DAY!
WELL, IT WAS RAINING AROUND 1 A.M. WHEN I WOKE YOUR DAD AND TOLD HIM IT WAS TIME TO GO TO ST. EARL'S.
MY WATER JUST BROKE!
©2016 ZITS Partnership. Dist. by King Features
WE GRABBED OUR HOSPITAL BAG, BUT WE DROVE OFF WITH MY PURSE ON THE ROOF OF THE CAR!
STOP!
SCREECH!
5/8
HE WAS FISHING MY WALLET OUT OF A STORM DRAIN WHEN THE CONTRACTIONS STARTED COMING FASTER.
HURRY!
zitscomics.com
THE OB/GYN WAS LATE, YOUR DAD PASSED OUT IN THE DELIVERY ROOM...
...ANYWAY, AFTER SEVENTEEN HOURS OF LABOR YOU WERE BORN.
MY MOM HAS AN ODD DEFINITION OF "WONDERFUL."
SCOTT and BORGMAN

July 24, 2016

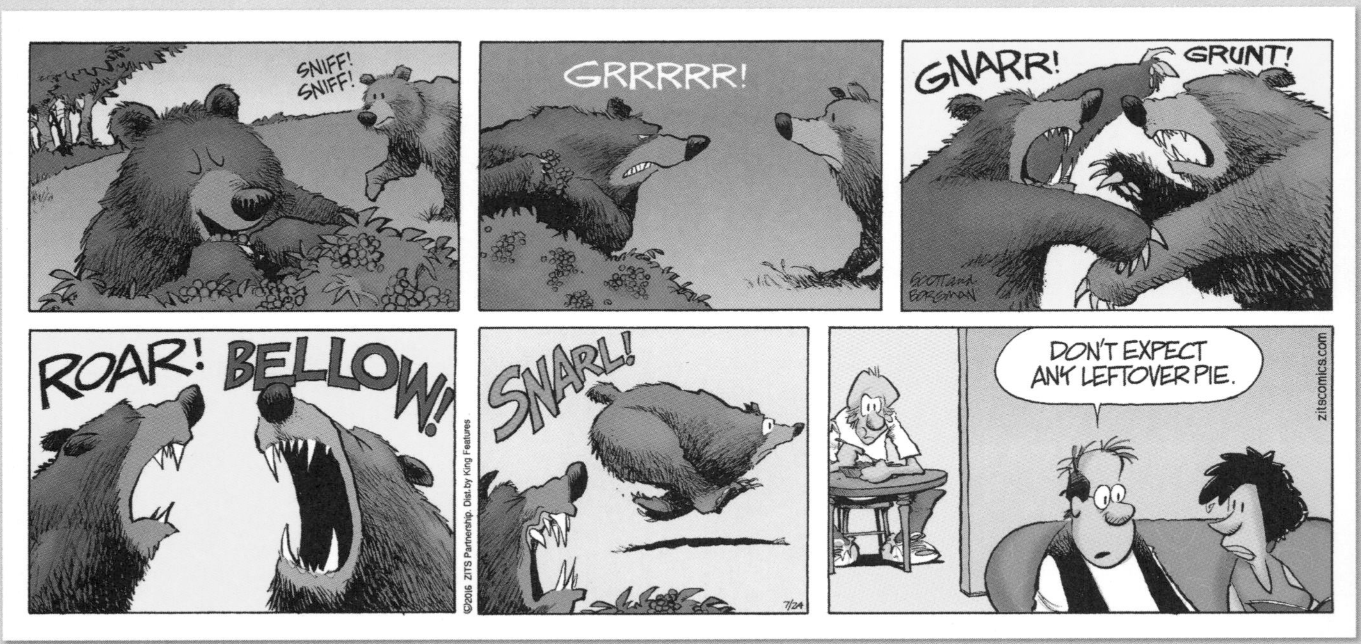
SNIFF! SNIFF!
GRRRRR!
GNARR!
GRUNT!
SCOTT and BORGMAN
ROAR!
BELLOW!
©2016 ZITS Partnership. Dist. by King Features
SNARL!
7/24
DON'T EXPECT ANY LEFTOVER PIE.
zitscomics.com

August 5, 2016

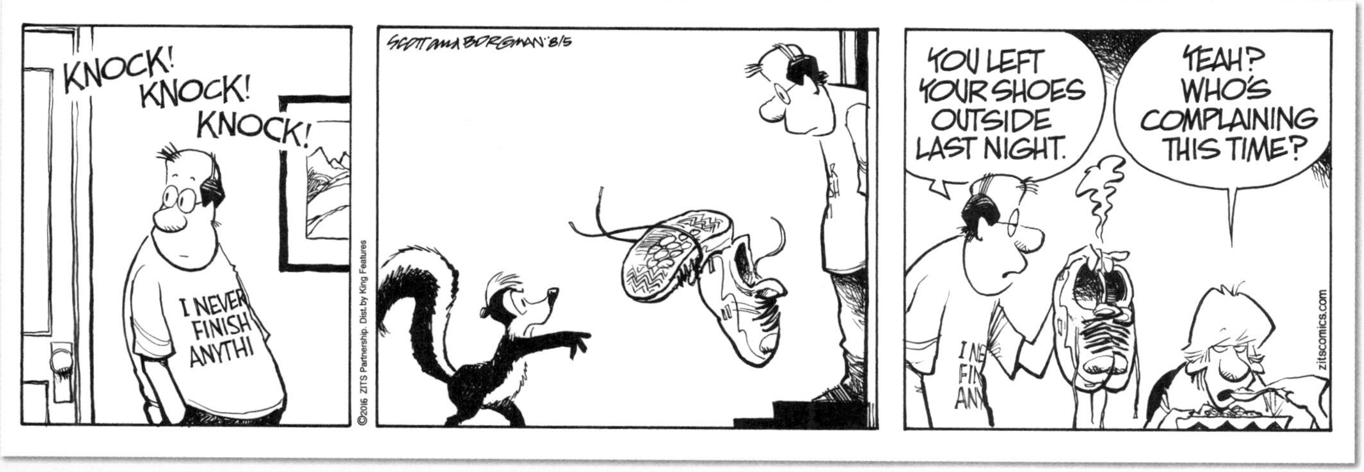
KNOCK! KNOCK! KNOCK!
I NEVER FINISH ANYTHI
SCOTT AND BORGMAN 8/5
©2016 ZITS Partnership. Dist. by King Features
YOU LEFT YOUR SHOES OUTSIDE LAST NIGHT.
YEAH? WHO'S COMPLAINING THIS TIME?
zitscomics.com

September 2, 2016

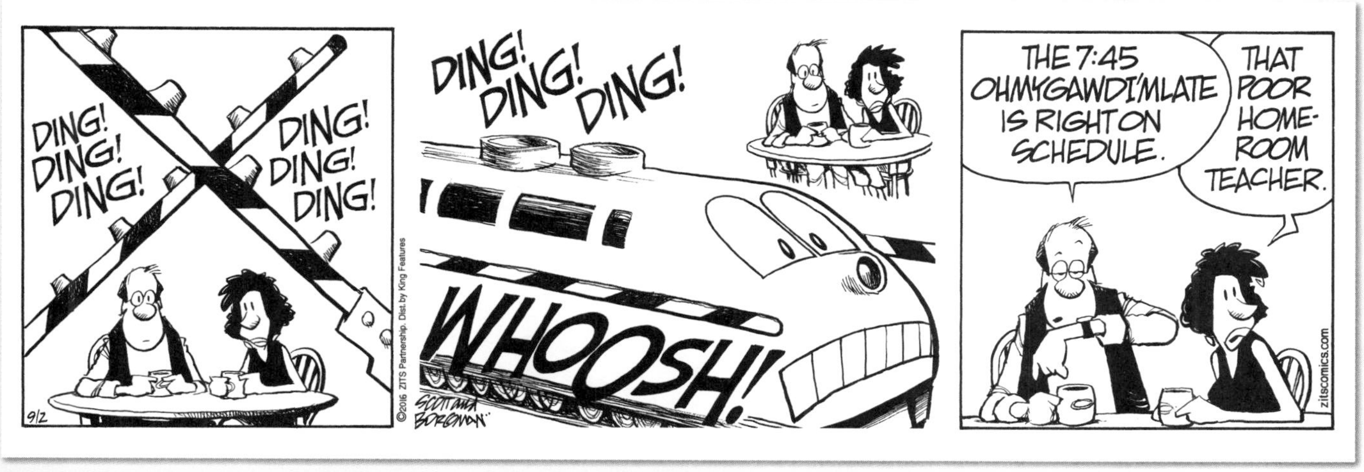
DING! DING! DING!
DING! DING! DING!
9/2
DING! DING! DING!
WHOOSH!
©2016 ZITS Partnership. Dist. by King Features
SCOTT AND BORGMAN
THE 7:45 OHMYGAWDI'MLATE IS RIGHT ON SCHEDULE.
THAT POOR HOME-ROOM TEACHER.
zitscomics.com

September 16, 2016

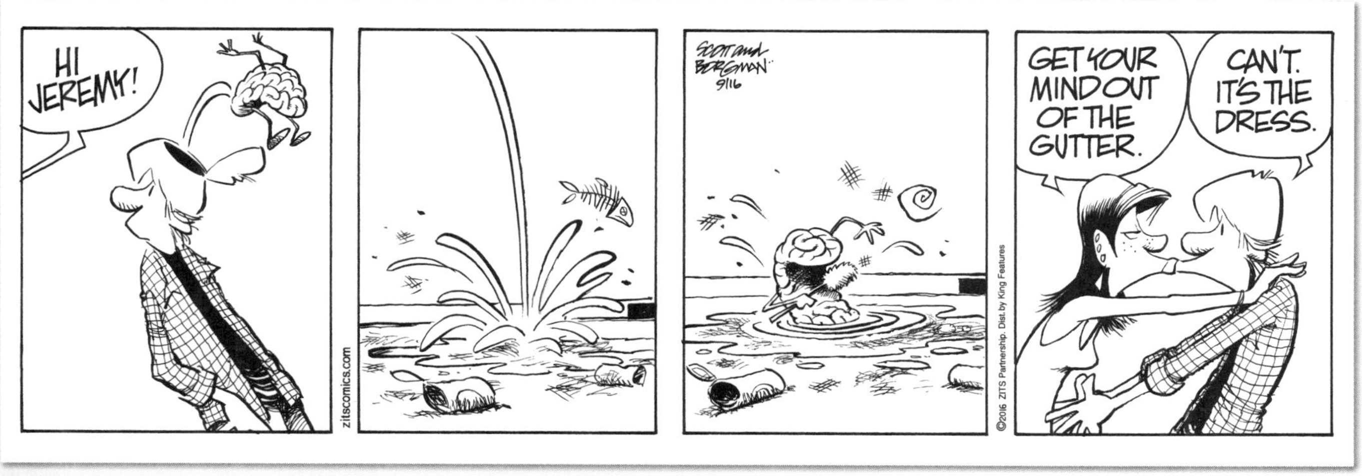
HI JEREMY!
zitscomics.com
SCOTT AND BORGMAN 9/16
©2016 ZITS Partnership. Dist. by King Features
GET YOUR MIND OUT OF THE GUTTER.
CAN'T. IT'S THE DRESS.

September 19, 2016

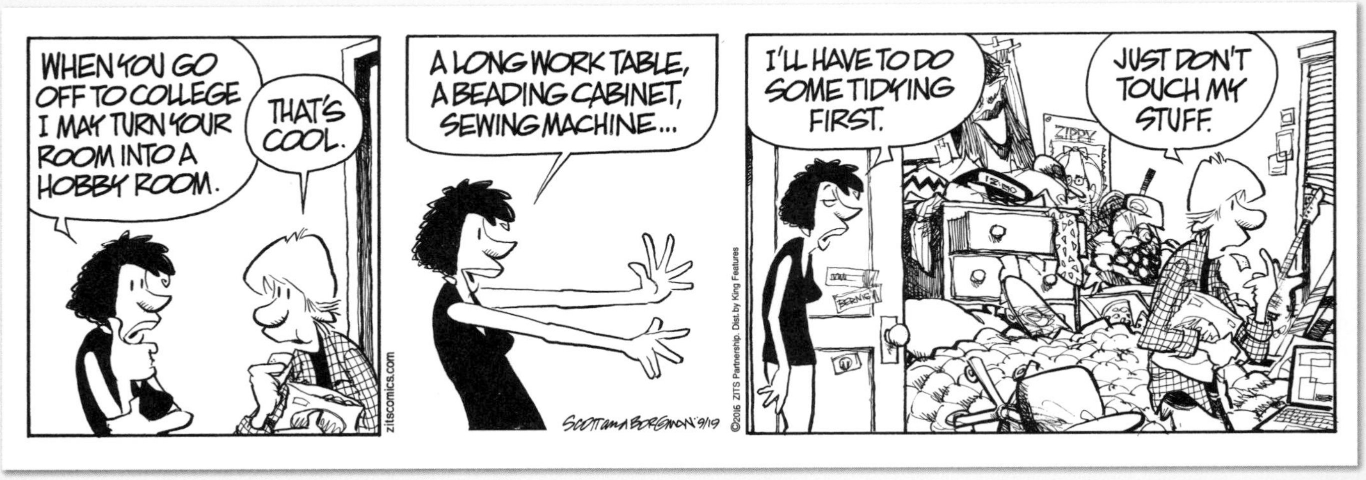
WHEN YOU GO OFF TO COLLEGE I MAY TURN YOUR ROOM INTO A HOBBY ROOM.
THAT'S COOL.
A LONG WORK TABLE, A BEADING CABINET, SEWING MACHINE...
I'LL HAVE TO DO SOME TIDYING FIRST.
JUST DON'T TOUCH MY STUFF.
zitscomics.com
SCOTT AND BORGMAN 9/19
©2016 ZITS Partnership. Dist. by King Features

September 28, 2016

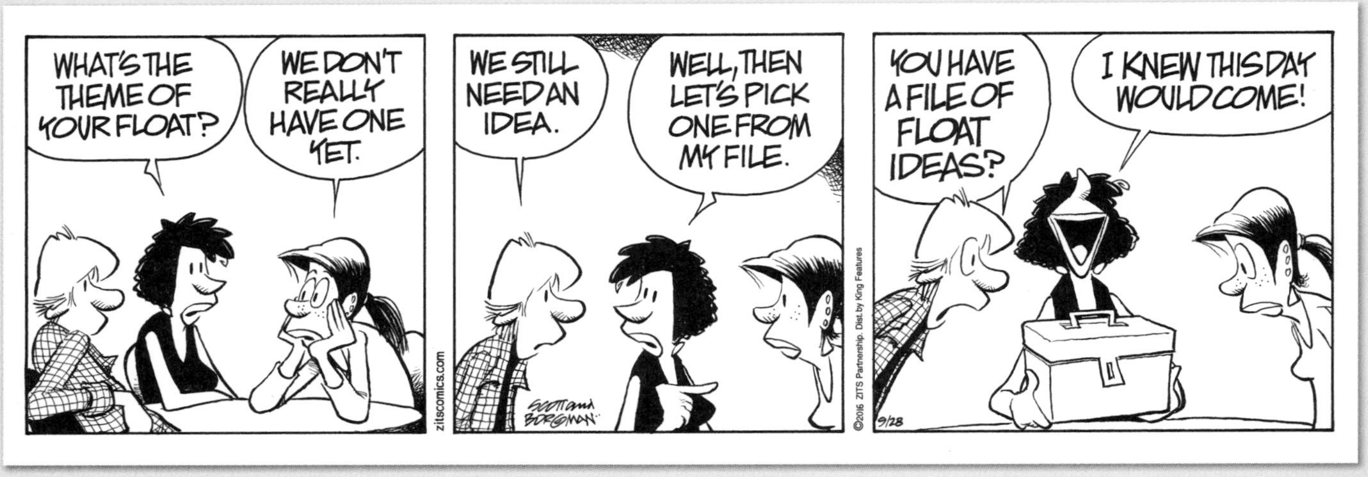
WHAT'S THE THEME OF YOUR FLOAT?
WE DON'T REALLY HAVE ONE YET.
WE STILL NEED AN IDEA.
WELL, THEN LET'S PICK ONE FROM MY FILE.
YOU HAVE A FILE OF FLOAT IDEAS?
I KNEW THIS DAY WOULD COME!
zitscomics.com
SCOTT AND BORGMAN
©2016 ZITS Partnership. Dist. by King Features
9/28

September 30, 2016

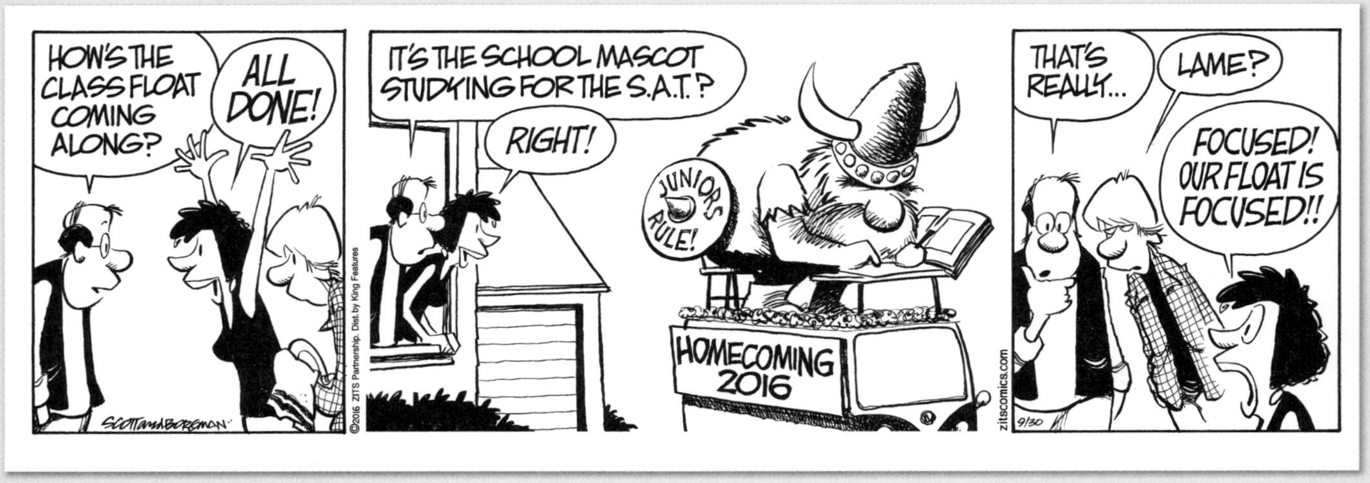
HOW'S THE CLASS FLOAT COMING ALONG?
ALL DONE!
IT'S THE SCHOOL MASCOT STUDYING FOR THE S.A.T.?
RIGHT!
JUNIORS RULE!
HOMECOMING 2016
THAT'S REALLY...
LAME?
FOCUSED! OUR FLOAT IS FOCUSED!!
SCOTT AND BORGMAN
©2016 ZITS Partnership. Dist. by King Features
zitscomics.com
9/30

October 3, 2016

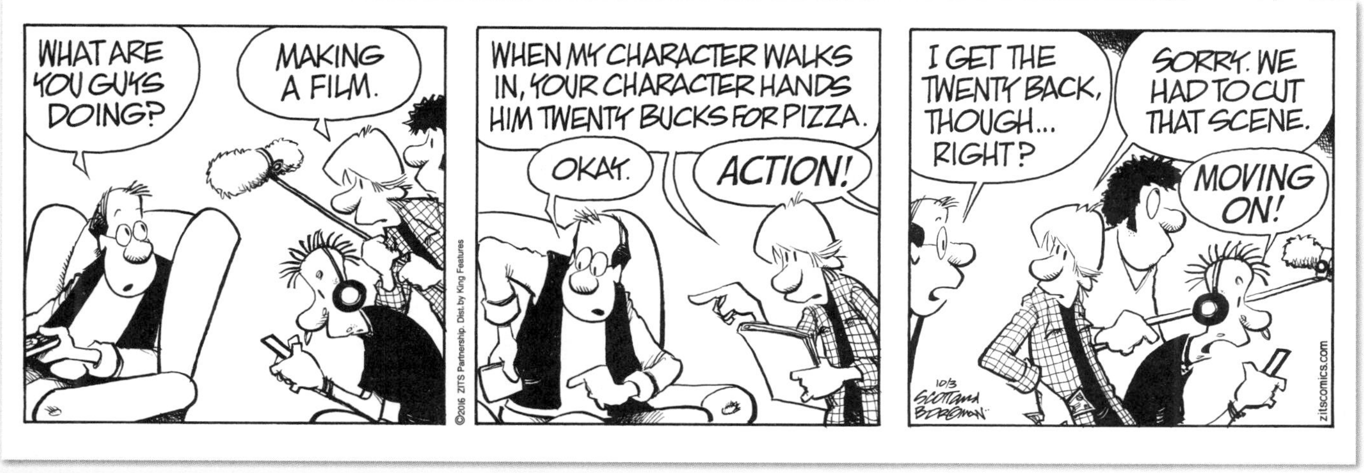
WHAT ARE YOU GUYS DOING?
MAKING A FILM.
©2016 ZITS Partnership. Dist. by King Features
WHEN MY CHARACTER WALKS IN, YOUR CHARACTER HANDS HIM TWENTY BUCKS FOR PIZZA.
OKAY.
ACTION!
I GET THE TWENTY BACK, THOUGH... RIGHT?
SORRY. WE HAD TO CUT THAT SCENE.
MOVING ON!
10/3 SCOTT and BORGMAN
zitscomics.com

October 12, 2016

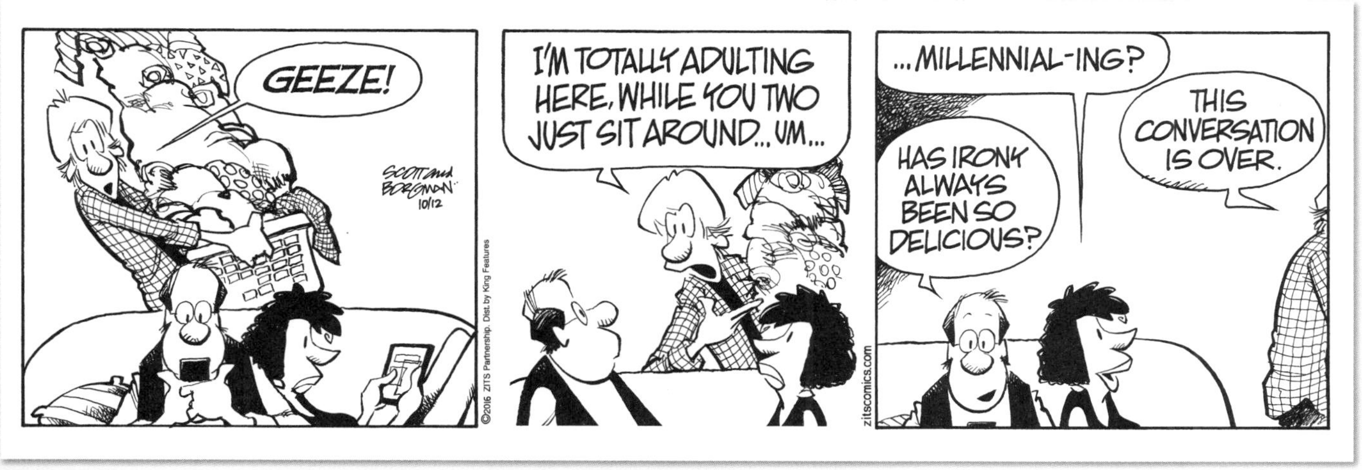
GEEZE!
SCOTT and BORGMAN 10/12
©2016 ZITS Partnership. Dist. by King Features
I'M TOTALLY ADULTING HERE, WHILE YOU TWO JUST SIT AROUND... UM...
zitscomics.com
...MILLENNIAL-ING?
HAS IRONY ALWAYS BEEN SO DELICIOUS?
THIS CONVERSATION IS OVER.

October 20, 2016

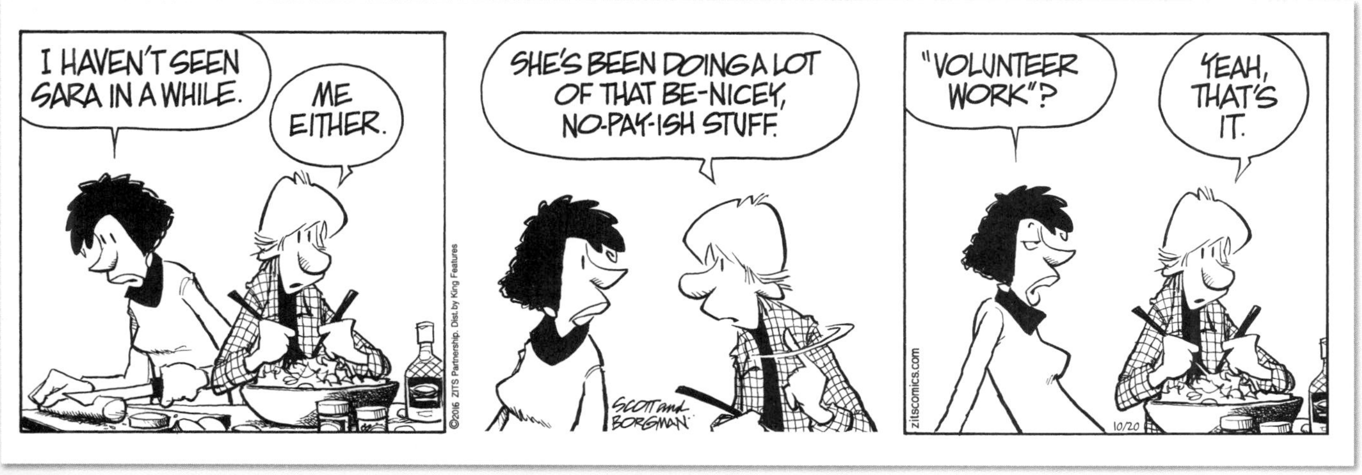
I HAVEN'T SEEN SARA IN A WHILE.
ME EITHER.
©2016 ZITS Partnership. Dist. by King Features
SHE'S BEEN DOING A LOT OF THAT BE-NICEY, NO-PAY-ISH STUFF.
SCOTT and BORGMAN
zitscomics.com
"VOLUNTEER WORK"?
YEAH, THAT'S IT.
10/20

September 25, 2016

HI GUYS. HOW WAS THE PARTY?
FINE
I GUESS
zitscomics.com
NO! (SOB!) IT WAS AWFUL!
YEAH. IT KINDA GOT OUT OF CONTROL.
I JUST TOOK CARE OF MY DRUNK FRIENDS ALL NIGHT!
9/25
SOME PEOPLE WERE REALLY WASTED!
GUYS WERE ACTING WEIRD AND I HAD TO HOLD WHITNEY'S HAIR BACK WHILE SHE BARFED IN THE TOILET FOR LIKE, AN HOUR!
THE WHOLE NIGHT WAS RUINED, THANKS TO A FEW STUPID PEOPLE!
IDIOTS!
©2016 ZITS Partnership. Dist. by King Features
WELL, WE'RE GLAD THAT YOU'RE BOTH OKAY!
AND WE'RE GOING TO PRETEND WE'RE SORRY YOU HAD TO GO THROUGH THAT.
SCOTT AND BORGMAN

October 16, 2016

SCOTT AND BORGMAN 10/16
Z
zitscomics.com
SPROING!
ZANG!
FWING!
BUPPITY BIPPITY BIPPITY BUPPITY
HI
WOOGA WOOGA
WOOGA WOOGA
ZIP ZIP ZIP ZIP ZIP ZIP ZIP ZIP
BZZZZZZZERT!
CAFFEINE JUST KICK IN?
SOME DAYS IT KICKS HARDER THAN OTHERS.
©2016 ZITS Partnership. Dist. by King Features

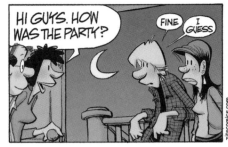

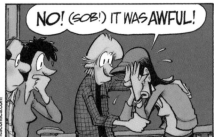

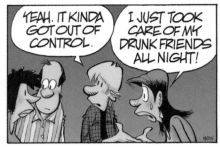

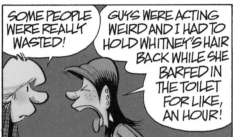

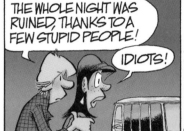

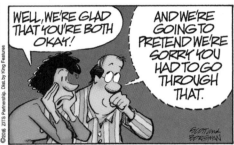

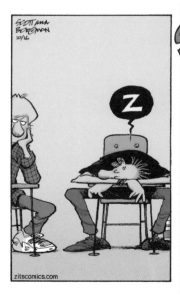

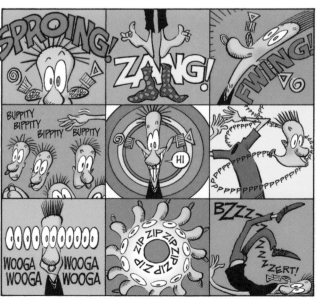

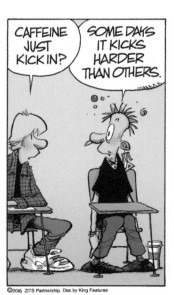

October 30, 2016

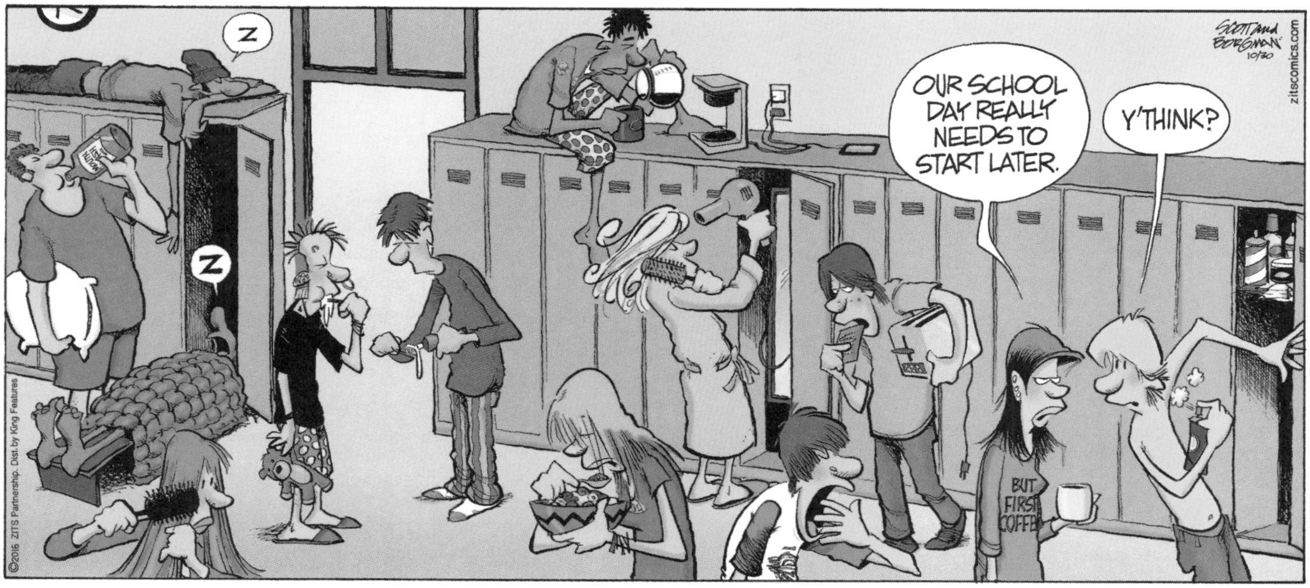
Z
Z
OUR SCHOOL DAY REALLY NEEDS TO START LATER.
Y'THINK?
BUT FIRST COFFEE
SCOTT and BORGMAN 10/30
zitscomics.com
©2016 ZITS Partnership. Dist. by King Features

November 6, 2016

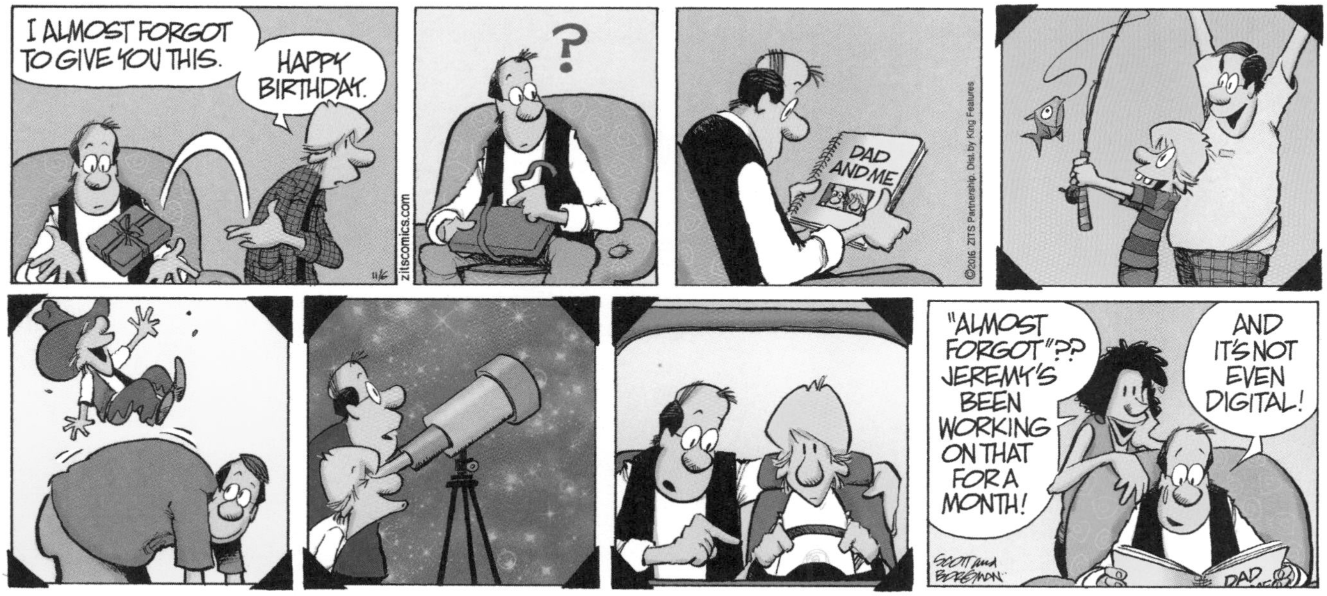
I ALMOST FORGOT TO GIVE YOU THIS.
HAPPY BIRTHDAY.
?
DAD AND ME
"ALMOST FORGOT"?? JEREMY'S BEEN WORKING ON THAT FOR A MONTH!
AND IT'S NOT EVEN DIGITAL!
SCOTT and BORGMAN
zitscomics.com
©2016 ZITS Partnership. Dist. by King Features

November 21, 2016

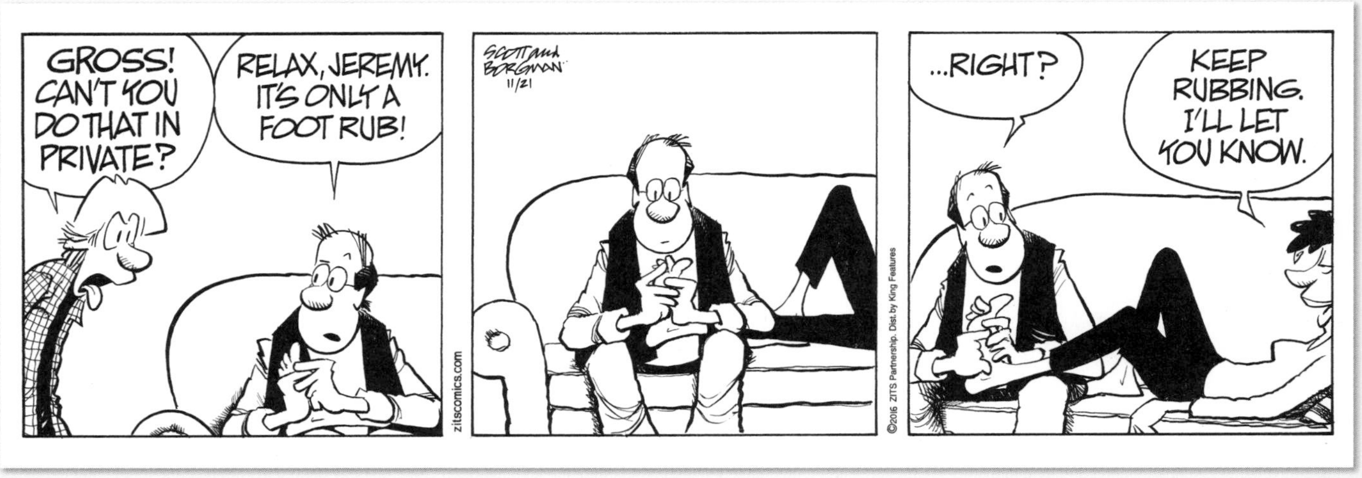
GROSS! CAN'T YOU DO THAT IN PRIVATE?
RELAX, JEREMY. IT'S ONLY A FOOT RUB!
SCOTT and BORGMAN 11/21
zitscomics.com
©2016 ZITS Partnership. Dist. by King Features
...RIGHT?
KEEP RUBBING. I'LL LET YOU KNOW.

November 29, 2016

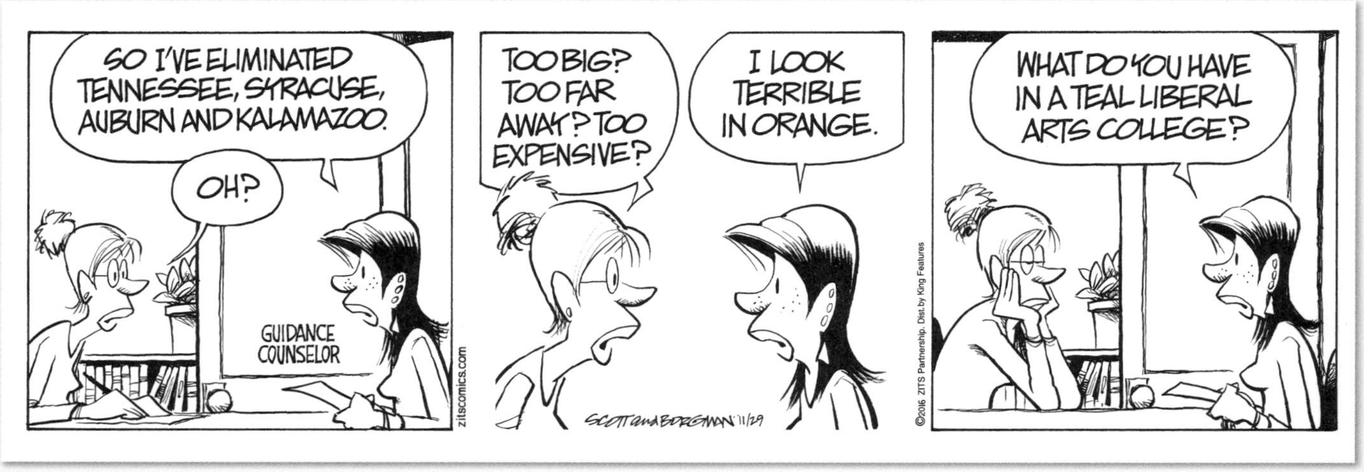
SO I'VE ELIMINATED TENNESSEE, SYRACUSE, AUBURN AND KALAMAZOO.
OH?
GUIDANCE COUNSELOR
zitscomics.com
TOO BIG? TOO FAR AWAY? TOO EXPENSIVE?
I LOOK TERRIBLE IN ORANGE.
SCOTT and BORGMAN 11/29
©2016 ZITS Partnership. Dist. by King Features
WHAT DO YOU HAVE IN A TEAL LIBERAL ARTS COLLEGE?

December 3, 2016

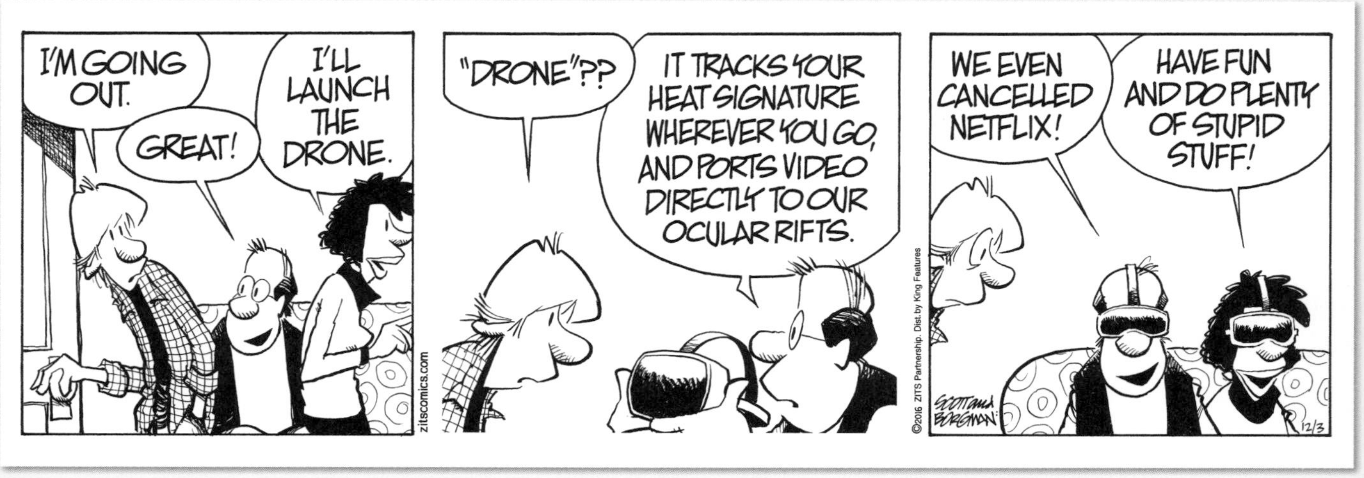
I'M GOING OUT.
GREAT!
I'LL LAUNCH THE DRONE.
zitscomics.com
"DRONE"??
IT TRACKS YOUR HEAT SIGNATURE WHEREVER YOU GO, AND PORTS VIDEO DIRECTLY TO OUR OCULAR RIFTS.
©2016 ZITS Partnership. Dist. by King Features
WE EVEN CANCELLED NETFLIX!
HAVE FUN AND DO PLENTY OF STUPID STUFF!
SCOTT and BORGMAN 12/3

November 27, 2016

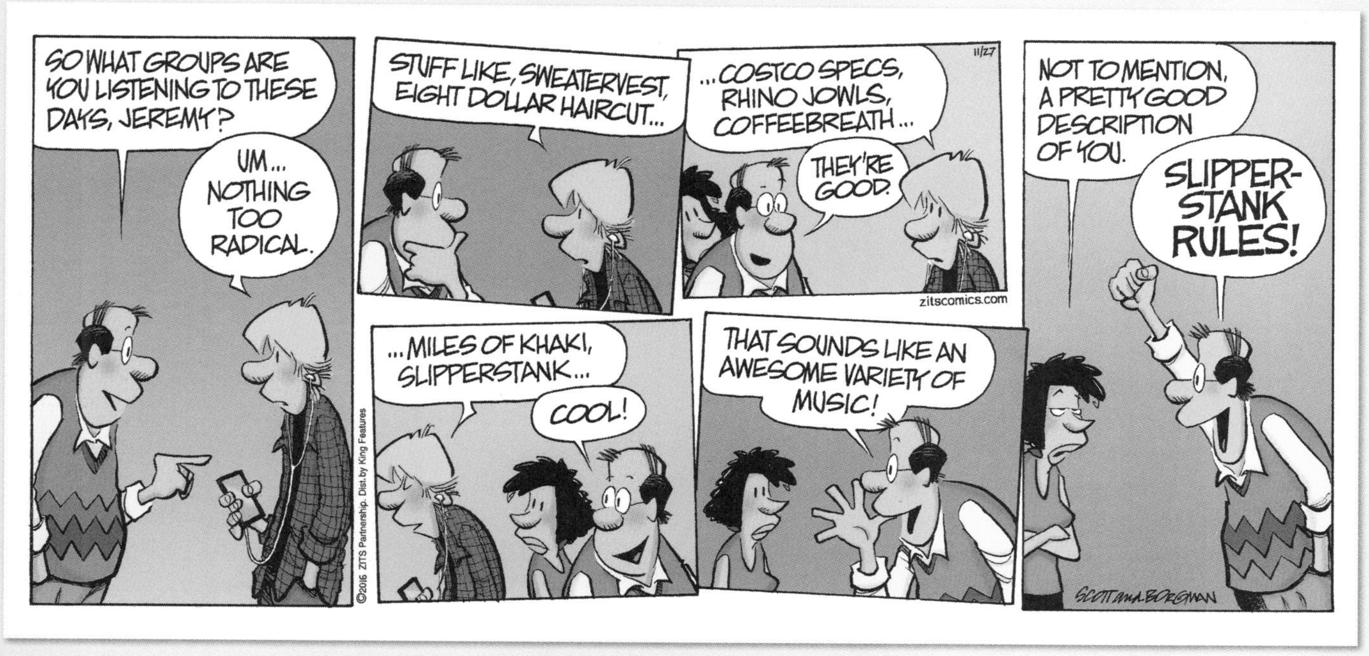
SO WHAT GROUPS ARE YOU LISTENING TO THESE DAYS, JEREMY?
UM... NOTHING TOO RADICAL.
©2016 ZITS Partnership. Dist. by King Features
STUFF LIKE, SWEATERVEST, EIGHT DOLLAR HAIRCUT...
11/27
...COSTCO SPECS, RHINO JOWLS, COFFEEBREATH...
THEY'RE GOOD.
zitscomics.com
...MILES OF KHAKI, SLIPPERSTANK...
COOL!
THAT SOUNDS LIKE AN AWESOME VARIETY OF MUSIC!
NOT TO MENTION, A PRETTY GOOD DESCRIPTION OF YOU.
SLIPPER-STANK RULES!
SCOTT and A. BORGMAN

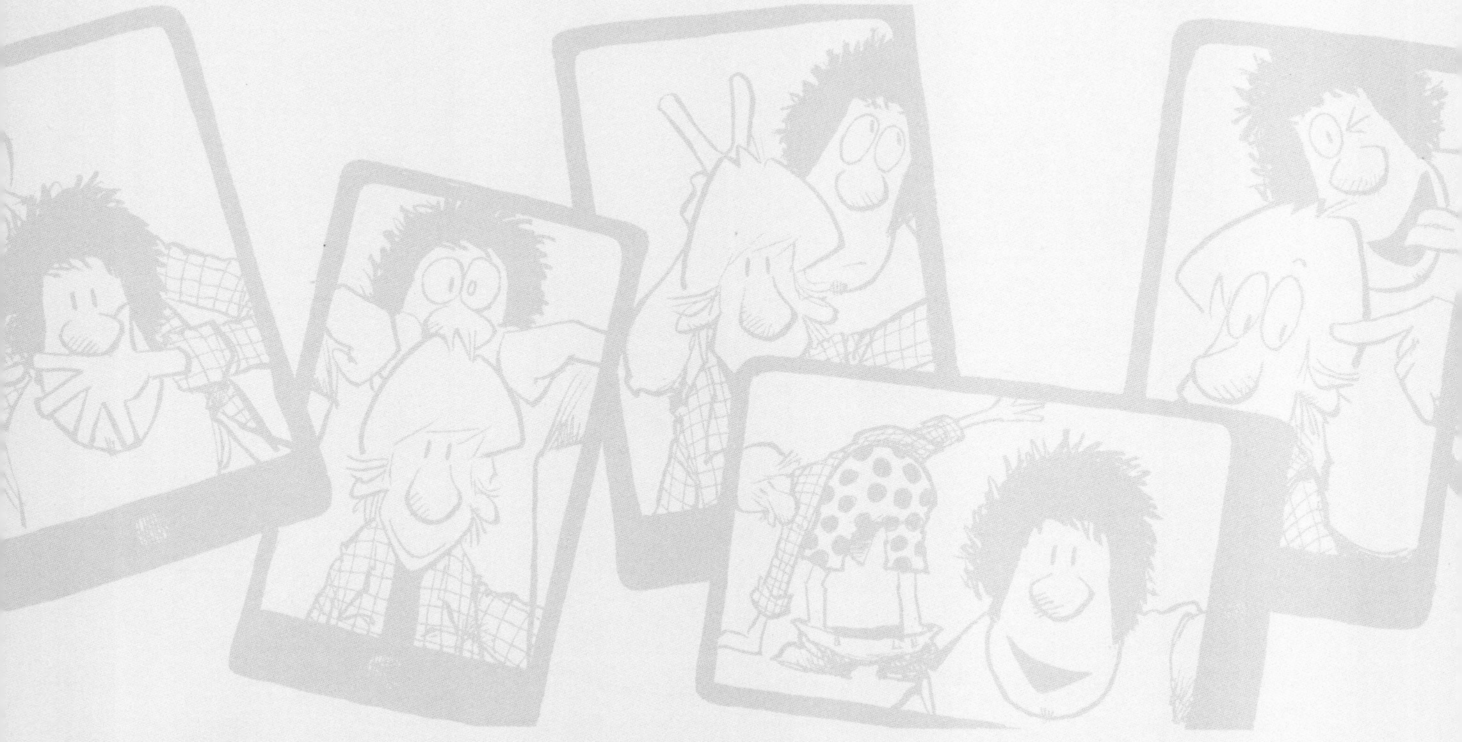

Does Jeremy Age?

Jerry Scott

Jeremy is aging in glacial time. We've given him one official birthday in the twenty years we've been doing the strip, and that was just to give him a driver's license and expand our canvas. Somewhere along the line we started referring to him as seventeen, so I guess we missed that party. I think we're done with birthdays now.

Research papers have been written about the philosophy of time passage in comic strips. Or maybe I just heard some guy in a bar yapping about it. I don't really remember, but that's not what's important here. What's important is that real time passes pretty fast, and things can zip by before you know it (e.g., anniversaries, deadlines, youth). Comic strip time needs to pass more slowly than real time because every strip is about something. Say you could divide the days of your life into two piles: The first pile would be the days in which something universally funny or interesting or annoying happened to you, and the second pile would be all the other days. I'm betting that the second pile would be a LOT bigger. Mine is. Well, Jim and I try to only write and draw the days of Jeremy's life from the first pile, so it takes lots of piles to get a year's worth of strips. Mathematically, the equation would be:

comic strip Time equals Life minus routine times Reader interest, or
$$csT = L - r \times Ri.$$

If Jeremy gets a couple of birthdays every twenty years, he'll turn twenty-one in forty years. Lucky kid. I wonder where we will be?

254